PENGUIN CLASSICS

MAGNA CARTA

DAVID CARPENTER is professor of medieval history at King's College London. He is a leading authority on the history of Britain in the central Middle Ages and author of *The Struggle for Mastery: Britain 1066–1284*. He has held lectureships at Christ Church, Oxford, St Hilda's College, Oxford, the University of Aberdeen, and Queen Mary College, University of London.

D1331453

C015861224

Magna Carta

With a New Commentary by
DAVID CARPENTER

PENGUIN BOOKS

PENGUIN CLASSICS

Published by the Penguin Group
Penguin Books Ltd, 80 Strand, London WC2R ORL, England
Penguin Group (USA) Inc., 375 Hudson Street, New York, New York 10014, USA
Penguin Group (Canada), 90 Eglinton Avenue East, Suite 700, Toronto, Ontario, Canada M4P 2Y3
(a division of Pearson Penguin Canada Inc.)
Penguin Ireland, 25 St Stephen's Green, Dublin 2, Ireland (a division of Penguin Books Ltd)
Penguin Group (Australia), 707 Collins Street, Melbourne, Victoria 3008, Australia
(a division of Pearson Australia Group Pty Ltd)
Penguin Books India Pvt Ltd, 11 Community Centre, Panchsheel Park, New Delhi – 110 017, India
Penguin Group (NZ), 67 Apollo Drive, Rosedale, Auckland 0632, New Zealand
(a division of Pearson New Zealand Ltd)
Penguin Books (South Africa) (Pty) Ltd, Block D, Rosebank Office Park,
181 Jan Smuts Avenue, Parktown North, Gauteng 2193, South Africa

Penguin Books Ltd, Registered Offices: 80 Strand, London WC2R ORL, England

www.penguin.com

This edition first published by Penguin Classics 2015
001

Commentary copyright © David Carpenter, 2015
All rights reserved

The moral right of the author of the commentary has been asserted

Set in 9.75/11.5 pt Adobe Sabon
Typeset by Jouve (UK), Milton Keynes
Printed in Great Britain by Clays Ltd, St Ives plc

ISBN: 978-0-241-95337-2

www.greenpenguin.co.uk

Contents

Preface

Runnymede today is an atmospheric and evocative place. The great meadow stretches out beside the Thames, and one can easily imagine it filled with the pavilions of King John and the tents of the barons during those June days in 1215 when Magna Carta was being negotiated. John ended the Great Charter with the statement that it was 'Given by our hand in the meadow which is called Runnymede, between Windsor and Staines, on the fifteenth day of June, in the seventeenth year of our reign', which meant that it was on 15 June 1215 that he authorized the Charter's writing out and sealing. The great jets taking off from London's Heathrow Airport often come up over Runnymede, and then turn to fly down its whole length, slowly gaining height as they disappear into the distance. It is as though they are carrying the Charter to the four corners of the world.

The Charter has indeed become one of the most famous documents in world constitutional history, regarded as a fundamental protection against arbitrary and tyrannical rule. In some ways, this illustrious history is as undeserved as it was unintended. Magna Carta, as originally conceived, certainly did not offer equal protection to all the king's subjects. It was, in many ways, a selfish document in which the baronial elite looked after its own interests. While, moreover, the Charter is usually regarded as firing its salvoes at the king, it was also (a major theme of this book) firing at sections of society. It discriminated against unfree peasants, who formed the largest section of the population. It also discriminated against women. It revealed tensions between barons and their knightly tenants. The towns, like the knights, got far less from the Charter than they might have hoped. Magna Carta shows the king's subjects in conflict with one another as well as in conflict with the king.

Yet Magna Carta did assert a fundamental principle. That

principle was the rule of law. Henceforth, the king was to be bound by law, the law the Charter made. He was thus restricted in a whole series of ways, for the Charter had no fewer than sixty-three chapters. Most significant of all were chapters 39 and 40. In chapter 40, the king was not to sell, deny or delay justice. Under chapter 39, no free man was to be imprisoned or dispossessed save 'by the lawful judgement of his peers' or 'by the law of the land'. These two chapters are still on the statute book of the United Kingdom.[1] To be sure, in 1215, it was only the 'free man' who benefited from chapter 39. It offered nothing, therefore, to the unfree peasant. The chapter still reads 'free man' today. In course of time, however, the chapter became more socially inclusive. Legislation in 1354 defined 'free man' as a 'man of whatever estate and condition he may be'. The legislation also made clear that treatment according to the law of the land meant treatment according to due legal process. Other legislation interpreted 'lawful judgement' by peers as meaning trial by peers (that is social equals), and so trial by jury.[2] While, moreover, chapter 39 read 'no free man', 'man' here, from the start in 1215, could be understood as meaning human being, and thus as applying to both sexes.[3]

In terms of the principles it asserted, therefore, the Charter was rightly called in aid by the parliamentary opposition to Charles I, and by the founding fathers of the United States of America. In the twentieth century it was appealed to by both Mahatma Gandhi and by Nelson Mandela.[4] It still features in political debates in Britain today. A *Guardian* newspaper leader in 2005, protesting about the proposed ninety-day detention period in terrorist cases, was headed 'Protecting Magna Carta'.[5]

That Magna Carta was to have an illustrious future hardly seemed likely in 1215. Little more than a month after Runnymede, John asked the pope to quash the Charter. His baronial opponents too seemed to abandon it. Giving up hope of restricting the king, they decided to replace him altogether and offered the throne to Prince Louis, the eldest son of the king of France. The result was a civil war, not the peace that Magna Carta was supposed to bring. When John died at Newark, during the night of 17–18 October 1216, as a great storm battered the town, his heir was his nine-year-old son, Henry III, while Louis controlled more than half the country. In this desperate situation, Henry's governors effected a complete change of policy. In order to tempt rebels into the young king's allegiance, they immediately issued, in the king's name, a new version of Magna Carta. They did so again in November 1217, having won the civil war, this time in order to consolidate the peace. And then Henry issued the Charter for a third and final time in 1225, in return for a grant of taxation. It was the 1225 Charter that became the definitive version. Confirmed many times under Henry III and his son Edward I, by the end of the thirteenth century it had achieved iconic status.

Given the significance of the Charter of 1225, it might be wondered why the 800th anniversary of Magna Carta is being celebrated in 2015 and not in 2025. Celebrations in 2025 will certainly be in order, but those in 2015 easily deserve first place. Although there are important differences, the Charter of 1225, in its spirit, detail and much of its phraseology, replicates the Charter of 1215. Without the 1215 original there would have been no 1225 version. This book is chiefly about Magna Carta 1215, although it also considers the impact of the Charter, in its various versions, in the thirteenth century.

I first encountered Magna Carta in 1968 in the chapter house of Oxford cathedral, a building, with its elegant lancet windows, which was being erected around the time John conceded the Charter. There I heard John Mason lecture on Bishop Stubbs' *Select Charters and Other Illustrations of English Constitutional History from the Earliest Times to the Reign of Edward the First*. This was no longer a popular course by the time I took it, having been eclipsed by one on the Crusades. As far as I remember, there were only one or two other students in the audience. Yet I found the lectures, which climaxed with Magna Carta, enthralling. The documents themselves illuminated both constitutional history and the whole changing nature of English society. When I complimented Dr Mason on the series, he modestly (too modestly I think) said that the lectures were actually those of his old tutor, Sir Goronwy Edwards, who had been taught by T. F. Tout, who in turn had been taught by Stubbs himself. The lectures were followed by one-to-one tutorials with John (although it was many years before I called him that), in which we worked through the documents, and I wrote gobbets on many of Magna Carta's chapter.[6] Subsequently, revising for finals back at Westminster (where my father was a canon of the abbey), I worked late into the evening in the abbey's muniment room, with its wonderful view over Henry III's great church. There I cross-referenced in my copy of *Select Charters* the chapters of Magna Carta with their equivalents in the Articles of the Barons, the Coronation Charter of Henry I, and the Charters of 1216, 1217 and 1225. I have used my annotated copy of *Select Charters* ever since, although it has now lost its cover and is in a very dilapidated state.

The 1960s proved to be a very exciting time generally and especially so for those starting work on Magna Carta. This was because the subject had been transformed by two great books by J. C. Holt. The first was *The Northerners: A Study in the Reign of King John*, which appeared in 1961. The second was *Magna Carta*, published in 1965 to coincide with the Charter's 750th anniversary. I acquired my copy of the latter on 27 March 1968, or at least that is the date I wrote into it. W. L. Warren, who in 1961 brought out a superb biography of King John, generously acknowledged that Holt's books had so altered the landscape that 'all earlier work [on the Charter] appears to be less than satisfactory'.[7] Although my book often differs from Holt, it does so in the context of a profound admiration and respect for his work. Unlike previous historians of the period, Holt started not with the king but with a vast amount of research into the histories of baronial and knightly families. He focused on the north because it was the northerners, as they were called at the time, who took the lead in the rebellion that led to Magna Carta. Holt thus gained a unique understanding of the complex ties of lordship, neighbourhood, friendship and family that held together the local society on which John's government impacted. He was also adept at deducing political ideas from statements in letters and law cases. And he expressed himself in what were often pithy and epigrammatic sentences: 'Sometimes Magna Carta stated law. Sometimes it stated what its supporters hoped would become law. Sometimes it stated what they pretended was law. As a party manifesto it made a party case with scant regard for fact or existing practice.'[8]

The impact and authority of Holt's work was such that for many years little was written about Magna Carta by anyone else. Indeed, when Holt brought out a second edition of *Magna Carta* in 1992, the major addition, a chapter on justice and jurisdiction, was the result of his own research.[9] Knowing a second edition was on the way, I had myself sent Holt a small list of mistakes that I had found in the first edition. A postcard came back in reply pointing out that I had got the date of John's death wrong in my *Minority of Henry III* (1990)! Nonetheless, when the second edition appeared, Holt did thank me in the preface for correcting errors 'which were still buried deep in the first edition'.

Reading the second edition, I was struck by the account of events at Runnymede, as I had not been for some reason before, although it was much the same as in the first edition. Holt (in common with many historians) took the view that 15 June 1215 was not the true date of Magna Carta. Instead he thought it was only finalized four days later on 19 June. I felt this hypothesis was mistaken, and the first chapter of my *Reign of Henry III* (1996) sought to vindicate the 15 June date. Let us hope I am right about that, otherwise the celebrations in 2015 will climax on the wrong day. Chapter 2 of *The Reign of Henry III* went on to offer a critique of Holt's new chapter on justice and jurisdiction. In a letter of reply, Holt, while not saying he agreed, congratulated me on the 'tough thinking' about the date of Magna Carta, and wrote that 'Cheney would have liked this, and Galbraith would have relished it'. High praise indeed! On the other hand, he thought that the chapter on justice and jurisdiction was 'almost totally misconceived as your brighter students will be able to tell you in a moment'. I was not persuaded by his comments, but this is a good example of how historians can look at the same evidence and come to different conclusions.[10]

This book differs from Holt in its interpretation of several individual chapters in the Charter.[11] More significantly, it also gives what is sometimes a very different narrative of the events of 1214–1215, quite apart from the actual date of the Charter. Where Holt was sceptical as to whether there had been a revolutionary meeting of the barons at Bury St Edmunds in 1214, I argue that one certainly did take place, but not at the time usually ascribed to it. I also argue that John was forced to make further concessions at Runnymede, having granted the Charter, something one can only appreciate after establishing its true date. I give a completely new account of how the Charter was implemented in the localities. In addition, I bring out the importance of the Oxford council in July 1215, and suggest it was there that John took the decision to abandon the Charter. The book also offers a fresh perspective on Magna Carta by using it as a window into the nature of, and tensions within, English society in the early thirteenth century.

Some of what I say has depended on new discoveries. I have, I hope, been able to prove that one of the four extant originals of the

1215 Charter, that preserved in the British Library and known as Ci, was sent to Canterbury cathedral, where indeed it remained until it was stolen in the seventeenth century. It should thus be known as the Canterbury Magna Carta. This exciting finding adds to our understanding of how the Charter was distributed and publicized. I have also discovered a copy of a letter in which King John sets out the terms of the treaty that he forced on William the Lion, king of Scots, in 1209. This reveals a stunning fact, hitherto unknown, namely that John was trying to assert overlordship over the Scottish kingdom. The Scottish involvement in Magna Carta and much else about Anglo-Scottish relations in the thirteenth century become clearer in this context. In the course of my research, I have attempted to collect and analyse copies of the 1215 Magna Carta made in the hundred years after Runnymede, something never done before. Many of these turn out to be variant texts, and seem in places to preserve drafts made at Runnymede. They help cast new light both on the course of the negotiations and on how knowledge of the Charter was spread. In Chapter 2, I provide a Latin text and translation of the Charter, which for the first time indicates how the conventional divisions into chapters do not always correspond with the divisions in the four originals.

Since Holt's second edition, much important work has been published about the reign of King John, Magna Carta, and the wider political and social setting. I hope I have put it to good use. We know far more about the Anglo-Norman realm, the scale of royal revenue, the development of parliament, the nature of the knightly class, the role of the king's household knights, the position of women and the structures of magnate power. We also know more about the intellectual climate of the period, to which John's archbishop of Canterbury, Stephen Langton, himself made a notable contribution. There is much about Langton in this book.

I owe a great debt to the Magna Carta Project, funded by the Arts and Humanities Research Council: http://magnacarta.cmp. uea.ac.uk. Its 'Principal Investigator', to use the official term, is Nicholas Vincent, of the University of East Anglia (UEA), while the co-investigators are Paul Brand of All Souls College, Oxford, Louise Wilkinson of Canterbury Christ Church University and David Carpenter of King's College London, that is to say myself. The original 'Researchers' were Hugh Doherty and Henry Summerson, with Hugh being replaced by Sophie Ambler on his appointment to a lectureship at UEA. The British Library is also involved, where Claire Breay and Julian Harrison are organizing a great Magna Carta exhibition for 2015. One focus of the project's research is to collect, analyse and publish on the project's website all the original charters and letters of King John, scattered as they are across many archives in Britain and abroad. Several hundred of these have now been found. Nicholas Vincent has also discovered, this time as a copy rather than an original, a baronial letter from 1215 that I have used extensively in my chapter on the enforcement of the Charter. The discovery was made one wet Friday afternoon in the Lambeth Palace Library, and I was lucky enough, through Nick's email, to get there in time to see it with him. A memorable moment! Another focus of the project is to write the first chapter-by-chapter commentary on the 1215 Charter since W. S. McKechnie's in 1905, and the first chapter-by-chapter commentary ever on the definitive Charter of 1225. The bulk of the work here is being done by Henry Summerson, and his commentaries are likewise appearing on the project's website. Henry and I have not always agreed about the meaning and significance of individual chapters, but, as my footnotes show, I am hugely indebted to his commentaries both for information and for interpretation. Many other scholars have helped by giving their advice on individual points and by reading sections and chapters of the book. I thank them all at the appropriate place.

Many celebratory events for the 800th anniversary of the Charter in 2015 have been planned and coordinated by the Magna Carta 800th Committee, chaired by Sir Robert Worcester: http://magnacarta800th.com/magna-carta-today/the-magna-carta-800th-committe. Much historical work, explaining the significance of the Charter, has been done by Nigel Saul of Royal Holloway College, and I have often been helped and entertained by discussing matters with him. Parliament's own celebrations in 2015 both for Magna Carta and for the 750th anniversary of the 1265 parliament of Simon de Montfort have been organized by Caterina Loriggio. I have been lucky enough to be on the relevant Speaker's Advisory Committee chaired by Lord Bew and Sir Peter Luff.

At Penguin I owe a great debt to my commissioning editor, Simon Winder, and to Anna Hervé, editorial manager of the Penguin Classics series, and Penelope Vogler, publicist. I am also greatly indebted to my copy-editor, Richard Mason, and to the proofreader Stephan Ryan. The book could not have been written without the

MA students at King's College London who have taken my MA course on Magna Carta over the years. Many of the ideas and approaches in the book have been developed and tested in our discussions.

David Carpenter
King's College London
June 2014

NOTES

1. See 'Magna Carta repeals': http://www.legislation.gov.uk/aep/ EdwIcc1929/25/9/contents. Chapters 39 and 40 of the 1215 Charter became chapter 29 of the definitive Magna Carta of 1225. The latter appears on the statute book in Edward I's confirmation of 1297. The other chapters still on the statute book are chapter 1, giving freedom to the church and announcing the concessions to the realm, and chapter 9, protecting the liberties and customs of London and those of other cities, boroughs, towns and ports, including the Cinque Ports. Although the other chapters have been repealed, this was often because, as Richard Godden has pointed out to me, their contents were covered by later legislation.

2. Thompson, *First Century*, pp. 90–92; Holt, *Magna Carta* (1992), pp. 9–10.

3. For the use of *homo* in this sense see *Glanvill*, p. 106, a reference I owe to John Gillingham.

4. This later history of the Charter is fully explored in the British Library's Magna Carta exhibition of 2015.

5. The *Guardian*, 5 November 2005: http://www.theguardian.com/ politics/2005/nov/05/terrorism.terrorism.

6. In the cards he sent me, John, who was a kind but quite shy man, avoided, or so I thought, signing off either as 'John' or as 'John Mason', by always scrawling his initials 'JFAM'.

7. Warren, *King John*, p. xiv.

8. Holt, *Magna Carta* (1965), p. 205; *Magna Carta* (1992), pp. 300–301.

9. Holt seems to have missed Thomas Keefe's important article 'Henry II and the earls'.

10. John Hudson, in his *Oxford History*, p. 853 note 47, observes that 'overall the differences of [Carpenter's] position and that of Holt are limited'. This is true when it comes to the course of justice under John. The debate chiefly concerned what happened under Henry III.

11. Holt told me he disliked talking of the 'clauses' of the Charter, and I have followed him in speaking of 'chapters'.

Note on the Text

The Text and Translation of Magna Carta

The Latin text and English translation of Magna Carta may be found between pp. 36 and 69.

Glossary of Terms

A glossary of terms found in Magna Carta is placed at the end of the book between pp. 461 and 470. This includes an explanation of pounds, shillings, pence and marks, for which see also p. 26.

References

In the endnotes, works by authors writing in the twelfth and thirteenth centuries appear for the most part under either the name of the author, or, in the case of chronicles where the author is unknown, under the place where the chronicle was written. Occasionally they are also cited under an abbreviated form of the title of the work. Record sources are cited by an abbreviated form of the published title, so *PR* for Pipe Roll and *F* for *Foedera*. Full references to all these sources can be found in the Bibliography. References to unprinted sources are given in full in the endnotes, where BL stands for the British Library and TNA for The National Archives at Kew. Secondary sources are cited by the surname of the author and a short form of the title, italicized in the case of books, placed within inverted commas in the case of articles. Full details may be found in the Bibliography under the name of the author.

Capitalization and Surnames

After some hesitation, I have employed lowercase for offices and institutions: so 'chancellor' and 'chancery'. As for surnames, where they refer to identifiable English places, the place is put in its modern form, preceded by 'of': so Robert of Ropsley (Lincolnshire). However, I have not applied the rule where it conflicts with established usage: so Hubert de Burgh not Hubert of Burgh (Norfolk). Where places cannot readily be identified (at least by me), I have used a contemporary form, preceded by 'de': so Laurence de Tybridge. Identifiable places in France are likewise put in their modern form, preceded by 'de': so Engelard de Cigogné (dép. Indre-et-Loire).

MAGNA CARTA

Magna Carta: The Documents

Magna Carta is a document approximately 3,550 words long, written in Latin.[1] 'Magna Carta' means in English 'Great Charter'. It was the Norman Conquest that replaced English with Latin as the language of record. Latin was thus the language of the huge number of documents produced by the government of King John. It was also the language of the monastic chroniclers who wrote the history of his reign. For the official version of Magna Carta to have been in other than Latin would have been inconceivable.[2]

Latin was not, however, the normal spoken language either of King John or of the barons and knights who shaped the course of events in 1215. That was French. In order to broadcast the Charter to such an audience, it was quickly translated into French, thus bringing us closest to the language used during the negotiations at Runnymede before it was turned by clerks into the lapidary Latin of the Charter. A later translation shows how Magna Carta was described in French: 'la graunt chartre des fraunchises' – 'the great charter of liberties'.[3] It was likewise in French that the two accounts of John's reign designed directly for consumption by the lay aristocracy were written.[4] It is here that one comes closest to the actual language used by King John, his remarks at turns cutting, at turns conciliatory, often fixing attention by a direct address or by the use of his favourite oath, 'Segnour ...', 'Ha, Robiert', 'par les denz Dieu' ('by the teeth of God').[5]

This does not mean that John and his nobles were ignorant of Latin, making the Charter, in its official form, a closed book to all but churchmen. John's father, Henry II, according to his clerk Walter Map, spoke Latin as well as French and was for practical purposes 'litteratus', which certainly meant he could read. The same was probably true of John and many of his barons and knights.[6] Barons might also speak English, at least to communicate with their social inferiors. Among the knights, English sat alongside French as a naturally spoken language. The peasantry, who formed the great bulk of the population, were exclusive English speakers. It indicates the circles in which the Charter moved that it was translated into French both in 1215 and several times later in the thirteenth century. It was not until 1300, as far as the evidence goes, that the Charter was proclaimed in English. The first written English translations only appear in the sixteenth century.[7]

WHENCE THE NAME MAGNA CARTA?

King John never described the charter that he issued at Runnymede in June 1215 as 'magna carta'. Nor, at the time, did anyone else. In the document itself and in letters issued soon afterwards, John spoke simply of his 'carta' ('charter'). So did the English bishops when they issued a letter authenticating the final text. When, in 1216, the rebel John de Lacy surrendered to the king, he forswore 'the charter of liberties which the lord king has granted in common to the barons of England'.[8] Contemporary chroniclers wrote in exactly the same terms.[9] How, then, did the term 'magna carta' come into being? The answer is that it came into being as a result of a clerk's second thought.

In November 1217, at the end of the civil war, the minority government of John's son, Henry III, issued a new version of the 1215 Charter, one that amended the version it had issued at the start of the reign in 1216. Alongside the new Charter, it also published a quite separate charter regulating the running of the royal forest. Some months later, in February 1218, the government ordered the two charters to be proclaimed throughout the country. No original of this order is known to survive, but a copy was made on the chancery close roll. As it first appeared there, the order reminded the sheriffs (the king's local agents) of a new clause 'at the end' which stipulated that all the unauthorized castles built during the war should be destroyed:

> you are to cause the charters to be observed in all points, and you are
> especially to implement, without any delay, what is placed at the end
> concerning the destruction of unauthorized castles, built or rebuilt

after the beginning of the war, according to what is contained in the
greater charter [*in maiori carta*].

Here the term 'greater charter' was being used to distinguish
Henry III's 1217 version of the 1215 Charter from the shorter
Charter of the Forest. The text in the close roll did not, however,
remain like this, for very soon afterwards the clerk made an alter-
ation. At the end of the entry, he crossed out 'in the greater charter'
('in maiori carta') and wrote instead 'in the same charter'. This
referred back to an insertion that he had made above the line
between 'at the end' and 'concerning the destruction of unauthorized castles'. The insertion was 'magne carte', which was 'magna
carta' in the genitive case, hence 'of magna carta'. The passage
about the castles was thus to be found 'at the end of magna carta'.
   The text now ran:

> you are to cause the charters to be observed in all points, and you are
> especially to implement, without any delay, what is placed at the end
> of magna carta concerning the destruction of unauthorized castles,
> built or rebuilt after the beginning of the war, according to what is con-
> tained in the same charter.

Almost certainly, the explanation for this change is that the clerk
was working from a draft of the order, which was subsequently
altered, and so he altered his copy to bring it into line. It is, therefore,
a scribal insertion above a line in the chancery rolls, prompted by
the second thoughts of a drafting clerk, that the name Magna Carta
enters history. It appeared not to proclaim the greatness of the
document but to distinguish it from its smaller Forest Charter
brother.[10]
   The future of the term 'magna carta' (it was rarely capitalized)
was far from assured. In 1225, when Henry III issued new versions of both charters, he did nothing to insert the term 'magna
carta' into the larger one. Instead he simply called it, as before, 'our
charter'. Thus, although the Charter of 1225 became the final and
definitive version of Magna Carta, the one with legal force, the
name by which it became known to history never actually appeared
in the document at all. Its establishment depended entirely on how
the Charter was described elsewhere. Here initially 'magna carta',
as the preferred term, had to vie with the 'maior carta' ('greater

charter') initially used in 1218. Thus the Charter of the Forest, in its 1225 version, referred to the liberties conceded not in 'magna carta' but 'in maiori carta'. Likewise, in a proclamation of 1225 the government referred to the liberties 'in the greater charter' and 'in the lesser charter' – 'in maiori carta', 'in minori carta'.[11] Neither 'maior carta' nor 'magna carta', however, seems to have penetrated the minds of contemporary chroniclers when they mentioned the Charters of 1225. At St Albans abbey, Roger of Wendover described one as a charter of 'common liberties' and the other as a charter about 'the liberties of the forest'.[12]

The term 'magna carta', however, remained in the field and gradually conquered. Henry III himself, in a letter of 1225 to the bishop of Durham, referred to the liberties conceded in 'our magna carta'.[13] In 1237, when Henry confirmed the Charters of 1225, he described them as his 'magna carta' and his 'charter of the forest'.[14] In the same way, Matthew Paris, who had by then taken over from Roger of Wendover as the chronicler at St Albans abbey, wrote of the king promising to maintain 'the liberties of magna carta'.[15] When the 1225 Charters were again confirmed in 1253, with the bishops solemnly excommunicating all who transgressed them, the term 'magna carta' is found in general use in both government proclamations and the accounts of chroniclers.[16] It was not universal. Contemporaries continued to speak of 'the charter of common liberties' or just the 'charter of liberties'.[17] Nonetheless, in 1297 and 1300, when Edward I confirmed again the 1225 Charters in widely circulated letters, he referred to 'the magna carta of the lord Henry, formerly king of England, our father, about the liberties of England'. A clerk at the exchequer drew a splendid picture of Edward, imposing in his crown, with a straight nose and big jaw, pointing to his order 'for the observance of the great charter' – 'pro magna carta observanda'.[18] The term 'magna carta' was now firmly fixed in the public mind. By this time too, one may be sure, 'great' was no longer simply a way of distinguishing it from the Forest Charter. It referred to the greatness of the Charter itself.

This gradual establishment of the term 'magna carta' was, however, establishment for the Charter of Henry III. 'Magna carta' was very rarely applied to the Charter of King John. Instead, when it was copied in the thirteenth century the latter document was given such titles as 'the charter of Runnymede', 'the provisions of Runnymede', 'the charter of King John which is called Runnymede', or indeed simply 'Runnymede'. In this, it was being brought into line with other legislation that was often associated with its place of issue. Thus legal collections might begin with 'the provisions of Runnymede', continue with Henry III's 'magna carta', and then have the statutes of Merton (1236), Marlborough (1267), Westminster (1275) and so on.

Against this tide confining the term 'magna carta' to the Charter of Henry III, there were, in the thirteenth century, just a few contrary streams. The chief was at St Albans abbey, where Roger of Wendover took the view, in fact erroneous, that Henry III's Charter of 1225 was identical to John's of 1215. This seemed all the more the case since the only text of the Charter that Wendover provided was one issued in John's name, although in fact it was a conflation of the Charters of 1215, 1217 and 1225. Likewise Wendover, or his source, had concocted a version of the Forest Charter which had it granted by John, rather than by Henry III.[19] It was hardly surprising, therefore, that in the 1250s Matthew Paris could describe the 1225 Charter as the 'magna carta of King John, which King Henry III swore to uphold . . .'.[20] It was doubtless in the same spirit that the Articles of the Barons (a precursor of Magna Carta) were catalogued in the muniments of the archbishop of Canterbury as 'the articles of the magna carta of liberties under the seal of King John'.[21]

These contrary views, did not, however, have much immediate purchase. The St Albans' texts, which contained Wendover's version of John's Magna Carta and of his Charter of the Forest, had very little circulation. Instead, the work by Wendover and Paris that did gain wide currency was the *Flores Historiarum*. This certainly had Henry, in the 1250s, confirming the 'magna carta which King John conceded', but the impact was rather lessened by the omission of any reference to John's Charter from the accounts of either 1215 or 1225, as also by the failure to provide any texts of the Charters at all.[22] The general view, exemplified by the lawyers of the Tudor period, remained that Magna Carta had begun with Henry III.[23]

It was in the later part of the sixteenth century that all this changed. In 1571 Archbishop Parker published Matthew Paris's *Chronica Majora*, which for John's reign was essentially Wendover's chronicle with Paris's additions. This exposed the historians Stowe and Holinshed, and the lawyers Coke and Selden, to the view that John's Charter was the same as Henry III's. For those reading Paris and Wendover, therefore, there appeared to be only one Magna Carta, that of King John. It had been conceived as a bulwark against John's tyranny. Now, it could be a bulwark against the tyranny of the Stuarts.

It was not until the work of the lawyer William Blackstone, published in 1759, that the versions of the Charter issued in 1215, 1216, 1217 and 1225 were finally distinguished, and their separate texts established. In the process, Blackstone showed that John had never issued a 'Charter of the Forest'. Blackstone, however, made no effort to deprive John's Charter of the name and status of 'Magna Carta'. His transcription of John's Charter was headed in capital letters 'MAGNA CARTA REGIS JOHANNIS'. Subsequent historians have all followed his lead, without feeling much need for excuse or even explanation. Indeed, the Charter of Henry III, which once held centre stage, has dropped into the background, receiving nothing like the study devoted to the Charter of King John. W. S. McKechnie's *Magna Carta*, first published in 1905, was thus, as the subtitle stated, 'A commentary on the Great Charter of King John'. So was J. C. Holt's classic *Magna Carta*, which was first published in 1965 to coincide with the 750th anniversary. This book is no different. It too places the 1215 Charter centre stage. Technically, to be sure, there was no 'Magna Carta' in 1215. The name had yet to be invented. Yet without the Charter of 1215, there would have been no subsequent versions and no definitive version of 1225. While the latter is not identical with John's Charter, it retains a large proportion of its contents. Contemporaries themselves recognized the importance of the 1215 Charter, for they copied it many times in the thirteenth century. When Matthew Paris finally obtained an authentic text, he strove to correct the botched version he had found in Wendover. When he described the Charter of 1225 as 'the magna carta of King John, which King Henry III swore to uphold', he was technically incorrect, but right in spirit. The Charter of 1215 is deservedly hallowed by the name Magna Carta.

THE AUTHORIZED TEXT

Was there a final, authorized text of Magna Carta in 1215? No such text was recorded on the rolls of the chancery to which we have referred, although they had reams of other business from

1215. Yet a final, authorized text there was. At the end of the Charter, John declared that the bishops would issue 'letters patent testimonial' to the 'aforesaid concessions'. These letters testimonial were in fact letters affirming and guaranteeing the final, authentic text of the Charter. We know this because, although no originals survive, one did reside in the royal exchequer in the early fourteenth century, when it was copied into a volume of important documents known as 'The Red Book of the Exchequer'.[24] The letter, as recorded there, was issued in the name of the archbishop of Canterbury, Stephen Langton, the archbishop of Dublin, six other bishops, and Master Pandulf, the representative of the pope. This imposing body of ecclesiastics had featured at the start of the Charter in the list of those on whose advice John said that he had acted. They now made public their 'inspection' of the Charter 'under this form', the whole text of the Charter being then set out. The aim of the inspection was made clear in the conclusion to the letter: 'so that nothing can be added or taken away or diminished from the foresaid form, we have placed our seals to this writing'.[25] The copyist of the letters testimonial made a few mistakes in his transcription. One was particularly silly, for he wrote of all who 'wish' ('voluerint') to swear to support the Charter being compelled to do so, instead of all who 'do not wish' ('noluerint').[26] Elsewhere, however, he was careful to correct his slips, so adding 'letters' above the line to correct an omission in chapter 14 and squeezing in the 'or' ('aut') that he had omitted in chapter 40. We can be confident that the letters testimonial of the bishops, bar a few obvious mistakes, preserve the final, authorized text of the Charter.

THE ENGROSSMENT AND SEALING
OF THE CHARTER

Although there was a single authorized text, there was no single original Magna Carta. Rather, John issued a number of originals, all with equal status. It is usual to call these originals 'engrossments', an engrossment being a document written out (or engrossed) so as to make a formal and legal record of a transaction. It is thus distinct from what is simply a copy of such a document, which in itself has no authority. John ended the Charter with the statement that it had been 'Given by our hand in the meadow which is called Runnymede, between Windsor and Staines, on the fifteenth day of June, in the seventeenth year of our reign'. The 'given by the hand' formula – 'data per manum' in the Latin – was usual in royal charters, and indicated when, where and by whom authorization had been given for the final engrossment. So John authorized Magna Carta at Runnymede on 15 June in the seventeenth year of his reign, which was 15 June 1215.[27] The engrossment was followed by the sealing, which gave the Charter its final authentication. One of the most often repeated errors about Magna Carta is that it was 'signed' by King John. The vision of John working his way through a pile of Magna Cartas, grimly scribbling his name at the end, is certainly attractive, but it is a fantasy. Royal documents at this time did not receive the king's sign-manual. Magna Carta, like all royal charters, was validated by attaching the king's seal, not his signature. It was the seal that distinguished the original engrossments from simple copies, accurate or otherwise. As the chronicler Ralph of Coggeshall put it, the Charters were 'of one tenor validated by the royal seal'.[28]

The sealing itself was the work of a special official, the bearer of the seal. He would have placed the silken cords or parchment tongue, with which the seal was to be attached to each Charter, into the sealing apparatus along with the soft wax that came in a variety of colours – white, green, red, yellow. The apparatus was then tightened so that it pressed the wax between the two halves of the silver deal die, and produced John's magnificent double-sided seal. The apparatus itself and its operator do indeed appear in some modern depictions of the scene at Runnymede.

THE NUMBER OF CHARTERS
AND THE SURVIVING ORIGINALS

Almost certainly some engrossments of the Charter were immediately written out and sealed. At the very least the baronial negotiators needed one as proof of their achievements. In the days and weeks that followed, more engrossments were produced for distribution around the country, a process which was still going on as late as 22 July. Just how many there ultimately were is a matter of debate.

If, as could be argued, each county got an engrossment, along with London and the Cinque Ports, then there were around forty Charters, beyond those made immediately at Runnymede. If on the other hand (as is argued in Chapter 12), the Charter was distributed not to the counties but to the bishoprics, the number produced was much smaller, being something upwards of thirteen.

Historians have long accepted that four original engrossments survive of the 1215 Charter. Two of these are now displayed in the British Library and were part of the stupendous collection of medieval documents made in the seventeenth century by Sir Robert Cotton. These are conventionally known as Ci and Cii. The other two engrossments are preserved at Lincoln and Salisbury, and belong to the cathedral archives. Like most documents in this period, all four Charters were written on parchment, a writing material prepared, by an elaborate process, from sheepskin. The four are different in shape and size. Ci and Salisbury are taller than they are broad. They thus have more but shorter lines of text than Cii and Lincoln, which are broader than they are tall. To be exact, Ci has 86 lines, Salisbury 76 lines, Cii 52 lines, and Lincoln (the most nearly square) 54 lines.[29] No particular significance attaches to these differences in dimension. It was normal for royal charters, and indeed for later versions of Magna Carta, to be issued in different shapes and sizes. Probably the clerks either took whatever size of parchment was at hand, or cut it themselves into the size with which they felt most comfortable.

The reasons for deeming the four Charters authentic are threefold. First, all are written in hands compatible with a date in the early thirteenth century; second, all have texts in their essentials the same as that found in the letters testimonial of the bishops; and third, and most important, all have evidence of sealing.

It has been asserted that Ci and Cii are the work of the same scribe, but this plainly is not the case.[30] In fact, all four Charters had different scribes, which is not surprising given the length of the document, and the numbers that had to be produced. According to a calculation by J. C. Fox, based on the testimony of 'an experienced law stationer' about rates of copying 'in an old engrossing hand', the Charter would have taken about eight hours to write out.[31] Ci, Cii and Lincoln are all in hands typical of clerks working in King John's chancery. The clerks were using, however, not the most formal chancery hand, such as that found in some royal charters, but one a step down, a quicker, more 'cursive' hand (to use the technical term for it) – again not surprising given the amount they had to write out. It may be that when the Magna Carta Project's collection of original King John charters has been completed and sifted, the hands of the three Magna Carta scribes will reappear in that corpus. They may also be found elsewhere, for such hands were certainly not confined to the royal chancery. The hand in the Salisbury Charter is different from those in the other three Charters. It is far more 'bookish' in form, being similar to those found in texts such as bibles and psalters, as opposed to royal documents. This, however, is no reason to doubt its authenticity, as has occasionally been done.[32] It would not be surprising, under the pressure of business after Magna Carta, if the king's clerks called in or were made to accept outside help. Of the four Charters, Lincoln's (in my view) is the most finely written. It is the only one where the clerk elegantly spaced out the words on the last line (as was sometimes done in royal charters) so as to make that line complete. In all the other examples, part of the last line is left blank. After the Lincoln Charter, simply as a work of art (as many royal charters are), comes Ci, and then the more workaday Cii. The Salisbury hand is the most formal and thus, to my mind, the least idiosyncratic and engaging.

The texts of the four originals are, as we have said, in their essentials identical. The variations are recorded in the notes to the Latin text of the Charter, which is given in the next chapter.[33] The most obvious difference is that the scribes of Ci and Cii mistakenly omitted some short passages, and had to write these in at the bottom of the Charter with an indication as to where they should go. There are three such corrections in Cii, and five in Ci, three of which overlap with those in Cii. The two original to Ci may be no more than the scribe correcting his own mistakes, but the three corrections that the two Charters have in common presumably arose from their being copied from a similarly misleading draft. A collation of the texts again shows the Salisbury Charter to be the odd one out, since it has over thirty readings not found in the other engrossments, over twice as many as in the Lincoln Charter, which has the next highest score. Nearly all Salisbury's differences, however, like Lincoln's, are minor and do not affect the sense. They arise from such things as the insertion or omission of individual words like 'et' and 'de', from variations in word order and from differences in tense, Salisbury often preferring the future indicative to the present subjunctive. There are only three mistakes in Salisbury which verge on the significant: namely the omission of 'elongatus' ('dispossessed') from chapter 57; the omission of the name of Henry, archbishop of Dublin, from chapter 62; and the statement, in chapter 61, probably through a slip of the pen, that breaches of the Charter should be referred to the king's justices, rather than his justiciar. None of these were as serious as the mistakes in Ci and Cii, and, if they were spotted, they were evidently considered not worth correcting. If the other variations were down to Salisbury's scribe, as opposed to being found in the draft from which he was working, they are no more than might be expected from an outsider unused to routine copying of royal documents. The overall impression is that all four engrossments were written carefully and with a proper sense of the Charter's importance. Certainly it was not a case of the scribes all going in different directions. Thus when either the Lincoln or Salisbury Charter did go it alone, the other engrossments and the bishops' copy nearly always agree against them.

We now come to the most important feature of the Charters, when it comes to judging their authenticity, namely their sealing.[34] Here Ci stands above the others. It is the only one that has preserved its seal, albeit now reduced by a fire in 1731 to no more than a diminished and featureless roundel of wax. The Cottonian sub-librarian, however, testified that he had seen the seal before the fire and recognized it as indeed King John's. The end of the parchment tongue that attached the seal to the Charter still protrudes from the wax, although the current attachment is the result of repair. The Lincoln Charter has no surviving seal but, by an arrangement so as to bear the weight of the seal, which is found in other royal charters (and probably once in Ci), the parchment is folded at the bottom. In the centre of the fold there are three holes in the form of a pyramid through which the cords holding the seal once ran. In the case of Salisbury, the seal was probably attached to the Charter by cords hanging from two holes rather than three. This would explain the two gashes in the parchment at the bottom of the Charter, which were made, one may suppose, when the seal was removed by a clumsy wrench. The Salisbury Charter has no fold, but that may well have been trimmed off at some point after the seal was removed.

Finally Cii. Here there is evidence of sealing because at the bottom of the Charter, in the centre, there is a slit, through which the seal tag would have run. The seal was thus attached in the same way as in Ci, rather than with the cords of the Lincoln and Salisbury Charters. Given its current situation, there is certainly insufficient parchment beneath the slit in Cii to create a fold for bearing the weight of the tag with the seal, but we have to remember that the Charter was probably cropped when it was bound into a volume of the Cotton collection.[35] Ci also has two smaller slits at its base, to the right of the central slit that had the tag. 'From their appearance,' Fox wrote, 'they might . . . be taken for the work of John's own hand – stabs with a knife or a dagger – the visible evidence of his fury against the barons.' They are, disappointingly, far more likely to be the result of incisions made by Robert Cotton's bookbinder.[36]

What of the origins and history of the four originals? The Lincoln Charter has 'LINCOLNIA' written twice on its back. Since the hand seems the same as that which wrote the actual text, this suggests the Charter was destined for Lincoln from the start. That it was kept in the cathedral archives is indicated by shelf marks on its back. It is also very likely to have been the source for the copy of the 1215 Charter found in the cathedral's fourteenth-century register.[37] The Lincoln Charter, more recently, has had an adventurous, not to say dangerous, time. It was sent to the USA in 1939 for the New York World Fair and, trapped across the Atlantic by the outbreak of hostilities, was exhibited at the Library of Congress in Washington. A scheme to give the Charter permanently to the USA having fallen through, it was returned to Lincoln after the war. It was subsequently toured around Australia, in the hope that it would make money for Lincoln cathedral. Since no money was made and the cathedral ended up in debt, Lincoln was perhaps lucky to get the Charter back. Before one of its last trips, I myself saw the specially made bomb-proof container in which it was to wing its way again across the Atlantic. The Lincoln Charter is now displayed not in the cathedral but in the castle, thus ending up ironically in the one place in 1215 where (as we will see) it was not meant to go.

The Salisbury Charter has had a less exciting history. It has no destination mark on its back, but seems to have remained in the cathedral archives throughout its history, although for a period no one could find it. As a result it did not contribute to the official text of the Magna Carta published in the *Statutes of the Realm* in

1810. It is now displayed in the chapter house as the centre of a Magna Carta exhibition.

We know virtually nothing about the provenance of Cii, save that Cotton acquired it in 1629 from a barrister, Humphrey Wyems.[38] Cotton's second Charter, Ci, is quite another matter.

THE CANTERBURY MAGNA
CARTA REVEALED

In May 1630, Sir Edward Dering wrote to Cotton from Dover castle (where he was lieutenant) as follows:

> I haue heere yᵉ Charter of K. John dat. att Running Meade: by yᵉ first safe and sure messenger itt is your's. So are yᵉ Saxon charters, as fast as I can coppy them: but in yᵉ meane time I will close K. John in a boxe and send him.[39]

If only an original of Magna Carta, let alone John himself, could be obtained so easily in a box today! At the Sotheby's New York auction in 2007, an engrossment of the 1225 Charter in Edward I's confirmation of 1297 fetched $21,321,000. The subsequent history of Ci has been sad indeed. Cii, Lincoln and Salisbury are all in reasonable condition, and perfectly legible, despite the darkened cabinets in which perforce they have now to live. Ci is quite different. It was first of all caught up in the great fire that swept through the Cotton collection in 1731. This, however, left the text perfectly legible, as is clear from an engraving made and marketed by John Pine in 1733, where the charter was attractively surrounded by the 'hand-coloured' shields of the Magna Carta barons. Despite his commercial interest and acumen, there is no reason to suppose that Pine's engraving was other than accurate. Indeed it was certified as such at the time, when only nine letters in the main text had to be supplied by reference to Cii.[40] The chief damage seems to have been to the seal, which appears featureless, although Pine's engraving shows it was then red, as opposed to its current darkish hue. All thus might have been well but for further intervention in 1834. The villain of the piece here, exposed by Andrew Prescott, was the restorer Hogarth. It was almost certainly his misplaced efforts that reduced Ci to no more than a parchment sheet on which hardly a single word is readily discernible.[41] How fortunate then that the text lives on in Pine's lovely engraving, showing Ci to have been, despite its corrections, a really beautiful exemplar of the Charter.

The fact that Ci was sent to Cotton from Dover castle has led to repeated suggestions that it was an engrossment despatched to the Cinque Ports, of which of course Dover was one. This idea seemed supported by the fact that a letter in John's name, dated 19 June 1215, was indeed sent to the officials of the Cinque Ports informing them of the peace 'which you can see from our charter, which we have ordered to be read and obeyed in your bailiwick'. The implication is that the officials of the Cinque Ports, like the sheriffs to whom the letter was also sent, were to receive engrossments of the Charter. In fact, however, there are reasons to believe that this never happened. Even if it had, Ci was not the Charter that was sent to the Ports. Instead its destination was Canterbury cathedral. The possibility that Ci had a Canterbury provenance was first put to me by Julian Harrison and Nicholas Vincent, this on the grounds that Sir Edward Dering had certainly obtained the Anglo-Saxon charters (which he likewise mentioned in his letter to Cotton) from that source.[42] Following up this suggestion, I had a brainwave, namely that of collating Ci, as found in the Pine engraving, with the copy of the 1215 Charter preserved in the late thirteenth-century Register E of Canterbury cathedral, a register that is still in the cathedral archives.[43] Was there any evidence that the text in Register E was copied from Ci? If there was, it would come close to proving that Ci was in the Canterbury archives at least in the late thirteenth century. I had not much hope of any very conclusive results, but I was wrong. As I went through the Charter it became clearer and clearer that the text in Register E was indeed copied from Ci.

The evidence is set out in Appendix II. It turns on certain mistakes and oddities in the E text, which are readily explicable if it was copied from Ci. Most conclusive of all is the passage where the scribe of E got to one of the sections in which Ci had omitted some words from its text and had added them in at the bottom. Here E's scribe became confused over just what needed to be included, and copied in text from the bottom of Ci belonging to a different insertion. He then realized his error, and had to start the passage all over again. These and other indications come close to proving that E was copied from Ci and thus, as I say, that Ci was in the archives of Canterbury cathedral in the late thirteenth century. One can offer several hypotheses as to how it got there, but by far the most likely is that it was sent there in 1215 itself, just as the engrossments now at Lincoln and Salisbury were probably despatched to their cathedrals. If this is right, three of the four known originals of the 1215 Charter were preserved from the start at cathedrals. The significance of this form of distribution we will discuss in Chapter 12.

THE UNKNOWN CHARTER AND
THE ARTICLES OF THE BARONS

What historians call the 'Unknown Charter' is a list of concessions said to have been made by King John. They are undated but probably represent baronial demands put together in the immediate period before Magna Carta. The name the 'Unknown Charter' derives from the document being indeed unknown to English historians before 1893. The Unknown Charter survives on a single sheet of parchment now preserved in the Archives Nationales in Paris, where it is classified as J.655. On the sheet, it follows a copy of the charter issued by Henry I after his coronation in 1100.[44] Both the Coronation charter and the Unknown Charter are written by the same scribe, who made some errors in both texts, some of which he corrected. Although it cannot be proved, my feeling is that he was copying a document in which the two were already together. As we will see, the Coronation Charter itself played a very important part in the build-up of baronial demands in 1214–15. Just when the copy was made we cannot know, but the hand, an everyday business one, is certainly compatible with a date in 1215 or soon afterwards. It is not at all impossible that the document entered the French royal archives as part of the material taken out of England by Prince Louis after he gave up his claim to the English throne in 1217.[45] Whatever the truth here, there is no reason to doubt the Unknown Charter's authenticity. Its twelve chapters are important evidence for the development of baronial demands in 1215. Doubtless there were other, similar schedules now lost. By the time negotiations began at Runnymede, however, all these had been consolidated into one comprehensive document, the Articles of the Barons.

The Articles of the Barons survive as an original document. By the middle of the thirteenth century, they were in the archives of the archbishop of Canterbury. Probably they were taken from Runnymede by Archbishop Langton himself.[46] The Articles remained in the archiepiscopal archives until the fall of Archbishop Laud in 1640, when with other documents they were spirited away to prevent their capture by his parliamentary enemies. After various travels, which they were lucky to survive, they finally reached the British Museum in 1769. They are now on display in the British Library alongside the Library's two originals of the 1215 Charter, Cii, and Ci or the Canterbury Charter as we will now call it. The Articles of the Barons consist of a single sheet of parchment with the heading 'These are the chapters which the Barons seek and the lord King concedes'. What 'concedes' really meant in this context we will discuss later. That John had, however, agreed the Articles in some way was made clear by one vital feature, a feature that gave them an authority which the Unknown Charter completely lacked. This was that, although not couched in any way as a formal charter issued in John's name, the Articles nonetheless bore his seal. This was attached by a parchment tongue inserted into the fold at the bottom of the document, much as was the case in Cii and the Cantebury Charter. The seal, made of white wax, is now detached and displayed separately. However, it was in place in an early nineteenth-century engraving. Judging from the hand, the Articles could have been written out by one of John's chancery clerks, although, as we have said, such hands are not exclusive to the chancery. The precise point at which John agreed the Articles is unknown, for the document is undated, but it was probably on 10 June, at the start of the final negotiations at Runnymede.[47]

Underneath the heading, proclaiming John's consent, the Articles contained forty-eight separate chapters, unnumbered but each beginning a new line, distinguished by a paragraph mark. These take up seventy-four lines. Then, after a four-line gap, there follows the security clause, in which twenty-five barons are permitted to force John to keep the Charter. This takes up another fourteen lines, making eighty-eight in all. Some of the chapters are couched in terms of what the king shall or shall not do. Others just state what is to be without reference to the king (so 'justice' is not to be denied). The Articles were the foundation for Magna Carta. All forty-eight of the chapters have corresponding chapters, or parts of chapters, in Magna Carta, often employing the same or similar phraseology.

COPIES OF THE 1215 MAGNA CARTA:
THE SURVIVAL OF DRAFTS

The Charter of King John was copied many times in the century after its concession. It is found (in whole or part) in chronicles, monastic cartularies and unofficial compilations made by lawyers of legislation and other legal texts known as statute books. Sometimes the copy was made, as in the case of Canterbury's Register E, from an original engrossment; sometimes it was made from another copy. One cannot always be sure which. Not all the copies, however, are of the final, authorized text. Instead, some seem to contain elements from drafts circulating at Runnymede.

One of the earliest copies of the Charter is that preserved in the cartulary of the leper hospital of Saint Giles at Pont-Audemer in Normandy. The copy is remarkable in being that of a French translation of the Charter. The copy itself is in an early thirteenth-century hand and must have been written within a few years of 1215. The translation was probably made in 1215 itself.[48] Another early copy of the Charter was that made by Roger of Wendover at St Albans. It dates to soon after 1225. Wendover did not, however, possess a complete text of the 1215 Charter. He had the beginning and the security clause at the end; for the rest he, or his source, inserted sections from the Charters of 1217 and 1225. Wendover's security clause, moreover, differs from that found in the Charter, notably by placing the castellans of four strategic castles under the orders of the twenty-five barons appointed to enforce the Charter. Wendover does not have a great reputation for accuracy, but he cannot have made this up. In all probability he was using a rival draft of the clause aimed at imposing tougher restrictions on the king.

When Holt brought out the first edition of his *Magna Carta* in 1965, Wendover's version of the security clause was the only known evidence for drafts. This was soon to change. In 1967, V. H. Galbraith published an article about a copy of Magna Carta which he had found in a late thirteenth-century statute book preserved in the Huntington Library in California.[49] This differed from the authorized version of the Charter in various ways and was, so Galbraith argued, in fact a draft. The absolutely key evidence here came in the chapter on fines and amercements, where the phraseology was far closer to that in the Articles of the Barons than it was to that in Magna Carta.[50] Again, this was not something a clerk could have made up. It seemed, therefore, that the Huntington copy preserved a version of the Charter in which some features of the Articles had yet to be changed into the form found in the authorized version of the Charter. Since the Huntington copy was given by the hand of King John on 15 June not at Runnymede but at Windsor, Galbraith argued that it was, in fact, the penultimate draft, being made before John moved later in the day to Runnymede for the last negotiations and the agreement of the final text.

Galbraith, on his return to England from America, seems to have made no effort to follow up his discovery by examining other copies of the Charter. In that sense he was like a tourist who looks at sights abroad but neglects those at home. To be fair, Galbraith had the excuse of age. He had retired from the Regius Chair at Oxford University back in 1955, hoping, vainly as it turned out, that A. J. P. Taylor might be his successor rather than Hugh Trevor-Roper. Holt himself was a great admirer of Galbraith (rightly so), but he too steered clear of the field of copies. In the second edition of his *Magna Carta*, published in 1992, he commented in an Appendix on Galbraith's findings (which he accepted), and observed that 'draft versions of the Charter constitute the most intriguing problem of all'. He also said there could be more of them, but then left it at that.[51]

I cannot claim any particular virtue myself in this area of historical endeavour. I became interested in copies of Magna Carta not to find drafts but to see the different ways in which it was divided up into chapters, the divisions often being more emphatic in copies than in the original engrossments. It was reading through a copy of the Charter in a cartulary of Peterborough abbey, preserved in the Society of Antiquaries in London, with this end in view, that I suddenly noticed chapters in a different order and text in different words from that found in the authorized version.[52] It was only then that I thought of Galbraith and started to compare his Huntington copy with the Peterborough one. Although most of Peterborough's variations were different from Huntington's, they did have one sovereign point in common, namely the text of the chapter on fines and amercements. In the Peterborough copy, as in the Huntington, this manifestly came from the Articles of the Barons rather than Magna Carta. There was also one other chapter (on the dismissal of John's foreign agents) where the Peterborough word order, here unlike Huntington's, seemed closer to that in the Articles than to that in the Charter.

Inspired by this finding, I set out to find more copies of the 1215 Charter with the idea of testing, by word-for-word collation, whether they were in fact copies of the authorized version. One thing quickly became apparent, namely not to trust statements in catalogues, for these sometimes claimed a copy as being of the authorized text when it turned out to be no such thing. Editors evidently had merely glanced at the text, instead of actually reading it through. The search for copies of the 1215 Charter remains ongoing but, at the time of writing, I have found over thirty examples from the hundred years after 1215.[53] Nearly half of these are of the authorized version, barring obvious mistakes. The others are variants, seven associated with St Albans, and one a unique single-sheet copy now in the Bodleian Library. Ten are all linked to the Huntington/Peterborough family through the treatment of the chapter on fines. There is, however, only one incomplete copy which follows Huntington in being 'given' at Windsor rather than at Runnymede on 15 June. All told the copies seem to preserve at least five different versions of the Charter. One cannot, of course, assume that all the variations derive from drafts. Some may be mistakes or improvements made in the process of transmission. Nonetheless, it is noticeable that they often occur in chapters that we know were changed during the negotiations at Runnymede. Arguably, the copies shed new light on the tense and tortuous debates that finally produced the Charter. They certainly suggest that unofficial texts made an important contribution to spreading knowledge about it.

Enough about the copies, illuminating although they may be. Let us now turn to the text of Magna Carta itself.

2

The Chapters, Contents and Text of Magna Carta

THE CHAPTERS OF MAGNA CARTA

Discussion of the contents of Magna Carta hinges on its separate chapters: 'chapter 40 says this', 'chapter 42 says that'. To aid such a discussion, in texts printed today, whether in Latin or in English translation, each chapter is numbered and starts a new paragraph. The original Charter was not like that at all. All the four engrossments were written out as continuous text without any numeration. In this they differed from the Articles of the Barons, where each of the 'capitula', although still unnumbered, began on a new line and started with a sign conventionally used to indicate a new item on a list.

The Charter did not follow this pattern, because there was no tradition of putting new paragraphs into royal charters. What the four engrossments did do, however, was to divide the contents up into what were effectively separate chapters by starting each new one with a prominent capital letter, although this was done less emphatically in the Salisbury Charter, given its formal book hand, than in the others. Sometimes, moreover, capitals of smaller, but still abnormal size, seem to indicate subsections within chapters. These divisions may reflect the way, until a late stage, drafts of the Charter were divided up into separate 'capitula', as in the Articles of the Barons. This in turn would reflect how the negotiations themselves were carried out article by article. When Magna Carta was copied out after 1215, the scribes often made the divisions clearer by starting each chapter on a new line and colouring in its first letter or paragraph marker. Only one attempt, as far as I have discovered, was made in these copies to number the chapters of the Charter and there the effort was abandoned before the end. The numbers were anyway being applied not to the final, authorized version but to one of the variant copies of the Huntington/Peter-borough family.[1]

The key moment in the numbering of the 1215 Charter came with Blackstone. In his book of 1759, he printed the Charter as a continuous text, and did not distinguish the start of new chapters with larger capital letters. But what he did do was to supply numbers to the chapters in the margin of his text, his total being sixty-three. Nearly all the later editions have kept to Blackstone's numbers, although Bishop Stubbs in his *Select Charters* did not divide up the security clause, and thus ended up with only sixty.[2] It is a curious fact, however, never apparently noticed, that Blackstone's chapter divisions do not exactly match up with those in the engrossments of the Charter, as indicated by their capitalization. This was partly because Blackstone had numbered the Articles of the Barons in order to relate the chapters in the Articles to the corresponding chapters in Magna Carta. Where a Magna Carta chapter either broke an Articles chapter into two, or ran two together, Blackstone occasionally ignored this and kept to the Articles' division. Equally, when a new section appeared in the Charter, he sometimes created a chapter for it, as with his chapter 19, even when the engrossments did not do so. Blackstone also made no effort to indicate where the engrossments, if not necessarily starting new chapters, certainly seem to indicate subsections within chapters. The resulting divergences are not of great moment, but are none-theless a pity, for they can obscure what is going on. The engrossments, for example, manifestly break what is chapter 27 in the Articles into two, rightly so because the bearing of the second part is completely changed, and in a way prejudicial to knights and under-tenants. Blackstone, however, presumably to retain the correspondence with the Articles, kept everything together as the Charter's chapter 37. It is, of course, too late now to undo Blackstone's numbering, but I mention the original divisions in the discussion that follows, and also indicate them in my text and trans-lation of the Charter.

Students studying the Charter are sometimes given the task (at least by me) of putting its chapters into a more coherent order. How far the Charter, as it stands, is organized logically is a question we will address when looking at the negotiations at Runnymede and the differences (some made to improve the organization) between the Articles of the Barons and Magna Carta. Here we will indicate briefly, by way of introduction, the Charter's main concerns, the dos and don'ts that it laid down for kingship. Those can be broken down into several broad interlocking areas, with individual chapters often bearing on more than one of them.

The Charter was above all about money. Its overwhelming aim was to restrict the king's ability to take it from his subjects. Another major thrust was in the area of law and justice. The Charter wanted to make the king's dispensation of justice fairer and more accessible, while at the same time preventing his arbitrary and lawless treatment of individuals. Overlapping with both these agendas was the issue of local government. Here the Charter sought to deal with the malpractices of the king's local officials, above all his sheriffs and foresters. There were chapters on London, and towns and trade, while the first chapter of all was on the church, one that arrived at a very late stage in the negotiations, despite coming right at the Charter's start. The Charter, as it hoped, thus set a new course for kingship in the future. It was also about redressing the injustices committed in the past. Several chapters set up procedures for doing that, and included among the beneficiaries both Llywelyn ab Iorwerth, the Welsh ruler of North Wales, and Alexander II, the king of Scots. Much thought went into how John's concessions might be enforced. The 'security clause' at the end of the Charter was easily its longest and most controversial chapter.

The chapters of the Charter set out the 'liberties' being granted by the king to his subjects, hence the way the 1215 Charter, like its successors, was called 'the charter of liberties'. John would have regarded these liberties very much as privileges that he had graciously conceded. His subjects would have baulked at such a description. For them the liberties were more in the nature of rights to which they were very much entitled, often by ancient custom. Indeed, when John conceded to London, in chapter 13, 'all its ancient liberties and free customs', he was manifestly merely conceding what Londoners had already. The issue was also blurred, at the end of the Charter, when John, in chapters 60 and 63, referred to 'these aforesaid customs and liberties' and 'the foresaid liberties, rights and concessions'.

There was one other key feature of the concessions John was making. They were, as he said thrice over, to be held from him and his heirs in perpetuity. The Charter for ever afterwards was to provide the fundamental law for the government of the kingdom.

THE CONTENTS OF MAGNA CARTA

The Preamble

King John started the Charter, having set out his titles, by greeting his subjects. He then fixed their attention (as was usual in royal charters) with a resounding and commanding 'Know', all the engrossments giving a big capital letter to the 'S' at the start of 'Sciatis'. The king went on to explain his reasons for acting, and on whose advice he had acted, after which there followed an impressive list of counsellors – bishops, barons and ministers. It is only at the end of this list (thus making a gigantic sentence) that we find out what John was actually doing.

The Church

'In the first place' – 'In primis' – John granted freedom to the church, demonstrating his good faith in so doing by reference to his earlier concession of freedom to elect bishops and abbots, which had been confirmed by Pope Innocent III. Blackstone naturally made this the first chapter of the Charter.

The New Start

Having privileged the church in this separate section, John then commenced the Charter all over again. 'We have also granted to all the free men of our kingdom, for us and our heirs in perpetuity, all the below written liberties.' Blackstone simply included this in his chapter 1 and it is always printed as such. That is fair enough on the basis of the Lincoln Charter and the copy in the letters testimonial, but the other engrossments have the kind of a capital here (for the 'C' in 'Concessimus', 'We have granted') that indicates the beginning of a new section. Later copies of the Charter went down the same path. This makes sense, for the Charter is clearly now making a new start.

What then were the areas in which John granted liberties to his free men?

Money

The pre-eminent concern, as we have said, was money, and before starting here, a word about money itself. In John's reign there was only one coin, the silver penny, of which there were 240 in the pound. 'Pound' itself was simply a term of account, a way of expressing a sum of money. The same was true both of 'shilling', of which there were twenty in the pound, making each worth twelve pennies, and of 'mark', which was two thirds of a pound, so 160 pennies or thirteen shillings and four pence. The Latin for pound was 'libra', for shilling 'solidus' and for penny 'denarius', hence the abbreviations l.s.d. Pounds, shillings and marks avoided the need for people to talk in large sums of pennies; but since pennies were the only currency, there was no avoiding transporting large numbers of them around, which was often done in great sacks and barrels. In July 1215 John acknowledged receipt of 9,900 marks in sixty-six sacks, which meant there were 24,000 pennies in each.[3] The king's annual revenue at the start of John's reign was around £22,000, or 5,280,000 pennies. John minted many silver pennies but never in his own name. His brother Richard had been equally nameless. Both continued to mint coins that bore on one side the name of their father 'Henry' placed around a sometimes crude image of a royal head. On the other side was a small cross and the name of the moneyer.

Returning then to the Charter, a raft of early chapters, nearly all those between 2 and 14, were concerned to restrict the money-getting operations of royal government. Within this group, chapters 2–8 regulated the highly lucrative rights that came from the tenurial relationship between the king and his earls, barons and other tenants-in-chief. So these chapters were about relief (an inheritance tax), wardships and the marriages of heirs, heiresses and widows. Later in the Charter, chapters 37, 43 and 53 dealt, at least in part, with particular aspects of related rights and demands.

With chapters 10 and 11, the Charter tackled another issue, that of debts owed to the Jews, one point being to prevent them accruing interest during minorities. Here too the king was involved because (as chapter 10 indicated) he might take debts owed the Jews into his own hands and extract the money for himself.

Chapters 12 and 14 were of the greatest importance, for they were about taxation in the form of 'scutages and aids'. Save on three specified occasions, these were only to be levied by 'our common counsel of the kingdom'. The assumption here was that counsel would lead to consent, so essentially this meant that taxation needed the consent of the kingdom.[4] Chapter 14 went on to set out the rules for convoking the assembly which could give that consent.

The king was not just owed money. He also had unpleasant ways of forcing people to pay up, notably by 'distraint', which involved the seizure of the chattels and land of the debtor and his sureties. This process chapters 9, 26 and 27 attempted to regulate and limit. Money was also an issue in the sections of the Charter that dealt with justice and local government.

Justice and the Arbitrary Treatment of Individuals

After the opening section of the Charter on money, there followed chapters 17 to 22 – about justice. Chapters 17 to 19 made the king's procedures for civil litigation more accessible, and also placed them under local control. Later, chapter 36 was likewise concerned to make the king's justice more available and free of cost, although here in the area of criminal jurisdiction. Conversely, chapter 34 aimed at preventing royal justice interfering with private courts. Chapters 20 to 22 were about 'amercements'. These were financial penalties for falling into the king's 'mercy', and arose when an individual was convicted before the king or his judges of some offence. Today they would be called fines. The aim of the chapters was to ensure they were kept at a reasonable level and assessed either by the victim's neighbours or, in the case of an earl or a baron, by his peers, that is, social equals. The related chapter 32 limited the king's ability to seize land as penalty for a felony.

Another section about justice comes between chapters 38 and 40. Chapter 38 prevented a bailiff, that is a local official, putting anyone 'to law', meaning essentially putting anyone on trial, on his sole accusation unsupported by witnesses. Chapters 39 and 40 are the most famous in Magna Carta, and are still part of the law of the United Kingdom today. Chapter 40 seemed to make a blanket promise of justice, speedy and free, to everyone.

To no one will we sell, to no one will we deny or delay, right or justice.

Chapter 39 dealt directly with the arbitrary treatment of individuals.

> No free man is to be arrested, or imprisoned, or disseised, or outlawed, or exiled, or in any way destroyed, nor will we go against him, nor will we send against him, save by the lawful judgement of his peers or by the law of the land.

Here 'disseised' meant dispossessed of property, whilst going against or sending against someone meant (if not exclusively) taking action against them by force of arms. I have preferred 'destroyed', as a translation of the Latin 'destruatur', to the more common 'ruined', since it better captures the sense of threat to life as well as property.

Local Government

After the section on justice between chapters 17 and 22, chapters 23 to 31 turned to local government and the malpractices of the king's local agents – sheriffs, bailiffs and constables of castles. Here chapter 25 had particular importance since it sought to limit the financial burdens placed by the king on the counties. Chapter 45 attacked on another front and insisted that the king's officials should 'know the law of the kingdom and wish to observe it well'. Chapter 50 went further and made the king dismiss various named sheriffs and castellans, all of them foreigners, from their bailiwicks, which meant their local offices.

The Charter was also concerned with the running of the royal forest. Chapter 44 sought to limit the jurisdiction of the forest justices, while chapter 47 reduced immediately the extent of the forest, with more to come, it was hoped, from chapter 53. Most promising of all for John's subjects, most poisonous of all to the king, was chapter 48, which empowered twelve knights elected in each county to investigate and abolish the malpractices of the king's local agents.

London, Towns, Trade, Measures and Movement

The chapter protecting London from arbitrary taxation and confirming its liberties is, in modern printings, split between chapters 12

and 13. One could argue the case, looking at the original engrossments, for making it a discrete chapter, or at least a subsection within
a chapter. What is certain is that all the engrossments started a new
chapter with the liberties and ancient customs of the other towns,
rather than tagging them on, as in modern printings, to the chapter
on London. Another chapter benefiting both London and other towns
was chapter 33, which removed fish weirs (an obstacle to trade) from
the rivers Thames and Medway and elsewhere throughout all England, unless at the seashore. Chapter 35 sought to establish uniform
measures of drink, corn and cloth throughout the country (corn
according to the measure of London), while chapter 41 allowed, save
in time of war, all merchants safety of travel, without suffering any
unjust exactions. The following chapter 42 gave freedom of travel to
everyone in and out of the kingdom, again save in time of war.

Appointments and Patronage

The Charter said that officials should know the law of the kingdom, and dismissed some named sheriffs and castellans. Apart
from that, however, it did nothing to control the king's choice of
his ministers, either locally or centrally. That could be seen as one
of its central weaknesses. The Charter was not much more restrictive when it came to the king's bestowal of patronage. Chapter 4 at
least meant that the king's appointees would lose control of wardships for maladministration. Chapter 6 was designed to prevent
heirs and heiresses in wardship from being 'disparaged' in marriage, which meant being married to those beneath them in social
rank. It also stipulated that the family should be informed of what
was planned. The idea was thus to make it more difficult for the
king to give marriages to whomever he wanted. The same was true,
more astringently, of chapter 8, which laid down that a widow could
no longer be forced into remarriage if she wished to live without a
husband.

Redress of Past Grievances

Two important chapters in the Charter, chapters 52 and 55, were
concerned to redress the wrongs suffered by individuals in the
past. Under chapter 52 those disseised (that is, dispossessed) of

their possessions by King John without lawful judgement of their peers would have them immediately restored. Under chapter 55 all fines and amercements imposed unjustly by John were to be pardoned. Amercements we have already encountered in the chapters that sought to limit their size and regulate their assessment. Fines were offers of money accepted by the king for concessions and favours. They might be more or less compulsory (so to recover the king's good will) or entirely voluntary (so for the right to set up a new market). Both chapters laid down that if disputes arose over the restorations and pardons, these were to be determined by the twenty-five barons named in the Charter's 'security of peace', that is the 'security clause', which is described below. Chapter 52 also put on the agenda the dispossessions committed by John's predecessors, his father Henry II and brother Richard I. John was to deal with these when he returned from or abandoned his prospective crusade. There was no postponement when it came to the hostages and charters which John had extracted as guarantees of peace and 'faithful service'. Under chapter 49, these were to be immediately returned.

The Welsh and the King of Scots

It was in the context of redress of grievances that the Welsh and Alexander, king of Scots, entered the Charter. Under chapter 56, Welshmen were immediately to be restored to lands and liberties taken by King John without judgement of their peers. The chapter also set up procedures to deal with any disputes over the process. Chapter 57 put the disseisins suffered by the Welsh at the hands of Henry II and Richard I on the agenda, while chapter 58 laid down that John was to restore the son of Llywelyn and the other Welsh hostages. Under chapter 59, John promised, with one qualification, to treat King Alexander, when it came to returning his sisters, hostages, liberties and rights, in the same way as, under the terms of the Charter, he was to treat the barons of England.

The Passing Down of the Concessions

The Charter was primarily aimed at the malpractices of the king and his ministers. It did, however, aspire to set the same standards for others. Thus chapter 60, the final one before the security clause, stated that all the customs and liberties which John had conceded to his men should be observed by everyone in the kingdom towards their men. There were other chapters too, like chapters 7 and 8 on widows, and chapter 15 on aids, which protected tenants from the demands of their lords. We will discuss in Chapter 4 the tensions within society the Charter thus revealed.

The Enforcement of the Charter

At the end of the Charter came the most sensational and revolutionary chapter of all. John declared that, wishing his concessions to be firmly maintained, he had offered the barons the following 'security'. This was that they might choose twenty-five of their number who were empowered, if necessary, to force him and his ministers to observe the liberties granted and confirmed in the Charter. They also had the power to put right any other wrongs. In this, the twenty-five were to act with 'the commune of all the land'. The word 'commune' here meant a sworn association. It was to be formed by 'all the land' swearing either voluntarily or, if necessary, under compulsion to obey the orders of the twenty-five in bringing the king to heel. Finally, the chapter concluded with John promising not to seek anything by which the Charter might be invalidated. Blackstone printed the security clause as a single chapter, but the engrossments broke it up, in slightly different ways, which shows the desire to make its elements as clear as possible. It was not quite the only device in the Charter by which the barons sought to ensure its enforcement. They also strove to reduce John's power of resistance. The key chapter here was chapter 51, under which John promised, after the peace, to dismiss all the foreign soldiers he had recruited. In the printed versions, this chapter is separated, as it is in the Articles of the Barons, from the preceding chapter, which dismissed some of John's foreign sheriffs and castellans from office. In fact, in two of the engrossments, and in the bishops' copy of the Charter, the two chapters are one, which strongly suggests that the dismissals, apart from removing unpopular local officials, were also seen as stripping John of military experts, as all these men were.

The Conclusion of the Charter

At the end of the security clause, in what is printed as chapter 62, John remitted his rancour and ill will, pardoned all transgressions committed since the start of the civil war at Easter 1215, and undertook that the bishops should issue letters testifying to the 'aforesaid concessions'. In fact, the engrossments, perhaps surprisingly, give little warrant for making this a discrete and single chapter, but they all agree in starting the final section of the Charter with what became chapter 63. Here John reiterated that the church should be free and stated that the men of the kingdom and their heirs were to enjoy the 'foresaid liberties, rights and concessions' in perpetuity. An oath, he continued, had been taken on his behalf and that of the barons for the observation of everything in good faith. In a normal charter, what would have followed next would have been a list of witnesses, but in Magna Carta these were stated to be as 'above said'. This referred to the counsellors John had listed at the start of the Charter. Magna Carta then concluded with the following statement:

> Given by our hand in the meadow which is called Runnymede, between Windsor and Staines, on the fifteenth day of June, in the seventeenth year of our reign.

The date of Magna Carta was thus 15 June 1215.

THE TEXT OF MAGNA CARTA

The Latin text and English translation of Magna Carta are here printed on facing pages. The Latin text comes from the Lincoln Charter since, of all the engrossments, it is the most finely written. It is also the engrossment whose history is most certain since 'LINCOLNIA', written twice on the back, almost certainly by the scribe of the Charter, shows it was intended for Lincoln from the start. The Latin text given here differs from previous printed examples in trying to indicate how the originals, by the use of capital letters of different sizes, were divided up into chapters, or sections within chapters. While the divisions, thus indicated, for the most part correspond with the numbered chapters set in stone since Blackstone's work of 1759,[5] there are differences, as we have seen. In both the Latin and English texts set out below, a line is left blank where the engrossments indicate the start of a new chapter or section, but only those given numbers by Blackstone are numbered. The largest capital letters found in the engrossments I have rendered in the Latin text as $\mathbf{N}$. Capital letters of less emphasis, but still of a size to indicate a division, appear as N. Where Blackstone made chapter divisions (so at chapters 19 and 51) that are questionable, then his number is placed in the body of the text. In making these divisions, I have not followed Lincoln exclusively, but have also taken into account the capitalizations found in Canterbury, Cii and Salisbury, although the capitals in the Salisbury Charter are throughout given less emphasis than those in the other three. I have also taken into account the capitalization found in the bishops' letters testimonial, which guaranteed the authentic text. Significant divergences in the capitalization between these sources are indicated in the footnotes. The symbol | in the Latin text indicates where the Lincoln lines end. I have used a larger font altogether to reflect the exceptionally large letters at the start of the Lincoln Charter. In the translation, following Holt, I indicate the equivalent chapters in the Articles of the Barons (AB) and the Charter of 1225 (1225).

In the footnotes, I have collated the Lincoln text with that found in the other three engrossments and the copy in the bishops' letter. Although of no great moment, this is the first published collation to use all five, since the Salisbury engrossment could not be found when the *Statutes of the Realm* text was published in 1810.[6] My collation indicates omissions, corrections and variations in word order. I have not, however, included the variations in the spellings of personal names place names and such words as 'pledges', 'carts', 'socage' and so on. I have also omitted some small slips in the bishops' copy, which were probably the result of mistakes made by the fourteenth-century copyist. Some significance may attach to a corrected omission in Canterbury and Cii, but apart from that the chief value of a collation is to show that the differences between the texts are minor. The engrossments were made, on the whole, with care.

Of previous published texts, Blackstone's is the Canterbury engrossment collated with the bishops' copy. That in *Statutes of the Realm* uses the Lincoln engrossment, and indicates all variations

with Canterbury, Cii and the bishops' copy in footnotes. It makes
no division into chapters and does not expand the abbreviations,
instead using a typeface that sought to reproduce them.[7] It also
sought to follow the original punctuation. The text below, in line
with current practice, expands the abbreviations and uses modern
punctuation. It seeks, however, to follow the text's use of capitals.
As in much other contemporary writing, this appears to have been
haphazard. It is also often ambiguous, especially where a letter
like 'w' has the same from in both upper and lower case. I have
used capitals less frequently than *Statutes of the Realm*, and usually
only where they seem quite clear. In the process, I may sometimes have been unfair to sheriffs, Wales and the Welsh where
I have generally gone for lower case: 'vicecomites', 'wallia' and
'walenses'.[8] In preparing the transcription, I have used a photo-
graph of the Pine engraving, the engraving of the Lincoln Charter
published in *Foedera*,[9] and photographs of Lincoln, Salisbury and
Cii. With the bishops' copy, I have been able to work directly on
the text in the Red Book of the Exchequer.[10] I have also photo-
graphed it.

   There have been many translations of the 1215 Charter, the
most widely used being J. C. Holt's, which is printed as an Appendix to his *Magna Carta*. (Holt's Latin text was Cii.)[11] The present
translation is in places perhaps a little more literal than Holt's but
is not fundamentally different from it or many others. In making the
translation, I have been helped immensely by both Daniel Hadas
and Henry Summerson's translation on the website of the Magna
Carta Project. The meaning of some of the technical terms and
obscure words found in the translation is explained in the Glossary at the end of the book (pp. 461–470).

MAGNA CARTA 1215

Johannes dei gratia Rex Anglie, Dominus Hibernie, Dux Normannie et Aquitanie, Comes Andegavie, Archiepiscopis, Episcopis, Abbatibus, Comitibus, Baronibus, Justiciariis, Forestariis, Vicecomitibus, Prepositis, Ministris et Omnibus Ballivis et Fidelibus Suis Salutem.

Sciatis nos intuitu dei et pro salute anime nostre et omnium antecessorum et heredum nostrorum, ad honorem* | dei et exaltacionem sancte ecclesie, et emendationem Regni nostri, per consilium venerabilium patrum nostrorum, Stephani Cantuariensis, Archiepiscopi Totius Anglie, Primatis et Sancte Romane ecclesie Cardinalis, Henrici Dublinensis Archiepiscopi, Willelmi Londoniensis, Petri Wintoniensis, Joscelini Bathoniensis et Glastoniensis, Hugonis Lincolniensis, Walteri Wigornensis, Willelmi Coventrensis, et Benedicti Roffensis Episcoporum; Magistri Pandulfi domini Pape Subdi | aconi et familiaris, et† fratris Eimerici Magistri Militie Templi in Anglia; et Nobilium virorum Willelmi Marescalli Comitis Penbrocie, Willelmi Comitis Sarresbyrie, Willelmi Comitis Warennie, Willelmi Comitis Arundellie, Alani de Galweia Constabularii Scotie, Warini filii Geroldi, Huberti de Burgo Senescalli Pictavie, Petri filii Hereberti,‡ Hugonis de Nevill', Mathei filii Hereberti, Thome Basset,| Alani Basset, Philippi de Albiniaco, Roberti de Roppelay, Johannis Marescalli, Johannis filii Hugonis et aliorum fidelium nostrorum:

---

* The font size down to this point reflects the large letters and capitals of the Lincoln Charter's first line.
† Canterbury, Cii and the bishops' copy omit 'et'. Salisbury has it.
‡ In Canterbury, Cii and the bishops' copy, the name of Peter fitzHerbert precedes that of Hubert de Burgh. Salisbury is as Lincoln.

John by the grace of God, king of England, lord of Ireland, duke of Normandy and Aquitaine, count of Anjou, to his archbishops, bishops, abbots, earls, barons, justices, foresters, sheriffs, reeves, ministers and all his bailiffs and faithful men, greeting.

Know that we, inspired by God and for the salvation of our soul, and for the souls of all our ancestors and heirs, for the honour of God and the exaltation of holy church, and the reform of our kingdom, by the counsel of our venerable fathers, Stephen archbishop of Canterbury, primate of all England, and cardinal of the holy Roman church, Henry archbishop of Dublin, William of London, Peter of Winchester, Jocelyn of Bath and Glastonbury, Hugh of Lincoln, Walter of Worcester, William of Coventry and Benedict of Rochester, bishops, Master Pandulf subdeacon and member of the household of the lord pope, and brother Aymeric, master of the knights of the Temple in England, and of the noble men, William Marshal, earl of Pembroke, William earl of Salisbury, William earl of Warenne, William earl of Arundel, Alan of Galloway, constable of Scotland, Warin fitzGerold, Hubert de Burgh, seneschal of Poitou, Peter fitzHerbert, Hugh de Neville, Matthew fitzHerbert, Thomas Basset, Alan Basset, Philip d'Aubigné, Robert of Ropsley, John Marshal, John fitzHugh, and our other faithful men:

1. In primis concessisse deo et hac presenti carta nostra confirmasse, pro nobis et heredibus nostris in perpetuum, quod Anglicana ecclesia libera sit, et habeat jura sua integra, et libertates suas illesas; et ita volumus observari quod apparet ex eo quod libertatem electionum, que maxima et |* magis necessaria reputatur ecclesie Anglicane, mera et spontanea voluntate, ante discordiam inter nos et Barones nostros motam, concessimus et carta nostra confirmavimus, et eam obtinuimus a Domino Papa Innocentio tercio confirmari; quam et nos observabimus et ab heredibus nostris in perpetuum bona fide volumus observari.

Concessimus† etiam omnibus liberis hominibus regni nostri, pro nobis et heredibus nostris in perpetuum, omnes libertates subscriptas, habendas et tenendas, eis | et heredibus suis, de nobis et heredibus nostris.

2. Si quis comitum vel baronum nostrorum, sive aliorum tenentium de nobis in capite per servicium militare, mortuus fuerit, et cum decesserit heres suus plene etatis fuerit et relevium debeat, habeat hereditatem suam per antiquum relevium; Scilicet heres vel heredes comitis de Baronia comitis integra per centum Libras; heres vel heredes baronis de Baronia integra per centum Libras; heres vel heredes | militis de feodo militis integro per centum solidos ad plus; et qui minus debuerit minus det secundum antiquam consuetudinem feodorum.

3. Si autem heres alicuius talium fuerit infra etatem et fuerit in custodia, cum ad etatem pervenerit, habeat hereditatem suam sine relevio et sine fine.

4. Custos terre huiusmodi heredis qui infra etatem fuerit, non capiat de terra heredis nisi rationabiles exitus et rationabiles consuetudines, et rationabilia servitia, et hoc sine destruc | tione et vasto hominum vel rerum.

*

* The Lincoln hand gets slightly smaller from this point onwards until the end of the Charter.
† Lincoln does not have a large capital for the 'C' in 'Concessimus', but I have followed the other engrossments, which do.

1. In the first place, have granted to God and by this our present charter have confirmed, for us and our heirs in perpetuity, that the English church is to be free, and is to have its rights in whole and its liberties unharmed, and we wish it so to be observed; which is manifest from this, namely that the liberty of elections, which is deemed to be of the greatest importance and most necessary for the English church, by our free and spontaneous will, before the discord moved between us and our barons, we granted and confirmed by our charter, and obtained its confirmation from the lord pope, Innocent the third, which we shall both observe and wish to be observed by our heirs in perpetuity in good faith.

We have also granted to all the free men of our kingdom, for us and our heirs in perpetuity, all the below written liberties, to be had and held by them and their heirs from us and our heirs. [1225, 1]

2. If any of our earls or barons, or others holding from us in chief by knight service, dies and when he dies his heir is of full age and owes relief, he is to have his inheritance by the ancient relief; namely the heir or heirs of an earl for a whole barony of an earl by a hundred pounds; the heir or heirs of a baron for a whole barony by a hundred pounds; the heir or heirs of a knight for the whole fee of a knight by a hundred shillings at most; and who owes less is to give less according to the ancient custom of fees. [AB, 1; 1225, 2]

3. If, however, the heir of any such one is underage and is in wardship, when he comes of age, he is to have his inheritance without relief and without fine. [AB, 2; 1225, 3]

4. The guardian of the land of an heir of this kind who is underage, is not to take from the land of the heir anything other than reasonable issues and reasonable customs and reasonable services, and this without destruction and waste of men or things.

*

Et si nos commiserimus custodiam alicuius talis terre vicecomiti vel alicui alii qui de exitibus illius nobis respondere debeat, et ille destructionem de custodia fecerit vel vastum, nos ab illo capiemus emendam, et terra committatur duobus legalibus et discretis hominibus de feodo illo, qui de exitibus respondeant nobis vel ei cui eos assignaverimus.

Et si dederimus vel vendiderimus alicui custodiam alicuius talis terre, et ille | destructionem inde fecerit vel vastum, amittat ipsam custodiam, et tradatur duobus legalibus et discretis hominibus de feodo illo qui similiter respondeant nobis* sicut predictum est.

5. Custos autem, quamdiu custodiam terre habuerit, sustentet domos, parcos, vivaria, stagna, molendina, et cetera ad terram illam pertinentia, de exitibus terre eiusdem; et reddat heredi, cum ad plenam etatem pervenerit, terram suam totam instauratam de carrucis et | waignagiis secundum quod tempus waignagii exiget et exitus terre rationabiliter poterunt sustinere.

6. Heredes maritentur absque disparagatione, ita† quod, antequam contrahatur, matrimonium ostendatur propinquis de consanguinitate ipsius heredis.

7. Vidua‡ post mortem mariti sui statim et sine difficultate habeat maritagium et hereditatem suam, nec aliquid det pro dote sua, vel pro maritagio suo, vel hereditate sua quam hereditatem maritus suus et ipsa | tenuerint die obitus ipsius mariti, et maneat in domo mariti sui per quadraginta dies post mortem ipsius, infra quos assignetur ei dos sua.

8. Nulla vidua distringatur ad se maritandum dum voluerit vivere sine marito, ita tamen quod securitatem faciat quod se non maritabit sine assensu nostro, si de nobis tenuerit, vel sine assensu domini sui de quo tenuerit, si de alio tenuerit.

---

* Canterbury and Cii have 'nobis respondeant'.
† Canterbury, Cii, Salisbury and the bishops' copy insert 'tamen' here.
‡ An emphatic 'V' only appears in Lincoln and the bishops' copy.

And if we commit the wardship of any such land to a sheriff or anyone else who ought to answer to us for its issues, and he causes destruction to the wardship or waste, we will take amends from him, and the land is to be committed to two law-worthy and prudent men of that fee, who are to answer for the issues to us or to him to whom we assign them.

And if we give or sell the wardship of any such land to anyone, and he then causes destruction or waste, he is to lose that wardship, and it is to be handed to two law-worthy and prudent men of that fee, who similarly shall answer to us as aforesaid. [AB, 3; 1225, 4]

5. The guardian, however, for as long as he has wardship of the land, is to maintain the houses, parks, fish ponds, ponds, mills and other things belonging to that land, from the issues of the same land. And he is to deliver to the heir, when he comes of age, his land fully stocked with ploughs and wainages according to what the time of the wainage will demand and the issues of the land will reasonably be able to sustain. [AB, 3, 35; 1225, 5]

6. Heirs are to be married without disparagement, provided however that, before a marriage is contracted, it is to be made known to the nearest kin of that heir. [AB, 3; 1225, 6]

7. A widow, after the death of her husband, immediately and without difficulty, is to have her marriage portion and inheritance, nor shall she give anything for her dower, or for her marriage portion, or her inheritance, which inheritance she and her husband held on the day of the death of that husband. And she is to remain in the house of her husband for forty days after his death, within which time her dower is to be assigned her. [AB, 4; 1225, 7]

8. No widow is to be distrained to marry while she wishes to live without a husband, provided however that she gives security that she will not marry without our assent, if she holds from us, or without the assent of her lord from whom she holds, if she holds from another. [AB, 17; 1225, 7]

9. Nec nos nec ballivi nostri saisiemus terram aliquam nec reddi-
tum pro debito aliquo | quamdiu catalla debitoris sufficiunt ad
debitum reddendum; nec plegii ipsius debitoris distringantur quamdiu ipse capitalis debitor sufficit ad solutionem debiti.

Et* si capitalis debitor defecerit in solutione debiti, non habens
unde solvat, plegii respondeant de debito; et, si voluerint, habeant
terras et redditus debitoris donec sit eis satisfactum de debito quod
ante pro eo solverint, nisi capitalis debitor monstraverit se esse
quietum inde versus eosdem plegios. |

10. Si quis mutuo ceperit aliquid a Judeis, plus vel minus, et
moriatur antequam debitum illud solvatur, debitum non usuret
quamdiu heres fuerit infra etatem, de quocumque teneat; et si debitum illud inciderit in manus nostras, nos non capiemus nisi
catallum contentum in carta.

11. Et si quis moriatur, et debitum debeat Judeis, uxor eius habeat
dotem suam, et nichil reddat de debito illo; et si liberi ipsius defuncti
qui fuerint infra etatem remanserint, provideantur eis necessaria
secundum | tenementum quod fuerit defuncti, et de residuo solva-
tur debitum, salvo servitio dominorum.

Simili modo fiat de debitis que debentur aliis quam Judeis.

12. Nullum scutagium vel auxilium ponatur in regno nostro nisi
per commune consilium regni nostri, nisi ad corpus nostrum redimendum, et primogenitum filium nostrum militem faciendum, et ad
filiam nostram primogenitam semel maritandam, et ad hec non fiat
nisi rationabile auxilium.

Simili modo fiat de auxiliis | de civitate Londoniarum.

13. Et civitas Londoniarum habeat omnes antiquas libertates et
liberas consuetudines suas, tam per terras, quam per aquas.

*

* Lincoln has 'et' here.

9. Neither we nor our bailiffs are to seize any land or rent for any debt, for as long as the chattels of the debtor suffice to pay the debt; nor are the sureties of that debtor to be distrained for as long as the chief debtor himself has sufficient for payment of the debt.

And if the chief debtor fails in the payment of the debt, not having the wherewithal to pay, the sureties are to answer for the debt. And if they wish, they are to have the lands and the rents of the debtor until satisfaction is given to them for the debt which before they paid for him, unless the chief debtor shows that he is quit against those same sureties in that matter. [AB, 5; 1225, 8]

10. If anyone has taken anything on loan from the Jews, more or less, and dies before that debt is paid, the debt is not to bear usury for as long as the heir is underage, from whomever he holds; and if that debt falls into our hands, we shall not take anything save the capital contained in the charter. [AB, 34]

11. And if anyone dies, and owes a debt to the Jews, his wife is to have her dower, and is to pay nothing of that debt; and if children of the deceased, who are underage, remain, their needs are to be provided for in keeping with the tenement which was the deceased's, and the debts are to be paid from the residue, saving the service of the lords. In a similar way, it is to be for debts owed to others than Jews. [AB, 35]

12. No scutage or aid is to be levied in our kingdom, save by the common counsel of our kingdom, save for the ransoming of our body, and the making of our first-born son a knight, and for the marrying a single time of our first-born daughter; and for these things there is only to be a reasonable aid. [AB, 32; 1225, 37]

In a similar way it is to be for aids from the city of London. [AB, 32]

13. And the city of London is to have all its ancient liberties and free customs, by both land and water.

*

Preterea volumus et concedimus quod omnes alie civitates, et burgi, et ville, et portus, habeant omnes libertates et liberas consuetudines suas.

14. Et ad habendum commune consilium regni de auxilio assidendo aliter* quam in tribus casibus predictis, vel de scutagio assidendo, summoneri faciemus Archiepiscopos, Episcopos, | Abbates, Comites, et maiores barones, sigillatim per Litteras nostras. Et preterea faciemus summoneri in generali, per vicecomites et ballivos nostros, omnes illos qui de nobis tenent in capite ad certum diem, scilicet ad terminum quadraginta dierum ad minus, et ad certum locum; et in omnibus litteris illius summonitionis causam summonitionis exprimemus; et sic facta summonitione negotium ad diem assignatum procedat secundum consilium illorum qui presentes | fuerint, quamvis non omnes summoniti venerint.

15. Nos non concedemus decetero alicui quod capiat auxilium de liberis hominibus suis, nisi ad corpus suum redimendum, et ad faciendum primogenitum filium suum militem, et ad primogenitam filiam suam semel maritandam, et ad hec non fiat nisi rationabile auxilium.

16. Nullus distringatur ad faciendum maius servitium de feodo militis, nec de alio libero tenemento, quam inde debetur.

17. Co | mmunia placita non sequantur curiam nostram sed teneantur in aliquo certo loco.†

18. Recognitiones de nova dissaisina, de morte antecessoris, et de‡ ultima presentatione, non capiantur nisi in suis comitatibus et hoc modo.

Nos, vel, si extra regnum fuerimus, capitalis Justiciarius noster, mittemus duos justiciarios per unumquemque comitatum per quattuor vices in anno, qui, cum quattuor militibus cuiuslibet comitatus

---

* Salisbury has 'aliter assidendo'.
† Canterbury, Cii, Salisbury and the bishops' copy have 'loco certo'.
‡ Salisbury here omits 'et' and has 'De' rather than 'de'.

In addition, we wish and grant that all other cities and boroughs, and vills and ports, have all their liberties and free customs. [AB, 32; 1225, 9]

14. And to have the common counsel of the kingdom for an aid to be assessed, other than in the three cases aforesaid, or for a scutage to be assessed, we will cause to be summoned archbishops, bishops, abbots, earls and greater barons, individually by our letters; and in addition we will cause to be summoned in general, by our sheriffs and bailiffs, all those who hold from us in chief, at a specified day, namely at a term of forty days distant at least, and at a specified place; and in all the letters of that summons, we will express the cause of the summons; and thus, the summons having been made, the business is to proceed on the assigned day, according to the counsel of those who are present, although not all those summoned come.

15. We will not grant henceforth to anyone that he may take an aid from his free men, save for the ransoming of his body, and the making of his first-born son a knight, and for the marrying a single time of his first-born daughter, and for these things there is only to be a reasonable aid. [AB, 6]

16. No one is to be distrained to do more service for the fee of a knight, or for another free tenement, than is owed therefrom. [AB, 7; 1225, 10]

17. Common pleas are not to follow our court but are to be held in some specified place. [AB, 8; 1225, 11]

18. Recognitions of novel disseisin, of mort d'ancestor, and of darrein presentment, are not to be taken unless in their counties and in this way.

We or, if we are out of our kingdom, our chief justiciar shall send two justices through each county four times a year, who, with four knights of each county, elected by the county court are to take the

electis per comitatum, capiant in comi | tatu et in die et loco comitatus assisas predictas. (19) Et* si in die comitatus assise predicte capi non possint, tot milites et libere tenentes remaneant de illis qui interfuerint comitatui die illo, per quos possint sufficienter juditia† fieri, secundum quod negotium fuerit maius vel minus.

20. Liber homo non amercietur pro parvo delicto, nisi secundum modum delicti; et pro magno delicto amercietur secundum magnitudinem delicti, salvo contenemento suo, et mercator eodem | modo salva mercandisa sua, et villanus eodem modo amercietur salvo waignagio suo, si inciderint in misericordiam nostram; et nulla predictarum misericordiarum ponatur nisi per sacramentum proborum hominum de visneto.

21. Comites et barones non amercientur nisi per pares suos, et non nisi secundum modum delicti.

22. Nullus clericus amercietur de laico tenemento suo, nisi secundum modum aliorum predictorum, et non secundum quantitatem beneficii sui ecclesiastici.

23. Nec‡ | villa nec homo distringatur facere pontes ad Riparias, nisi qui ab antiquo et de iure facere debent.

24. Nullus vicecomes, Constabularius, Coronatores, vel alii ballivi nostri, teneant placita corone nostre.

25. Omnes Comitatus, et§ Hundredi, Trethingii et Wapentachii¶ sint ad antiquas firmas absque ullo incremento, exceptis dominicis maneriis nostris.

---

* Only Salisbury could be read as starting a new chapter here. Canterbury and Cii have 'et'.
† Canterbury, Cii and the bishops' copy have 'judicia sufficienter'. Salisbury is as Lincoln.
‡ Salisbury here has 'Nulla' rather than 'Nec'.
§ Canterbury, Cii, Salisbury and the bishops' copy omit 'et'.
¶ Canterbury, Cii and Salisbury all have 'Wapentakii et Trethingi'. The bishops' copy follows Lincoln.

aforesaid assizes, in the county court and on the day and in the place of the county court. [AB, 8; 1225, 12] (19) And if on the day of the county court, the aforesaid assizes cannot be taken, enough knights and free tenants are to remain from those who attended the county court on that day, that judgements can be effectively made, according to whether the business is great or small. [AB, 13; 1225, 12]

20. A free man is not be amerced for a small offence, and only in accordance with the degree of the offence; and for a great offence, he is to be amerced according to the magnitude of the offence, saving his livelihood, and a merchant in the same, way saving his merchandise, and a villein is to be amerced in the same way saving his wainage, if they fall into our mercy. And none of the aforesaid amercements are to be imposed save by the oath of upright men of the neighbourhood. [AB, 9; 1225, 14]

21. Earls and barons are not to be amerced save by their peers, and only in accordance with the degree of the offence. [1225, 14]

22. No clerk is to be amerced in respect of his lay tenement, save according to the manner of the others aforesaid, and not according to the quantity of his ecclesiastical benefice. [AB, 10; 1225, 14]

23. No vill nor man is to be distrained to build bridges at river-banks, save those obliged to do so from ancient times and by law. [AB, 11; 1225, 15]

24. No sheriff, constable, coroners or other of our bailiffs are to hold pleas of our crown.
[AB, 14; 1225, 17]

25. All counties and hundreds, ridings and wapentakes, are to be at the ancient farms without any increment, except our demesne manors. [AB, 14]

26. Si aliquis tenens de nobis laicum feodum moriatur, et vicecomes vel Ballivus | noster ostendat litteras nostras* patentes de summonitione nostra de debito quod defunctus nobis debuit, liceat vicecomiti vel Ballivo nostro attachiare et inbreviare catalla defuncti inventa in laico feodo ad valentiam illius debiti, per visum legalium hominum, ita tamen quod nichil inde amoveatur, donec persolvatur nobis debitum quod clarum fuit;† et residuum relinquatur executoribus ad faciendum testamentum defuncti; et‡ si nichil nobis de | beatur ab ipso, omnia catalla cedant defuncto, salvis uxori ipsius et pueris rationabilibus partibus suis.

27. Si aliquis liber homo intestatus decesserit, catalla sua per manus propinquorum parentum et amicorum suorum, per visum ecclesie distribuantur, salvis unicuique debitis que defunctus ei debebat.

28. Nullus constabularius vel alius ballivus noster capiat§ blada vel alia catalla alicuius nisi statim inde¶ reddat denarios aut respectum inde habere | possit de voluntate venditoris.

29. Nullus constabularius distringat aliquem militem ad dandum denarios pro custodia castri si facere voluerit custodiam illam in propria persona sua vel per alium probum hominem, si ipse eam facere non possit propter rationabilem causam; et si nos duxerimus vel miserimus eum in exercitum, erit quietus de custodia secundum quantitatem temporis quo per nos fuerit in exercitum.**

30. Nullus vicecomes, vel Ballivus noster, vel aliquis | alius capiat†† equos vel carettas alicuius liberi hominis pro carriagio faciendo, nisi de voluntate ipsius liberi hominis.

---

* Salisbury omits 'nostras'.
† Canterbury, Cii, Salisbury and the bishops' copy have 'fuerit'.
‡ Cii and the bishops' copy have 'Et' here.
§ Salisbury has 'capiet', here and elsewhere preferring the future indicative to the present subjunctive found in the other engrossments and the bishops' copy: Fox, 'Originals', p. 330.
¶ Salisbury places 'inde' after 'reddat'.
** Canterbury, Cii, Salisbury and the bishops' copy have here 'exercitu'. Salisbury also places 'fuerit' after 'exercitu'.
†† Salisbury has 'capiet'.

26. If anyone holding a lay fee from us dies, and our sheriff or bailiff shows our letters patent for our summons of a debt which the deceased owed us, it is to be permissible for our sheriff or bailiff to attach and write down the chattels of the deceased found in the lay fee, to the value of that debt, by view of law-worthy men, provided however that nothing is removed from there until the debt which was clear is paid to us. And the residue is to be left to the executors to make the will of the deceased; and if nothing is owed us by him, all the chattels are to pass to the deceased, saving for his wife and children their reasonable shares. [AB, 15; 1225, 18]

27. If any free man dies intestate, his chattels are to be distributed by the hands of his nearest relations and friends, under the supervision of the church, saving to each person the debts which the deceased owed him. [AB, 16]

28. No constable or other bailiff of ours is to take the corn or other chattels of anyone, unless he immediately gives money for this, or is able to have a delay with the consent of the vendor. [AB, 18; 1225, 19]

29. No constable is to distrain any knight to give money for the guard of a castle, if he wishes to perform that guard in his own person, or through another upright man, if he himself cannot do it for a reasonable cause. And if we lead or send him in an army, he will be quit of the guard, according to the amount of time he will have been in the army by our order. [AB, 19; 1225, 20]

30. No sheriff or bailiff of ours or anyone else is to take the horses or carts of any free man for carriage, save with the consent of the free man himself. [AB, 20; 1225, 21]

31. Nec* nos nec ballivi nostri capiemus alienum boscum ad castra, vel alia agenda nostra, nisi per voluntatem ipsius† cuius boscus ille fuerit.

32. Nos non tenebimus terras illorum qui convicti fuerint de‡ felonia nisi per unum annum et unum diem, et tunc reddantur terre dominis feodorum.

33. Omnes kidelli decetero deponantur penitus de Tamisia, et | Medewaye,§ et per totam Angliam, nisi per costeram maris.

34. Breve quod vocatur precipe decetero non fiat alicui de aliquo tenemento unde liber homo possit¶ amittere curiam suam.

35. Una mensura vini sit per totum regnum nostrum, et una mensura** cervisie, et una mensura bladi, scilicet Quartarium Londoniense, et una latitudo pannorum tinctorum et Russetorum et Halbergettorum, scilicet due ulne infra listas. De ponderibus autem sit ut de me | nsuris.

36. Nichil detur vel capiatur decetero pro brevi inquisitionis de vita vel menbris, sed gratis concedatur et non negetur.

37. Si aliquis teneat de nobis per feodifirmam, vel per socagium, vel per burgagium, et de alio terram teneat per servitium militare, nos non habebimus custodiam heredis nec terre sue que est de feodo alterius, occasione illius feodifirme, vel socagii, vel burgagii; nec habebimus custodiam illius feodifirme, vel socagii, vel burgagii, nisi ipsa feodifirma | debeat servitium militare.

*

* Salisbury runs straight on here with 'nec'.
† Salisbury has 'illius'.
‡ Salisbury omits 'de'.
§ Canterbury, Cii and the bishops' copy insert 'de' before 'Medewaye'. Salisbury is as Lincoln.
¶ Canterbury, Cii, Salisbury and the bishops' copy put 'possit' after 'amittere'.
** Salisbury omits 'mensura'.

31. Neither we nor our bailiffs shall take wood belonging to another person for castles, or for our other affairs, unless with the consent of him whose wood it is. [AB, 21; 1225, 21]

32. We will not hold the lands of those who are convicted of felony, save for one year and one day, and then the lands are to be returned to the lords of the fees. [AB, 22; 1225, 22]

33. All fish weirs are henceforth to be removed completely from the Thames and the Medway, and through all England, save at the seashore. [AB, 23; 1225, 23]

34. The writ which is called precipe is not to be made out henceforth to anyone for any tenement whereby a free man could lose his court. [AB, 24; 1225, 24]

35. There is to be one measure of wine through all our kingdom, and one measure of ale, and one measure of corn, namely the quarter of London, and one width of tinted cloths, and russets and haubergets, namely two ells within the borders. Moreover, for weights it is to be as for measures. [AB, 12; 1225, 25]

36. Nothing is to be given or taken henceforth for a writ of inquisition concerning life or limbs, but it is to be given without payment and not denied. [AB, 26; 1225, 26]

37. If anyone holds from us by fee farm, or by socage, or by burgage, and holds land from another by knight service, we will not have wardship of the heir nor of his land which is of the fee of another, by reason of that fee farm, or socage, or burgage, nor will we have wardship of that fee farm or socage or burgage, unless that fee farm owes knight service.

*

Nos* non habebimus custodiam heredis vel terre alicuius, quam tenet de alio per servitium militare, occasione alicuius parve serianterie quam tenet de nobis per servitium reddendi nobis cultellos, vel sagittas, vel huiusmodi.

38. Nullus ballivus ponat decetero aliquem ad legem simplici loquela sua, sine testibus fidelibus ad hoc inductis.

39. Nullus liber homo capiatur, vel inprisonetur, aut dissaisiatur, aut utlaghetur, aut exuletur, aut aliquo modo | destruatur, nec super eum ibimus, nec super eum mittemus, nisi per legale iuditium parium suorum vel per legem terre.

40. Nulli vendemus, nulli negabimus, aut differemus, rectum aut† justitiam.

41. Omnes mercatores habeant salvum et securum exire ab‡ Anglia, et venire in Angliam,§ morari et ire per Angliam, tam per terram quam per aquam, ad emendum et vendendum sine omnibus malis toltis, per antiquas et rectas consuetudines, preterquam in tempore guerre, et si sint de terra | contra nos guerrina, et si tales inveniantur in terra nostra in principio guerre, attachientur sine dampno corporum et rerum, donec sciatur a nobis vel capitali justiciario nostro quomodo mercatores terre nostre tractentur, qui tunc invenientur in terra contra nos guerrina; et si nostri salvi sint ibi, alii salvi sint in terra nostra.

42. Liceat unicuique decetero exire de regno nostro, et redire salvo et secure per terram et per aquam, salva fide nostra, nisi tempore guerre per aliquod breve tempus, | propter communem utilitatem regni, exceptis inprisonatis et utlaghatis secundum legem regni, et gente de terra contra nos guerrina, et mercatoribus de quibus fiat sicut predictum est.

---

* All the engrossments and the bishops' copy start a new chapter here.
† Salisbury has 'vel'.
‡ Canterbury, Cii, Salisbury and the bishops' copy have 'de' here.
§ Canterbury, Cii, Salisbury and the bishops' copy add 'et' here.

We will not have wardship of the heir or the land of anyone, which he holds from another by knight service, by reason of any small serjeanty which he holds from us by the service of rendering to us knives, arrows or things of that kind. [AB, 27; 1225, 27]

38. No bailiff is henceforth to put anyone to law on his sole accusation without trustworthy witnesses brought forward for this. [AB, 28; 1225, 28]

39. No free man is to be arrested, or imprisoned, or disseised, or outlawed, or exiled, or in any way destroyed, nor will we go against him, nor will we send against him, save by the lawful judgement of his peers or by the law of the land. [AB, 29; 1225, 29]

40. To no one will we sell, to no one will we deny or delay, right or justice. [AB, 30; 1225, 29]

41. All merchants are to be safe and secure departing from England and entering into England, and staying and going through England, both by land and by water, to buy and sell, without any evil exactions, according to ancient and right customs, save in time of war, and if they are from a land at war with us. And if such are found in our land at the beginning of the war, they are to be attached without damage of body and goods, until it is known by us or our chief justiciar, how the merchants of our land are treated, who then are found in the land at war with us, and if ours are safe there, the others are to be safe in our land. [AB, 31; 1225, 30]

42. It is to be allowable for anyone henceforth to depart from our kingdom, and return safely and securely, by land and by water, saving our faith, save in time of war for some brief time, for the common utility of the kingdom, except those imprisoned and outlawed according to the law of the kingdom, and people from a land at war with us, and merchants for whom it is to be as aforesaid. [AB, 33]

43. Si quis tenuerit de aliqua escaeta, sicut de honore Wallingeford', Notingeham', Bolonie, Lancastrie, vel de aliis escaetis, que sunt in manu nostra, et sunt baronie, et obierit, heres eius non det aliud relevium, nec faciat aliud nobis servitium* quam faceret baroni si baronia illa esset | in manu baronis; et† nos eodem modo eam tenebimus quo baro eam tenuit.

44. Homines qui manent extra forestam non veniant decetero coram justiciariis nostris de foresta per communes summonitiones, nisi sint in placito vel plegii alicuius vel aliquorum qui attachiati sint pro foresta.

45. Nos non faciemus justiciarios,‡ constabularios, vicecomites, vel ballivos, nisi de talibus qui sciant legem regni et eam bene velint observare.

46. Omnes | barones qui fundaverunt Abbatias, unde habent cartas Regum Anglie, vel antiquam tenuram, habeant earum custodiam cum vacaverint, sicut habere debent.

47. Omnes foreste que afforestate sunt tempore nostro, statim deafforestentur; et ita fiat de ripariis que per nos tempore nostro posite sunt in defenso.

48. Omnes male consuetudines de forestis et warrennis, et de forestariis et warrennariis, vicecomitibus, et eorum ministris, Ripariis | et earum custodibus, statim inquirantur in quolibet comitatu per duodecim milites iuratos de eodem comitatu, qui debent eligi per probos homines eiusdem comitatus, et infra quadraginta dies post

---

* Canterbury, Cii, Salisbury and the bishops' copy read 'nobis aliud servitium'.
† Cii has 'Et' here.
‡ Salisbury inserts 'vel' here.

43. If anyone dies who holds from any escheat, as from the honour of Wallingford, Nottingham, Boulogne, Lancaster, or from other escheats which are in our hand, and are baronies, his heir is not to give us other relief, nor to do us other service, than he would do to the baron if that barony was in the hand of a baron; and we will hold it in the same way as the baron held it. [AB, 36; 1225, 31]

44. Men who live outside the forest are not henceforth to come before our justices of the forest through the common summonses, unless they are in a plea, or the sureties of some person or persons who have been attached for the forest business. [AB, 39; 1225 Forest Charter, 2]

45. We will not make justices, constables, sheriffs or bailiffs, save from those who know the law of the kingdom and wish to observe it well. [AB, 42]

46. All barons who have founded abbeys, for which they have charters of the kings of England, or ancient tenure, are to have custody of these when they become vacant, as they ought to have. [AB, 43; 1225, 33]

47. All forests which have been afforested in our time are to be immediately deforested; and it is to be the same for riverbanks which through us in our time have been placed in enclosure. [AB, 47; 1225, 16; 1225 Forest Charter, 3]

48. All evil customs of forests and warrens, and of foresters and warreners, sheriffs and their ministers, riverbanks and their keepers, are to be immediately inquired into in each county by twelve sworn knights of the same county, who are to be elected by upright men of the same county, and within forty days after

inquisitionem factam, penitus, ita quod numquam revocentur, deleantur* per eosdem. Ita quod nos hoc prius† sciamus vel justiciarius noster, si‡ in Anglia non fuerimus.

49. **O**mnes obsides et cartas statim reddemus que liberate fuerunt nobis ab Anglicis in securitatem pacis vel fide | lis servitii.

50. **N**os amovebimus penitus de balliis parentes Gerardi de Atyes§ quod decetero nullam habeant balliam in Anglia; Engelardum de Cygoyny, Andream, Petrum et Gyonem de Cancellis,¶ Gyonem de Cygoyny, Galfridum de Martiny et fratres eius, Philippum Marc', et fratres eius, et Galfridum nepotem eius, et totam sequelam eorumdem; (51) et** statim post pacis reformationem amovebimus de regno omnes alienigenas milites, Balistarios, servientes | stipendiarios, qui venerint cum equis et armis ad nocumentum regni.

52. **S**i quis fuerit dissaisitus vel elongatus per nos sine legali iuditio parium suorum, de terris, castellis,†† libertatibus, vel iure suo, statim ea ei restituemus; et si contentio super hoc orta fuerit, tunc inde fiat‡‡ per juditium viginti quinque baronum, de quibus fit mentio inferius in securitate pacis.

*

* Above 'deleantur' in Canterbury there is a sign in the form of a line with a diamond-like shape at the end that refers down to the foot of the Charter where we find the same sign followed by '<u>deleantur</u> per eosdem ita quod nos hoc sciamus prius vel Justiciarius noster si in Anglia non fuerimus', the passage 'per eosdem . . . fuerimus' having been omitted in the text. The underlining of passages so as to draw attention to them was common practice, and was here employed to help mark the place where the insertion should go. The passage 'per eosdem . . . fuerimus' is also added at the foot of Cii, having likewise been omitted from the text, although the 'per' seems now lost as is any sign of '<u>deleantur</u>'.
† Canterbury and Cii (in the passage they add at the bottom) and Salisbury and the bishops' copy place 'prius' after 'sciamus'.
‡ Salisbury inserts 'nos' here.
§ Atyes and the names that follow are spelt in a variety of different ways.
¶ Cii has 'Petrum et Gionem et Andream'.
** Lincoln and the bishops' copy have 'et' here. Canterbury, Salisbury and Cii have 'Et', although only in the last two does it suggest a new chapter or subsection of a chapter.
†† Canterbury has 'castallis'.
‡‡ Salisbury has 'fiet'.

the inquiry has been made, they are to be wholly abolished by them, so that they are never revived, provided that we, or our justiciar, if we are not in England, know about it beforehand. [AB, 39]

49. We will immediately return all hostages and charters which were given to us by Englishmen as security for peace or faithful service. [AB, 38]

50. We will remove completely from their bailiwicks the kinsmen of Gerard d'Athée, so that henceforth they shall hold no bailiwick in England: Engelard de Cigogné, Andrew, Peter and Gio de Chanceaux, Gio de Cigogné, Geoffrey de Martigny, and his brothers, Philip Marc and his brothers, and Geoffrey his nephew, and all their following. [AB, 40] (51) And immediately after the restoration of peace, we will remove from the kingdom all alien knights, cross-bowmen, serjeants, mercenaries, who have come with horses and arms to the harm of the kingdom. [AB, 41]

52. If anyone has been disseised or dispossessed by us, without lawful judgement of his peers, of lands, castles, liberties or his right, we will restore these to him immediately. And if a dispute arises about this, then it is to be dealt with by the judgement of the twenty-five barons of whom mention is made below in the security of peace.

*

De omnibus autem illis de quibus aliquis dissaisitus fuerit vel
elongatus sine legali iuditio parium suorum, per Henricum | Regem
patrem nostrum vel per Ricardum regem fratrem nostrum, que in
manu nostra habemus, vel que alii tenent, que nos oporteat war-
antizare, respectum habebimus usque ad communem terminum
cruce signatorum; exceptis illis de quibus placitum motum fuit vel
inquisitio facta per preceptum nostrum, ante susceptionem crucis
nostre.

Cum autem redierimus de peregrinatione nostra, vel si forte
remanserimus a peregrinatione nostra, statim inde plenam iustitiam
exhibebimus.

53. Eundem* autem | respectum habebimus, et eodem modo, de
iustitia exhibenda de forestis deafforestandis† vel remansuris forestis,
quas Henricus pater noster vel Ricardus frater noster affores-
taverunt, et de custodiis terrarum que sunt de alieno feodo, cuiusmodi
custodias hucusque habuimus occasione feodi quod aliquis de
nobis tenuit per servitium militare. Et de Abbatiis que fundate fuerint in feodo alterius quam nostro, in quibus dominus feodi dixerit se
ius habere. Et cum redierimus, vel si reman | serimus a peregrinatione
nostra, super hiis conquerentibus plenam iustitiam statim
exhibebimus.

54. Nullus capiatur nec inprisonetur propter appellum femine de
morte alterius quam viri sui.

---

* In Canterbury, there is another sign in the form of a line with a diamond-like
shape at the end above 'Eundem'. It refers down to the foot of the Charter where
we find the same sign followed by 'Eundem autem Respectum habebimus, et eodem
modo de Justicia exhibenda', 'et . . . exhibenda' having been omitted from the text.
The same passage 'Eundem . . . exhibenda' appears at the foot of Cii, where there is
the same omission.
† At the foot of Canterbury, in the Pine engraving, we find 'De forestis deafforestandis
vel remansuris forestis', 'vel remansuris forestis' having been omitted from the text. In
drawing attention to the omission, Canterbury relies on the sign at the start of the
chapter before 'Eundem' (see note above). 'De forestis deafforestandis vel remansuris
forestis' also appears at the foot of Cii, 'vel remansuris forestis' having likewise been
omitted from the text. In Canterbury 'De forestis deaffore' was actually destroyed by
the fire of 1731 and was supplied in the Pine engraving by reference to Cii; see BL
Cotton Charter XIII 31b; and above, pp. 15–16.

Concerning, however, all those who have been disseised or dispossessed without lawful judgement of their peers by King Henry, our father, or by King Richard, our brother, which things we have in our hand, or which others hold, which we ought to warrant, we will have respite until the common term of crusaders; except for those things concerning which a plea has been moved or an inquest made by our order, before the receiving of our cross.

When, however, we return from pilgrimage, or if by chance we remain behind from our pilgrimage, we will then immediately give full justice. [AB, 25]

53. We shall have the same respite, and in the same way, concerning the giving of justice with regard to forests to be deforested or forests to be retained, which Henry, our father, or Richard, our brother, afforested, and concerning the wardship of lands which are of the fee of another, wardships of which kind we have had hitherto by reason of a fee which somebody held from us by knight service; and concerning abbeys which have been founded in the fee of another, not our own, in which the lord of the fee says he has right. And when we return, or if we remain behind from our pilgrimage, we will immediately give full justice on these things to the complainants. [1225 Forest Charter, 1, 3]

54. No one is to be arrested or imprisoned through the appeal of a woman for the death of anyone other than her husband. [1225, 34]

55. Omnes fines qui iniuste et contra legem terre facti sunt nobis-cum, et omnia amerciamenta facta iniuste et contra legem terre, omnino condonentur, vel fiat inde per iuditium viginti quinque baronum de quibus fit mentio inferius in securitate pacis, vel per iuditium maioris partis | eorumdem, una cum predicto Stephano Cantuariensi Archiepiscopo, si interesse poterit, et aliis quos secum ad hoc vocare voluerit: et si interesse non poterit, nichilomi-nus procedat negotium sine eo. Ita quod, si aliquis vel aliqui de predictis viginti quinque baronibus fuerint in simili querela, amove-antur quantum ad hoc iuditium, et alii loco eorum per residuos de eisdem viginti quinque,* tantum ad hoc faciendum electi et iurati substituantur.†

56. Si nos disseisivimus vel elongavi | mus walenses de terris vel libertatibus vel rebus aliis, sine legali iuditio parium suorum,‡ in anglia vel in wallia, eis statim reddantur; et si contentio super hoc orta fuerit, tunc inde fiat in marchia per iuditium parium suorum, de tenementis anglie secundum legem anglie, de tenementis wallie secundum legem wallie, de tenementis marchie secundum legem marchie. Idem facient walenses nobis et nostris.

57. De omnibus autem illis de quibus aliquis walensium dissaisi-tus fuerit | vel elongatus§ sine legali iuditio parium suorum, per Henricum regem patrem nostrum vel Ricardum Regem fratrem nostrum que nos in manu nostra habemus, vel que alii tenent que nos oporteat warantizare, respectum habebimus usque ad communem terminum crucesignatorum, illis exceptis de quibus placitum motum fuit vel inquisitio facta per preceptum nostrum ante susceptionem crucis nostre. Cum autem redierimus, vel si forte remanserimus a peregrinatione nostra, statim eis inde plenam iusticiam | exhibebi-mus, secundum leges walensium¶ et partes predictas.

---

* Here and elsewhere Salisbury renders 'viginti quinque' as 'xxv'. It also places 'eisdem' after 'xxv'.
† Salisbury has 'substituentur'.
‡ In Canterbury, above 'suorum', there is a sign ÷ that refers down to the right-hand foot of the document where we find marked out by a similar sign 'parium suorum in Anglia vel in Wallia', 'in Anglia vel in Wallia' having been omitted from the text.
§ Salisbury has 'Walensis' and omits 'vel elongatus'.
¶ Salisbury has 'Wallie'.

55. All fines which have been made with us unjustly and against the law of the land, and all amercements made unjustly and against the law of the land, are to be completely remitted, or dealt with by the judgement of the twenty-five barons of whom mention is made below in the security of peace, or by the judgement of the greater part of them, together with the aforesaid Stephen, archbishop of Canterbury, if he will be able to attend, and with others whom he wishes to call with him for this. And if he will not be able to attend, nonetheless the business is to proceed without him, provided that if any person or persons from the aforesaid twenty-five barons is in such a plea, they are to be removed just for that judgement, and others in place of them, chosen and sworn just to make that judgement, are to be substituted by the rest of the twenty-five. [AB, 37]

56. If we have disseised or dispossessed Welshmen of lands, or liberties or other things, without lawful judgement of their peers, in England or in Wales, those things are to be immediately restored to them. And if a dispute arises about this, then it is to be dealt with in the March by judgement of their peers, concerning tenements in England according to the law of England, concerning tenements of Wales, according to the law of Wales, concerning tenements of the March, according to the law of the March. Welshmen shall do the same for us and our men. [AB, 44]

57. Concerning, however, all the things of which any Welshman has been disseised or dispossessed, without lawful judgement of his peers, by King Henry, our father, or King Richard, our brother, which we have in our hand, or which others hold which we ought to warrant, we will have respite until the common term of crusaders, those things excepted concerning which a plea has been moved or an inquest has been made by our order before the receiving of our cross. When, however, we return, or if by chance we remain behind from our pilgrimage, we will then immediately give full justice to them according to the laws of the Welsh and the foresaid parts. [AB, 44]

58. Nos reddemus filium Leulini statim, et omnes obsides de wallia, et cartas que nobis liberate fuerunt in securitatem pacis.

59. Nos faciemus Alexandro Regi scottorum de sororibus suis et obsidibus reddendis, et libertatibus suis, et jure suo, secundum formam in qua faciemus aliis baronibus nostris Anglie, nisi aliter esse debeat per cartas quas habemus de Willelmo patre ipsius,* quondam rege scottorum; et hoc erit per | iuditium parium | suorum in curia nostra.

60. Omnes autem istas consuetudines predictas et libertates quas nos concessimus† in regno nostro tenendas quantum ad nos pertinet erga nostros, omnes de regno nostro, tam clerici quam laici, observent‡ quantum ad se pertinet erga suos.

61. Cum autem pro deo, et ad emendationem regni nostri, et ad melius sopiendam discordiam inter nos et barones nostros ortam, hec omnia predicta concesserimus, volentes ea integra et firma§ stabilitate in perpetuum gaudere,¶ facimus et conce | dimus eis securitatem subscriptam; videlicet quod barones eligent** viginti quinque barones de regno quos voluerint, qui debeant pro totis viribus suis observare, tenere, et facere observari, pacem et libertates quas eis concessimus, et hac presenti carta nostra confirmavimus. Ita scilicet quod, si nos, vel justiciarius noster, vel ballivi nostri, vel aliquis de ministris nostris, in aliquo erga aliquem deliquerimus, vel aliquem articulorum pacis aut securitatis transgressi fuerimus, et delictum ostensum | fuerit quattuor baronibus de predictis viginti quinque baronibus, illi quattuor barones accedent†† ad nos vel ad justiciarium nostrum, si fuerimus extra regnum, proponentes

---

* Salisbury has 'eius' not 'ipsius'.
† Canterbury has 'concessissimus'. Salisbury, Cii and the bishops' copy are as Lincoln.
‡ Salisbury places 'observent' after 'quantum ad se pertinet'.
§ Salisbury has 'firma et integra'.
¶ Above 'gaudere' in Canterbury, there is a sign ∴ referring down to the right-hand foot of the Charter, where we find marked out by a similar sign 'gaudere in perpetuum', 'in perpetuum' having been omitted from the text. In the Pine engraving, 'gaudere' is not here underlined. Salisbury also has 'gaudere in perpetuum' as opposed to 'in perpetuum gaudere'.
** 'eligant' appears in Canterbury, Salisbury, Cii and the bishops' copy.
†† 'accedant' appears in Canterbury, Cii and the bishops' copy. Salisbury is as Lincoln.

58. We will return the son of Llywelyn immediately, and all hostages from Wales, and the charters which have been delivered to us as security of peace. [AB, 45]

59. We will deal with Alexander, king of Scots, concerning the restoration of his sisters and hostages, and his liberties and his right, according to the form in which we will deal with our other barons of England, unless it should be otherwise by reason of the charters which we have from William, his father, once king of Scots, and this will be by judgement of his peers in our court. [AB, 46]

60. All these aforesaid customs and liberties, moreover, which we have granted to be held in our kingdom, as much as it pertains to us towards our men, all the men of our kingdom, both clerks and laymen, are to observe, as much as it pertains to them, to their men. [AB, 48; 1225, 37; 1225 Forest Charter, 17]

61. Since, moreover, for God and for the reform of our kingdom and for the better quieting of the discord arisen between us and our barons, we have granted all the things aforesaid, wishing these things to enjoy a complete and firm durability in perpetuity, we make and grant them the below written security: namely that the barons shall choose twenty-five barons of the kingdom, whom they wish, who should with all their strength observe, keep and cause to be observed, the peace and liberties which we have granted to them, and have confirmed by this our present charter, so namely that if we, or our justiciar, or our bailiffs, or any of our ministers, offends against anyone in any way, or transgresses any of the articles of peace or security, and the offence is shown to four barons of the aforesaid twenty-five barons, these four barons shall go to us or our justiciar, if we are out of the kingdom, putting

nobis excessum;* petent ut excessum illum sine dilatione faciamus emendari. Et si nos excessum non emendaverimus, vel, si fuerimus extra regnum, justiciarius noster non emendaverit infra tempus quadraginta dierum computandum a tempore quo monstratum fuerit nobis vel justiciario nostro† si extra regnum fuerimus, predicti | quattuor barones referant causam‡ ad residuos de illis§ viginti quinque baronibus, et illi viginti quinque barones cum communa totius terre distringent et gravabunt nos modis omnibus quibus poterunt, scilicet¶ per captionem castrorum, terrarum, possessionum, et aliis modis quibus poterunt, donec fuerit emendatum secundum arbitrium eorum, salva persona nostra et Regine nostre et liberorum nostrorum; et cum fuerit emendatum, intendent nobis sicut prius fecerunt.

Et quicumque voluerit de | terra, iuret quod ad predicta omnia exequenda, parebit mandatis predictorum viginti quinque baronum, et quod gravabit nos pro posse suo cum ipsis, et nos publice et libere damus licentiam iurandi cuilibet qui iurare voluerit, et nulli umquam iurare prohibebimus.

Omnes autem illos de terra qui per se et sponte sua noluerint iurare** viginti quinque baronibus, de distringendo et gravando nos cum eis, faciemus iurare eosdem de mandato nostro, sicut predictum est.

Et si aliquis de†† vigin | ti quinque baronibus decesserit, vel a terra recesserit, vel aliquo alio modo impeditus fuerit, quominus ista predicta possent‡‡ exequi, qui residui fuerint de predictis§§ viginti quinque baronibus eligant alium loco ipsius, pro arbitrio suo, qui simili modo erit iuratus quo et ceteri.

*

* Salisbury adds 'et' here.
† Salisbury has 'justiciariis nostris'.
‡ Canterbury, Cii, Salisbury and the bishops' copy all add 'illam' after 'causam'.
§ 'illis' is omitted in Canterbury and Salisbury.
¶ A capital 'S' marks out the 'Scilicet' in Salisbury.
** Salisbury has 'predictis' before 'xxv' (its rendering of 'viginti quinque'). The bishops' copy absurdly reads 'voluerint' rather than 'noluerint'.
†† Salisbury and the bishops' copy have 'predictis' here.
‡‡ The bishops' copy has 'possint'.
§§ 'illis' rather than 'predictis' appears in the bishops' copy.

before us the transgression; they shall seek that we cause that transgression to be redressed without delay. And if we do not redress it, or, if we are out of the kingdom, our justiciar does not redress it, within the time of forty days to be counted from the time when it is shown to us or our justiciar, if we are out of the kingdom, the aforesaid four barons are to refer the cause to the rest of those twenty-five barons, and those twenty-five barons, with the commune of all the land, shall distrain and distress us in all ways they can, namely by the taking of castles, lands, possessions, and in other ways as they shall be able, until it is redressed, according to their judgement, saving our person and those of our queen and our children. And when it is redressed, they shall obey us as they did before.

And whosoever of the land wishes, is to swear that for the executing of all the aforesaid things, he shall obey the orders of the foresaid twenty-five barons, and that he will distress us with them according to his ability, and we publicly and freely give licence to swear to anyone who wishes to swear, and to no one will we ever prohibit swearing.

All those, however, of the land who do not wish of their own accord and spontaneously to swear to the twenty-five barons, concerning distraining and distressing us with them, we shall cause these same to swear by our order, as is aforesaid.

And if any of the twenty-five barons dies, or departs from the land, or in any other way is impeded, so that they are the less able to carry out the foresaid things, those who remain of the aforesaid twenty-five barons are to choose another in his place, according to their decision, who will be sworn in the same way as the others.

*

In omnibus autem que istis viginti quinque baronibus committun-
tur exequenda, si forte ipsi viginti quinque presentes fuerint, et
inter se super re aliqua discordaverint, vel aliqui ex eis summoniti
nolint vel neq | ueant interesse, ratum habeatur et firmum quod
maior pars eorum qui presentes fuerint, providerit, vel preceperit,
ac si omnes viginti quinque in hoc consensissent. Et predicti viginti
quinque iurent quod omnia antedicta fideliter observabunt, et pro
toto posse suo facient observari.

Et nos nichil impetrabimus ab aliquo, per nos nec per alium, per
quod aliqua istarum concessionum et* libertatum revocetur vel min-
uatur. Et si aliquid tale impetratum fuerit irritum sit et inane et
numquam | eo utemur per nos nec per alium.

62. Et† omnes malas voluntates, indignationes, et rancores, ortos
inter nos et homines nostros, clericos et laicos, a tempore dis-
cordie, plene omnibus remisimus et condonavimus.

Preterea omnes trangressiones factas occasione eiusdem‡ dis-
cordie, a Pascha anno Regni nostri sextodecimo usque ad pacem
reformatam, plene remisimus omnibus, clericis et laicis, et quantum
ad nos pertinet, plene condonavimus.

Et insuper, fecimus eis fieri | litteras testimoniales patentes Domini
Stephani Cantuariensis Archiepiscopi, Domini Henrici Dublinen-
sis Archiepiscopi,§ et Episcoporum predictorum, et Magistri
Pandulfi, super securitate ista¶ et concessionibus prefatis.

---

* The bishops' copy has 'vel' not 'et'.
† Lincoln does not begin a new section here.
‡ The bishops' copy has 'huius' not 'eiusdem'.
§ Salisbury omits Henry, archbishop of Dublin.
¶ Salisbury has 'illa'.

In all the things, moreover, which are committed to these twenty-five barons to be dealt with, if by chance these twenty-five are present, and disagree among themselves on any thing, or if any of them, having been summoned, should not wish or should be unable to attend, what the greater part of those who are present provide or order, is to be treated as ratified and binding, as if all the twenty-five had consented to this. And the aforesaid twenty-five are to swear that they will faithfully observe all the aforesaid things, and to the best of their ability will cause them to be observed.

And we will obtain nothing from anybody, by us nor by another, by which any of these concessions and liberties may be revoked or diminished; and if any such thing is obtained, it is to be invalid and void, and we will never use it, either through ourselves or through another. [AB, 49]

62. And all ill will, indignation and rancour which has arisen between us and our men, clerks and laymen, from the time of the discord, we have fully remitted and pardoned to everyone.

In addition, all transgressions perpetrated on occasion of the aforesaid discord, from Easter in the sixteenth year of our reign, until the restoration of peace, we have fully remitted to all, clerks and laymen, and as much as it belongs to us, have fully pardoned.

And, moreover, we have caused to be made for them letters patent testimonial of lord Stephen, archbishop of Canterbury, of lord Henry, archbishop of Dublin, and of the aforesaid bishops, and of Master Pandulf, on this security and the aforesaid concessions.

63. Quare volumus et firmiter precipimus quod anglicana ecclesia libera sit et quod homines in regno nostro habeant et teneant omnes prefatas libertates, jura, et concessiones, bene et* in pace, libere et quiete, plene et integre, sibi et | heredibus suis, de nobis et heredibus nostris, in omnibus rebus et locis, in perpetuum, sicut predictum est.

Juratum est autem, tam ex parte nostra quam ex parte baronum, quod hec omnia supradicta bona fide et sine malo ingenio servabuntur.†

Testibus supradictis et multis aliis.

Data per manum nostram in Prato quod vocatur Runimed' inter Windleshor' et Stanes | Quintodecimo die Junii, Anno Regni Nostri Septimodecimo.‡

---

* Salisbury omits 'et' and has 'omnes' after 'concessiones'.
† Canterbury, Cii, Salisbury and the bishops' copy have 'observabuntur'.
‡ In Lincoln the words from 'Quintodecimo' are spaced out so as to fill the whole of the last line. Cii has 'Decimo septimo'.

63. Wherefore, we wish and firmly command that the English church be free, and that the men in our kingdom have and hold all the aforesaid liberties, rights and concessions, well and in peace, freely and quietly, fully and completely, for them and their heirs, from us and our heirs, in all things and places, in perpetuity, as is aforesaid.

Moreover, it has been sworn both on our part and on the part of the barons, that all these things abovesaid will be observed in good faith and without evil intent.

Witnesses the abovesaid and many others.

Given by our hand in the meadow which is called Runnymede, between Windsor and Staines, on the fifteenth day of June, in the seventeenth year of our reign.*

---

* On the back of the Lincoln Charter, in the bottom left- and the bottom right-hand corners, the word LINCOLNIA appears in capital letters probably in the same hand as that which wrote the body of the Charter. Also written on the back in a contemporary hand is 'Concordia inter Regem Johannem et Barones per concessionem libertatum ecclesie et regni anglie', 'The Concord between King John and the Barons in return for the concession of the liberties of the church and the kingdom of England'.

3
King John and the Sources
for His Reign

John was the youngest son of King Henry II and Eleanor of Aquitaine. He acceded to the throne of England, on the death of his brother Richard the Lionheart, in 1199. Yet he was far more than simply king of England. At its start Magna Carta proclaimed him also 'lord of Ireland, duke of Normandy and Aquitaine, count of Anjou'. In an important respect, even this panoply of titles failed to reflect John's power, for it suggested nothing of his dominance over Wales and Scotland. It was that which provoked the Welsh rulers and the king of Scots, Alexander II, to ally with the barons in 1215. There were chapters in their favour in Magna Carta, making it a British, not just an English, document. Nor were the other dominions irrelevant to what happened in 1215. Quite the reverse. The rebellion had no footing in Ireland, and the 1215 Charter was not sent there, but John's quarrels with some of his greatest barons had major Irish dimensions.[1] Even more important, indeed absolutely crucial, was the continental empire. How right that Normandy, Aquitaine and Anjou stand in large letters on the first line of Magna Carta, as though weighing down all the rest! The financial burdens placed on England to defend and recover the continental empire were the single most important cause of Magna Carta. Had John been content with ruling England and dominating Britain and Ireland, there would have been no Charter.

The assemblage of territories proclaimed in John's title was put together by Henry II. Henry began to rule in Anjou and Normandy in 1151. Anjou he had inherited from his father, Geoffrey, hence the way that historians refer to the dynasty as that of the Angevins, while calling the dominions under their rule the Angevin empire. Henry's title to Normandy, as to England, came from his mother, Matilda, daughter of Henry I (r. 1100–1135), and thus a granddaughter of William the Conqueror. In 1152 Henry II's marriage to Eleanor of Aquitaine brought him her extensive duchy, which embraced both Poitou and Gascony. Then Henry, ending at last the long civil war, forced King Stephen to accept his claim to the throne of England, becoming king on the latter's death in 1154. More was to come, for Henry's intervention in Ireland in 1171–2 created the dynasty's lordship there. He conferred it on John, who, at the start of his reign, added 'lord of Ireland' to the royal titles.

The continental dominions, Normandy, Anjou and Aquitaine, were held as fiefs from the Capetian king of France. They might be liable to forfeiture for any breach of the homage and service that was owed him. In the early years of Henry II's reign, the likelihood of any such sentence being enforced was negligible, given the weakness of the Capetian king, Louis VII (r. 1137–80). Everything began to change with the accession of Philip II, later called Augustus, in 1180. His burning aim was to weaken, and, if possible, destroy the Angevin empire. Gradually he built up the resources to do so. He also proved a master at exploiting divisions within the Angevin family. When Henry died in 1189, only two of his sons by Eleanor of Aquitaine remained alive, Richard and John. Richard succeeded to England and to all the continental possessions, and then left immediately on crusade. During Richard's absence in the Holy Land, and then in captivity in Germany, John first challenged the government in England and then laid claim to the throne. Philip Augustus, meanwhile, overran much of Normandy. Richard, on his return in 1194, having put down what was left of John's revolt, spent the following years on the continent in a fierce struggle to recover what he had lost. He had great success, yet failed to put the frontiers of Normandy back to their state in 1189.[2] Then, in 1199, Richard's dramatic career was abruptly ended. Laying siege to the castle of Chalus-Chabrol in the Limousin, he left his tent one evening on a tour of inspection. With characteristic but fatal self-confidence, he had not donned his armour. He was carrying a shield, but then failed to duck behind it in time when an arrow winged its way towards him from the battlements. The arrow bit deep into his shoulder, its extraction was botched, the wound festered, and Richard died on 6 April.[3] He was childless. There were two candidates for the succession, John himself and his nephew Arthur, the son of John's deceased older brother Geoffrey of Brittany. Arthur, however, was only twelve, and had few supporters among the Anglo-Norman barons. John was able to secure

Normandy and England without difficulty. In 1200, by the Treaty of Le Goulet, King Philip accepted his succession to all the continental dominions. Of the disasters that soon followed, we will say something in Chapter 7. They culminated in 1203–4 with John's loss of Normandy and Anjou. He spent much of the next ten years exploiting England in order to gain the resources to win the empire back. The financial exactions of Angevin government were already unpopular in 1199. Now the situation seemed many times worse. The result was Magna Carta.

The needs of the Angevin empire cannot be seen in isolation from the system of government that fed them and the structure of the society on which that feeding impacted. Both are reflected powerfully in the Charter, as we will see in Chapters 4 to 6. Equally important were the political ideas, discussed in Chapter 8, that set the standards by which the king's rule was judged. Important too was the character of the king. John's government would have been unpopular whatever his character, given the level of his exactions. Yet had he been a better man, he might well have got away with them. Without the intense hostility to him as a person, there would have been no revolt and no Magna Carta.

The Charter itself can seem very personal to King John. His name is its first word, the 'J' in some of the engrossments and later copies being elongated and decorated. The words 'we' and 'our' – 'nos' and 'noster' – appear no fewer than 139 times in the text. At its end, John 'gives' the Charter with his own hand. And then, hanging beneath all the originals would have been John's seal. There he appeared, on one side, sitting elegantly crowned and holding orb and sword, while on the other side he was astride his horse, in armour, brandishing his sword, and with a shield bearing the lions of England. The seal gave a wonderful picture of kingship's majesty and might. How ironic that it should authenticate a charter that was designed to diminish both!

The Charter also suggested something of the menacing contradictions in John's character. At its start, John said that he was acting for the honour of God, the health of his soul, the exaltation of holy church and the reform of his kingdom. Noble sentiments, which did not come altogether falsely from his lips. They were certainly not invented just for the Charter, for John often explained his actions in such terms. Yet the Charter also suggested John's other side. Under chapter 62, he remitted 'all ill will, indignation and rancour' between himself and his men, angry feelings from which might flow the arrest, imprisonment, outlawry, dispossession, exile and destruction mentioned in chapter 39. The Charter also testified powerfully to the belief that John was utterly untrustworthy. Hence the way the security clause gave such extraordinary coercive powers to the twenty-five barons and the commune of the land if John broke the agreement. Suspicion also hovered over John's sincerity as a crusader, hence the way the Charter envisaged that he might never in fact set out. And John's promise at the end of the Charter to seek nothing by which it might be invalidated revealed all too clearly the suspicion that he intended to do just that. John's character was far from straightforward, which was one reason why he was so dangerous. He was perfectly capable of acting in what appeared to be a gracious and consensual manner. He frequently said he wished to uphold law and custom. On the other hand, he could equally behave in ways that seemed utterly unacceptable. The better one knew him, the more one detected the malevolence behind the smile and the knife beneath the cloak.

John was in his early thirties when he came to the throne in 1199 and late forties at the time of Magna Carta, having been born in England in 1166 or 1167. We know little of his physical appearance. Over his tomb in Worcester cathedral lies an effigy of the king made from dark, rather forbidding Purbeck marble. It gives John a short beard, a clipped moustache and a smallish, almost delicate face with prominent cheekbones. Although presumably finished in time for the removal of John's body to its new tomb in 1232, there is no reason to think that it bears a likeness to him.[4] The tomb itself was opened in 1797, when some grey hairs were discernible under the covering of the head, a covering that disappointingly was not removed. The teeth in the displaced upper jaw were good, and the bones of the right foot were well preserved 'on two or three of which the nails were still visible'. Some teeth, a thumb bone and a shoe from the tomb are displayed in the British Library's Magna Carta exhibition. The body measured five foot six and a half inches, so John, for the time, was of reasonable height.[5] When, therefore, Gervase, a monk of Canterbury, writing of early in the reign, spoke of John's 'smallness of body' – 'corporis parvitatem' – he was probably referring to the slightness of his frame. Later, given his good appetite, for which there is ample evidence, he probably put on weight. The St Albans chronicler, Matthew Paris, has a former servant of John, in the course of narrating a very fanciful story, describe him as 'strong in body, not tall, but rather compact'.[6]

How then can we get a feel for what John was like? The answer is through the works of contemporary writers and through the records of royal government. This chapter explores John's personality as seen through the lens of both, thereby also providing an introduction to what are the most important sources for the Magna Carta period. The contemporaries who wrote about King John have not received a good press, being often judged both prejudiced and inaccurate. Yet it is remarkable how many accounts were written by men who either saw John at close quarters or had information from those who did. Such sources often preserve what seem authentic and intimate pictures of John in action and conversation. They can take us close to the king.

JOHN BEFORE HIS ACCESSION: GERALD OF WALES AND ROGER OF HOWDEN

We get a first glimpse of John in the writings of Gerald of Wales, a prolific and prejudiced author, sometime royal clerk, and aspirant to the bishopric of St David's.[7] Gerald accompanied John to Ireland in 1185, and gave an account of the expedition in his *Conquest of Ireland*, which was finished four years later. At this time, Gerald was still broadly a supporter of the royal house. His picture of John betrays the contradictions that were to become familiar. Gerald has John falling at his father's feet and begging 'in a most laudable fashion it is said' to be sent not to Ireland but on crusade to Jerusalem. This was certainly no easy option, but it was to Ireland, by decision of his father Henry II, that John went. There his young and irresponsible entourage showed its contempt for the native rulers by pulling their beards, 'which were large and flowing according to the native custom'. Such offensive conduct was one reason, Gerald believed, for the failure of the expedition.[8]

John's reputation in the ensuing years was further blasted by his rebellion against his father. It was Gerald, in a later dyspeptic phase, who gave the vivid picture of Henry, on his deathbed, turning his face to the wall when learning of the treachery of his youngest and favourite son. This was followed by John's rebellion against his brother Richard while the latter was absent on crusade and then in captivity. The most detailed account of these years is given by Roger of Howden, another royal clerk, but one whose writings, compared to Gerald's, are measured and self-effacing. Howden preserves Richard's contemptuous reflection on John's treachery: 'my brother John is not a man to conquer a land if there is someone to resist him with even a meagre degree of force'.[9] Yet Howden also has John, after his rehabilitation on Richard's return in 1194, fighting loyally and successfully against the king of France, as well as clearing himself of further charges of treachery. Indeed, in 1196, John and the mercenary captain Mercadier, having captured the bishop of Beauvais, returned to Richard 'gloriously triumphant'.[10]

RALPH OF COGGESHALL

This mixed but far from wholly negative picture is continued in the chronicle of Ralph of Coggeshall, a monk and, from 1207, the abbot of the Cistercian monastery of Coggeshall in Essex. Ralph's narrative of the years 1199–1201 was written very soon afterwards, and certainly before the disasters of the loss of Normandy in 1204 and the Interdict pronounced on England in 1208 by Pope Innocent III.[11] Coggeshall was not a court insider like Gerald of Wales and Roger of Howden, but when it came to narrating John's quarrel with the Cistercians, he was almost certainly an eyewitness.

When the Cistercians, standing on their rights of exemption, refused to pay a tax levied on England in 1200, John 'in anger and fury' ordered the sheriffs both by word of mouth and by letters to do as much damage to them as they could. They were to deny the Cistercians any 'justice' or assistance and refer everything to him. After the intervention of his chancellor, the archbishop of Canterbury, Hubert Walter, John withdrew these 'cruel' orders, but he then brushed aside, as far too small, the payment of 1,000 marks that Hubert suggested for a settlement, and gave orders to his foresters to expel all Cistercian-owned animals from his woods. When a great council met at Lincoln in November 1200, the Cistercian abbots did not go in procession to greet the king, for fear of being turned away by his attendants and excluded with ridicule from the royal hall. John, meanwhile, refused to listen to another attempted intervention by Hubert Walter: 'My lord archbishop, I beg you not to enrage me today, because I propose to be bled.'

In the end, however, after the archbishop had talked to John as he came out from Mass, the abbots were allowed to prostrate themselves before the king, and were then given access to his chamber. There John left them standing as he twice withdrew for private discussion with ministers and bishops, before Hubert Walter himself, on John's command, pronounced a settlement. The Cistercians were restored to the king's favour, no mention was made of the tax and John promised to found a monastery of the order (which he did later at Beaulieu). When, in return, the abbots forgave all the damages that they had suffered, John prostrated himself humbly at their feet, his face covered with tears, while the monks in their turn fell to the ground, 'seeing such great humility and reverence from the king'. The abbots, Coggeshall, concluded, 'were filled with immense joy and gave manifold thanks to God, who had so inclined the mind of the king to mercy and reverence for their order'.[12]

John here seems very different from the ignorant, ineffectual youth portrayed by Gerald of Wales and dismissed by Richard. He is hands on and intimidating, as kings needed to be, yet he also takes counsel and changes course, coming out of a quarrel with his reputation enhanced, indeed as one guided by the hand of God. All this is not dissimilar to John's conduct in his quarrel, in 1201-2, with the abbey of St Augustine, Canterbury, over the patronage of the church of Faversham. Here, according to the abbey's account, John in a fury threatened to burn Faversham church down and all inside it. He certainly issued orders that led to the church's blockade, the violent extraction from it of the abbot and some monks, and the seizure of St Augustine's estates. Then, however, with the pope becoming involved, sentences of excommunication flying round and the monks offering money for a settlement, John calmed down and asked advice from Hubert Walter. The archbishop, in a long and nuanced letter, counselled a climb-down. His conclusion was that it was John's agents, rather than John himself, who had profited from the seizure of the estates: 'for as to you it may be said on this matter that you *have shaken the bushes and others have caught the birds*'. Clearly John was someone to whom a leading counsellor could write frankly and fully. Apart from deciding to take the offered money, John acted on the advice. 'And thus he who had formerly been the most cruel persecutor of this monastery became its patron and protector', the abbey's account concluded.[13]

John's record early in the reign won favourable comment in matters of greater moment. Thus Coggeshall welcomed the peace John made with Philip Augustus in 1200, hoping this would end the terrible financial exactions that had been needed to finance Richard's wars.[14] Gervase of Canterbury (who finished writing in 1210) was also impressed by the peace. If it led the 'malevolent and envious' to call John 'softsword', that was only because 'by prudence more than war, he had obtained peace everywhere'.[15]

THE LIFE OF ST HUGH OF LINCOLN

There was, of course, no peace, or not for long. In 1204 Philip Augustus completed his conquest of Normandy and Anjou. After that John was soon embroiled in his quarrel with the papacy, which saw his excommunication and England being laid under an Interdict.[16] There is one intimate account of John written during this time, written in fact in 1213, so before Magna Carta. This comes in the Life of Hugh of Avalon, the bishop of Lincoln between 1186 and 1200, who was canonized in 1220. The *Life of Saint Hugh* was the work of his chaplain, Adam of Eynsham, and is one of the greatest biographies by an acolyte ever written, quite worthy to stand beside Boswell's *Life of Johnson*. Inevitably, Adam's account of the start of John's reign is prejudiced by later events. Bishop Hugh is made to rumble the king's character and foresee the disasters that were to come. Yet Adam, in his position by Hugh's side, was extremely well informed. Once the later veneer is removed, he can actually show John as much like the 'good' king revealed by Ralph of Coggeshall.[17]

Thus at Chinon, just after Richard's death, seeing Bishop Hugh approaching, John spurred his horse forward in his eagerness to meet him, leaving all his companions behind. The pair met again a few days later, at the abbey of Fontevrault, where both Henry II and now Richard were buried. Standing under the great Last Judgement portal, Hugh, as a dreadful warning, pointed up to kings being dragged down to Hell, only for John to point up to the kings on the other side, joyfully ascending to Heaven, with the assurance that he would be among their number. Next year, when Hugh was dying, John dismissed his attendants and sat alone for a long time beside his bed, 'saying many kind words'.

Mixed in with such conduct, however, was other behaviour that seemed utterly inappropriate and disrespectful. Thus John boasted to Hugh that a stone set in gold, which he wore around his neck, would preserve all his dominions from harm. This prompted the natural response that John should put his trust not in magical gems but in the Lord Jesus Christ. A little later, John scandalized the bishop by seeming for a moment about to pocket the twelve gold coins of his offering at Mass. And then, to cap it all, being hungry and wanting to eat, he sent three messages asking the bishop to conclude the sermon and hurry on with the service. The *Life of Saint Hugh* also reported the laughter and levity of John's entourage during his investiture as duke of Normandy. Turning round to join in, John dropped the lance that had been placed in his hands – not a good omen.

John's contradictory treatment of Bishop Hugh has parallels with his conduct in Jocelin of Brakelond's Life of Samson, abbot of Bury St Edmunds, which was finished soon after 1202. Here John won golden opinions by going at once, after his coronation, on a pilgrimage to Bury. He then spoiled the effect by giving the monks not the great offering that they expected but a single silken cloth which he had borrowed from the abbey's sacrist, and never paid for.[18]

Adam of Eynsham's *Life of Saint Hugh* is the last significant testimony to John's personality actually written in his reign. The other relevant works come from the decade after his death. One of these, an account of Hugh of Northwold's election as Samson's successor at Bury, written by a Bury monk and eye witness, gives a fascinating impression of John in 1214 and 1215, and we have saved it for our narrative of these years. Here let us look first at an account of the reign by a writer known as the Anonymous of Béthune.

THE ANONYMOUS OF BÉTHUNE

It is hard to think of a more unappetizing name than 'the Anonymous of Béthune' for the author of what is a superb and unique account of the Magna Carta period. This is found as part of a larger work, conventionally entitled 'The History of the Dukes of Normandy'.[19] At the heart of the portion that concerns us is a circumstantial narrative of events between 1213 and 1217. This is combined with a character sketch of King John, and a much vaguer account of episodes in his reign prior to 1213, notably John's expedition to Ireland in 1210 and the fall of the Briouze family. The work is enlivened by numerous anecdotes, vivid scenes, and quotations from John's actual conversations. Since the author is unnamed he is called 'the Anonymous'. Since he was in the entourage of Robert de Béthune (judging from the number of times Robert appears), he becomes 'the Anonymous of Béthune'.

The author had every reason to be well informed. He was writing at the latest soon after 1220. Between 1213 and 1216 his master, Robert de Béthune, was intermittently in England in John's service. Indeed, he was there for the weeks either side of Magna Carta. Our author was almost certainly with his master and thus an eyewitness to what he narrates. Given the level of detail, in such matters as dates, he must also have taken notes at the time. Robert was the younger son of the lord Béthune in Artois and Dendermonde in Flanders. He and his associates were regarded and regarded themselves as Flemings. Robert had, however, inherited land in 1214 (on his father's death) in no fewer than five English counties.[20] With numerous connections with the great English and Anglo-Norman barons, he was far from being an outsider. The Anonymous wrote for Robert de Béthune's entertainment (hence in French), and the amount of detail about warfare doubtless reflects Robert's soldierly interests. There was also a political agenda. Although never openly avowed, the way the narrative switches focus in the middle of 1216 strongly suggests that Robert, at this point, had switched sides and entered the service of Prince Louis on his arrival in England, having been offered the throne by the rebels. The portrait of John as 'bad' thus justified this conduct. That does not make it any the less believable.

The Anonymous acknowledged John's lavish hospitality and his generosity in giving robes to his knights. But the overall picture was negative indeed:

He was a very bad man, more cruel than all others; he lusted after beautiful women and because of this he shamed the high men of the land, for which reason he was greatly hated. Whenever he could, he told lies rather than the truth. Her set his barons against one another whenever he could; he was very happy when he saw hate between them. He hated and was jealous of all honourable men; it greatly displeased him when he saw anyone acting well. He was brim-full of evil qualities.[21]

Here then we meet two of the key charges against John: his cruelty, and his tampering with the wives and daughters of his barons. The Anonymous gives an example of the second in relaying Robert fitz-Walter's claim that John had tried to seduce his daughter, the wife of Geoffrey de Mandeville.[22] He gives an example of the first in a graphic account of the murder of Matilda de Briouze and her eldest son. Although the Anonymous does not make the connection, here John had form, for he had also been responsible for the murder of his own nephew Arthur.[23] Arthur had come into John's hands in 1202 and been imprisoned first at Falaise and then at Rouen. The annals of Margam abbey in south Wales give the only circumstantial account of what happened next:

> In the tower of Rouen, after dinner on the Thursday before Easter [3 April 1203], when he was drunk and possessed by the devil, [John] killed him with his own hand, and attaching a great stone to the body, threw it into the Seine.[24]

The Margam story probably came from William de Briouze, Matilda's husband. He was in Rouen at the time, but is obviously a hostile source. That, however, John, in one way or another, murdered Arthur, there can be little doubt. The murder was not necessarily unpremeditated. Ralph of Coggeshall had heard of an earlier plan to blind and emasculate Arthur when he was at Falaise.[25] Arthur, as we have said, had little support in England, but Louis, son of Philip Augustus, thought the murder worth harping on in his manifesto when he invaded England in 1216.[26] According to the St Albans abbey chronicler, Roger of Wendover, Matilda de Briouze herself refused to surrender her sons as hostages on the grounds that John had wickedly murdered Arthur.[27]

If the murder of Arthur was bad enough, that of Matilda de Briouze and her eldest son seemed far more shocking, for it struck at the heart of a great baronial family, with wide lordships in Ireland, Wales and England. The course of the family's quarrel with King

John we will trace in Chapter 7. It ended in 1210 with Matilda and William de Briouze junior being starved to death. There was nothing unpremeditated about that. The Anonymous's account registers the full horror of this atrocity:

> He imprisoned Matilda and her son at Corfe and ordered that a sheaf of oats and one piece of raw bacon be given to them. He did not allow them to have any more meat. After eleven days, the mother was found dead between her son's legs, still upright albeit leaning forward against her son's foot. Her son, who was also dead, was found sitting straight, bent against the wall. So desperate was the mother that she had eaten her son's cheeks.[28]

So far so terrible, yet when the Anonymous gets to his narrative of 1213 and portrays John close up, the picture is rather different. We see a king acerbic certainly but also quite able to take counsel and act in a rational and appropriate manner.[29] Thus when, in 1213, Robert de Béthune comes to court to seek help for the embattled Ferrand, count of Flanders, John is welcoming and well informed: 'I know exactly what you want.' He calls in his counsellors, and agrees to send out the earl of Salisbury, the result being the destruction of the French fleet at Damme. Next year, when Robert announces the arrival of the count in England, and asks why John (at the Tower of London) is not at once riding to meet him, John appears to mock:

> Hear the Fleming, he does think his lord the count of Flanders is a great man.[30]

But when Robert replied that 'by Saint James', he certainly was, John laughed, summoned his horses and outrode his entourage in his haste to get to Canterbury. On arrival he went straight to the count's hostel and, with the count waiting outside in the road, dismounted to salute and kiss him. Inside, John was affability itself and invited the count to dine with him on the next day, when their alliance would be sealed. It is difficult to think John could have handled this better.[31] Here is very much the king who, as the Anonymous observed, treated Robert de Dreux, when captured later in 1214, 'most honourably', allowing him to hunt and hawk.[32] On balance, therefore, the Anonymous's picture of John between 1213 and 1215 was a positive one.[33]

THE LIFE OF WILLIAM MARSHAL

The same could not be said for the second great work written for
aristocrats who had actually participated in the events of John's reign,
namely the life of William Marshal. William was a younger son of a
middle-ranking magnate who had lands in Wiltshire and Berkshire
and was marshal of the royal household. Born around 1147, and
with no prospect of an inheritance, William had made an awesome
reputation as a knight on the French tournament circuit, French
because France, not England, was the centre for such chivalric enter-
prises.[34] He eventually entered the service of Henry II, where he
combined his reputation as a fighting knight with that of a counsellor
and military strategist. On Henry's death, King Richard married William to a stupendously wealthy heiress, thus transforming him into
one of the greatest barons in the Anglo-Norman world, lord of Leinster in Ireland, Chepstow in Wales and Longueville in Normandy. At
the start of his reign, John went further and accepted William's claim
(through his wife) to the earldom of Pembroke. Despite much provocation, William never rebelled against King John and is named in
Magna Carta as the first of the 'noble men' on whose advice John
said that he had acted. On the king's death in October 1216, William
became regent for his son, the nine-year-old Henry III, despite being
around seventy. He held the post until shortly before his death in May
1219, winning the war for the young king, and sealing with the papal
legate the new versions of Magna Carta issued in 1216 and 1217.

   In the mid-1220s William's sons decided that this extraordinary
life should be made known and preserved. So they commissioned a
poet to write it in what turned out to be no fewer than 19,214 lines
of rhyming French verse. The *History of William Marshal*, as it is
called, is a cardinal text for the ideals and actions of chivalric knights.
It is equally so for the factual course of events. William's family and
entourage took great pains to see that the poet was well informed.
Key testimony came from the Marshal's former steward, John of
Earley, who witnessed many of the crucial passages between John
and the Marshal. The vivid picture of the king is thus well sourced.

   The portrait of John has a few redeeming features. The immensity
of his victory at Mirebeau in August 1202 (described later) is brought
out, even if the fruits are then thrown away. In one passage John
seems concerned over the health of one of the Marshal's younger

sons (Richard), kept as a hostage; and there is pathos in the account of the king on his deathbed, when he asks the Marshal's pardon and begs him to assume the regency of the kingdom. Occasionally the pleasant face the king could adopt is acknowledged:

> he reverted to his former habit
> of displaying friendliness [*bele chiere*]
> in [the Marshal's] company
> as if he bore no grudge against him
> or was angry with him.[35]

It is, however, made very clear that such friendliness was duplicitous, assumed merely when the king needed the Marshal's support.[36] The general thrust of the *History* is to substantiate the Anonymous's view that John was 'brim-full of evil qualities'. There is a subtext here, not very different from that in the work of the Anonymous. The Marshal was loyal, but his eldest son, William Marshal junior, perhaps with his father's connivance, joined the rebels and was one of the twenty-five barons commissioned to enforce the Charter. Nothing is said about his rebellion in the *History*, but clearly, as the chief patron of the work, William Marshal junior would have welcomed evidence to justify his conduct. John himself would certainly have defended his own treatment of the Marshal. Should William not have been more grateful for becoming earl of Pembroke at the start of the reign? Was he not guilty of trickery and disloyalty in striking a deal with Philip Augustus, and thus keeping his Norman lands after John's loss of the duchy?[37] And yet, when all allowances have been made, the picture in the *History*, supported by much circumstantial detail, remains a powerful and for the most part convincing indictment of the king.

The *History* does not mention directly the murders of Arthur or Matilda de Briouze, but it certainly agrees with the Anonymous's charge of cruelty, notably in John's treatment of the prisoners taken at Mirebeau:

> When the king arrived in Chinon,
> he kept his prisoners in such a horrible manner
> and in such abject confinement
> that it seemed an indignity and a disgrace
> to all those with him
> who witnessed his cruelty.[38]

It was not just at Chinon that the prisoners suffered. The Margam annals mention twenty-two noble and gallant knights taken at Mirebeau being starved to death at Corfe castle.[39]

An aspect of his cruelty was John's readiness to lie in the cause of giving pain. One day, riding out from Guildford, John summoned the Marshal up to him and announced news from Ireland. In a great conflict there, the Marshal's knights had apparently been victorious, but some had been killed, including John of Earley. It was all made up, but until he learnt the truth, the Marshal was left 'greatly aggrieved at heart'.[40]

The conflict in Ireland illustrates another characteristic mentioned by the Anonymous, namely the way in which John 'set his barons against one other whenever he could'. Thus, in Ireland, the king did all he could to exploit and exacerbate the tensions between his governor there, Meiler fitzHenry, and the Marshal. He also made strenuous efforts to undermine the loyalty of the Marshal's men. During these quarrels, the *History* shows the difficulties of being a great man at court. Between his bursts of 'good cheer', the king could treat the Marshal so coolly that no one would speak to him.[41] And in such situations, we see again the John who loved to mock. In one confrontation, when the court was in a field overlooking the sea at Portsmouth, waiting to embark for Poitou, John stomped off to one side with his entourage, leaving the Marshal virtually alone:

> The king, from where he was standing,
> looked at the scene and was greatly pleased by it,
> and he said: 'That is how I want it.
> He really is richly counselled.
> The Marshal has nobody there
> with him in his deliberations,
> from amongst all those he wanted to be present,
> except Henry fitzGerold
> and that mangy John of Earley . . .'[42]

The king had reason for his anger. The Marshal was refusing to join the expedition, being unwilling to fight against the king of France, to whom he had done homage for his Norman lands. Yet to seek to humiliate the Marshal in this way, in an episode that clearly burnt deep and was long remembered, was neither wise nor kingly.[43]

The men John went off with, while taunting the Marshal, were not his barons but his 'bachelors'. These were his household knights, some of good birth, some not, who had taken a special oath of loyalty to the king and, usually without great landed estates, were totally dependent on his favour. It was one of these, John of Bassing-bourn, who acted as John's spokesman against the Marshal.[44] Later, in another episode, it is a man of similar status, Gerard d'Athée, a knight from the Touraine, and very much one of John's creatures, who is seen in the *History* going into the king's chamber after dinner, with Meiler fitzHenry, to discuss the Marshal's affairs, while the Marshal himself is left outside, cold shouldered. It was with people such as Bassingbourn and Athée that John felt most comfortable, people who would laugh sycophantically at his jokes and, without question, do his bidding. Athée himself was dead by 1215, but his name appears in Magna Carta chapter 50, where John was made to dismiss his relations from office.

The *History* shows something else about John, namely the way he could swing from over-confidence to under-confidence, from ill-judged arrogance to exaggerated fears and suspicion. The king owed much of his victory at Mirebeau to William des Roches, but in the flush of that success he fobbed William off, telling him first to meet up with him at Chinon, then at Le Mans:

> . . . day by day the king's arrogance [*orguels*] grew
> and grew, a fault which does not allow those in its grip
> to see reason but brings them down.

John thus saw no need to honour his promises to des Roches, and the result was the latter's defection to the king of France, and the undermining of John's position in Anjou.[45] Next year, John seems very different. Sensing treason everywhere, the *History* gives a graphic picture of his flight from Normandy, steeling away in the morning before people were up, avoiding the main roads and prom-ising he would return, while leaving everyone suspecting that he would not. The reason for such conduct was clear:

> A man who does not know whom he has to fear,
> and who always thinks he is in an inferior position,
> is bound to fear everybody.[46]

Ralph of Coggeshall's verdict was the same on these events. John 'always feared betrayal by his men'.[47] No wonder the king so often tried to secure loyalty by the taking of hostages.

COGGESHALL'S CONTINUATION AND THE CROWLAND CHRONICLE

Ralph of Coggeshall's account of the later stages of John's reign, that is from 1212, was written after John's death in 1216, in much the same period as the work of the Anonymous and the *History* of the Marshal. It is of the first importance as evidence for the Magna Carta period, but lacks the intimate picture of the king at work found in the portion finished soon after 1201. What is clear is that Coggeshall's view of John has completely changed. The catalyst was probably the Interdict, during which the Cistercians were major sufferers. Thus Coggeshall's hostility to the king was now set, albeit expressed in clipped remarks rather than set-piece denunciations. Thus he stigmatized John's 'violent' exactions from the English church, his resort to fraud, 'as was his custom', his cruel threats at the siege of Rochester in 1215, and his tearful, terrified and shameful retreats after Prince Louis' invasion. To seek mercy from John was to seek 'mercy from the unmerciful'.[48] Coggeshall gives an eerie and lurid account of John's death in Newark castle during the night of 17–18 October 1216, and adds that 'many horrible and fantastic visions were told by many people afterwards, the tenor of which we will forgo describing here'. His readers would have known what this meant. The visions were of John suffering the torments of Hell.[49]

A second major account of John's last years is found in what is often called 'the Barnwell chronicle', this for no better reason than that a copy of it once belonged to Barnwell abbey in Cambridge. In fact, thanks to the work of Cristian Ispir, there can be no doubt that the original text was written by a monk at Crowland abbey in southern Lincolnshire, and it will be called the Crowland chronicle in this book.[50] Getting into its stride around 1212, the chronicle offers what is generally agreed to be the most perceptive analysis of John's last years. The chronicle has none of the unremitting hostility to the king found in Coggeshall. It recognizes the domination he achieved for a while over Britain, the popularity of his concessions in 1212 and 1213, and the advantages gained from his submission to the pope. On the other hand, in its final comments, the chronicle observes that John favoured foreigners and oppressed his native subjects, being deserted by them at the last. John was 'a great but unlucky prince' – 'princeps magnus sed minus felix'. Like Marius, he experienced both types of fortune – the reference being to Gaius Marius, the seven-times consul and triumphant general who, at the end of his life, suffered exile and then engulfed Rome in a bloody civil war.[51] This measured view is striking and may be explicable. The abbot of Crowland between 1190 and 1236 was Henry de Longchamp. The family was Norman but Henry spent most of his life in England, having been a monk of Evesham before becoming abbot. He owed his promotion to his brother, none other than John's great enemy in the 1190s, William de Longchamp, bishop of Ely, Richard's chancellor. Henry had, therefore, reasons to dislike John. Yet when, early in the reign, he saw John at close quarters, this in the course of Crowland's great dispute with Spalding abbey, he found him perfectly reasonable. The king 'graciously' promised to show the abbot 'the fullness of justice', and though he postponed the case again and again, and took money from both sides, he ultimately came down in Crowland's favour, having taken advice from 'the wise men of his court'.[52] The monks of Crowland knew that John was not all bad.

ST ALBANS ABBEY: ROGER OF WENDOVER AND MATTHEW PARIS

At St Albans, Roger of Wendover did not complete his account of John's reign until 1225 at the earliest. That account was then copied and embellished after 1235 by his successor as the St Albans house chronicler, Matthew Paris. Given the circumstantial detail that Wendover offers, he must have been working from a draft or from notes made close to the events he describes, although this did not free him from invention and error. Neither Wendover nor Paris is of much value when it comes to an assessment of John's character, but their works were important in fostering the picture of John as a cruel, godless tyrant. Thus it is Wendover who has the

story of how John tortured to death Geoffrey, archdeacon of Norwich, by having him pressed to death in a leaden cope, his crime
being disloyalty during the Interdict. Here, however, there was at
least some truth behind the story, for the sober annals of Dunstable record how Geoffrey of Norwich (not the archdeacon) died
in prison at Bristol, having suffered a long and grievous 'martyrdom'. A Reading abbey source has him being starved to death
there.[53] Matthew Paris, however, was certainly ascending into the
world of pure fantasy when, having heard the tale from one of the
supposed envoys, he described an embassy John sent to the emir of
Morocco offering to convert the kingdom to Islam. Paris copied
Wendover's famous account of John's death in which the king's
fever is exacerbated by pigging himself one night on peaches
(would there be peaches in October?) and new cider. He then con-
cludes with a much-quoted verse:

> England is still fouled by the stink of John,
> The foulness of Hell is defiled by John's foulness.[54]

THE RECORD SOURCES

In making use of the writings of contemporary writers, scholars
are, of course, utilizing a source with a long pedigree behind it.
When they also use the records of royal government, they are using a
source that, in good part, is sensationally new. It is at the start of
John's reign that the full orchestra of government records begins to
play with a pounding force. These records allow the history of
John's reign to be written in a level of detail impossible for any previous period of English history. In understanding those records, and
the government that produced them, there are also two remarkable books both written in the reign of Henry II. One of these,
called the *Dialogus de Scaccario*, was by Henry's treasurer, Richard fitzNigel, and explains the workings of the exchequer. The
other, named *Glanvill* after Henry's chief justiciar, Ranulf de Glanvill, does the same for the new legal procedures introduced in Henry's
reign, which were at the heart of the common law. Both the *Dialogus*
and *Glanvill* are extraordinary achievements, full of professional
pride for the systems they describe with such passionate precision.[55]

The *Dialogus* and *Glanvill* are about how things ought to work, at least in the eyes of their authors. How government actually did work (and how society responded to it) is shown by the gigantic corpus of royal records. From 1155 there is a continuous annual sequence of pipe rolls that record the exchequer's annual audit of the money owed the crown. Then, from 1199, many rolls survive on which the chancery recorded the charters and letters issued by the king, as also the offers of money to him for concessions and favours. From the 1190s there are also the rolls recording pleas in the king's courts. Thanks to the labours of nineteenth- and twentieth-century editors, nearly all this material has been published. On a rough count, for John's reign it runs to some 8,650 printed pages of various shapes and sizes, all of it indexed, albeit to variable standards. Even this does not exhaust the corpus of government material, for only now, under the Magna Carta Project, are John's original charters and letters (as opposed to the copies on the chancery rolls) being collected, analysed and published.

The records produced by the chancery, exchequer and law courts show the great power of the governmental machine in John's hands. They also shed light, sometimes oblique, sometimes direct, on his character. To be sure, many of the king's letters, copied and thus preserved on the chancery rolls, were about routine matters and were the work of ministers, sometimes explicitly so. Where the king was directly involved, he probably gave general instructions about the form of the letters, rather than dictating them word for word, but he could still give vigour to their phraseology. One picture in the Marshal *History* takes us close to how things worked:

> The king said to his chancellor:
> 'Make all haste to carry out the task.
> Prepare these letters forthwith,
> with explicit wording aimed
> at all those holding land from me,
> to the effect that, if they fail to come to England,
> they will not hold so much as a foot of land
> from me in the whole of England.'

Some letters, therefore, may well catch John's own emphatic words, as where miscreants are to be 'hanged from the nearest oak', or Jews are to be protected since 'even if we give our peace to a dog, it ought to be inviolably observed'.[56]

Above all, the records show John's tremendous grasp of detail. He was always thinking around the angles of the problems he faced, in the process sometimes revealing all too clearly his anxiety that things might go wrong. The wording of a charter is altered by his 'special order'; a prisoner is to be kept in a deep dungeon; knights sent to garrison a castle are not to go into the surrounding country; prisoners are to be released although not named in his letter (he doesn't know their names); payment of a debt is to be delayed until he can come to the exchequer and see from its rolls exactly how much is owed; if he is right in thinking an instalment of a pension has been paid twice over, then it is to be adjusted accordingly; houses and lands are to be taken away because he has been deceived by lies about the size of a debt; Engelard de Cigogné is to bring Robert de Dreux to Winchester provided he can safely leave the castles in his custody; if he cannot, he should give the job to reliable men.[57] These examples involve relatively small matters, but the same attention to detail was displayed in matters of more significance, notably in devising punishments and in setting often excruciating terms for the repayment of debts. The Oxfordshire baron Henry d'Oilly was to pay off a debt of £1,015 at 100 marks a year. If he did not keep the terms, in an oft-used threat, he was to lose all he had paid.[58]

The letters also testify to positive sides of John's kingship, amply justifying the Anonymous's claim that he was an expansive host. With such alimentary extravagance, John hoped to enhance the morale of his entourage, conciliate those who came to court and by holding great feasts with erstwhile enemies demonstrate that quarrels were at an end. For John it seemed especially grievous that someone 'who ate my bread' should betray him.[59] The records also hint at a human side of the king. He allows the hostage son of Robert de Ros to spend the winter with his parents, although he wants him back at Easter. Sometimes the threats themselves were jokes, as when John sent his minister William Brewer a fat deer, and told him he would not get another unless he carried out the accompanying order.[60] The letters can express what seems like genuine friendship:

> Know that we are safe and well ... we are coming into your area soon and are thinking about you concerning the hawk, and although we have been apart from you for ten years, on our arrival it will not seem to us more than three days.

This was addressed to the German knight Theodoric Teutonicus, whom John had made constable of Berkhamsted. The hawk was probably a gift of Theodoric to the king.[61] John could also write letters full of fulsome praise, none more so than when thanking William Marshal for his support in Ireland in 1212. Here John concluded by responding to the Marshal's anxieties about his hostage son. The king offered to entrust the boy to John of Earley, volunteered to buy him a much needed horse and robe (although wanting to be repaid), and denied that he had the least intention of sending him to Poitou. Indeed, he had heard nothing about the idea until it was mentioned by one of his ministers.[62]

The rolls recording the lawsuits that were heard at John's court likewise show his activity in a favourable light.[63] John thus declares that cases should be decided according to custom, reason and 'the counsel of his barons'. He is frequently consulted by his judges ('speak with the lord king') even over minor cases. In one, he makes a ruling in favour of one Emma, daughter of Holfrid, who was seeking a mere eight acres of land as her inheritance. Doris Stenton, reviewing this material, felt such involvement, even in difficult times, 'demonstrates a singular strength of character, a genuine "stabilitas", which is wholly admirable whatever view is taken of King John as a man'.[64]

The records, on the other hand, also go some way to support allegations of impiety. Two rolls recording John's day-to-day expenditure during the regnal years 1209–10 and 1212–13 (apart from revealing the king's regular baths) are full of offerings to the poor as acts of penance. Thus John frequently fed a hundred paupers because he dined twice on a Friday, supposedly a day of abstinence. Five hundred paupers benefited when, instead of fasting, he ate fish and drank wine on the feast of the Adoration of the Holy Cross.[65] Other occasions for almsgiving were when John went hunting or hawking on a church festival. One Holy Innocents' Day, he gave a penny apiece to 350 paupers, this being fifty for each of the seven cranes taken by his hawks.[66] The less than pietistic atmosphere at court is also reflected in the way John fed paupers because of the food and drink transgressions of his ministers, one beneficiary being Thomas Basset, who was named as a counsellor in Magna Carta.[67] On the other hand, the fact that John felt the need for acts of penance at all shows he was not wholly irreligious. He also fed paupers for reasons other than his own transgressions, for example for the souls of his father Henry and brother Richard. When his mother died in 1204, he arranged for the feeding of over two thousand paupers each day throughout the summer.[68] If he asked Bishop Hugh to hurry up his sermon so he could go and eat, it was surely because he had fasted before the service.[69]

The records have something to say about John's recreations. We have just seen him as a hawker. Indeed his hawking helped provoke a couple of the chapters in Magna Carta.[70] He was also a great hunter with hounds. John's hunt 'shadowed' his itinerary and could rise to as many as 300 greyhounds, nine other hunting dogs and sixteen boarhounds, with sixty-four handlers, an impressive sight as they went past.[71] The rolls also record payments of John's gambling debts and occasionally mention his mistresses. In 1212 a chaplet of roses was sent to John's 'friend' from a manor of the chief justiciar, Geoffrey fitzPeter.[72] More sinister is an entry concerning the wife of John's chief forester, Hugh de Neville. The 'fine rolls' for 1204–5 record her as offering the king '200 chickens so that she might be able to lie one night with her lord, Hugh de Neville'. Interpretations of what was going on have varied, but the most likely explanation is that the wife was John's mistress and the two of them were joking about what a night back with Hugh was worth; the answer was a ridiculous 200 chickens. The joke was made all the more humiliating for Hugh by putting him down as surety for the delivery of a hundred of the chickens.[73] Hugh was to desert John in 1216, although he had little to hope for in the rebel camp. Another, even more high-profile desertion was that of John's half-brother, William Longespee, earl of Salisbury (an illegitimate son of Henry II). The French court had a simple explanation for that. While Longespee was in French captivity in 1214, John had seduced his wife.[74]

How in the end to balance all this up? It is tempting to agree with John Gillingham's pithy conclusion that John was a 'shit'. This was said in a radio debate in which my unpalatable task was to defend the king! Yet a defence can be made. John was energetic, intelligent, astute, imaginative, informed and a master of detail. He was sensitive to behavioural expectations, and, when he felt like it, could appear pious and penitent, courteous and considerate, a king eager to act justly (if for money) and ready to take advice. John also faced immense problems. He inherited a monarchy already unpopular and an empire already seriously under threat. The Crowland chronicler, even at the end of the reign, thought of John as a great prince, if an unlucky one. One can, however, see the force in a Gillingham-type verdict. If the testimony of Wendover and Matthew Paris can be discounted, it is much harder to set aside, whatever their agendas, the character sketch by the Anonymous of Béthune and the picture that emerges from the Marshal *History*. That they were written after John's death merely increases their force. The record was now complete. Those who really got to know John realized that behind the sometimes acceptable exterior there lay a fractured personality, suspicious, untrustworthy, aggressive and cruel. John, as we have seen, seems to have got on best with subordinates, who did what they were told. It is no accident that the greatest show of affection in his letters is precisely to one such man, Theodoric Teutonicus. The king felt much less easy with those more his equals, and probably did not like their company. In one telling episode (for which one of his letters is evidence), he tried to persuade William Marshal to leave court and go and visit his estates until the next meeting of the king's council. (The Marshal, knowing the dangers of absence, refused to go.)[75] Whereas John's good characteristics were assumed, his bad ones were part of his very being. When he was pleasant to the Marshal and the Flemings, he was so out of calculation. When he cast aside William des Roches, and murdered Matilda de Briouze, he gave vent to real feelings.

It is also far from clear that John's character began well and then deteriorated under the pressures created by the loss of Normandy. If he acted sensibly in his quarrels with the Cistercians and St Augustine's, Canterbury, early in the reign, that is not so different from how he appears at work in the Anonymous of Béthune's account between 1213 and 1215. Equally, the negative sides of John's character can all be seen before 1204: his delight in mockery; his cruelty; his arrogance; his fearful suspicions; his unseemly conduct (Adam of Eynsham's stories here cannot be entirely made up). What happened is that after 1204 these characteristics operated in a far more hostile environment created by absolutely novel financial exactions. John's character itself would not have provoked the rebellion that led to Magna Carta. Nor would his financial exactions. It was the two together that were unsupportable.

How John became like this one can only speculate. Did his conspiracies against his father and brother make him always expect treatment in like coin? Had he been damaged as a youngest son, treated by Richard with contempt, and for long holding only the remote lordship of Ireland? The nickname 'Lackland' ('sine terra') was contemporary, as (unfairly) was 'softsword'.[76] Did his slight frame, in early life, make him feel inferior to macho knights such as William Marshal? Whatever the causes, for the Anonymous of Béthune, even John's perfectly reasonable treatment of the Flemings could not erase his reputation as an evil man. On his death-bed, William Marshal was equally explicit. Turning to the young Henry III, and clasping his hand, he expressed the hope that he would grow up to be a worthy man. If, on the other hand, he followed the path of 'any criminal ancestor' ('alcun felon ancestre'), then 'I pray God that he does not give you long to live'. The 'criminal ancestor' was, of course, King John.[77]

QUEEN ISABELLA

Magna Carta begins with King John. It ends, in the security clause, with his queen and children. No mention is made of their names, but their persons, like that of the king, are to be spared in any actions taken by the twenty-five barons. John married Isabella of Angoulême, then at most in her early teens, in 1200, his first marriage to the countess of Gloucester having been annulled. John thereby gained Isabella's rich and strategic inheritance of Angoulême. Beyond that, Isabella certainly fulfilled her primary role of providing John with an heir.[78] Her first child, born in October 1207, was a son, the future Henry III. She went on to produce another son and three daughters. Despite John's mistresses, marital relations continued throughout the reign, and Isabella was pregnant with her last child, Eleanor (the future wife of Simon de Montfort), at the time of John's death in 1216.[79]

The St Albans chroniclers provide two stories about Isabella. One, from Wendover, was that John dallied in her company while Normandy fell in 1204. That, of course, is ridiculous.[80] The other, from Matthew Paris, is that the envoy sent to Morocco told the emir that John had her many lovers strangled on her bed.[81] If so, she certainly paid John back for his infidelities, although with unfortunate results for the lovers. But of course the story is even more unbelievable than

Wendover's. Both chronicle and record evidence suggests that Isabella resided in a series of royal castles, where she was doubtless carefully guarded. At a critical moment in November 1214, by an order typical of John's micro-management, Theodoric Teutonicus was told, once he had sufficient knights (doubtless for a guard), to take Isabella to Berkhamsted by a specified route. A month later, Theodoric was ordered to go with her to Gloucester, and 'keep her there in the chamber in which our daughter Joan was born'.[82]

It does not sound as though Isabella had much say about these arrangements, and that would have been par for the course. She had been crowned and anointed with much display. Isabella was queen 'by the grace of God', just as John was king. As queen, the expectation was that she would play a role as an intercessor and peacemaker. Yet, there is no evidence that John involved her in political or any other decisions. Even when she must have been in her twenties, he denied her the traditional revenues of queenship, and treated Angoulême as his own. Isabella's later career shows she was a woman of hard and high spirit. After John's death, denied any role in the minority government, she left her five children, returned to Angoulême, and produced another family with her second husband, Hugh de Lusignan. She never forgot her queenly status and was 'killed' (as she put it) when made to stand in the chamber of the king of France like some 'fatuous servant', while the royal family lolled on the bed. When her husband went on to entertain the French at Lusignan, she ransacked the castle, took all her goods back to Angoulême and kept Hugh waiting outside for three days before she would see him.[83] How Isabella must have wished to treat John in the same way! That she did try to stand up to him is suggested in one story preserved by the Anonymous. With the French overrunning the continental possessions, John tried to reassure her:

> My lady, don't worry . . . I know a corner where you won't have to watch out for the king of France for ten years, not for all his power.

This was Isabella's reply:

> Indeed, my lord, I really think you are keen to be a king who is mated in a corner.[84]

If this reflects the nature of their conversations, one can understand why Isabella had so little influence over her husband. After
she left England, she mentioned him in not a single one of her
charters.[85]

KING JOHN AND CORFE CASTLE

This chapter has concentrated on the written sources for John's
reign. It is a pity that so little survives of the physical environment
in which he lived, all the more so since John was a master of
manipulating space, as the contemporary accounts of him at work
show. He moved discussions between halls, chambers, chapels and
chapter houses, in a kind of ritual of the rooms. With different spaces
came different audiences, as John first took counsel from one
group, then another – 'you, you, you, the rest wait outside' –
before announcing his decisions or having them announced. We
have no evidence for dining arrangements, but these too were part
of the ritual. Hoi polloi ate (and slept) in the hall, while the king
himself, save at great feasts, ate with the favoured few in his chamber. An invitation to the chamber meal showed you were 'in'. If
you were excluded, you knew you were 'out'.

Fortunately, one building does survive to give an impression of
the environment John created for this theatre. It is Corfe castle,
on which he spent over £1,400.[86] John was at Corfe in nine years
of his reign. He made three visits in 1215. In 1216 he was there
for a month as he prepared for what turned out to be his final
campaign. John was acutely aware of the different gradations of
Corfe's architectural layout. In 1215 the privileged prisoner Robert de Dreux was to be entertained in the castle's hall and allowed,
if he wished, to enter the keep, but nothing was said about the
more private apartments.[87]

The castle on which John lavished such attention was built on
an extraordinary natural mound, sticking up in a cleft between
two ranges of the Purbeck hills. John strengthened the castle
because it had great strategic significance, controlling the harbours
of Poole and Wareham. He also wanted it to be utterly secure, a
place where he could keep his prisoners, and house his wife and
sons. And John also wanted the castle to impress. A visitor arriving
at Corfe came up from the little village and entered through the

gateway of the castle's outer bailey. Having dismounted, he then walked up the steep incline and passed through a second gateway, from where he saw the great palisaded ditch dug, on John's orders, to protect the middle and inner bailey. The middle bailey John had strengthened with new wall towers, making the whole ensemble resemble the most famous of all contemporary castles, Richard I's Château Gaillard. In the middle bailey was the king's hall where Robert de Dreux was to be entertained. To progress further, the visitor had to go on and up into the inner bailey, where he could enter, as Robert was permitted to do, the towering twelfth-century keep, and reflect on those who had starved to death in its dungeons. He had still not reached the king's own private apartments. John had built these at the very highest point of the castle. To reach them, you had to climb a covered stone stairway leading to the middle stage of a three-storey tower, from which doorways opened left to the king's chapel and right into his 'great chamber'. And what a chamber! For John, after the might of the rest of the castle, had gone not for size but for delicacy and sophistication. Built like the rest of the apartments in beautifully cut stone, the chamber was lit by long lancet windows, four on either side, each rising from window seats. From the windows on the eastern side, standing above the castle's outer wall, there were magnificent views towards the Dorset coast. In the great chamber, the king's clerks, counsellors and cronies mingled, waiting to be called into another room, or for the king to come out from it. For the great chamber was not the end of this set of apartments. Beyond it (alas now lost) was an even more extraordinary room, called quite probably by John himself 'La Gloriette'. The name seems to have derived from a twelfth-century *chanson de geste*, in which a Saracen palace called La Gloriette has, among other wonders, 'a fantastical marble tower with fixtures in gold and silver including silver windows'. How John's inner chamber resembled that we do not know, but evidently it did.[88] It was here, if he could get past the ushers, that a baron could at last bow down before John himself, a king doubtless bejewelled and dressed in magnificent robes, playing perhaps with a new sword or crown, and poring over some of the many treasures of gold and silver he kept at the castle. Was the baron awed and inspired to do John's bidding? Or did he see through the outward show, to John's real personality? Probably he did.

4
Magna Carta and Society: Women, Peasants, Jews, the Towns and the Church

At the start of Magna Carta, John greeted his clerical and lay magnates, his ministers and 'his faithful men' – 'Fidelibus Suis' – and informed them of what he was doing. He was thereby announcing the Charter to all the men of the kingdom, since each adult male was expected to take an oath of fealty to the king, thus becoming his 'faithful man' – 'fidelis'. Likewise at the end of the Charter, in the security clause, it was 'everyone' – 'omnes' – or all men who were to swear the oath to support the twenty-five barons in their work of maintaining the Charter. All adult males were thus potentially part of the 'commune of all the land' ('commune' meaning sworn association), which the oath created.[1]

Contemporaries could regard the Charter in the same way. The annals of Dunstable described it as being about 'the liberties of the kingdom of England'. Later it was often called a charter of 'common liberties'.[2] This meant it was 'common' in the geographical sense in that it applied to all the country (whereas the later Forest Charter was only relevant to forest areas), but the Charter also carried at least a tinge of being common in the sense of everyone sharing in its benefits. Nor on the face of it was that untrue. Some of the chapters seemed to have a universal reach. 'To no one will we sell, to no one will we deny or delay, right or justice', ran chapter 40.

THE ECONOMIC FRAMEWORK

The people of Magna Carta's England lived in an age of economic expansion.[3] All historians would agree that the population of England rose very considerably in the hundred or so years either side of the Charter, before it was slashed by the Black Death. There would be much less agreement over precise figures, especially for the 1200s, which are situated in a statistical vacuum between the data that come from Domesday Book in 1086 and the 'Hundred Roll' survey of 1279. A high estimate for the early thirteenth century would be 4.5 million people, a low one 3 million. Perhaps around 3.5 million might be the safest bet. The rising population was accompanied by urban and commercial expansion. Many new towns were founded, and old ones grew in size. The town population may well have increased faster than that in the countryside, reaching by 1300 at least 10 per cent of the whole.[4] There was a gigantic increase in the money supply, and a new network of markets and fairs was introduced.[5]

Just where the reign of John fits into this picture of general expansion is, however, far from clear. Indeed, it could be argued that the economy in his time suffered a series of shocks, some being the results of his policies, some not. There were certainly at the start of John's reign some years of very rapid inflation, in which prices tripled or more than tripled. Although they then fell back, prices never returned to their old levels. The most important price of all, that of wheat, fluctuated, after 1207, at something more than twice its level before 1200.[6] The causes of the inflation have been much debated, but the most immediate factor was probably a series of bad harvests that pushed up the price of corn. Ralph of Coggeshall specifically blamed the high prices of 1205, which he contrasted with those in the reign of Henry II, on the freezing weather that had destroyed the crops.[7] Chroniclers also commented on the bad weather of 1201 and the famine of 1203.[8] Another factor, purely monetary, was arguably the release of large numbers of coins because hoarders had decided to spend their money, having lost confidence in a much clipped currency and being fearful of losing out in a recoinage, which indeed was introduced in 1205.[9] Over the longer term, the failure of prices to return to their old levels was probably due to the flow of silver into the country from Flanders in order to pay for English wool. This inflation took place, moreover, despite the deflationary pressures resulting from the money sent overseas for the defence and then recovery of the Angevin empire. A large amount of money was also taken out of circulation as John, after 1204, built up the treasure needed to finance his continental schemes.[10] Trading patterns, meanwhile, must have been disrupted both by the loss of Normandy and Anjou in 1203–4, and the conflict with France that continued thereafter. This indeed is reflected in Magna Carta's chapter 41 with its concern, if war broke out, for the treatment of foreign merchants in England and English merchants abroad, the implication being that hitherto they had been arrested and their goods seized.

John's reign in this perspective might seem then to combine bad harvests, inflation, shortage of coin, disruption of trade and a general decline in productivity, all making his exactions the more grievous. Magna Carta becomes the result of an economic crisis. P. D. A. Harvey indeed remarked that 'no landmark in English constitutional history was more clearly brought about by economic change than Magna Carta'.[11] Yet it is impossible to be sure of this interpretation. The harvests in 1213 and 1214 were actually good, and prices tumbled from the high levels of some earlier years.[12] The year 1215 was thus very different from 1258, when a great political revolution, stripping John's son, Henry III, of power, took place at a time of dearth and starvation, following a harvest failure. The sums John was able to raise from barons even late in his reign hardly suggest that they were strapped for cash. With surplus corn to sell on the rising market for agricultural produce, lords might anyway be shielded from the inflation. Many towns in John's reign were prosperous enough to offer him money for exemption from tolls and the right to answer directly for their revenues at the exchequer.

It is anyway impossible to generalize across society, since economic developments affected different groups in different ways. The economy might expand, for example, without bringing any benefit to the peasants who formed the bulk of the population. The Charter itself reflected deep divisions in England society, divisions between men and women, free and unfree, lords and towns, lords and tenants, Christians and Jews, and church and state. It was, moreover, far from being a mere passive reflection of the status quo. On the contrary, the Charter was, in places, an aggressive document, which sections of society sought to use against each other. It is usual, when looking at that society, to focus on the earls, barons and knights. This is understandable, given that it was this elite which forced the Charter on the king. John himself and the contemporary writers often described the rebels simply as 'the barons'. But such concentration also conceals what the Charter tells us, sometimes by its silence, about everyone else. Earls and barons formed a tiny elite one hundred or so strong. Of knights there were several thousand. The population was several million. This chapter, therefore, concentrates on those whom the Charter more or less left out, namely women, peasants, Jews and towns, before concluding with the church. Earls, barons and knights appear in the chapter that follows.

WOMEN

If the population in John's reign was 3.5 million, then there were around 1.75 million females, of whom perhaps half would have been under fifteen, so 875,000 adult women, and around the same number of adult males.[13] No women are mentioned by name in Magna Carta. The queen appears in the security clause but is left anonymous. Also anonymous are the sisters of the king of Scots, Alexander II, who feature in chapter 59, although they are named in John's letter announcing the 1209 Treaty of Norham; it was under this treaty that they came into his hands.[14] By contrast, the Charter names John and thirty-eight other men. The words 'man' and 'men' – 'homo' and 'homines' – appear nineteen times in the Charter. 'Woman' – 'femina' – appears once, and in a chapter (54) that reduces the power of women over men. There are two references to the 'widow' – 'vidua' – and two to the widowed 'wife' – 'uxor' (chapters 7, 8, 11 and 26). To be sure, the word 'homo' could certainly be used at this time to mean simply a human being. Women, therefore, were protected by many of Magna Carta's chapters. Indeed, it may be that the murder of Matilda de Briouze, alongside her eldest son, was one strand behind chapter 39's insistence that no free man be 'destroyed' save by the lawful judgement of his peers or by the law of the land. Yet chapter 39, if it embraced women, also ignored them. When it said that there should be no outlawry save by judgement or by law, it was dealing exclusively with men. A woman was not outlawed, she was 'waived', which meant she was abandoned as a 'waif'. This had the same consequences (a waived woman like an outlawed man could be killed on sight) but also reflected a fundamental difference between men and women. Whereas women did have rights over property (although less than those of men), they had hardly any public functions. Thus whereas all adult males, as we have seen, swore fealty to the king, women in general did not. There was no need for them to do so since, in theory, every woman was under the protection of, and could be answered for by, a man, be it father, husband or lord. Since, therefore, there was no oath of fealty making women generally 'in law', they could not be 'outlawed', and hence they were 'waived'. The only women who took an oath of fealty to the king were those who did so as part of an act of homage performed to the king (an act discussed more fully in the next chapter). The number of women in this category was small, since it was confined to heiresses who held their land directly from the king and did homage when they entered their inheritances – did homage, that is, if they were unmarried (usually being widows). If they were married, their husbands perfomed homage for their lands. Only when the husband died was the heiress called on to do so. Since, therefore, the great majority of women did not swear fealty to the king, they were technically not even among the king's 'fideles' to whom the Charter was addressed.

This imbalance corresponded to the position of women in male-crafted law, custom and wider thought.[15] 'Women differ from men in many respects, for their position is inferior to that of men', opined the great book on the laws of England known as *Bracton*, much of which was written in the couple of decades after John's death.[16] The subordination of women was partly justified biblically, going back to Eve's role as Adam's serpentine temptress. Other female failings (in the view of the mid-thirteenth-century Oxford friar John of Wales) were garrulity, sloth and ostentation in dress and makeup.[17] Walter Map, writing in the 1180s, equated women with one thing, namely 'malicia' – 'malice'.[18] How necessary then the injunction in Ephesians 5:22–3: 'Wives should be subject to their husbands as to the Lord, since the husband is the head of the wife as Christ is the head of the Church . . .'! Women were also frail. When, in 1249, Ughtred Smith, of Buteland in Northumberland, pulled an arrow out of his head before going home, it was 'so that my wife may not see it, for she would perhaps grieve over much'.[19] Strong man, weak woman.

Women then had a very limited public role. They did not sit on juries, and only very exceptionally held any kind of office. If, under chapter 39 of the Charter, free women were entitled to judgement by their peers, that judgement would have been given exclusively by men. When Magna Carta was redrafted in 1216, it was made clear that a woman could not remain in the house of her late husband if it was a castle. The 1216 Charter was issued in the middle of a civil war, but the clause remained in place in the later versions issued in time of peace. Evidently castles were not for single women. The Charter, however, shows that women *did* have rights over property. Chapter 7 laid down that, on the death of their husbands, widows should have free entry into their inheritances, marriage portions and dowers. The Charter was thinking pre-eminently here of those at the top of the social scale, namely the daughters and widows of the king's baronial and knightly tenants-in-chief; but its stipulations also applied downwards, that is, to the daughters and widows of the knights who held from the tenants-in-chief themselves.[20] This was why, if a widow wanted to remarry, she needed, under chapter 8, to get the consent of whomever she held her land from, whether it was the king or a lord. Under King John, widows had certainly not entered their dowers, marriage portions and inheritances free of charge; but that they were entitled to them, under existing law and custom, was not disputed. The Charter was concerned to secure free entry into those properties, not establish the principle of entry itself. When it came to inheritances, a woman's rights were inferior to a man's. She only inherited her parents' property in default of a brother. And whereas, by the operation of primogeniture, an eldest brother would inherit everything, with women there was no primogeniture and sisters divided the inheritance. This is why chapter 2 of the Charter spoke of the 'heir or heirs' of earls, barons and knights, the heirs here being women. It was also why the chapter implied that baronies and knights' fees might not be 'whole', which would be the result of their division between heiresses. When they were not heiresses, women might still have land in the form of a marriage portion given by their natal families. And, on the death of their husbands, they were entitled to a dower, carved out of his estates. The 1217 version of the Charter defined this as a third of the estates held by the husband in his lifetime, unless a smaller amount had been agreed.[21]

A woman, therefore, might have property, but her chances of actually controlling it were limited. For much of the time it was controlled by men. In the law as stated by *Glanvill*, a female heiress could not enter her inheritance unless she was married. If unmarried at the time of her father's death, then, even when of full age, she remained in the wardship of her lord, until he married her off.[22] A male heir, by contrast, escaped from wardship and gained his inheritance as soon as he attained his majority. The 1216 Charter gave the age for that as twenty-one. In practice, most heiresses were married off either by their fathers or, if they came into wardship, by their lords, long before they reached that age. In the case of daughters of tenants-in-chief, the lord was the king. When Magna Carta laid down that 'heirs' (of both sexes) were to be married 'without disparagement', it was designed to stop lords, and above all the king, from marrying off heiresses in their wardship to those of lower social rank. In marriage a husband had control of his wife's inheritance and could alienate it as he wished. The Charter acknowledged as much. The inheritance it allowed a widow to recover was the inheritance as held at the time of her husband's death.

It was only after a husband's death that this picture changed. As widows, women could themselves control their inheritances, marriage portions and dowers. The Charter, in saying that these properties should be entered without difficulty and without charge, was designed to make it all the easier for widows to obtain them. When it came to widows obtaining their dowers, the Charter was also putting them in a stronger position than some translations have indicated. In Holt's, for example, it is said that the widow 'may stay in her husband's house for forty days after his death, within which period her dower shall be assigned to her'. The 'may stay' here could be taken to imply that staying is just a possibility open to the widow. But there is very little in the Latin to justify the 'may'. Rather, the present subjunctive is jussive, as it is in the other verbs in the chapter, and is much better translated as 'is to stay'. In other words, the widow is absolutely not going to be disturbed, until the forty days are up, by king, lord, family or whomever.[23] The Charter also offered two further protections for widows. In chapter 11, if a husband died owing money to the Jews, or anyone else, the widow was both to get her dower and pay nothing of the debt. Under chapter 26, although this only applied to widows of tenants-in-chief, widows were guaranteed a reasonable share of their late husband's chattels as against the demands of the executors of his will.

If widows remarried, however, their property became again subject to their husband's control, but at least the Charter, in chapter 8, prevented them from being forced into a second union. As unmarried widows, women could also litigate, and indeed many did so both over their dowers and over property alienated by their husbands from their inheritances. Unmarried widows were thus very much public figures in the king's courts. Indeed, they had all the more opportunity in this area under the demands of 1215. The protection offered widows, when it came to the free entry into their dowers, marriage portions and inheritances, was not merely for the future. There was also the intention of redressing the grievances of the past. Under chapter 37 of the Articles of the Barons, all fines made for dowers, marriage portions and inheritances, unjustly and against the law of the land, were to be remitted.[24] If there was any dispute (as was quite likely), it was to be judged by the twenty-five barons of the security clause and Archbishop Langton. There were numerous widows with grievances over just such fines. If they secured redress by authority of the twenty-five barons, they were exploiting the most revolutionary feature of the Charter.

It is natural to think that the chapters in favour of widows in the Charter owed a good deal to the demands of their male relatives, and there must be truth in that. No son wanted to see his mother, with all her lands, taken off by some second husband. It was far better that she remained single, in which case the son himself might hope to profit from her lands. Women, however, were far from being mere pawns in the hands of men. Before 1215 they had been active in securing, in return for money, precisely the kinds of concessions that they were to gain in Magna Carta. Government records show no fewer than 149 widows in John's reign offering money to the king for the right to stay single or marry whom they wished, offers that were sometimes also for entry into their lands and the wardship of their children.[25] Holt has called such proffers 'one of the first great stages in the emancipation of women'.[26] It seems inconceivable that all the women in question were being manipulated by men. John, of course, could not care less one way or the other. All he wanted was his money, and the offers show that women had plenty of it. In 1214 Margaret, widow of Robert fitzRoger, promised the queenly sum of £1,000 for the right to stay single and other concessions. Her offer was clearly at her initiative, for it was actually aimed in part at her son: she was to have her dower, even if he did not wish to give it to her. This pointed to a common cause of friction. Since a widow's dower had to be carved out of her late husband's lands, it diminished, until her death, the amount to be inherited by the heir, whether her son or anyone else. The offer also shows how determined Margaret was to litigate in order to right perceived injustices. Thus John agreed to give her justice in his court over her claims to her inheritance, part of it alienated, she believed, by her two former husbands.[27] Women might also hope to benefit from the famous chapters about justice in the Charter. Chapter 39 might not refer to 'waiving', but free women could still be protected from unjust disseise under its terms. Indeed, Isabella, countess of Arundel, later upbraided Henry III for the way, in his dealings with her, he had breached this very clause.[28] This was also a society which accepted that noblewomen could hold public office at least in the few cases where they had inherited a title to it. John himself accepted the claim of Nicola de Hay, as her father's heir, to be castellan of Lincoln, and she was determined to do the job in person. The *History* of the Marshal shows her in command there during the great siege in 1217 that helped determine the outcome of the civil war. By this time she had wider authority, for John, on the day of his death, made her joint sheriff of Lincolnshire.[29]

At the lowest level of society, the Charter had nothing to say about the property of the unfree, male or female, since, as we will see, that was entirely a matter for the lord. Women as a whole, however, did feature in the Charter, which brings us to the one chapter, chapter 54, where the word 'woman' – 'femina' – appears. This was a chapter introduced, for reasons we will see, at Runnymede itself.[30] The background to the chapter was the way in which women, whatever their status, were permitted in courts of law to appeal, that is accuse, individuals of crime. Whereas a man could bring appeals for a whole range of crimes, a woman, in the legal theory as set out in *Glanvill*, was limited to accusations of two kinds.[31] The first was for the killing of her husband, where she had personally witnessed the deed – with the husband, in the conventional phraseology, dying in her arms. The second was for rape and injury to her body. One factor underlying these restrictions, quite apart from the usual prejudices, was the view that women had an unfair 'procedural advantage'. They could not be challenged to back up their accusations in a trial by battle, and so, with less to lose, might bring their charges irresponsibly, either on their own account or because they were being manipulated by men.[32] Chapter 54 did not deal with these restrictions directly, but limited the power of women in a related area. Thus it directed that no one was to be arrested or imprisoned on the appeal of a woman for the death of anyone other than her husband. In other words, if a woman *did* make an appeal for the killing of someone other than her husband, the accused was not to be imprisoned prior to trial, as would have been the case if the accuser was a man. Instead, as was probably the practice for crimes other than homicide, whatever the gender of the accuser, he could give sureties for coming to court and answering the charge. Women, as accusers, therefore, were being put on a lower plane than men.

Chapter 54 could, however, have been worse. It clearly implied that women *were* making appeals for homicides other than those of their husbands. It limited the pre-trial consequences of such accusations but did nothing to stop them, or other appeals, by enforcing *Glanvill's* rule. Indeed, plea roll evidence, both before and after 1215, shows that the restrictions on women's appeals were far from routinely enforced by the king's judges. What is equally clear is that appeals brought by women formed a large part of the business of judges when they toured the counties. There were over seventy such appeals brought before the judges in Lincolnshire in 1202. The great majority of the appeals, moreover, seem to have come from women of peasant background. Here there was no distinction between the free and the unfree. That was certainly not the case elsewhere in the Charter.[33]

THE PEASANTRY: UNFREE AND FREE

In the 1200s, on a very rough estimate, about 90 per cent of England's population were peasants, so approaching some 3.15 million souls – men, women and children – if the total population was around 3.5 million. Within this group the balance between peasants who were free and unfree varied both as between neighbouring manors and as between different parts of the country, and there is simply not the evidence to be precise about it. A classic study by the Russian historian E. A. Kosminsky (who survived the purges by putting in dutiful references to the works of J. Stalin) showed that in six Midlands counties for which there was evidence in the 1279 Hundred Roll survey, the ratio between the unfree and free peasantry was 62 per cent to 38 per cent in terms of land held, and 58 per cent to 42 per cent in terms of number of households.

In other parts of the country, however, notably in East Anglia and the north, there was certainly a much higher proportion, indeed a preponderance of free peasants.[34]

The Latin texts that mostly describe their condition had a whole variety of words for peasant, including 'villanus', 'servus', 'rusticus', 'nativus', 'custumarius' and 'bondus'. Although some of these words could be used in a looser sense, they usually carried the implication that the individual was unfree. A sokeman, on the other hand, was a free or freer peasant. Fortunately, there is no need to spend time agonizing over definitions. We know from numerous surveys of manors, not least the 1279 Hundred Roll survey, the type of person whom contemporaries described as peasants, using one of the above terms.

In such surveys lists of unfree peasants (most often described as villeins) frequently show them holding either a whole or a half virgate of land from their lord. A virgate varied in size; it could be thirty acres, twenty-four acres, or less. Land, of course, varied in productivity. Half a virgate in one place might be worth as much or more than a virgate somewhere else, but probably most peasants with half a virgate and upwards could support their families largely from their land. Beneath the villeins, another group often listed (still clearly unfree) were the 'cottarii' – 'cottagers'. These were smallholders with at best a few acres of land (the amount is rarely stated). In return for their land, both these groups of peasants owed the lord a combination of money rents and agricultural labour services; for villein virgaters, the latter might involve supplying two men, who would work for the lord a couple of days a week for most of the year, and every day in harvest time.

The peasants described as sokemen can be found in surveys holding as few as five acres of land and, more typically, as much as half a virgate or a virgate. They answered for money rents, and if they owed labour services, these were usually light compared to those of villeins. Manorial surveys also often have lists of 'free tenants'. These were men who answered exclusively for money rents. Some had substantial holdings that placed them above the general run of the peasantry, but many others had land of equivalent size to that held by villeins and cottars. Apart from being legally free, and answering exclusively for rents, they must often have been in a very similar economic condition.

The framework governing the life of the peasant, especially the unfree peasant, was very often that of the manor, although these came in many forms, shapes and sizes. Sometimes they were coterminous with another unit of local society, the 'villa', mentioned in chapter 23 of the Charter, which is conventionally translated 'vill' but in many cases equated to a village. Many villages, on the other hand, had more than one manor. In the thirteenth century, lords retained most of their manors in hand – 'in demesne' – rather than renting them out. Chapter 25 of the Charter mentioned the king's own 'demesne manors', while a new chapter (26) in the Charter of 1217 safeguarded the demesne carts of lords from seizure, which meant the carts that they had on their demesne manors. With an in-hand manor, lords cultivated for their own profit a large part of the land within what were usually two or three big fields around the village centre. This area was also called the 'demesne', being the in-hand part of a demesne manor. The labour services owed by the unfree could be used to work the demesne, although paid labour was often employed as well. In Kosminsky's analysis of the 1279 survey, 32 per cent of the land was demesne, as against 40 per cent villein land and 24 per cent peasant freeholdings.[35] This just shows the inequalities that existed, for of course the number of lords ran into thousands, and the number of peasants (who anyway had to work for the lords) into millions. Even a large peasant holding of thirty acres was small compared to the 250 acres that might typically be held in demesne in a medium-sized manor, and great lords had many manors.

By 1215 the king's judges had developed a very clear test to decide who was unfree, and used the words 'villein' and 'servus' – 'serf' – in a technical legal sense to describe someone in that condition. The test had several components, but the most vital was whether the peasant (or his ancestor) had performed agricultural labour services of any significance to the lord in return for his land. The king's judges were very clear about the consequences of unfreedom. Villeins could not leave the manor without the lord's consent. They had to pay the tax called 'merchet' to marry off their daughters. Villeins could be sold with the land 'like oxen and cows'. They had no recourse at all to the king's courts in any matter concerning their land and services. These were entirely matters for the lord to determine. As the law book *Bracton* put it, a villein 'cannot know in the evening the service to be rendered in the morning. [He] is bound to do whatever he is bid.'[36]

The economic position of the peasantry in the thirteenth century has been much debated in the so-called 'standard of living controversy'.[37] According to one view, the rising population was outrunning the ability of the land to support it, and creating a proliferation of peasant smallholders living on the edge of subsistence. A key calculation here is that, in average conditions, a peasant family needed at least ten arable acres to subsist simply from its land. Kosminsky's figures chillingly suggest that over 40 per cent of the peasantry were smallholders who fell below that level. Indeed, it has been estimated that around 1300 this was true of 60 per cent of peasant households.[38] To survive at all, smallholders had to find other sources of income, most notably from wage labour. That might provide enough to get by in normal times, but not when prices went up with bad harvests. Then there might be widespread starvation. Some historians, however, have sought to qualify this bleak picture, which in any case relates more to the later thirteenth century than it does to the reign of John. In some parts of the country, peasants could exploit resources of forest and meadow, outside the arable fields. The ten-acre calculation is itself based on figures from the productivity of lordly demesnes, whereas productivity on peasant land, which was literally a matter of life and death, might have been much higher. Where peasants lacked access to ploughs, they could, with plenty of family labour, prepare their lands for sowing all the more fruitfully by spade.[39] Yet, whatever the truth in this debate, no one would dispute that the English peasantry were poor and disadvantaged. They needed all the protection in Magna Carta they could get.

There was no reason, in theory, why the free peasantry should not benefit directly from the Charter. As free men, under chapter 20, they were protected from excessive amercements (fines in modern parlance), whether imposed by the king or their lords; in chapter 39, they were protected from unjust dispossession. They might also gain from chapters 17 to 19, which aimed to expedite civil litigation in the king's courts. This was more than mere form, for the plea rolls recording such business show many of apparently peasant status litigating over small amounts of land. The Charter turned a much more negative face to the unfree, indeed it was deliberately designed to do so. The unfree were among the king's *fideles* to whom the Charter was announced, but the concessions were not actually given to them. John, at the start, made his grant to 'all the free men of our kingdom', so not to the unfree at all. The bishops, in their letters testifying to the Charter's authorized text, described it as being granted to 'the earls, barons and free men of England'. True, in chapter 63, it was 'the men in our kingdom' who were to enjoy the concessions, but it went without saying that these men were free. The point was clear in chapter 60's stipulation that 'all the men of our kingdom' should observe the concessions to their own men. The unfree had no men.

The Charter did nothing at all to challenge the basic restrictions of unfreedom. On the contrary, it reinforced them, making it very clear that the unfree were indeed subject to the will of their lords. The only chapter in which villeins appeared by name, and where they gained protection, was not what it seemed. This was chapter 20 on amercements. It laid down that amercements imposed on free men and merchants should fit the crime. They should not be so large as to affect a free man's 'contenementum', which meant his means of livelihood, and a merchant's merchandise, which came to the same thing. The chapter then continued:

> and a villein is to be amerced in the same way saving his wainage,
> if they fall into our mercy. And none of the aforesaid amercements
> are to be imposed, save by the oath of upright men of the neigh-
> bourhood.

'Wainage' here means the things necessary for the villein to be able to make a living, in other words his crops under cultivation, seed corn, ploughs and plough teams.[40] It was thus the equivalent of 'contenementum' and merchandise. On the face it, therefore, villeins here are being treated like everyone else. Indeed, the plural in the passage quoted above, 'if they fall into our mercy', might seem to imply that the 'if' qualification applies to the free men and merchants in the early part of the chapter just as much as to villeins at the end. In other words, all three groups are only protected from amercements imposed by the king.[41] Indeed, the chapter has sometimes been translated to make this all the clearer with 'If they fall into our mercy' being placed at its start to govern all that follows. But it is plain that the qualification 'if they fall into our mercy' was meant to apply only to the villein. Had the Charter meant to lump free men, merchants and villeins together here, it would have made that clear, as it did in the immediately following passage, which said that 'none of the aforesaid amercements' were to be imposed save by the oath of upright men of the neighbourhood. The confusion that could arise from the 'if they fall into our mercy' being plural rather than singular was eliminated in the Charter of 1216, and its successors. There the 'they' was changed to 'he', so the passage now read 'if he falls into our mercy', thus clearly referring only to the villein. In the engrossments of the later Charters, moreover, the section 'and a villein . . . if he falls into our mercy' is often punctuated as a separate and discrete clause. This change was anticipated in the very early French translation of the 1215 Charter, where again 'if they fall' appears as 'if he falls'.[42] Either the translator had sensed the correct meaning or he was working from an engrossment where the singular in fact occurred. The point of all this is that the lords wished to protect their villeins from amercements imposed by the king, while remaining free to impose whatever amercements they liked themselves.

There is one other striking feature about this clause on villeins. The qualification 'if he falls into our mercy' (as it should have read) does not appear in the equivalent chapter in the Articles of the Barons (9). It was thus inserted into the Charter at Runnymede itself. Evidently lords had realized that, left as it was, the chapter gave blanket protection to villeins. That would not do, hence the change. The doing down of villeins in the chapter and the separation of them from everyone else was thus highly deliberate. Even at Runnymede, in the midst of tense negotiations with the king, lords were thinking of how to entrench their authority over the unfree peasantry. That is a measure of how important the issue seemed to be.

Just how aware the drafters of the Charter were of chapter 20's implications for the peasantry is shown in a change made to it in the new version of the Charter which was issued in 1217. The 1215 Charter, probably inadvertently, had left the king in a worse position than his lords. They could impose whatever amercements they liked on their own villeins. The king, on the other hand, could not, for there was nothing to indicate that his own villeins were not protected by the chapter if they fell into his mercy. In 1217 this was put right through the introduction of another qualification to the chapter.[43] The villeins who were to be protected from excessive amercements imposed by the king were to be 'other than our own'. In other words, the king now gained the same let-out as lords and could do what he liked, as far as the Charter was concerned, when amercing his own villeins. In the 1215 Charter itself, the king had already gone some way to asserting his authority over his own peasants. Chapter 25 had exempted the king's demesne manors from the limitations on the money that could be taken from the counties. The king was thus free to impose heavier burdens on his manors, which meant of course heavier burdens on his peasant tenants.

After the section on amercements, chapter 23 went on to protect men and vills from being distrained to work on bridges, other than when such work was customary, the protection of 'men' rather than just of vills being added at Runnymede itself. This certainly offered something to unfree peasants. That the chapter spoke of 'men' rather than 'freemen' shows that the lowest sections of society were involved. The chapter was there, however, because lords were acting in their own interests. Their aim was to prevent their peasants being dragged away from their proper duties by work on the king's bridges. Failure to carry out such work also rendered men and vills liable to amercement, and it was on the issue of amercements that the chapter in the Articles of the Barons had focused, which is why it appears after the section on amercements, a place it kept in the Charter itself. To enforce bridge work was an ancient royal right.[44] It was, however, one which John had exploited in a new way for the bridges needed for his hawking.[45]

What then of the clutch of chapters about justice between 38 and 40? Chapter 38, in insisting that no bailiff (and not just a bailiff of the king) should put 'anyone' 'to law', and thus on trial, on his own unsupported accusation, seemed in theory to benefit everyone. This made the contrast with 39, the Charter's most famous chapter, all the starker. Here it was 'no free man' not 'no man' who was to be protected from unjust imprisonment, disseisin and outlawry. The implication here was not that lords could outlaw their villeins as they liked. Outlawry was a public process for the county courts. Nor really could lords imprison their villeins. But what they could do was to disseise them of their land. That was a vital power, and to reserve it was the reason why the chapter protected the free man but not the man who was unfree. Lords, as far as the Charter was concerned, could disseize the latter as they liked. This was made even clearer in a slight revision to the chapter in the Charter of 1217, where it now stated that no free man was to be disseised of his 'free tenement'. This gave lords even more scope because it meant a free man *could* be disseised of land he held in villeinage, which meant land to which villein customs, such as labour services, were attached. For free men to take on such land was risky because it could involve being dragged down into personal unfreedom, but with land in short supply, many took the risk.

And so to chapter 40. 'To no one [*nulli*] will we sell, to no one will we deny or delay, right or justice.' Surely, here at last, the Charter was offering justice equally to free and unfree alike. Unfortunately not. If a villein accused his lord of felony and sedition (not a very likely occurrence), it is true the king was bound to hear him. But it was the law itself that denied villeins any rights against their lords, and thus any justice from the king, in matters concerning land and services.

Lords, judging from the Charter, were thus very concerned to single out their unfree peasants and keep them in their place. But why so? After all, in practice lords did not make regular use of the full range of their powers; they did not usually dispossess their peasants, or make them work 'at their bidding'. Sometimes lords were ready to convert labour services into money rents, even to grant villeins outright freedom. They also allowed (as later records show) peasants themselves to assess the amercements imposed in manorial courts, much in line with the stipulation in the Charter that they should be assessed by local men.[46]

It is, however, very clear why the powers affirmed in the Charter were so important. The early thirteenth century was a period when the rural economy was being transformed. Lords, aware that there was more profit to be made from land in the expanding economy, were reducing the areas that they had out at rent, and increasing the size of their demesnes, with the aim of cultivating them directly and having large grain surpluses to sell. But at the very time when lords wished to assert more control over their manors, there were forces making it more difficult to do so. The rising population was creating pressure to subdivide peasant holdings. Along with an increasing money supply, it was also generating a peasant land market.[47] Lords, in the face of entrenched manorial customs, might find it more difficult to increase the burdens on their peasants than legal theory implied. Failing the testing of the issue in court, there could be considerable uncertainty as to where the line between free and unfree should be drawn. A peasant might appear as a sokeman in one survey and a villein in another. There were sokemen free sokemen 'gersumarii' sokemen, bond sokemen, villein sokemen and serf sokemen, a variety of names that suggests the struggle of sokemen to assert their freedom on the one hand, and of lords to deny it on the other.[48] In addition, free men, as we have said, might take land to which villein services were attached. In these challenging circumstances, lords felt it was absolutely necessary to hold the line and retain their package of powers over the unfree. Those powers seemed vital for disciplining their peasant workforce and keeping control of what was going on in the manor. The Charter thus became an instrument of lordship that asserted the fundamental division between the free and unfree. It protected the unfree from the king, only to place them all the more firmly under their lords.

What made this lordly victory all the more significant was that it cut across a current which suggested it might have been otherwise. Unfree peasants could certainly be regarded as very much part of the realm. John enlisted everyone, free and unfree alike, in his scheme of national defence in 1205, just as everyone was enlisted to enforce the Charter.[49] Peasants, free and unfree, were involved in the running of local government, having to give evidence at coroners' inquests and at local courts. There was also the idea that the king should indeed protect unfree peasants from their lords. This emerges in the discussion, found in the *Dialogus de Scaccario*, as to why the king could take possession of the chattels of villeins when they were convicted of an offence. Was this not surprising, the *Dialogus* asked, given that such chattels were the property of the lord? The answer was that if lords got the chattels in such circumstances, they might be encouraged to trump up charges against their villeins. So the king, 'entrusted by God with the care of all his subjects', had protected villeins from the 'greed' of their lords, by laying down that the chattels should belong to him.[50] The unfree gained no protection from the greed of their lords in Magna Carta.

THE JEWS[51]

Chapter 10 laid down that if anyone died owing money to the Jews, the debt should not gather interest during the minority of the heir. In addition, if a debt owed the Jews came into the hands of the king, then he would only take the principal of the debt (the 'catallum'), in other words he would not exact the accumulated interest. Chapter 11 went further, protecting both a debtor's widow, as we have seen, and underage children. The latter were to have the necessary requirements for their support, and only then was the debt to be paid from what remained.

In John's reign there were probably not many more than five thousand Jews in England, and they were confined to the major towns. That there were chapters about them in Magna Carta, nonetheless, shows the central part they played in the economic life of the country. The reason, as the Charter showed, was that Jews were moneylenders; indeed, given the church's ban on Christian usury, they were the main source of credit. The borrowers ranged across society: free tenants, even of peasant status, knights, barons, earls, bishops and monastic houses. The debts of great men could run into hundreds, even thousands of pounds, with this business being in the hands of a small number of Jewish plutocrats, whose town houses excited awe and envy. The interest rate could run at one or two pence in the pound per week, so 22 per cent or 44 per cent a year. The Jews were not only resented because of their moneylending. They were also persecuted for their religion. A combination of both factors led to an appalling massacre of the Jews in York in 1189.

Given such powerful enemies, why was the Charter not more radical? Why did it not seek to ban interest on debts altogether, or even expel the Jews from the country as finally happened in 1290? The answer lay partly in an acknowledgement that the Jews were indeed useful as sources of credit, and partly in the way they were protected by the king. This was not an issue on which John would give way. The fact was that the Jews were a vital source of profit for the crown. There were a whole variety of ways in which debts owed the Jews could come into royal hands, whereupon the king could then exact them for himself. In addition, the king could tax the Jews at will. The reason was that the king regarded them as his own property. As a legal work of the mid-twelfth century, known as the *Leges Edwardi Confessoris* (*The Laws of Edward the Confessor*), put it, 'the Jews themselves and all their possessions are the king's'.[52] John, like his predecessors, thus put the Jews under his 'special protection', and gave them a series of privileges. He was furious when they were maltreated in London. His resulting letter to the mayor and sheriffs, saying that his peace should be observed even if given to a dog, showed his contempt for the Jews, but also his determination to protect them.[53]

LONDON, TOWNS AND MERCHANTS[54]

London is the only town mentioned by name in Magna Carta. The Charter stipulated that the aids (that is, taxes) levied on London by the king were to be taken in the same way as those imposed on the rest of the kingdom, which meant that they were to be 'reasonable' in size and agreed by the 'common counsel of the kingdom'. London was also to have all its ancient liberties and free customs by both land and water. In modern printings of the Charter, the first of these provisions is tacked onto the end of chapter 12, the second made to start chapter 13. Looking at the original engrossments, there would be a case for joining them together in an exclusive chapter on London itself, and that is how they appear in one early copy of the Charter.[55] Chapter 33 of the Charter, following again the Articles, also met one of London's major demands (one already conceded in royal charters), namely that fish weirs should be completely removed from the Thames and Medway. In chapter 35 'the quarter' of London was to be adopted as the standard for measures.

London's exclusive place in the Charter is absolutely understandable. It had played a central part in the rebellion against King John. Indeed its mayor was one of the twenty-five barons of the security clause. Already in the 1150s, London could be described as 'the queen of the whole kingdom'.[56] One reasonable estimate of its population in the early thirteenth century is around 40,000, having doubled in the previous hundred years. It was many times larger than its nearest rivals Bristol, Winchester, Norwich and York.[57]

Situated in a low river basin, sheltered by the friendly protecting hills around Blackheath, Brockley and Hampstead, London owed its pre-eminence to its location. Its place on the eastern side of the country opened it to merchants from the continent who, sailing up the Thames, could unload their wares, not in some channel port but well inland. The bridge, the most seaward over the river, meant that from London one could travel both north and south. Vessels could also navigate upstream as far as Lechlade in Gloucestershire.

In the second half of the twelfth century, the exchequer moved from Winchester to Westminster, confirming London as the country's governmental capital. With the might of the Tower controlling the city, and with William Rufus's gigantic hall at Westminster providing a magnificent setting for feasts and assemblies, London was the chief seat of England's monarchy.

The power and aspirations of the Londoners had long been recognized in concessions made to them by the king. These were the 'ancient' liberties that Magna Carta confirmed. They facilitated trade by freeing the citizens from tolls, and also allowed them to elect their own sheriffs. In the crisis of 1191, during King Richard's absence on crusade, the Londoners had gained from John and the magnates of the kingdom the right to form a 'commune', which meant a sworn, self-governing association, headed by its own elected mayor.[58] Neither Richard on his return, nor John on his accession, actually confirmed the commune, but they probably acquiesced in its existence. In 1206, during an episode that reveals the social tensions in the city, John complained that 'the superiors' of London were exploiting 'the common people' at his expense. Nonetheless, he still accepted the city's self-government, for he ordered the leading citizens, 'the barons', to elect twenty-four of their fellows to put matters right. In 1215 itself, little more than a month before he conceded Magna Carta, John granted the 'barons' of the city the right to choose their own mayor.[59]

The Charter also recognized the importance, albeit nameless, of 'all other cities and boroughs, and vills and ports', when it confirmed 'their liberties and free customs'. Indeed, the original engrossments all have a new chapter beginning with this clause, rather than joining it onto chapter 13 on London. The most important of these towns did indeed have liberties to defend, since between 1100 and 1215 over seventy had acquired royal charters granting various privileges, sometimes similar to those enjoyed by London. In the charters, the towns were described as cities, boroughs or vills, so corresponding to the terminology in Magna Carta. Sandwich, Dover, Hythe, Romney and Hastings formed the Cinque Ports, with Rye and Winchelsea associated towns. The recipients of the grants were called citizens, burgesses or simply men. They held their property by burgage tenure, referred to in chapter 37 of the Charter, which meant in return for rent and with freedom of alienation.[60] The wealth of the towns came from both trade and manufacture. The Charter, in one of its few non-partisan chapters (35), tried to facilitate both by standardizing measures of wine, ale, corn and cloth. It also, in chapter 41, gave merchants safe transit to, from and within England, free from all 'evil exactions'. The importance of the merchants was seen equally in chapter 20, which treated them as a separate class alongside free men and villeins, when laying down that they should only be amerced saving their 'merchandise'. That the merchants in England might be foreign, as, equally, English merchants might be in foreign parts, was clear in chapter 41, in which John established regulations about what should happen to both groups in the event of a 'land at war with us'. The use of 'land' here, rather than kingdom, reflected that merchants, such as those from Flanders, might not come from a kingdom at all.

Much trade was, of course, internal to England, including that in corn, which was only imported in times of dearth. Ale was even more local, for it had to be consumed soon after it was brewed. The different cloths mentioned in the Charter – the dyed cloths, russets and halbergets in chapter 35 – were manufactured at many centres in England. A thirteenth-century doggerel mentioned the scarlets of Lincoln, the halbergets of Stamford, the russets of Colchester and so on.[61] High-quality cloth was also imported, above all from Flanders, the centre of the European cloth industry. England's chief import, however, was wine. With the loss of Anjou, in 1204, this came more and more from Gascony, routed through its great port of Bordeaux. England's chief export was wool, above all to Flanders to supply its cloth industry. The duty on exported sacks of wool was to be the foundation of the English customs, and just why it was not introduced before 1275 is one of the mysteries of English royal finance.[62] Since the cloth Flanders sent to England did not balance the value of the wool it imported, it paid for much of the wool in cash, in silver, which was a major factor in the stunning increase in England's money supply in the thirteenth century.

At first sight, London and other privileged towns seem to be very much getting their due in the Charter, even against other sections of society. Thus the removal of fish weirs (as an obstacle to trade passing up and down rivers) impacted on the lords who had weirs on their own sections of river. Later, in compliance with this chapter of Magna Carta, among the weirs destroyed were those of Richard, earl of Cornwall.[63] In other ways, however, towns got much less than they had hoped for, indeed less than they had solicited in the Articles of the Barons. There tallages and aids imposed both on London and on other cities with liberties were to require the common consent of the kingdom. Here, in terms of principle, the real prize was control over tallage. The king might acknowledge that taxes in the form of aids required some form of consent, however nebulous that consent might be in practice, hence the way the Charter, as we will see, tried to define the assembly which should give it. Tallages, on the other hand, the king claimed to levy on his towns at will. That they should henceforth require consent would thus have been a major gain. But in Magna Carta the reference to tallage was dropped. Instead just aids required common consent and only those imposed on London, not the other towns. There was another chapter where more might have been done for towns. Chapter 25 prevented the king increasing the fixed payments (called 'farms') due from his counties and hundreds, but no similar restrictions were imposed on town farms. The towns would certainly have welcome that for John was very much in the business of increasing their farms.[64]

John himself must surely have fought hard to keep tallage and town farms out of his concessions, arguing that his opponents had no business to interfere with his rights over his own property. That the barons did not make a stand on the issues was, however, also because of self-interest and self-regard. If Magna Carta prevented the king tallaging his towns and increasing their farms, then the barons also might be subject to the same restrictions in towns subject to their lordship. The earl of Chester, for example, was accustomed to take regular taxes from his burgesses of Coventry.[65] There was a related danger. When the king tallaged his towns and manors, lords too could profit because they were usually allowed to tallage any of their properties that had once been the king's. When, therefore, Alan Basset, one of John's counsellors named at the start of the Charter, reached an agreement with his burgesses of High Wycombe, he reserved the sums he might levy 'when the king and his heirs tallage their demesnes through England'.[66] In keeping tallage out of the Charter, therefore, the magnates and king were making common cause against the towns. There was also a degree of social prejudice against towns, townspeople and trading. The baronial leaders would have agreed with the *Dialogus de Scaccario* when it criticized knights who had so far 'degenerated from the dignity of their status' as to make money from trade.[67] In 1236 the

Statute of Merton thought heirs might be disparaged if they were married either to burgesses or to villeins.[68] Significantly, although the mayor of London was one of the twenty-five 'barons' in the security clause, in none of the lists of the membership is he given a name.

All this helps to explain the very striking way in which London was excluded from any role in the assembly that was to give the common consent of the kingdom to taxation. This was true whether the assembly was to consent to aids levied on the kingdom as a whole or aids levied on London. The same assembly was to deal with both and, as defined in chapter 14, it was to be composed entirely of tenants-in-chief. The archbishops, bishops, abbots, earls and greater barons were to be summoned individually and the other tenants-in-chief generally, through the sheriffs. As noted, the mayor of London was one of the twenty-five 'barons' of the security clause. The king called the leading citizens his 'barons', but there is no suggestion that they would have been summoned either personally or generally under Magna Carta's arrangements. What makes this all the more pointed is that London had been involved in great political decisions in the past. Londoners had played a key role in the accession of Stephen in 1135, claiming that it was their right and privilege to choose the king.[69] In 1191, during King Richard's absence on crusade, they had joined with John and the bishops and barons in deposing William Longchamp, as governor of the kingdom, putting the archbishop of Rouen in his place. This was the moment when the Londoners were granted their commune.[70] There was also a feeling among Londoners that their consent *should* be sought, along with that of the kingdom, when it came to taxation. Thus a schedule of city demands from John's reign includes one stating that tallages are to be abolished save when authorized 'by common consent of the kingdom and the city'.[71] The implication was clearly that if a tallage was to be levied on the city, then the Londoners would need to be part of the national assembly which consented to it. The Londoners probably also thought that they should be present when such an assembly consented to an aid, whether one paid just by London or by London as part of a general aid levied on the kingdom. Such representation, however, was not something that the barons of 1215 were prepared to contemplate. It was only in 1265, when the government was controlled by Simon de Montfort, that representatives of the towns were summoned to parliament.

THE CHURCH AND CHURCHMEN

Churchmen seem, in the Charter, to play a far larger part in the life of the realm than do townsmen. The archbishops, bishops and abbots *were* to receive personal summonses to chapter 14's national assembly. Stephen Langton, archbishop of Canterbury, together with seven other English bishops, were all mentioned by name at the start of the Charter as those on whose advice John had acted. It was the same men, in chapter 62, who were to issue letters testifying to the Charter's authentic text. Magna Carta, in its very first chapter, guaranteed the freedom of the church, and confirmed John's previous concession over free elections. Chapter 22 preserved clerks from unjust amercements. Magna Carta also revealed the position of the pope both as head of the church and as overlord (thanks to John's concession in 1213) of the kingdom. Thus the preamble listed Master Pandulf, a *'familiaris* of the lord pope' – meaning a member of Pope Innocent III's household – as one of John's counsellors, while chapter 1 mentioned Innocent's confirmation of John's charter granting free elections. The Articles of the Barons, in their turn, had tried to prevent John seeking anything from the pope that might undermine the Charter.

This place accorded to churchmen was absolutely natural. It stemmed in part from the deep-rooted idea that the bishops in general, and the archbishop of Canterbury in particular, should be the king's counsellors in both spiritual and temporal affairs. Innocent III himself opined that bishops should be 'loyal to the king, profitable to the kingdom, and capable of giving counsel and help'.[72] The place of the church in the Charter also stemmed from its great wealth. Some of the bishops of the seventeen English dioceses had incomes that equalled or exceeded those of the greatest earls. The same was true of the greater abbots (of St Albans or Westminster, for example). At the time of Domesday Book in 1086 over a quarter of the land in England was in the hands of the church, and the share had increased considerably since then with the foundation of new monasteries, especially those of the Cistercian order. Much of this land, moreover, was held directly from the king in return for the same military and other services (described more fully in the next chapter) as were owed by earls and barons. The church, as a landholder, therefore, benefited like everyone else from the chapters in the Charter which sought to restrain the abuses of the king's local officials, and reduce the area of the royal forest.

There was also, however, a vast range of ecclesiastical activity governed by the church's own procedures and canon law, the latter the sum of pronouncements by the pope and church councils down the ages. One of the most remarkable narratives from John's reign is an account of Evesham abbey's struggle against its lecherous abbot and the jurisdictional claims of the bishop of Worcester. Written by the monk Thomas of Marlborough, who played a leading part in the affair, it runs to over 130 printed pages in a modern edition and gives graphic accounts of journeys to Rome and decisions by the pope and his delegated judges.[73] King John hardly appears once. This separation between church and state is seen in the very first chapter of the Charter where the concession to God of the freedom of the church is made quite distinct from the concessions to the realm. The precise boundary between ecclesiastical and secular jurisdiction had long been contentious, and Magna Carta illustrates something of the uneasy divide. The secular court had jurisdiction when the right to appoint a parish priest to a living (one claimed by many lords) was disputed. Indeed, the relevant legal action, that of 'darrein presentment', was one of those made more available under chapter 18 of the Charter. Ecclesiastical courts, on the other hand, had jurisdiction over Church revenues to which no secular services were attached, so tithes and land held 'in free alms'. Thus, in chapter 22, the amount of an amercement imposed on a clerk was to be determined according to the value of his 'lay tenement', not his ecclesiastical benefice. Over the latter the king had no authority. The Charter also made a nod towards the Church's claim to oversee the administration of a dead person's property, the point being so that it could then ensure the fulfilment of charitable bequests. Chapter 27 thus said that the goods of someone who died intestate should be distributed by his nearest relations and friends 'under the supervision of the church'.[74] The church did not, however, use the Charter to strengthen the division between secular and ecclesiastical jurisdiction, although it often complained of its breach. The Charter thus did not try to reaffirm the concession made by Henry II after the dispute with Thomas Becket, which freed clerks accused of crime from trial and punishment in secular courts. Just why the Charter was not more of an ecclesiastical document will emerge when we look at the role of Archbishop Langton in the events of 1215.[75]

5
Magna Carta and Society: Earls, Barons, Knights and Free Tenants

The Charter gives no information about the relations between lords and their villeins. By contrast, it provides a great deal of information about the relations between the king and his leading men, namely the earls, barons and others holding their land directly from him, holding, that is, from him 'in chief' – 'in capite' – as it was put in chapters 2 and 14 of the Charter. These 'tenants-in-chief', as historians call them, formed an elite group, above the many others who held their land not from the king, but from the tenants-in-chief themselves. To regulate relations between the king and his tenants-in-chief was a central thrust of Magna Carta. The tenants-in-chief were thus at the heart of the Charter. They were also, as the Charter saw it, at the heart of the kingdom. They alone, under chapter 14 of the Charter, were to give the common consent of the kingdom to taxation. The most important of the tenants-in-chief, the earls and greater barons, were to receive individual letters of summons; the rest were to be summoned generally by the sheriffs. At the end of the Charter, it was twenty-five barons, chosen by the barons themselves, who were to enforce its terms.

The land held by a tenant-in-chief from the king was often called a 'feodum', a word, translated as 'fief' or 'fee', which appears thirteen times in the Charter. And it is from 'feodum' that historians have often labelled the tenurial structure based on the fee as 'feudalism'. Chapter 2 of the Charter highlights a major division within the tenants-in-chief, between, that is, the earls and barons on the one hand and knights on the other. Chapter 14 makes a different division between earls and greater barons, and the rest of the tenants-in-chief. Included among the greater barons were the ecclesiastical magnates, the archbishops, bishops and abbots, for they too held land direct from the king on comparable terms to their lay colleagues.

It was assumed in the Charter that fees were hereditary, as

indeed they generally were. When the Articles of the Barons, in its chapter 1, stated that 'heirs shall have their inheritance after the death of their ancestors . . .', the issue was not the succession itself but the amount to be paid for it. At the start of the relationship between the king and a tenant-in-chief was the act of homage. This is not mentioned in the Charter, although it does feature in chapter 3 of the Charter of 1216 and its successors. Homage took place when a new tenant succeeded. The tenant would kneel down, place his two hands between the hands of the king and declare 'I become your man for the tenement which I hold of you, and I will bear you fealty in life, limb and earthly honour.'[1] This act established a much stronger and more intimate bond than that involved in a simple oath of fealty, for it was directly related to loyalty in return for land, as fealty was not. It also created a mutual bond, so that the ceremony of the hands symbolized the king's protection of his man and the man's subjection to his king. The ceremony was supposed to take place in a public space, so in a church, chapel or hall, and have a numinous quality. It meant every tenant-in-chief began his career with a very personal encounter with his king, and was thereafter bound into a mutual relationship with him.

While the 1215 Magna Carta said nothing about homage, it was very clear about the other ingredients in the relationship. One was the counsel the king could and should receive from his tenants, as the Charter testified when it came to taxation in chapters 12 and 14. Another was military. Chapter 2 mentioned that the tenants-in-chief held 'by knight service'. The same chapter also referred to 'the whole fee [*feodum*] of a knight'. This meant a fee for which the service of one knight was owed when the king summoned out his army. A knightly tenant-in-chief might indeed owe the king the service of one knight. The returns to an inquiry from 1166, on the other hand, show many earls and barons owing the king anything between twenty knights and a hundred.[2] An alternative form of military service was that of garrisoning a royal castle. Chapter 29 was concerned to prevent John demanding a double ration – both garrisoning a castle and appearing in his army. An addition in the 1217 version of the Charter (chapter 29) made it explicit that the army service in question was 'for the fee' for which it was owed.

Chapter 29 also demonstrated the way in which military service could be commuted to money, when directing that if a knight wanted to serve personally or through a deputy, rather than give money in lieu, he should be allowed to do so. Giving money in lieu had long been common. For each of his many campaigns, John raised a tax called 'scutage'. This is referred to in chapters 12 and 14, which tried to ensure that it was levied only by common consent. 'Scutage' was paid at a fixed rate according to the number of fees held by the tenant-in-chief, and thus the number of knights he owed. (Scutage itself – 'scutagium' in Latin – means shield.) If the scutage was £2 a fee, a baron with eighty fees would owe £160. Whether a tenant-in-chief led a contingent of knights, or gave scutage instead, depended on a personal agreement with the king, as did, in practice, the precise numbers actually brought to the host. The nominal service based on fees determined scutage but not any longer, if it ever had, the actual size of the contingents. These could be much smaller, which was a reflection of the costs involved.[3]

Other features of the relationship between the king and his tenants-in-chief likewise stand out in the early chapters of the Charter. There was the payment made when the new tenant entered his estate. The Charter stipulated this should be a fixed sum, called a 'relief', and not some arbitrary fine. There were the 'aids' (essentially taxes) of chapters 12 and 14, which the king could raise for ransoming his body (as King Richard had done), knighting his eldest son and the marrying on one occasion of his eldest daughter. And then in chapters 3, 4 and 5 there were the king's rights of wardship over an heir who was underage. (The Charter of 1216 added to chapter 3 that the age of majority was to be twenty-one.) These rights meant the king held the fee of the heir (male or female) and received all its revenues during the minority. Alternatively (as chapter 4 said), he could give or sell the custody to someone else. The Charter went on, in the next chapter, namely chapter 6, to state that 'heirs' were to be 'married without disparagement', that is not to those below them in social rank. The king also had power over the widows of tenants-in-chief, hence the statement, in chapters 7 and 8, that widows should not have to pay to get their lands after the death of their husbands, and should not be forced into remarriage. Another chapter, 26, shows the special vulnerability of the widow and children of a tenant-in-chief when he died (the 'children' here implies there was no heir of age), for it tried to stop the king's agents arbitrarily seizing chattels on the excuse that the deceased tenant-in-chief had owed money to the crown.

The status and military mien of the great tenants-in-chief are displayed in the effigies on their tombs and the images on their seals. The Purbeck marble effigies of William Marshal, earl of Pembroke, and William Longespee, earl of Salisbury (King John's half-brother), both survive, the one in London's Temple Church, the other in Salisbury cathedral. Longespee's effigy shows him with his hand on his sword, his body encased in chain mail protected by a great shield on which dance the six lions of his coat of arms. The might of these men stands out in the castles sited at the centre of their fees. At his seat at Framlingham, Roger Bigod, earl of Norfolk, one of the twenty-five barons of the security clause, rebuilt the castle with no fewer than thirteen towers around its curtain wall.[4]

What kind of numbers then are we dealing with when it comes to earls and barons? Earls are easiest to count because they are always given their title, and had probably received it at a formal ceremony. In the Latin of the Charter, this made the lord a 'comes', while, in the French translation, he is a 'conte' – a 'count'. It was only in English that he would have been called an 'earl', but that is how conventionally all historians describe these men. Thanks to the formal ceremony needed to enter the honour, one either was an earl or one wasn't. In John's reign they usually numbered around a dozen. There were seven earls among the twenty-five barons elected under the Charter's security clause, while John was able to name four at the start of the Charter among his advisers. He might have added Ranulf, earl of Chester, and his ally, William de Ferrers, earl of Derby, had they not been absent from Runnymede.[5] Barons are harder to count, because, although a baron did homage for his barony, he did not actually use 'baron' as a title. In addition, the estates constituting the 'whole' baronies of chapter 2 of the Charter were never clearly defined before 1215. Afterwards, they had to be, in order to decide who owed the £100 relief stipulated by the Charter. Often using this later evidence, I. J. Sanders in his study of English baronies between 1087 and 1327 was able to list 102 of them, although he then added another forty-eight 'probable baronies'. Nearly all of these baronies were in existence before 1215, although far from all were in being at any one time. As for the knightly tenants-in-chief who held not baronies but knights' fees, there were perhaps between three to four hundred of them.[6]

The average baronial income, drawn from a sample group

taken from between 1160 and 1220, was about £200 a year and the median was £115, but seven barons had incomes of over £400. In one year between 1211 and 1212 the king's officials were able to raise, after necessary expenses, around £1,000 from the lands of the underage John de Lacy. Probably that was the kind of income enjoyed by many of the earls, although later in the century, when we have more figures, some earls had incomes of several thousand pounds a year. By way of comparison, King John's annual income from England at the start of his reign was about £22,000. The wage of a labourer working on one of the king's buildings was one and a half or two pennies a day. A woman labourer received one penny, so 240th of a pound.[7]

Both earls and barons presided over the same kind of estate. That point emerges from the phraseology of the Charter where earls succeeded not to an earldom but to the 'barony of an earl', which in terms of its structure was no different from the barony of a baron. Although nearly all the earls were earls of a county, or the chief city of a county, this entitled them to no more than a fairly modest annual payment from the county's revenues. The only exception was Chester, where the earl had all the king's rights in Cheshire itself. The earldom was thus an honorary position, although one coveted, for the honour was great. Between the earls and greater barons, and the other tenants-in-chief, there was, however, a fundamental difference in the structure of their fees. True, all of them derived the bulk of their income from land, from the demesne manors that they kept in hand. But the earls and greater barons also had manors, parts of manors and other properties, held from them by their own knightly tenants, whereas minor barons and knights holding in chief did not, or did not on anything like the same scale. In 1166 William de Ferrers, earl of Derby, listed forty-seven such tenants.[8] It was the total package, demesne manors and tenanted lands, that made up the hereditary fee of the earl or baron. Sometimes, as in chapter 43, which dealt with some fees in the king's hands, this was called not the baron's fee but his 'honour' (his estate).

Within the baronial fees or honours, the great majority of significant tenants in the early thirteenth century were knights, and their relationship with their baronial lord replicated that between the baron and the king. This was made very clear in respect of homage in chapter 3 of the Charter of 1216, which directed that, in the case of an underage heir, the lord (so not just the king) was to take his homage before receiving the wardship. The relationship is also illuminated in chapter 43 of the 1215 Charter, dealing with baronies in the king's hands. This stipulated that the king should receive relief and other services from the tenants as if the barony was still held by the baron. The other services would have included aids and knight service, as chapters 15 and 16 of the Charter showed. They would also have included scutage, so that, when levied by the king, the baron recouped it from his knightly tenants. In addition, lords controlled wardships and marriages of underage heirs, and had rights over the remarriage of widows. Thus, under chapter 8, a widow had to give security that she would not remarry without the king's assent, if she held her land from him, or 'without the assent of her lord from whom she holds, if she holds from another', a perfect laying out of the tenurial hierarchy. Lords also held a court (sometimes called by historians 'the honorial court') for their tenants by military service, and defended its authority in chapter 34 of the Charter. Such courts had jurisdiction over disputes around both possession of the fees and the services owed the lord. The courts might become a focus of loyalty and community. They were also a way for the lord to make money from amercements.

KNIGHTS

Knights were absolutely central to key features of the Charter. True, they were only named directly as the beneficiaries of two chapters, and these were limited to knightly tenants-in-chief. Chapter 2 regulated relief due from the heir or heirs of a knight, and chapter 29 allowed knights to garrison castles in person, and protected them from having to do both garrison and army duty. Chapter 43, too, benefited knights, although again only those holding their land from the king, when it regulated the relief and other services within honours that had come into the king's hands. It was in the chapters on justice and local government that the general body of knights, not just those holding from the king, came into their own. Under chapter 18, the king was to 'send two justices through each county four times a year' to hear the common-law legal actions, called assizes, which determined disputes over property. These judges were not to act alone. They were to hear the cases with four knights of the county, elected by the county court.

This was a striking recognition of the legal expertise and self-confidence of the knights. Evidently, they felt quite able to sit along-side the king's judges. In addition, in what Blackstone wrongly made a new chapter (19), it was laid down that sufficient knights and free tenants were to stay behind for judgements to be made, if the business could not be finished on the day of the meeting of the county court. The role of knights was revealed even more remarkably in chapter 48 of the Charter. Under its terms, twelve knights in each county, elected by 'upright men of the same county', were to investigate the abuses of the king's local officials and then, within forty days, abolish them. The knights thus had virtually a free hand in the reform of local government. Just how central this chapter was to the whole settlement was shown on 19 June 1215, when, as a condition of the peace, John had at once to set the work of the knights in motion.[9] According to the calculations of Kathryn Faulkner, there were around 4,500 men accepted as knights in early thirteenth-century England, accepted that is for the purpose of sitting on juries and performing various administrative and judicial tasks. A large county such as Yorkshire had an estimated total of 238 knights; a small one such as Surrey, 90 knights.[10] A few hundred of these knights would have been tenants-in-chief of the king, and direct beneficiaries of chapters 2 and 29. The rest would, for the most part, have been tenants of the earls, barons, bishops and abbots. As we have seen, the terms on which they held from their lords replicated those on which those lords held from the king. In respect of landed wealth, a survey of fifty-seven Oxfordshire knights from the 1220s shows that five had four or more manors, and thus incomes approaching baronial proportions. Some of these knights had their own tenants by knight service for whom they held courts.[11] Many of the knights who star in Holt's study of northerners come from this upper band of the class.[12] Their influence helps to explain why chapter 34, protecting private jurisdiction, was drawn widely and spoke of the courts of free men, not just of the courts of barons. Below this upper level there were, in the Oxfordshire survey, twenty knights with two or three manors; twenty-five with one manor of reasonable size; and seven with smaller properties. A Bedfordshire survey from a few years earlier suggests a much higher proportion of knights in the last category, with over 50 per cent having less than a whole fee, although fees are an uncertain guide to actual property.[13] Later in the thirteenth century, when the level was put at the bare minimum required, an income of £15 a year was deemed sufficient to render one liable to take up knighthood.[14] Probably, in John's reign, most knights with two reasonably sized manors or equivalent properties would have been above that level; those with one manor of reasonable size might have been at that level; those with less, below it.

The knights in John's reign thus covered a very broad social spectrum. From a core of knights with one or two manors, the group reached up to those of baronial wealth, and down to those not much different from the free tenants sitting above the peasantry. In the upper levels of society, both kings and barons had long become knights through a formal ceremony in which they were girded with the sword of knighthood. Increasingly, aping their superiors, this was also true of the wealthier county knights. Whether, however, the general run of those described as knights in John's reign had gone through a ceremony may be doubted. Probably men were accepted as knights on juries and in other local government roles because they in some way looked the part. This could cause arguments as to who exactly was a knight. The abbot of Crowland in the 1190s complained that four 'knights' who had testified against him were actually 'low fellows' ('viles'), 'not of the knightly order nor girt with sword'. Indeed they did not hold their lands by knight service. One of them could not even speak French.[15] That the king sometimes ordered inquiries to be made by belted knights shows that not all knights were belted.

In the decades after Magna Carta, there was a rapid decline in the number of knights. In response to attitudes such as the abbot of Crowland's, the view became established that only those who had gone through the ceremony could be regarded as holding the honour.[16] Since the ceremony was expensive (the aspiring knight needed to have the necessary equipment), only the upper levels of the old knightly class took up the honour. The expense is shown in Magna Carta itself where the knighting of an eldest son was one of the occasions on which both king and lords could levy an aid. In 1216 John gave someone ten marks or a horse worth the same amount 'in aid of his knighting'.[17] In John's reign, however, we still have the 'old' knightly class, and that did nothing to diminish its power. In a sense, it had the best of both worlds, the new and the old. On the one hand, there were belted knights very conscious of their status and importance. Yet, on the other hand, on juries and in other local roles, these men, without any formal distinction of status, worked alongside knights of much lesser estate. Indeed, just where knights stopped and free tenants began was not at all clear. Society was less stratified and arguably more cohesive than it became later. The Charter itself did not stipulate that the knights in chapters 18 and 48 needed to be belted, and thus did nothing to accelerate the development of a knightly elite. It also envisaged an easy cooperation and interchange between knights and free men, thus reflecting the lack of any clear division between those who were and were not knights. The Charter had two men running wardships where the Unknown Charter had four knights. Under chapter 19, it is knights and free tenants together who are to stay behind to assist judgements in the county court.

The knights of John's reign were certainly militarily active, hence their importance in the rebellion of 1215. They could all have performed the army service and castle guard expected of the knightly tenants-in-chief in chapter 29. The same men were equally busy in local affairs. Many knights in John's Irish army of 1210 can be found sitting on grand-assize juries. The knights were well qualified for the roles assigned them in Magna Carta. Under the procedures of the grand assize, which determined the right to land, twelve knightly jurors, chosen by four knights, gave the verdicts. Panels of four knights were regularly appointed to investigate the excuses of those who did not turn up in lawsuits, and also to 'bear the record' of proceedings in the county court either before the king or before his judges at Westminster. The king was employing knights in a whole raft of roles across local government: as sheriffs, coroners, keepers of manors and forest officials. Lords were employing them too, notably as their stewards. Matthew Paris described the knight Laurence de Tybridge, steward of St Albans abbey, as 'a man most handsome in body, eloquent, wise and knowledgeable about civil pleas'. The vigour with which he stood up for St Albans in one dispute earned him the hatred of the great baron Robert fitzWalter.[18]

The roles assigned to the knights in chapters 18 and 48 of the Charter were part of a wider campaign, well under way by 1215, for local men to control local offices.[19] The strength of feeling is brilliantly highlighted by a case in the Somerset county court in 1204 recorded by twelve knights of the county. Here Richard Revel upbraided the sheriff for being an outsider while he and his father were 'native men and gentlemen of the country' – '*naturales homines et gentiles de patria*'.[20] In Lincolnshire, no fewer than twenty-nine local men stood surety for the 500 marks offered for the sheriffdom by the major county knight Thomas of Moulton.[21] The men of Cornwall, and of Somerset-Dorset (a joint sheriff-dom), both offered John over 1,000 marks to have sheriffs chosen from their number, who would be resident in their counties.[22] The men of the counties who made such offers could include bishops and barons as well as knights, but knights were at the heart of such groups. Indeed, bishops and barons, thinking they could look after themselves, sometimes refused to be involved.[23] It was knights who led the resistance in Devon when the sheriff seemed to be breaking the county's charter. In December 1214 twelve knights apiece from Cornwall, Devon and Somerset came to the king to negotiate about the concession of further 'liberties'.[24]

The stipulation that the knights in chapters 18 and 48 be locally elected thus responded to local society's desire to control the personnel of the king's government in the shires – 'self-government at the king's command', as the historian A. B. White put it.[25] In chapter 18 it is clear from the context that the county court is to be the body electing the four knights sitting with the judges. (In Latin, the word '*comitatus*' can mean both 'county' and 'county court'.) Chapter 48, where the twelve knights reforming abuses are to be elected by '*probos homines eiusdem comitatus*', is more ambiguous, and the words are usually translated as simply 'upright men of the same county'.[26] However, John's letter of 19 June 1215, setting chapter 48 in motion, shows that the county court was again to be the forum.[27] A newly discovered letter also shows the elections were to take place in each county before four knights appointed by the twenty-five barons of the security clause.[28]

The county courts usually met once a month, but little survives from this period to show exactly how they worked.[29] That, how-ever, knights were central to their procedures, there can be no doubt. It is panels of knights who routinely bear the record of cases in the county court before the king or the judges at Westminster; in 1212 it is knights who are arrested for making false judgements in the Gloucestershire county court; in the Herefordshire court, a year before, a case is postponed because the knights are in disagreement and too few are present; in Suffolk, in 1213, money is to be paid over at the county court 'before the knights'; in Oxfordshire, in

1222, 'nearly all the knights' of the county court 'rise up' in protest against a particular judgement.[30] Just how many knights routinely attended the court we cannot know. There was probably a small-ish core at the forefront of its business, as there was when it came to sitting on grand-assize juries. The Gloucestershire case suggests that it was a clique of knights who were managing the judgements. On the other hand, important business may well have brought in larger numbers. The framers of chapter 48 cannot have known precisely who would constitute the 'upright men' of each county, charged with elections. There cannot have been any doubt, however, that they would be largely synonymous with the county knights.

None of this means that earls and barons lacked influence in the county court. The knights were their tenants, and many were also their stewards. Indeed, those who attended the court are some-times described as 'stewards and knights' or 'knights and stewards'. In a case in the Lincolnshire court, in 1226, knights of the county, rallying in defence of a chapter in Henry III's Magna Carta, threat-ened a steward who had stepped out of line with telling his lord about his behaviour.[31] Barons could also appear in the county court in person. Yet it would be equally wrong to think that the county court was simply dominated by great lords. In 1220 the baron Roger de Montbegon, who was also one of Magna Carta's twenty-five barons, swept furiously out of the Nottinghamshire court when he found the majority opinion against him.[32] The Oxfordshire knights who rose up against a court judgement in 1222 were not acting for a great baron or barons; there were none in the county. Instead, the knights were standing together against the over-mighty sheriff, Falkes de Bréauté, and his agents.[33] Clearly, the balance of power varied between counties, depending on the local political geography. That the twenty-five barons in 1215 ordered the elections to take place before four nominated knights was partly to protect the process from the sheriffs, who presided over the county courts. It also meant that indirectly they hoped to have some influence over the elections themselves. But the twenty-five only went so far. They did *not* say the four knights, as in the grand assize, should actually make the election. That would have been contrary to the terms of the Charter.

FREE MEN AND FREE TENANTS

Magna Carta reached out to a much broader section of society than that composed of earls, barons and knights. John granted the Charter, as we have seen, to 'all the free men of our kingdom'. Indeed, free men were apparently a far more privileged group than earls and barons, having seven chapters in the Charter devoted specifically to their interests, whereas the latter (like knights) only had two.[34] In some cases, it is true, 'free men' meant essentially earls, barons and knights. There can have been few outside that number who held the courts belonging to free men whose jurisdiction was protected in chapter 34. Indeed, a later gloss on the clause described it as dealing with the courts of 'magnates'.[35] On the other hand, free men are sometimes manifestly distinct from the earls and barons, notably in the chapters on amercements (20 and 21) where the two groups are given separate treatment. In other cases, 'free man' would seem, in theory at least, to embrace all sections of society above the unfree peasantry. This was true of chapter 27, which directed that 'if any free man' died intestate, his chattels were to be distributed by his 'closest kin and friends'. It was also true of chapter 30, under which no official was to take the horses and carts of 'any free man', save 'with the consent of the free man himself'; the consent of the free man was an empowering concept. And, of course, under chapter 39 it was 'no free man', not just no earl, baron or knight, who was not to be proceeded against save by the lawful judgement of his peers or by the law of the land.

Free men were a wider group than the free tenants, who in chapter 19 were to stay behind with the knights to hear the assizes. A free tenant by definition held land, a free man might not, for he could be a merchant, a professional soldier or a craftsman. All free tenants were free men, but not all free men were free tenants. Free tenants themselves were divided according to the terms on which they held land, as the Charter made clear in chapter 16. They could owe service for the fee of a knight or 'for another [kind of] free tenement'. Chapter 37 revealed that the latter might include tenements held in fee farm, or in socage, which meant essentially tenements held in return for different kinds of rent.[36]

Free tenants holding land for rent included a very large slice of the peasantry. They also included a far more significant group,

governmentally and politically, one whose importance helps to
explain why the chapters in the Charter on free men and free tenants appeared at all. This is a group hard to define, and very little
studied by historians, but one recognized by contemporaries when
they spoke, as in chapter 19, of free tenants separate from knights
but nonetheless cooperating with them. These free tenants formed
a hinge between the general run of the peasantry free and unfree,
on the one hand, and the knights on the other. They are best seen
in the groups of twelve men called on to staff the juries representing the local government division of the hundred. Such juries were
vital institutions, for they gave evidence about events in the hundred to the king's judges on their visitations to the counties. In
terms of personnel, the juries probably overlapped with the men
who took a leading part in the business of the hundred court,
attended the county court and staffed the numerous common-law
juries. (It was only the juries of the grand assize that were confined
to knights.) When the personnel of these hundred juries can be
studied for later years of the thirteenth century, at the bottom of
the scale they comprise men who in terms of the size of their
landed holdings seem of peasant status. At the top of the scale
there can be some knights. In between these two groups, and
forming the social core of the juries, were men who held between
thirty and a hundred or so acres. Their land might be in a contigu-
ous block or scattered between several holdings. It might be all in
hand, or party held by tenants. In the Hundred Rolls, jurors from
Blackbourn hundred in Suffolk include those with 32, 56, 64, 86,
110, 129, 145, 180 and 320 acres. The average holding was
79 acres.[37] In such groups, some members were rising socially
from the ranks of the peasants, others descending (often as younger
sons with small provision) from the ranks of the knights.[38] In the
early thirteenth century, the number of those on such juries passing for knights would have been larger, given the later decline in
knightly numbers. But many of the jurors, even in the 1200s,
would have been below the knightly level, and have just been
regarded as free tenants. It was through these juries, indeed, that
the jagged and uncertain line between knights and non-knights ran,
as did too the divide between those who could speak both French
and English and those who were only English speakers. The abbot
of Crowland complained, as we have seen, that one of the knights

who swore against him had no French, and that must increasingly have been the situation as one went down the social scale.

The role in local affairs of the kind of 'hinge' men on the juries, above the general run of peasants but beneath the knights, can be sensed in various provisions in the Charter. Thus if a wardship is pillaged, it is to be entrusted to 'two law-worthy and prudent men of that fee' (chapter 4). If common-plea business cannot be finished on the day of the county court, then sufficient free tenants as well as knights are to remain so that judgements can be made (chapter 19). When amercements are imposed on free men, villeins and merchants, their amount is to be determined by 'the oath of upright men of the neighbourhood' (chapter 20); and when the sheriffs or bailiffs make lists of the chattels of deceased tenants-in-chief, they are to do so 'by view of law-worthy men' (chapter 26).

King John himself was very aware of the importance of the kind of men found on the hundred juries, and they were probably the main target of resounding ceremonies in 1209. In great meetings throughout the country, climaxing at one before John himself at Marlborough, mass acts of homage to the king were performed by free men. These men were not swearing loyalty to him in return for land that they held from him, as in a normal act of homage. The great majority, after all, held no land from the crown. But John knew what he was doing, for the one person to whom homage could be done, where land was not involved, was the king. Of course, these men cannot all have knelt down before the king and placed their hands in his. Probably, while taking their oaths, they raised their hands rather like the salutes at some fascist rally. The ceremony symbolized John's protection of the men and their subjection and obedience to him. It was the reciprocity of the bond thus created, absent in a mere oath of fealty, that explained how the ceremony could be regarded as one of homage. John had recognized the military power of this group in his ordinance for the defence of the realm in 1205. It enlisted knights and also 'serjeants' and 'others holding land', 'serjeant' here probably describing free tenants just beneath the rank of knight.[39]

FAMILY, FRIENDSHIP AND
NEIGHBOURHOOD

The vision of England in chapter 14 of the Charter was of a kingdom divided up into, and dominated by, the fees of the earls, greater barons and ecclesiastical tenants-in-chief. These were the men who were personally summoned to the assembly giving the kingdom's common consent to taxation. They can answer for the kingdom, the implication seems to be, because by commanding the loyalty of the tenants in their fees, collectively they answer for everyone in the kingdom. There was some truth in this vision, but not the whole truth. Magna Carta's England is England, but only because other chapters hint at a more nuanced and complex picture from that found in chapter 14. In the first place, there were other ties beyond those in the vertical relationship running down between king, barons and their tenants.

The Charter is very clear about the importance of the family. The chapters protecting widows, wards, children and heirs were very much there at the behest of the family groups to which they belonged. That was made plain in chapter 6, which said that before heirs could be married, their closest kin were to be informed of the proposed union. Chapter 3 of the Articles of the Barons had gone further and demanded that the marriages should take place with the closest kin's 'counsel'.[40] Likewise, under chapter 27 of the Charter, if a free man died intestate, his chattels were to be distributed by his nearest relations and friends. Families could be united in their actions, and the brothers Thomas and Alan Basset, and Peter and Matthew fitzHerbert, stood shoulder to shoulder at the start of the Charter among John's counsellors. They could also be divided, although the divisions were not always what they seemed. It was surely to keep a foot in both camps that William Marshal, earl of Pembroke, remained loyal to King John, being named first among John's lay counsellors in the Charter, while his eldest son was one of the twenty-five barons of the security clause. The twenty-five included two Bigods and two Clares (in both cases father and son), among many other ties of kinship.

The chapter on wills also mentioned 'friends' as well as family.

Ties of friendship could be given visual expression. On his dashing seal, Robert fitzWalter displayed the coat of arms of Saer de Quincy, earl of Winchester, thus proclaiming their military, political and personal alliance. Saer on his seal repaid the compliment. Nor did this just apply to the men, for Saer's wife, Margaret, likewise featured fitzWalter's coat on her seal.[41] Friendships might develop from meetings at court or on campaign. They could also grow from ties of neighbourhood. There was a crucial neighbourhood dimension to the 1215 rebellion in the role played by men from the north, 'the northerners' of Holt's classic book. Particularly in the early stages of the revolt, that was the name often given by contemporary writers to the rebels as a whole. Later, the uprising became much wider, and the twenty-five barons of the security clause were balanced in favour of those from the eastern and home counties. But still eight of its number had large interests in the north.[42] It was doubtless the northerners who secured at Runnymede the inclusion of the ridings of Yorkshire and Lincolnshire among the local government units from which the king was not to take more than the fixed annual payments of their 'ancient' farms.

Working for royal government on local juries and inquiries itself solidified groups of neighbours. The Charter directed, in chapter 20, that amercements were to be assessed 'by the oath of upright men of the neighbourhood'. Groups of kinsmen, friends and neighbours were equally solidified by the pressures of royal government. One way in which that happened is shown in chapter 9 of the Charter. This sought to prevent the sureties of a crown debtor from being distrained to pay his debt, when the debtor could still pay himself. If the sureties were forced to pay, they could have the debtor's lands and rents in compensation. It was routine for King John to demand sureties from a debtor. When he finally turned on the great northern baron William de Mowbray, and demanded that he pay an astronomical debt of 1,740 marks, his sureties included seven great barons, six of them from the north, all of whom had to go surety for specified amounts.[43] As chapter 9 in Magna Carta shows, this system could create tension between the debtor and his sureties, but it might also generate a community of interest and incipient action. Four of Mowbray's pledges and the son of another appear with him among the twenty-five barons of Magna Carta's security clause.

SOCIAL CHANGE

Ties of family, friendship and neighbourhood existed alongside ties of tenure and could indeed support them. But the tenurial hierarchy itself was far less clear-cut than the simple division into earls, barons, knights and free tenants might seem to imply, as indeed the Charter again hinted. At the very top, there was uncertainty about the position of earl, for John and his predecessors were very far from admitting that the honour was always hereditary. Indeed, even in Magna Carta the earl was to owe relief for the 'barony of an earl', so not actually for an earldom at all. As we will see, this may well have been a contentious issue at Runnymede itself.[44]

There was also ambivalence over the position of baron. Chapter 2 of the Charter, in fixing the relief of tenants-in-chief, made a division between barons succeeding to baronies and knights succeeding to knights' fees. There was nothing novel in that. The distinction is found in both the *Dialogus de Scaccario* and in a list of the tenants-in-chief in Shropshire made by its sheriff in 1212.[45] Yet John could also describe someone who only held one knight's fee as his 'baron', which suggests that the term could still be used for any tenant-in-chief of the crown.[46] It was equally employed by great lords to describe their own knightly tenants. 'I now wish to consult my barons,' said William Marshal.[47]

Even if one did try to draw a line between tenants-in-chief holding baronies and tenants-in-chief holding knights' fees, how logical in terms of wealth would it always be? That some barons might be men of no very great importance is clear from chapter 14 of the Charter, in which only greater barons were to receive personal summonses to its national assembly.[48] There was equally a problem the other way round, created by the wealth and importance of those who held only one or two fees from the crown and so could scarcely qualify as barons at all, let alone greater barons. A case in point is William of Huntingfield. He was one of the twenty-five 'barons' of Magna Carta's security clause, yet he only held one fee (at Mendham in Suffolk near Huntingfield) from the crown. Much of his wealth came from other properties, including seven fees held from the honour of Eye.[49] Men such as Huntingfield were rising in society from knightly backgrounds, often through royal service, and augmenting their inheritances through purchases, and gifts from great lords and from the king. Alan Basset, one of the coun-sellors John named in the prologue to Magna Carta, was a self-made man, a younger son, who put together an estate of baronial propor-tions, including the manors of High Wycombe and Woking, which he received from the king.[50] Thomas Basset, Alan's elder brother (although both were younger sons), illustrates another point, namely how quickly families could rise and fall. By the time of his death in 1220, he too had built up a great estate, including, as a gift from King John, the manor of Headington outside Oxford, but leaving no son, the estate was split between his three daughters. Thomas's branch of the Bassets had come and gone in a gener-ation. It would have been a moot point whether Huntingfield and the Bassets were entitled to the personal summonses to the national assembly envisaged in Magna Carta's chapter 14.[51] The same would have been true in the case of Simon of Kyme. He was a leading figure in Lincolnshire from the 1190s. He had his own following, including the Lincolnshire knight Peter of Beckering, yet of his thirty or so fees, only two were held in chief.[52] At least Huntingfield, Kyme and the Bassets did hold in chief, and would have been summoned under the terms of chapter 14. Yet there were many of equivalent or near equivalent status who would have been ignored altogether since they held nothing from the king.[53]

In this fluid situation, the Charter attempted a piece of social cementing. Chapter 2 fixed for the first time the size of a baronial and knightly relief. For the first time, therefore, it became necessary to decide who held by barony and who held by knight's fee, for the two groups were to owe reliefs of different sizes. From one point of view, those who fell on the baronial side lost out, for they had to pay a larger relief. But the gain was that they would now be part of a group very clearly separated, in terms of status, from those below them. They were to form a new elite, as David Crouch puts it, the 'king's barons, the nobles closest to the crown'.[54] The Char-ter also confirmed and improved the privileges that went with baronial status. Chapter 21 of the Charter thus laid down that earls and barons were to be amerced by their peers, which meant their social equals. This separated earls and barons from everyone else, free men, merchants, villeins and clerks, who were to be amerced by men of the neighbourhood. This privilege in the Char-ter built on existing practice, for prior to 1215, if an earl or a baron was convicted of an offence before the king's judges in the localities, the amercement was assessed not before the judges but at Westminster by the exchequer.[55] The aim of the Charter, therefore, was to prevent this happening and ensure that earls and barons were amerced by themselves, in the process making them all the more of an exclusive group.[56]

Another privilege affirmed by the Charter was that relating to national assemblies. Under chapter 14, as we have seen, it was only earls and greater barons who were to receive personal summonses to the councils empowered to give the kingdom's consent to taxation. The other tenants-in-chief were to be summoned generally, through the sheriffs. Here then the great men of the realm were not even content with a division between the baronage and the rest. They set the bar for personal summonses higher, so that only greater barons would get them. Those who were not tenants-in-chief, of course, would not be summoned at all. Probably chapter 14 reflected what had long been existing practice. It responded to the idea that the duty to give counsel was an obligation involved in tenure, and thus especially something which fell on the king's own tenants.[57] Yet, given the changing nature of society, might not the Charter have included 'magnates' within the assembly, thus ensuring the presence of great men who were not tenants-in-chief? The answer was a resounding no! Instead, the Charter pulled up the drawbridge and sought to wall in the status quo. By enshrining the existing system, its aim was to ensure that national assemblies remained exclusive and exclusionary bodies.

In this area, however, Magna Carta was becoming out of date at the very time that it was promulgated. There were simply too many men around who were not technically barons, but whose wealth and status justified a personal summons. While, in the course of the thirteenth century, it was indeed a personal summons to parliament that created a parliamentary peerage, it was not a peerage defined by those who held baronies. It was defined by those whose wealth and status seemed to necessitate a summons.[58] The problem with chapter 14's vision of the realm was revealed near the end of the Charter, in the very provision where it seemed again to be recognized. Under chapter 60, all the liberties that John had conceded to be held in the kingdom:

as much as it pertains to us towards our men [*nostros*], all the men [*omnes*] of our kingdom . . . are to observe, as much as it pertains to them, to their men [*suos*].

As is usual in translations of the Charter, I have inserted here 'men' after 'our', 'all' and 'their', since this is how the chapter was certainly understood. The king's men were his tenants-in-chief and pre-eminently his earls and barons. At first sight, then, we have here the traditional 'feudal' hierarchy, with the king making concessions to his tenants-in-chief, which they then pass down to their own men. But this is not what the chapter says. Instead of John stating that 'our men [*nostros*]' are to observe the concessions in the Charter, he says that 'all the men [*omnes*]' of the kingdom are to do so. The tenurial hierarchy has, therefore, been invaded by a body completely un-tenurial in its structure. When Henry III referred to this chapter in 1234, he said it was his archbishops, bishops, earls, barons and 'other magnates' who were to obey the Charter.[59] The king thus recognized that there were 'magnates' quite on a par with his comital and baronial tenants-in-chief. No such recognition was made when it came to deciding who should be summoned to the national assembly in 1215. In that sense Magna Carta was a deeply conservative document.

THREATS TO THE BARONIAL FEES

Earls and barons faced another problem, namely that of maintaining authority within the landed estates which made up their 'fees' or 'honours'. Here we should think of the fees not as a neat set of 'feudal pyramids', but as a range of hills such as that around Wastwater in Cumberland, all of different shapes and sizes, with one merging into another, and with rocks and boulders frequently slipping off the sides into gullies and the lake. The vastly different size of baronies is revealed in the returns to the inquiry of 1166, where some owed the service of sixty or more knights, and some fewer than ten.[60] The fees of barons, moreover, did not exist in some steady state, for they were liable to come into the king's hands either through forfeiture or through failure of heirs. That had happened to the honours of Wallingford, Nottingham, Boulogne and

Lancaster, as chapter 43 of the Charter shows. Fees were also liable to division. The statement in chapter 2 about relief being due for a 'whole barony' reflected the fact that baronies were sometimes no longer 'whole'. Division could especially come about through the marriage of heiresses, which the Charter sought to regulate in chapter 6. If there was a single female heir, the honour remained whole. Both William Marshal and William Longespee had been set up by marriages to such coveted women. But if there was more than one female heir, then the barony would be split between them, as happened to the honour of Leicester in John's reign. This was why chapter 2 of the Charter spoke of the heir 'or heirs' of baronies, the latter being heiresses or the descendants of heiresses. As chapter 6 also indicated, another dynamic was the king marrying an heiress to someone of lower social status, the 'disparagement' that the chapter tried to prevent.[61]

In maintaining the loyalty or at least the obedience of their knightly tenants, a great deal then depended on the history of the fee and whether it had remained whole or been split apart. Much depended too on its geographical contours. Manifestly, a lord would have more control over his tenants if they lived close to one of his main residences. The success of the Ferrers earls of Derby in retaining the service and loyalty of their tenants owed a great deal to the compactness of their honour and the proximity of the fee to its centre at Tutbury in Staffordshire.[62] The loyalty between lord and tenant could be very real, as is clear from chapter 4 of the Charter. There a wardship, pillaged by the agents of the king, was to be handed over to 'two law-worthy and prudent men of that fee'. The 'men of the fee' had their own interest in preventing the wardship being exploited, but the implication was also that they could be trusted to look after the interests of their future lord. The mutual bond established by homage and tenure set standards of conduct. The knight Richard de Vernon justified his rebellion in the 1260s by saying that 'in the whole time of the war he followed his lord, Robert de Ferrers, earl of Derby, from whom he held his land and to whom he had done homage'. Many knights in the 1215–17 civil war would have justified their conduct in similar terms.[63] It was likewise how the Marshal expected his tenants in Ireland to behave, when he called upon them to show loyalty in return for the fees that they had been given.[64]

There were, however, forces working to unravel the tenurial

bond. One, of course, was that knights played a major role in the running of local government for the king. A lord might welcome it when one of his knights was thus employed, but he had also to reckon with the independence they obtained. The development of the common law also meant that under-tenants could easily litigate in the courts of the king, rather than in those of their lords, a threat that chapter 34 of the Charter tried to do something about.[65] Another destabilizing factor was the way knights might hold from more than one lord. That was less true of the middle-ranking knights who held only one manor, but it was increasingly common further up the knightly scale. The Charter itself bears witness to the tensions produced when this other lord was the king. Thus chapter 37 shows that the king was usurping wardships which belonged to 'the fee of another' by knight service, on the grounds that the tenants also held from him by rent or some other form of service. The equivalent chapter in the Articles of the Barons (27) made it even clearer that this was a case of usurping the wardships of knightly tenants, for it spoke of John taking 'the custody of the knights of the fee of another'. Chapter 53 in the Charter also put on the agenda the whole question of how the king took the ward-ship of lands 'which are of the fee of another', when the tenants also held from him by knight service. In the king's view this was a prerogative right, but that it was raised in the Charter, if only as a matter to be dealt with at the end of John's prospective crusade, shows how irritating it was thought to be.[66] At Runnymede itself two of the great baronial leaders, Eustace de Vescy and Gilbert de Gant, complained about John usurping wardships that, they claimed, belonged to their fees.[67] Equally damaging were the con-flicts when service and wardships were claimed by rival lords. In 1211 Vescy himself was involved in one such case, and it was the subject of much later litigation.[68]

In these difficult circumstances, the attitude of great lords was itself ambivalent. On the one hand, they wanted to employ whom-ever they liked in their service. The king had the right to do that, as the *Dialogus de Scaccario* affirmed.[69] It was vital for lords to do the same. If they became stuck in some honorial straitjacket, they might end up with a very inferior entourage. Thus William Marshal's fol-lowing contained very few tenants, and was rarely rewarded with grants of land.[70] The search for good service was a dynamic and disruptive force in society. Great lords were also far from dependent on tenants and honorial courts for their local power. As we will see in the next chapter, many had control of the local government division of the hundred and claimed the right to hang thieves on their own gallows. Yet, for all this, lords remained very much in the business of preserving the integrity of their fees, and the service of their tenants. Quite apart from the military service they could expect, their rights when it came to aids, scutages, reliefs, wardships, and the marriages of heirs and widows were valuable as sources of both money and patronage. When it came to controlling the fee, however, lords faced problems from the tenants themselves. No ambitious knight wished to be stuck with a lord who could do him no good, whatever the bond of homage. Knights in Oxfordshire therefore deserted their ineffectual baronial lord, Henry d'Oilly, and entered the service of the coming man, Thomas Basset of Headington, sheriff of the county from 1202 to 1214. They also entered the service of the king and litigated in his courts, despite d'Oilly's attempts to preserve the jurisdiction of his own.[71] The competition for good lordship was just as disruptive a force as the competition for good service.

There were also tensions within the fees arising from the demands that lords made of their tenants. Barons and knights had much in common. They could all agree about keeping the unfree peasantry in its place. They could all agree about the chapters in the Charter limiting the king's financial exactions and insisting that he acted justly. When, in 1219, the great baron Gilbert de Gant argued, in the Lincolnshire county court, that he had suffered unlawful disseisin, the whole court rallied behind him and Magna Carta. They 'cried out with him and for him, and for themselves and for the common liberty of all the kingdom conceded and sworn'.[72] There remained, however, a clear difference of interest between the great majority of knights, holding up to one or two manors, and with few or any tenants holding by knight service, and the greater barons who had many manors and many knightly tenants. The Charter shows how ruthlessly the king exploited his tenurial rights, and there were surely 'bad lords' who did the same. That such men disparaged heirs in marriage and laid waste to wardships is clear from later legislation.[73] Evidence for the lord–tenant relationship in John's reign is limited, but there are two remarkable documents that shed light on the matter. One is a charter, issued sometime between 1207 and 1209, by the great northern baron Peter de Brus, making a series of concessions to the knights and free tenants of his wapentake of Langbargh in the north Yorkshire moors. Knights and free tenants are, of course, precisely the group we find in chapter 19 of the Charter, staying behind to attend judgements in the county court. Under the Brus charter, no one was to be put on trial at the wapentake court save in 'reasonable' fashion and 'by consideration of the wapentake', which anticipated chapter 38 of the Charter. Brus also conceded that any penalties were to be assessed according to the means of those convicted and the nature of the offence; so chapter 20 of Magna Carta. Indeed, both charters used the same word for the offence: 'delictum'. And finally, Brus put his concessions into a charter, and described them as 'liberties', which were to be held 'in perpetuity', all like Magna Carta. Brus had just bought the wapentake of Langbargh from King John for 400 marks. He still owed 1,300 marks of his fine made in 1200 to acquire the nearby lordship of Danby. The knights and free tenants had every reason to expect, and probably were already experiencing, his oppressive rule.[74] The Brus charter does not stand alone as testimony to tensions between lords and men. After Magna Carta, Ranulf, earl of Chester, was faced perhaps by a revolt, certainly by a series of demands from his 'barons of Cheshire', baron here meaning his major tenants in the county. Ranulf refused some of what was asked, but conceded much in what became known as the Cheshire Magna Carta. The issues between Ranulf and his barons replicated in part those between the barons of England and the king. So the eighteen chapters of the Cheshire Charter included provisions about amercements, widows, marriages (to be without disparagement), military service and the inheritance tax called 'relief'.[75]

SOCIAL DIVISION IN THE CHARTER

Did any of these tensions between lords and tenants surface in Magna Carta? They were certainly not the Charter's major theme. It is usually viewed, pretty well exclusively, as a document aimed at the king. Indeed, when it came to the treatment of tenants, the baron seemed to set the standard for the king to follow. Thus chapter 43 of the Charter directed that if an honour came into the king's hands, the king should hold it as the baron had held it. He should demand no other services from the tenants than those given to the baron if the barony 'was in the hand of a baron'. Good baron, bad king.

This is not, however, the whole story. In other parts of the Charter, both in what is put in and in what is left out, there are clear signs of conflict. Earls and barons were taking shots at knights and under-tenants, knights and under-tenants were shooting back at earls and barons. Earls and barons, therefore, made quite sure that chapters 2–5 on relief and wardship were exclusively for themselves and other tenants-in-chief. While chapter 8, forbidding the enforced remarriage of widows, did apply to under-tenants, here lords inserted a safeguard, on the same lines as the safeguard inserted by the king: widows needed the consent of their lord if they wanted to remarry, just as widows of tenants-in-chief needed the consent of the king.

The tensions thus suggested reached a head in chapter 15. There the king promised that he would not grant 'anyone' permission to levy an aid from his free men save for the ransom of his body, the knighting of his eldest son and the marrying on one occasion of his eldest daughter. The aid was also to be 'reasonable'. The chapter referred to 'anyone' probably out of recognition that some major knights might seek aids from their tenants, but the main target was undoubtedly the baron. Indeed, in the Articles of the Barons, the equivalent chapter (6) simply stated that 'the king will not allow any baron to take an aid from his free men' save on the three specified occasions. The chapter in Magna Carta promised major gains for under-tenants.[76] John had frequently ordered them to give aids to their lords on other than the Charter's specified occasions, notably to help pay their lord's debts to the crown.[77] There is some evidence of the ill feeling thus created. When William de Mowbray sought to levy an aid to pay his debts, the religious houses holding from him protested.[78] In 1206 or 1207 the tenants of Robert de Mortimer refused to pay an aid to sustain him 'in the king's service in Poitou'. Aids, they said, had only been customary for themselves and their ancestors on three occasions.[79] Since these were the very occasions later permitted in the Charter, under-tenants were evidently well aware of their rights.

Chapter 15 in the Charter did not merely restrict the instances on which aids could be levied. It also implied that, without permission from the king, lords could not impose aids even on the three customary occasions. This was very different from the situation in *Glanvill*, where lords were allowed to levy aids without royal sanction, even for making war, provided they had the consent of their courts. Lords, under John, often secured writs from the king in order to facilitate the levying of an aid. Now, without such writs, they were not to levy aids at all.[80] At the behest of under-tenants, the Charter seemed to be weakening the lord's authority over his fee.

Chapter 16 was also designed to benefit under-tenants. It laid down that 'no one' was to be distrained to do more than the service due either 'for the fee of a knight, or for another free tenement'. The position of this chapter, right after chapter 15, and its phraseology – 'fee of a knight', 'free tenement' – suggest that its main beneficiaries were intended to be knights and free tenants who were being forced to perform other than customary services by their lords or the king.[81] The scope of the chapter, moreover, was widened during the negotiations at Runnymede, since 'another free tenement' does not appear in the Articles of the Barons. Its inclusion meant that the large numbers of free tenants who held by rent rather than by knight service were now included among the beneficiaries. The Charter does not specify the kinds of extra services that lords might demand, but they probably included military service and scutage, about which there is considerable evidence of dispute over what was due.[82] An issue that became important in the reign of Henry III was that of attendance at private courts. It was the subject of major legislation in 1259 and may already have been a grievance in 1215.[83] That chapter 38 of Magna Carta prevented bailiffs in general (they were nor specified as those of the king) from putting people on trial on their own unsupported allegations suggests tensions over the running of private courts. A related grievance was that of the amercements levied in private courts, often for non-attendance. Here chapter 20 of the Charter was relevant, for it dealt with amercements in general and thus protected free men (although not villeins) from unjust amercements levied in the courts of lords as well as those of the king. When a writ was introduced in the 1260s enabling legal actions to be brought under the terms of the chapter, private courts were the target.[84]

Between chapter 16 on the service due from fees and other free tenements, and chapter 20 on amercements, came chapters 17 to 19 on the common pleas. More than any other chapters of the Charter, they reveal a society far from dominated by great lords. Were modern historians to have a go at drafting the Charter without knowledge of its contents, they might well conceive a clause preventing the common-law actions encroaching on the courts of lords. The chapter would thus have paralleled chapter 34, which restricted the issue of the writ 'precipe' if it had that effect. That barons would have liked such a chapter is suggested by a striking passage in the Anonymous of Béthune. This has John agreeing in 1215 that the barons could have 'all high jurisdiction [*hautes justices*] in their lands'. The king, in fact, had agreed no such thing. The point is that the Anonymous, so close to baronial feeling, thought that he had or should. It is unlikely that the barons in 1215 were hoping for 'high jurisdiction' in the sense of establishing control over all criminal justice. That was never on the agenda. What they hoped to do was to protect their courts and jurisdictions from the challenges of the common law.[85]

The detail of the common-law procedures which generated this ambition will be explained in the next chapter. Here it is enough to say that they were hugely popular with knights and free tenants, who were their chief users and beneficiaries, and who, sitting on the juries, actually decided the cases. Much of the litigation was between social equals, often over small properties, but the procedures had the potential to take cases from the court of the lord into the court of the king, as well as weakening the lord's power over his tenants more generally. Yet the Charter, instead of trying to restrict their use, made the procedures more available. Chapter 17 thus did not allow such pleas to 'follow' the king's court, and insisted they be heard in a fixed place. Chapter 18 laid down that the king's judges were to come to each county four times a year to hear the most popular of the assizes. The procedures were also, as we have seen, made subject to local control, by stipulating that the judges were to sit with four knights elected in the county court.

At the end of the Charter, its benefits seemed finally spread over all society. Chapter 60, as we have seen, stated that all men were to pass down to their own men the concessions which they had received from the king. The 'all men', of course, as the king made clear in 1234, were essentially the lay and ecclesiastical magnates of the kingdom. Under the terms of the Charter, they had thus to obey, within their fees, the chapters on relief, wardships, the marriages of heirs and the rights of widows. It was with a sure political eye that the government of Henry III constantly reminded his magnates of this chapter. It was the one that gave the Charter value to under-tenants.[86]

Knights and under-tenants, therefore, were able to make gains from the Charter, sometimes to the disadvantage of their lords. Yet the Charter was also very much shaped by lords, anxious to affirm their authority over their tenants. Chapter 60 itself implied that under-tenants were less subject to royal authority than the men of the king, and were dependent on their lords for the full enjoyment of the Charter. Chapter 26 also testified to the control that lords expected to have over their fees. Here, if a tenant-in-chief died, leaving a widow and children, the sheriff was prevented from seizing his chattels on the pretext of debts owed the crown. No similar protection was offered on the death of an under-tenant. This was because, when an under-tenant died, it was the lord, not the sheriff, who had entry into the estate. Chapter after chapter in the Charter was designed to protect the interest of what it called 'the lord of the fee'. Thus chapter 8 stipulated that a widow could not marry without 'the assent of her lord from whom she holds', if she held from other than the king. Chapter 11 laid down that during minorities, debts were to be paid to Jews 'saving the service of the lords'. Chapter 32 ensured the 'lords of the fees' should recover the lands of their tenants convicted of felony after the king had held them 'for one year and one day'. Chapter 34 prevented the king, at the request of litigants, from removing cases from the courts of 'magnates' (as a later description of the clause put it) through the issue of the writ of 'precipe'. In chapter 53 John also promised to give justice, when he returned from or abandoned his prospective crusade, where 'the lord of the fee' was claiming rights over an abbey founded on his fee. This was linked to chapter 46, which ensured that all barons should have custody of the abbeys of their foundation when they were vacant.[87] Chapters 37 and 53 tried to deal with the issue of encroachments by the king on the rights of wardship, while chapter 10 helped lords exploit more freely estates so held. Under this chapter, debts owed the Jews were no longer to gather interest during minorities, whether the heir held from the king or anyone else. Lords wanted the provision because, if they had an heir in wardship, they were bound pay his debts. Thus, in 1213, Roger Bigod, earl of Norfolk, one of the twenty-five barons, had to pay £20 towards the Jewish debts of the heirs of William de Pirnhow.[88] The chapter only benefited the heir himself if the lord did fail to pay. Then, under its terms, the heir would no longer be hit, on coming of age, by all the interest. The chapter thus again suggests tension between lord and tenant. Just as the Charter was an instrument of lordship to discipline the unfree peasantry, so equally it was an instrument of lordship to control the fee. That continued to be the case in later versions of the Charter, as we will see.[89]

Lords thus protected themselves and their fees by what they put into the Charter. They also did so by what they left out. It is often said, and rightly, that Magna Carta owed a great deal to the 1100 Coronation Charter of Henry I. Yet the contrast between the way the two charters deal with the interests of under-tenants is striking. In his regulations on relief, wardships and the marriage of heirs and widows, Henry I insisted twice over that his barons should make equivalent concessions to their men.[90] There was nothing of that kind in Magna Carta, the tenants of barons having to rely on the blanket provision on passing down the concessions in chapter 60. The £5 relief for a knight's fee in chapter 2 was simply for tenants-in-chief. Although there is some indication that a £5 relief for a knight's fee was the accepted figure for under-tenants before 1215, enshrining it in Magna Carta would have made the custom all the stronger. The fact that the £5 relief appears in the Cheshire Magna Carta shows that under-tenants felt the need for such protection.[91] They would also have valued the Charter making clear that its provisions on wardships applied to lords as well as the king. It was left to the 1275 Statute of Westminster to do that.[92]

There is an equally extraordinary contrast between Magna Carta and Henry II's 1176 Assize of Northampton. This gave protection to the free tenant by laying down that on his death, his heirs should remain in possession of his fee, and have his chattels to carry out his will. If the heir was underage, he was to do homage to the lord, thus safeguarding his eventual entry into the inheritance.[93] None of these provisions surfaced in Magna Carta. Indeed, chapter 26, which did something to preserve the chattels of a deceased lord for the execution of his will, was quite specifically limited to tenants-in-chief. We can be pretty sure that there were demands for the Charter to give more to under-tenants in these areas, for the version of 1216 did just that.[94] There were other omissions in Magna Carta. In chapter 29, knights were only protected when the king, not when their lords, sought to impose a double dose of castle guard and army service. In chapter 31, it was only the king who was prevented from seizing wood for a castle or for other business. Likewise, in chapter 37 it was only those who held by socage and other rents from the king who were protected from claims to wardship, not those who held in the same way from tenants-in-chief. In 1221 Henry, earl of Warwick, found himself sued for trying to assert rights of wardship over an heir who held from him in socage. He lost the case, but no thanks to Magna Carta.[95] There was also a telling change made to the end of chapter 37 as between the Articles of the Barons and Magna Carta. In the former the equivalent chapter (27) had protected free men from losing the privileges of knighthood because they held any land from the crown by non-knightly service. In Magna Carta this clause was scrapped in favour of protecting not the tenants but the lords. They were not to lose their rights of wardship over such men.

The omissions are equally striking when it comes to the inquiry into local government by the twelve knights in each county, commissioned in chapter 48. There were precedents for such inquiries. In 1170 Henry II had mounted one, called by historians the 'Inquest of Sheriffs'. Despite its name, it inquired not merely into illicit exactions of the sheriffs but also into those of the earls, barons and knights. Did Magna Carta follow this precedent? No, it did not. Its inquiry in chapter 48 was simply into the 'evil customs' of the ministers of the king. The security clause was similarly limited. It dealt with breaches of the Charter by the king. No procedure was laid down for dealing with breaches by the barons themselves, although they too, of course, under chapter 60, were supposed to obey the Charter. In much the same way, when we get to the Charter of 1217, chapter 42 sought to prevent shrieval extortion at the hundred court. Nothing was said about the extortions of the bailiffs when such courts were controlled by lords, as was often the case.[96]

Again this background, it hardly comes as a surprise that, under chapters 12 and 14 of the Charter, the assembly called on to give the kingdom's consent to taxation, in the form of scutages and aids, was one composed entirely of tenants-in-chief. The earls, greater barons, bishops and abbots, as we have seen, were to receive individual summonses. The rest of the tenants-in-chief were to be summoned generally through the sheriffs. It is true that the control over scutage met a particular grievance of under-tenants, since it was from them that great lords recouped, or tried to recoup, what they owed the king. Knights also had a potential voice in the tax granting assemblies themselves since they would have featured among the few hundred lesser tenants-in-chief summoned through the sheriffs. Although there was a long precedent for the summoning of such tenants, the confirmation of their presence in the Charter constituted a knightly victory.[97] It was a precursor to the formal summons to parliament of knights representing the counties. Yet precursor was all it was. Those summoned under Magna Carta *were* solely the lesser tenants-in-chief of the crown. They came for themselves. They had no representative function. The thousands of other knights and free tenants in the counties, just like the burgesses in the towns and the magnates who did not hold from the crown, were completely unrepresented in the assembly envisaged in 1215. It could have been different. Indeed, knights may well have demanded that it should be different. After all, an early thirteenth-century account of King Arthur, written by the poet Lawman in English for a knightly audience, has him summoning to his assembly at Caerleon in south Wales 'the knights and all the free men who were in the land at all' as well, of course, as the bishops, earls and barons.[98] In 1213 John himself summoned four knights from every county to come before him at Oxford 'to discuss with us the affairs of our kingdom'.[99] He had already summoned to the Oxford council both his barons and groups of knights from each county. Almost certainly the latter were his knightly tenants-in-chief. He was now reaching out to a wider constituency and creating a more representative assembly. It was an example the barons in 1215 conspicuously failed to follow. In the Charter itself, the counties were to elect knights to sit with the king's judges and hold the inquiry into local government. Why not also have the counties elect knights as representatives at national assemblies? But if these were blocks from which knightly attendance at such meetings might have been constructed, they were left in the builder's yard. It was to be different in the next great crisis that shook England. In 1258 the knights inquired into the malpractices of both king and lords. In 1259 the legislation dealt first of all with the way lords had forced men to attend their courts. In 1265 Simon de Montfort summoned both knights from the counties and burgesses from the towns to his parliament.

6
Magna Carta and the Structure of Royal Government

On his accession in 1199, John declared that he had come to 'the rule of the kingdom of England' 'by hereditary right, divine mercy, and the unanimous consent and favour of the clergy and people'.[1] All three sources of authority were reflected in the Charter. Chapters 52, 53 and 57 mentioned both of John's immediate predecessors, his father, King Henry II, and his brother King Richard, from whom he had inherited the throne. The Charter also looked to the future, for it was granted by John for himself and his heirs in perpetuity. Heirs, moreover, direct heirs, John had – hence the way the security clause exempted his queen and children from any kind of personal attack. John had named his sons Henry and Richard, thus linking together the dynastic past with its hoped-for future. In his last illness, in 1216, John begged the pope's help in securing what he called 'the perpetual hereditary succession' of his dynasty.[2]

John was not fantasizing when he claimed 'the unanimous consent and favour of the clergy and people' at his accession. He was referring to the moment in the coronation ceremony when, asked whether they wanted him to rule, the assembled throng had shouted their assent. It was these acclamations at William the Conqueror's coronation in 1066 that had led his Norman soldiers, outside Westminster abbey, to think a coup was taking place.[3] John was happy to proclaim this popular assent in 1199. In Magna Carta it was turned against him, not on the issue of succession to the throne, although that was to come, but over taxation that was only to be levied by 'the common counsel of the kingdom'.

The 'divine mercy' that made John king was proclaimed in the Charter, both in his titles at the start and on his seal: he was king 'by the grace of God'. It was that status which had at least something to do with the immunity from personal attack allowed him in the security clause. John had become king by God's grace at the coronation when, shorn of his royal robes and dressed only in a silk tunic and open shirt, he was consecrated with holy oil by the archbishop of Canterbury, Hubert Walter.[4] This, more than the actual crowning, was the spiritual climax of the ceremony, hence the service was called the king's consecration as much as his coronation. The anointing was biblical in origin, as the service showed in its references to Samuel's anointing of King David. It did not give the king any priestly qualities. That was made very clear in a long discussion on the subject written later in the century by Robert Grosseteste, a contemporary of John, and the greatest scholar of his age. But what the anointing did do, as Grosseteste went on to say, was to pour into the king all the blessings of the Holy Spirit.[5] Truly, the anointing made John king by the grace of God.

The traditional coronation oath indicated what was expected of the king. Before the anointing and crowning, in what was very much a pact with his people, John had sworn 'that all the days of his life he would give peace and honour and reverence to God and holy church and its ordinances; that he would exercise right, justice and equity to the people committed to him; and that he would abolish evil laws and perverse customs; and he would make good laws and keep them without fraud and evil intent'.[6] John would not have quibbled with this view of his task, although he might have questioned what were good and bad laws and customs. The 'exaltation of holy church' (as the Charter put it), the maintenance of peace, the dispensation of justice, the protection of everyone's rights – these had always been integral to kingship. John would also have added another central thrust to his duties, indeed he may have taken an oath to that effect at his coronation. This was to preserve and recover the rights of the crown.[7] That imperative, given that he would lose so much of his right with the fall of Normandy and Anjou, overshadowed the reign.

John, then, was king 'by the grace of God'. In general terms, his duties were clear. Yet there was no way he could carry them out without an effective administrative structure. Such a structure he certainly possessed. Indeed, it was arguably the most impressive at that time in Europe.

THE COURT

At the heart of government was the king himself and his surrounding court. When John, in chapter 17 of the Charter, conceded that 'common pleas' were not to 'follow' his 'court' but were to be heard in a fixed place, he meant 'court' as formed by the whole body of counsellors, ministers, knights, clerks and domestic servants who were with him. The court was, as the chapter implied, itinerant. Indeed, John's breakneck itinerary (examined in the next chapter) was a vital feature of his rule. The court was also large, probably never less than several hundred strong. Walter Map, one of Henry II's clerks, spoke indeed of many thousands being there. Map noted that the personnel of the court was constantly changing, so that if he returned after a period of absence he could feel a stranger. Yet in structure it remained the same. 'It is a hundred-handed giant, who if he be all maimed, is yet all the same, and still hundred-handed; a hydra of many heads.'[8] The court embraced another body, known as the king's 'household' (in Latin 'domus' or 'familia'), to which knights, clerks and domestic servants belonged. It also had within it a series of defined offices, each integral to John's rule. These were the chancery, the chamber with the wardrobe, and the departments that supplied the household's food and drink.[9]

THE CHANCERY

English royal government was driven by documents. It was through them that John conferred patronage, made proclamations, spent money, dispensed justice, and generally issued the orders on which his rule depended. From the court, there were always messengers setting out for near and far, with documents of different types and purposes directed to bishops, abbots, earls, barons, knights, sheriffs, justices, exchequer officials and so on. The court was like a beacon shooting out its rays in all directions, sparking the targets into life. The men at court who wrote the king's documents were clerks. Their head was the chancellor, a position that dated back to before the Norman Conquest. The great seal, authenticating the documents the chancery issued, and worked by its own keeper, was likewise under the chancellor's authority. Not all chancellors performed their duties in person. In 1215, however, the chancellor, Richard Marsh, was very much hands on. He was soon to combine the post (a usual career move) with a bishopric, in his case Durham. Most of the charters during his period of office ended with the statement that they had been 'given by the hand of Richard Marsh our chancellor'. Magna Carta, however, was given instead by the hand of King John, testimony to its importance and the barons' desire to pin him to it.[10]

The body to which the writing clerks belonged was called 'the chancery', although the term only came into use gradually in the twelfth century.[11] How many clerks there were both over the reign as a whole and at any one time is impossible to say. The Magna Carta Project, in bringing together and distinguishing the hands of the original charters and letters of King John, will establish some minimum figures, but only minimums, for very few of the numerous less formal letters have survived. Three different hands, typical of the chancery, were responsible for three of the four originals of the Charter, and there seem at least another four hands at work in 1215, so that provides a minimum establishment of around half a dozen. But almost certainly the number of clerks was much larger than that.[12] There were occasions when John's speed of movement meant he was separated from the chancery staff, or at least from the staff with the seal, and used his 'small seal' or 'privy seal' – 'parvum sigillum', 'privatum sigillum' – to authenticate documents instead. This was the case during his dramatic dash to Bury St Edmunds in 1214, and in the days before his arrival at Runnymede in the following year.[13] The chancery, however, seems in general to have followed the king's itinerary. It had not gone out of court and become established at Westminster, as was to happen in the following century.

By John's reign the types of documents issued by the chancery had achieved a set form. All had one cardinal feature in common, namely a final clause that indicated when and where the king or a minister had authorized their issue. In terms of hierarchy, at the top of the scale were the charters in which John made solemn and significant grants of land or rights, usually in perpetuity. Magna Carta is the grandest of these, although it differs from most charters both in being given by the hand of the king rather than the chancellor or a chancery official, and by listing the men on whose counsel the king had acted at the start, rather than having them as witnesses at the end.

Next down in importance were letters patent. These, like charters, had the seal hanging down from the bottom of the document, attached by a tag or (more rarely than in charters) a silken thread, and were thus open or 'patent' rather than being closed up by the sealing. They might be addressed, like charters, to everyone in the realm, although as befitted a less solemn document, the litany of archbishops, bishops, earls and barons might be omitted. They could also be addressed to individuals, or to groups such as the men of a county. Letters patent differed from charters in other ways. They lacked both the 'given by the hand' clause and a list of witnesses, being normally witnessed simply by the king or an individual minister. Letters patent were used to issue proclamations, make appointments, and also give important orders of a public nature. It may have been by letters patent that the greater barons were to be summoned to the assembly mentioned in chapter 14 of the Charter, although it could equally have been by letters close.

Letters close were the final type of document issued by the chancery. Like letters patent they ended by simply being witnessed by the king or a minister, but they differed in being 'closed'. This meant that they were folded and tied up with a strip of parchment cut from the bottom, and the seal, or what was usually just a dab from it, was placed across the tie. These letters were the administrative maids of all work and were addressed in great numbers to the king's agents, telling them to do this and that. Also in the form of letters close were the 'writs' (in Latin 'breves'), which initiated legal actions. These had to be obtained by litigants from the chancery. Two of them featured in the Charter, the writ of 'precipe' in chapter 34, and the writ for an inquiry into matters 'concerning life or limbs' in chapter 36. It was likewise writs in the same form, issued in great numbers, that initiated the common-law assizes mentioned in chapter 18 of the Charter.

The production of these documents did not end the labours of the chancery clerks. Surviving from John's reign are a series of rolls on which they recorded the charters, letters patent and letters close that they were issuing, with new sets of rolls being begun at the start of each new regnal year.[14] John's reign began with his coronation on Ascension Day 1199, and since Ascension Day varies in date according to the date of Easter, he was actually the only king in English history who had regnal years of unequal lengths. Some of the rolls have wonderful headings in large capital letters proclaiming their identity. Given the small proportion of original charters and letters that survive, it is from the copies on the rolls that we can appreciate the scale of chancery output, and through the dating clauses trace John's itinerary often on a daily basis. In the close rolls alone for the period May 1204 to May 1205 (which John spent entirely in England), around 940 writs and other items of business are recorded. This, moreover, was only a fraction of the letters close that were issued, for the standardized writs initiating the common-law assizes were never enrolled. In June 1215 itself, Magna Carta was not enrolled. John had no desire to record a document extracted from him by force. But the chancery rolls do record five other charters, 135 letters close and over 150 letters patent. In the previous month a special keeper of the rolls had been appointed, one William Cucuel, a nickname that may refer to his cuckoo-like speech or behaviour. Was it on John's instructions that a few weeks later the clerk writing the patent roll included the little greeting 'I salute you William Kukke Wel'?[15]

THE CHAMBER AND WARDROBE

Alongside the chancery, the most important office with the king was his chamber. The chancery sent out the king's letters, the chamber received and sent out his money. Both were vital for the operation of royal government. The chancery letters communicated the king's orders. The chamber money supplied the force behind them.

In origin the chamber was simply the room where the king slept. One of its men was 'the porter of the king's bed'.[16] Its head, the chamberlain, could be a layman. Hubert de Burgh, named at the start of Magna Carta as 'seneschal of Poitou', had held the post earlier in the reign. Later, the most senior chamber clerk, before he went on to be chancellor, was Richard Marsh. What he and his fellows did was to receive, store and spend the money that the king carried with him. This money could come from the exchequer (of which more soon), from local officials, from individual debtors and from the great stores of cash that John assembled in castle treasuries. At Easter 1213, 8,000 marks were received from the treasury at Salisbury.[17] It seems probable that the chamber officials often stored their money not in the chamber itself but in the king's 'wardrobe', which also contained his jewels, clothes, and general bag and baggage. At major royal castles and houses, chamber and wardrobe may have had set rooms; elsewhere they used whatever space was offered. With overlapping personnel, there was often not much distinction between them.[18]

No written authorization seems to have been needed for expenditure out of the chamber-wardrobe. It must have been agreed to orally by the king, which shows his closeness to the officials concerned. However, the clerks did keep a detailed record of the daily expenditure, and this gives a remarkable insight into the range and extent of their activities.[19] In the regnal year May 1209 to May 1210, the money going out (sometimes just transfers into castle treasuries) was all carefully added up and amounted to around £8,000, which would have been a third of the king's total income at the start of the reign.[20] This, moreover, does not include the amounts spent on food and drink, which was probably the same again. Later in 1210, the chamber-wardrobe financed John's army in Ireland, and totalled its expenditure at over £11,400.[21] In the year May 1212 to May 1213, it supplied 10,000 marks to John's ally, Otto, the Roman emperor, and gave money to Flemish knights, sailors of the fleet at Portsmouth, and serjeants and foot soldiers going to the war in Wales. Money also went for work on castles, notably at Corfe, Dover and Nottingham, and on a plethora of gifts and payments to envoys and messengers, one of the latter bringing six amputated heads of Welshmen to the king at Rochester. There was also a great deal of expenditure on things personal to the king: on his gloves, furs, boots, robes (including a dressing gown and a nightgown), jewels, swords, bleeding, baths, urinals and gambling debts.

THE FOOD AND DRINK DEPARTMENTS

John was famous for his lavish hospitality, and the offices that obtained and prepared the food and drink must often have been hard at work. Of these, the most important were the kitchen, which cooked the meat; the dispensary, which baked the bread; and the buttery, which supplied the drink, ale for the general run of servants, wine for the king and his courtiers and guests. Later, when records survive under John's son, Henry III, they show that the cost to the departments of acquiring, by either cash or credit, the food and drink served could average out at between £15 and £20 a day, the minimum annual income required to be a knight. On a great feast day, the cost could be over £200, the annual income of a wealthy baron. At the very least, John must have equalled these sums.[22] They understate, moreover, the total value of the daily servings, since much of the wine was acquired by special buyers at Southampton and Bristol, while supplies also came from the king's own manors and huntsmen, and from the purchases made by local officials. For John's Christmas at Windsor in 1213, the sheriff of Kent, Reginald of Cornhill, was to provide twenty tuns of good and new ordinary wine, both French and Gascon (a tun held 252 gallons), four tuns of best wine, red and white, for the king's own table; 200 pigs' heads, with all the pickled pork, 1,000 hens, 50 pounds of pepper, 2 pounds of saffron, 100 pounds of good fresh almonds and 15,000 herrings; as well as spices for making sauces, two dozen towels and 1,000 ells of linen for table-cloths. Other officials were to provide 200 more pigs' heads, 15,000 more hens, 10,000 salted eels, and all the pitchers, cups and dishes needed for the feasts.[23] All of this was over and above what was paid for by the food and drink departments themselves.

The money to pay for the departmental purchases came from the chamber-wardrobe, but it did not necessarily come at once. Instead, the departments could exploit the king's right of 'prise', or 'purveyance', namely his right of compulsory purchase on a promise of paying later. In the case of wine, indeed, the king was allowed to take a certain amount from each ship at special low rates. Under Henry III, the departments, and the purchasers of wine, ran up great debts.[24] John may here have had a cleaner record. The issue of purveyance does occur in Magna Carta. Under chapter 28 the king's constables and bailiffs were not to take anyone's corn or other chattels unless they paid for them immediately or were able to get a delay with the consent of the vendor. This chapter, however, seems to relate to the activities of constables of castles and local officials, rather than to the officials of the household. Given that John was cash rich, he may have more or less paid his way. That was just as well. His near permanent presence in England after 1204, compared with his brother Richard's almost total absence, had the potential to make purveyance for the royal household a very major issue. At least this was one bad box John did not tick.

CHAPEL AND ALMONRY

The clerks of the king's chapel performed the king's daily Mass, although there is no evidence John took much delight, unlike Richard, in their singing. On great ecclesiastical festivals, the clerks also sang, as they had under John's predecessors, the ceremonial hymns, beginning 'Christus vincit', which cried out for Christ and the saints to bring the king victory and salvation. They had to work less hard than under John's son, Henry III, who multiplied the occasions on which the hymns were sung many times over.[25] There is equally little sign in the records of the lavish expenditure on vestments, chalices and other liturgical artefacts so characteristic of Henry. John did, however, have a relic collection, housed in coffers, around which he would sometimes order that candles burn through the night.[26] John's almoner (in 1209–10 the abbot of Bindon in Dorset) was a busy man, for he distributed John's daily alms of 36 pence (enough to feed that number of paupers), and also fed the hundreds of paupers as atonement when John, among other things, ate heartily on fast days.[27]

TRANSPORT

Carts, carts, carts. The cost of hiring them, repairing them and feeding the horses to pull them runs through the records of the chamber-wardrobe. Carts were, of course, essential for transporting the whole bag and baggage of a household which hardly remained anywhere for more than a few days.[28] In 1212 it took ten or more carters and twenty-five horses to pull the long carts holding John's bed and all the money, clothes and jewels of his wardrobe. Another ten carters with eighteen carthorses were needed for the kitchen, pantry and buttery. The stable establishment that looked after the carthorses and the elegant palfreys, on which the king and his entourage rode, was thus a major element of the household. The number of 'stable boys', as they are called, could rise to over seventy, and the number of horses being fed to nearly a hundred.[29] These numbers, moreover, exclude the horses and carts of the chancery staff, which seem to have been funded from the chancellor's own revenues. If John's household largely paid its way when it came to hiring carts, that was hardly true of his local officials. Chapter 30 of Magna Carta forbad sheriffs and bailiffs from taking the horses and carts of any free man without his consent. The new version of the Charter of 1216 went further and said that payment should be according to the 'ancient' rates: 10 pence a day for a cart with two horses and 14 pence for a cart with three.

THE STEWARD OF THE HOUSEHOLD AND THE HOUSEHOLD KNIGHTS

The head of the king's household was the steward, and there was usually more than one in office at any one time. They were men of knightly status who, like John's steward William de Cantilupe, built up estates of baronial proportions. They played a major, although varying, role in securing the king's food and drink.[30] They were also at the head of the king's household knights.

The knights 'de familia regis', as they were called, seem to have numbered at any one time around a hundred, although they were far from being all at court at any one time.[31] They gave kingship its punch, forming the posses when John wished, in the words of the Charter, to 'go against' someone and vent his 'ill will, indignation and rancour'. When John heard that the great baron Robert fitz-Walter was laying siege to Binham priory in Norfolk, he despatched at once a group of household knights and armed serjeants to arrest him. They were very disappointed to discover that he had fled.[32] Some knights remained mere military heavies, but others, such as John of Bassingbourn, with more ambition and ability, became counsellors, diplomats, sheriffs and castellans. Having taken a special oath of loyalty to the king, which included the obligation to report anything said against him, they acted as his eyes and ears. At court, they were the men John liked most to be with and whom he could rely on for support.[33] Several of the counsellors named at the start of Magna Carta were or had been household knights – the Basset brothers, for example, and Robert of Ropsley. Thomas Basset combined his position at court with a long spell as sheriff of Oxfordshire. With his brother Alan, he was to lead a decisive charge at the battle of Lincoln in 1217.

THE CHIEF JUSTICIAR

Only one minister was superior to the chancellor. This was the chief justiciar.[34] The post appears in four chapters of the Charter and is mentioned on no fewer than seven occasions. In chapter 18 it is the king, or if he is out of the kingdom, 'our chief justiciar' who is to send judges round the country to hear the assizes. In chapter 41 king or chief justiciar are to learn how English merchants are treated abroad. In chapter 48 the 'justiciar' (the 'chief' was often omitted) in the king's absence is to be informed before the knights abolish the evil customs in the counties. And then, in the security clause, it is the justiciar, if the king is abroad, who is to redress breaches of the Charter. These chapters give a clear idea of the justiciar's role. It was to act as governor of the kingdom during the king's absences. On such occasions, it was normal for the king to address his orders to the justiciar alone rather than direct to officials in England. The justiciar then issued his own letters, sealed with his own seal, passing the orders on. He could also issue letters, dealing with a wide variety of issues, on his own initiative. The justiciar went on his own journeys around the country and also presided at the exchequer, of which he was the head. When the king was in the country, as John was for the most part after 1204, the justiciar's role was more circumscribed, but he continued to act as the king's chief minister, sometimes at court, sometimes at the exchequer.

COUNSEL AND COMMON COUNSEL

There is no evidence that John ever had a formal council of ministers, with a defined membership, bound together with a special oath. That would have been contrary to his whole style of government, in which he took advice, as it suited him, from shifting and shifted groups of ministers and magnates. The personnel of those at court, as Walter Map recognized, was constantly changing. Ministers retired or fell from favour, left court on embassies or, in times of tension, took personal command of castles and sheriffdoms. At the same time, people were coming to court in search of concessions and favours. Those simply wanting the writs that initiated and furthered common-law litigation could get these from the chancery without involving the king at all. Those wanting something more, to buy a wardship, for example, or recover the king's benevolence, would need to get through to the king in person. This was where the courtiers proved their worth and made their profit. Very few coming to court in disfavour had the courage and confidence of Bishop Hugh of Lincoln, who brushed aside William Marshal's warnings and offers of mediation, and insisted on going straight into King Richard's presence, where he seized his cloak and shook him into a good humour. In 1215 the prospective abbot of Bury St Edmunds had the justiciar, Peter des Roches, make his case. Des Roches failed (perhaps not trying very hard), but still pocketed his bribe.[35]

At its fullest, the king could bring together at court the great and good of the land in a formal assembly. Here the court expanded like a great bellows before contracting when the council was over. Magna Carta referred to a national assembly in chapters 12 and 14, when it said that taxes were not to be levied save by the 'commune consilium' of the kingdom. The Charter here was slightly ambiguous as to whether it was referring to an assembly itself, 'the common council of the kingdom', or to what such an assembly could do, namely give the kingdom's 'common counsel', the Latin 'consilium' being capable of either meaning. Probably it meant the latter, hence my translation, like most others, has here 'counsel' rather than 'council'. But it was really a distinction without a difference. Those summoned to give the 'common counsel' of the kingdom in chapter 14 became once assembled the kingdom's 'common council'. Great assemblies of the kingdom had long been described as 'councils', 'general councils' and 'great councils'. In the second half of the twelfth century they were occasionally called 'parliaments', the name that was to become established in the reign of Henry III. The Anonymous of Béthune, writing in French (from which the word came) had the opponents of King John in 1214–15 coming together in 'a parlement' and agreeing to a 'parlement' with John at Staines. In 1244 a chancery clerk, looking back to 1215, wrote of 'the parliament of Runnymede'. It had long been traditional to summon the king's tenants-in-chief to such assemblies, with the greater barons receiving a personal summons. Chapter 14 of the Charter was thus trying to solidify what was customary, although the custom, as we have seen, was fast moving out of line with social reality.[36]

THE EXCHEQUER AND THE
KING'S REVENUES

So far we have been talking about institutions of government that for the most part travelled with the king. The greatest office of all, however, was mostly resident at Westminster, meeting probably (as it did later) in chambers either side of the entrance to William Rufus's great hall. This office was the exchequer. The exchequer is Magna Carta's elephant in the room. It is not mentioned in the Articles of the Barons, the 1215 Charter or its successors. Yet its presence hangs over all the Charter's financial clauses. Although the itinerant chamber-wardrobe spent a good proportion of the king's revenues, it did not raise the revenue itself. That was the job of the exchequer. So was the annual auditing and hearing the accounts of all the money owed the king. The exchequer sent a large proportion of the money that it raised to the chamber-wardrobe, but it could also spend it in other ways on the king's orders, as well as store it in its central treasury, or send it to one of the treasuries John established in castles around the country. With its precise procedures, voluminous records and utter determination to raise the money due the king, the exchequer was far and away the mightiest instrument of government that John possessed.

The first certain reference to the exchequer is in 1110. The name derived from the chequered cloth on which the annual audit of the debts owed the king took place. The results of the annual audit, county by county, were recorded on a great document later called the pipe roll, because rolled up it looked like a pipe. The first surviving roll belongs to the financial year 1129–1130.[37] The head of the exchequer was the chief justiciar, while beneath him, often in day-to-day charge, was the treasurer of the exchequer. It was the treasurer Richard fitzNigel who wrote the *Dialogus de Scaccario* in the reign of Henry II.[38]

While Magna Carta says nothing about the exchequer, it gives a very full impression of the revenues that it had to collect. The most traditional and staple of these came from the county 'farms', which the Charter sought to regulate in chapter 25. The county farm was a fixed sum of money (usually several hundred pounds) for which the sheriff of the county answered at the exchequer every year. To make up the farm he could draw on the revenues from the king's own lands in the county, the 'demesne manors', that is, which are also referred to in the chapter. The farm, too, came from a range of traditional payments, such as 'sheriff's aid', and from the proceeds of pleas and exactions in the county and hundred courts. The exactions in the hundred courts were regulated in chapter 42 of the 1217 Charter. The county farm could also be derived, from the individual farms of its component local government divisions, namely 'the hundreds, ridings and wapentakes' mentioned in chapter 25 if, that is, they were leased out.

The aim of chapter 25 was to prevent the king increasing the county farms and the subsidiary farms of hundred, riding and wapentake. It excepted, however, from the restriction the king's demesne manors. Some of these contributed directly to the county farm, and so that element of it could still be increased. By 1199, many other demesne manors, after appropriate deductions, had been removed from the farm and were accounted for separately by the sheriff or another keeper. Also accounted for separately, often by their men, and forming another staple part of the king's income, were the farms due from the king's cities and boroughs. That neither these nor the farms due from the king's demesne manors were restricted in Magna Carta was partly at least due to an acceptance that the king's own personal properties were a matter for him, in a way other revenues were not. The Charter likewise said nothing about tallage, which was a tax levied at the king's pleasure on his cities, boroughs and demesne manors. The Articles of the Barons in chapter 32 had mentioned tallages, but their attempt to have those levied on London and other privileged cities made dependent on the common consent of the kingdom never made it into the Charter itself.[39]

Another part of the king's private demesne was the royal forest. In the large areas of the country within the royal forest, and thus subject to forest law, this meant that amercements could be imposed for poaching or hunting deer and boar. They could also be imposed for damaging the actual growth of the forest through the 'purpresture, waste and assart' mentioned in chapter 4 of the Forest Charter of 1217. Purpresture was putting up buildings and enclosures; waste was cutting down trees; and assart was clearance for the creation of new arable land. The king asserted that these amercements, because of the special status of the forest, were entirely a matter for him, and were not subject to the usual customary constraints. Hence the *Dialogus de Scaccario* stressed that the law of the forest, in contrast 'to the common law [*communi iure*] of the kingdom', depended on the arbitrary will of the king alone: 'solius regis arbitrio'.[40] The Charter did not deal explicitly with forest amercements, but they were presumably covered by the amercements regulated in chapters 20–22.

Equally part of the king's 'own' were the Jews, whom he could tallage as he wished. There was not even a suggestion in 1215 that these tallages, unlike the ones imposed on London and other towns, should be made subject to the common consent of the kingdom, although in fact such tallages pressed down indirectly on all who owed the Jews money. After all, the only way the Jews could pay the taxes was to get money in from their debtors. The king could also find many reasons for taking the assets of Jews, which were essentially the debts that were owed them, into his own hands. As a result, the debtors ended up owing their money to the crown. Chapter 10 of the Charter sought, in that case, to reduce the king's potential profit. He was only allowed to exact the original debt, rather than the debt plus interest.

The Charter gives a full picture of the revenues derived from the tenurial relationship between the king and his tenants-in-chief, the 'feudal' revenues, if one likes, derived from relief, wardships, the sale of marriages and impositions on widows, all of which were the concern of chapters 2 to 8. This same relationship brought the king profit from the church, since, after the death of bishops and abbots, he had custody of the lands that they held from the crown until a new appointment was made. Magna Carta said nothing about this directly. However, the duration of such vacancies would have been limited by John's earlier charter promising free and speedy elections of bishops and abbots, which Magna Carta confirmed in chapter 1. The 1216 Charter, however, extended to ecclesiastical vacancies the same protections from exploitation that Magna Carta gave to secular wardships.

Chapters 12 and 14 of the Charter revealed the king's income from scutages and aids, although these could be very different things. Scutage, as we have seen, was paid by tenants-in-chief in place of providing the king with military service. An aid could likewise be a payment owed by the tenant-in-chief to the king as part of his tenurial obligations. The Charter tried to limit the occasions it was due to the ransoming of the king's person, the knighting of his eldest son and the marrying once of his eldest daughter. Aids, however, could also be general taxes paid by everyone in the realm, and these, levied as a percentage of everyone's rents and movable property (chiefly corn and farm animals), could bring in sums incomparably greater than anything in the form of scutage. Before 1215, there was already a feeling that such aids required the consent of the kingdom. Indeed, when levying his great aid of 1207, John claimed, however spuriously, that consent had been given.[41]

The profits of justice had long made a major contribution to royal revenue and on these the Charter was eloquent. Chapters 20 to 22 dealt with amercements, the financial penalties for falling into the king's 'mercy', as the result of being convicted of some offence, either before the king's judges or the king himself. Chapter 32 showed that the king was entitled to hold for a year and a day the lands of those convicted of felonies (serious crimes). Although this was not mentioned in the Charter, he was also entitled to the chattels of outlawed and executed criminals. Chapter 36 showed the payments that might have to be made for writs. Chapter 40 issued its famous blanket ban on the sale of justice.

One of the most lucrative sources of royal revenue were 'fines', which the Charter dealt with in chapter 55. These were offers of money accepted by the king for concessions and favours, and could be made in many of the areas mentioned above. On the one hand, they could be entirely voluntary, so for a wardship, or for a writ to start a legal action. On the other hand, they could be pretty much compulsory, as when they were made to obtain the king's forgiveness and benevolence. The Articles of the Barons had sought to redress unjust fines made for dowers, inheritances and marriages. The Charter went further and demanded redress of all unjust fines without any qualification.

These revenues were not, of course, of equal incidence or value. The county 'farms' came in every year, and were an absolute staple.

Other revenues were more occasional; those from ecclesiastical vacancies and wardships depended on death; those from judicial and forest amercements depended very largely on the periodic visitations of the king's judges. Great taxes, on the kingdom itself, or on the Jews, could transform the king's finances but they could not be levied very often. In the financial year covering John's accession (so that from Michaelmas 1198 to Michaelmas 1199), the king's cash revenue, as calculated by Nick Barratt from the pipe roll, was some £22,183. This breaks down as follows: county farms 14.6 per cent; royal demesne manors outside the farm, and farms of cities and boroughs, 11.6 per cent; judicial revenues 29.5 per cent; feudal revenues (payments for reliefs, marriages and wardships) 10.9 per cent; scutage 10.7 per cent; tallage 10.9 per cent; forest 5.4 per cent; Jews 2.3 per cent. These are not untypical figures for early in the reign, although there was no revenue from ecclesiastical vacancies. In 1200–1201 that was worth £1,165 and in the next year £1,582. Later in the reign, large sums were raised from general taxation and taxation on the Jews, while there were also increasing revenues from the royal forest.[42]

The exchequer's work of raising the king's money began every year with the preparation of what were called the 'summonses'. These were lists of the debts that the sheriff of each county had to collect. The lists would begin with the county and other farms, and then go on to all the debts owed by individuals. When Magna Carta in chapter 26 spoke of the sheriff showing 'our letters patent of summons' for a debt owed the king by a deceased tenant-in-chief, it was referring to this annual list.[43] These letters patent for our summons, like a whole range of letters close about getting in the revenue, were issued, in the king's name, by the exchequer itself and sealed with its own seal. The seal was kept by the chancellor of the exchequer, hence the name of that office. The exchequer, therefore, had the power to take independent action. It used that power to devastating effect when ordering debts to be gathered in by distraint.

The exchequer knew what debts to put on the list of summonses in various ways.[44] It included recurring farms and old debts from the record of the last audit on the pipe rolls or from other related material. As for new debts arising from amercements, the exchequer was sent regular lists of those imposed before the king, before the court at Westminster and before the king's judges in the counties. It also received on a roll (called the originalia roll) the list of fines accepted by the king as he travelled the country. These had been recorded by the chancery on fine rolls of which the originalia rolls were a copy. Although, therefore, the king was personally involved in accepting fines, he handed them over to the exchequer for collection and audit, which just shows the central part it played in the workings of royal finance. Of course, the king could always fasten on a particular debt and order that it be paid into the chamber-wardrobe rather than the exchequer. However, when he did so, he informed the exchequer, so that it could make due allowance for the payment when the debt was audited. The only occasions when the exchequer was bypassed altogether was when the king took over the total management of a debt, or when a fine was paid cash down, immediately and in full into the chamber-wardrobe. As far as can be seen, this did not happen very often.

The sheriff, when he received the summonses, had then to set about collecting the money. If a debtor did not pay, then the sheriff could enforce payment by the distraint mentioned in chapters 8, 9, 16, 23 and 29 of the Charter. This involved seizing and selling the debtor's chattels, which would chiefly be his corn and animals. If these did not suffice, the Charter acknowledged that land and rents might be possessed; and after that the sheriff could turn to the resources of the debtor's sureties. Chapter 26 of the Charter implied that sheriffs, on the death of tenants-in-chief, had simply gone in and seized whatever they liked on the excuse of some debt, without bothering over its size.

The sheriff collected most of the money personally, but it was permissible for a baron to make his own payments, with the sheriff just notifying him of the amount owed.[45] The payments were due in two instalments each year, at Easter and Michaelmas, and were made into a branch of the exchequer called the exchequer of receipt or lower exchequer. This was presided over by two chamberlains of the exchequer, an hereditary position. One of the chamberlains, Warin fitzGerold, although he does not have his title there, appears among John's counsellors in the preamble to the Charter. As a receipt for each individual payment, the sheriff and other payees received a tally. This was a wooden stick on which the amount of the payment was recorded in notches. The stick was then split down the middle, with half being kept by the exchequer and half by the payee. For identification purposes, the nature of the debt and the amount of the payment was also written on both the halves.

The exchequer of receipt kept its money in its 'treasury', and only dispensed it as ordered by special letters close sent by the king to the treasurer and chamberlains. These letters (called 'writs of liberate') might order the exchequer to send money to the king, where it would be paid into the chamber-wardrobe, or spend it in a whole variety of other ways. It was really just a matter of convenience whether the king paid for something with money from the chamber-wardrobe, the exchequer treasury, the castle treasuries or the funds in the hands of the sheriffs and other local officials.

The actual work of hearing the accounts, as of preparing the summonses, was done by the upper exchequer or exchequer of audit. After Michaelmas each year, in a long procession that lasted sometimes until the following Easter or beyond, each sheriff came before the upper exchequer to account for the debts which he had been summoned to pay in the previous year, so at the previous Easter and Michaelmas. The exchequer went through the list of summonses and the sheriffs handed over their tallies as proof of payment, the exchequer matching up the proffered half with the half it had kept. At the same time the sheriffs proffered any writs that had ordered them to spend revenue locally, so that due allowance could be made for that too. If baronial stewards had paid in money for their masters, then they would also attend the audit and go through the same procedure. The audit itself was done on the exchequer cloth where counters in the form of silver pennies were set out representing each individual debt. Beneath them were placed counters representing the amount paid or allowed against it. The latter were then subtracted from the former, revealing what was still owed. The state of play on the debts was then recorded on the pipe rolls, with the debtors being quit or left still owing. If the sheriff had failed to raise money and could show it was not his fault, he might be ordered to distrain more vigorously for the sums outstanding. If it was his fault, he could be subject to imprisonment, as might the stewards of barons if they too had defaulted.

In John's reign we see the pipe rolls in their full pomp. As printed by the Pipe Roll Society, all of them down to 1211 have more than 200 pages, many over 250. On a rough count, a typical roll contains more than 4,500 names of people, places and institutions, most of them owing money to the king. The rolls reveal John's success in increasing his revenues, as also the pressure he was placing on individuals. They show just how the grip of the exchequer ranged from top to bottom of society: from lay and ecclesiastical barons owing gigantic sums, through knights and townsmen, down to peasants and peasant communities amerced in numerous ways by the king's judges.

Not all the king's revenues are revealed in the pipe rolls. They show nothing about the flow of treasure from Ireland, which may well have averaged out at over £1,000 each year. In terms of English revenues, they have nothing about the great tax of 1207, although we know its yield from another record source. Nor do the pipe rolls contain records of the taxation imposed on the Jews. This is because such taxation was the responsibility of a sub-branch of the exchequer, with its own records, called the exchequer of the Jews. The latter was also responsible for collecting the debts owed the Jews that had come into the king's hands. When these were large and owed by great men, they were sometimes placed under the main exchequer and appear on the pipe rolls, but the great majority of such debts stayed under the exchequer of the Jews. Since its records hardly survive for this period, the precise yields of Jewish taxation, and of Jewish debts in royal hands, will never be known, a big gap in our knowledge. The emergence of the exchequer of the Jews was linked to a reform of 1194 that sought to regulate the whole process of Jewish moneylending. Henceforth, the contracting of loans was to be limited to major towns under the oversight of two Christians, two Jews and two clerks of the Jewish exchequer. Each town had a chest (an 'archa') in which a copy of the charter recording each loan was deposited, the other copy being kept by the Jew. This is the 'charter' referred to in Magna Carta, chapter 10, where it says that if a debt owed to a Jew came into the king's hands, he would only extract the capital sum, 'catallum', found in the charter, in other words he would not extract interest. All this bureaucracy made it easier for the king to protect the Jews and also to extract their money both through taxation (for the king could find out exactly what resources there were to tax) and through debts taken into his own hands.

LOCAL GOVERNMENT

'All counties and hundreds, ridings and wapentakes, are to be at the ancient farms without any increment', ran chapter 25 of the Charter, thereby laying bare the basic structure of royal government in the localities. For administrative purposes, England was divided up into counties. There were thirty-eight of these of very different sizes, ranging from the tiny Rutland to the gigantic Yorkshire. Counties were subdivided into smaller administrative divisions called hundreds or wapentakes. Of these there were around 630. Yorkshire and Lincolnshire, given their size, were also divided into groups of wapentakes, the ridings of chapter 25.

It was a tribute to the power of royal government in the twelfth century that nearly all the counties were under the control of sheriffs appointed and dismissed by the king. In other words they had not fallen under the control of earls or hereditary sheriffs.[46] The sheriffs make nine appearances in the Charter, being saddled with a series of dos and don'ts. It was the malpractices of the sheriffs and forest officials that were to be investigated in chapter 48. Three of John's sheriffs were named among those who were to be removed from their offices in chapter 50. Apart from their role as debt collectors, the sheriffs also had major responsibilities in the field of justice and law and order. The Crowland chronicler described them as providing peace for local people as well as carrying out the business of the 'fisc'.[47] The sheriffs thus presided over the county and hundred courts, arrested and hanged criminals, empanelled common-law juries and implemented judgements.

As the king's chief officers in the shires, the sheriffs received a stream of orders on a multiplicity of subjects. Under chapter 14 of the Charter, for example, they were to summon the lesser tenants-in-chief to a national assembly. They were continually being told to spend the money they were collecting on a range of purchases and payments, instead of paying it into the exchequer. The resulting allowances on the pipe rolls are a remarkable testimony to the range of their activities. Some sheriffs were great regional commissars, controlling wardships (as chapter 4 of the Charter indicated), escheats, royal manors and castles, as well as several counties. Most sheriffs had as their main base the royal castle in the county town.

The king's castles, 'the bones of the kingdom' as they were called, were a vital source of royal power.[48] In 1214 there were ninety-three of them, which was roughly half the number of baronial castles.[49] A castle's strategic purpose, as John indicated when he ordered one to be built in Dublin in 1204, was to project power outwards, thereby controlling a town or strategic area.[50] John also used his castles to hold his prisoners and house large amounts of treasure. Some castles were under sheriffs, others under separate constables. The Charter told of the measures to maintain the castles. Chapter 28 forbad constables and bailiffs from taking anyone's corn or other chattels without immediate payment, unless the vendor consented to the delay. The Charter of 1216, however, allowed a delay in payment where the corn and chattels had been taken from the vill where the castle was situated.[51] Chapter 31 of the 1215 Charter stipulated that bailiffs were not to take wood for castles, save with the permission of the owner. Chapter 29 dealt with the garrisoning of castles and allowed knights, if they wished, to serve personally or provide an 'upright man' as a deputy, as opposed to being forced to give money in place of service.

THE ADMINISTRATION OF
THE ROYAL FOREST

When Magna Carta commissioned its inquiries into the malpractices of the king's local officials, in chapter 48, the list of those officials was headed not by the sheriffs but by the king's foresters.[52] Without an extensive administrative apparatus, there was no way that the king could make money for offences against the forest law. The Forest Charter of 1217 was not bothered at all with what it called the king's 'demesne woods', the forest that is on his own manors and properties. The trouble was that the royal forest and forest law extended much further than that and enveloped woods and lands held by bishops, abbots, earls, barons, knights and free tenants. This was why the Unknown Charter, in its chapter 10, demanded privileges for knights who had their woods in the king's forests. In John's reign there was royal forest in twenty counties. It embraced large parts of Cumberland, Yorkshire, Lancashire, Nottinghamshire, Derbyshire, Berkshire, Hampshire and Wiltshire, and all of Essex. In total it covered about a third of the kingdom.[53] Its main purpose was not to provide kings with areas for hunting, although they certainly were great huntsmen. It was to provide them with money.

The individual forests were administered by chief foresters, some of them hereditary, who were liable to dismissal and ferocious punishment, usually financial, for any failures in their duty. They in turn employed numerous subordinate officials who preyed on the local population. One aim in chapter 7 of the 1217 Forest Charter was to limit the number of such pests. There were also groups of officials (often local knights) called 'regarderers', who monitored the bounds of the forest, and 'verderers', who made records of the offences committed. The activities of these officials were coordinated at forest courts, and they were all subject to the chief justice of the forest. For much of John's reign this was Hugh de Neville, named in the preamble of the 1215 Charter, although without his title, perhaps by design, for it was hardly one that brought him honour. The Charter, in chapter 44, did refer to the forest 'justices', or judges, and it was from their periodic visitations of the forest counties, often led by the chief forester, that the great bulk of the revenue came. The judges tried those accused of offences and imposed the amercements. Where the offenders were important, they might be amerced directly by the king. The judges also made money by summoning men to attend their sessions even though they lived outside the bounds of the forest. If such men did not turn up, they were amerced. In reaction, chapter 44 of the Charter laid down that no one living outside the forest had to attend unless they were involved directly or indirectly in a plea. The penalties were not only financial, however. Those for offences against the protected beasts of the forest, the deer and boar, could be corporal, probably because many poachers were peasants with few resources worth amercing. The Unknown Charter had John conceding that no man was to lose life or limb for an offence against the beasts of the forest. The Anonymous of Béthune liked to think that this was in the Charter itself, but in fact it had to wait until the Charter of 1217.

THE KING'S JUDICIAL COURTS

The royal forest was an unmitigated disaster for the king's subjects. It had no benefits for them. The king's dispensation of justice, in part at least, could be looked at in a different light. At the local level, there were two public courts presided over by royal officials, those of the county and the hundred or wapentake. The Charter of 1217, in chapter 42, regulated both. The former were to meet once a month, unless a longer interval had been customary. As for the latter, the sheriff was only to hold the especially well-attended sessions, called the 'tourn', twice a year, at Easter and Michaelmas. How often the hundred courts should meet beyond the tourn became a matter for dispute. The government in 1234, trying to settle the issue, said the sessions had been fortnightly under Henry II, but now might be once every three weeks.[54] The overlapping jurisdiction of both the hundred and the county courts embraced minor disputes over land, debts and distraint, as well as criminal cases of a type that did not involve breaches of the king's peace.

Above the local courts of county and hundred, there were other superior types of royal court. One was held, nominally at least, in the king's presence, 'coram rege', wherever he was on his journeys. Another was presided over by the king's judges at Westminster. There were also courts of varying jurisdictions held by the king's judges when they visited the localities. In chapter 59 of the Charter, John agreed that the claims of 'Alexander, king of Scots' should be settled 'by judgement of his peers in our court'. Given that these claims were of great moment, this was clearly a court that would be presided over by the king himself and where great barons (Alexander's peers, for he held an English barony) would be present to give judgement. The Articles of the Barons were thinking of the same court when they laid down in chapter 25 that those disseised unjustly by Henry II and Richard should have 'right without delay by judgement of their peers in the court of the king'. This was also the court in which disputes between the barons themselves would be heard. Chapter 17 of the Charter indicated something else, when it directed that 'common pleas' should not follow the king's court but be heard in a fixed place.[55] In other words, John's court at court, if one may call it that, had heard not merely cases involving great men, but also quite routine civil litigation of the common-pleas variety. In those cases, it would have been presided over by the king's professional judges rather than by the king personally, unless he was especially interested in a case, as sometimes he was.

The Charter of 1215 did not specify where the fixed place for common pleas to be heard might be. Its 1217 successor was more informative since it referred, in chapters 14 and 15, to cases being heard by 'the justices of the bench'. The bench, until suspended by King John, usually sat at Westminster, and, presided over by professional judges, heard a whole raft of disputes about property. The king's judges also went on visitations (or 'eyres') of various types around the counties. One type is shown in the judges who were to visit the counties to hear the common-law assizes under chapter 18 of the Charter. These were eyres entirely for civil pleas. The king's judges also came to hear criminal pleas, when they tried the cases of those imprisoned in county gaols. Most impressive of all, as a manifestation of royal justice and power in the localities, were the great 'all pleas' eyres. Here the judges heard both criminal and civil pleas and also carried out investigations into the king's rights. These visitations are often called by historians 'general eyres', both because of the scope of their jurisdiction and because they were usually arranged as part of circuits that covered the whole country. In a large county, such eyres could mean thousands of people being concentrated together before the king's judges.[56]

PEACE AND CRIMINAL JUSTICE

The Charter twice referred to the peace that would end the civil war. It also, in chapter 49, referred to the 'peace or faithful service' that John had sought to obtain by taking hostages. Here, then, it was interpreting peace as the opposite of rebellion and civil strife. Chapter 42 of the 1217 Charter, on the other hand, was thinking of peace in the law-and-order sense when it made arrangements so that 'our peace shall be kept'. The maintenance of the peace in both these senses was a fundamental duty of kingship. At the local law-and-order level, it was intimately linked to the 'pleas of our crown' mentioned in chapter 24 of the Charter, since these gave the king a near monopoly over the trial and punishment of serious crime, over that is, the homicide, affray, premeditated assault, burglary, rape, (serious) theft and arson that John had listed in 1201 as 'those things which belong to our crown and justice'.[57]

Chapter 42 of the 1217 Charter linked together three basic

elements of local law enforcement when it said, rather incomprehensibly for modern readers, that 'the view of frankpledge shall be held so that the peace is kept and the tithing is full'. The tithing was a group of ten or twelve adult males, usually unfree, who were sworn to keep the peace and guarantee the good behaviour of their fellows. Supposedly all the unfree population south of the Humber were grouped in tithings and it was these that the sheriffs checked at Michaelmas each year, in the hundred or wapentake courts at their 'view of frankpledge' – 'frankpledge' here being simply another word for the tithing. The sheriffs, in so doing, had many opportunities for imposing penalties on the tithing groups – for example, when men failed to arrest criminals, or when they had given false evidence or evidence not in the proper form.[58] It was unjust exactions on such occasions that chapter 42 sought to restrain, as it also sought to limit the tourn to two a year.

The Articles of the Barons in 1215 had demanded that sheriffs should not interfere in the pleas of the crown without the coroners. It was the coroners, introduced in 1194, and usually county knights, whose duty it was to make a record of the pleas of the crown, and in so doing to hold inquests into all cases of death other than by obviously natural causes. The Articles implied that the sheriffs were usurping the function of the coroners in this area when it said that, without them, they were not to interfere with the pleas of the crown. The Charter itself, in chapter 24, was concerned with a wider usurpation, and laid down that sheriffs, constables, coroners and bailiffs were not to hear the pleas of the crown. There had been a time when sheriffs heard pleas of the crown routinely in the county and hundred courts, but increasingly in the twelfth century this had become the prerogative of the king's judges sent to the counties. Stopping the sheriffs hearing such pleas was probably an issue on which, in normal circumstances, the king could see eye to eye with his critics.

When the judges arrived in a county, a man could accuse or 'appeal' an individual of any of the offences coming under the heading of 'pleas of the crown'. The rights of women in this area were more restricted, as we have seen.[59] The great majority of crimes, however, came before the justices not through private appeals but through a system of public accusation. Twelve jurors from each hundred or wapentake (chosen by knightly electors) were charged with revealing the cases of serious crime since the last visitation. They also gave evidence about usurpations of the rights of the crown. Chapter 38 of the Charter, which said that no bailiff was 'to put anyone to law', meaning essentially to put anyone on trial, by his own, unsupported accusation 'without trustworthy witnesses', was designed in part to ensure the use of such juries. Guilt or innocence could be determined by the ordeal of hot iron or water, by the swearing of oaths by supporters of the accused, and also, in cases of appeal, by trial by battle. However, there was pressure for more rational procedures, and chapter 36 of the Charter laid down that the 'writ of inquisition concerning life or limbs' should be conceded freely. This meant that someone accused of a serious offence, essentially a plea of the crown, for which the penalty was death or mutilation, could obtain a writ that ordered his case to be heard by a jury. From 1218 onwards, after the Fourth Lateran Council in 1215 had banned attendance of the clergy at ordeals, the use of juries became general practice.[60]

The usual punishment in the thirteenth century was death by hanging, although it had earlier been mutilation. The great majority of criminals, however, were not brought to justice. Instead they fled and were outlawed. Chapter 42 of the Charter excepted those 'outlawed according to the law of the kingdom' from those allowed free exit and entry into England. Some of those envisaged here were doubtless magnates outlawed for political crimes, but the great majority would have been absconding criminals. Nearly all of these, judging from the value of their chattels, were of peasant status.

Criminal justice brought great financial profit to the crown, as we have seen – profit from the chattels of criminals, and, as the Charter indicated, from the right to hold their lands for a year and a day. There were also numerous amercements imposed on tithings, juries and local communities, for offences real or concocted. When the Charter, in chapter 20, laid down that villeins were to be amerced, saving their wainage, by upstanding men of the neighbourhood, it had in mind above all the amercements imposed at the eyre.[61] For local society, any benefits brought by the eyre's maintenance of the peace seemed far outweighed by the financial burdens. The great increase in the numbers of those suffering such burdens, as revealed in the financial accounts of the eyres on the pipe rolls, is a striking indication of how far royal power had advanced after 1154 and how it dug down deep into society.

CIVIL JUSTICE

Thrice in the Charter, in chapters 52, 53 and 57, John promised to give 'full justice' to those complaining of abuses committed by himself or his predecessors. The king equally had a duty to give justice to everyone (or everyone who was free) in their disputes with each other. As he put it in 1210, 'we desire justice according to the custom of our kingdom of England to be shown to all who complain of wrongdoing'.[62] If the wrongdoing involved breaches of the peace, then that came under the criminal side of the king's jurisdiction. If, on the other hand, it involved disputes over lands, rights and other properties, then there was a whole set of other legal actions, developed under Henry II, which could bring such cases before the king's justices.[63] The most famous of these, as in chapter 18 of the Charter, were called 'assizes'. Resort to the new assizes was entirely voluntary. Although there was an established rule, set out in *Glanvill*, that anyone claiming a free tenement held by another had to begin the action with a writ obtained from the king, the case could then proceed by a variety of procedures in a variety of courts.[64] That so many people did resort to the assizes is, therefore, a sure indication of their value.

The most important of the new procedures were those mentioned in chapter 18 of Magna Carta. This laid down that the king was to send two justices to each county four times a year to hear 'recognitions of novel disseisin, of mort d'ancestor and of darrein presentment'. A recognition, used interchangeably in the chapter with 'assize', meant a legal action culminating in the verdict of a jury. The recognitions in question were open to the free but not to the unfree. They could be used by women, although married ones needed to litigate with their husbands. Novel disseisin dealt with cases where a plaintiff claimed that he had been disseised, that is dispossessed, unlawfully of a free tenement, free tenement here meaning land and or other property held for free as opposed to villein services. The assize could also be brought if a free tenement had been encroached on by the erection of a bank or making of a road. The offence had to have been relatively recent, hence 'novel disseisin'. 'Mort d'ancestor' was a remedy for those who claimed that they had been denied succession to an inheritance in land.

Darrein presentment, much less frequently used, dealt with disputes over the right to appoint a clerk to a church living, usually a parish church.

All three assizes were commenced by securing a writ from the chancery or, if the king was out of the country, from the chief justiciar. This writ was one 'of course' – 'de cursu' – which meant that it was standard form, cheap and issued automatically. When Magna Carta in chapter 36 asked that the writ of inquisition concerning life or limbs be given without payment and not denied, it was asking for such writs to be likewise ones 'of course'. It was not literally true that such writs were free, since they probably cost 6d, so the equivalent of four days' wages for a labourer.[65] There were other costs, including those of actually going to court to get the writs, but still they were probably within reach of all but the very poorest of free tenants.

The writ ordered the sheriff to summon a jury of twelve free and lawful men from the neighbourhood of the land in dispute to come before the king's judges on their next appearance in the county to give the verdict in the case. In novel disseisin, the jury had to determine whether the plaintiff had been disseised of the land unjustly and without judgement, the criteria for unjust disseisin being usually a disseisin made without the judgement of a court. In mort d'ancestor, the jury had to answer two questions. Was the plaintiff the nearest heir of the deceased person from whom he was claiming to inherit? Did the deceased actually die in possession of the land being sought 'as of fee'? The 'as of fee' here meant that the land had been held with some vestige of hereditary right and not simply for a term of years, nor at the lord's pleasure. If the jury found for the plaintiff, then the justices would give judgement in his favour, and issue a writ in the king's name (but witnessed and sealed by the senior judge) ordering the sheriff to put him in possession. The defendant would then be amerced, as would an unsuccessful plaintiff. The amercements, however, at least in routine cases, were not so large as to deter litigation.

Novel disseisin and mort d'ancestor were far and away the most popular of the new legal actions, but others were developed on comparable lines dealing with a range of further issues, one of the most used being that open to widows trying to recover their dowers. There was also a more elaborate procedure, much used in

John's time, called the grand assize, in which juries made up of twelve knights determined the question of ultimate right to land, as opposed to just answering the narrow questions put to them in the other assizes. All these actions were the same, or 'common', throughout the country, from Cornwall to Cumberland. They were thus at the heart of the 'common pleas' to which Magna Carta referred in chapter 17, and by extension at the heart of what contemporaries called 'the common law'. These actions could be used by great men in their litigation, but the bulk of the litigants (as one can see from the plea rolls that survive from the 1190s) were lesser men, knights and free tenants. They might be litigating upwards against lords or downwards against tenants, but equally a good deal of the litigation, often over very small amounts of land, was between neighbours on much the same social level.

The appeal of the actions to wide sections of society is understandable. The writ setting them off was routinely available at a small cost. The decision was in the hands of a local jury as opposed to being determined by oath swearing or trial by battle. Indeed, the rationality of the new procedures was one of their merits canvassed in *Glanvill*.[66] The case was heard in a court presided over by the king's judges as opposed to the court of a lord or the court of the hundred or wapentake presided over by the sheriff. And the whole procedure could be speedy. Indeed, speed was specifically aimed at in novel disseisin, where the jury was to give its verdict even if the defendant did not turn up, whereas other litigation could be dragged out ad infinitum by a whole series of non-appearances.

The new procedures appeared very differently from the perspective of great barons, for they had the potential to harm their jurisdictional control over their tenants. If two tenants by knight service were in dispute over who should rightfully hold land from a particular lord, then the lord was bound to think that the proper venue for the case was his own honorial court.[67] Equally, the lord would think that his court was the proper forum for any dispute between himself and a tenant over failure to perform services or over the succession to a fee. With the new procedures, however, it was easy for litigants to remove cases from the court of the lord. In an action over right, the defendant could do so by putting himself on the grand assize. At least such a case would have started in the lord's court, but if the issue was simply one of disseisin, then a writ of novel disseisin would take the case at once before the king's judges, bypassing the lord's court altogether.[68] If the disseisor had the lord's favour, or indeed was the lord himself, the plaintiff had every reason to do just that, thereby escaping a court that must always have been dominated by the lord's interests.[69] The fear of comeback from a novel disseisin action must also have deterred lords from disciplining tenants by simply seizing their land without legal process.[70] As for the assize of mort d'ancestor, this too started the case from scratch before the king's judges. So much the better for the plaintiff if it was the lord himself who was denying him entry into his inheritance. Lords inevitably now found it more difficult to prevent the succession of an unwelcome tenant. One comment on a particular decree of Henry II probably reflects well enough the lordly view of developments as a whole: 'the king had made an ordinance in his kingdom, which caused the barons of the country much harm, whereby each lost his court by a false oath'.[71]

OTHER COURTS AND STRUCTURES
OF GOVERNMENT

Courts held by great lords for their tenants by knight service were not the only private courts. All lords of manors held manorial courts for their peasant tenants, courts that dealt with such matters as succession to the tenements and disputes over services, as well as minor cases of disorder. Such manorial courts, unmentioned in Magna Carta, were entirely under the jurisdiction of the lord. Lords could also enjoy some share of the king's jurisdiction, either through a specific grant from the king or through long usage. These 'liberties', as they were called, included 'infangenthief', which gave the lord the right to try, and execute on his gallows, a petty thief taken red handed on his property. The liberty could be attached to a manorial court. It could also be attached to a hundred.[72] In 1215 perhaps some 250 of the roughly 630 hundreds and wapentakes were in private rather than royal hands. The balance across the country was uneven. Nearly all the hundreds were private in Devon, Oxfordshire and Sussex. Nearly all were royal in Warwickshire and Lincolnshire. Many hundreds had long been in the hands of bishops and abbots. Others were held by great secular lords. Indeed Magna Carta comes in the middle of the period in which lords were busily securing grants of hundreds from the king. Here they gained some compensation for the inroads of the common law. John made fifty-five such grants, mostly to lay lords, Henry III made 108. William de Ferrers, earl of Derby, started John's reign with no private hundreds. By the end of it he had six, three through an inheritance, three by grant of the king. Thomas Basset, likewise, gained from John the hundreds of Bullingdon and North Gate outside Oxford. He also had the hundred, 'my hundred', of Colyton in Devon.[73] The rights of lords in private hundreds varied. In some the sheriff still entered and shared the profits. In the most privileged, he did not enter at all and handed the king's writs (so those summoning juries, executing verdicts and collecting debts) to the bailiff of the lord.[74] In most private hundreds it would be the lord's bailiff who presided over the hundred court and heard the view of frankpledge every Michaelmas, although one would never have thought so from chapter 42 of the 1217 Charter, which dealt simply with the exactions of the sheriff. Equally exempt from the jurisdiction of the sheriffs were many of the privileged cities and boroughs mentioned in chapter 13 of the Charter. They had the right to choose their own officials, who presided over the town court and answered directly to the exchequer for the farm.[75] The Londoners had the right both to choose their own sheriffs and, by John's concession in 1215, their mayor.

Lords certainly derived power, money and status from their manorial, liberty and honorial courts. Sometimes the same meetings carried out all three types of business and the courts tended to merge together, which made them all the more impressive. The relationship between the liberties and royal government has been much debated by historians. From one point of view, they can be seen as fitting naturally and harmoniously into a hierarchy of courts, with the king's at the top.[76] Certainly the king had no objection to liberties as such and was often prepared to grant them away to make money or reward service, as did John and Henry III. Those with private hundreds, such as the abbot of Bury St Edmunds, were very aware that they could be confiscated by the king, and ran them in that light.[77] The procedures in private courts, moreover, often imitated those found in the courts of the king. Yet, on the other hand, for judges, sheriffs and officials of the exchequer, the liberties were a pain in the neck. Again and again sheriffs explained their failure to raise debts and produce litigants and jurors on the grounds that they had handed the order to a private hundredal bailiff who had then done nothing about it. In the 1270s and 1280s Edward I made a determined effort to check 'by what warrant' all the liberties were held.[78]

THE KING'S MILITARY FORCES

The unpopularity of John's rule, and the exigencies of his situation, placed a premium on one ultimate source of power, a power that stood behind everything he wished to do. This was his ability to use force. In its highest degree, force meant armies, armies with which the king might put down revolts in England, dominate Britain and Ireland, and maintain and recover the continental possessions. John in one way was permanently armed. He had at any one time around a hundred household knights, who could form the core of royal armies. He also had military forces in the localities, for all the sheriffs and castellans had under their command crossbowmen and serjeants, whom they paid from local revenues, varying the numbers up and down according to the situation. When he was forming an army, John supplemented his household knights in two main ways. For all his campaigns, he summoned his tenants-in-chief to provide him with knights, as they were obliged to do by the terms of their tenure. John also summoned the knights holding from baronies that had come into his hands.[79] Whereas many tenants-in-chief were allowed to pay scutage in place of service, many others did indeed come personally with their due contingents. Such contingents, however, were far smaller than those on which scutage was owed. The great northern baron Gilbert de Gant owed scutage on over sixty fees, yet was expected to bring to royal armies only six or ten knights.[80] How this discrepancy between nominal obligation and actual performance had come about is obscure, but it certainly preceded John's reign.[81] It may in part have been a quid pro quo for the service lasting longer than the customary forty days. Even in producing these reduced contingents, however, John's tenants-in-chief often did not pay their way. Instead, for their maintenance during a campaign, for example in Ireland in 1210 and Poitou in 1214, they received money in the form of loans from the king. Loans left open whether the service was being performed as part of a tenurial obligation, but since John rarely asked for the money back, he was in practice paying wages. It was with wages, straight out, that the king recruited the second type of force that strengthened his armies, namely paid knights recruited from abroad, notably from Flanders and Brabant, both great sources for mercenary soldiers.

Essentially then, if John wanted to muster and maintain armies of any size, he had to pay for them. For much of the reign, given his buoyant finances, he was able to do so. Indeed, he may well have invented the loan system that he used to support his forces.[82] In contemporary terms, he was certainly able to raise armies of some size. The one that he took to Ireland in 1210 consisted of around 800 named knights and 1,500 serjeants and crossbowmen. Even in December 1215 just one of John's field armies included forty-seven household knights, and another 403 knights mostly recruited from the continent. The knights were divided up into 'constabularies', each about twenty-five strong, which gives a good indication of how the force was organized. One of these constabularies was commanded by the Anonymous of Béthune's patron, Robert de Béthune.[83]

In an ideal world John should never, of course, have needed an army to put down internal revolt. His keeping of the peace and dispensation of justice should have justified his exaction of revenue and insistence on his rights. His subjects would see the need for the second, the extraction of revenue, in order to enjoy the first, the keeping of the peace. Unfortunately, by 1215 it was very hard to see any such balance in the rule of King John. Hence the need for Magna Carta.

7

The Rule of the King: John and His Predecessors

The structure of royal government placed formidable power in the king's hands, both to do good and to do ill. How the ill, in the view of the king's subjects, came to predominate is the subject of this chapter. Its focus is primarily on the rule of King John, yet his predecessors too must shoulder some of the blame. That was the view at the time. According to Ralph of Coggeshall, the barons demanded that John 'abolish the evil customs ... which both his father and brother once introduced, together with the abuses which he had added'.[1]

HENRY I (r. 1100–1135) AND HIS 1100 CORONATION CHARTER

Coggeshall thus pointed the finger at Henry II and Richard I as well as John. Yet he could easily have gone further back. Immediately after his coronation in 1100, Henry I had issued a Charter abolishing the evil customs that had oppressed the kingdom.[2] These, as the Charter went on to make clear, were the customs of Henry's brother, William Rufus, and even his father, William the Conqueror. When the opposition in 1214–15 demanded that John confirm Henry's Charter, it was not for merely symbolic reasons. It was because the Charter, in its details, covered matters that still seemed very relevant. Many of the grievances against John, therefore, had much earlier roots. The 1100 Charter, like Magna Carta, dealt with such issues as relief, wardships, marriages and the rights of widows. It also dealt with debts, wills, amercements and the royal forest, which again were all subjects of concern in Magna Carta.

Henry I certainly did not keep his promises in the 1100 Charter. Indeed, his financial exactions, as revealed in the pipe roll of 1130, were not, in real terms, far short of John's.[3] Yet Henry's successor, his nephew Stephen, was not made to repeat Henry's Charter on his accession in 1135. The reason was that, given Stephen's character, his baronial background and the political situation, a charter restricting him seemed hardly necessary. With the collapse of royal power in the ensuing civil war, as Stephen was challenged for the throne by Henry's daughter, Matilda, and then by her son, the future Henry II, individual barons concentrated on extracting charters, making concessions to themselves. A charter making concessions to the kingdom as a whole was not on the agenda.

HENRY II (r. 1154–1189)

Henry II was a bully with brains and brawn. His overriding aim in England was to rebuild royal power after its disintegration under his predecessor. That he certainly achieved. Up to a point, the way Coggeshall linked Henry, when it came to evil customs, with Richard and John was unfair. After all, in developing the legal actions of the common law, Henry did more than any king in the medieval period to create a solid base for monarchy – a base that reached out beyond the baronage to the knights and free tenants who were the main users and beneficiaries of the procedures. Magna Carta attacked many aspects of royal rule. The one thing it did not attack were the common-law assizes that Henry had introduced. Indeed, between chapters 17 and 19, it made them more available. The king was not, therefore, to be reduced to a mere feudal overlord. His justice was in demand.

There was also, around the time of Magna Carta, a feeling that things had been better under Henry. Thus the 1217 Charter, in three places, tried to put back the clock to what had been 'customary' in his time, customary that is when it came to the enclosure of riverbanks (chapter 20), the levying of scutage (chapter 44) and the sheriffs' exactions in the hundred courts (chapter 42). Clearly Henry's government had acquired a golden glow. That was understandable. The work of Thomas K. Keefe has shown that, with some exceptions, Henry placed limited financial pressure on his earls and greater barons. Keefe's conclusion was that the contest between monarchy and baronage over administrative abuses and financial exactions which led to Magna Carta had hardly begun in Henry's reign.[4]

This is not, however, the whole story. In 1173–4 Henry II faced a massive revolt against his rule.[5] In some ways, this was very different from the revolt that produced Magna Carta. At its heart was a conflict between Henry, on the one side, and his sons and their mother, Eleanor of Aquitaine, on the other. The English barons who joined the revolt, themselves in a minority, put together no general manifesto and hoped their wrongs would be righted simply by the benevolent rule of Henry's eldest son, also called Henry. He was known as 'the Young King', following his coronation in 1170 with a view to his acting as his father's deputy in England. Yet the grievances of the earls of Chester, Ferrers, Norfolk and Leicester over claims to castles, lands and rights, and over heavy fines and amercements, were very comparable to those of the rebels of 1215. Although, moreover, Henry II had earls as leading ministers, he was reluctant to create new earldoms and refused to accept that old ones were 'in their essence hereditary'.[6] During the 'anarchy' of Stephen's reign, there had been a proliferation of earldoms and the expansion of their local power. Henry was determined to put a stop to it. There were twenty-three earls at the start of his reign. By its end there were twelve, and only the earl of Chester had control of the local government in his shire. Grievances over this were still there under John. Gilbert de Gant's claim to be earl of Lincoln, recognized by Prince Louis in 1216, went back to a grant of King Stephen that Henry II had refused to recognize.[7] Royal policy with regard to earldoms was closely related to policy over castles. Here Henry's actions, both at the start of the reign and after the 1173–4 revolt, were a major factor in shifting the ratio between royal and baronial castles from 1 to 5 in 1154 down to 1 to 2 in 1214.[8] Against this background, it is not surprising that Magna Carta, in chapter 52, put on the agenda the disseisins of Henry II as things to be dealt with after John returned from or decided not to go on his prospective crusade. The Articles of the Barons had gone further and demanded that those disseised by Henry should have 'right' without delay, by judgement of their peers, in the king's court.[9]

The demands of 1215 revealed another aspect of Henry's rule, namely his administration of the royal forest. When John, in 1215, offered to remedy the 'evil customs' of his father 'by the counsel of his faithful men', the forest would have been top of the agenda.[10] Everyone agreed that the extensive boundaries, which made it such a burden to wide sections of society, had been the work of Henry's notorious chief forester, Alan de Neville. His forest eyre in 1175, partly designed as punishment for the rebellion, produced debts worth an exorbitant £12,305, far more than the total of any later eyre.[11] De Neville would doubtless have claimed that he was merely restoring the bounds of the forest to their extent in 1135, before the losses of Stephen's reign. Whether or not that was true, when the Unknown Charter in 1215 called for the deforestation of Henry II's afforestations, it made no distinction between his restorations and creations *de novo*. All the areas he had brought within the bounds of the forest were to be removed from it, and thus no longer to be subject to forest law. In the liberated areas people could now hunt freely, cut down trees, erect buildings and create new arable land without fear of punishment. If implemented, the demand would have reduced the royal forest to little more than the king's demesne woods. John evidently put up a stiff resistance to this demand, and, in Magna Carta, only conceded the immediate deforestation of his own afforestations, which were insignificant compared to his father's.[12] It was left to the Forest Charter of 1217 to return to the charge, and abolish the afforestations of Henry II once they had been established by knightly jurors.

There was, of course, one final stigma to Henry's rule, the murder of the archbishop of Canterbury, Thomas Becket, in his own cathedral. This terrible event appalled Christian Europe and within three years Becket had been canonized by the pope. Henry claimed that he had no murdering intent. His words, spoken in anger, had been taken all too literally by the knights who carried out the deed. But the murder, nonetheless, seemed to encapsulate his dynasty's capacity for rancour and malevolence, the very things John promised to forgo at the end of the Charter. If, moreover, Becket cast a shadow over the dynasty, he was a shining light for conscientious churchmen, demonstrating all the courage, endurance and ultimate sacrifice that might be necessary to protect the liberty of the church. For no one was this more true than John's own archbishop, Stephen Langton. He enhanced the image of Becket's murder on the seal of the archbishop, like Becket he spent his exile at the Burgundian monastery of Pontigny, and in 1220, in a great international ceremony, he translated Becket's body from its old shrine to its splendid new one in Canterbury cathedral.[13]

RICHARD I (r. 1189–1199)

If anyone could rescue the reputation of the dynasty, it was Henry's successor, his son Richard. (The Young King had died in 1183.) Henry had failed to go on crusade, hence the misfortunes of his last years, thought Roger of Howden. Richard, on the other hand, both went to the Holy Land and won eternal fame there through feats of arms. For Ralph of Coggeshall, Richard had another saving grace – his ostentatious piety. He delighted in the divine office, and did not hurry through it so that he could attend to business or have a meal. He adorned his chapel with precious vestments and rewarded its choral clerks with many gifts, sometimes conducting their singing and indeed joining in with it. In Coggeshall's view, Richard's general treatment of the church was also commendable. He appointed suitable churchmen as bishops and abbots and did so quickly, not prolonging vacancies so he could take the revenues.[14] Initially, moreover, Richard's rule had not been financially oppressive. He had certainly raised large sums at the start of his reign, but that had been partly achieved by selling off lands and rights.

Here, however, the chronicler William of Newburgh was critical. In granting away so much, was Richard not showing a 'lack of care' for his kingdom? Indeed, had he not said, 'I would sell London if I could find a suitable buyer.'[15] Nowhere was Richard's self-confident irresponsibility clearer than in his treatment of John. John was already lord of Ireland, and count of Mortain in Normandy. Richard now married him to Isabella, countess of Gloucester, whose inheritance included the lordship of Glamorgan. Richard also gave him six royal castles and total control of seven counties, so that their revenues completely disappeared from the pipe rolls. Having thus empowered John, he then provoked him. It is here that Arthur first enters the picture. Born in 1187, Arthur was Richard and John's cousin, the son of their deceased brother, Geoffrey, by his marriage to Constance, the heiress to Brittany. On his way to the Holy Land, Richard suddenly recognized Arthur as his heir. The aim was to seal an alliance with Tancred, the ruler of Sicily, under which Arthur was to marry Tancred's daughter.

Not surprisingly, John was furious. In a series of confrontations, he overthrew William Longchamp, whom Richard had left behind as governor of England, and gained recognition as Richard's successor. Then, when Richard, in December 1192, was captured on his way back from his crusade, eventually becoming a prisoner of the Emperor Henry VI, John announced that his brother was dead, and did homage to the king of France, Philip Augustus, for the continental dominions. Philip proceeded to overrun a large part of Normandy.

Richard finally arrived back in England in March 1194. He quickly extinguished the embers of John's revolt, and then spent the rest of his reign on the continent. There, in warfare against King Philip, he recovered much of Normandy and reasserted authority more widely over the Angevin dominions. During this period, Richard certainly 'cared' for England but he cared chiefly for its money, money he desperately needed to support his continental wars. The years between 1194 and 1199 marked a significant ratcheting up in the financial demands that led ultimately to Magna Carta.

Richard's revenue from England between 1194 and 1198, as calculated by Nick Barratt from the pipe rolls, averaged some £25,000 a year, this against a little over £23,000 averaged by Henry II in the last eight years of his reign.[16] Richard's pipe roll revenue, however, was on top of all the money he raised from England to pay his ransom to the emperor. Just how much of the £90,000 eventually handed over came from England, as opposed to Normandy and John's other dominions is unknown, but it must have been a significant proportion of it. A tax was levied in England in 1193–4 at a quarter value of everyone's rents and movable property. There was a precedent for this in the 'Saladin tithe', levied in 1188 to support the crusade proclaimed by the pope following the fall of Jerusalem the previous year, but then the rate had been a tenth. The quarter of 1193–4 was the highest rate of taxation in medieval England. The levy should obviously have raised more than the £57,000 of John's great tax of 1207 when the rate was only a thirteenth, although the collection in 1207 may have been more efficient. One can at least be sure that if the yield from Richard's tax could be added into his total revenues between 1194 and 1198, then it would boost their annual average to way over the £25,000 revealed by the pipe rolls.[17]

Richard's ordinary revenues, leaving aside the tax, were also achieved despite a significant decline in easy money from crown land. Over the course of the twelfth century, the great stock of land in the king's hands at the time of Domesday Book had dwindled, being given away to reward service and buy support. The results are graphically laid out in the pipe rolls where the county accounts have long lists of deductions from the farm because of 'land given away'. The losses had been particularly severe during the turmoil of Stephen's reign. Henry II had tenaciously retained the land that was left and indeed reversed some of the losses. Richard, on the other hand, in the great sell-off at the start of his reign, undid his father's work 'virtually overnight'.[18] The result was that John inherited a royal demesne worth over £2,000 a year less than in 1189. Had this land still been there, it would have helped mitigate some of the grievances that led to Magna Carta. Revenue from crown land was politically uncontentious, coming from selling the crops and taking the rents of the peasants, hence the way chapter 25 of the Charter exempted the king's demense manors from the restrictions placed on money raised above the county farms. Once the demesne was lost, the difference had to be made up by exploiting more unpopular sources of revenue.

Richard's government had done that in ways very much reflected in the demands of 1215. Indeed, even before the meeting at Runnymede, John had volunteered to extirpate Richard's 'evil customs' as opposed to offering merely to take counsel about those of Henry II.[19] In 1194 Richard's government imposed increments above the farm of many counties. This meant that the sheriffs had to account first for the farm and then an additional fixed sum, 'the increment', demanded above it. Such additional exactions were specifically banned in chapter 25 of the Charter. In 1198 there was an oppressive forest eyre, and a drive against widows: forty were forced to offer a total of 1,689 marks for permission to stay single or marry whom they wished. The forcing of widows into remarriage would be banned under chapter 8 of Magna Carta.[20] Richard also extracted inheritance payments way above the Charter's £100 'relief' laid down for a barony: the 'fine to inherit' of the Gloucestershire baron Robert of Berkeley was £1,000; that of the great baronial leader in 1215, Eustace de Vescy, was 1,300 marks.[21]

Richard's magnates also felt threatened by arbitrary disseisins, unjust fines and denial of justice, all things that the Charter stood against. Robert de Ros was disseised of his lands for allowing a

French prisoner to escape and had to offer 1,200 marks to get them back; Walter de Lacy offered 3,100 marks to recover the king's benevolence and seisin of his lands; the Lincolnshire lord Simon of Kyme was penalized to the tune of 1,000 marks for allowing foreign ships and merchants to depart from Boston fair in Lincolnshire.[22] When Roger Bigod offered King Richard 1,000 marks to succeed to the earldom of Norfolk, included in the fine was the concession that Roger's brother, Hugh, should not be placed in any of the lands of their father save 'by judgement of the king's court made by his peers'. The implication was that if fortune's wheel swung Roger down and Hugh up, then Richard might simply transfer the lands from one to the other without legal process. The matter did not end there. A few years later, Roger offered 100 marks not to be disseised of lands claimed by Hugh save by judgement of the king's court. The offer was accepted by Hubert Walter as chief justiciar, in charge of the home government, only for Richard to intervene from overseas and bump the fine up to 700 marks.[23] Richard's disseisins remained of concern in 1215 and they were treated in the same way as those of Henry II. Thus, under the Articles of the Barons, the victims, with certain qualifications, were to secure redress without delay by judgement of their peers in the king's court, although under chapter 52 of the Charter the issue was postponed until the termination of John's prospective crusade.

Coggeshall gives a vivid picture of Richard in the last years of his reign. When petitioners came to court, they could glimpse him with his private entourage, affable and relaxed, enjoying games and jokes. But when they approached his presence, they found a king whose menacing glares, violent gestures and ferocious words made him seem every bit a raging lion.[24] Coggeshall's verdict of the reign was despairing:

> No age can remember, no history can record any preceding king, even those who reigned for a long time, who exacted and received so much money from his kingdom, as that king exacted and amassed in the five years after he returned from captivity.[25]

It was in the light of Richard's malpractices, as well as Henry's, that John's supporters in England, before his accession, promised the assembled earls and barons that he would restore everyone to their rights, if they accepted him as king.[26]

JOHN AND THE CHURCH

John on his accession in 1199 was very aware of his brother's unpopularity. Indeed, eager, as he said, to abolish 'evil customs', he immediately reduced the excessive charges Richard had imposed 'by will rather than reason' for issuing charters and letters.[27] When John made peace with the king of France and settled an early quarrel with the Cistercians, agreeing to found what became Beaulieu abbey in Hampshire, Coggeshall thought a new age was dawning.[28]

It was not to be. John's tumultuous and tempestuous quarrel with the church was a centrepiece of his reign, and had a major influence on the content of Magna Carta. Chapter 1 of the Charter set the church free. In doing so, it followed the Coronation Charter of Henry I, but it also went further. John, as testimony to his good faith, referred to another charter. This, as he said, was a charter conceding 'the liberty of elections, which is deemed to be of the greatest importance and most necessary for the English church'. John was here referring to his charter of November 1214, which he had reissued in January 1215. It had then been confirmed by Pope Innocent III, as Magna Carta said in chapter 1.[29] The liberty of elections meant that bishops should henceforth be chosen, without royal interference, by the cathedral monks or clergy, while abbots would be elected by their monks. As a result, conscientious churchmen hoped that prelates would no longer be secular-minded royal servants, but men committed to their spiritual mission. They would also, under the terms of the November 1214 charter, be elected quickly, thus dealing with a second great evil, namely the way that the king kept bishoprics and abbeys vacant so that he could take their revenues. Admittedly John, a master at qualifying his concessions, was still allowed, under the terms of the charter, to refuse consent to elections, if he could show 'a reasonable and legitimate cause'. Nonetheless, the charter was a great triumph for the church, which was why it was confirmed in Magna Carta.

John granted his freedom of election charter in November 1214 because of immediate political pressures, as we will see. But the concession was also in partial settlement of his more general quarrel with the church. That quarrel had begun with the death of his archbishop of Canterbury, Hubert Walter, in 1205. Walter had been just the kind of archbishop that kings liked. An efficient and resourceful administrator, he had grown up in government service. He believed in reform of the church, and was the first archbishop to place Becket's martyrdom on his seal. But he was also happy to combine the archbishopric with the justiciarship under Richard and with the chancellorship under John, the total reverse of Becket. John wanted another archbishop like him, and thought he had the man in John de Grey, bishop of Norwich. But the monks of Canterbury, the electoral body, were not unanimous in their choice, some going instead for their sub-prior. The dispute was referred to the pope, Innocent III, who, in 1206, ordained a fresh election and ensured the votes went to Stephen Langton. Langton was a professor at the University of Paris. His lectures and commentaries on the Bible, and his division of it into chapters, had built him a towering reputation. John was amazed and infuriated by the choice. University professors did not swim into his orbit very often and he did not know this one. That Langton was English (as the pope stressed) counted for little beside his lecturing for twenty years in the capital of John's greatest enemy, the king of France. The contrast with Hubert Walter, whose learning was ridiculed but whose loyalty was absolute, could not have been more stark. The custom that the king should influence the election of the archbishop had been flouted.

John, therefore, refused to accept Langton. Henry II and Richard might well have done the same. John could not be blamed for his predicament. He was just unlucky, the victim of growing papal authority and Pope Innocent's determination to assert it. In March 1208, with John obdurate, Innocent imposed an Interdict on England. In November 1209 he followed this up with the personal excommunication of the king:

> Oh what a horrible and miserable spectacle it was to see in every city the sealed doors of the churches, Christians shut out from entry as though they were dogs, the cessation of divine office, the withholding of the sacrament of the body and blood of our Lord, the people no longer flocking to the famous celebration of saints' days, the bodies of the dead not given to burial according to Christian rites, the stink infecting the air and the horrible sight filling with horror the minds of the living.[30]

This was Ralph of Coggeshall's description of the Interdict imposed on France in 1200. His comments on the much longer English

Interdict were so heated that after John's reconciliation with the church he excised them.[31] The reconciliation, however, took some time in coming. John would not give way, although nearly all the English bishops went into exile, a remarkable testimony to papal authority. In retaliation, John seized the revenues of the church, making as much as £100,000 from them. The Cistercians suffered in particular. Coggeshall's hopes for John's reign had been utterly dashed.[32] They were also dashed in another area.

THE LOSS OF NORMANDY

At the start of his reign, in 1199, John had secured Normandy and England without difficulty. Much more problematic were Anjou and Maine, Maine being the frontier county between Anjou and Normandy, with its great city of Le Mans where Henry II had been born. In these areas, John's nephew, Arthur, based in his mother's province of Brittany, had much support. He was also supported by King Philip Augustus. Yet John beat off their challenge. In May 1200, by the Treaty of Le Goulet, Philip recognized his title to all the continental possessions, and accepted that Arthur should hold Brittany from John as duke of Normandy. Ralph of Coggeshall looked forward to an age of peace in which the terrible financial burdens imposed by Richard's wars might cease.[33] Later in the year, John seemed to strengthen his continental position further. That August, his union with Isabella of Gloucester having been annulled (although he kept her lands), he married Isabella of Angoulême, thus gaining possession of her strategically placed county in south-western France. Here, however, there was a difficulty, for Isabella was already betrothed to the greatest of all the Poitevin nobles, Hugh de Lusignan, count of La Marche. Receiving no compensation from John, Hugh appealed to the court of King Philip for justice. When John failed to appear to answer the charges against him, he was sentenced to forfeit all the continental possessions. In July 1202 Philip followed this up by taking Arthur's homage for all those possessions, barring Normandy. Philip was determined to have Normandy for himself.[34]

At first, there seemed little likelihood of Philip making this a reality. Arthur had set off at once for Poitou, the strategic county between Gascony and Anjou, and besieged the castle at Mirebeau, where John's mother, Eleanor of Aquitaine, now in her seventies, was valiantly upholding her son's cause. John acted with decision. He covered the eighty miles between Le Mans and Mirebeau in forty-eight hours, and, arriving on 1 August 1202, won a comprehensive victory, capturing Arthur and the Lusignans as well.[35] It was a false dawn. In 1203 King Philip conquered Anjou and Maine. In 1204 he completed the conquest of Normandy, taking Rouen on 24 June. He then went on to secure much of Poitou. John retained two great and grim castles between Tours and Poitiers, namely Chinon, defended by Hubert de Burgh, and Loches, by Gerard d'Athée, both men who were named in Magna Carta. But in 1205 these castles too, deprived of help, were captured, despite a long and determined defence. Further south, with John's authority weakened by the death of Eleanor of Aquitaine in April 1204, King Alfonso VIII of Castile invaded Gascony. He had married Eleanor, a daughter of Henry II and Eleanor of Aquitaine (so John's sister), and maintained that Gascony should come to him as her dowry on Eleanor of Aquitaine's death. It was not until 1206 that John was able to launch an expedition with the aim of reversing his losses. He managed to expel Alfonso's forces from Gascony, and then got as far north as Angers, before retreating in the face of King Philip's army. In October 1206 a truce between John and Philip left the latter in control of Poitiers, and all his conquests north of the Loire, so Anjou, Maine and Normandy.

In just a few years, the Angevin empire had been destroyed, thus transforming the European balance of power. Most crucial of all was the loss of Normandy itself. In terms of resources, it was by far the most valuable of the continental possessions, with revenues much the same as England's. Its loss was not entirely John's fault. At the level of the knightly society, the ties between England and Normandy had long been weak. In the twelfth century, of the seventy leading families in Warwickshire and Leicestershire, only seven held lands in Normandy, and all but one had lost them by 1200.[36] Defending the continental possessions was also going to be far more difficult for John than for Henry II. Philip Augustus (r. 1180–1223) had a ruthlessness and political ability that his easy-going father, Louis VII (r. 1137–80), completely lacked. His supreme aim was the destruction of the Angevin empire. Henry II's resources had dwarfed those of the French kings. By the early 1200s that was no longer the case, for French revenues had been increasing very fast. In terms of their total resources, the two kings John and Philip were now just about evenly matched. While, moreover, Philip's money came from a compact royal demesne adjoining the Norman frontier (Rouen is only eighty-five miles from Paris), much of John's had to be transported from England across the Channel.[37] John had also inherited Norman defences far weaker than they had been in 1189. During Richard's captivity, Philip had made advances in the frontier region, which Richard, for all his valour, never totally reversed. In particular, Philip held onto the mighty castle of Gisors, rebuilt by Henry II to defend the frontier along the river Epte. The French king now controlled much of the Norman county of the Vexin to the west of the river.[38] In order to fill the gap, Richard built his stupendous castle at Les Andelys on the Seine, which he called Château Gaillard, but this showed all too clearly that the old frontier had been lost.[39]

For all these problems, John should have made a much better fist of defending his empire. After all, there remained a substantial body of Anglo-Norman landholders with every interest in keeping England and Normandy together. If kingdom and duchy came under separate and warring rulers, these landholders were highly likely to lose their lands in one or the other. Of the 199 Norman tenants-in-chief in 1172, some 107, or their descendants, held lands on both sides of the Channel in 1204.[40] Likewise (and the two groups overlapped) many of the greatest English barons, including the earls of Pembroke, Chester, Warenne, Arundel, Clare and Hereford had substantial interests in Normandy. John should have been able to mobilize these men to support the duchy's defence. His failure effectively to do so was due to the speed of events, which in turn owed much to his own mistakes and conduct.

There were reasons for John's marriage to Isabella of Angoulême, but it was a mistake, a product of arrogant over-confidence, not to conciliate and compensate Hugh de Lusignan afterwards. The same characteristics were displayed in John's treatment of William des Roches. To William, the dominant magnate in Anjou, he owed much of his victory at Mirebeau, but he then broke his promise to take William's advice over what to do with Arthur.[41] The result was William's defection and the unravelling of John's hold on Anjou and Maine. This in turn undermined the loyalty of nobles in southern Normandy, who decided to throw in their lot with their neighbours in Maine and Anjou.[42] Meanwhile, John's cruel treatment of the prisoners taken at Mirebeau tarnished his reputation – and then came the disappearance of Arthur and rumours of his murder. In September 1203 Arthur's stepfather, the ruler of Brittany, Guy de Thouars, deserted, which meant John had to divert resources to defend the Norman/Breton frontier. John also failed as a diplomat, for he was unable to maintain the alliances with the counts of Flanders and Boulogne, on which Richard had relied. John's rule should have been most secure in central Normandy between Bayeux and Rouen, but here too he made fatal mistakes. He appointed a series of unpopular seneschals, and stationed his mercenary captain, Louvrecaire, not on the frontiers but at Falaise, where he behaved as though he was in enemy territory.[43] And then finally there was John's own personal conduct. It is surely extraordinary that when Philip began his final conquest of Normandy in the summer of 1203, John never once confronted him in the field. He made a single, half-hearted attempt to relieve the siege of Chateau Gaillard, which came to nothing. In the end he slunk out of Normandy in December 1203, like a thief in the night. He was thus not there at all when Chateau Gaillard and Rouen fell next year. John presumably calculated that he lacked the forces to put up any resistance, but this was in large part due to his own failure of nerve. The situation would have been very different under Richard.

The loss of Normandy was a watershed in John's reign and on the road to Magna Carta. Even today, looking at where John's charters and letters were issued before 1204 – Chateau Gaillard, Rouen, Caen, Bayeux, Le Mans, Angers, Poitiers, Chinon – one has a sense of shock at the places and the power that had been lost. John could not possibly let them go. His overriding aim became to increase his English revenues and build up the treasure needed to recover his continental possessions. The grievances he thus created were the single most important cause of the Charter. A great treasure, to buy allies and hire soldiers, was certainly necessary, for the recovery of Normandy, in particular, was always going to be problematic. King Philip was now much richer thanks to its revenues. His rule there was firmly based. He brought the duchy peace, introduced new French lords, and also provided opportunities for existing families, often of second rank.[44] For his campaigns in both 1206 and 1214, John had to land far to the south at La Rochelle in Poitou. Since he had lost both Anjou and Maine to the north, he would have to advance through hostile territory merely to enter Normandy.

This raised another problem, one revealed in the demands of 1215. A significant number of barons had lost lands in Normandy in 1204. But few if any had stakes in Poitou or Anjou. If John's campaigns were confined to those areas, as in fact they were, then those disinherited in Normandy had little to gain from them, hence the resistance to John's campaign in 1214 and the 'Poitevin' scutage levied to support it. In 1215 the Unknown Charter demanded that overseas service be confined to Normandy and Brittany, so it was not to be owed for Poitou, Anjou or Gascony at all.

John also made less profit than might have been expected from the tenurial revolution consequent on the loss of Normandy. Both Philip and John quickly decided that it was impossible to serve two masters. Those Anglo-Norman landholders who remained in Normandy, subject to King Philip, thus had their lands in England confiscated by King John, and vice versa.[45] Very few imitated William Marshal's success in keeping his lordships in both the kingdom and the duchy. In his case, both kings calculated that they had more to lose than to gain from breaking with him. John, for his part, knew that to evict the Marshal from his Welsh and Irish lordships would take a major campaign, which was the last thing he wanted in 1204. Nonetheless, the Marshal's refusal to join the 1206 expedition against King Philip showed how right John was to force the choice on everyone else. The result was that John gained a great windfall from the confiscations in England. He was careful not to use this land in any major way to compensate those who had lost their Norman estates. That, he knew, would diminish enthusiasm for the eventual campaign of recovery. Instead, he gave significant amounts to such leading servants as Geoffrey fitzPeter, Thomas and Alan Basset, William de Cantilupe and Peter de Maulay. These gifts were only held at John's pleasure. He could revoke them at any time, as he might want to do if he was tempting Normans back into his allegiance. Nonetheless, the beneficiaries, threatened with such losses, must have had mixed feelings about Normandy's recovery. John's best policy might have been to retain the lands in his own hands and run them for profit, thus alleviating some measure of his financial problems. That he was unable to follow such a course suggests the weakness of his position. He needed to use the lands to consolidate his core support. In that, he set a pattern for the future. The lands of the Normans were the great bank on which kings of England drew for patronage in the thirteenth century.

JOHN'S ITINERARY

In amassing his treasure, John had one great advantage over his predecessors. He could be far more hands on. Henry II had spent roughly half his reign in his continental possessions. Richard, apart from a few months in 1189 and 1194, had been entirely absent from his kingdom. John, after his return to England in December 1203, was there almost continuously for the rest of his reign, apart from campaigns in France in 1206 and 1214, in Ireland in 1210 and Wales in 1211.[46] In so far as John had favourite residences in England, they were at his castles and houses in the southern half of the kingdom. In that respect he was repeating the pattern of his predecessors, going back to Anglo-Saxon times. At the top of John's list was London, where he largely divided his time between Westminster, the Tower and (taking it over during the Interdict) the archbishop's palace at Lambeth. Then came Winchester, Marlborough, Clarendon, on the hill above Salisbury, and Woodstock, just north of Oxford. Yet none of these locations saw John stay there for long. In his sixteen-year reign, he spent 376 days in London and only 176 at Winchester. Windsor castle saw him in residence for about a hundred days. That he had to spend two weeks there between 9 and 25 June 1215, while Magna Carta was negotiated and peace established, testified to the quite exceptional importance of the business, as it also suggests how frustrated and impatient John must have been with it.

For the most part, John's itinerary was characterized by its ceaseless movement. In his sixteen-year reign, according to the calculations of Julie Kanter, he travelled some 79,612 miles, at an average of 12.5 miles a day. He rarely stayed anywhere long, averaging thirteen changes of location a month. Some 43 per cent of his time was spent in stays of just two or three days' duration; only 12 per cent in stays of a week or more. Not surprisingly, as John hawked, hunted and hurried along his way, he could become separated from his slow-moving baggage wagons. Hence he was not with them in 1216 when they were lost trying to take a short cut across an estuary of the Wash.[47] Although John spent the bulk of his time in the southern half of his kingdom, he knew England north of the Trent far better than any of his predecessors. He visited it in every year of his reign save the ones in which he was largely abroad. This is why Nottingham equals Windsor as his sixth most favoured residence, and also why the northerners played such a large part in the rebellion against him.[48] Several of these visits were related to the affairs of the king of Scots, which also drew north John's son, Henry III. But while Henry went straight there and back, thankful to return to his southern comforts, John took the opportunity to go on long tours of the northern counties. A life of such restless movement was unnecessary simply for the purposes of governing England. The itinerary of Henry III was far more sedentary. But that, John would bitingly have observed, was one reason why his son was so weak and poor.

John's travelling was, as we will see, closely linked to his raising of money. In that sense it lay behind many chapters in the Charter. It was also linked to some chapters more directly. This is most obvious with chapter 17, which directed that common pleas were not to follow the court but be heard in a fixed place. Clearly for litigants to have to chase after so mobile a king must have been infuriating. The Charter also dealt with another problem created by John's itinerary, although here not in so many words. This was the problem caused by the hawking to which the king, like many of his predecessors, was addicted.[49] The place for hawking was riverbanks, where the cranes, herons and ducks that the hawks targeted were found. Indeed, the very word for hawking, in both French and Latin, derived from the word for riverbank. The king's hawking had not been an issue under the absentee Richard. It very much was an issue under John. His near permanent presence in England and the wide areas over which he travelled exposed the country to royal hawking as never before. This was the background to chapter 47 of the Charter, which laid down that all the enclosures placed around riverbanks during John's time were to be removed. The 1217 Charter went further and sought to restore the enclosures to their state under Henry II. The men responsible for keeping the riverbanks were also unpopular and were brought within the investigation into local government abuses commissioned by chapter 48 of the Charter.

John's hawking also lay behind chapter 23 of the Charter limiting the obligation to build bridges at riverbanks. Bridges were a necessary adjunct of hawking because, whereas hawks themselves brought their victims back in their talons, falcons, the more prized sporting birds, knocked their prey down, making it necessary to

follow with dogs to retrieve the spoil. For that, bridges were necessary. In 1214 one official was allowed 60s for the costs of making
twenty bridges for the king's hunting.[50] What seems to have happened under John is that the ancient obligation to work on bridges
was extended to work on the numerous temporary structures being
constructed for the king's hawking. One can imagine villagers being
press-ganged to follow the king to carry out such work, much to the
annoyance of their lords, hence the chapter in the Charter. The
importance of the issue is seen in the way the chapter was refined at
Runnymede itself. The Articles of the Barons, in chapter 11, had
laid down that 'no vill' was to be amerced for failing to build
bridges, save in places where such work was lawfully due by ancient
custom. Perhaps members of the court itself, on its travels, had
been amercing villages for failing in such work. In Magna Carta,
chapter 23 added 'nor man' to 'No vill', thus protecting individuals
as well as villages. It also dropped the reference to amercements
and instead, getting to the heart of the issue, forbad enforced building of bridges altogether, save where the people were bound to it
'from ancient times and by law'.

The issue of the riverbanks and their bridges was clearly deeply
felt. It paled, however, before the grievances that arose from John's
financial policies.

JOHN'S REVENUES

John's task in increasing his revenues was made the harder and more
opprobrious by something for which he was not to blame, namely
the great inflation. As we have seen, prices tripled at the start of his
reign, before settling back to at least twice their former level.[51] John
had to run faster just to stand still. He also had to run down a bump-
ier track than his barons. The bulk of their income derived from
land. By selling their corn surpluses they could profit from the rising
market for agricultural produce. John, with a far smaller proportion
of income coming from land, thanks to the alienation of royal
demesne during the course of the twelfth century, could take advantage to a correspondingly smaller extent. He had to exploit his
subjects instead. This was not helped by any sense that the inflation justified John's exactions. Contemporaries were aware that

prices fluctuated with the harvest, not that there was a general inflationary trend. When the Charter fixed the baronial relief at £100, it was not with any awareness that, in real terms, £100 was worth half as much as twenty years before, nor that its value might be further whittled away by more inflation in the future.

In these difficult circumstances, as Nick Barratt has shown, John's success in raising his income and getting ahead of inflation was stupendous.[52] He invented no new sources of revenue. Rather, he exploited old ones to an unprecedented extent. Although a start was made in 1204, especially with the county farms (as we will see), it was from 1207 onwards that John really tightened the screw. The failure of the 1206 French campaign had shown the measure of the task and the need for enormous resources to meet it. John's English revenues averaged £24,000 a year between 1199 and 1202, so they were less than Richard's between 1194 and 1198 if we add in the large sums raised by the tax to pay the ransom. Coggeshall, of course, had thought Richard's revenues utterly rapacious, but in the second half of his reign John in cash terms (and it was cash that counted in public perception) far outstripped them. If we simply take those revenues for which there is record evidence, then between 1207 and 1212 they averaged £49,000 a year, so twice as much as at the start of the reign. If we make the guess that a £40,000 tallage imposed on the Jews in 1210 produced at least £30,000 (which is not at all unlikely), then the average rises to £54,000.[53] If we add in £100,000 worth of church revenues that John gained during the Interdict (itself an official figure), then the average reaches a stupendous £71,000. By 1214, John had saved up a treasure of £130,000. The income did not, of course, accrue in any average way. There was a great spike from the tax of 1207 (producing £57,000), which made the rise in ordinary revenues thereafter the more grievous. In all this, even by the £54,000 figure, John had got ahead of inflation, increasing his income in real terms compared to its level at the start of the reign. In real terms, he was making more even than Henry I in 1130, although Henry had been a king of fabled wealth, with a much higher proportion of his income flowing in effortlessly from royal land. If we include the Interdict revenues, then arguably John's exactions, in the words of Nick Barratt, 'represent the greatest level of exploitation seen in England since the Conquest'. Whether John was making more in real terms than Richard between 1194 and 1198, depends on the amount of money raised for the ransom. What is certain is that John's exactions seemed even less acceptable than those of his brother. Under Richard, there was a real sense that payments towards the ransom, however burdensome, were made in a good cause. There was no good cause under John. No wonder the central thrust of Magna Carta was to restrict his revenues.[54]

The Charter responded exactly to the detail of John's exactions.[55] Counties were to be 'at the ancient farms without any increment', declared chapter 25. That meant the sheriffs would no longer have to answer for the increments above the ancient farms, worth some £713 a year, imposed by Richard in 1194.[56] Chapter 25 was also designed to stop another way in which John tried to get more money from the counties. The background here was the realization that the revenue at the disposal of the sheriffs to pay the farm and increments still came to considerably more than both. One reaction would have been simply to impose additional increments, but in 1204 John tried something more ambitious. He made a considerable number of sheriffs 'custodians', who were to account every year for *all* the revenue behind the farm. As a result, between 1204 and 1212, the sheriffs owed the exchequer on average an additional £1,400 each year. The income for which the sheriff of Yorkshire accounted in 1212 was nearly double that of 1204 and treble that of 1199.[57] Since the new revenue over and above the existing farms and increments was described as 'profit', and chapter 25 was only specific about banning increments, it has been thought that the 'profits' were left untouched.[58] That was not the case. A sheriff who answered for profits was answering, in reality, not for any farm but for all the revenue that he received. In effect, the farm had been abolished.[59] Thus when the Charter said that counties were to be held 'at the ancient farms', John's profits were directly targeted. And no wonder, for they had baleful consequences for local society. Sheriffs answering for all their revenues had nothing left for their own support. John made no effort to give them salaries, as happened later. So the sheriffs made money illicitly, exploiting the 'miserable provincials' in ways the Charter tried to stop. They seized chattels, wood and carts, and threatened people with trial on their own unsupported allegations, without indictment by a jury, doubtless receiving bribes for letting off those accused.[60]

If the sheriffs were oppressive, so were the king's judges. Their visitations of the counties produced an average of £3,680 a year for the exchequer between 1209 and 1212 as opposed to only £955 on average over each of the previous five years. When the judges came on general eyres to hear all pleas, the bulk of the money derived not from the common-law civil litigation, but from the criminal side of their jurisdiction. Here the king received the chattels of outlaws and convicted criminals, and profited from the amercements imposed on peasants and peasant communities; hence the protection over amercements offered to villeins, at the behest of their lords, in chapter 20 of the Charter. The chapter on amercements was also thinking of the special eyre staged in the autumn of 1210 with a brief to root out and punish a whole range of 'transgressions'. The amercements were large, those of 30 to 100 marks being common.[61] Whether they were imposed by the oath of 'upright men of the neighbourhood', as the Charter demanded, one may doubt. They surely did not meet the Charter's criteria of matching the scale of the offence. Indeed, that the Charter used the word 'delictum' for 'offence', rather than the narrower 'felony' or 'crime', may be because it better covered the range of 'transgressions' punished on the 1210 eyre.[62] Here John was offending an important group in society, for many of the victims were county knights who acted as jurors and local officials, the very men on whom local government depended. Wimar of Bassingbourn, for example, who was hit with an amercement of 100 marks, was a leading figure in Cambridgeshire, where he and twenty-six other knights later joined the rebellion.[63]

The Charter also dealt directly with the burden of the royal forest. Under chapter 47, John was immediately to deforest everything that he himself had brought within the forest's bounds. This was not nearly as good as getting rid of Henry II's afforestations, but was still important in some parts of the country. A Dorset jury from 1225 was to allege that John had afforested the whole of the Purbeck area around Corfe castle.[64] The Charter also addressed the issue of the forest eyres. In chapter 44 only those who actually lived within the forest had to attend, unless they were connected with a plea, the point being to reduce the numbers being amerced for non-attendance.[65] The forest eyres between 1207 and 1212 raised on average £1,648 a year, as opposed to averaging £487 annually in the six previous years. The total imposed between 1207 and 1210, at £8,738, was more than double that demanded between 1198 and 1201. The eyre of 1212 alone imposed penalties totalling £5,504. Here the amercements were entirely decided by the will of the king. For lower sections of society, that will might be expressed by the forest judges, but for those more important, with more to give, John could intervene directly. The abbot of Furness was thus amerced 500 marks 'by mouth of the king'.[66] The forest eyre seemed particularly oppressive in the north, where the amount owed from Yorkshire in 1212 was as much as £1,498.[67] Some 300 marks of this was due from an amercement imposed on the abbot of St Albans 'by will rather than any reason', as he later said, this for failing to answer the summons of the judges to appear before them. Given that the abbot had no land in Yorkshire, this was precisely the abuse that the Charter sought to end.[68]

Even more burdensome than the royal forest were the taxes or 'aids' that John levied. These were paid by everyone in the country, or at least by everyone who had anything worth taxing, free and unfree alike. One tax above all made a major contribution to John's escalating revenues after 1204, and helped provoke chapters 12 and 14 of the Charter. This was the great tax of 1207. The writ setting its collection in motion shows all too well the bureaucratic tentacles of John's government. The tax was to be paid by 'every layman of all England of whomsoever's fee he may be'. No lord's authority over his fee was thus to stand in its way. The rate was to be a thirteenth of the value of both rents and movable chattels (the latter being chiefly corn and animals), and was to be assessed by a group of 'judges' sent to each county. These were to write down the names of each hundred in the county, and each parish within the hundred, so that they could be sure of answering for every vill. Before the judges, and in a way they thought best suited the king's 'profit', the stewards of the earls and barons were then to swear to the value of their lords' rents and goods, while everyone one else was to swear to the value of his own. Anyone guilty of concealment or false valuation was to lose all his chattels and be thrown into prison. Having assessed the tax, the judges were to send copies of their rolls recording the results to the sheriffs, who were to collect the money. They were then to bring the rolls to the king. None of this was mere parchment talk. The great tax of 1207 produced the gigantic sum of £57,000.[69]

This is an official figure sent to John himself by those hearing the accounts of the tax. How it compares with the sums raised by Richard's tax of 1193–4, the Saladin tithe of 1188 and a seventh on movable chattels that John himself raised in 1203 we do not know, for there is no record evidence. There is little sign that large sums came from John's tax of 1203.[70] The great tax of 1207, therefore, was not without precedent, but there had been nothing like it for thirteen years. No wonder the Charter insisted in chapters 12 and 14 that aids were only to be levied with the common consent of the kingdom.

The tax of 1207 hit all sections of society. The documents of 1215 also testified to how John had oppressed particular interest groups. Most important here were London and the towns. Magna Carta in chapter 12 directed that aids levied on London needed the common consent of the kingdom. The Articles of the Barons had gone further and subjected to common consent tallages as well as aids, and those levied not just on London but other 'cities' with liberties. The Charter, in chapter 13, protected both the liberties of London and those of 'all other cities and boroughs, and vills and ports'. That the towns should want protection was not surprising given the large sums of money John had taken from them in the form of tallages, amercements and fines. Some of the fines were made voluntarily in order to secure privileges. Others were not. The men of the Cinque Ports had to offer 1,000 marks to recover the king's benevolence.[71] The burdens became particularly heavy after 1204. In 1208 London's various debts were brought together in a lump sum of £1,500, which was paid off in three years. Then in 1211, London gave 2,000 marks as a gift to the king, as well as another £1,000 to clear off old debts. In 1214 came a tallage of 2,000 marks.[72] London, of course, became the great seat of the rebellion against John. In the north, Lincoln and Carlisle were equally rebel bases, the former occupied by the barons, the latter by the king of Scots, Alexander II. Both towns had suffered severely from John's exactions. From Lincoln, John after 1207 demanded some 2,750 marks in tallages, amercements and fines for his benevolence.

John also levied very heavy tallages on the Jews. In 1207 he demanded a tenth of all the debts that were owed them.[73] Then in 1210 he imposed tallage of £44,000 on them.[74] When payment was not immediate, the Jews were arrested and their assets seized. Roger of Wendover tells the story of Isaac the Jew of Norwich having a tooth knocked out each day until (with seven down) he agreed to pay 10,000 marks. He certainly promised to pay 10,000 marks, at a mark a day, to be released from prison.[75] These pressures did not merely impact on the Jews themselves. They also impacted on their Christian debtors. It was from the latter that the Jews had to get the money to pay the king. If they failed, then the king, as he did in 1210, could take the debts into his own hands, and collect them for himself. In 1207 every Jew had to send in a list of his debtors, so John henceforth had a total view of the Jewish portfolio and his potential income from it. Just how many debts eventually came into his hands we do not know, but the numbers were certainly large. Here again John was delving down into the county society of knights and free tenants. A surviving roll of 1213, recording payments to the king from debts owed the Jews, has receipts from 71 individuals in Lincolnshire and 164 in Norfolk and Suffolk. The victims, like those in other counties, had been made to compound for their debts and were paying them off in instalments. Although the payments seem quite modest, on a knightly or less than knightly income they were still significant. The Lincolnshire knight and future rebel Peter of Beckering had to pay £2.[76] Those owing Jewish debts to the king also included some of the greatest men in the land. Gilbert de Gant, for example, a leader of the rebellion in Lincolnshire, owed 1,200 marks, which in 1211 he was told to pay off in two years. On failing to keep the terms, he forfeited a 300-mark pardon and the debt went back up to 1,500 marks.[77]

What made this all the worse is that John apparently abolished the protection that tenants-in-chief had once enjoyed against interest on Jewish debts accruing during their minorities. This protection is implied in a charter that Richard I issued in 1190, confirming one of his father's. It does not reoccur in the charter that John granted the Jews in 1201.[78] There was, of course, no question of John paying interest or capital on Jewish debts owed by minors in his custody. But whereas before, that had just left the minor, on coming of age, to clear any debt as owed by his father, now he would have to pay all the interest which had accumulated as well. The Jewish assets from which the king might hope to profit were thus commensurately increased. This was why the Unknown Charter, in its chapter 11, followed by the Articles of the Barons and Magna Carta, sought to restore the situation to what it had been under King Richard, when it stated that no interest should accrue during a minority.[79]

The Charter also sought to deal with another grievance. In the past, when a debt owed the Jews was taken by the king, he expected to be paid all the interest which had accumulated down to that point.[80] When, therefore, one sees a Jewish debt in the pipe rolls, the amount may well be both capital ('the catallum') and interest, although this is very rarely stated. In one case, an exchequer memorandum shows what this could involve. So Simon of Kyme's debt of £1,272 was £853 in capital and £419 in interest.[81] The aim of chapter 10 of the Charter was to limit the king, when he took possession of a debt, simply to the 'catallum'. To be sure, in one interpretation of the chapter, the king's concession is merely seen as applying to the narrow case of debt taken into his hands during a minority.[82] This is because the stipulation that the king should only take the 'catallum' follows on immediately from the same chapter's demand that interest on Jewish debts should not accumulate during minorities. Yet it is pretty clear that the concession was understood as applying to all Jewish debts in royal hands. Thus in 1212, eager to be conciliatory in a moment of crisis, John had ordered the sheriffs to summon before him all those who owed him Jewish debts. He wished, he said, to give them relief by henceforth only demanding the 'catallum'. In other words he would now forgo the interest.[83] How far this concession was ever implemented we do not know, but it seems almost certain that the aim of Magna Carta was to enforce it. The radicalism of the Charter's chapter on the Jews has, therefore, been underestimated. It would have meant (as one can see from the case of Simon of Kyme) a very great reduction in the value of the Jewish debts in the king's hands. Not surprisingly, the concession was left out of later versions of the Charter. Also removed with it was the less contentious demand that Jewish debts should not accumulate interest in minorities. Later, King Henry III renewed this concession. He never renewed the concession limiting himself just to the 'catallum'.

These exactions made John's government deeply unpopular with many sections of society. It was, however, the king's tenants-in-chief who bore the heaviest burdens. They put their concerns right at the start of the Charter in the chapters that dealt with John's exploitation of his tenurial rights. Under chapter 2, the relief of earls and barons was to be £100. John had charged Nicholas de

Stuteville 10,000 marks. Under chapter 3, no relief was to be paid when a ward came of age and inherited his lands. John de Lacy, constable of Chester, had been in wardship yet in 1213 still had to agree to a fine of 7,000 marks to gain his inheritance and secure various other concessions.[84] These are but the most spectacular examples of exactions that in general were way above the limits envisaged in the Charter. The same fine roll that has John de Lacy's offer has five fines of 500 marks to enter inheritances, and one (linked to other concessions) of 2,000 marks. John's conduct was equally at odds with the Charter's stipulation that £5 should be the relief for a knight's fee. Thus in 1207 he charged the Lincolnshire knight and future rebel William of Well 50 marks to inherit a single fee, although an inquiry had shown that its annual value was only £7 10s.[85] Knights holding from honours in the hands of the crown were particularly vulnerable, as chapter 43 of the Charter suggests. Thomas Huscarl, another future rebel, had to offer 100 marks to inherit the three fees that his father held from the honour of Wallingford.[86]

John also made large amounts of money from wardships, either selling them off or running them through his own officials, hence the way chapters 4 and 5 of the Charter laid down detailed regulations to prevent the wardships being laid waste. It was such exploitation that raised no less than £1,319 from John de Lacy's lands from just one year in the king's hands in 1211–12. Cattle were sold off, manors were tallaged and an increment imposed above their farms.[87] Similar tallages were imposed during the minority of Walter de Beauchamp of Worcester. Later, John sold this wardship to the marcher baron Roger de Mortimer for £2,000, only in 1214 to threaten to take it away if he did not keep to the terms. The Charter recognized the danger that those, such as Mortimer, who had bought wardships would lay them waste in order to pay off the king and make money for themselves. It thus added to the Articles of the Barons a whole new section, regulating the conduct of such guardians. Walter de Beauchamp would certainly have welcomed the new stipulations. While still underage, he went with John to Poitou in 1214. Fearful of what was happening to his estates, he secured an order telling Mortimer not to commit waste.[88]

The regulations on wardships in the Charter were related to those governing John's treatment of the widows of his tenants-in-chief. One can see why these were necessary. In 1212 Hawisia, countess of Aumale, had to offer 5,000 marks, paying £1,000 at once, to have her inheritance, her dower and the right to stay single, all things she would have got free under Magna Carta.[89] This was but the most exorbitant example of payments that under John were routine and heavier than before. In Richard's reign there were sixty-eight fines from widows of tenants-in-chief for permission to stay single or marry whom they wished. The average value was £114. In John's reign there were 149 fines with an average value of £185. Although John sometimes paid lip service to the principle of consent, the pressures he brought to bear on widows are clear. In 1208, he stipulated that if Avelina, widow of Osbert de Long-champ, did not wish to marry Walter of Tew (a knight of the royal household), Walter was anyway to have her inheritance. In the end, Avelina had to offer 500 marks, 100 marks more than Walter, to escape the marriage.[90]

Another area where John pressed down on his tenants-in-chief was that of scutage, the payment in place of military service. The Unknown Charter sought to limit it to one mark per knight's fee. If more was wanted it had to be taken by the 'counsel' of the barons. Magna Carta went beyond this and achieved a blanket control over scutage. Henceforth, under chapters 12 and 14, both its incidence and its rate were to be made subject to the common counsel of the kingdom. The Charter's demands were completely understandable. Henry II had levied eight scutages in thirty-four years; Richard had levied three in ten years; John levied eleven in sixteen years and at higher rates than before. Henry II never levied a scutage at more than 26s 8d a fee. Two of John's scutages, in 1210 and in 1214, were at 40s. Alongside his scutages, John also demanded fines from his tenants-in-chief to avoid serving personally on the campaigns.[91] And he made money in other ways. Roger Bigod, earl of Norfolk, one of the twenty-five barons of the security clause, paid no less than £893 between 1210 and 1212 for the privilege of paying scutage for his lifetime on only the 60 fees that he acknowledged rather than on 120 fees as John was demanding.[92]

When it came to the actual payment of their debts, barons, as the *Dialogus de Scaccario* explains, enjoyed special privileges. The sheriff informed them of the amount due, but did not collect it. Instead, a baron, or his steward, could answer directly at the exchequer. At the start of his reign, John was already tightening up the procedures here. If stewards failed to answer for the debts of their lords, they were to be imprisoned, and the money owed was to be raised from the lord's chattels.[93] Later in the reign, the screws were tightened in another way. The exchequer put a lot of work into amalgamating into one lump sum the debts owed by an individual, which had hitherto been scattered through various county accounts in the pipe rolls. It thus became easier to see the total position, and act upon it. Money from these grouped debts brought in £7,830 in 1209–10, ten times more than in 1205.[94] When the debts of the earl of Clare (one of the twenty-five barons of the security clause) were brought together in 1208, they totalled £1,229. He was then pardoned £229 and told to pay off the balance in three years. If he failed he would lose the pardon.[95] Another great rebel, Peter de Brus, had to liquidate his debts at £400 a year.[96] John's changing attitude to baronial debt is seen in the 2,000 marks owed by William de Mowbray. Since 1201 it had more or less slept on the pipe rolls. Then, in 1208–9, he was told to pay off the debt at £100 a year and had to find sureties (many of them later rebels) guaranteeing that he would do so. For the next two years he more than kept the terms.[97]

These pressures squeezed under-tenants as well as tenants-in-chief. Indeed scutage could hit the former more heavily than the latter. Although not always easy to collect, a baron, if he paid scutage, had the right to recoup it from his undertenants. If he campaigned personally, as many did, and was thus exempt, he could take a scutage from the tenants who did not accompany him. When it came to his debts, a baron might be allowed to levy an aid on his tenants to help pay them. A large debt, like Mowbray's, also fanned out its burdens through the system of sureties.[98] The long lists of such guarantors are a striking feature of John's fine rolls. No wonder chapter 9 of the Charter sought to protect them. The same chapter sought to regulate the processes of distraint. The records of the exchequer show just how routine this was, with the clerks just putting the letter 'D' against the debts that were to be subject to it.[99] One may be sure the sheriffs were far from observing the orderly process, set out in the Charter, by which they were to distrain on the chattels and then the lands of the principal debtor, before turning to the assets of the sureties. There was certainly nothing orderly about the way John pounced on the chattels of deceased tenants-in-chief, on the pretext that they had owed him money, a practice which chapter 26 of the Charter tried to prevent.[100] On Roger de St John's death, leaving a minor as his heir, he owed nothing at all to the crown, but the sheriff still seized £35 of his chattels.[101] When Gilbert Basset, lord of Bicester, died, although his exchequer debts were trivial, John made £365 by seizing his money and selling his chattels.[102]

However much John depended on his ministers, he was very active in raising his own money. One reason why he travelled so frenetically and extensively was to seek out those who might give money voluntarily for favours, or involuntarily for forgiveness. The resulting bonanza is recorded in the fine rolls. In 1199–1200, at the start of his reign, John went on a great tour of the kingdom, taking in the north, and in the process he extracted fines worth some £41,000. This total was never approached again, but the annual sums offered thereafter were still substantial: in 1204–5, £18,000; in 1207–8, £22,000.[103] Given that John's revenue at the start of his reign averaged some £24,000 a year, one can see just how significant these fines were. The money did not come in at once, and the fines of 1199–1200 provided a revenue stream for years to come. John was very involved in the process of collection. The exchequer's records show him being consulted again and again about the treatment of individual debts.[104] He could draw them in simply to make money. He could postpone or pardon them as a form of favour. He could foreclose on them as a form of punishment. They were monarchy's greatest asset as a source both of revenue and of political control. They were also its greatest danger. The rebellion of 1215 was 'a rebellion of the king's debtors'.[105]

THE WRIT 'PRECIPE' AND
THE COMMON PLEAS

We saw in the last chapter how the development of the common-law legal procedures were a threat to baronial courts and jurisdictions. There was nothing the barons could do about that when it came to the two most popular of those actions, novel disseisin and mort d'ancestor. On the contrary, they were made more available in the Charter. But the barons did do something about another threat, namely that posed by the writ 'precipe'. Chapter 34 of the Charter banned the issue of the writ if it might cause a free man to 'lose his court'. The beneficiaries here – free men – theoretically covered a large group, but the essence of the chapter (as a later comment on it said) was to protect the courts of 'magnates'.[106] In the form found in *Glanvill* the writ 'precipe' was addressed to the sheriff, and told him to 'command' – 'precipe' – A to return land to B, which B complained A was withholding from him. If A did not, then he was to be summoned before the king or his judges to justify his inaction. The expectation was that A would not comply, so this was a way of moving the case into the king's court. The lord's court was thus bypassed in cases where it would otherwise have been the forum, so where A and B held from the same lord, or where A was the lord himself. It is difficult to believe that the chapter in Magna Carta was simply there to spare lords the bother of resorting to the procedure (which did exist) for the recovery of their courts in such circumstances. Rather, it suggests a much deeper resentment at the way the writ had been used under John to encroach on lordly jurisdiction. When *Bracton* said that while actions of right could be brought in the king's court, 'it ought not to happen against the will of lords, as used to be done by precipe', it was referring back to the situation before 1215. Around forty writs of precipe were purchased from the king in the pipe roll of 1203–4, some of them covering issues other than the right to land. Large numbers were also purchased in 1213–4.[107]

In the development of the common law there was, of course, a great opportunity for kingship. If the new procedures threatened the barons, they delighted the knights and free tenants. By expanding the common law and making it more available, John could win such groups to his cause and undermine his baronial opponents. Yet, in a crucial period of his reign, instead of playing this strongest card, John threw it away. Between 1209 and 1214 he virtually shut down both the judicial bench at Westminster and the eyres in the counties, apart that is from the punitive eyre in the autumn of 1210.[108] Probably John was worried about rival centres of authority during the Interdict and wanted everything under his control. He thus decided that common pleas were now to follow his person and be heard by the court *coram rege*. However much John tried to ease the path of litigants, the condemnation in chapter 17 of Magna Carta is sonorous and decisive. It tells us all we need to know about the unpopularity of the policy. Common pleas henceforth were not to follow the king's court but were to be heard in a fixed place. This meant they were to be heard either before the bench or before the king's justices in the localities. The latter, under chapter 18, were to visit each county four times a year to hear the assizes, with four knights of each county elected in the county court. John recognized the importance of knights and free men. In 1213 he summoned four knights from each county to come before him at Oxford.[109] But he had failed to conciliate such groups by offering them his justice. Had he done so consistently over his reign, he might well have fended off the rebellion of 1215.

MANIPULATION, SALE AND
DENIAL OF JUSTICE

In the minds of John's subjects, his financial exactions were intimately linked to another failure as king, namely his manipulation, sale and denial of justice.[110] 'To no one will we sell, to no one will we deny or delay, right or justice', John promised in chapter 40, the shortest and most emphatic in the Charter. John's fine and pipe rolls have numerous offers of money to secure 'justice', 'judgement' and other favours in law cases. Some of these, smallish in size, were for no more than hurrying things along, and were pretty innocuous. They were little different from the routine offers of a mark or two for the writ 'pone', which gave a 'place' for the hearing of a case before the king, the justices of the bench at Westminster or the justices in the localities. There were thirty-three such offers on the fine roll of 1207–8. But other fines were for much larger sums and effectively were bribes.[111] Justice seemed to depend not on what was just but on what one could pay. Robert of Berkeley offered 100 marks, in an unspecified case, 'to have his reasonable judgement by his peers', and Maurice de Gant 100 marks for the king to 'help him to have his right in those things which he claims'.[112] Gilbert de Gant followed up the purchase of a writ to begin his action against Agnes de Rupe, with an offer of 100 marks for 'judgement' in the case. John was very ready to accept competing offers. The great debt of William de Mowbray had itself arisen from a fine of 2,000 marks 'to be treated justly according to the custom of England' in a lawsuit being brought against him by

William de Stuteville. Mowbray needed to bid high because Stuteville had himself offered £2,000 for, among other things, 'right' in the case.[113] The Anonymous of Béthune described Mowbray as 'most valiant' but 'as small as a dwarf'. His small frame must have seethed with indignation at his treatment by King John. In the event, Mowbray was forced into an unfavourable settlement and still had, as we have seen, to pay the money.[114] It was equally possible to give money simply to stop a case and thus in effect deny justice to one's opponent. Gerard de Furnivall promised a cool £1,000 to end the lawsuit that Nigel de Luvetot was bringing against him.[115] One could also promise a win bonus. In 1199 William de Briouze, seeking to make good claims to Totnes in Devon, offered '£100 if he lost, 700 marks if he won'.[116]

The grievances of barons over the administration of justice were related to a fundamental difference between the treatment of their cases and the treatment of the cases of the general run of the free population. The litigation of the latter, according to the forms of the common law, went through, for the most part, quickly and cheaply. The king had scant interest in the general run of cases, for they had no political bearing. Here, if he interfered, which was rarely, he might well be influenced by abstract considerations of justice and even of 'pity'.[117] Nor, on the whole, did he exploit such cases for profit. The routine writs initiating the procedures cost 6d. The amercements (unlike those on the punitive eyre of 1210) were usually of reasonable size. It was quite different for barons. The earl of Clare had to give the king £100 for a writ of mort d'ancestor.[118] Even worse, when barons were litigating against each other over land held in chief from the king, the venue had to be the court that followed the king, the court *coram rege*. This was presided over by professional judges. When common-law business came before them, they could give judgements in the normal way, following the verdict of local juries, although getting such juries before the itinerant court was always a struggle. In important cases between tenants-in-chief, by contrast, it seems probable (although evidence here is sparse) that the king himself and any others he summoned would be present, at least at key sessions. The king's aim, in such cases, might simply be to drag them out. Hence the need to make offers to secure justice and judgement, and the way in which chapter 40 forbad the deferral of justice. If there was a conclusion, it might take the form of a settlement, and not necessarily a fair one. If there was a judgement, the court might give it, perhaps after the verdict of a jury from the neighbourhood of the land in dispute, or perhaps having itself weighed the case so that verdict and judgement were effectively rolled into one.

Cases between barons, therefore, were directly subject to the will of the king. Although a writ became available during John's reign ('precipe in capite'), which enabled such litigation to be commenced, it certainly did not then run through according to the set forms of the common law.[119] Justice before the king was inseparable from politics, patronage and profit. It was subject to all kinds of delays and manipulations. Even when, as could happen, litigation *coram rege* seems to have been decided according to law, there was usually a political subtext. It was surely to discipline a baron with whom he was increasingly at odds that Robert fitzWalter, in a case involving rights over Binham priory, was condemned to pay damages to St Albans abbey. Sometimes, in the litigation *coram rege*, John's hand is very clear. In a dispute over possession of Caldbeck in Cumberland, he accepted offers of £136 from Alexander of Caldbeck and £306 from Robert de Courtenay. Alexander knew he was beaten, and told the judges that he was no longer seeking a jury to decide the case, 'because it did not please the king that he should have it'. That was the end of the matter. If John could stop cases, he could also start them. In 1212, in order to bring pressure to bear on Geoffrey fitzPeter and his son Geoffrey de Mandeville, he encouraged Geoffrey de Say to began an action for their Mandeville inheritance. Just how directly John was involved here is shown by his personally providing the court with the names of Say's attorneys.

When chapter 40 of the Charter said that the king was not to sell, deny or delay justice, it was thinking above all of how he had treated his tenants-in-chief. When chapter 39 said that no one was to be deprived of property or otherwise punished 'save by the lawful judgement of his peers or by the law of the land', the implication was that judgement by peers should be the proper procedure in the court *coram rege*. Robert of Berkeley was making the same point in his fine to have 'his reasonable judgement by his peers'. His aim was both to ensure there was judgement and to prevent its being given by a court packed with household knights and ministers, as nearly happened to William Marshal on one occasion.[120] The desired link between the court *coram rege* and judgement by peers was also shown in chapter 25 of the Articles of the Barons, which stipulated that those disseised unjustly by Henry and Richard should receive 'right', 'by judgement of their peers in the court of the king'. Likewise under Magna Carta, chapter 59, King Alexander (as a baron of England) was to receive judgement by his peers in the king's court when it came to deciding the merits of John's claims against him.

A complicating factor in cases where barons were seeking justice was that they often stemmed from, or were related to, acts of injustice, or perceived injustice, by the king himself. Thus Maurice de Gant's fine was also to have justice concerning 'his rights', which were in the king's hands.[121] One type of right that John denied concerned earldoms. He refused to accept that they were necessarily hereditary. Even men he acknowledged as earls were sometimes denied the traditional annual payment associated with their office (known as 'the third penny') from the revenues of the counties from which they took their title. That payment was not worth much, but it nonetheless carried prestige. John gave it to Saer de Quincy for Hampshire, when making him earl of Winchester, but not to Earl David for Cambridgeshire and Huntingdonshire. An inquiry of 1205 into whether David ought to have the third penny led to nothing. It was only in 1215 itself, in a bid to retain his support, that John gave way to David on the issue.[122] Even worse off were the de Vere earls of Oxford, or earls as they thought they should be. Aubrey de Vere had entered his inheritance in 1194. It was another ten years before he was recognized as earl of Oxford, this after offering John 200 marks for the favour. The offer was also in order to have the third penny of the county, but the third penny never properly materialized. On Aubrey's death in 1214, his brother Robert had to offer the king 1,000 marks to enter the inheritance, but this did not include the earldom. It was only at Runnymede that the earldom and the third penny were conceded. Equally aggrieved was Geoffrey de Mandeville, son of Geoffrey fitzPeter, John's chief justiciar and earl of Essex. After his father's death in 1213, Geoffrey complained that John had neither invested him with the earldom nor given him the third penny of the county.[123]

In all this one needs to be fair to John. Henry II and Richard had been sticky over earldoms and had equally accepted offers of money for justice. Under John, however, thanks to his presence in the kingdom, legal actions before the court *coram rege* played a part in baronial life that they had never done under Richard, when there had been no such court in England. If this made the king's justice more accessible, it also subjected litigation all the more to the royal will. To be fair again, cases between great men, quite apart from their political ramifications, could be highly complex. In tangled webs of family history and royal intervention, stretching back over generations, it was often difficult to see where right did actually lie. There was also an element of hypocrisy about the offers of money. Those making them wanted not justice but victory, yet when victory was not obtained, they complained of injustice. John's problem was that he sacrificed his reputation as a righteous judge without any commensurate political benefit. His manipulation of justice had created far more enemies than friends. His division of the Percy inheritance, fair or unfair, and its accompanying litigation, won him the loyalty of William de Percy, but this was far outweighed by the alienation of William's uncle, the great Yorkshire baron Richard de Percy, who was to play a leading part in the rebellion and become a member of Magna Carta's twenty-five.[124] Worse still, John's intervention in lawsuits often failed to secure the loyalty of either party. William de Mowbray and Nicholas de Stuteville (William de Stuteville's heir), Gerard de Furnivall and Nigel de Luvetot, Geoffrey de Say and Geoffrey de Mandeville all joined the rebels. Robert fizWalter's treatment in his action against St Albans was one factor in his rebellion, yet at St Albans the king was regarded much like rat poison.

ARBITRARY RULE

Offers of money for right and justice at least implied there were standards of conduct that the king acknowledged. But there were other areas, as the Charter indicated, where John's rule seemed to move entirely to the motions of his will. One of these, deeply resented, was the taking of hostages. Under chapter 49, John was to restore all hostages taken as 'security for peace or faithful service'. The taking of hostages was an old practice, but under John it became almost a system of government – government by hostage. In 1208, fearful that the pope would absolve his subjects from their allegiance, John, according to Roger of Wendover, demanded hostages from all those he suspected of disloyalty.[125] He took a fresh round of hostages after the plot against him of 1212. One of those targeted, Earl David, was summoned to a council in 1214 'as you love your hostages and whatever you hold of the king'.[126] The sensitivity and seriousness of the issue is seen in the space devoted to it in the *History of William Marshal*. It described in detail how John successively demanded as hostages the Marshal's eldest son, his second son and then five knights, including John of Earley, several of whom were harshly treated in captivity.[127]

Another feature of John's arbitrary rule was the exaction of fines to assuage his anger and recover his good will. In the 1207–8 fine roll, the total offered under this heading was £5,580. This came from twelve individual fines, which had hit barons, churchmen, towns and local society. The men of Cornwall offered 200 marks; the disgraced sheriff of Hampshire, Roger fitzAdam, offered 1,000 marks, with over 700 local men acting as his pledges.[128] The amounts actually paid in to the exchequer from such fines 'rose dramatically' in the second half of the reign, totalling in 1209, £2,252, in 1210, £3,414 and in 1211, £2,731.[129] To be fair, such fines were not unprovoked. Usually the offences were unspecified, but the victims had obviously done things to incur the king's wrath, and kings had to be good punishers. The 1,200-mark fine of Roger de Cressy, later a leading rebel in East Anglia, was for marrying an heiress without the king's permission.[130] Whether, however, the amounts involved were reasonable or reasonably imposed was another matter. The Charter had such penalties in mind when it laid down that John was to forgive all fines made with him 'unjustly and against the law of the land'.

There was a close link between these fines and chapter 21 on amercements. When it came to amercements, earls and barons were particularly subject to the king's will. Their litigation against each other had to take place in the court *coram rege*, where of course the king could in practice impose whatever amercements he liked. If, on the other hand, a baron was convicted of an offence before the king's judges in the counties, then the custom before 1215 was for the amercement to be imposed by the chief officials of the exchequer.[131] Given that these included such royal henchmen as Peter des Roches and William Brewer, such amercements were essentially determined by the will of the king. Some baronial amercements were hefty. The great northern rebels Eustace de Vescy and Robert de Ros suffered ones of 300 marks; the earl of Clare's amercement for a disseisin was 500 marks.[132] It is perfectly true that such amercements were often pardoned in whole or in part by the king. Some from the start were reasonable in size. But the threat of arbitrary punishment was always there; hence the need to offer fines for the king's benevolence to escape such punishment. One can see this happening in the case of Ruald fitzAlan, the constable of Richmond in Yorkshire. He gave 200 marks to escape the amercement coming his way for refusing to cooperate with the 1207 tax.[133] It was this threat which the Charter sought to remove when it said that earls and barons should be amerced by their peers, which meant amerced by themselves. That this was the same as being amerced by 'the barons' of the exchequer, as the chief officials there were called, would have been fiercely denied.

Fines for the king's grace were also prompted by acts of arbitrary disseisin, or dispossession. Thus the Gloucestershire baron Robert of Berkeley had to offer 2,000 marks 'to have his lands and his castle of which he was disseised because of the benevolence of the king', 'benevolence' here, of course, meaning lack of benevolence.[134] Like the chapter on amercements, chapter 39 of the Charter, forbidding disseisin save by judgement of peers, or otherwise by the law of the land, was thus intended to remove the threat behind such fines for the king's grace. It was also dealing with one of the most fundamental characteristics of John's rule. As Henry Summerson writes, 'disseisin had become a well-nigh automatic reaction on the part of the king and his agents to any misdeed or suspicious act which came to their attention'.[135] In 1204 John issued orders for the seizure of the lands of Ranulf, earl of Chester, suspecting him of dealings with the Welsh ruler Gwenwynwyn of Powys. At the same time the king disseised the northerner Roger de Montbegon (one of Magna Carta's twenty-five barons in the security clause) for failing to come to court. Next year it was the turn of another northerner, also a member of the twenty-five, Robert de Ros.[136] In 1207 John's first move against Ruald fitzAlan was to seize Richmond castle. In the fine roll of 1207–8 there are thirteen fines made to recover land seized into the king's hands, probably by similar acts of will. Occasionally, John even admitted his lawless conduct. In 1213 he ordered Geoffrey de Lucy to be restored Newington in Kent if disseised of it 'simply by our will' rather than by 'the judgement of our court'. Ten years later a jury stated that Geoffrey had indeed been disseised of all his lands 'because the king was angry with him'.[137]

Sometimes disseisin was the consequence of indebtedness. When Nicholas de Stuteville had to offer 10,000 marks so he could succeed to the lands of his brother, John retained the castles of Knaresborough and Boroughbridge as security for payment. Given the impossibility of paying such a sum, possession of the castles had been John's object in the first place. The Stutevilles regarded this as an act of arbitrary disseisin.[138] John de Lacy, having agreed to pay 7,000 marks for his inheritance, must have regarded John's retention of Pontefract and Donington castles in the same light. Equally blatant was the way John confiscated the honour of Trowbridge from Henry de Bohun, earl of Hereford, on a cleverly arranged legal technicality, and ignored his efforts to recover it. John then allowed William Longespee, earl of Salisbury, who had hitherto made little progress in his lawsuit for the honour, to simply take it over. Henry's son later described this as disseisin 'by will and without judgement'.[139] It was precisely such disseisins of lands, castles, liberties and rights, made 'without lawful judgement of peers', that John promised to correct under chapter 52 of the Charter. Under its terms nearly half the twenty-five barons of Magna Carta's security clause recovered lands and rights, including Bohun, who regained Trowbridge.[140]

Great barons were not the only victims of arbitrary disseisin. Knights who held from honours in the king's hands were equally vulnerable, as they were also when it came to relief, scutage and military service.[141] William fitzEllis, a tenant of the honour of Wallingford, had been amerced 20 marks for swearing a false oath on a jury.[142] This was not his only grievance. At Runnymede itself he was restored to the manor of Oakley, having complained that John had disseised him 'by will without judgement'.[143] The fall of a lord often meant trouble for his dependants and followers. When John deprived Earl David of Godmanchester in 1212, he disseised David's tenants in the manor.[144] Likewise, when John turned on Roger de Cressy, he seized the lands of his associate, the knight William fitzRoscelin. William protested his innocence, but still had to offer 60 marks and a good hawk to get his lands back.[145] How the king's will penetrated into the county courts is shown in a Somerset case from 1204. There the sheriff was informed secretly of the king's order to arrest and imprison a clerk present in the court. When the sheriff tried to do so, he was resisted by the county knights on the grounds that there should be no arrest 'without judgement'.[146]

Arbitrary disseisin was hardly invented by King John. The Articles of the Barons and Magna Carta were also concerned with the disseisins of Henry II and King Richard. The Charter adjourned their consideration until John completed or abandoned his prospective crusade.[147] It was John's own disseisins that cried out for immediate remedy, and remedied they were to be under chapter 52, while chapter 39 sought to prevent such actions in the future. These two chapters were among the most important in the Charter. They sought to end the king's arbitrary rule.

THE KING'S MEN

John's government was not merely unpopular for what it did. It was also unpopular because of the men who did it. John's agents, or at least some of them, were loathed because of their ruthless conduct. They were also envied because of their rewards. Yet such men often stood in fear of the king, and felt they had been poorly treated, receiving less than their just deserts.

The lay counsellors whom John listed at the start of the Charter were not very different from the kinds of men employed by his predecessors, under whom, indeed, many had begun their careers. Of the laymen listed, there were four earls, William Marshal, earl of Pembroke, William Longespee, earl of Salisbury (an illegitimate son of Henry II), William de Warenne, earl of Surrey (although usually styled, as in the Charter, earl of Warenne), and William d'Aubigné, earl of Arundel. There then followed, after Alan of Galloway, constable of Scotland, eleven men, many of them from knightly backgrounds. Several had begun their careers as household knights. Several came from families with long traditions of royal service: Warin fitzGerold, first of the eleven, had followed his brother and father in the hereditary position of chamberlain of the exchequer; Hugh de Neville, John's chief forester, was the grandson of Henry II's chief forester, the odious Alan;[148] Hubert de Burgh and Thomas and Alan Basset, like William Marshal, were younger sons who had started out with their fortunes to make. Ties of family were evident within the group. Thomas and Alan Basset were brothers, so were Peter and Matthew fitzHerbert. John Marshal was the illegitimate son of William's older brother. There were also ties of faction. William Marshal was close not just to

John Marshal, but also to the Bassets.[149] If only we knew more about the sleeping arrangements in the halls and chambers used by the courtiers, we would probably see such ties mapped out in the sharing of space and beds. None of this worried John. He took such groupings for granted and manipulated them to his advantage, placating or punishing a great minister through the treatment of his men.

The Charter shows John's counsellors at court, but they equally acted on the king's behalf in the localities as castellans and sheriffs. Indeed, of those named at the start of the Charter, the earls of Pembroke and Salisbury, Hubert de Burgh, Peter and Matthew fitzHerbert, Thomas Basset, Robert of Ropsley, John Marshal and John fitzHugh had all been sheriffs, sometimes for long periods and in clusters of counties. Such men did not run their counties personally. They employed under-sheriffs to do that. But they wielded great local power, partly because of their direct line to the king, partly because they were usually allowed to keep the money that they could raise above the farm. They thus had plenty of resources to garrison royal castles and hire troops to sort someone out. The lay counsellors whom John names at the start of the Charter, however, were not in general among his most hated officials. Only four of them appeared in Roger of Wendover's list, thirty-two strong, of the king's evil ministers: the earl of Salisbury, Hugh de Neville (not surprisingly since he is named as chief forester) and bringing up the rear, Thomas Basset and Peter fitzHerbert (a marcher baron through his father's marriage).[150] Salisbury, Basset and fitzHerbert would have been indignant at their inclusion. All were praised in the *History of William Marshal*. FitzHerbert demonstrated the best chivalric standards when, in a tense episode at court, he refused to sit next to 'the traitor who has failed his lord', referring here to a knight who had let down William Marshal. Thomas Basset, from an old local family, took several Oxfordshire knights into his service during his long stint as sheriff of the county.[151] The Marshal's own absence from Wendover's list suggests that others took him at his own valuation, or at least knew of his quarrels with John.[152] Another of the king's counsellors at the start of the Charter, Philip d'Aubigné, was later to win fame as a crusader.[153]

The picture of relative respectability is not very different if we glance at John's judges.[154] The same men can be found at different times sitting in the court at Westminster (the bench), the court *coram rege*, and the courts on eyre. Seventeen feature with sufficient frequency to be regarded in some way as professional judges. Only two appear in Wendover's list, Geoffrey fitzPeter, who as chief justiciar frequently presided at the bench and *coram rege*, and William Brewer. Both feature not so much for being judges as for their more general roles in John's government. Brewer was a baron of the exchequer and a highly unpopular sheriff of Somerset and Dorset. When the men of the two counties offered money to have a local man as sheriff, they added 'except William Brewer'. Later, in the minority of Henry III, Brewer was to argue that Magna Carta was invalid as having been extracted from the king by force.[155] The majority of the judges achieved nothing like this prominence or unpopularity. They were mostly laymen, from knightly backgrounds, who had learnt their law in local administration, or occasionally as pleaders and attorneys in the courts. Several had entered the king's service through connections with great ministers like fitzPeter or Hubert Walter. The judges were not particularly close to John and received limited rewards. Some, as we will see, joined the rebels. They were certainly out to make as much money as possible for the king from the criminal pleas, but their treatment of civil pleas, when great men were not involved, may well have been according to the rules and standards found in *Glanvill*. It was John himself who was responsible for the manipulation and sale of justice.

What then was wrong with John's ministers? In the list of his episcopal counsellors at the start of the Charter, one name stands out, like a lighthouse flashing danger: the name of Peter des Roches, bishop of Winchester. Peter came from the Touraine, and was probably related to the Anjevin magnate, William des Roches, whom John cast off with such disastrous results in 1202.[156] Des Roches began his known career under King Richard, and went straight on into John's service, in 1205, being made bishop of Winchester. John knew his man:

> The warrior of Winchester
> Presides at the exchequer
> Indefatigable at accounting
> Indolent at the scripture
> Revolving the king's roll.

Thus ran one lampoon.[157] This was unfair. Des Roches was an enthusiastic founder of religious houses, but he was also at the heart of John's financial policies, and was the one bishop to remain at the king's side during the Interdict. Magna Carta did not explicitly demand his removal from the justiciarship, but his removal was soon to follow.

Des Roches was also intimately connected with the one group of ministers whom the Charter, in its chapter 50, did dismiss, laying down indeed that they were henceforth to hold no bailiwicks in England.[158] These were the kinsmen of Gerard d'Athée, of whom no fewer than eight were named, the most prominent (both featuring with Gerard on Wendover's list) being Engelard de Cigogné and Philip Marc.[159] Gerard himself (who was dead by 1215) was, like des Roches, from the Touraine. (Athée-sur-Cher and Cigogné are both within fifteen miles of Tours.) After his capture at Loches, John ransomed Gerard (using 1,000 marks from the fine of the Cinque Ports) and brought him to England.[160] There he can be found at court (glimpsed going into John's chamber in the History of the Marshal), but his pre-eminent role, like that of his kinsmen, was in the localities. When the Charter said that Gerard's crew were to be dismissed 'from their bailiwicks', it was thinking above all of their sheriffdoms, castles and other custodies. In the Welsh marches, Gerard played a key role in bringing down William de Briouze. With his hands full there, in 1208 he passed on the custody of Nottingham castle and the sheriffdom of Nottinghamshire-Derbyshire to Philip Marc. He passed on Bristol castle and the sheriffdoms of Gloucestershire and Herefordshire to Engelard de Cigogné. When the king's judges visited Gloucestershire in 1221, they discovered that Gerard and Engelard had heard pleas of the crown (forbidden by Magna Carta) and had pocketed around 385 marks in a whole series of extortions.[161] The exactions of the clerk Matthew de Cigogné from various religious houses 'through the violence and multiple oppression of Engelard de Cigogné, sheriff of Gloucestershire, his brother', called forth a protest in 1213 from Archbishop Langton himself.[162] None of this mattered much to John. Engelard and Gio de Cigogné (another brother, this one named in the Charter) had arrested and seized the chattels of two Gloucestershire knights because they 'had spoken ill of King John'.[163] That was why they were in office.

The contempt in which Gerard's family were held is seen in the

Charter's demand for them to be dismissed 'and all their follow-ing', the word here for 'following' – 'sequela' – being often used for the families of peasants.[164] Such contempt is equally seen in the way neither the Articles of the Barons nor the Charter were both-ered by the precise names of the lesser members of the group and seem indeed to have named one man twice over.[165] The presence of such officials explains very well the desire in the counties to have local men as sheriffs. It explains too the demand in the Charter's chapter 45 that sheriffs should know and mean to observe the law of the kingdom, or as the Articles put it more potently, the law of the land. No one could say Gerard and his lot knew that.[166]

Perhaps because they were foreign, and complete outsiders, only Gerard's 'following' were actually dismissed in the Charter, but there were others hardly less unpopular. Wendover listed two of John's great agents in the north, Philip of Oldcoates, from 1212 the sheriff of Northumberland, and Brian de Lisle, who held Knaresborough, Boroughbridge and the Peak. Wendover also named the knights Robert and Henry of Braybrook, a father and son team, who were in succession sheriffs of Northamptonshire and Bedfordshire-Buckinghamshire. Neither was particularly close to the king, but they raised large sums of money from their coun-ties as profits for the exchequer. It was to men like them, rather than courtier sheriffs, that John turned to execute his profits pol-icy. As sheriffs, they might be less effective in standing up to great barons, and governing a county in times of storm, than Philip Marc or Engelard de Cigogné (who were allowed to keep the prof-its), but they were perfectly able to raise the sums from the general run of the population on which the profits depended.

John's men were thus unpopular for what they did. They were also envied for what they received. The king had a great deal to give, as the Charter showed. There were the wardships, and mar-riages of heirs, heiresses and widows, dealt with between chapters 4 and 8. Among those named at the start of the Charter, both William Marshal and William Longespee owed their earldoms and estates to marriages to great heiresses. At a lesser level, Hugh de Neville gained an heiress from King Richard, as did Robert of Ropsley from John.[167] 'No widow is to be distrained to marry while she wishes to live without a husband,' said chapter 8 of the Charter. Well yes, but Warin fitzGerold and Hubert de Burgh had both profited from marrying widows, who were also heiresses.

Aside from wardships and marriages, the king could give patronage from land that had come into his hands, such as the honours in chapter 43 of the Charter. Alan Basset thus obtained Mapledurwell in Hampshire and what became Berwick Bassett in Wiltshire, manors forfeited by Adam de Port for treason back in 1171.[168] Servants could also be fed both from the lands of the Normans, as we have seen, and from the royal demesne manors mentioned in chapter 25. Despite its depletion over the previous century, John was still prepared to make grants from the royal demesne in hereditary right, although usually in return for a money rent. It was on such terms that John gave High Wycombe to Alan Basset and Headington to Thomas Basset, placing these trusties astride the strategic road between London and Oxford.

While not accepting that they were necessarily hereditary, John could be generous when it came to earldoms. At the start of his reign he recognized the claims of William Marshal, William de Ferrers and Henry de Bohun to respectively the earldoms of Pembroke, Derby and Hereford. In a new creation, in 1207 he made Saer de Quincy earl of Winchester. There was also more to royal favour than just outright gifts. It could ease a man's passage in lawsuits, and in many other areas. 'It is just that we do better for those who are with us than those who are against us,' John remarked in one letter.[169] With his cynical political intelligence, he understood very well the need for the carrot as well as the stick. There was never, however, too much carrot. John acted in the spirit of his grandmother, the Empress Matilda, whose counsel for training men was the same as for training hawks: keep them hungry.[170] Patronage had to be earned. John gave his household knights robes and their maintenance at court, but not regular salaries.[171] Those starting off, like Godfrey of Crowcombe, had to serve in hope of reward, and work their passage towards grants of lands, usually at first held not in hereditary right but at the king's pleasure.[172]

With his great barons too, John kept things back, even from those for a while in his favour. He did not acknowledge Saer de Quincy's claim to the castle of Mountsorrel nor William Longespee's to the castle of Salisbury. When becoming earl of Derby, William de Ferrers had to resign claims to cherished parts of the Peverel inheritance. Henry de Bohun, on becoming earl of Hereford, had to resign claims to the inheritance of Miles of Gloucester.[173] In some cases John had done enough. The patronage received by the earls of Pembroke, Chester and Derby was at least a factor in their remaining loyal, although with Derby it was a close-run thing.[174] On the other hand, John's treatment of the earls of Salisbury, Winchester and Hereford (in Hereford's case culminating in the confiscation of Trowbridge) were among the reasons for their rebellion. There were other barons, of course, such as William de Mowbray, who had seen none of John's favour. They were simply harried to pay debts, and denied, as they thought, right and justice. It was easy, moreover, to feel appalled at some of those who did receive John's patronage. Take the case of Peter de Maulay. He came from the border country between Poitou and the Touraine, and was another of Peter des Roches's protégés featuring on Wendover's list.[175] The terms in which he is described by the Anonymous of Béthune show baronial astonishment at his trajectory:

> This Peter de Maulay had been an usher of the king; but then his career grew so much that he became a knight and constable of Corfe, and so powerful that he fought against the earl of Salisbury.[176]

In fact, Maulay became far more than a mere knight. His marriage to a great baronial heiress established him as lord of Doncaster in Yorkshire. His sureties in 1214 for the massive 7,000 marks that he offered in return included not one of the northern barons who were later to join the rebellion.[177] This was just the kind of marriage that the Charter forbad when it said, in chapter 6, that heirs should be 'married without disparagement'. It was not merely outsiders who were offended by Maulay's rise. John also gave him, from the lands confiscated in England from Normans who had taken the French allegiance, the strategic manor of Upavon in Wiltshire in the heart of Basset and Marshal territory, thus characteristically creating divisions between his own men.

John did not merely set his own men against each other. He also made quite sure they stood in fear of himself. If they stepped out of line, or failed in some way, they could expect heavy punishment. Again there were precedents for this under Richard and earlier kings, but that did not make such penalties any the less resented. They help explain why even some of John's closest servants turned against him. A case in point was Hugh de Neville, who ultimately rebelled in 1216. John's probable seduction of his wife was not Hugh's only grievance. In 1212 he had to offer

6,000 marks to recover the king's benevolence, having allowed two prisoners to escape, and having failed to account properly for his administration of the royal forest.[178] John's heavy hand could also fall on his household officials. So Philip de Lucy offered 1,000 marks to recover the king's benevolence, after failing in his duties as clerk of the chamber.[179] The threatened punishments were not only financial. In 1212, when Peter de Maulay was so mad as to disobey a royal order (especially grievous from someone John thought was his creature), his sureties undertook that, if he misbehaved again, they would hand over his body for any punishment which John wished to inflict. Eight of the sureties (seven leading ministers, including Hugh de Neville, and the son of an earl) also agreed that they would subject themselves to a whipping. All had to issue charters to that effect. John wanted it on record.[180] If there was any truth in the later rumour that Maulay was involved with the murder of John's nephew Arthur, he knew what punishment to expect.[181]

Ultimately, John's regime collapsed because it had too narrow a base. Its enemies among barons and knights had come to far outnumber its friends. It had ceased to command any kind of general consent. The demand in chapters 12 and 14 of the Charter that John levy scutages and aids with the common consent of the kingdom could have applied to his rule as a whole. As it was, the way John levied the great tax of 1207 foreshadowed the lack of consent that would bring him down. Aware that the tax could not be justified on the grounds later allowed in Magna Carta (to ransom his body, to knight his eldest son or marry off his eldest daughter on one occasion), John claimed it had been agreed by 'the common counsel and assent of our council at Oxford'. But what did that mean? It might be no more (as was to be said of Edward I in 1297) than people standing around nodding assent in the king's chamber.[182] Later, perhaps sensing the inadequacy of the formula, John claimed the tax had been agreed by 'the archbishop [of York], the bishops, abbots, priors and magnates of our kingdom'. The claim was specious since the archbishop of York actually resisted the tax. At most, around thirty days' notice was given for the council at Oxford where the tax was imposed, not the forty days demanded by Magna Carta. The council itself lasted only a day and a half. None of this suggests it was well attended or was the forum for much debate or agreement. Probably the consenting group was composed of little more than the king's ministers.[183] It is easy, then, to understand why the Charter gave exact instructions about how the tax-granting assemblies should be convened. Even the stipulation that the 'cause' of the assembly should be expressed in the writ of summons was relevant to 1207, when John had sprung on the outsiders present the claim that the tax was needed to defend the kingdom and recover his rights, although there was no imminent threat of invasion and the eventual campaign of recovery was years away. Later taxes of this kind were usually accompanied by major concessions from the government. Indeed, the next great tax, that of 1225, was conceded in return for the definitive issue of Magna Carta. In 1207 John offered nothing in return. The whole procedure in 1207 showed what was wrong with John's rule. It took far too much and it gave far too little.

KING JOHN AND THE BRITISH ISLES

Magna Carta was not exclusively an English document. It had important chapters dealing with the grievances of the Welsh rulers and the king of Scots, Alexander II. While Ireland only featured in John's titles at the start, it was central to his quarrels with some of the greatest baronial families. All this was related to John's domination of the British Isles. The Crowland chronicler, writing of the situation in 1211, declared that there was no one in Ireland, Scotland or Wales who did not obey the king of England, something achieved by none of his predecessors.[184] In respect of Scotland, a striking new discovery has indeed revealed just how far obedience was expected to go. None of this was at odds with John's primary aim after 1204 of recovering his continental possessions. It was vital to prevent disloyalty and disturbance in Britain and Ireland disrupting those continental plans.

There was also more to it than that. John knew the British Isles better than any of his predecessors. He had been lord of Ireland since 1177, and understood how his authority and revenues there might be increased. As for Wales, John's first marriage in 1189 had made him lord of Glamorgan and he retained the lordship until 1214, despite the marriage's annulment in 1199. After the loss of Normandy in 1204, he visited Wales or the Welsh marches in every year down to 1211. He wished to sharpen his authority over the

Welsh rulers and expand the areas under his direct control, both at their expense and, if they stood out of line, that of the great marcher barons, at times playing off one against the other. In Scotland, John remembered the overlordship of the kingdom that his father, Henry II, had established by the Treaty of Falaise in 1174, following William the Lion's capture during the great rebellion. In 1189 King Richard, intent on raising money for his crusade, had allowed King William to buy back Scotland's independence, but John was far from regarding that as the last word. Secondary ambition it may have been, but he very much aspired to be ruler of Britain and Ireland.

DOMINATION OVER WALES

When it came to the Welsh chapters in Magna Carta, John was not the only king being attacked. The Articles of the Barons sought redress for Welshmen disseised, without judgement of their peers, by both Henry II and Richard of land in England, Wales or the March. In the Charter itself, however, treatment of these disseisins was postponed until John returned from or abandoned his prospective crusade. It was only his own disseisins that were to be dealt with.[185] John was also, under the Charter, to return all the hostages 'from Wales' and the charters (containing the details of unpalatable submissions) that had been given him as 'security of peace'. The kind of thing the Welsh rulers complained of is exemplified by John's treatment of Gwenwynwyn ab Owain, the ruler of southern Powys. In 1208 Gwenwynwyn had attacked Peter fitz-Herbert's lordship in Brecon. In revenge, John seized his lands and placed him under arrest until he handed over twenty hostages. Unless he came up with the first twelve within eight days, the king was to be 'able to do with his body as he wills'.[186] This was no idle threat. When John arrived at Nottingham in 1212, he had twenty-eight boys, Welsh hostages, hanged before he tasted food.[187] The chivalric rules that acted as some restraint on John in England (where he mistreated hostages but did not kill them) had far less purchase in Wales.[188]

The only Welsh ruler actually named in Magna Carta was the greatest of them all, Llywelyn ab Iorwerth. Under chapter 58 the king was immediately to release his son, and deliver his hostages and charters, along with all other hostages and charters taken from the Welsh. Early in John's reign, seeing off rivals from within his family, Llywelyn had established his mastery over the whole of Gwynedd from the Dee to the Dyfi. He titled himself 'prince of North Wales', a title John accepted. In 1205 Llywelyn was allowed to marry John's illegitimate daughter, Joan. Good relations did not last. John was furious when Llywelyn scavenged away some of the territories of Gwenwynwyn. In 1211 John invaded Gwynedd, penetrating as far west as Bangor. There, with Joan interceding with her father, Llywelyn came to terms. To have John's grace and benevolence, he surrendered for ever the eastern half of Gwynedd between the Dee and the Conwy. If he did not have an heir by Joan (as seemed likely, for they were childless), then, on Llywelyn's death, the king was to have all his remaining lands. Meanwhile, Llywelyn was to surrender his illegitimate son, Gruffudd, and deliver as many hostages as John wished. These terms were all embodied in a charter that Llywelyn was forced to issue.[189] One can see very well why its return was demanded under chapter 58 of the Charter. At best the treaty truncated Gwynedd, at worst, if Llywelyn and Joan were childless, it would bring Gwynedd to an end. When it came to Scotland, John was equally ambitious, although here his aim became not to end the kingdom but to subject it to his overlordship.

THE SUBJUGATION OF SCOTLAND

In the first phase of his reign, John had left King William the Lion largely alone, contemptuously brushing aside his long-standing claims to Northumberland, Cumberland and Westmorland. In 1209 the situation changed. The initial dispute seems to have been over the security of the border, where William, to John's anger, pulled down a castle recently built at Tweedmouth. This brought John north in April of that year. He was already, according to one Scottish chronicle, making 'unheard of demands ... inconsistent with the liberties of the Scottish kingdom'.[190] Probably he was already seeking Scotland's subjection. When his demands were rejected, John returned south, while negotiations continued. There was then a major escalation of the crisis. John heard that William was trying to use the marriage of one of his daughters to seal an alliance with Philip Augustus.[191] In July he set off again for the northern border. According to a contemporary Scottish narrative, John had with him around 13,000 Welsh foot soldiers, 1,500 knights from England, and 7,000 crossbowmen and Brabantine mercenaries. The numbers are impressionistic but show John had mustered an overwhelming force. King William, old, sick and unprepared, was in no condition to resist. In August 1209 he agreed to the Treaty of Norham.

Just what the Treaty of Norham contained has long been debated by historians. The problem is that two of the main accounts, although derived from contemporary sources, are filtered through much later Scottish chronicles. Fortunately much of the mystery can now be solved. I have discovered a letter of John himself setting out the main features of the treaty. This survives as a copy in one of the many cartularies of the Benedictine abbey of St Augustine at Canterbury. This particular cartulary probably dates from the mid 1320s. The hand has copied the letter with much other material from John's reign, some of it concerning the affairs of the abbey, some of general political interest. Since the letter is addressed to 'all faithful men in God', and thus was intended as a general proclamation, there is no problem about its reaching St Augustine's. That it is genuine there can, I think, be no doubt. The Latin text and a translation are given in Appendix I.[192]

In the letter, John indicates that King William himself is to remain in his existing state of homage. This was the homage that he had done to John in 1200, and was almost certainly just for his lands and rights in England, so for the lordship of Tyndale, and the earldom of Huntingdon which was held from him by his younger brother David.[193] With William's son, however, the eleven-year-old Alexander, it was quite different. Alexander, the letter said, 'has done us homage as William, king of Scotland, did homage to the lord Henry, king of England, our father'. Everyone knew what that meant. It referred to the great ceremony at York in 1175, following the 1174 Treaty of Falaise, when King William had done homage to Henry II 'for all his tenements and namely for Scotland'. His homage was followed by that of the chief men of Scotland. All this was in fulfilment of the Treaty of Falaise, which had been forced on King William, following his capture during the great rebellion against Henry the year before.[194] Technically, of course, Alexander could not in 1209 have done homage for the kingdom, since it was still held by his father. Presumably some form of words was found to get round this. Perhaps Alexander did homage for Scotland as his father's heir. Whatever the precise arrangement, the implication was completely clear. Once Alexander succeeded, he would then do homage for the kingdom in a great ceremony replicating that at York in 1175.

The shattering nature of this concession is reflected in the way Alexander's homage was treated in Scottish sources. The only completely contemporary source, the Melrose chronicle, written between 1211 and 1214, ignores the homage altogether, but says that the settlement was 'against the wishes of the Scots'.[195] If the Scottish narrative specifying the size of John's armies gave the full facts about the homage, they were too much for the patriotic Walter Bower, writing in the fifteenth century, through whose chronicle the narrative has been filtered to us. Bower here abandons the narrative, and prefers the account in another chronicle, the *Gesta Annalia*. This is based on contemporary sources, but was probably doctored around 1285.[196] It actually makes out that the homage was advantageous to Scottish independence. William thus resigned his English lands and rights to Alexander, who did homage for them to John, this as part of an agreement that henceforth it was the heir to the Scottish throne who would do homage to the king of England. In other words, the king of Scotland himself would no longer owe homage to the king of England at all. That John agreed to anything like that in 1209 is inconceivable.

The homage was not the only humiliating feature of the 1209 agreement. The letter, here broadly in agreement with the chronicle sources, explains that William had handed over to John his two daughters, Margaret, his first-born, and Isabella. Margaret was to be married to John's eldest son, Henry, once he reached the age of nine or ten, or before. (He was currently not yet two.) Isabella was then to be married a year or two later, in such a way as to give honour to both John and the king of Scotland. John, therefore, had scotched any plans to use the marriages of the two daughters to make alliances with the king of France or anyone else. There then followed the only things in the letter advantageous to the Scottish royal house. There was a pledge of mutual assistance, and a promise from John to help Alexander secure the throne on his father's death. He would help him 'as his man', meaning as someone who owed homage for the kingdom. Within this context, William and Alexander were to retain all their liberties and dignities and their claims to the three northern counties. At least they had not been made to resign the latter, although equally they had made no progress towards their realization.

Some further provisions in the treaty, for which there is documentary evidence, were left unmentioned in John's letter. John agreed not to build a castle at Tweedmouth, so that at least was a Scottish gain.[197] On the other hand, William had to hand over around thirteen hostages, and promise to pay 15,000 marks for John's benevolence. In 1189 only 10,000 marks had been needed to recover Scotland's independence. This time the money was essentially to buy off invasion and conquest.[198]

In 1212 John strengthened his hold over Scotland yet further, helped by the fact that William and Alexander were now facing internal revolt.[199] In February he met William again at Norham, and the agreements of 1209 were probably reaffirmed. In addition, William conceded that within six years John could marry Alexander, 'as his liege man', to whomever John wished, provided that Alexander was not disparaged.[200] The concession was completely at odds with any idea of Scottish independence. John's overlordship of the kingdom could not have been more clearly demonstrated. Next month, Alexander, now fourteen, came south and was knighted by John in London. He returned with Brabantine mercenaries to help put down the revolt of Guthred, son of Donald mac William.[201] William himself was now sixty-nine and ailing. John's great day when Alexander would succeed and do homage for the kingdom was approaching. To make sure of it, John started to build up a party in Scotland. He gave a pension to Robert de Londres, an illegitimate son of King William, who had a high position at the Scottish court.[202] He also granted Alan of Galloway, constable of Scotland, a great fief in Ulster.[203] His main considerations here were Irish, but Alan's power would also help in Scotland in the crucial period after William's death.

This new account of Scottish politics has direct relevance to the Scottish chapter in Magna Carta. The precise meaning of chapter 59 will be discussed later, but it covered the return of Alexander's sisters and the hostages, and thus reacted directly to the way they had been handed over in the Treaty of Norham in 1209.[204] Here, and when it came to the question of Alexander's rights and liberties, it laid down that he was to be treated in the same way as 'our other barons of England'. For Alexander this made a crucial point.

The only relationship between himself and King John was as 'a baron of England'. He was not in any way a subject king. As far as he was concerned, the 1209 treaty was dead.[205]

IRELAND AND THE BREAKING
OF THE BRIOUZES

John's policies in Ireland also helped shape the events that led to Magna Carta. Nowhere did he demonstrate more clearly the frightening power of his monarchy and his ability to break even the greatest baronial families.

Ireland, like Wales, was ideally suited to a master of manipulation such as John. He could play off the native rulers in the west (nominally in his allegiance) against the baronial lords in Munster, Leinster, Meath and Ulster. He could deal with men from each group both directly and through his justiciar based in Dublin, who controlled the areas subject immediately to royal rule. In the first part of the reign, the justiciar was Meiler fitzHenry, the great enemy of William Marshal. John's policies towards both the native rulers and the baronial lords often depended on his fortunes elsewhere in his empire. He cosseted or caned them as it suited his wider purpose, while always seeking to increase his income. In 1203 John thus ordered the justiciar to take over the best ports and villages in Connacht, and invest the revenues in building castles, founding new villages and doing everything possible for royal 'profit'.[206] It was likewise with the aim of making money that John in 1207 instituted the first Irish coinage. He also built new castles at Dublin and Athlone, established the procedures of the English common law and achieved a large and lasting expansion in the areas under direct royal control.

At the heart of John's dealings with the baronial lords in Ireland were his relations with William de Briouze.[207] William was lord of Briouze in Normandy, Bramber in Sussex, and Radnor and other lands in the marches of Wales. Very close to John at the start of his reign, Briouze was rewarded in 1202 with a grant of 'the honour of Limerick' in northern Munster. His presence there, John hoped, would help control an area contested with the native rulers. Characteristically, however, John kept something back, namely the city of Limerick itself, allowing Briouze at most to act there as royal custodian. Control of the city, therefore, became a great bone of contention between Briouze and the justiciar, Meiler fitzHenry. Another was created in 1206 when Meiler began to assert royal control over parts of Munster, in the process encroaching on Briouze's lordship. With relations deteriorating, John opened up a new line of attack, one that also taught a general lesson to his barons about the need to pay their debts.[208] Briouze had promised 5,000 marks for the grant of Limerick, which he was supposed to pay off at 1,000 marks a year. By 1207, disappointed over Limerick city, and thinking perhaps that John was not serious, he had cleared no more than 700 marks.[209] John, however, was now very serious indeed. In 1208 he started to compel payment by distraining on Briouze's chattels. When Briouze resisted, all his lands and castles in England and Wales (where Gerard d'Athée was the agent) were seized into the king's hands. Briouze fled to Ireland, with his wife, Matilda, and William, his eldest son.

In Ireland, Briouze was harboured by William Marshal, lord of Leinster, and the brothers Walter and Hugh de Lacy, respectively lords of Meath and Ulster. Walter was Briouze's son-in-law, and they were close collaborators. Since John had ordered Marshal and the Lacys to hand Briouze over, he could not possibly let this defiance pass. In 1208 an expedition to Ireland had already been on the agenda, after Marshal and the Lacys had worsted Meiler fitz-Henry. In 1210 John finally went there, taking a great army. By the time he sailed, Briouze had left Ireland, and was little more than a fugitive. The expedition was now about disciplining his Irish supporters. William Marshal wisely submitted, and retained his lands, but Walter and Hugh de Lacy were expelled from Meath and Ulster. John was much less successful in his dealings with the native kings, but he had demonstrated his power over the baronial lords in stunning fashion.[210] The corollary was also a massive increase in John's power in Wales, where Walter de Lacy's Ludlow and all the Briouze lordships came into his hands.

William de Briouze had left Matilda and their son William in Ireland. They had then gone to Scotland, only to be captured there and brought to the king. Matilda de St Valery, as she styled herself, using her family name, was easily the most famous woman of her age. John's own account of his quarrel with her husband shows that William and Matilda were very much a team, and gives a vivid picture of her courage and resourcefulness. Gerald of Wales praised Matilda's household management and her acquisition of property. The Anonymous of Béthune recorded her boast that she had 12,000 milking cows and so much cheese that it would support a besieged garrison of 100 men for a month, and still leave some to throw from the battlements. Matilda would know because in the 1190s she had defended the Briouze castle of Painscastle from an attack by the Welsh, whereafter it was always called 'The castle of Matilda'. John himself called her Matilda de Hay, probably because she also commanded at the Briouze castle at Hay-on-Wye. According to Roger of Wendover, Matilda refused to hand over her sons to John as hostages, remarking that she knew what John did to boys in his custody, a reference, of course, to his murder of Arthur. The story may be apocryphal but it catches her spirit.[211] According to the Anonymous of Béthune, Matilda was 'a beautiful lady, most wise, most worthy and most energetic. She was never absent from any of her husband's councils. She carried on warfare against the Welsh in which she conquered a good deal.'[212]

John's destruction of this celebrated woman and her son through starvation was a hideous crime. Its impact on baronial opinion can be gauged from the horrific and piteous account in the Anonymous of Béthune.[213] It was not as though William junior was himself unknown. He was already of full age, active in running the family estates and married to a daughter of the earl of Clare.[214] He was 'one of us'. The murders seemed more terrible than that of Arthur, who was a figure remote from the English baronage. They brought John's violence and cruelty close to home.

After his return from Ireland, but before Matilda's murder, John issued a long account of his quarrel with the Briouzes. It is an extraordinary document, and cannot be entirely specious, for it was witnessed and thus in a sense vouched for by many earls and barons who were later to rebel, including William de Briouze junior's father-in-law, the earl of Clare.[215] Plainly, John felt he had some explaining to do, a measure of the anxiety and criticism provoked by his conduct. Yet the document is as much a warning as an excuse. One purpose is to demonstrate the utter ruin awaiting those who cross the king. William de Briouze himself ends up as an outlaw, and thus liable to be killed on sight. (In the event he died in exile in France in 1211.) Matilda, at the last, is forced to promise 50,000 marks simply for the life and limbs of herself and her family. When the king's ministers come to her in prison to demand the first instalment, all that she has is a pathetic £16 and a few pieces of gold. The implication is that her life is now forfeit. And how had all this come about? Because Briouze failed to pay his debts. The need for baronial debtors (of whom Clare was one) to pay up was made chillingly clear.[216]

While issuing this warning, John is at pains to show that he has acted perfectly lawfully. William de Briouze has been outlawed according to 'the custom of England'.[217] Matilda's agreement with John has been confirmed by earls and barons in attendance. Briouze has been distrained to pay his debts according 'to the custom of the kingdom and the law of the exchequer'. John's opponents were thus set a challenge. What were the standards by which the king could be judged and brought to account?

8

Standards of Judgement

In general terms, John's government was considered extortionate and unjust. But what were the contemporary standards that informed and validated this judgement? When I first lectured on Magna Carta, I used to say that it was bereft of political ideas. I was right in that it has no long prologue justifying the restrictions it was placing on the king. Yet, in other respects, I was quite wrong, since ideas of law, justice, judgement, custom, counsel, consent and reasonable conduct run through the Charter like the shells in a shaft of Purbeck marble.

THE IDEAS IN THE CHARTER

At first sight, it was individuals, alone and defenceless, who benefited from the Charter. Its concessions, after all, were granted to individuals, 'to all . . . free men'. Yet these men were part of and protected by a wider entity: the kingdom.[1] The word 'kingdom' – 'regnum' – appears twenty-one times in the Charter and is fundamental to it. The kingdom was a physical, geographical entity that one could enter, exit and travel within. If the king left it, the chief justiciar took over its government. Within it there was to be one measure for cloth, food and drink.[2] The kingdom was also a living entity that possessed its own law – the 'lex regni' – and could give its common consent to taxation.[3] Things could be done for its harm and also for its 'reform' and 'utility'.[4] The kingdom possessed its own people. The free men to whom the Charter was granted were not so isolated after all; they were the free men of 'our kingdom', just as the barons were the barons of the kingdom.[5]

At the end of the Charter, in chapter 60, John declared that his concessions were to be held 'in our kingdom'. This avoided saying that they were to be held 'by' the kingdom but came close to it. In fact, that was very quickly how the Charter was regarded. The Dunstable annalist called it a Charter 'concerning the liberties of the kingdom of England'.[6] On the back of the Lincoln original, it is described in a contemporary hand as a 'Concord between King John and the Barons' achieved by 'the concession of the liberties of the church and the kingdom of England'. Henry III himself in 1255 wrote of 'Magna Carta' as being 'about the liberties conceded to the generality [*universitas*] of England'.[7]

John claimed throughout the Charter that the kingdom was 'his' kingdom. Indeed that seemed inherent in the very word 'kingdom'. Yet the Charter testified powerfully to the view that the kingdom had been harmed by the king and was now extracting the much needed 'reform' – 'emendatio' – from him. Some translations of the Charter seem to capture this sense of the kingdom apart from the king by rendering 'regnum' not as 'kingdom' but as 'realm'.[8] This foreshadows the universal translation of the 'communitas regni', which ranged itself against John's son, Henry III, as 'community of the realm' rather than 'community of the kingdom'. 'Realm' has some contemporary warrant. When the Coronation Charter of Henry I was translated into French in John's reign, 'regnum' appears as 'reaume', the word from which the English 'realm' derives.[9] 'Reaume' is also found in French translations of the 1225 Charter.[10] There are, however, problems. There is no indication in John's reign that 'reaume' – 'realm' – carried the nuances with which it is invested in 'the community of the realm'. Rather it seems synonymous with another French word, 'regne', the English equivalent of kingdom. It is 'regne' not 'reaume' that appears throughout the French translation of Magna Carta probably made in 1215 itself. Apart from one appearance of 'reaume', 'regne' is also found throughout a later French translation.[11] 'Kingdom' has, therefore, been preferred in the translation given in this book.

The Charter, however, certainly had a word that indicated a political entity, similar to the kingdom but separate from the king. The word was 'land'. 'Land' appears ten times in the Charter. In chapter 41 it is innocuous. It speaks of the treatment of merchants 'in our land', rather than kingdom, so as to balance merchants from lands that might be at war with the king, the point being that not all such merchants necessarily belonged to kingdoms. Elsewhere, however, the use of 'land' in the Charter carries a high political charge. It comes in the most aggressive clauses in the Charter where the king is being coerced and his arbitrary conduct challenged. It is thus the 'commune of all the land', formed by a universal oath, that is to aid the twenty-five barons of the security clause in keeping John to his promises, not the 'commune of the kingdom'. John is to proceed against free men only by lawful judgement of their peers or 'the law of the land'. He is to forgive all fines made unjustly 'and against the law of the land'.[12] Moreover his officials, under chapter 42 of the Articles of the Barons, are to know 'the law of the land' and mean to observe it. John managed to get 'land' here changed in Magna Carta (chapter 45) to 'kingdom', but in the contemporary French translation this is the one place where 'regnum' does not become 'regne'. Instead it appears as 'land' – 'la terre'. Either the translator sensed the intention of the Articles or he was working from an engrossment where the change had not been made.[13] The point in all these cases was to assert that there was an entity coterminous with the kingdom but separate and in a way older than it. There is no indication that the land is the king's. The implication is rather that the land, the elemental land, with its own law and people, had been there before kings and kingdoms. It was to this that everyone belonged when they formed the community of the land to enforce the Charter against the king.

The Charter also asserted something else, something so obvious that it is easy to forget its significance. The kingdom, the land, was England. This Englishness of the Charter is another of its chief characteristics. The Charter has fourteen references to England and three to the 'English church' – 'Anglicana ecclesia'. Merchants are to be allowed to go 'from England', 'into England', 'through England'. Fish weirs are to be removed from the rivers 'through all England'. The kinsmen of Gerard d'Athée are no longer to hold office 'in England'.[14] England also possesses its own law, and its own barons, 'our ... barons of England' as John puts it.[15] It was but a small step to see the Charter as being granted, as Henry III later put it, to the *universitas* of England.

In the Charter, the choice of 'England', as opposed to 'kingdom' or 'land', is not pointed in the same way as is the choice between 'kingdom' and 'land'. We hear of 'the law of England' in chapter 56 so as to distinguish it from 'the law of Wales'. Yet the Englishness of the charter still reflected something of great importance against which John and his government were tested. By the early thirteenth century there remained an elite group of barons who had land in both England and Normandy.[16] They are found both among John's counsellors at the start of the Charter and among the twenty-five barons who were to enforce it. The earls of Pembroke, Warenne, Arundel, Clare and Hereford, and William de Mowbray and Robert de Ros, all fall into this category. Such men, before 1204, had travelled constantly back and forth across the Channel, much like the king. They were just as likely to have been born in Normandy as in England. In terms of their nationality, if and when they thought about it, this elite probably regarded themselves as Anglo-Norman. John himself had been born in England, but whether he felt English is doubtful. His brother Richard, likewise born in England, certainly did not. 'You English are too scrupulous,' he once exclaimed, before threatening to send his mercenary captain, Mercadier, to sort someone out.[17]

By the early thirteenth century, this Anglo-Norman baronial elite were in a tiny minority. The great bulk of the political community of barons and knights were born and held their lands exclusively in England. England was their 'land'. The strength of the English tide can be seen in the way the *History of William Marshal* tried to stress the Englishness of its hero.[18] William was born in England, but he made his career on the continent and became a great Anglo-Norman baron. His son, the patron of the *History*, was born in Normandy, and for that reason led the Norman contingent at the battle of Lincoln in 1217. Yet a major theme of the *History* is how the Marshal, as a loyal 'Englishman' – 'uns Engleis' – saved England from the French invasion of 1216–17. When he becomes regent there is no better man 'in England'. Before the battle of Lincoln he exhorts the army to defend 'our land' from the French. His ultimate demise is 'bad for England'. The *History* also gloats at the hundred Frenchmen eaten by dogs, whom the English had killed between Winchester and Romsey during the 1215–17 civil war.[19] To be sure, English national feeling, as revealed in the *History*, a work of the mid-1220s, was accentuated by civil war and the politics of Henry III's minority.[20] Such tensions were there, however, before 1215. As far back as 1189, the appointment of the Norman, William Longchamp, as Richard's chancellor had been criticized on the grounds that he was an obscure foreigner.[21] The Melrose chronicle's accusation that John oppressed his subjects with foreign soldiers and gave patronage to aliens was made in or soon after 1218, and thus before the crises of Henry's minority.[22] The complaint that John was generous to foreigners and trusted more in aliens than his own people was made by the well-balanced Crowland chronicler.[23] One may well believe Ralph of Coggeshall when he says that in 1214 the nobles of the kingdom grumbled when the alien, Peter des Roches, was appointed over them as justiciar. Under chapter 50 of the Charter John was to remove from office Peter's countrymen, the Tourangeau relations of Gerard d'Athée. As the chapter said, heaving with emotion, 'henceforth they shall hold no bailiwick in England'. In some of the engrossments of the Charter, there is no division between this chapter and the next, which removed from the country all 'alien' soldiers who had come 'to the harm of the kingdom'. In the mind of the Charter, Gerard's kin were equally aliens who had harmed the kingdom. The whole Englishness of the Charter set a standard by which John was found wanting.

The kingdom, the land, England, then, had possessions and could suffer harm. Of the possessions, by far the most important were law and custom. More than anything else it was these that should protect the people from harm. The 'law of the kingdom', the 'law of the land', and 'the law of England' appear six times in the Charter. No one was to be proceeded against save by judgement of their peers or the law of the land; those imprisoned and outlawed according to the law of the kingdom were not to be allowed back into the kingdom; officials were to know the law of the kingdom and mean to observe it; fines and amercements made unjustly and against the law of the land were to be quashed; disseisins suffered by the Welsh in England were to be judged by 'the law of England'.[24]

The law of England was not a law laid down in legislation. As *Glanvill* declared, 'the laws of England are not written'. Rather, they were the legal rules that governed the conduct of justice in the courts. When it came to the local courts of shire and hundred, these rules were so many and various that they could not, *Glanvill* thought, be written down. Other rules, however, worked out by the king's judges or promulgated by the king in council, were 'in frequent and general use throughout the kingdom'. It was these that formed the principal subject of *Glanvill*, and lay at the heart of the common law.[25]

Defined like this, there was not much distinction between law and custom. Indeed *Glanvill* was described as a treatise 'on the laws and customs of the kingdom of England'. 'Custom' itself appears five times in the Charter, and on three occasions it is affirmed as 'ancient'. Clearly the antiquity of the custom was thought to give it a special strength. Tenants-in-chief were thus to succeed on payment of 'the ancient relief', and be treated according to 'the ancient custom of fees'. London was to have its 'ancient liberties and free customs', as were all other cities, boroughs, vills and ports. Merchants were to be allowed to buy and sell 'according to ancient and right customs'. In addition, vills and men were not to build bridges save when obliged to do so 'from ancient times and by law'. The counties were to be held at their 'ancient farms'. Where lords were the patrons of abbeys through 'ancient tenure', they were to have custody of them during vacancies.[26]

Under the shelter of law and custom, men could expect above all 'justice'. John thus promised not to deny, delay or sell justice, and to give 'full justice' on several issues when he returned from or abandoned his prospective crusade.[27] Justice was itself closely linked to 'judgement', which makes twelve appearances in the Charter, on seven occasions as judgement by peers.[28] It was by something closely akin to judgement, '*arbitrium*', that the twenty-five barons of the security clause were to decide whether John had put right his transgressions and breaches of the Charter.

There was another key idea that informed much of the Charter: the idea that exactions should be 'reasonable'. In the case of wardships, in chapter 4, custodians were only to exact 'reasonable issues and reasonable customs and reasonable services'. In chapters 12 and 15, aids imposed on the kingdom and on under-tenants were to be 'reasonable'. Knights, in chapter 29, were to be allowed to send substitutes to perform castle guard if they could show 'a reasonable cause'. Although the word itself was not used, when chapter 20 laid down that amercements should match the means of the offender and the nature of the offence, it was in effect calling for them to be 'reasonable'. If all this was obeyed, what individuals above all should enjoy were their 'rights'. At the start of the Charter, the church was to have its 'rights in whole'. Later chapters (52, 53 and 59) addressed the grievances of those, including the king of Scotland, whom John had deprived of their rights. In chapter 40 John promised to deny no one 'right or justice'.

Magna Carta, therefore, was full of ideas about the standards that John should meet. Those standards, however, did not apply to the king's subjects in the same way and in the same measure. At its broadest, the king promised justice to everyone. Some of his concessions in the areas of local government would indeed have lightened the burdens on all his subjects. Yet there was a fundamental difference between what was available to the free and the unfree. The king offered his justice to the former in their disputes over rights and property, but not to the latter. There was also a fundamental difference when it came to the king's tenants-in-chief. With these men, the king had a unique relationship. It was founded on the mutual bond between lord and tenant, in which, as *Glanvill* put it, 'the lord owes as much to the man on account of lordship as the man owes to the lord on account of homage, save only reverence'.[29] The Charter applied ideas of ancient custom and reasonable practice to the ingredients of the relationship, so to relief, wardships and marriages. It also testified, in its chapter on taxation, to the counsel that was owed by tenants to their lord. The Charter, therefore, set standards for John as both king and lord. It was because he had failed as both that Magna Carta was necessary.

THE ORIGINS OF THE IDEAS

Many of the basic concepts in Magna Carta were very old, and part of a general European inheritance. In the Bible, where Saul was only one example of a tyrannical king, judgement and justice were frequently linked together:

> Behold the days come, saith the Lord, that I will raise unto David a
> just branch, and a king shall reign and will be wise, and shall execute
> judgement and justice in the land.

So ran Jeremiah 23:5. Such ideas were elaborated in a long tradition of thought stretching back to Augustine and to Gregory the Great. The maxim, 'the king is so named from acting justly' – 'rex a recte agendo vocatur' – often quoted in the twelfth and thirteenth centuries, came from Isidore of Seville (560–636). To read Janet Nelson's study of 'bad kingship' in the early Middle Ages is to enter an ideological world very similar to that of

England in the early thirteenth century.[30] Thus the later Carolingian kings were accused, like King John, of being arbitrary, wilful and tyrannical. They had deprived men of their property 'against the law' and had aggressively and inventively extorted their wealth; all this instead of acting justly and reasonably, for the 'utility' of their subjects, by the 'common counsel' of their 'faithful men'. In the eleventh century King Conrad II of Germany protected knights from arbitrary disseisin by laying down that they were not to be deprived of their lands 'save according to the constitution of our ancestors and the judgement of their peers'.[31] The principle of judgement by peers, when it appeared in chapter 39 of the Charter, was, therefore, centuries old.

As for the mutual obligations involved in lordship, these were set out very fully in the early eleventh century by Fulbert of Chartres in a letter to the duke of Aquitaine. The 'faithful man' – 'fidelis' – to be worthy of what he held from his lord, had to display loyalty in a whole series of ways, 'and the lord in all these matters should behave in the same way towards his *fidelis*'. Both would be equally 'perfidious and perjured' if they failed in their obligations.[32] Fulbert's ideas too had deep roots, being influenced by the writings of Isidore of Seville, Archbishop Hincmar of Rheims (806–82) and Carolingian capitularies.[33] The ideas also had a long future. Around 1200 Fulbert's letter was inserted into a mid-twelfth-century Lombard compilation known as 'The Book of Fees', which in turn was incorporated, in the thirteenth century, into the fundamental statement of Roman law known as the 'Corpus Iuris Civilis'.[34]

England had long been part of these wider European developments. A key standard by which kings could be judged was the oath they swore at their coronations. This had appeared for the first time in West Frankia in 877, and was introduced a century later in England for the coronation of Edgar in *c.* 960 or 973.[35] In essence the oath bound the king to protect the church, maintain the peace and give justice, and it was easy to think that John had not done that. Indeed, when he was reconciled to the church and his excommunication was lifted in 1213, John had to renew his oath.[36] There were also the standards that kings set themselves in charters which they issued at the time of their coronations. It has been plausibly argued that the Coronation Charter of King Cnut is preserved in one of his law codes. It covers the malpractices of local officials, the rates of heriot (different from but in some ways akin to relief) and the right of 'widows and maidens' not to be forced into marriage. 'The journey towards Runnymede' had already begun.[37]

The journey had gone a lot further by the time of the 1100 Coronation Charter of Henry I. Henry's Charter became very well known, and, as we will see, was paraded before King John in 1214-15. Indeed, so as to be more accessible to the secular aristocracy, around that time it was translated into French.[38] The charter showed how old ideas about lordship had become channelled into the new tenurial structures created by the Norman Conquest. The Conquest had created a society in which all land was held from the king by his tenants-in-chief with attendant rights and obligations.[39] Thus the Coronation Charter, after a first chapter, like Magna Carta, on the church, went on to regulate the relationship between the king and the barons, earls and others 'who held' from him, thus dealing with the levying of relief, and the treatment of wardships, marriages and widows. In all this it anticipated Magna Carta.

The political unit governed by the 1100 Coronation Charter is the 'regnum' – 'the kingdom' – just as it is in Magna Carta. The word appears six times in what is a short Charter of only fourteen clauses. Sometimes it is the king's kingdom, 'my kingdom', but twice it is 'the kingdom of England', in a sense separate from the king. It is thus 'the kingdom of England' that has been oppressed by the unjust exactions of Henry I's predecessor, William Rufus. The 1100 Charter was equally clear about the standards that should obtain in the kingdom. It makes three references to 'right' – 'rectum' – and seven to 'justice' – 'justicia'. Things 'unjust' and done 'unjustly' in the past were to be 'just' and done 'justly' in the future. The Coronation Charter does not refer to 'judgement', unlike Magna Carta, but 'judgement by peers' was as well known in England as it was in Germany. It appeared both in Henry I's treaty with the count of Flanders in 1101 and in a legal work from his reign, known as 'The Laws of Henry I'. The latter added that the peers were to be from 'the same province' as the person judged, thus anticipating Magna Carta's demand that amercements should be imposed by 'upright men of the neighbourhood'.[40] The Coronation Charter makes no reference to 'reasonable' exactions, but the idea underlay the stipulation that penalties should be 'according to the nature of the offence'. Most striking of all was the emphasis in the 1100 Charter on the king ruling with counsel. Henry thus promised to give heiresses in marriage and retain forests in his hands with 'the counsel' or 'common counsel' of his barons. Indeed, he had come to the throne, 'by the common counsel of the barons of all the kingdom of England'. There was, therefore, no conceptual step involved when Magna Carta demanded that taxation should only be levied 'by the common counsel of the kingdom'.[41] Indeed, had not John's resistance been stronger, the Charter might well have demanded such counsel across a broader range of issues.

In the final promise of his Coronation Charter, Henry I said that he would maintain the laws of Edward the Confessor along with the changes made by William the Conqueror 'by the counsel of his barons'. In fact, there were no written laws of Edward, and the promise, if it had any reality, meant simply that Henry would maintain the laws and customs which were thought to have operated in Edward's time. Around the middle of the twelfth century, however, someone decided to make up for this lack, and produced a work of thirty-five chapters entitled the *Leges Edwardi Confessoris* (*The Laws of Edward the Confessor*). This was quickly accepted as the real thing, and the work became popular. Alongside the Coronation Charter of Henry I, it was flourished in John's face and became therefore another standard by which his kingship was judged.

The importance of the *Leges Edwardi* was not in the precise and sometimes archaic procedures that they described for maintaining the king's peace. Rather, it lay in reinforcing the picture, however apocryphal in the case of William the Conqueror, of a king ruling with the counsel and consent of his people, and indeed accepting the law as they defined it. Thus at the start of the *Leges Edwardi* we hear how King William 'by the counsel of his barons' summoned 'from all the counties of the country English nobles' so that he could learn their customs. These he finally accepted 'by the counsel and at the request of the barons'. William seems here to be taking the advice of a baronial assembly, but actually the *Leges Edwardi* also showed something else of relevance to 1215, namely that the political community, by which the king should be guided, was not simply a baronial one. Having described the convening of the English nobles on the advice of his barons, the *Leges Edwardi* set out a second stage in the procedure. Twelve men were to be 'chosen from each county of the entire country, to declare on oath their laws and customs'.[42] The parallel is obvious with chapter 48 of Magna Carta, in which twelve sworn knights are to be elected in each county to investigate and abolish 'all evil customs'. There is also a link here with the 1100 Charter, for that taught the same lesson about the breadth of the political community. Henry thus made direct concessions to the 'knights' when it came to the payment of the geld, and twice insisted that the barons pass on what they were getting from him to their own men.[43]

KING ARTHUR AND HIS KNIGHTS

In the second half of the twelfth century these ideas about good kingship were to be supported, invigorated and elaborated by momentous developments in European literature and learning. Around 1140 Geoffrey of Monmouth published his *History of the Kings of Britain*. The work virtually invented King Arthur and was a phenomenal success. It was translated by the poet Wace from the original Latin into French verse, and thus made more accessible to the secular nobility. It inspired the romances of Chrétien de Troyes. Its impact at the highest level is shown by the way John's nephew was named Arthur. In England, knowledge of Arthur also reached down to the level of knightly society. One of the most remarkable works produced in John's reign, or soon after, is a translation of Wace into English by the poet Lawman. One manuscript says that Lawman lived at Areley in Worcestershire 'with the good knight', which gives the best indication of the audience for which the work was produced.[44]

The trouble with Arthur was that he set impossible standards for kings.[45] He conquers much of Europe and performs many individual deeds of derring-do. He is open handed in gifts of land, gold and silver to his knights. He is also, especially in Lawman, a consensual ruler with a real concern for law, justice and the welfare of his people. Far more than in Geoffrey of Monmouth or in Wace, Lawman's Arthur reaches out to the men of the shires, summoning to his great assembly at Caerleon earls, bishops, knights and 'all the free men who were in the land at all'. Indeed, in protecting

'God's people', Arthur orders 'all the knights to give just decisions', although being very clear that the tillers of the soil must stick to their work! Arthur is also distinguished for his humanity: he blushes red and white with emotion when hearing of the death of his father. And though a fierce punisher of traitors and criminals, he is also merciful, summoning back those, 'whether great or mean', who have forfeited their lands, so that they can 'have their own again'.[46]

How could John, of all people, measure up to this standard? Of course, everyone knew that the chivalric ideal was an impossible dream. There was no 'world of limitless kingly wealth', where treasuries emptied by giving could quickly be replenished by the riches from further conquests, so that generosity and bravery chimed together.[47] The *History of William Marshal* wrestled with the problem in the case of Henry the 'Young King', the eldest son of Henry II. In imitation of Capetian practice, the Young King had been crowned king in 1170 during his father's lifetime, but this hardly moderated his irresponsibility. His open-handed generosity left behind a trail of debts that the more prudent William Marshal, as his leading knight, had to settle. Yet in the end the Young King still seemed to epitomize all the virtues of 'chivalry'. Recording his death (in 1183), the *History* lamented the end of the 'courtesy, prowess, debonaireté, and largesse' that had dwelt in his heart.[48] John did try. He could be courteous. He could give. But there was always something false and calculating about it. And no one could say John had much 'debonaireté' about him, that calm, charm and good cheer which was the opposite of anger.[49]

What made this worse was the example of King Richard. He had been everything a king should be when it came to prowess. John certainly could act in war with both dash and determination. He showed the former at Mirebeau in 1202, the latter during the long siege of Rochester in 1215. But he was never credited with feats of personal gallantry. To describe him as 'softsword' after the Peace of Le Goulet in 1200 was unfair, for there was much to be said for the settlement, but the description had an element of truth.[50] In both 1203, faced with the loss of Normandy, and in 1216, faced with Prince Louis's invasion, he seems to have lost his nerve. Richard, when he wanted, could also be the epitome of courtesy and debonaireté. When the garrison of Nottingham surrendered to him in 1194, it feared punishment in life or limb. Instead

Richard, 'compassionate, gentle and full of mercy', set a fair ransom on their heads. The Marshal *History* commented:

> the more a worthy man [*prusdom*] has the advantage,
> the more he should show his worth by desisting
> from doing harm and from acts of cruelty.

That was Richard. On the other hand:

> ... when a bad man has the advantage,
> cruelty and outrage are the consequences.

That obviously was John. He was a 'malveis home' (bad man), not a 'prusdom' (worthy man).[51]

There was here a wider context. The garrison at Nottingham feared for their lives. Everyone accepted that the penalty for breaking faith with one's lord could be corporal, the loss of life or limb. Yet, whatever the theory, nobles were rarely killed in battle or, if captured, executed for treason. Warfare and politics from the corporal point of view were fail-safe. Armour prevented nobles being killed in the normal course of fighting. When unable to fight on, the convention was to offer to surrender, and surrenders were nearly always accepted. One reason for that was the prospect of ransom; a captured lord was worthless dead, but worth a great deal alive. Another reason was that nobles simply were not killed for political crimes. They were imprisoned or disinherited, although often only temporarily. But they were very rarely executed. Here the reasons were partly chivalric – the 'courtesy' due to a conquered opponent – and partly pragmatic, growing from the conditions of the Anglo-Norman realm.[52] There was little point executing a great noble in England when that might stir up revolt among his kin in Normandy or elsewhere on the continent. Henry I, after capturing his elder brother Robert in 1106, kept him thereafter in comfortable confinement. The *Dialogus de Scaccario* noted with admiration how few of those who rebelled against Henry II in 1173–4 suffered loss of possessions, and none lost their rank or life. It was much the same in 1194.[53] John's cruelty to prisoners, and his murders of Arthur and Matilda and William de Briouze junior, thus seemed completely outside the conventions of the age.

ACADEMIC THOUGHT: THE 'IUS COMMUNE' AND THE STUDY OF THE BIBLE

Alongside the flourishing of chivalric literature, there were the momentous developments in academic learning. At their centre was the systematic study of canon and Roman law: the blend of the two was called the 'ius commune'. The foundation for study of the canon law was Gratian's *Decretum*, or *Concordance of Discordant Canons*, which was published in Bologna around 1140. The foundations of Roman law were the great legal collections of the Emperor Justininian, his *Digest*, *Code* and *Institutes*. In pursuit of the new learning, many Englishmen went abroad to the emerging universities of Bologna and Paris. The new learning could also, by the end of the century, be found at schools in England, at Oxford, Lincoln, Northampton and elsewhere. One of the most popular works of Roman law, a cheap summary of the *Digest* and *Code* for poor students, hence its title, *The Book of Poor Men* (*Liber Pauperum*), was written by Vacarius, who had come from Bologna to teach in England in the 1140s.[54] Virtually all the mantras about law and custom, justice and judgement, counsel and consent, reason and rationality, could be supported from texts in both canon and Roman law.

Within this context one work was particularly influential, the *Policraticus*, written by John of Salisbury, who was a friend and counsellor of Thomas Becket and who finished his career as bishop of Chartres. John portrayed the state as an organism, indeed as a human body, governed by reason. The prince was a ruler who upheld the laws and liberty of the people. The tyrant was a ruler who trampled on the law and oppressed the people.[55] None of these ideas were new, but the *Policraticus* gave them wide publicity. Their influence can be seen in the allegation of the Waverley abbey chronicle that under John 'instead of law there was tyrannical will'. The accusation of tyranny and lawlessness is equally found in the chronicles of Crowland, Margam and Melrose.[56]

In the hierarchy of academic life, at the very summit stood the study of theology, which meant above all the study of the Bible. Central to this work was the circle of the great Paris theologian Peter the Chanter, of which John's archbishop of Canterbury,

Stephen Langton, was part. Langton's own views are revealed in his sermons, and his commentaries on the Bible.[57] Like those of the circle in general, they frequently touched on day to day questions of social and political life. When, therefore, Langton's diocesan statutes in 1213–14 prohibited the receiving of bribes for the deferral or acceleration of justice, he was doing more than merely reiterating what was found in earlier ecclesiastical legislation. He would have had in mind the discussion in Peter's circle, which condemned the taking of bribes but acknowledged that judges needed to be properly paid, the kind of sensible balance typical of the school, and of Langton himself.[58]

We will question later whether Langton played a direct part in the evolution of the opposition programme in 1214–15, but he certainly believed in the Charter, and, once it was promulgated, did all he could to support it. Langton believed in royal power. It was necessary to protect the church and give peace to the people.[59] In origin, however, royal power was not divinely ordained. Unless exercised within prescribed limits it could be oppressive. God, Langton noted in his commentaries on Deuteronomy, had warned the people of Israel against having a king. 'Tyrannical exactions' lay in store if they insisted. Langton also stigmatized 'modern kings, who collect treasure not in order that they may sustain necessity, but to satiate their cupidity'. Demands that went 'beyond necessity' were 'evil'.[60] Langton had given thought about how to keep kings in check. In his commentaries, again on Deuteronomy, he commended the injunction that kings should secure an exemplar of the law from the priests and read it assiduously.[61] Another gloss, from a commentator in Langton's circle, explained that the prophet Samuel:

> announced the law of the kingdom, that is to say what [the king] ought to exact from his people, and what the latter ought to give him, and he laid down this charter [*ipsam scripturam*] before the lord, that is to say in a holy place, in order that if the king came to demand more from his subjects, he would be condemned by this charter.[62]

The parallels with Magna Carta seem very clear.

ENGLAND: THE LESSONS TO BE LEARNT
FROM ROYAL GOVERNMENT

Ideas about good rule did not merely come from chivalric literature and academic thought. In England they were also inculcated by the king himself. Henry II and his sons proclaimed their concern for the welfare of the kingdom. They said they had acted with counsel and consent. They demanded that their subjects, in their disputes with one another, should act justly and with judgement. They insisted, in all kinds of contexts, that things should accord with 'reason' and 'the custom of the kingdom'. At the very start of his reign, John abolished the fees that Richard's chancery had demanded 'more by will rather than by reason'.[63]

Both *Glanvill* and the *Dialogus de Scaccario* make many statements about law and custom that anticipate chapters in Magna Carta. This is true of the £5 relief for a knight's fee;[64] the forbidding of relief when land had been in wardship;[65] the stipulation that land in wardship should be returned 'stocked';[66] the protection offered to widows over obtaining their dowers and share of their husband's chattels;[67] the regulations on distraint and sureties;[68] the injunction that aids should be 'reasonable';[69] and the ideas about amercements matching the offence ('delictum'), and not destroying the transgressor's 'contenementum'.[70] A proclamation by King Richard in 1190, meanwhile, foreshadowed the Charter's provision about Jewish debts not gathering interest during minorities. A concession by John foreshadowed its limitation of the king to the principal sum when Jewish debts came into his hands.[71] The theory and sometimes the practice of summoning national assemblies before 1215 laid the foundations for the Charter's chapter on the subject.[72] Many government measures and pronouncements envisaged a kingdom of England with its own people and laws, whose safety and 'common utility' needed to be considered.[73]

In all this, one powerful instructor was the assize of novel disseisin, which developed in the years after 1166. The key question for the jury was whether the complainant had been disseised of property 'unjustly and without judgement'. Large numbers of knights and free tenants were using the assize. They also staffed the juries deciding the cases. The idea that the king himself should act up to the principles of the assize and disseize no one without judgement was inescapable. Essentially, what happened in 1215 was that the kingdom turned around and told the king to obey his own rules.

IMPACT

There is plenty of evidence that the ideas just discussed influenced attitudes and actions. While the substance of the law set out by *Glanvill* was indigenous, the way it was categorized and described was influenced by Roman examples, for example in the division between criminal and civil pleas and the discussion of the different types of dower.[74] The author of the *Dialogus*, Richard fitzNigel, eventually bishop of London, scoffed at the schoolmen who made their learning all the more exclusive by wrapping it up in complex and obscure language. He, by contrast, would write not about 'subtilia' but 'utilia'. Yet fitzNigel framed the *Dialogus* in the form of a university debate between a master and a pupil, and made sixty-two references to the Bible, and thirty-seven to classical and patristic texts, including several to Roman law.[75]

The impact of the 'ius commune', and more directly the canon-law element within it, was resoundingly clear in chapter 1 of Magna Carta. The chapter set the church free and proclaimed the papal confirmation of John's charter of November 1214 promising freedom of elections, freedom that is for the church itself to elect its bishops and abbots. The 1100 Coronation Charter had equally promised freedom to the church, but had said nothing about elections. That was a measure of how far the church's power and its law had advanced in the intervening hundred years. Magna Carta also reflected canon law in other ways. Thus, in chapter 22, clerks were to be amerced according to the value not of their ecclesiastical benefices but of their lay property, which recognized the canon-law principle that clerics did not hold benefices as personal possessions. Likewise, in chapter 27, the goods of those who died intestate were to be distributed 'under the supervision' of the church, which recognized the growing claims of the church in testamentary matters. Here Magna Carta was advancing beyond both the 1100 Charter and the Unknown Charter, which said nothing about the church's supervision. The law, as it was being defined by the church, also impacted very much to John's benefit when it was decided in chapters 52, 53 and 57 that he should enjoy the 'crusader's respite'. He could, therefore, delay dealing with the abuses of his father and brother until the end of his prospective crusade.

As for the other chapters of the Charter, Professor Helmholz has worked through no fewer than twenty-three of them, demonstrating parallels with the *ius commune*.[76] Sometimes this is a case of the *ius commune* confirming long standing principles. Magna Carta prevented widows being forced into re-marriage. So did the putative Coronation Charter of King Cnut. But the idea was reinforced by the stress placed on free consent by both Gratian and Pope Alexander III (1159–81). If Langton's diocescan statutes strengthened the view that there should be a chapter forbidding the sale and deferral of justice in Magna Carta, that justice should not be sold was acknowledged in the *Dialogus*. That it should be expeditious was a central aim of the common law. Indeed, Ranulf de Glanvill himself, as Henry II's chief justiciar, boasted that justice in royal courts was far quicker than in those of the church.[77] In other cases, the *ius commune* seems to have influenced the English law set out in *Glanvill*, which then found its way into Magna Carta. An example is the protection offered to sureties found in chapter 9 of the Charter.[78] In a few cases, the *ius commune* arguably helped the drafters of Magna Carta actually extend English law and practice. *Glanvill* averred that amercements should not damage the victim's means of livelihood, his 'contenementum', which was precisely how Magna Carta put it in chapter 20 when dealing with free men.[79] But neither *Glanvill* nor any other source before 1215 extended, as Magna Carta does, the principle to protecting a villein's 'wainagium', that is his means of cultivation, so his crops under cultivation, seed corn, ploughs and plough teams. Is there, however, a link here with a chapter in Justinian's *Codex*? There, slaves who do ploughing, ploughs and plough oxen are all protected from seizure for debt, if that would delay the payment of taxes.[80] In the *Codex*, the point is to protect agricultural labourers so that their lords can pay taxes to the state. In Magna Carta, it is to protect them, and thus their lords, from amercements imposed by the state. But the one stipulation may have helped shape the other.[81]

In the decades before Magna Carta, many of the ideas behind it can be seen in action. The turmoil that followed King Richard's absence naturally enhanced the need for counsel and consent. The new form of government in 1191 was agreed by bishops, earls, barons and indeed the citizens of London. The gigantic tax for Richard's ransom, paid by everyone in the kingdom, was likewise levied 'by common assent', although being for ransoming the king's body, such consent was not strictly necessary. As Maddicott observes, the principle that national taxation needed general consent, established by the grant of the crusading tax ('the Saladin tithe') of 1188, was thus confirmed.[82] Protection was also sought against arbitrary dispossession. In the peace treaty of 1191 lay and ecclesiastical magnates, knights and free tenants were to be deprived of their lands and chattels only 'by judgement of the court of the king according to legitimate customs and assizes'. They were not to be disseised simply by 'will' of the king's ministers.[83] Around the same time, Roger Bigod was offering his fine not to lose his inheritance 'save by a judgement of the court of the king made by his peers'. Bigod's fine is just one of many where people offer money for concessions that they would later get free of charge in Magna Carta. Such fines show the political mind of the king's subjects. They were very aware of the standards they wished to regulate their relations with the king. They were also aware that, for money, they could have them applied. What was obtained individually before 1215, and for money, was obtained generally and by the pressure of rebellion in Magna Carta. The pipe rolls and fine rolls are thus full of offers of money for justice and judgement, 'reasonable' shares of inheritances, 'reasonable' dowers and freedom for widows to marry or stay single. One baron defined a 'reasonable' relief as one of £100, just as in the Charter, although since he had to pay 100 marks in order to secure it, what he ended up with was hardly 'reasonable'.[84]

Equally telling are the concessions obtained by communities. The men of various counties gave large sums of money to remove the royal forest, get rid of increments and have sheriffs who were local men.[85] Numerous towns secured charters that conceded them liberties and confirmed ancient customs, or customs they liked to think were ancient. John himself granted at least seventy charters to over fifty towns. These were the urban liberties and free customs that Magna Carta confirmed in chapter 13. The town charters anticipated Magna Carta in having amercements assessed by local men, and giving freedom of trade 'through all England'. They conceded that officials could be elected by 'the common counsel' of the town, and laid down that such officials should monitor the provost (also elected) and ensure that he treated rich and poor alike rightly and justly. King Richard's charter to London abolished the fish weirs on the Medway and the Thames, just as did chapter 33 of the Charter.[86]

There also striking examples of under-tenants anticipating the demands of Magna Carta. The tenants of Robert de Mortimer were clear they owed aids only on the three occasions that the Charter was to specify.[87] Peter de Brus's knights and free tenants in his wapentake of Langbargh in north Yorkshire secured concessions that foreshadowed the Charter's regulations about both bringing men to trial and penalties matching the offence. Indeed, the word for offence – 'delictum' – is the same as in the Charter. Brus's concessions were embodied in a charter and described as 'liberties' to be held 'in perpetuity'.[88] Here one can see under-tenants developing an agenda of demands both against the king and against their lords.

The way ideas were moving against the Angevin kings is seen in a series of early thirteenth-century additions made to a London legal collection containing copies of the *Leges Edwardi Confessoris* and related texts. 'Right and justice ought to reign in the kingdom rather than perverse will; law is always what does right; for will and force and violence are not right', ran one such passage.[89] Another interpolation in the same collection showed how the same principles might apply at the local level. Thus in the hundred court nothing was to be taken 'save by law and reason, by the law of the land and justice, and by judgement of the court, without deceit'.[90] There was a close connection between London and the rebels. One of the baronial leaders, Robert fitzWalter, was lord of Baynard's castle in the city. These ideas, therefore, were almost certainly circulating in baronial circles.[91] There was nothing original about them. They could have been written under the Carolingians. What is striking is that someone in London, in the early thirteenth century, thought such assertions were sufficiently important and timely to deserve interpolation into a legal collection. He had a very good reason, for while the *Leges Edwardi*, in their original form, showed that the king should accept the law as revealed by his people, they said nothing about the conflict between law and will. It was with a sharp appreciation of how John actually operated that the interpolator dealt with that issue, giving the *Leges* and its associated texts teeth and bringing them up to date. That is a measure of what John was up against.

JOHN'S DEFENCE

By 1215, therefore, the basic ideas of how the king should rule, as found in the Charter, were the reverse of novelties. They were part of the very fabric of English society. John in the 1200s was judged by far more exact and exacting standards than Henry I had been a hundred years before. Old ideas about good and bad kingship had been strengthened by the literature and learning of the twelfth century and by the precepts and procedures of royal government. These standards challenged old abuses, like punitive fines, arbitrary disseisins and the taking of hostages, which John was now practising on a new scale. They challenged financial exactions which, after the loss of Normandy, were being carried to altogether unprecedented heights. John's rule was becoming very different from that of his father and brother. What he desperately needed was to provide it with an ideological rationale, which could justify what was in effect a new monarchy. One reason for Magna Carta was his failure to do so.

Neither John nor his predecessors ever really tackled a central criticism of their rule, namely the way that their acts of will seemed contrary to law. When the 1191 agreement said that men must be deprived of land by judgement and not by will, it then, in deference to the absent Richard, added that they could also be disseised 'by the order of the king'. This admitted the king's reserve of power, but did nothing to justify it. It stood there brazen, undefended and indeed undermined by the immediately preceding appeal to judgement. There were weapons to hand, both in the Bible and in Roman law, from which a new theory of monarchy might have been constructed. Yet the agents of royal government did no more than pull them from their scabbards only to hastily resheathe them. *Glanvill* itself quoted the famous maxim found at the start of Justinian's *Institutes*, 'the will of the prince has the force of law'. But instead of elaborating and glorying in the principle, *Glanvill* hurried on to say that the laws of England were those things 'settled in council on the advice of the magnates and with the supporting authority of the prince'. John himself could invoke the 'common utility of our kingdom', but he never, like Edward I, observed that 'for the common utility by his prerogative, the king is in many cases above the laws and customs used in his kingdom'.[92]

John could also speak of his 'necessity', but unlike Henry III's queen, he never declared that 'all things belong to the prince in cases of urgent necessity'.[93]

In all this, John got little help from his professional judges. Some of them might well be venal. Ralph of Coggeshall gives a vivid picture of the judge Osbert fitzHervey in Hell, being forced to swallow and then regurgitate burning coins. Yet these were men steeped in the principles and practices found in *Glanvill*. They would all have ascribed to the declaration made by the justices visiting Lincolnshire in 1218: 'we are bound to give justice to all, rich and poor alike, without exception of persons'. Another of John's judges, the knight, and later rebel, John of Guestling, was a tenant of the archbishop of Canterbury, and became close, having left John's service, to Archbishop Langton. In a charter that he issued to local men about the mutual exploitation of marshland, he limited the amercements which could be imposed by his court to two shillings, very much in the spirit of Magna Carta.[94] If there was going to be a tract justifying, indeed celebrating, absolutism, it would surely be the *Dialogus*, written by the king's own treasurer. But not a bit of it, or at least not much of it. The *Dialogus* certainly got off to a good start. With a smattering of quotations from the Gospels, it declared that:

> with all due reverence, we must subject ourselves and give obedience to the powers ordained by God, for all power comes from God. Therefore it is proper to serve kings who surpass all others ... It is not for the king's subjects to question or condemn his actions. For princes, whose hearts and consciences are in God's hand, and to whose sole care God himself has entrusted his subjects, stand or fall by divine, not human, judgement.[95]

After this ringing passage, however, the *Dialogus* then continued in a more cautionary vein. 'Let no one flatter themselves they can misbehave with impunity.' God, here quoting the Book of Wisdom, would 'punish the powerful with powerful torments'. And of course, the Last Judgement portals, like that shown to King John at Fontevrault by Bishop Hugh, often featured kings among those being dragged down by gruesome devils into the jaws of Hell. The *Dialogus* might preach non-resistance, but it did not justify arbitrary rule. Historians often scoff at contemporary references to the law of the exchequer, suggesting it was more or less the same as the will of the king. In John's exchequer, under Peter des Roches and William Brewer, it may well have been. Yet it is quite clear that the *Dialogus* did not look at it in that way. While acknowledging that the king's wealth might come by 'his arbitrary will' – 'voluntatis arbitrio' – as well as by law, it hardly seemed comfortable with the fact. The procedures or 'laws' of the exchequer, it explained, were for the king's 'utility', but 'saving equity'. They would ensure that the king got his dues and everyone their 'right'. No one should be offended by the procedures of the exchequer, provided 'they do not stray from the path of what is established by law'. The *Dialogus* also averred that the king ought not to revoke his gifts and pardons, a principle which constituted a vital barrier against tyranny since it meant that the lands and rights granted by royal charter were safe. The king could not just regret his concessions and overturn them.[96]

The problem for the king was partly that the biblical and Roman law texts did not give any consistent message. The Bible might show the king as the lord's annointed, but it also gave plenty of examples of kings who had gone to the bad, and indeed (as in the case of Saul) had been removed. Roman law asserted both that the ruler was above the law, and that he was bound by it. It stressed both the prince's role in making law and also the people's. The tendency of legal teaching in England, as revealed in Vacarius's *Liber Pauperum* and related texts, was to play down the absolutist elements in Roman law. Thus a gloss on the maxim that one should not dispute the ruler's acts read 'This is not true when the prince does anything by himself without the suggestion of anyone, for in that case it is permissible to dispute his act.' 'The vigour of the law comes from custom and the will of the people', ran another gloss.[97]

Rhetoric under John and his predecessors certainly emphasized the king's elevated status. *Glanvill* wrote of 'your highness', the *Dialogus* of 'your excellency'.[98] Actions could be stigmatized as against 'the royal dignity and excellency', or as offences 'against the royal majesty'.[99] John also enhanced the dignity of his kingship through his lavish hospitality and burnished its image through his expenditure on crowns, swords, jewels, clothes and buildings. One of the swords in his treasury was called 'Tristan' after that 'swashbuckling hero' of chivalric romance. We have seen the extraordinary apartments he built for himself at Corfe castle.[100] Yet John failed, in any decisive way, to improve the image of monarchy on the silver penny, although it was far more familiar than any other. In the recoinage of 1205, he neither placed his own name on the coins (the king was still 'Henry') nor gave the king's head a proper crown. It was left to John's son, in his recoinage of 1247, to assume a crown and stamp his own name, 'Henricus III' or 'Henricus tercius', on the coins.[101]

At the heart of John's defence were very traditional ideas. He challenged his opponents on their own ground, by arguing that his demands were ancient and customary, while it was they who were acting wilfully and unjustly. Thus the pope, back on John's side in 1215, opined that the king's 'ancient' right to scutage was being denied 'without judgement' by a baronial act of 'will'. In the same year, John summoned Wallingford honour knights to garrison its castle, as they were 'anciently accustomed'.[102] In some cases, John had every right to deny the existence of the 'ancient customs' that were being appealed to. Chapter 2 of the Charter made out that the 'ancient' relief of an earl or a baron was £100, but both *Glanvill* and the *Dialogus* agreed that the sum was determined by the king's pleasure and was subject to whatever could be negotiated. The exchequer's pipe rolls show that that was indeed the actual practice.[103] A different point could be made about chapter 25, which said that the counties should be held at their ancient farms, without any increment. Certainly the farms were 'ancient', but it was surely perfectly 'reasonable' for the king to try to exact sums above them, given the increasing population and wealth of the country. And what of the forest? That it should extend no further than at the start of the reign of Henry II was the demand, but was that 'reasonable' given all the losses of royal forest under Stephen? In all these things, it was surely John's critics who were the innovators. Magna Carta might be trying to subject the king to law, yet in many cases it was not ancient law but the law that the Charter itself was making.

John also sought to exploit one of the most basic strands of royal authority, namely the loyalty and service due from men who had done him homage and sworn him fealty. Again and again, John harped on these bonds and tried to strengthen them. He did so in 1205 when facing invasion, in 1209 in the great oath of Marlborough, and, on several occasions, in 1215.[104] It was his natural reaction in any moment of crisis. As Thomas Bisson has remarked, 'John lived by oaths.'[105] John saw the crises he faced as crises of lordship, caused by the failure of his men to live up to their obligations. They were solvable by insisting that the obligations be fulfilled. Thus John demanded that William Marshal and Walter and Hugh de Lacy should surrender William de Briouze 'in the faith they are held to us, as they are our liegemen'. The consequences of breaching faith were made very clear by John's threats against the Marshal in 1206, uttered for him by John of Bassingbourn. 'I cannot see or understand why or how anyone should hold land if he fails his lord in his hour of need.'[106] John was here exploiting powerful ideas. True, those who remained loyal usually had strong material reasons for doing so. John's unpopular castellans and sheriffs had nowhere else to go. The alliance between the Welsh rulers and the rebels gave the marcher barons, including Ranulf, earl of Chester, and William Marshal, strong grounds for remaining on the royal side. The Marshal had also to consider his position in Ireland, where he had many enemies and the rebellion had no footing. Yet the duty of loyalty to one's lord, which runs throughout the *History of William Marshal*, was far more than poetic rhetoric. The Marshal himself saw his career in those terms. In a letter of 1216 the young Henry III described how the Marshal 'had always stood faithfully and devotedly by our father when living, and now adheres constantly to us . . . having proved himself as gold in the furnace'.[107] Likewise, Reginald of Cornhill, as sheriff of Kent, acknowledged that he should make an annual payment in alms for 'the glorious king of England':

> as I am a faithful man [*fidelis*] of the lord king and have done him homage nor ought I to want his honour or utility ever to suffer, particularly in those things which especially belong to the preservation of his body and soul.[108]

Rebellion could seem dishonourable. The *History of William Marshal* makes no reference to that of William Marshal junior. The Anonymous of Béthune likewise passed over his patron's desertion of John.[109] Some of John's enemies may well have wrestled with their consciences before taking the final step into rebellion. But the trouble was they did take the step. There was a whole array of arguments to justify rebellion and indeed deposition, as we will see.[110] And John provided so many material reasons to embrace them. Reginald of Cornhill's son, another Reginald, who followed his father as sheriff of Kent, himself rebelled in 1215. He had been made to offer 10,000 marks to have his father's lands and be forgiven his debts.[111]

John, like his predecessors, also stressed his absolute, overarching duty to preserve and defend his own rights, the rights of 'my' crown, or the rights of 'my' kingdom.[112] This was a constant theme in his dispute with the monks of Bury St Edmunds between 1213 and 1215 over the appointment of their new abbot. 'Welcome my lord abbot elect, saving the rights of my kingdom' was his greeting on one occasion. 'What do you want me to say to you?' he angrily asked on another. 'I have to consider myself and my crown before you and your honour.'[113] Linked to the idea of the crown was the argument that the king could do as he liked with certain possessions which were peculiarly 'his own'. John evidently deployed the argument to some effect in 1215, for the king's demesne manors were exempted from the Charter's restrictions, in chapter 25, on the raising of revenue from the counties and hundreds. He would also have deployed it to defend his right to tallage both the Jews and royal towns as he pleased.[114]

Such ideas, however, were not without danger. Was there any connection between the rights of the king and the welfare of his subjects? John did not suggest so when he demanded support for the recovery of Normandy simply 'as you love us and our honour' 'in our most urgent need'. All John offered in return was to give a good hearing to his subjects when they brought 'their affairs' before him. He could not have shown more clearly that his 'affairs' were quite separate from theirs.[115] Sometimes John did strike a more inclusive note. In 1205, facing invasion, he summoned his magnates to discuss 'our great and laborious affairs and the common utility of our kingdom'. Likewise, the tax of 1207 was for 'the defence of our kingdom and the recovery of our right'.[116] In 1213, with another invasion threatening, the king summoned barons, knights and all free men to Dover to defend 'our head, their heads and the land of England'.[117] John could also indicate how his interests and those of the kingdom were connected. 'You should defend our rights because we are bound to defend yours,' he opined in one proclamation.[118] Such rhetoric had an impact. Interpolations in the *Leges Edwardi* collection included one about the obligation to serve the king 'for the protection of the kingdom'. On the other hand, another interpolation stressed the duty to muster in defence of 'the honour and utility of the crown of the kingdom', which almost suggested the kingdom had wrested the crown from the king, and had its own interests separate from his.[119]

Even at its best, John was doing nothing to justify the arbitrary features of his rule. Indeed, his basic line was simply to pretend that they did not exist. His government was consensual and congruent with the law:

> We do not wish that you should be treated henceforth save by law and judgement, nor that anyone shall take anything from you by will, nor that you be disseised of your free tenements unjustly and without judgement.

So ran one proclamation to Ireland.[120] Thus John's letters, like the legal rulings and decisions of his judges, frequently stressed that he was acting reasonably, according to the law and custom of the kingdom.[121] When John acted against the monks of St Augustine's, Canterbury, he claimed that they were challenging the dignity of the crown, and violating the law of the kingdom, while he, in ejecting them from Faversham church, was acting 'on the advice of our nobles according to the custom of the kingdom'.[122] John's long and detailed account of his proceedings against William and Matilda de Briouze was in exactly the same vein.

John's arguments have convinced the greatest Magna Carta historian of the validity of his case. Holt has declared that John and his predecessors 'were normally able to take action against the recalcitrant by lawful and accepted procedure'. 'John's conduct of affairs was not in the main unlawful or contrary to custom.'[123] In Holt's perspective, John's rule was thus broadly congruent with Magna Carta chapter 39, the more especially since the chapter offered treatment according to 'the law of land' as an alternative to judgement by peers.[124] The immediate precursor of the clause was an offer of John himself in the days before Magna Carta. In a letter issued on 10 May 1215, he promised the barons that he would not arrest, disseize or go against them by force or by arms 'save by the law of our kingdom or by the judgement of their peers in our court'.[125] There was certainly much in the law of the kingdom that John could exploit. The Charter itself accepted, in chapter 9, that chattels and land might be seized to compel the payment of a debt. In law suits, property could likewise be seized and people arrested in order to compel attendance at court. The law also permitted pre-trial arrest in criminal cases, as the Charter acknowledged in chapter 54 when it said that no one was to be arrested and imprisoned on the accusation of a woman for the death of anyone other than her husband. In a criminal cases before the justices in eyre, guilt or innocence, was usually determined not by judgement of a jury but by the ordeal. Yet it is very unlikely that in 1215 'the law of the kingdom' was seen as weakening the force of judgement by peers and giving the king some kind of leeway. John made the offer to conciliate his enemies, and probably in answer to their demands. The barons altered 'the law of our kingdom' to 'the law of the land', the latter both more independent of the king and more respectful of local custom, and then incorporated 'by judgement of their peers or by the law of land' into the Articles of the Barons and thence into Magna Carta. The law of the land was seen as tightening not loosening the bonds around the king. It meant he should rule in concert with his nobles, for *Glanvill*, as we have seen, insisted that the laws of England were made by the magnates and the prince together. The law of the land might represent no more than a general sense of what was right and customary, but that made it all the easier to accuse John of contraventions. It could also be seen as offering quite specific protections. It allowed an individual to defend himself by trial by battle, as the Marshal wished to do in 1206.[126] It meant the process of outlawry must follow proper customary procedures (a major issue given the outlawries of William de Briouze and later Robert fitzWalter and Eustace de Vescy.) And it meant, unless there were other local customs, that pre-trial arrest should take place after accusation by a private individual or a jury, here overlapping with chapter 38 which insisted that a bailiff was not to put anyone 'to law' and so on trial on his own unsupported accusation.

John's problem was that however much he said his conduct was lawful, no one at the time believed him. His subjects were far less persuadable than Holt. With his arbitrary conduct and financial exactions, John was creating a new type of kingship, but a kingship new in its actions, not in its justifications, a kingship of great physical power without any kind of ideological support. John was reduced to telling everyone that it was just kingship as of old. The whole political community knew this was untrue. It had plenty of standards by which to judge John, and in essence, like the annals of Waverley abbey, it judged him a tyrant. The question for John's enemies became what to do about it, and how to justify what they wished to do.

THE EUROPEAN CONTEXT

Some answers to that question were being given elsewhere in Europe, where ideas similar to those in England were being elaborated in legislation, embodied in concessions made by rulers and appealed to by those in opposition to the king. Magna Carta certainly did not stand alone.[127] In the Spanish kingdom of León and Castile, legislation covered the rights of widows, royal courts meeting in fixed places, due legal process, judgement of peers and the levying of taxation, all issues found in Magna Carta.[128] Rulers were also making detailed concessions. In 1205 King Pedro II of Aragon drew up for his subjects in Catalonia a charter (probably never promulgated) that granted privileges in the areas of 'taxation, administrative practices, justice and coinage'. In the process he promised that local officials should be knights of the land, chosen by 'the counsel of the magnates and wise men of that land'.[129] How English local society would have liked that in Magna Carta! Then, in December 1212, Simon de Montfort issued the Statute of Pamiers for the state which he was founding in Béziers and Carcassone after victory in his crusade against the Albigensians. The Statute ran to over forty chapters. Many of these dealt with relations with the heretics. But the Statute, having begun like Magna Carta, by protecting the rights and liberties of the church, also made justice free, limited the obligation to perform military service, gave safeguards against imprisonment, allowed French widows, magnates and heiresses to marry among themselves without permission, and upheld French customs of inheritance for barons, knights and burgesses. There was even some protection for men against the 'malice' of their lords.[130] Given that Simon de Montfort, as we will see, was canvassed in 1212 as king of England, if John was deposed, it is highly likely that this example was known to English barons.[131] What then could they do to resist John in England?

9
Resistance, 1212–1215

There were plenty of reasons to judge John's rule oppressive and tyrannical. The question was what to do about it. Signs of an answer were already apparent in the first part of the reign. In 1205, according to Gervase of Canterbury, after the king had convened the 'magnates of England' at Oxford, they 'compelled' him to swear to uphold the 'rights [*jura*] of the kingdom of England' 'with their counsel'. John, in return, extracted an oath from the earls and barons that they would give him their due service. We know no more about this episode, which was probably related to the scheme for national defence against invasion that John promulgated a few days later.[1] It reveals, however, two key elements in the revolt of 1215: first, the ability of the barons to take collective action against the king; and second, the way that action was in support of a political programme, however vague and insubstantial. There seems here to have been a major advance from the situation under Stephen, when the barons had pressed their individual claims upon the contestants for the throne and extracted their own individual charters of concession. The rebels of 1173–4 probably hoped for similar individual solutions. The barons in 1215 certainly obtained redress of their own individual grievances, but they did so under procedures set up by a Charter conceded to the kingdom. The Charter also laid down general rules of conduct for the king from which all barons might hope to benefit. This change from individual to collective remedy had above all been produced by the pressures and abuses of royal government. These had given the barons a community of interest in their resistance to the crown.

THE PLOT OF 1212

If the episode in 1205 suggests a course was being set that would eventually lead to Magna Carta, in 1212 it took a radically different direction. The barons conspired not to make John respect the rights of the kingdom, but to get rid of him altogether. The first crack in John's authority had come in Wales. There, in the summer of 1212, Llywelyn formed a coalition of Welsh rulers, including the maltreated Gwenwynwyn of southern Powys. They were strengthened by an alliance with Philip Augustus, and soon informed him that they had wrested 'a great part of the land and the strongest castles from the yoke of English tyranny'.[2] Llywelyn himself certainly recovered all the land between the Conwy and the Dee which he had ceded in the treaty of 1211. John could not possibly let this go. Quite apart from his loss of territory, the alliance with King Philip set a pernicious example. John, therefore, mustered an army for another Welsh campaign. Only then, while he was at Nottingham in mid-August, on his way to the rendezvous at Chester, did he hear of a conspiracy against him.

When John took action against one ringleader of the conspiracy, Robert fitzWalter, it was for plotting 'our death, betrayal and imprisonment'.[3] The forthcoming campaign, when the king would be surrounded by treacherous barons and Welsh enemies, could clearly facilitate 'something happening' on those lines. With John out of the way, the aim then, according to a story that reached the Dunstable annals, was to give the throne to the great French noble Simon de Montfort, lord of Montfort l'Amaury near Paris. He had just carried the papal banner in the campaign against the Albigensian heretics in the south of France, and had a claim (which John had briefly recognized) to the earldom of Leicester.[4]

As soon as he heard of the plot, John called off the campaign, dismissed his baronial army and hurried foreign mercenaries to his side.[5] Only two magnates were directly fingered as conspirators, fitzWalter himself and Eustace de Vescy. FitzWalter was lord of Dunmow in Essex and Baynard's castle in the city of London. Vescy was lord of Alnwick in Northumberland. Each had many knightly tenants. Both ranked among 'the most high men of England and most powerful'.[6] There may have been something deeply personal about their revolt. FitzWalter when in exile in France alleged that John had tried to seduce his daughter.[7] According to a story current in the late thirteenth century, John had likewise made advances on Vescy's wife.[8] There were also material grievances. Vescy's had begun with his 1,300-mark fine to enter his inheritance in 1190. Under John, having made several offers for justice and judgement, he was amerced 300 marks for losing one lawsuit, and then lost another in which he was trying to establish his overlord-ship over a knightly tenant. The 300 marks were pardoned, but in a writ attested by Peter des Roches – and Peter did not do such things for free. Meanwhile Vesci owed money to the Jews.[9] In themselves, many of these were small things, but they mounted up.

Compared to the darkly formidable Vesci, Robert fitzWalter appears a far more dashing and dramatic figure. On his silver seal die, we see him galloping along, in a great helmet, brandishing his sword, the heraldic devices proclaiming his alliance with Saer de Quincy, earl of Winchester.[10] The two together had defended the castle of Vaudreuil in Normandy in 1203, and had lived down the apparently ignominious circumstances of its surrender. FitzWalter had one clear material grievance, over Hertford castle, which John had given him and then, in 1209, taken away. FitzWalter's right to the castle was to be recognized at Runnymede.[11] In one story, told by the Anonymous of Béthune, when John threatened to hang fitz-Walter's son-in-law during a quarrel at court, fitzWalter riposted 'You would hang my son-in-law! By God's body you will not. You will see 2,000 laced helms in your land before you hang him.'[12] At St Albans abbey, fitzWalter was remembered for laying siege to Binham priory in an attempt to assert his rights as its patron, mak-ing John cry out 'Is he or me king in England?' Matthew Paris caught the essence of the man:

> There was scarcely an earl in England who was his equal. He was vigorous in arms, courageous and proud, abounding in many posses-sions, of noble birth, with numbers of powerful relations, supported and strengthened by a multitudinous affinity.[13]

In 1212 there must have been more conspirators than simply Vescy and fitzWalter, although they clearly escaped discovery. Vescy and fitzWalter themselves were apparently unconnected and came from different parts of the country. John suspected another northern baron, Richard de Umfraville, and also Earl William de Warenne, lord of Conisbrough in Yorkshire and Lewes in Sussex. (His sister had been John's mistress.) There was clearly a British dimension to the plot, just as there was to the rebellion in 1215. Indeed, according to one story, it was Joan, John's illegitimate daughter, the wife of Llywelyn, who warned her father what was afoot. Another story was that the leak came from the Scottish court.[14] Eustace de Vescy's wife, the recipient of John's alleged attentions, was an illegitimate daughter of William the Lion, king of Scots, and it was to Scotland that Vescy fled. Another suspect was King William's brother, Earl David of Huntingdon.

The opportunities offered by the campaign in Wales were doubtless the immediate trigger for the 1212 plot. Behind it lay the transformation of royal government that John had effected since 1205, above all in the area of financial exactions. One can sense both the mounting grievances, and the beginnings of collective action, in the groups of supporters who rallied behind individual barons as sureties for the payment of their gigantic debts. By 1212, moreover, the murders of Matilda and William de Briouze junior must have been well known. One of those who came under suspicion was Earl Richard de Clare. He had to hand over as a hostage his daughter Matilda, who was William's widow.[15] The year 1212 also saw an exigent forest eyre and a threatening inquiry into land tenure. John had launched the latter on 1 June. He wanted information about the fees that were held from him in chief, and alienations made from them which might impair the service owed the crown. The returns in some counties were extraordinarily detailed (in Lincolnshire, in a modern edition, they run to forty-four printed pages). They covered the holdings of many later rebels, barons and knights. In fact, the knightly jurors gave little information about alienations and often stoutly denied that there had been any to the king's detriment. With the disintegration of his political position, John never acted on the results. Yet the intention of penalizing alienations or bringing them back under royal control must have been alarmingly clear.[16]

Just exactly what was planned by the conspirators in 1212 we do no know. Presumably, at some point, a great council would have met to offer the throne to Montfort or someone else. This is what happened in 1215, after the failure of Magna Carta, when the barons chose Louis, the eldest son of King Philip of France, in John's place.[17] Ideas about removing tyrannical kings were certainly around. John of Salisbury illustrated the terrible ends met by tyrants, and said it was 'equitable and just' to kill them.[18] There was also a famous example in the past of the pope sanctioning the removal of kings. Outlawed with Robert fitzWalter in 1212 was the canon of St Paul's, Gervase of Howbridge. Gervase was surely familiar with the *Leges Edwardi*, of which there was a text in London. This told how the pope had sanctioned the transfer of the kingship from the Merovingians to the Carolingians, the former having so signally failed to defend church and people.[19] Simon de Montfort, singled out as John's successor, was probably familiar with Carolingian precedents. His son was later to tell Henry III that he deserved to be imprisoned like the Carolingian king Charles the Simple.[20]

In fact, Innocent III never went as far as deposing John, but it was easy to believe, or manufacture the belief, that he had or was about to do so.[21] Archbishop Langton had urged the knights of the realm to defend the church with their swords, and made clear that John's subjects would be absolved from their fealty if he persisted in his disobedience.[22] Innocent himself in a letter of April 1211 had threatened John with 'ruin' if he did not repent.[23] What that meant was very clear. The year before, Innocent had absolved the subjects of John's nephew and ally, the Emperor Otto, from their allegiance and forbidden them to obey him.[24] The justification for the Welsh revolt against John in 1212 was the belief that Innocent had absolved the Welsh rulers from their allegiance to John and had urged them to make war on him.[25] Simon de Montfort himself perfectly fitted this scenario. Having led the crusade against the Albigensian heretics, he was a favourite son of the church. A great baron, would he not also be sympathetic to baronial aspirations? Indeed, in December 1212 he was to issue for his state of Béziers and Carcassonne provisions that, in protecting the rights of his subjects, anticipated Magna Carta.[26] There could be no greater contrast to King John and no more suitable replacement.

CONCESSION AND OPPRESSION, 1212–1214

John was profoundly shocked by the plot of 1212. In January 1213 he went north and reached Alnwick, in order, as he said, to ensure his hold over 'the northern part of England'.[27] Running into

1213, he made a series of concessions designed to re-establish his position. He treated widows with more leniency, reformed the administration of the forests, promised to demand only the capital in debts owed to the Jews, and abandoned his policy of extracting profits from the counties. He also dismissed some of the northern sheriffs, and, 'moved' by the complaints against them, mounted an inquiry into their activities.[28] The concessions were deliberately designed to appeal to knights and free tenants as much as to earls and barons. Indeed, the latter were specifically excluded from the measure on the Jews.[29] John knew what he was about. The Crowland chronicler thought his concessions were worthy of 'memory and praise', and several of them were affirmed and elaborated in Magna Carta.[30]

John also settled his great quarrel with the papacy. The catalyst here was the threatened French invasion of 1213. Philip Augustus had decided to invade at a great council held at Soissons early in April. What he represented as a pious enterprise, designed to avenge the injuries to the church, was in reality a pre-emptive strike against John's continental campaign, plans for which were now reaching completion. If Philip, as he intended, could put Louis, his eldest son, on the English throne, he would end the Angevin threat once and for all, and make the Capetians supreme in Europe. Accordingly, an army was summoned, a fleet was assembled and Louis issued a charter subjecting himself, if he became king of England, to his father's 'will and counsel' in various matters, one being what was to happen to John if he were captured.[31] In response to this grievous threat, John mustered a great army in Kent and took action against French shipping. On 30 May a naval force under the earl of Salisbury destroyed the French fleet at Damme in Flanders, thus eliminating the threatened invasion.[32]

It was while the two armies were facing each other across the Channel that John reached his settlement with the pope. He had already been weakening in his refusal to accept Stephen Langton as the papally imposed archbishop of Canterbury, but he had continued to haggle over the extent of compensation due to the church. Now he gave way and on 13 May 1213 bowed to the papal terms. Two days later, he went even further and made England a papal fief. On 20 July, in a ceremony at Winchester, sealed by a great feast, John tearfully prostrated himself before the bishops and was absolved from his excommunication by Langton himself.[33] John also sought to appease individual bishops. Immediately after his absolution, he granted Langton and his successors the keepership of Rochester castle, thus meeting a long-standing Canterbury grievance.[34] Next year, as partial compensation for the church's losses during the Interdict, John also offered Langton half of a 20,000 mark fine he was extracting from Geoffrey de Mandeville. This fine, as we will see, was one of John's most notorious exactions. If Langton accepted money, he would be benefitting from John's oppressive rule. Yet accept it Langton did. How John must have laughed. He had compensated the church and compromised the archbishop all in one go. The cynicism with which he doubtless regarded pietistic and prating prelates like Langton seemed amply justified.[35] In fact, not for the last time, John had miscalculated. Langton himself did not feel compromised in the least. If he hesitated over taking money from so tainted a source, he took it in the end with a clear conscience. The needs of the church must come first. In 1215, Langton steered his own course and placed the welfare of the kingdom, as he saw it, above any narrow allegiance to the king.

Quite apart from losing half of the Mandeville fine, the settlement with the church was expensive. How much John repaid of damages put at £100,000 is unknown. In terms of hard cash, he certainly handed over at least £25,000.[36] More serious was the political cost, for John had to accept the return to England of Eustace de Vescy and Robert fitzWalter, who had cleverly linked their cause to that of the church. Both played central parts in the coming rebellion, Vescy being the only noble who earned a personal letter of rebuke from the pope.[37] Making England a papal fief was also thought by many to be humiliating. Indeed it seemed to fulfil the prophecy of the hermit Peter of Wakefield that John would not reign beyond his fourteenth year, which ended on Ascension Day 1213. John spent the day holding an open-air feast, before having Peter dragged from Corfe castle to Wareham and there hanged. Many, however, said that handing the kingdom over to the pope had made the prophecy come true. For all these disappointments and disadvantages, John's settlement with the church was still a masterstroke. It meant that henceforth the pope stood steadfastly behind him. Without that support, he would not have survived. Innocent's support was given material shape by the presence in England for over a year from September 1214 of a papal legate, Nicholas of Tusculum. He was there to lift the Interdict, having ensured proper compensation for the church. He also undermined Langton's authority and seemed to favour the rights of the crown more than the liberties of the church.[38] On his departure, Pandulf, the papal 'familiaris' – a member of the papal household and thus someone very close to Innocent – remained in England, and was named, of course, as one of John's counsellors in Magna Carta.

For all John's concessions, when they returned to England both Vescy and fitzWalter found a simmering pot just waiting to be stirred. However justified in John's eyes, his treatment of the conspirators could seem further evidence of his tyranny, involving as it did a fresh round of hostage taking and disseisins. In May 1212, so even before the plot, John had confiscated Godmanchester in Huntingdonshire, one of Earl David's richest manors. He admitted at Runnymede that this was a disseisin committed 'by our will without judgement'. Equally disseised were twelve of David's tenants, a good example of how John's arbitrary conduct impacted at the level of knightly society. After the plot, David was made to give his son as hostage, and, under threat of siege, surrender his castle of Fotheringhay.[39] Although John had to accept back Vescy and fitzWalter, he made sure to pull down Alnwick castle and Baynard's castle first.[40]

There was also, almost certainly, criticism of the processes by which fitzWalter, Vescy and earlier William de Briouze had been outlawed. In fitzWalter's case one part of the customary process had undoubtedly been followed. FitzWalter had been summoned to four successive county courts (in Essex) and had been outlawed by judgement of the court on failing to turn up. Another part, however, had been violated. According to the law and custom on outlawry, proceedings had to be initiated, not by order of the king, but through an accusation made by the 'fama patrie', which probably meant by the indictment of a jury. Yet it is clear that in the outlawry of fitzWalter, proceedings had been begun by a royal order. The very writ to the sheriff of Essex was enrolled on the close roll. No mention was made of the 'fama patrie'. When chapter 39 of the Charter said that no free man should be disseised or outlawed 'save by the lawful judgement of his peers or by the law of the land', it was thinking, among other things, of the disseisins and outlawries following the conspiracy of 1212. Indeed, the stipulation about the 'law of the land' had particular relevance to outlawry where the correct procedures, as we have seen, required indictment by a jury and a summons to four successive county courts.[41]

Quite apart from his treatment of the conspirators, John had continued to bear down heavily on baronial families.[42] The new offers made to the king in the pipe roll of 1213–14 included William de Monte Canisio's 2,000 marks to have his inheritance and be quit of debts to the Jews, William fitzAlan's 10,000 marks to have the land of his father, and Robert de Vere's 1,000 marks to enter the lands of his brother. Despite this large fine, he was still denied the earldom of Oxford. The same pipe roll shows John de Lacy still owing 4,200 marks of the 7,000-mark fine for his inheritance, as security for which John had retained his castle of Pontefract. Meanwhile, John continued to exploit widows in ways that would be clean contrary to the Charter. Margaret, the widow of Robert fitzRoger, thus agreed to pay £1,000 to have her dower and inheritance and not be forced into remarriage. Sibilla of Ewyas Harold, the widow of Robert de Tresgoz, offered 800 marks for much the same privileges, only for John then to sell her remarriage for £1,000 to the Welsh marcher lord Roger of Clifford. John continued to exploit down on the towns, slapping a 2,000-mark tallage on London.[43] And he continued to disseize 'by will', taking Trowbridge from Henry de Bohun, earl of Hereford, and giving it to William Longespee, earl of Salisbury, a lawless act that was to be reversed at Runnymede.[44]

This period also saw one of John's most extraordinary impositions, namely the fine, already alluded to, made by Geoffrey de Mandeville. Geoffrey was the son of John's justiciar Geoffrey fitzPeter, who had died in 1213. He had, however, taken the surname Mandeville, his father having made good on a controversial claim through marriage to the old Mandeville earldom of Essex. Mandeville's first wife was the daughter of Robert fitzWalter, and, if there was any truth in the story, the subject of John's libidinous attentions.[45] On her death, Geoffrey agreed to pay the colossal sum of 20,000 marks to marry Isabella, countess of Gloucester, the Isabella whose union with John had been annulled so that he could marry Isabella of Angoulême. The countess's inheritance, which included Glamorgan, was rich, even though John held back the title of Earl of Gloucester, but there was no way that

Mandeville could pay the 20,000 marks in the stipulated ten months. John's aim was simply to place Mandeville in his power, and make as much money as he could from him. The Dunstable annals stated that Mandeville entered the marriage unwillingly, as surely was the case. He had agreed to it because of a promise (unfulfilled) that he would now be recognized as Earl of Essex. More importantly, if Geoffrey did not go ahead, John was threatening him with the loss of the whole Mandeville inheritance, this through the revival of the claims of the Says, which Geoffrey fitzPeter had defeated in order to secure the inheritance in the first place. No wonder this monstrous fine, as the Crowland chronicler recognized, became a major issue in 1215. It was a classic example of the fines made unjustly and against the law of the land that the Charter, in chapter 55, insisted John must remit.[46]

DIPLOMACY AND DEFEAT, 1212–1214

While John was settling with the pope, resisting French invasion and struggling to retain authority in England, he was also labouring to build up the continental alliances that would enable him to recover his lost empire. The defection of King Richard's allies, the counts of Flanders and Boulogne, had been a major factor in the fall of Normandy. John would not make the same mistake again.

There was much in the international situation that John could exploit, beginning with the predicament of the emperor of the Romans, Otto of Brunswick. Otto was John's nephew, the fruit of the marriage between Henry the Lion, duke of Saxony, and Matilda, daughter of Henry II. As emperor, Otto both ruled in Germany and claimed authority in Italy. In asserting such claims, he had, however, quarrelled with Pope Innocent. In 1210 Innocent called on the German princes to depose him and elect as king of Germany, Frederick, king of Sicily, the young son of Otto's predecessor, the Emperor Henry VI. In March 1212 Frederick set off for Germany. In December he was elected king by his supporters and crowned. Since Frederick was heavily backed by Philip Augustus, Otto and John became natural allies, all the more so since John had the money that Otto desperately wanted. In May 1212 John joyfully proclaimed their alliance. It was an alliance that also included Renaud Dammartin, the count of Boulogne. Ousted by

Philip, Dammartin now offered his homage to John, who restored him to his lands in England. Negotiations were also in train with Ferrand, count of Flanders, the count of Holland, and the dukes of Limberg and Louvain. John was building up a great coalition against France's northern frontier.[47]

Tantalizing possibilities were also emerging for a great alliance in the south. There political structures had been transformed by the success of Simon de Montfort and his French army in the crusade against the Albigensian heretics. The first phase had concluded in 1209 with Montfort establishing himself as lord of Béziers and Carcassonne. In the cause of resisting the French advance, this made natural allies of Raymond VI, count of Toulouse, and King Pedro of Aragon. The two were also, therefore, natural allies of King John. Raymond was John's brother-in-law, having married (thanks to King Richard) a daughter of Henry II, Joan. Pedro, after his destruction of Moslem power in Spain at the battle of Las Navas de Tolosa in July 1212, was free to challenge Montfort, rather than, as he had done hitherto, compromise with him. In 1212 and 1213 envoys were going back and forth between John and both Raymond and Pedro.

With his northern alliance falling into place, and his southern one at least in the air, John in 1213 was eager to be off. He summoned an army to muster for a continental campaign in March, only then to abandon his plans when faced with the threat of a French invasion. With that over, buoyed up by his settlement with the church, he summoned another army for August. The summons met a hostile reception, especially in the north of England. Resistance was fortified by the argument, set out later in the Unknown Charter, that military service overseas was only owed in Normandy and Brittany, so not in Poitou, where John's campaign necessarily must begin. As a measure of his determination, John embarked anyway and got as far as Jersey, before accepting that he lacked the requisite forces to continue.

Once back in England, John in late August set off for the north in order to punish those who had disrupted his plans. This was the moment for a decisive intervention by Archbishop Langton. He hurried after John, caught up with him at Northampton and warned him not to attack his opponents without having first secured a judgement against them.[48] John continued to the north, but then decided on negotiations. At the start of November 1213 he met certain northerners at Wallingford and promised to observe their 'ancient liberties'. The agreement quickly collapsed. On 7 November John ordered the knights from each county previously summoned to a meeting at Oxford to come armed, while the barons were to come unarmed – apparently an attempt to use the one to intimidate the other. At the same time John reached out to a second group of knights, summoning to the assembly four knights from each county to discuss with him the affairs of the kingdom.[49]

It is in the resistance to the continental campaign of 1213 that the 'northerners' first appear in contemporary narratives as taking the lead in the opposition to King John. They are, of course, the subject of Holt's classic book. Contemporaries did not use the term with any geographical precision but they would certainly have seen as 'northerners' men from Lincolnshire, Nottinghamshire and Derbyshire, as well, of course, as men from Yorkshire, Northumberland and Cumberland. John's government had lain heavy on these areas through the exploitation of the royal forest and the oppressions of the sheriffs. Philip Marc (dismissed from office under Magna Carta) was sheriff of Nottinghamshire and Derbyshire. John retained the loyalty of some magnates with interests in the north. He had a grip on Westmorland through Robert de Vieuxpont, to whom he granted the sheriffdom in hereditary right. Ranulf, earl of Chester, was lord of Richmond in Yorkshire, and William, earl of Warenne, was lord of Conisbrough in the same county. But there were many more northerners at the heart of the opposition to the king, notably Eustace de Vescy, William de Mowbray, Richard de Percy, Roger de Montbegon, Nicholas de Stuteville, Gilbert de Gant, Peter de Brus – and, at a later stage, Robert de Ros and John de Lacy.

In individual terms the grievances of these men were little different from the grievances of men elsewhere in England. But they were given a special edge by the way the north, under John, had felt the direct hand of kingship as never before. Henry II only visited the north on eleven occasions during a reign of thirty-five years. Richard took a brief look at Sherwood forest (he liked it), and went no further north. John, by contrast, penetrated northern counties in every year of his reign save the four when he was largely abroad. On what were sometimes long tours of inspection, he extracted large sums in fines for favours and benevolence. All this impacted on a baronial society that, in some ways, was more self-contained and cohesive than elsewhere in England. Many of the northern barons had compact baronies and limited interests further south. They rallied behind each other, acting as sureties for the enormous amounts of money they owed the king. At the same time, the northern barons gained strength and independence through their proximity to Scotland and connections with the Scottish court. At the very least, Scotland could be a bolt-hole. At most, the king of Scots might ally with them against King John. And there was one final factor. The northern barons had leadership, leadership from Eustace de Vescy. He was at the centre of the plot of 1212 and later, as we have said, was singled out for reprimand by the pope. It was Eustace above all, one may suspect, who rallied the north against the king.

After his abortive settlement with the northerners, John continued his preparations for his continental campaign. He finally set sail in February 1214. By this time his position was weaker than the year before. In September 1213, Simon de Montfort had won a comprehensive victory against King Pedro and Raymond of Toulouse at the battle of Muret.[50] Pedro, refusing to surrender, had been killed. His demise was caused, his son later thought, both by bad tactics and by a judgement of God for having lain with a woman before the battle.[51] Raymond of Toulouse escaped and came to England. He returned home in January 1214 with, it was said, 10,000 marks, but his power was broken.[52]

The rest of John's plans, however, were well laid and very much intact. In January 1214 he received the homage of Ferrand, count of Flanders, who had come to England with the counts of Holland and Boulogne. They then returned to Flanders with an English force under the earl of Salisbury. John, meanwhile, landed at La Rochelle in Poitou on 15 February. The strategy, of course, was to force Philip Augustus to divide his forces between north and south and defeat them individually. Despite opposition to the campaign, John had with him, apart from a large number of foreign mercenaries, a good body of tenants-in-chief of baronial and knightly status as well as household knights.[53] As in Ireland in 1210, John supported such men by giving them loans. At first all went well. John secured Poitou, if not Poitiers itself, and in May 1214 he received the homages of the Lusignans, thus at last smoothing over the offence of his marriage. In June he crossed the river Loire and by 17 June he was at Angers, capital of Anjou, the ancestral home of his dynasty. Here, however, he was still over eighty miles from the Norman frontier. It was the nearest he got. From Angers, John moved south-west and laid siege to the castle at La Roche-aux-Moines. It was there that Louis, King Philip's eldest son, came to meet him in battle array. John was eager to fight. The Lusignans and their Poitevin allies were not. It was one thing to ride with John and take his money. It was quite another to risk everything in a battle. Deserted by his allies, John abandoned the siege of La Roche-aux-Moines on 2 July and fled south. By 9 July he was back at La Rochelle. From there he addressed an all too revealing letter to the earls, barons, knights and faithful men of England. His claim that all was going well was immediately contradicted by an appeal for them to join him. They could then help him recover 'his' rights and conquer 'his' land, which showed plainly that no one else's rights and lands were involved. John added that those who felt they had incurred his 'indignation' could put matters right by joining him. Clearly he recognized very well the ill feelings back in England. How sensitive the point was is revealed by the way the letter was redrafted so that 'indignation' replaced the original 'rancour of mind', perhaps because it carried a stronger sense of justified disapproval.[54] It was 'rancour', however, as well as 'indignation', that chapter 62 of Magna Carta got John to remit. The truth was that John's campaign was over. It had been a complete failure. Everything now depended on his northern allies.

A full muster of John's allies, with Otto at their head, had taken place at Valenciennes in northern France in July.[55] Everyone was there and confidence was high. King Philip mustered his own forces at Péronne. The confrontation eventually took place on 27 July outside the village of Bouvines in the much fought-over borderland between France and Flanders. It was a close-run thing. At one point, King Philip was caught by the hook of a halberd and dragged to the ground, before being rescued by his bodyguard. In the end, however, he won a total victory. Otto fled. The counts of Flanders and Boulogne, together with the earl of Salisbury, were taken prisoner.

Bouvines is rightly regarded as one of the most decisive battles ever fought. It established Frederick II in Germany, ended the Angevin empire, assured the supremacy of France and led to Magna Carta. John arrived back in England on 13 October 1214. His treasure in money was gone. His revenue was collapsing. That revealed by the pipe roll of 1214 was £25,700, less than half the level of two years before. Individual barons, such as William de Mowbray, were ceasing to pay their debts.[56] John's prestige was in tatters. All his work of ten years lay in ruins.

The animosity towards John, which he had acknowledged in his letter of 9 July, had also been aggravated by events in his absence. A significant number of northerners had refused to go with him to France and had also refused to pay the scutage, which was fixed at the high rate of £2 a fee. In Yorkshire, it could not be collected at all. In November the pope wrote to Eustace de Vesci warning him not to obstruct the king's agents in the performance of their duties. Probably it was Eustace who led the opposition.[57] All this was made worse by John's new chief justiciar, Peter des Roches, bishop of Winchester. In place of the cautious and emollient Geoffrey fitzPeter, so keen to be accepted as a member of the high nobility, the government was now run by an arrogant, abrasive, armour-plated foreign prelate (he was later in the thick of the battle of Lincoln) who was very ready to push John's policies to the limit. Des Roches had Vescy's chattels seized for his failure to pay the scutage, and he threatened consequences for Earl David's hostages if David failed to attend a meeting. Des Roches was equally domineering in the localities.[58] When a group of Devon knights resisted the sheriff in defence of their charter of liberties, he descended on Exeter, and threatened the sheriff with loss of life and chattels if he failed to defend the rights of 'the crown'.[59] No wonder that Ralph of Coggeshall declared 'the nobles of all the kingdom complained that an alien man was placed over them'.[60]

The political narrative after John's return to England in October 1214 has two main strands. The first is the way John's opponents evolved the programme that became Magna Carta. Here one cardinal fact had transformed the situation since the attempted deposition in 1212. This, of course, was John's settlement with the church. The king now seemed to the pope a wonderful example of 'the boundless and infinite goodness of God which makes just men of transgressors and turns sinners into saints'.[61] Where now was the excommunicated tyrant whom the pope was urging everyone to resist? Since John's new status made it much harder to contemplate his deposition, his opponents looked to other remedies. Their detailed development we will explore in the next chapter.

The second strand is the way John's enemies mustered the force necessary to coerce the king. It is here that we come to another cardinal point, which shaped both the events of 1215 and the nature of the Charter. John was gravely weakened when he got back to England in October 1214. His enemies saw their chance, and were concerting action even before his return. Yet the king remained a formidable opponent. As the start of the Charter showed, he retained the loyalty of the earls of Pembroke, Salisbury, Warenne and Arundel, as he did also that of the earls of Chester and Derby. While he increasingly lost control in the shires, his castles remained firmly in his hands, many garrisoned by his ruthless foreign agents. Although John's cash mountain was gone, he still had thousands of pounds with which to hire foreign mercenaries.[62] In England, during the whole period down to Magna Carta, he was never defeated in the field. The Charter was thus a negotiated document. It might have looked very different had it been dictated to John on his knees.

THE OATH

The first and most crucial task of John's opponents was to form themselves into an association, a corporate body that could hold together in defiance of the king. It needed to be of a type that could expand but not contract, stopping members coming and going as they pleased as though held together merely by a rope of sand. All this was achieved by an oath. The great oath that led to Magna Carta is little discussed by historians, yet its importance is clear. The pope fulminated against the 'sworn associations' formed against the king, while John in 1215 gave letters of conduct to rebels 'withdrawing you from the oath and confederation made against us'.[63]

No formal text of the oath is known, although one may come to light – a great discovery waiting to be made. The oath was probably developed from earlier 'confederations and sworn associations' made during the Interdict, to which Innocent III refers. There was almost certainly an oath taken by the conspirators of 1212, while Ralph of Coggeshall in 1213 refers to what was clearly another sworn association, having just narrated the attempted settlement with the northerners that November: 'nearly all the barons of England confederated together to protect the liberty of the church and all the kingdom'.[64] This links very well with the fullest description of the oath, as it was in 1215, which appears in the Welsh chronicle the *Brut*:

All the leading men of England and all the princes of Wales made a
pact together against the king that not one of them without his fellow
would have from the king either peace or alliance or truce until he
restored to the churches their laws and their rights which he or his
ancestors had before that taken from them, and also until he restored
to the leading men of England and Wales the lands and the castles
which he had taken from them at his pleasure without either justice
or law.[65]

That the oath had a clause preventing members making a separate
peace is confirmed by the Southwark and Merton annals' description of the confederation between the barons and the Londoners.[66]
That the oath began with the church was to be expected, and helps
explain how Robert fitzWalter, as general of the rebel forces, could
style himself 'marshal of the army of God and holy church'. That
it had clauses about the restoration of lands and castles taken law-
lessly by the king fits exactly with chapter 52 of Magna Carta.

THE MEETING AT BURY ST EDMUNDS

A confederation binding men together in support of a political
programme was worth little unless it incorporated, or sat alongside, an agreement to impose that programme by force. Everyone
knew that John would never give way willingly. The crucial meeting at which resort to force was agreed is described by Roger of
Wendover and took place in 1214 at Bury St Edmunds in Suffolk.
The precise date is discussed below. According to Wendover, the
earls and barons, having gathered at Bury for a 'colloquium', came
before the high altar and swore that, if the king refused to accept
the Coronation Charter of Henry I and the laws of Edward the
Confessor, they would withdraw from their fealty and make war
on him, until he made the desired concessions in a sealed charter.
They also agreed to press their demands on the king after Christmas and meanwhile provide themselves with horses and arms.[67]

Holt is highly sceptical about this account, for which Wendover
is the only source.[68] Credence is not helped by later elaborations.
On the north-east pier of the presbytery at Bury, a tablet proudly
proclaims:

NEAR THIS SPOT
ON THE 20TH NOVEMBER A. D. 1214,
CARDINAL LANGTON & THE BARONS
SWORE AT ST EDMUND'S ALTAR
THAT THEY WOULD OBTAIN FROM
KING JOHN
THE RATIFICATION OF
MAGNA CHARTA.

WHERE THE RUDE BUTTRESS TOTTERS TO ITS FALL,
AND IVY MANTLES O'ER THE CRUMBLING WALL;
WHERE E'EN THE SKILFUL EYE CAN SCARCELY TRACE
THE ONCE HIGH ALTAR'S LOWLY RESTING PLACE –
LET PATRIOTIC FANCY MUSE AWHILE
AMID THE RUINS OF THIS ANCIENT PILE.
SIX WEARY CENTURIES HAVE PAST AWAY;
PALACE AND ABBEY MOULDER IN DECAY –
COLD DEATH ENSHROUDS THE LEARNED & THE BRAVE –
LANGTON – FITZ WALTER – SLUMBER IN THE GRAVE,
BUT STILL WE READ IN DEATHLESS RECORDS HOW
THE HIGH-SOUL'D PRIEST CONFIRM'D THE BARONS' VOW;
AND FREEDOM, UNFORGETFUL STILL RECITES,
THIS SECOND BIRTH-PLACE OF OUR NATIVE RIGHTS.

J.W. DONALDSON, Scripsit.   J. MUSKETT, Posuit, 1847.

Wendover would doubtless have been delighted to hear his *Flores Historiarum* described as a 'deathless record', yet in fact he neither gave a precise date for the assembly nor said that Langton was present at it. Indeed, he named none of the participants. Neither lapidary effusions nor Holt's reservations, however, should prevent us accepting the gist of Wendover's narrative. The arguments in its favour are far stronger than have ever been appreciated, in part, as we will see, because of one fundamental misunderstanding.

Wendover completed his account of this period around ten years after the events described. He can make egregious mistakes, including conflating John's Charter with those of Henry III. Yet it is equally clear that these mistakes are set in a narrative which, given its precision and dates, must have been written fairly close to the events. Indeed, his account of the Bury meeting follows a date for John's return to England, namely 19 October, which is only six days too late.[69] There is nothing in the account of the Bury meeting that is clearly false, and indeed it links perfectly with the events of January 1215 when the barons did indeed appear in arms and press their demands on the king.

The misunderstanding which has blighted previous discussion is the assumption that the meeting took place on 20 November. This is grounded on Wendover's statement that the barons, as cover for their real intentions, came to Bury as if 'for the sake of prayer'. What better day, then, to come to Bury 'for prayer' than the feast day of St Edmund itself, that is, 20 November. Yet, of course, it was perfectly possible to come to Bury for prayer on other occasions. John himself made six visits, none on the day. Given his reputation for impiety, perhaps that is not much of a guide, but even his pious son only timed two of his many pilgrimages to coincide with the feast itself. More important in undermining the 20 November date is what Wendover actually says. Having stated that John returned to England on 19 October, he affirms that the Bury meeting took place 'around the same time' – 'sub eadem tempestate'. Wendover, then, thought the gathering took place not on 20 November but about a whole month earlier. That seems far more likely on political and prudential grounds. Rather than waiting until John was at home and at large, the barons wisely planned their meeting as soon as they heard rumours of his return, and of course in the full knowledge of his defeat at Bouvines. The meeting then took place around the time of that return, so sometime around (following Wendover's date) 19 October.

Once this date is accepted, much else falls into place.[70] Out in Poitou, Hugh of Northwold, abbot elect of Bury, had won John's favour. He had good reason to hope that when John returned to England, his election would be speedily confirmed. In the event, both Hugh and John arrived back on the same day, 13 October. Hugh went straight to Bury, which he reached on 24 October, and then returned south to see the king. All seemed set fair, for, between 18 and 20 October, John had issued a letter protecting the abbey's possessions and looking forward, 'God willing', to a solution of the quarrel. Yet when Hugh met John in London on 28 October, the mood was totally different. John now accused him of stirring up 'rebellion' – 'bellum'. Holt argued that this meant no more than

Hugh's opposition to John's wishes over the election; it seemed unlikely that it referred to any political rebellion in England, since that had yet to gather steam. This second point is disposed of once we accept the re-dating of the meeting. 'Bellum' in any case seems a strong word to use for the dispute over an abbatial election, however important. What had happened is that, by 28 October, John had heard of the Bury assembly. No doubt the news came from his own local officials. It also came from John's supporters within the convent, who set off to see him as soon as Hugh got home. One of them told John directly that Hugh was 'working in every way and with all his strength to deprive you of the royal crown'.[71] In accusing Hugh of stirring up rebellion, John was thus charging him with involvement in the Bury meeting. If the meeting took place before Hugh's return to Bury, that charge was, of course, unfair, but fairness was never John's strongest suit. If, on the other hand, it occurred around the time of Hugh's brief stay at the monastery, then John might very reasonably have thought him complicit. Whatever the truth here, Hugh vigorously denied the charge, and John then backed down: 'I did not say this with reference to you in particular, but on account of certain others.' Evidently, John accepted that the meeting had not been with Hugh's connivance or consent. Nonetheless, he still despatched a fiery letter to the monks saying that Hugh was in deep disfavour.

What happened next was equally remarkable. Leaving London on 1 or 2 November, John made a dramatic dash to Bury, which he reached on 4 November. He took his privy seal instead of his great seal, which he left behind in London with Peter des Roches. John had promised, soon after his arrival in England, to visit Bury and settle the matter of the election, but he now came in very different circumstances. His decision was taken in haste, for as late as 25 October he was planning a tour of Kent, taking in Rochester, Canterbury and Dover.[72] That Hugh, on his return, went straight to Bury, and then came south with the abbey's charters, shows that he had no expectation of an imminent royal visit. John's aim now was not primarily to settle the issue of the election, which in fact was not settled. The main motive was to stamp royal authority on the place of the rebellious assembly. John's anxieties are clear from other orders. On 30 October he despatched archers to boost the garrisons of Corfe and Nottingham, increased the forces under the command of Engelard de Cigogné, the sheriff of Gloucestershire

and Herefordshire, and told Theodoric Teutonicus, at Berkhamsted in Hertfordshire, to attend diligently to the castle's custody and
keep him frequently informed about its state. Then, on the way to
Bury, he ordered Theodoric to conduct the queen to Berkhamsted
castle under armed guard, and by a prescribed route. Meanwhile,
in London, on 4 November, Peter des Roches ordered a payment in
connection with writs that the papal legate had made out 'against
those sworn together', in other words against those sworn together
at the recent gathering.[73]

At Bury, John had with him the earls of Winchester and Norfolk, and probably also Robert fitzWalter and Geoffrey de
Mandeville – all of course future rebels – so he made an impressive
show of his support.[74] When he entered the chapter house, the
sword was carried before him by Philip of Oldcoates, the sheriff of
Northumberland. Its edge was directed not just at the abbey but
at those who had so recently defied the king. When one of John's
supporters among the monks begged that 'the royal majesty may
flame out in anger "with powerful arm and mighty hand"' against
its adversaries', John left the reply to Oldcoates: 'O, man, fenced
in as you are on every side with the king's peace, you need not be
afraid'.[75] This reassurance summed up very well the wider purpose
of John's descent on Bury.

John remained at Bury merely for a day. The birds had flown
and he had made his point. On 5 November he was on his way
back south. He remained, however, acutely suspicious. While at
Bury he had refused to release William Marshal's hostages, despite
the intercession of the earl of Norfolk, agreeing only that one
could be exchanged for two others.[76] All this is the background to
the major concession that John made in London on 21 November.
At the New Temple, he issued his famous charter giving the church
freedom of elections. This was the charter that was to be confirmed in the first chapter of Magna Carta. John, therefore, after
the shock of Bury, was desperately trying to bind the church to his
side. The issue of elections was a particularly live one, given that
six bishoprics and thirteen abbeys had been left unfilled during the
Interdict and needed new pastors appointed.[77] However hedged
around, the charter, in legislating for speedy elections, also promised a great reduction in the king's revenues from vacancies. John
followed up the charter with a personal concession to Archbishop
Langton, for it was on 22 November that he gave Canterbury the

overlordship of the bishopric of Rochester. There is no evidence that Langton was at the Bury meeting. Almost certainly he was not. But to it he owed these great victories. In issuing his charter granting free elections, John tried to do something else, namely show that the kingdom was united behind him. Of the thirteen witnesses to the charter, five were to be named in Magna Carta as John's counsellors, while four were among the twenty-five barons of the security clause.[78]

Who then was at the Bury meeting? Into early 1215, sources continued to describe the insurgents as northerners, and they probably made a major contribution to the assembly. This is confirmed by the striking appearance at Bury of Philip of Oldcoates. As sheriff of Northumberland, Oldcoates is very rarely found at court. On 27 October John had written to him as though he were still at his northern post.[79] Yet, a few days later, he suddenly turns up, bearing the sword before John, in the Bury chapter house. Most probably, Oldcoates had come south in the wake of the insurgents in order to monitor their activities. The northerners, however, were clearly keen to widen the basis of their support, hence the choice of Bury for the meeting. One London chronicler later observed that the barons in 1215 were described as northerners, 'although they came from divers parts of the kingdom of England', and increasingly that became the case.[80] A government record from January 1215 described Roger de Cressy as one of 'the Northerners' who were against the king, but, in fact, his main interests were in East Anglia. Cressy may well have been at the Bury meeting.[81] John, however, still had Saer de Quincy at his side. He was the one layman, apart from Oldcoates, to be with him in the chapter house, and was the custodian of the Marshal hostages. Despite the statement in the Bury tablet, the presence with John of fitzWalter, like that of Mandeville and Norfolk, argues against their participation, but one cannot be sure. They may have come to make their excuses and explanations.

THE RESORT TO ARMS

In accordance with the plans laid at Bury, when the 'magnates' appeared before John at the New Temple in London in January 1215 they came in military array. The pope later described them as making their demands 'arrogantly and disloyally by force of arms'.[82] Just how close the situation was to civil war is shown by the way 'all those' who had come before the king with 'grievances' were given the king's 'peace', until another meeting at Northampton, as well as safe conducts guaranteed by Archbishop Langton, seven bishops and four loyalist earls. While fitzWalter, Mandeville and the earl of Clare were still sufficiently persona grata to attest royal charters in January, none of the great northern barons did so, apart from Robert de Ros.[83] The demands put at the New Temple centred on the Coronation Charter of Henry I, quite probably with some extra provisions tacked on. John's response was to condemn these 'novelties', and call for a general oath of fealty together with assurances (embodied in individual charters) that such demands would never be raised again. The meeting ended in stalemate. All that could be agreed was to postpone the issues until the meeting at Northampton, which was fixed for 26 April.[84]

There was now a hiatus as both sides appealed to the pope, a measure of the extraordinary role he had assumed in English politics since John had made him overlord of the kingdom. John, on his side, had cleverly prepared the way. During the New Temple meeting, he had reissued his charter conceding free elections to the church, and sent it to Innocent III for his confirmation.[85] John's envoy, Walter Mauclerc, at the start of a long career in royal service, arrived in Rome on 19 February, although delayed 'by a great illness'. The envoys of the insurgents, clerks of Eustace de Vescy and another great northerner, Richard de Percy, arrived at the start of March. In a letter to the king, Mauclerc explained that he had been unable to see their letters, but had learnt their gist. The barons certainly mounted a powerful case, and may well have hoped to change Innocent's mind. They claimed that the northerners were now joined by 'all the barons of all England'. They also challenged John's new status as a papal favourite, claiming that it was their own struggles for the church's liberty at papal command which had forced him to submit and make England a papal fief. They themselves were only demanding their 'ancient liberties' conceded by the charters of John's ancestors and confirmed by the king's own oath, probably a reference to the oath that he made on his absolution.[86]

During this hiatus, John took another step that was meant to bolster his position. On 4 March, Ash Wednesday, and so at the start of Lent, he took the cross in St Paul's cathedral, and committed himself to go on crusade.[87] From now on (one can imagine him thus at Runnymede), he wore on his shoulder a white cross that proclaimed his new status. John thus hoped to gain the protections of a crusader, which might allow him to shelve some of the complaints against him, as indeed happened in Magna Carta.[88] He had also bound himself yet more closely to the pope. For Innocent, the king was now threefold blessed: he had restored liberty to the church, subjected his kingdom to the papacy, and then taken the cross so that he could 'liberate the land which Christ had purchased with his own blood'. God would now 'on earth secure and confirm the throne of the kingdom to you and your heirs, and in heaven the righteous judge will give you a crown of glory which fadeth not away'. By the same token, as Innocent made clear, the obstruction offered to John's holy purposes by the recalcitrant barons was all the more illegitimate.[89]

John was now in a confident mood, and very ready to amuse himself by playing cat and mouse with Bury's still unconfirmed abbot elect. When the two met riding in Sherwood Forest, towards the end of March, Hugh dismounted, went down on his knees and begged John to confirm his election. John was gracious, raised him up, welcomed him as abbot and spoke to him lengthily in private, although always 'saving the rights of my kingdom'. But next day, when Hugh sought another audience after Mass, he was fobbed off and told to speak to William Brewer. Brewer then upbraided Hugh for showing contempt for the king's liberties, and told him to come before a council that was to meet at Oxford on 6 April. There John refused to accept the election unless he was given money (which Hugh refused on Langton's advice), and then postponed the whole matter until the return of the envoys sent to Rome to protest about elections being held 'in contempt for my liberties'. On the same day, John ordered for himself five tunics to wear under his armour and five banners with his coat of arms, trimmed with gold.[90] John celebrated Easter Day, which fell on 19 April, at the New Temple in London. A few days later he made the traditional payment to the clerks of his chapel who had sung the 'Christus vincit' in his presence:

Christ conquers, Christ reigns, Christ rules, hear O Christ,
To the king of the English, crowned by God, salvation and victory.[91]

How John must have hoped that would now come true. He was quickly disabused.

John had been too clever by half. His taking the cross only provoked the barons, who thought rightly that he had acted merely to 'defraud them of their proposals'.[92] There was soon further provocation in the letters of 19 March in which the pope gave his judgement. There is a puzzle over when the letters arrived in England. Pope Innocent himself, in his later narrative of events, seems to indicate that it was after the baronial defiance of the king that took place on 5 May. This seems rather late, given that the journey between England and Rome could take about a month, and this was certainly a letter of some urgency.[93] The Crowland chronicler has the letters arriving when John was in and around Oxford, which was between 7 and 13 April. This is impossibly early. There is nothing, however, impossible about the letters having become known in England during Easter week, which was the week of 19–26 April. Probably, in any case, the likely tenor of the letters was already known from earlier reports sent by the baronial envoys. If so, the intelligence must have been a major factor in the great escalation of the crisis, which now took place.

Pope Innocent put his judgement into three letters, one to John himself, one to the barons of England and one to Langton and his suffragans.[94] John was urged, 'as he hoped to have his sins remitted', to treat the barons kindly and listen to their just petitions. The barons were to make their claims not by force of arms but 'in humility and loyal devotion'. Langton and his suffragans were blamed for failing to support the king and for giving the impression that they favoured the barons. The pope now denounced all 'conjurations and conspiracies' on pain of excommunication.[95] The letters made it absolutely clear that the barons could receive no help from him. The idea that they should approach John humbly and witness his God-given change of heart was ludicrous. They had now either to put up or shut up. They put up. It was during Easter week that the barons mustered in arms at Stamford in Lincolnshire, a famous tournament ground. Previously the barons had been individually in arms. Now they were gathering an army, with which they marched from Stamford to Northampton. There was, of course, no question of meeting John there on 26 April as agreed back in January. Instead, the rising gained new force with the northerners, as the rebels were still called, being joined by Robert fitzWalter, Geoffrey de Mandeville and Giles de Briouze, bishop of Hereford. FitzWalter styled himself 'marshal of the army of God and holy church in England', an ambitious attempt to retain the status of fighting for the church, despite the papal condemnation. Bishop Briouze was a younger son of the murdered Matilda, and now heir to the family lordships. In March, John had actually restored these to the bishop, only then to create a fresh grievance by demanding 9,000 marks in return.[96]

On Monday, 27 April, now at Brackley in Northamptonshire, another tournament ground, the insurgents, through the good offices of Archbishop Langton and William Marshal, sent John a schedule setting out their demands. According to Roger of Wendover, these were an amalgam of the Coronation Charter of Henry I and the *Leges Edwardi*. More probably, they were an early draft of the Articles of the Barons. The fact that they were divided up into 'capituli' just like the Articles, and that the barons wanted them sealed by the king, as the Articles eventually were, supports this idea.[97] John's violent reaction is thus understandable. The demands, he angrily declared, would make him a slave; why did they not ask for his kingdom? Yet John also now made an attempt at conciliation.[98] He offered to abolish the evil customs introduced by himself and his brother Richard, and deal with those of his father Henry 'by the counsel' of his 'faithful men'. This might seem fair enough, but it was a pathetically vague response to the detailed concessions being demanded. It was also all subject to appeal to the pope. Not surprisingly, the barons rejected the offer. John next asked Langton to excommunicate the insurgents under the terms of the 19 March papal letter. The archbishop refused. He used the conventional excuse of knowing the mind of the pope, which meant that, in his judgement, Innocent would have written differently had he known the real situation.[99] The truth was that Langton would do nothing that threatened to escalate the crisis. He would not side with the barons, but equally he would not condemn them. That in itself, however, was enough. The archbishop's passivity may well have encouraged their next decisive step.

DEFIANCE

On 5 May 1215, at Reading, a monk formally defied John on behalf of the barons and returned their 'homages'.[100] In justifying what in effect was rebellion, this was a vital step. In the thought of

the period, any breach of faith to a lord could be judged as treason; '*seditio*' and '*proditio*' was the contemporary word. There
could be no more blatant example of that than the taking up of
arms. Equally, it was universally accepted that the penalty for treason was loss of life or limb, so execution or mutilation. Yet it was
also accepted that a tenant, in cases of deadly enmity, could defy
his lord and return or renounce his homage and the obligations
that went with it – the '*diffidatio*'.[101] Having done that, he could
then take up arms without breaking faith to his lord. He no longer
had a lord. He was free from any taint of treason.[102]

From one point of view, in escaping the consequences of rebellion, the '*diffidatio*' only went so far. It might cleanse the insurgents
from the taint of treason in their own eyes, but hardly necessarily
in those of the king. The king might simply ignore the defiance and
treat those who issued it as traitors. Even if he accepted that a 'diffidatio' was the proper procedure, and indeed defied his opponents
himself, it was not because he wished to place the war on some
gentlemanly footing in which both sides fought according to Mar-
quess of Queensbury rules – quite the reverse. He wished to be free
from all rules. The insurgents would become his enemies whom he
could attack and kill without let and hindrance. The medieval 'diffidatio' therefore led, in theory at least, into a lawless jungle where
warfare and politics could be nasty and brutish, not into a neat
playing field where they were sanitized and controlled. In theory,
but not in practice. In practice, it was rare for nobles to be killed
in battle, for when unable to fight on they were allowed to surrender. It was unheard of for nobles to be executed for political
crimes.[103] Even John was not expected to break these rules of conduct. That was not the least reason for the readiness to take up
arms against him. The rebels were not wrong in this calculation.
In the whole of the 1215–16 civil war, John executed not a single
noble.

Having defied the king on 5 May, the barons marched from
Brackley to Northampton. Lacking siege engines, they failed to
take it, but this was the first open act of warfare. John now shifted
his ground, if only a little, by putting flesh and bone on his earlier
proposals. On 9 May, at Windsor, he issued a charter, addressed to
'all the faithful of Christ'. It was pointedly not addressed to all his
faithful subjects, for many of these were no longer faithful, but at
least John acknowledged that they were still faithful Christians.

John's offer was that the 'complaints and articles' being pressed upon him should be considered by four barons chosen by himself and four chosen by 'the barons against us', with the pope as head 'above them'. John would then abide by whatever they decided. Next day, in a further act of conciliation, John promised that, until the work of the arbitrators was completed, he would not seize, dispossess or make war upon the barons 'save by the law of our kingdom or by judgement of their peers in our court', here of course anticipating chapter 39 of the Charter.[104] At the same time, John tried individual acts of conciliation and promised to deal, by judgement of his court, with the exorbitant fines imposed on both Geoffrey de Mandeville and Bishop Briouze.[105]

John may well have hoped that this proposal would lead to some minimal concessions, after which peace would be restored. Given that the pope would have the last word, there was little danger in the king having to concede too much. The barons thought so too. The proposal led nowhere. John's reaction was aggressive. On 12 May he ordered the lands of his enemies to be seized by the sheriffs.[106]

THE FALL OF LONDON

An event now occurred that changed the situation completely. Early on 9 May 1215, before he left for Windsor, John had been at the London Temple. There he agreed that a 1,100-mark loan which he had received from the Templars, to finance the bringing of 200 knights to England, could, if necessary, be repaid from his gold in their custody.[107] John also took steps to secure the loyalty of the Londoners, issuing a charter free of charge allowing them the right to elect annually their own mayor.[108] The conciliation of the Templars succeeded. The master of the Temple was at Runnymede by John's side and is named as one of his counsellors in Magna Carta. The conciliation of the Londoners failed. It may be that John offered them too little. Certainly he was soon outbid by the rebels, who, in the Articles of the Barons, made the levying of tallage on the city subject to the common consent of the kingdom. On 17 May, while the citizens were still at Mass, or pretended to be, a party of barons clambered up some steps placed outside the walls in the course of their repair, and got into the city, where they opened the gates to their fellows. John still held the Tower, but his forces there were insufficient to regain control of the capital. His view was that the Londoners had surrendered the city 'of their free will'. They certainly sealed an alliance with the rebels, got their demands into the Articles of the Barons and had their mayor as one of the twenty-five barons of Magna Carta's security clause.[109]

The loss of London was a hammer blow for John. Its financial resources were now at the disposal of the rebels. Its walls now protected them from any danger of attack. London, if properly defended, was virtually impregnable, for it was far too large to besiege. And properly defended it was, for the barons immediately placed guards on the walls.[110] There was no way now that John could easily win the civil war. He was also damaged in another way, for the loss of London meant the closure of the exchequer at Westminster.[111] It had hitherto been at work hearing the accounts of the 1213–14 financial year. Those for Yorkshire were heard after 5 March 1215, since a pardon issued to John de Lacy on that day was included in the pipe roll.[112] How much revenue was actually arriving into the exchequer was another matter. On 5 May John had wanted to repay the Templars their 1,100 marks from the first moneys received by the exchequer, only for the Templars to insist the loan be secured on the king's gold.[113] They obviously thought no money was coming in. Once London had fallen, the exchequer's seal and some of its rolls were taken to Reading abbey. Other rolls were left behind at Westminster, where next year they fell into the hands of Prince Louis. John, recognizing the treasury was empty, ceased to issue writs ordering the exchequer to pay out money.[114]

After the fall of London, the river of supporters joining the rebels now became a flood. The rebellion had expanded way beyond its original northern base. Of the twenty-five barons eventually named in Magna Carta's security clause, only eight could be described as northerners. Barons from the eastern and home counties predominated. The twenty-five included seven earls and three sons of earls. Nearly all the rest, apart from the mayor of London, were great barons.[115] The fact that the eldest son of William Marshal was on the side of the barons shows the weakness of the king's position. The Crowland chronicler noted how young men were attracted to the rebel cause, wishing to make a name for themselves through deeds of arms, sometimes pulling their fathers in

with them.[116] John could name as many earls among his supporters, but the rest of those who appeared as his counsellors at the
start of the Charter hardly compared in terms of status with the
twenty-five barons of the security clause.

SCOTLAND AND WALES

The gathering rebellion in England posed a difficult choice for
Alexander II in Scotland.[117] Alexander had succeeded to the throne
on the death of his father, William the Lion, in December 1214. It
was a time of acute anxiety. Alexander knew full well that John
would now expect him, under the terms of the 1209 Treaty of
Norham, to do homage for the kingdom. He had, therefore, every
reason to welcome the baronial revolt and the collapse of John's
power. On the other hand, he had to be careful. If he joined the
barons and John crushed them, the consequences for his country
would be disastrous. Alexander, until June 1215, also had his
hands full in Scotland dealing with the rising of Guthred macWil-
liam. In Magna Carta, the constable of Scotland, Alan of Galloway,
is named at the start as one of John's counsellors. This, however, is
less significant of Alexander's attitude than it might seem. Alan,
ruling Galloway as virtually his own kingdom, spent little time at
the Scottish court and was essentially an independent potentate
whom John had drawn to his side in 1212, notably by encourag-
ing him to conquer Ulster after the expulsion of Hugh de Lacy. By
contrast, Alexander's uncle, Earl David of Huntingdon, joined the
rebels, despite John's belated grant of the third penny of the earldom.[118] David was old and sick, but his actions were more than
symbolic, for his illegitimate son, Henry, was active in the baronial
cause and was later captured at the battle of Lincoln in 1217. It
was he who, at Runnymede, recovered Godmanchester.[119] As for
King Alexander himself, he was certainly abreast of baronial intentions. He welcomed his brother-in-law Eustace de Vescy to court in
March 1215, and Saer de Quincy, earl of Winchester, probably now
playing a double game, in April. No fewer than five members of
Magna Carta's twenty-five barons (the earls of Hereford, Oxford
and Winchester, and Eustace de Vescy and Robert de Ros) were
Anglo-Scottish landowners, and thus in Alexander's allegiance as
well as John's. My own view is that Alexander had made promises to

the baronial leaders, and had agreed to join them when the time was right. Hence the concessions to him in the Articles of the Barons and Magna Carta. Both the Crowland and Dunstable chroniclers had heard of such an alliance.[120] Of course, that still left open the possibility for Alexander that the time might never be right.

The situation in Wales was very different, for here the rebels did get very material help for their cause. John had done his best to shore up his position after the disasters of 1212. He hurried William Marshal into the custody of Cardigan and Carmarthen. From 1213 he also began to restore Walter de Lacy to his Welsh lordships and finally, on 12 April 1215, returned Ludlow castle to him.[121] The king also dangled before him the prospect of restoring his estates in Ireland. Bolstered in this way, in the early months of 1215, John tried to draw Llywelyn and his allies into negotiations, but to no avail. Both the Dunstable and Crowland chroniclers report the alliance between the barons and the Welsh rulers. The *Brut*, as we have seen, goes into its details. Around the time of the fall of London, Llywelyn seized Shrewsbury, while further south the Welsh aided the Briouzes in recovering the family lordships in and around Brecon. John retained the loyalty of many marcher barons, but the uprising disabled them from giving him much help in England. Apart from William Marshal and Peter fitzHerbert, none feature among the king's counsellors in the Charter.[122]

THE KNIGHTS

After his return to England in the autumn of 1214, John had sought to outflank his baronial opponents by winning over knights, nowhere more so than in the West Country, a particular centre, as we have seen, of local feelings and independence. In December John ordered the sheriffs of Somerset, Devon and Cornwall to send him twelve knights from each of their counties to discuss possible concessions over the royal forest. One result was a fine of 1,200 marks made in April 1215 by the men of Cornwall for deforestation and other liberties. Exeter, however, on which Peter des Roches had descended the year before, was still to be a centre of the rebellion. In the south-west generally the revolt was to be less one of great barons than of county society.[123]

There were two ways in which knights could participate in the rebellion. One was by joining the main baronial army that gathered at Stamford and swelled thereafter. The other was by participating in local activity, where they might challenge the king's government in the shires. The general impression is that knights joined the rebellion in large numbers. According to Wendover, 2,000 mustered at Stamford, a figure that is far from impossible.[124] By mid-May, knights from the honour of Trowbridge were throwing in their lot with their ousted lord, the earl of Hereford, against his replacement, the earl of Salisbury.[125] Around the same time, a Cambridgeshire knight, Jocelyn of Stukeley, was probably in the rebel camp, for he was given letters of safe conduct. He is earlier found as a grand-assize juror, custodian sheriff of Cambridgeshire-Huntingdonshire, steward of the abbot of Ramsey and briefly a justice at the bench.[126] He gives some idea of what John was up against. At Runnymede itself, we now know from Nicholas Vincent's discovery, the barons appointed four knights in each county to help implement the terms of the Charter, and presumably all these knights were already on the rebel side. Their names survive for Kent and are typical of the middle and upper levels of the knightly class, ranging from those who sat on local juries to those of virtually baronial wealth and status.[127]

Lists of rebels from a few counties drawn up in 1216 and 1217 confirm this impression of extensive knightly participation in the revolt.[128] In 1216 John was told by his local agents that 'the whole county' of Herefordshire and 'all the knights' of Shropshire had been against him, although the rebellion had much less purchase in Staffordshire. One striking fact about the rebel knights, when we have their names, is the numbers who appear on grand-assize juries. In other words, the rebellion had penetrated far deeper than just the elite of the knightly class, who were above such work. In Yorkshire, among those returning to the king's allegiance in 1217, Hugh Thomas found forty-six such knights, and thought many more were of comparable status. Kathryn Faulkner found thirty from Northamptonshire, and twenty-seven from Cambridgeshire. A Rutland return has five knights who sat together on a grand-assize jury in 1211. A short list of Leicestershire rebels, with only six names, included two grand-assize jurors.[129] A Gloucestershire list has around a dozen.

Knightly conduct in this period was governed, in varying degrees, by ties of lordship, neighbourhood and friendship, as well as by personal grievances and political ideas. The force of lordship was certainly strong. The loyalist earls of Chester and Derby kept the rebellion out of their key lands. On the other side, the great northern rebels, Holt concluded, were followed by their particular tenants 'almost to a man'. In Herefordshire the county rebelled with Bishop Briouze in the early summer of 1215 but returned with him to John in the autumn.[130]

It would be a great mistake, however, to conclude that the knights in 1215 were mere puppets. They were quite able to push their own agendas, even against their lords. The knights of Cheshire extracted from Earl Ranulf the Cheshire 'Magna Carta'. Ralph of Coggeshall's impression was that the knights of the loyalist earls and barons deserted to the opposition, which was an exaggeration, but it suggests the flow of the tide.[131] Indeed, outside Cheshire, in Earl Ranulf's honour of Richmond, which he had only acquired in 1205, there were many rebels, as there were in the Fossard barony in Yorkshire, into which Peter de Maulay had been intruded. Some knights may well have pushed their lords into rebellion. One suspects that was the case with Oxfordshire's ineffectual baron Henry d'Oilly. The four knightly tenants who joined him were all active in local government and two had been to Ireland in King John's army of 1210.[132] The baron Roger de Cressy and the knight William fitzRoscelin clearly formed a team. They both had their lands seized when Cressy quarrelled with John in 1207. From Easter 1215 they were running Norfolk and Suffolk together, with fitzRoscelin acting as Cressy's under-sheriff. He was well qualified to do so since he had already been the county's under-sheriff in 1211.[133] The rebellion in Shropshire clearly had much to do with the fitzAlan lords of Clun, labouring under a 10,000-mark relief, but two of their tenants, Vivian of Rosshall and Thomas de Costentin, both grand-assize jurors, were singled out from the other, unnamed knights in the list of rebels, and were clearly influential men.[134] In other areas such as Cambridgeshire and Northamptonshire where there were few dominant lords, many knights were able to choose their own course, and, as we have seen, numbers of them did so in favour of rebellion.[135]

Many of these knights have careers and backgrounds that can be traced in detail, although there is not the space to do that here. In Rutland, first on the list was the grand-assize knight Thomas de

Hotot, whose descendants compiled a family cartulary with copies of the 1217 Forest Charter, the 1225 Magna Carta and John's charter submitting the kingdom to Pope Innocent III.[136] In Leicestershire, first up was another grand-assize juror, Ralph de Martinwast, from a very prominent knightly family in the county.[137] One of the Gloucestershire knights, William de Parco, had been arrested, along with several other leading knights (they were knicknamed 'big shots' ('buzones')), for allegedly giving false judgements in the county court. Another Gloucestershire knight certainly had his own opinions as well as a direct interest in chapter 50 of Magna Carta, dismissing from office the relations of Gerard d'Athée, including Gio de Cigogné. This was William de Mara, who was arrested by Gio for speaking ill of King John.[138]

Conspicuous among knights acting for themselves were those holding from baronies in the hands of the king. Many from within the honours of Tickhill in Yorkshire and Peverel in Nottinghamshire joined the rebels. In April and May 1215, John sent out urgent orders to ten knights in the honour of Wallingford about garrisoning Wallingford castle. Half of those thus harried are later found in rebellion. Another Wallingford knight, William fitzEllis, had his grievances over unjust disseisin remedied at Runnymede itself. Doubtless such men pressed for chapter 43 of the Charter with its protection for those holding from such honours, those of Wallingford and Nottingham (so Peverel) being mentioned by name.[139]

By far the longest list of rebels is that from Gloucestershire, with some eighty-one names. About a third of these, in Adrian Jobson's analysis, are of men whose rebellion and indeed whose very existence is otherwise unknown.[140] Many of the unknown probably came from the ranks of the non-knightly under-tenants, as did a good proportion of those for whom some property can be found but without evidence that they were knights. This suggests that the rebellion embraced the kind of free tenants found on the hundred juries, whose importance we have already discussed.[141] In Rutland and Leicestershire, the sheriff made some effort to indicate a level of involvement beneath the knights, since he also gave the names of fourteen rebel 'serjeants'. Probably these were substantial free tenants of less than knightly status. At the muster at Stamford, besides the 2,000 knights, Roger of Wendover likewise mentioned that there were 'serjeants' both on horse and foot. Detailed inquiries into the rebels of the 1215–17 civil war, like those surviving for the civil war of 1263–7, would probably have revealed the very considerable social depth of the rebellion against the king.[142]

THE LAST STEP TO RUNNYMEDE

John had now to accept that he was losing authority throughout the country. From Easter in 1215, Norfolk and Suffolk were together controlled by Roger de Cressy and William fitzRoscelin.[143] Herefordshire, as we have seen, had gone with the defection of Bishop Briouze. In the West Country, Exeter was briefly occupied. A large part of Northampton was burnt in a conflict between the townsmen and the castle garrison. In London, the Tower was attacked, while a northern army, hearing of events further south, occupied Lincoln in Whitsun week (7–14 June).[144]

Major defections also continued, including those of two great northerners, Robert de Ros and John de Lacy, whom John had struggled to keep on side. Lacy had gone with John to Poitou and taken the cross with him on 4 March in St Paul's cathedral. He had then been pardoned all his debts. John still thought Lacy was loyal on 31 May. Probably he was already with the rebels. At Runnymede, Lacy, like Ros, became one of the twenty-five barons of Magna Carta's security clause.[145] Even worse was the defection of Saer de Quincy. He too had taken the cross with John on 4 March and was still thought to be loyal on 6 May. Yet on 25 May he was the only baronial negotiator named in a safe conduct that John issued. Given his alliance with Robert fitzWalter, Saer, one may suspect, had long been in baronial counsels.[146] John had been generous in making him earl of Winchester, but had then denied him the castle of Mountsorrel, leaving him an earl without a castle, almost as bad as a knight without a horse. Saer's throwing off the mask of fealty to his king was a major gain for the barons, since he knew John's government from the inside, having been for a while a baron of the exchequer. As his role on 25 May suggests, he probably played a large part in the negotiations at Runnymede. When he finally re-entered the allegiance of John's son, Henry III, in 1217, the clerk recording the fact on the close rolls wrote in the margin: 'I will hate as long as I am able; if not, unwillingly, I will love.'[147] No other baron provoked a comment.

With his situation thus deteriorating, John executed a fundamental change of course. On 16 May, the day before the fall of
London, he was still offering the insurgents just a truce.[148] But on
25 May (while at Odiham) the safe conduct he gave to Saer de
Quincy was to treat about 'peace', which clearly meant a settlement that would lead to peace. Evidently the king was now
engaging seriously with the baronial demands. John followed up
the safe conduct of 25 May with another two days later, allowing
Archbishop Langton to come to Staines, again to treat of 'peace'
between the king and the barons.[149] Quite probably, the envisaged
location was already Runnymede. In these circumstances, the
king's offer on 29 May to submit the demands of the barons to the
pope was merely going through the motions for papal consumption. John knew very well there was no way forward on that
basis.[150] On 8 June, now at Merton priory, he issued another safe
conduct to last until 11 June for those coming to Staines on behalf
of the barons 'to make and secure peace'.[151] The negotiations at
Runnymede were about to begin.

10

The Development of the Opposition Programme

While the insurgents had been turning the screws on the king, they had also been developing the programme that they wished him to agree to. There is much that is unknown about this process. There were probably many schemes of reform in play at the same time. The scheme found in the Unknown Charter is the only one that survives. In the broadest terms, however, the trajectory seems clear: from the liberties of the kingdom and the laws of Edward the Confessor, on to the Coronation Charter of Henry I, the Coronation Charter with additional demands, the Articles of the Barons and then Magna Carta itself.

ANCIENT LIBERTIES AND THE LAWS
OF EDWARD THE CONFESSOR

According to Roger of Wendover, before John was absolved in 1213 he swore to abolish evil customs, judge justly, give everyone their rights and uphold the laws of his ancestors, especially those of Edward the Confessor. Coggeshall too has John swearing to uphold 'ancient liberties'.[1] Respect for 'ancient liberties' was likewise the basis of John's abortive settlement with the northerners in November 1213. Whether these were fleshed out in any detail we do not know. As for the laws of Edward the Confessor, Wendover continues to feature them, with the 1100 Charter, in the baronial demands of 1214–15. The two are also linked together in the Welsh chronicle known as the *Brut*.[2] If John did take an oath in 1213 to uphold the laws of the Confessor, he probably saw it as no more than a generalized promise of good government. But the opposition could regard it as rather more tangible because, as we have seen, there was an actual text of the *Leges Edwardi Confessoris*. It showed the king accepting the laws of the kingdom as enunciated both by his nobles and by twelve men chosen from each county. The additions made to the London version of the *Leges* in John's reign stressed the king's obligation to govern not by will but by counsel and judgement. Other interpolations in the same collection which would have appealed to local society laid down that exactions in the hundred court were to be reasonable and according to the law of the land.[3]

The *Leges Edwardi* were, therefore, well worth laying before the king, yet they hardly restricted his rule in any kind of detailed and effective way. They included nothing at all about relief, wardships, or marriages of heirs and widows, issues that so exercised the barons. Indeed, for the most part, John could probably have agreed easily enough to the actual text. It was not general principles of good rule that his enemies needed to assert (to which John would always give lip service), but the detail of how they should operate. Not surprisingly, therefore, the *Leges Edwardi* gradually faded into the background. They are not mentioned by the Crowland or Coggeshall chroniclers and even in Wendover's account are soon eclipsed by the Coronation Charter of Henry I.

THE 1100 CORONATION CHARTER OF HENRY I

The demand that John should confirm the Coronation Charter of Henry I represented a quantum leap in the opposition programme, and this in two ways. First, John was no longer to make just vague promises, for the 1100 Charter covered in detail the treatment of relief, wardships, marriages and widows, issues that the *Leges Edwardi* so signally neglected. Indeed, on these matters the 1100 Charter directly influenced the order as well as the content of the Articles of the Barons, and thence of Magna Carta, since, in all of them, relief, wardship and marriages come at the start. In addition, the 1100 Charter's stipulation that penalties should be 'according to the degree of the offence' anticipated a similar stipulation (both use the same word 'modum' for 'degree') in the Articles.[4] The 1100 Charter might also appeal to knights and under-tenants, since it made concessions to knights (over the subject of the geld) and was specific that the barons should pass the concessions on relief, wardships, marriages and widows down to their men.[5] In general, it was far more fit for purpose than the *Leges Edwardi*.

There was a second way in which the 1100 Charter was instructive, a way obvious but important: it suggested that John should be bound to concessions embodied in a charter. That idea coincided with academic thought, as seen in the writings of Archbishop Langton and the school of Peter the Chanter.[6] It also, of course, coincided with long-standing practice, in which kings had made concessions by charter to individuals, towns, counties, ecclesiastical institutions and the church, the most conspicuous example of the last being John's 1214 charter granting free elections. Many of these grants, moreover, just like Magna Carta, were to be held from the king and his heirs 'in perpetuity'.[7] There was also a well-known European example of a written constitution binding a ruler, namely in Simon de Montfort's 1212 Statute of Pamiers.[8]

The importance of the 1100 Charter is shown by the way in which no fewer than four versions, all with slightly different texts, were circulating in John's reign. One of these was in London; another was at St Albans abbey; another was that copied out with the schedule of additional demands called by historians the Unknown Charter. Another again was translated into French, along with the coronation charters of Stephen and Henry II. Evidently they too were being inspected.[9] The fact of the translation shows, of course, the desire to make the charters easily accessible to French-speaking barons and knights. The charters of Stephen and Henry were brief affairs but gave added status to the 1100 Charter that they could be read as confirming. Indeed, the Bury chronicler, narrating the story of his abbot's election, thought that the whole quarrel in 1215 was caused by John trying to annul the Coronation Charter of Henry I, which his father had confirmed.[10]

When and how the 1100 Charter entered the political narrative has long been debated. According to Roger of Wendover, it was Langton himself who introduced the barons to the charter at a gathering at St Paul's cathedral in August 1213. Langton believed in the principle of binding the king to a charter, but there are reasons to be sceptical here about Wendover's story. While his dating of the St Paul's assembly is accurate, he himself gives a health warning when it comes to Langton's role: it is merely 'as rumour says'.[11] When Wendover admits that, alarm bells should be ringing. They should also be set off by his further statement that Langton, at this point, joined the baronial confederation and promised, when the moment came, to help fight for its liberties to the death. Nothing in the record of the period suggests that Langton actually threw in his lot with the barons in this way. In contrast, Ralph of Coggeshall, the Crowland chronicler, the Anonymous of Béthune and the *Brut* have the 1100 charter appearing on the scene a year later, after John's return from France, and none of them associate Langton with it.[12] There was certainly a copy of the Coronation Charter in the Canterbury archives, but there was no need for Langton to produce a text in some magical way, since, as we have seen, other copies were about. While the translation of the 1100 Charter mentioned above comes from a text like that at Canterbury, there are reasons to think that this version originated at Westminster, since it interpolates into the witness list the name of Westminster's abbot, Gilbert Crispin.[13] Canterbury, moreover, apparently had no copy of the coronation charters of Stephen and Henry II, which were also translated, while both of these were to be found in London.[14] Probably Wendover knew no more than that the 1100 Charter came onto the agenda at some point before 1215, and decided to pin it on Langton and the 1213 council. One cannot rule out the possibility that Langton drew attention to the 1100 Charter but his doing so was neither as dramatic nor as decisive as Wendover makes out. As for the timing, my view, like Holt's, is that the 1100 charter was only seriously pressed on John after his return to England in October 1214.[15] It is at this point, by the same token, that the more general idea of binding John to a charter enters the discourse.

For all its utility, the 1100 Charter was no total solution to the problem of 1215. Much of it was out of date. It dealt with geld, now more or less obsolescent (it is not mentioned in Magna Carta), and said nothing about scutages and aids. It directed that the forests were to be kept as under William the Conqueror, but how did that relate to the forests under John? And what was the use, save as an example, of the chapter that pardoned (with some exceptions) all debts owed to William Rufus?[16] There was also a whole range of concerns about law, legal administration and local government with which the 1100 Charter did not deal at all. More was needed.

THE UNKNOWN CHARTER

One attempt at providing more is seen in the document called by historians the Unknown Charter.[17] Here twelve additional concessions allegedly made by King John were appended to a copy of the 1100 Charter. Since it is certain that John never made the concessions in question, what we have here are essentially a series of demands which were being canvassed by John's opponents. It is a pity that the Unknown Charter cannot be dated, for it would help show just when the programme was moving beyond the 1100 Charter. A good case can be made for thinking that this was quite early, precisely because the 1100 Charter is so inadequate. That the Unknown Charter has nothing about London suggests it pre-dates the fall of the city on 17 May 1215. That it starts by making John agree not to arrest anyone without judgement suggests it may pre-date his promise to that effect issued on 10 May. Such a demand would fit well with the New Temple meeting in January, when John's opponents must have feared violent retribution. If the demands in the Unknown Charter were put to John at the New Temple, one can easily understand why he dismissed the baronial proposals as 'novelties'.[18]

The Unknown Charter was drawn up very much with reference to the 1100 Charter. Thus it too has the issues of relief, wardships and marriages at the start, and echoes its phraseology about wills.[19] But where it covered the same ground it brought the provisions up to date in ways that often anticipated the Articles of the Barons and Magna Carta. Thus heiresses were now to be married 'without disparagement'; widows were to stay in their late husband's house for forty days while their dower was assigned them; relief was not to be charged if the estate had been in wardship; and property held in wardship was not to be pillaged.[20]

In other areas, the Unknown Charter went beyond the 1100 Charter altogether. Thus John, right at the start, promised to arrest no one without judgement, to receive nothing for doing justice and to commit no injustice, the essence of the Charter's most famous chapters. The penultimate chapter, again anticipating the Articles and Magna Carta, laid down that interest on debts owed to Jews was not to accrue in a minority. The Unknown Charter also dealt with the highly contentious issue of overseas service, stipulating that it was only due in Normandy and Brittany – so not in Poitou as in 1214. The next chapter fixed scutage at one mark per knight's fee, as opposed to the three marks John had taken in 1214. These were radical demands, as was the chapter on the royal forest, which directed that everything made forest by John, Richard or Henry II was to be deforested. This was to virtually to remove the royal forest from large parts of the country.

These demands clearly form an important bridge between the 1100 Charter and the Articles of the Barons. Holt points out that seven chapters of the Unknown Charter have corresponding chapters in Magna Carta.[21] Arguably, a better figure is nine because the grievances over scutage, and indirectly over overseas service, were in some ways met in Magna Carta's chapters 12 and 14. The Unknown Charter, however, had nothing on London, towns and trade. It had nothing on grievances of the Welsh and the Scots. It had nothing on redress of past injustices or how the concessions might be enforced in the future. It had nothing about the workings of the common-law assizes and the running of local government. Under-tenants would have welcomed the restrictions on scutage and the privileges granted to 'knights' within the royal forest, but the Unknown Charter appears, for the most part, a narrowly baronial document. John is said to make the concessions to 'my barons' or to 'my men', so to his tenants-in-chief.[22] There is no statement that the concessions are to be passed on by the barons to their own men. When we reach the Articles we are in a different world.

THE ARTICLES OF THE BARONS

The advance in the opposition programme between the Unknown Charter and the Articles of the Barons is nothing short of sensational. The Unknown Charter has twelve chapters. The Articles of the Barons has forty-eight, followed by the lengthy security clause (chapter 49). The Unknown Charter had no input into the phraseology of the eventual Charter. The Articles are the foundations for it as they are also of its order. Indeed, they were drafted with the eventual Charter in mind since it is referred to, in chapters 1 and 49, on three occasions.

The Articles covered a much broader range of issues than both the Unknown Charter and the Charter of 1100. Legal procedures, local government, London, towns, merchants, the king of Scots and the Welsh all appear as issues. Scutages and aids had now to be levied with the common consent of the kingdom. A great deal of thought has gone into the question of enforcing the concessions, with twenty-five barons in the security clause being empowered to do so. Thought has also gone into the redress of past grievances, thus opening up a highly contentious area. Under chapter 37 of the Articles, amercements, and fines for dowers, inheritances and 'maritagia' (meaning both marriage portions and marriages), made unjustly and against the law of the land were to be completely remitted, or the issue was to be decided by the judgement of the twenty-five barons of the security clause, along with Archbishop Langton and those he wished to bring with him. This dealt with the grievances of widows, forced to offer large sums to gain their dowers, marriage portions and inheritances. It covered the gigantic fine of Geoffrey de Mandeville to marry Isabella, countess of Gloucester. And it covered all the fines, some colossal in size, for inheritances which John had exacted in place of reasonable reliefs. The Articles also sought to remedy unjust disseisins. Under chapter 25, those disseised by John without judgement of lands, liberties and rights were to have their property immediately restored, something of relevance to a great many of the insurgents. If there was any dispute, it should again be submitted to the twenty-five barons. As for those disseised by Henry II or Richard, they were to have judgement without delay by their peers in the king's court, unless, that is, John secured the exemptions of a crusader, in which case judgement would be passed by Langton and the bishops.

The very fact of the Articles testifies to the cohesion of the opposition. It had held together and combined what were probably many schedules of grievance into a single powerful document. The Articles are undated and just how they came into being is difficult to say. The 'schedule' that the barons sent to John from Brackley in Northamptonshire on 27 April, demanding it be sealed (as the Articles of the Barons eventually were sealed), may have been an early draft.[23] Quite probably, John engaged seriously with the Articles from 25 May, when he gave Saer de Quincy a safe conduct to come and treat about peace. As we will see in the next chapter, there are reasons for thinking that the king sealed the final version on 10 June at Runnymede, thus indicating his acceptance of the Articles as the basis for the coming settlement. How the opposition moved from a document like the Unknown Charter to the Articles is unclear, but quite probably the demands grew as the confederation grew. Indeed, to some extent one can see that happening. The chapters on London and merchants have the appearance of being inserted into an existing document, presumably after the baronial seizure of the capital in May 1215. In chapter 9 on amercements, therefore, the section on merchants is tagged on at the end after villeins, an order, defying social status, that was reversed in Magna Carta.[24] Likewise, the issue of London's tallages was added, quite logically, to the end of chapter 32 on taxation, while the chapters on merchants, and on entry and exit from the kingdom, were put either side in what became chapters 31 and 33. The chapter on getting rid of the fish weirs from the Thames and Medway, which replicated concessions made to London in royal charters, was inserted more randomly as chapter 23, where it broke up what would have been a coherent section dealing with the king's administration of justice.

That the chapters on the Welsh and the king of Scots come very near the end of the Articles suggests they too were added after the barons had made their alliance with the Welsh rulers, and had come to an understanding with Alexander. The importance of the Welsh alliance is reflected in the substantial nature of the concessions demanded. Under chapter 44, Welshmen disseised by John of their lands, liberties or rights in England or Wales were to be immediately given them back 'without plea', which meant without any challenge. Here they had done better than their English counterparts, for whom (in chapter 25) the possibility of a challenge, obviously by John, was recognized. Chapter 44 went on to say that Welshmen who had been disseised 'without judgement of their peers' by Henry II or Richard were to receive justice in the same way as the English, which meant under the procedure set out in chapter 25 – although this was to be according to the law of England, Wales or the March, depending on where the lands were situated. (The March was the borderland between Wales proper and England.) Chapter 45 directed that Llywelyn's son, taken under the terms of the treaty of 1211, was to be returned, as were all Welsh hostages and charters of security. Here, however, there was a qualification, for John evidently claimed that under his charters (presumably those covering the treaty of 1211) he was not bound to make these restorations. His claims here were to be decided by Langton and those he wished to bring with him.[25]

As for King Alexander, in chapter 46 John promised to treat his
liberties and his rights 'according to the form' in which he was
going deal with 'the barons of England', although here too there
was the qualification about whether things should be different
because of the charters that John possessed. John's newly discovered
account of the 1209 Treaty of Norham gives these stipulations
fresh meaning. Under the treaty, John was expecting Alexander to
do him homage for the kingdom of Scotland. The implication of
the Articles of the Barons, by contrast, was that the treaty was
dead. The only relationship that Alexander now had with John
was as another baron of England. Thus the liberties and rights that
Alexander was seeking, one may suspect, concerned not Scotland
itself, but his claims to the three northernmost English counties,
claims which had been reserved under the 1209 treaty. He was
now seeking to hold the counties from the English king, like any
other baron. Since Alexander's claims were to be treated like those
of the other barons of England, that meant, under the Articles'
chapter 25, they would be judged either by the twenty-five barons
or by Alexander's peers in the king's court.[26] The chapter on Alexander also dealt with his hostages, which were almost certainly
those taken to guarantee the 1209 treaty. These too were now to
be treated like those taken from English barons, which meant,
under chapter 38, that they were to be returned. Here too the saving clause applied: 'unless it should be otherwise by the charters
which the king has'. John evidently was trying to assert that the
1209 treaty still had validity.

Most important of all, in moving from a largely baronial document such as the Unknown Charter, was the influence of the
knights who were joining the rebel army in large numbers and
obstructing the king's agents in the shires. Knights were steeped in
the workings of the law, and had plenty of experience in extracting
concessions about the running of local government from the
king. They could draw inspiration from the Coronation Charter of
Henry I, with its direct concession to knights over geld. Indeed, the
version of the Coronation Charter most closely linked to the
demands of 1215, that attached to the Unknown Charter, is one
which includes a blatant appeal to the knights. Henry, in making his
concession over geld, hopes that 'as my kindness is the more felt by
them, so they may be faithful to me'.[27] Some knights may have
known of the twelve men in each county declaring the law in the

Leges Edwardi, and the interpolations in the same London collection about the exactions in local courts, and the sheriffs being elected 'in full folkmoot'.[28] Further afield, King Pedro had conceded that his officials in Catalonia should be elected knights.[29] Knights also had experience of extracting concessions from their lords, as the charter of Peter de Brus shows. There was also the example of the 1100 Charter where the barons were to pass on the concessions over relief, marriages and widows to their men.

Viewed from this perspective, the knights would have seen a document like the Unknown Charter as deeply disappointing. They must also have had reservations about the first chapters of the Articles of the Barons, which dealt with relief, wardship, marriage of heirs and the rights of widows. These completely lacked the injunctions about barons passing down the concession to their men found in the equivalent chapters in the Coronation Charter of Henry I. True, the Articles simply refer to 'heirs' and 'widows' without any indication of their tenurial status, so they could be taken as referring equally to tenants-in-chief and under-tenants. But that the chapters on relief and wardship were intended to apply to the relationship between the king and his tenants-in-chief was shown by the way they were redrafted at Runnymede. Barons may well have wanted the same to be true of the chapter on the marriage of heirs, since in the Articles it had been part of the wardships chapter. Baronial concern to control their tenants is revealed in the way a chapter in the Articles was redrafted. This was chapter 17, which prevented a widow being forced into remarriage. It was certainly aimed at both king and lords, and for that reason provided a safeguard for both. It thus insisted that a widow needed to get the consent of the king, or the lord from whom she held, if she wished to remarry. This chapter seems out of place in the Articles, where it comes after chapter 16 on wills, rather than more logically after chapter 4 about the rights of widows over their properties. Probably, the chapter had initially lacked the saving clause and, when redrafted to include it, dropped out of its original place. In Magna Carta it was put back there.

If knights were indeed disappointed with the early schemes of baronial reform, there may well have been parallels in 1215 with events at the revolutionary parliaments of 1258–9. At Oxford in 1258, the great men had likewise mustered with large numbers of knights, and that explains why the so-called 'Petition of the

Barons' in fact covered far more than baronial interests.[30] At the Westminster parliament of October 1259 a body of knights, described as 'the community of the bachelry of England', protested that the barons had only looked after their own interests and done nothing for 'the utility of the republic'. The result was the speedy publication of the Provisions of Westminster, with their early clauses dealing with grievances of under-tenants about being forced to attend the courts of their lords.[31] Was it comparable knightly pressure that shaped the nature of the Articles? Thus, after the chapters on relief, wardships and marriages, come a series of consecutive chapters, beginning with chapter 6, dealing with the interests of under-tenants, sometimes as against their lords.[32] One reads chapter 6 with a start. After all, the heading of the Articles is 'these are the chapters which the Barons seek'. Yet chapter 6 is specifically aimed at 'the baron'. The king is not to give him permission to take an aid from his free men save on the three specified customary occasions. What on earth is going on? The answer most probably is that this was a chapter on which knights and under-tenants insisted. Chapter 7 was in the same vein and laid down that no one was to do more service for the fee of a knight than was owed: a general statement, but clearly very much in the interest of under-tenants against their lords. Chapter 8 moved on to the major concern of knights and free tenants over the working of the common-law assizes, and called in the knights elected by the county court to sit with the king's judges. And then came the chapter on amercements, beginning with those levied on free men. How little the earls and barons were concerned with these chapters is shown by the way they were not mentioned at all within them. A special chapter about the amercements imposed on earls and barons had to wait until Runnymede.

After the chapters on amercements in the Articles, there follows a run of chapters, between 11 and 21, very much in the interests of knights and under-tenants, for they dealt with local government and local officials. Here chapter 14 banned the increments above the farms of the counties (and by implication too the whole policy of profits), thus echoing the concession that the men of Somerset and Dorset had obtained from the king. The same chapter stipulated that the sheriffs were not to interfere with pleas of the crown without the coroners. The provision thus focused, not on the abuse of the sheriffs hearing the pleas of the crown instead of the king's judges, but on their ignoring the coroners, whose job it was to keep a record of crown pleas, as well as hold inquests on dead bodies. Since coroners were county knights, probably elected by their fellows, the Articles were making sure the sheriffs did not here escape local supervision.[33] Only one of these chapters (chapter 16) had any equivalent in the Unknown Charter, and that was now made socially more comprehensive. Dealing with those who died intestate this chapter benefited 'any free man', whereas in the Unknown Charter (chapter 5) the benefit had only been for tenants-in-chief.

Knights and under-tenants were also protected against both king and lords by chapter 28 on accusations by bailiffs and chapter 29, which preserved a free man from arrest and disseisin save by judgement of his peers or by the law of the land. It was only in the second part of the chapter, when it came to 'going against' anyone, that it became simply a promise made by the king. Chapter 30, forbidding the sale, delay and denial of justice, was similarly general in its application. Both chapters contrasted with their equivalents at the start of the Unknown Charter, which only concerned the conduct of the king. Other chapters in the Articles benefited knights and under-tenants more directly. Thus chapter 27 ensured that free men did not lose the privileges of knighthood because they held some kind of non-knightly tenure. Chapter 34, which prevented interest on Jewish debts accruing in minorities, plainly embraced under-tenants, for it concerned the heir 'from whoever he holds'. It was again much broader than the equivalent chapter in the Unknown Charter, chapter 11, which was limited to tenants-in-chief. Chapter 35, which ensured that widows and children were still provided for when Jewish debts were paid during minorities, likewise applied to under-tenants, so much so that here lords put in another safeguard. Such debts were to be paid 'saving the service of lords'. Chapter 36 protected the knightly under-tenants in honours, such as Wallingford, that were in the king's hands.

In the Articles another run of chapters on local government began with chapter 39. This chapter itself limited the range of those who had to appear before the justices of the forest, and then went on to commission the inquiry of the twelve knights in each county into the abuses of the king's officials. The inquiry placed tremendous power in the hands of the knights. They were not simply to inquire into what was wrong; they were also to put it right. And they were to be chosen not by the barons, but by the county court.[34] Chapter 39 is followed by another chapter of concern to knights and local society. This dismissed the relations of Gerard d'Athée, who were sheriffs of Gloucestershire, Herefordshire, Nottinghamshire and Derbyshire. We have seen how this chapter must have pleased the rebel knight William de Mara, arrested by Gio de Cigogné for bad-mouthing King John. Athée's clan were also military experts, so the next chapter called for the dismissal of all the foreign soldiers whom John had brought to England. Then the Articles returned again to local issues, and laid down that sheriffs and other officials should know the law of the land and mean to observe it. Since such a law might vary according to the region, the chapter carried the implication that the sheriff should be a native of his county.

The Articles concluded in chapter 48 by stating that everyone should observe towards their men those liberties which the king was giving to his men. All the concessions, therefore, were to be passed down to under-tenants. The chapter thus provided some compensation for the absence of any similar injunctions within individual chapters earlier in the Articles. No equivalent statement is found in either the Coronation Charter or the Unknown Charter.

Knights certainly got less than they might have hoped for from the Articles. The stipulation that the sheriffs should know the law of the land was something, but a poor substitute for the concession, bought from John by some counties, that they should be local knights. There was no suggestion that the sheriffs should be elected by the county court, although such elections were conceded when it came to the knights in chapters 8 and 39 (chapters 18 and 48 in the eventual Charter). Knights and under-tenants were also given no opportunity in either the Articles or the Charter to complain about their lords, whether to the twelve knights in each county or to the twenty-five barons of the security clause. The opportunity to make such complaints, along with locally elected knightly sheriffs, had to wait until the reforms of 1258–9.[35] Nonetheless, even with these qualifications, the baronial demands, as represented in the Unknown Charter, had been transformed. The Articles were far more representative of the wider realm.

The Articles were a fair copy, but the clerk may well have been working from a difficult document with interlineations, and attachments, produced by the additions and changes we have described. He may sometimes have failed to see where a clause should go. He may sometimes have made his own decisions about both the sequence and the breaking up into chapters, as when he tacked onto chapters 14, 35 and 39 new sections with a rather uneasy 'and that'.[36] There was a logic to much of the arrangement, especially in the first half of the document, although Magna Carta improved upon it. Thus the chapters on amercements lead naturally to the chapters between 11 and 21 on local government, since the first here was about the amercements of villages for failure to perform bridge work. The intention to do something about measures at chapter 12 may have come at this point because of the amercements imposed on local communities when the measures were false.[37] One puzzles as to why chapters 29 and 30, demanding judgement by peers and forbidding the sale and denial of justice, appear relatively low down in the Articles, and thus likewise in Magna Carta, whereas in the Unknown Charter they come first. Perhaps the Articles wished to follow the 1100 Charter and thus began with reliefs and wardships. Perhaps the chapters dropped from their original place because of debates over wording. Whereas John's letter of 10 May, as an alternative to judgement by peers, mentioned treatment 'by the law of our kingdom', the Articles, more evocative and independent of the king, have treatment 'by the law of the land'. There were to be further changes to both chapters at Runnymede itself .

THE INPUT OF KING JOHN

Holt has suggested that the Articles were 'not produced in a purely baronial gathering but by both sides in concert'. Indeed, they were 'the work of a small committee slowly reaching common ground over a period of a fortnight'.[38] Assuming that serious negotiations began on 25 May, when Saer de Quincy was given his safe conduct to treat of 'peace', there was certainly time for such work before John, probably on 10 June, agreed to the Articles as the basis for the final settlement. But there was not much common ground. True, there were parts of the Articles that John might see as advantageous. He had much to gain from making common-law litigation more accessible, for he could thus win the favour of knights and free tenants. For the same reason, he might welcome the stipulation that everyone must pass the concessions down to their own men. In getting such chapters into the Articles, knights and free tenants should have had John's full support. These, however, were small compensations. John must have regarded the great bulk of the Articles as utterly unpalatable. He had originated none of the proposals. The heading of the Articles was quite right. 'These are the chapters which the Barons seek and the lord King concedes.' John was engaged essentially in an exercise of damage limitation. Here he achieved something, but far less than he might have hoped.

In the area of damage limitation, John scored one major victory. The Unknown Charter had demanded the deforestation of whatever Henry II, Richard and John had made forest. Here it was the afforestations of Henry that counted most. Yet the Articles of the Barons said nothing about Richard and Henry, and only called for the removal of John's afforestations. That the subject was long disputed may explain why the chapter about John's afforestations is at the end of the Articles, as though until the last moment the barons hoped for more.

In some other areas, John seems to have modified the detail of the demands. The Articles accepted that his charters might affect the restorations due to the Welsh and the king of Scots (chapters 45 and 46); that redress for those disseised by Henry and Richard might be affected by his privileges as a crusader (chapter 25); and that John might challenge whether disseisins, fines and amercements in his time were unjust (chapters 25 and 37). In all these cases procedures were set up to deal with such contingencies. The Articles exempted John's demesne manors from the restrictions on county revenues (chapter 14). They left the size of relief to be decided in the Charter, presumably because there had been no agreement about it. John won a victory when it came to wardships. The Unknown Charter had demanded that they be run by four knights of the fee. Although the knights were to answer for the issues to the king, this still meant that he could neither sell wardships nor exploit them through his own agents. The Articles of the Barons, by contrast, left John quite free to give wardships to whom he liked, only saying that the guardians should lose them if they committed waste. John won another victory, although it was a pyrrhic one. The Unknown Charter had banned service overseas save in Normandy and Brittany, and had fixed the rate of scutage at one mark per knight's fee. Neither of these demands appeared in either the Articles or the Charter. Yet that on scutage was unnecessary, because it had been replaced by a far more radical demand.

The Unknown Charter had allowed the king to levy a scutage higher than a mark 'by counsel of the barons of the kingdom'. In the Articles, this was transformed into the demand that no scutage was to be levied at all save by the kingdom's common counsel. Magna Carta went on to make clear that this counsel covered the rate as well as the incidence of scutage. The barons had thus gained total control of the tax. That was certainly a grievous intrusion into the rights of the crown, since the king had hitherto levied scutage without any consent, deeming it due under the tenurial obligations of his tenants-in-chief, if they did not send their actual military service. The chapter in the Articles (32) also had a bearing on overseas service. John was not stopped from demanding this, but the barons did gain the power to prevent him levying a scutage to support it, which, in practice, came close to the same thing. These defeats were grievous enough. They paled into insignificance beside the monstrosity of the security clause.

THE SECURITY CLAUSE

Having set out John's concessions, the Articles left a four-line gap and then continued, 'Here is the form of the security for the observation of the peace and the liberties between king and kingdom.' The gap has led to the idea that the security clause, as it is called by historians, was initially intended as a separate document, but this was certainly not the case by the time of the Articles, for they leave a detail in the clause to be settled 'in the charter'.[39]

The security clause was indeed momentous. It represented by far the most revolutionary, as also the most original, part of the Articles and the eventual Charter. John's detailed concessions could all be seen as extensions of those made by Henry I in 1100. There was no way the security clause could be seen in that light. The form of its coercion of the king had no precedent. V. H. Galbraith was right to say it represented 'the most fantastic surrender of any English king to his subjects'.[40] It was seen in those terms at the time. The Anonymous of Béthune (whose patron at this point was on John's side) thought there were good things in the Charter, but described with astonishment (and with some exaggeration) the powers assumed by the twenty-five barons. While not referred to specifically, such powers underlay the comments on the events of

1215 made in a contemporary poem copied into the Melrose chronicle. This acknowledged John's tyrannical rule, but nonetheless began by saying that:

> England has ratified a perverse order;
> Who has heard such an astonishing event be asserted in verse?
> For the body aspired to be on top of the head;
> The people sought to rule the king.[41]

Under the terms of the security clause, the barons were to choose twenty-five of their number. These were, as the Articles had already indicated, to sit in judgement on the king's unjust disseisins, fines and amercements, if there was any dispute over their immediate reversal. In the security clause itself, the twenty-five were given a wider brief. This was to ensure, with all their strength, that 'the peace and the liberties which the king has conceded and confirmed in his charter' were observed. If the king or his ministers offended 'anyone in anything' or transgressed any of the 'articles of peace or security', the victims were to complain to four of the twenty-five. The four would then bring the complaint before the king. If he did not redress the grievance, with a term to be decided in the Charter, then the four were to go to the rest of the twenty-five, and the twenty-five, 'with the commune of all the land', would then distrain and distress the king in every way they could, namely by taking his castles, lands and possessions, until the wrong, in their opinion, had been righted. At that point, everyone would obey the king as before. The clause then went on to explain the oath that would form 'the commune of all the land', before returning to the twenty-five and dealing with substitutes, majority verdicts and an oath of office. Finally, summing up the total distrust which made the whole clause so necessary, there was the stipulation that John should give security, through charters of the archbishop, the bishops and the papal representative Pandulf, that he would seek nothing from the pope which would overturn the agreement.

One striking feature of the clause, rarely commented upon, is that it gave the twenty-five a broader remit than simply that of enforcing the Charter. They were also to hear complaints if the king or his ministers offended 'anyone in anything'. This extraordinary provision meant they could take cognizance of anything they liked, and gave them virtually a permanent brief to monitor the activities of royal government. Voices were evidently raised to give the twenty-five even more power. The Anonymous of Béthune thought they were to choose the 'bailiffs of the land'. One draft of the Charter had them choosing the castellans of strategic castles.[42] John evidently beat that off, but what was there was bad enough. True, if the king did offend, then the procedure gave the chance of reform. When the four barons brought the complaint to his attention, he would have the opportunity to put matters right. If, however, he failed to do so, 'within a reasonable time to be determined in the Charter', there were no similar stages in the ratcheting up of punishment. Their whole weight crashed down at once on his head. Whereas chapter 5 of the Articles laid down that John's debtors should be distrained first by their chattels and only if that failed, by their lands, in the security clause the twenty-five were to seize at once the king's castles, lands and possessions. It was, moreover, entirely up to the twenty-five to decide when John had put matters right, and everyone could obey him as before.

To enforce all this, the twenty-five enlisted the 'commune of all the land'. This was formed by an oath to be taken by everybody, which is why 'communitas' in the Latin is always translated as 'commune', meaning a sworn association. The oath was itself astonishing. Unlike the later oath of 1258, which was to uphold the reforms of that year, it was an oath, not to uphold the Charter, but to obey the orders of the twenty-five in harming the king. The oath thus established the twenty-five in a permanent relationship with the people of the kingdom, with the oath of loyalty to them standing now alongside the oath of loyalty to the king. Another corollary was that anyone who broke the oath could in effect be accused of breaking faith to the twenty-five and be liable to attack in body, lands and chattels. This indeed was precisely what John's northern agent, Brian de Lisle, was threatened with later, if he refused to obey a judgement of the twenty-five returning Knaresborough castle to Nicholas de Stuteville.[43] Truly, John was now to be only half master in his kingdom.

The significance of the oath is shown by the curious double-handed provision over its swearing. One could either do so voluntarily, or be made to do so by the king. On the face of it, the barons were here taking a remarkable risk, for a common way of nullifying an oath was to say it had been taken under duress. There was no similar provision over coercion in the oath of 1258.[44] That the barons nonetheless ran the risk shows the importance which they attached to getting everyone to swear. They hoped, of course, since the oath had to be sworn anyway, it would be sworn voluntarily. They were also asserting something about the sheer status of the oath. It was in effect being made a condition of belonging to 'the land'. In was thus absolutely on a par with the oath of fealty taken to the king, which likewise everyone had to swear, willingly or not, to be a member of the kingdom.

A chief aim of the security clause was to enable the twenty-five and the commune of the land to attack the king without any taint of treason. In other words, they had the legal right to attack John's possessions while the king had no legal right to do anything in return. Since John had sanctioned their actions, they would not be breaking their oaths of fealty to him. There was no need now to issue any kind of formal defiance. Yet while the security clause clearly worked legally, it is hard to see how it could work practically. The idea that John would sit quietly by while his lands were seized, and his castles besieged, was fanciful, as was the idea that afterwards everyone would obey him as before. Many historians have thus seen the clause as impracticable, which is to miss the point. The security clause was conceived from the start as the medieval equivalent of a nuclear deterrent. The point was to threaten John with such massive and immediate retaliation that complaints brought to his attention were bound to be redressed. If they were not, the security clause had already failed. At the very most, it would help justify baronial action against the king. Even that possibility, when it came to it, the barons did not exploit. When John reneged on the Charter, they turned to an altogether different remedy and chose another king.

Underneath the umbrella of the security clause's deterrent, the barons had every intention of making the twenty-five do their work, hence the rules about majority verdicts and the election of a new member if one died. This was to be no temporary commission. Indeed, it would last as long as the Charter itself, and since that was to be in perpetuity, the twenty-five were to have a permanent place in the life of the kingdom.

How then was this remarkable plan of coercion and redress conceived? That is not easy to say, for it is so original. There is nothing like it earlier not merely in England but further afield. Here there are no parallels in Spanish jurisprudence.[45] The most likely explanation is that the security clause was indeed an original conception of the opposition, bringing together a series of different threads. The process of petitioning the king to put right acts of injustice, either committed by himself or his predecessors, was well established. John himself responded to such complaints, sometimes after a judicial inquiry. It was thus that he righted a disseisin of King Richard, and cancelled one of his own charters which he had been deceived into granting.[46] Equally well established were ideas about barons sitting in judgement; that after all was what was involved in judgement by peers. The monitoring role of the twenty-five also had parallels with the councils found in town constitutions. Under the charter John granted to Northampton, four men of the borough, chosen by common counsel, were to ensure that the provost, the chief town official, treated justly both poor and rich alike.[47] In 1200 twenty-five Londoners were elected to counsel the mayor.[48] In 1206 John himself ordered the barons of London to elect twenty-four of their fellow citizens to carry out reforms. The oath the twenty-four took still survives.[49] As for 'the commune of all the land', formed by a general oath, that was clearly modelled on 'the commune of the kingdom' formed to resist invasion by the oath of 1205.[50]

The idea of legitimate resistance had itself many roots. It was a familiar part of the debate in monastic communities when they were quarrelling with their abbots. At Evesham in John's reign, the monk Thomas of Marlborough observed that while civil and canon law forbad subordinates from bringing accusations against their superiors, they were allowed to do so in certain circumstances. He then went on to bring a series of charges against his licentious abbot.[51] In the secular world, it was, as we have seen, accepted that a vassal, suffering acts of injustice, might renounce his allegiance and make war on his lord. This was closely related to the idea of 'legitimate feud', where there was the necessity for a just cause, a proper complaint, the opportunity for the offender to make reparation, and where 'the proper goal was a restored balance of some kind'.[52] In Magna Carta, however, there is no need for any act of defiance, resistance being sanctioned by the king himself in the law laid down in the Charter. The appeal to law can be seen in a case from the kingdom of Jerusalem. In 1198, when Ralph, lord of Tiberias, was accused of treason by the king, he claimed protection under a law known as the 'Assise sur la ligece', and demanded a judgement by his peers in the king's court. When this was refused, his peers withdrew their service from the king and offered to maintain Tiberias in his rights.[53] Admittedly, the offer of support to Tiberias never materialized, and it is unclear what it was supposed to involve. It was not in itself sanctioned by the 'Assise', of which Tiberias was advancing only one possible interpretation. Nonetheless, in this case resistance was being justi-fied in the light of what was at least alleged to be a written law. A closer parallel to Magna Carta comes from Hungary, for here resistance was indeed legitimized by the king in his own charter. The thirty-one chapters of the Golden Bull, issued by King Andrew II in 1222, dealt with such issues as inheritance, dower, local offi-cials, taxation, dispensation of justice, national assemblies, military service outside the kingdom, and arrest and 'destruction' (the same word as in Magna Carta) without lawful process. At the end, the king conceded that if he or his successors acted contrary to the concessions, then 'by the authority' of the bull, the nobles had the right to resist and contradict him and his successors 'without stain of infidelity'.[54] Unlike Magna Carta, the Golden Bull gave no details about the nature of the resistance envisaged, so its sanctions were much weaker than those of the security clause.[55] Nonetheless, resistance, if the king contravened his concessions, was here being permitted by the king himself. There were connec-tions between England and Hungary in the early thirteenth century and Magna Carta may well have influenced the Golden Bull. It was probably also a case of similar problems spawning similar solutions.

In England, there was before 1215 at least the idea that mag-nates had a duty to restrain or limit the king. Gervase of Canterbury thought that 'the magnates of England' had done that in 1205 when they 'compelled' John to take an oath to preserve the rights of the kingdom 'with their counsel'.[56] In the great book on the laws and customs of England known as *Bracton*, largely written in the 1220s and 1230s, two views about resistance were canvassed. One was that the king must be left to the judgement of God. The other was that the 'universitas' of the kingdom should correct his acts of injustice 'in the king's own court'. An even more extreme state-ment was that the barons ought to 'put a bridle' on a lawless king. There was no suggestion that if this happened they ought to defy him and withdraw their allegiance. These sentiments were prompted by the 1233-4 rising against Henry III, a rising in defence, it could be thought, of Magna Carta.[57] The judge William of Raleigh, who was probably responsible for this passage in *Bracton*, was a protégé of the Pattishall dynasty of professional judges. In May 1215 Simon of Pattishall, John's senior judge, had his lands seized for joining the rebels. He protested his innocence, but did not make his peace until the following December.[58] Pattishall had material reasons for flirting with the rebellion, but one wonders whether his views on Magna Carta and the security clause laid the foundations for Raleigh's sentiments about the events of 1233–4.

In sum, the security clause drew on procedures for petitioning the king, the principle of judgement by peers, the monitoring activities of town councils, the 1205 'commune of the kingdom', and the violent actions that followed acts of defiance. But that violence was sanctioned not by any 'diffidatio' but by the king himself in his own charter. Whereas defiance was potentially a one-way process, for the king had no obligation to accept that it legitimized resistance, now he was bound to accept that resistance was legitimate, for he had sanctioned it himself in his own charter. That was the original trick that made the security clause so empowering.

Why finally the number twenty-five? There was some precedent here in the London council of 1200. The London council of 1205 was likewise twenty-five if the mayor was included. Twenty-five involved a goodly number of barons, and ensured (if they all turned up) that decisions could be taken by a majority, as the clause envisaged. It was, therefore, better than the even number of twenty-four, although that was a familiar number in some legal and biblical contexts. The number twenty-five also featured in biblical exegesis, although not always favourably.[59] Augustine, in a well-known homily, commenting on passages in St John's Gospel, argued that the number twenty-five signified the law, although he then went on to say that this law lacked perfection as it preceded the Gospel. In fact, thirty was the perfect number. The number twenty-five would hardly have appealed to Archbishop Langton. He equated the twenty-five men 'with their backs toward the temple of the Lord' in Ezekiel (8:16) with the carnal priests who rejected Christ. This is but one of many indications that Langton had little to do with the Articles of the Barons.

THE ROLE OF ARCHBISHOP LANGTON

Historians have long debated the role played by Archbishop Langton in shaping opposition demands between 1213 and 1215. On the one hand, he is seen as introducing the barons to the Coronation Charter of Henry I, having a major input into the Articles of the Barons and being responsible for the way the Charter reaches out beyond the selfish ambitions of a baronial elite. On the other hand, led by Holt, he has been seen largely as a peacemaker and go-between. There are persuasive reasons for thinking that the second view is the more correct.[60]

There is no doubt that Langton's political ideas put him in general sympathy with the Charter.[61] He had practical experience of John's tyranny, having seen his Canterbury estates ravaged in the Interdict. He knew the evils perpetrated by Gerard d'Athée's kin, having lamented the 'violence and great oppression' of Engelard de Cigogné as sheriff of Gloucestershire.[62] Langton may well have inspired the oath that John took at the time of his absolution to respect ancient liberties and customs. In 1213 all accounts agree that the archbishop urged John not to proceed against the northerners without judgement and lawful process. On the other hand, there are, as we have seen, good reasons for doubting Wendover's story that Langton introduced the barons to the Coronation Charter at St Paul's in 1213 and became a 'capital consenter' to the baronial league thereafter.[63] Whether or not he had any role in circulating the charter, the clear testimony of the Crowland and Coggeshall chronicles is that, in 1215, Langton was essentially an intermediary between the two sides. John's complaint against him, echoed by the pope in plaintive letters, was that Langton had refused to condemn the barons, not that he had openly taken their part. Essentially, the archbishop was trying to hold the balance even, and not aggravate the situation.[64]

The best evidence that Langton had no input into the development of the baronial demands in 1215 lies in the documents themselves. The Unknown Charter is an entirely secular creation, and has nothing on the church. Indeed, whereas Magna Carta, in chapter 27, laid down that if a free man died in intestate, his nearest relatives and friends were to distribute his chattels 'under the supervision of the church', the Unknown Charter, in its equivalent chapter (5), says nothing about the church's role. An omission of far more moment occurred in the Articles of the Barons. In their initial order and content, the Articles followed the 1100 Charter, save that they completely left out its first chapter on the church. It was not even as though the Articles said that the church would be introduced in the eventual Charter, as it did about some other matters. Evidently, the barons had no expectation that there would be a chapter on the church, yet they must have been very keen to include one. After all, defence of the church featured in their oath of association, and Robert fitzWalter styled himself 'marshal of the army of God and holy church'. That the church did not appear was almost certainly because Langton would not allow it.

Further evidence that Langton distanced himself from the Articles lies in the very evidence that features, at first sight, to show exactly the reverse. Langton appears in no fewer than five chapters of the Articles, surely proof that his hand lay heavy upon them.[65] Nearly all the roles assigned him were in response to difficulties that John was making or was expected to make. Thus if the king was to have the delay enjoyed by other crusaders on the disseisins committed by his father Henry and brother Richard, then Langton and the bishops were to take over and give judgement on the cases.[66] If there were disputes over pardoning fines, then the archbishop was to join the twenty-five in judging them (chapter 37). And again, Langton was called in to give judgement on whether John's charters would enable him to avoid the concessions demanded by the Welsh and the king of Scots. Finally, in the security clause, John was to get charters from Langton, Pandulf and the bishops guaranteeing that he would seek nothing from the pope by which the Charter might be overturned.

All this seems to show Langton deep in baronial counsels, and helping directly in the stand against the king. Yet the fact is that every single one of the references to Langton in the Articles was altered in the Charter. The reason, it may be suggested, was that the barons were asking Langton to do things which, once he engaged with the Articles at Runnymede, he either refused to do or agreed to do in a more qualified fashion. The most striking instance of this, one which has devastating consequences for the view that Langton was involved with the Articles, comes at the end of the security clause. There Langton and his fellow ecclesiastics were supposed to issue charters guaranteeing that John would seek nothing from the pope to overturn the Charter. Langton could not possibly have done anything of the kind. He would thus have been placing a barrier between John and the pope, a pope who was the king's temporal overlord as well as his spiritual father. Langton would have known that there was no quicker way to destroy the eventual Charter and himself, in some great explosion of papal anger, than to assent to that. Had he been involved with the Articles, he would have said at once that the demand was impossible. When he did engage at Runnymede, the demand was scrapped. How the other clauses were also altered at Runnymede we will see in the next chapter.

Langton had several reasons for acting at arm's length. One was practical. If he threw in his lot with the rebels, he would destroy his role as peacemaker. Another was ideological. Langton, at the start of the Interdict, had urged the kingdom's knights to protect the church with their swords. But the situation in 1215 was quite different, for John was now reconciled to the pope. While, in his biblical exegesis, Langton argued that disobedience to an unjust command might sometimes be legitimate, he never thought in terms of outright rebellion. He averred that if people knew that the ruler was trying to execute someone unjustly and without judgement, then they were bound to liberate him, but such an obligation could hardly stretch to justifying the rebellion of 1215.[67] Indeed, the pope pointed out that it was the barons who were trying to deprive John of his rights 'without judgement'.[68]

Once, therefore, the barons took up arms against John, which they did from the start of 1215, there was no way Langton could help develop their demands. When the king began serious negotiations after 25 May, the situation changed, but Langton still held aloof. It was only after John had made his position completely clear by sealing the Articles that the archbishop became involved. None of this means that Langton's attitude was unimportant for the growing insurgency. He was close to Eustace de Vescy; indeed, his steward, Elyas of Dereham, appears as Vescy's agent.[69] Through such channels, Langton's sympathy for the barons must have been clear, hence the role they hoped he would play in the Articles. His attitude also made it easier for his tenants to join the rebels. Three out of the four knights appointed by the baronial leaders to enforce the Charter in Kent were Canterbury tenants and close to the archbishop. All three witnessed an important agreement he made over

Rochester castle in 1213.[70] Most vital of all was Langton's refusal to launch sentences of excommunication. The rebellion would have had far less impetus had he succumbed to the pressure to do so.

THE COMMUNITY OF THE REALM[71]

Even without the first chapter on the church, the Articles of the Barons seemed far more than a mere baronial document. The chapters on amercements covered free men, merchants, villeins and clerks. The position of the knights in local government was fully recognized. All sections of society benefited from the limitations on taxation and the exactions of the sheriffs. All, in theory, were enlisted by the oath in the security clause to defend the Charter. How had this come about? One view is that it was the result of various interest groups getting their agendas into the Charter, as far as their power allowed, as well as lower sections of society benefiting when their interests happened to coincide with those of their superiors. Another view is that the baronial leaders felt a sense of responsibility for the realm as a whole. Thus Susan Reynolds has written:

> The barons of Magna Carta spoke – and presumably spoke more or less sincerely – on behalf of the community of the realm, not because they thought most of its members were their equals but because they did not. It was the accepted duty of the great men of any kingdom to represent the rest.

These different views about the role of idealism and self-interest in 1215 are not mutually exclusive, and weighing the balance between them is difficult, since we cannot see into the minds of the baronial leaders. There is a contrast here with the revolution of 1258 when we have abundant evidence for the uneasy relationship between principle and profit in the career of Simon de Montfort. How one wishes one could say the same for Saer de Quincy and Robert fitzWalter! Under King Stephen the barons had fought for themselves and extracted individual charters of concession, dealing with their own particular grievances. In 1215, by contrast, the barons certainly thought of themselves as representing the kingdom, a kingdom whose existence and interests are evoked so often throughout

Magna Carta. It is thus the baronial tenants-in-chief who answer for the kingdom when it comes to taxation. It is likewise twenty-five barons, leading the 'commune of all the land', who are to enforce the Charter. That the king should have a 'care' for all his subjects, even those who were unfree, had long been accepted. The idea is found in the *Dialogus de Scaccario*, in William of Newburgh and in the picture of the realm in Lawman's *Brut*.[72] Might not the baronial leaders have felt in the same way? At the start of Magna Carta, John said that he was acting for 'the reform of our kingdom'. Was that not really the barons speaking? Archbishop Langton might not have influenced the detailed development of opposition demands, but his ideas could still have informed baronial thinking. One of his fundamental concepts was that secular authority derived from the church broadly defined as the congregation of the faithful, both clerks and laymen. Might there then, John Baldwin asks, be a connection between that idea and the baronial view of their programme as 'representing the community of the realm'?[73]

Baronial leadership was accepted at the time by contemporary commentators. On the back of the Lincoln engrossment of the Charter, it was described as 'the Concord between King John and the Barons in return for the concession of the liberties of the church and the kingdom of England'. In 1205 Gervase of Canterbury could write of the 'magnates of England' demanding that John preserve the rights of the kingdom 'with their counsel'. There must be some truth in all this. After all, barons, knights, free tenants, churchmen and townsmen had all suffered from John's oppressive rule. They surely felt a solidarity in standing against it under baronial leadership. It was this 'equality of oppression' that made Magna Carta 'the classic statement of regnal solidarity against a king'.[74]

Yet this perspective, if pushed too far, is hard to square with the cold detail of the Articles and the Charter. The barons' claim to represent the realm can there seem merely a cover and support for their own interests. Magna Carta certainly stipulated that 'even an unfree man should be punished only in proportion to his offence'. Yet, as we have seen, this clause was specially drawn so as to exclude the unfree from any protection against their lords.[75] There was not much care for the unfree peasant there, although they made up a large proportion of the population. The barons believed certainly in justice and judgement, but most strongly when it came to themselves. One can hardly agree with the premise that they had 'relatively little seigniorial jurisdiction to protect'. Throughout, the Charter tries to preserve the interests of 'the lord of the fee'.[76] Self-interest too, at the expense of the wider realm, is clear in what the Articles of the Barons and the Charter left out. So, in contrast to the inquiries of 1170 and 1258, the twelve knights had no brief to deal with the malpractices of lords. And although the Charter was to be obeyed by everyone, not just the king, it was only against the king, under the terms of the security clause, that it was to be enforced.

The most immediate beneficiaries from the work of the twenty-five would clearly be the barons themselves. When the clause spoke of the barons choosing twenty-five of their number to do all they could to preserve 'the peace and liberties which the king has conceded *to them*' (my italics), it gave the game away. As events were to show, many of the baronial leaders were ready with their grievances; hence the way in which chapter 37 of the Articles stipulated that a member of the twenty-five must stand down if his own fine or amercement was being considered. Although the twenty-five made great efforts to see that the oath of allegiance to them was taken, this was in good measure to ensure that the Charter was enforced for their own benefit. Even against the king and his ministers, no real thought had gone into enabling lower sections of society to complain about breaches of the Charter. It was always going to be easier for barons and major knights to find four of the twenty-five than for those further down the social scale. To have made the Charter enforceable for the general body of free tenants, suffering the abuses of the sheriffs and foresters would have required a permanent group of knights in each county, with the brief of hearing and redressing all complaints. Something like that, however, had to wait until 1300.[77] This job could, in 1215, have been given to the twelve knights elected in each county to investigate and abolish local abuses. Instead, they had but a temporary commission, and not one that included judging breaches of the Charter. The fact was that the twenty-five were determined to stand alone as enforcers of Magna Carta, in the process ensuring it was not in any way enforced against themselves. Here they would not resign power to the knights. This was the same thinking that led to the assembly conceived at Runnymede for giving common consent to taxation being one entirely of tenants-in-chief.

When it came to the church, the baronial leaders in 1215

certainly wished to include it in their programme, and eventually succeeded in doing so. But one doubts whether they felt much solidarity with the church's demands over freedom of election and the length of vacancies, the subject of John's November 1214 charter, confirmed in Magna Carta. Indeed, the Articles, in chapter 43, actually protected the rights of barons to have the custody of vacant abbeys of their foundation. Here the Charter was preserving for barons rights that it was reducing for the king. Robert fitzWalter, one is reminded, had taken violent action to assert his prerogatives as patron of Binham priory.[78]

Fundamentally, the opposition programme developed from the narrowly baronial schemes, like that in the Unknown Charter, to one with much a wider scope for hard material reasons. As Holt put it, 'the society in which the battle for Magna Carta was fought and won was not one in which the great tenants-in-chief dominated the political scene completely'. The concern in the Charter for other sections of society was 'an act recognizing social facts'.[79] The baronial leaders needed support. They included the demands of the knights and under-tenants, London and the towns, the Welsh rulers and the king of Scots, in order to get it, as those groups joined up. At the same time, however, the great barons sought to limit such demands where they encroached on their own interests.

Although John, in the negotiations, had modified some of the opposition demands, he was still having to swallow a very bitter pill. He had been brought to this pass by the fall of London in May 1215 and the rapidly deteriorating situation in the country. He would now see what the negotiations at Runnymede would bring.

11

Runnymede

On Monday, 8 June 1215, King John issued letters of safe conduct allowing the baronial envoys to come to Staines for the establishment of peace. The safe conduct was to last until the end of Thursday, 11 June.[1] Although the letters only mention Staines, almost certainly the meeting place was meant to be Runnymede, the 'meadow of Staines', or 'the meadow between Windsor and Staines', as it was called. Runnymede had several advantages for the final negotiations. It was probably a traditional meeting place, 'mede' of course meaning meadow, while the 'Runny' was related to the Anglo-Saxon word for 'counsel' and 'consultation'. Runnymede was a discrete area, bounded on one side by the Thames and on the other by Cooper's Hill. It could only be approached from two directions, along the road by the Thames, so the king, based at Windsor, would come from the north-west, and the barons, at Staines, from the south-east. Given the way the Thames winds, Windsor was south of the river whereas Staines was to the north, with the only convenient crossing place being Staines bridge. Both sides could, therefore, think their bases were secure from attack.[2] According to the account of the election of Abbot Hugh, on Tuesday, 9 June, John himself arrived at Windsor with Archbishop Langton in his company.[3] Hugh arrived on the same day, and was soon discussing his business with Langton. When the king came up and sought to pass between them, Langton introduced Hugh as 'abbot of St Edmunds', and begged for the whole dispute to be now concluded. 'Let him,' John replied, 'come to us tomorrow in the meadow of Staines where by God's grace and the aid of your merits, we will attempt to settle the matter.'

On the next day, Wednesday, 10 June, 'when [Hugh]', in the words of the Bury account, 'had come and waited for a long time in the meadow which is between Windsor and Staines, after much discussion and messages from nobles sent by the king, at length the king admitted the abbot into his grace with a kiss'. The delay was because John had much more to deal with on this first day at Runnymede than the abbatial succession at Bury. The negotiations with the barons had begun. They were to lead to John authorizing Magna Carta on Monday, 15 June, and the re-establishment of peace on Friday, 19 June with the rebels once more entering the king's allegiance. John continued to do business at Runnymede until 23 June, whereafter he spent two days at Windsor and then departed for Odiham and Winchester.

Ralph of Coggeshall gives a splendid picture of the scene at Runnymede, where the barons 'gathered with a multitude of most famous knights, armed well at all points, and they remained there, having fixed tents. But the king with his men dwelt in the same meadow in pavilions.'[4] The contrast here was doubtless between the pavilions of the king that reached high, like circus tops, towering above the smaller but multitudinous tents of the barons and knights, which stretched out across the meadow. John, however, was far from spending all his time at Runnymede. The Charter itself and a letter of 18 June are the only documents he authorized there before the peace on 19 June. All the other royal letters between 10 and 19 June were witnessed by him at Windsor, which evidently remained his base and where he almost certainly spent the night.

This was hardly surprising. John had given a safe conduct on 8 June to 'all those who come on behalf of the barons'. The implication was that it would only be baronial representatives who would come to Staines and thence to Runnymede. In fact, as Coggeshall's account shows, nothing like that happened. The insurgents came in large numbers and occupied Runnymede itself. It became an armed camp. That put pressure on John to go through with the Charter and indeed make more concessions. It also held out other threats. Might there be some sudden assault, perhaps in the middle of the night, in which John would find his pavilions surrounded by the men from the tents? Accordingly, John spent no more time at Runnymede than he could help. It was only once the peace was proclaimed on 19 June that he began to witness letters there on a more regular basis. By the same token, of course, the barons were not going to negotiate at Windsor, where they would have been in the power of the king.

Just how the final negotiations that led to the Charter were conducted we do not know. Most probably they were in the hands

of a small group of representatives from either side, such as those
John had envisaged coming 'on behalf [*ex parte*] of the barons' in
his letters of safe conduct. Doubtless John's chief advisers were
those he named in the Charter itself. For the barons, the negotiators presumably included the leading members of the eventual
twenty-five. Saer de Quincy was almost certainly prominent since he
was the only person specifically mentioned in John's letter of safe
conduct issued on 25 May. In a treaty over London, which dates
to around 19 June, eleven barons are named, the first five names
appearing in the same order in a letter that was issued by the
twenty-five around the same date. The five were Robert fitzWalter,
bearing his title Marshal of the Army of God, Richard, earl of
Clare, Geoffrey de Mandeville, calling himself earl of Essex and
Gloucester, Roger Bigod, earl of Norfolk, and Saer himself, all
men with deep and obvious grievances against the king. Both
sides, of course, would have been accompanied by clerical staffs.
There were doubtless plenary meetings, perhaps in a special neu-
tral tent, which one can imagine becoming famous in the course of
the discussions. There must also have been meetings of the individual teams, with messages and drafts of chapters going to and fro
between them.[5] Coggeshall speaks of peace being finally agreed
through the intervention of Langton and several unnamed bishops
and barons. That the negotiations proceeded chapter by chapter is
shown by the way the engrossments, while abandoning the paragraphs of the Articles, nonetheless indicated the start of new
chapters with prominent capital letters.

As he was in the much lesser matter of the election of Abbot
Hugh, John himself must have been very involved, sometimes
delivering his own views directly, sometimes hiding behind the
arguments of ministers. He could still turn on the charm. After he
had given Hugh the kiss of peace at Runnymede on 10 June, he
sought him out again and said, 'Father abbot, I have now one final
request for your kindness to fulfil; let us not be without your company at table, since the divine mercy has this day restored you to
my favour.' The abbot thus dined with the king at Windsor, and
afterwards they sat together in John's chamber on the royal bed,
'talking of many things'. When, however, the sacrist of Bury came
in, and, on bended knees, welcomed the admission of the abbot,
John, 'as though in fury of spirit', turned on him with an oath: 'By
the Lord's feet, but for you I would have admitted him to my

favour six months ago.' This was disingenuous since, until forced to back down, John had welcomed everything the sacrist had done to resist the election. In the same way in his dealings with the barons, John doubtless alternated between affability and anger, conciliation and obstruction.

Back at Windsor on the afternoon or evening of 10 June, John did not merely dine with Abbot Hugh. He also issued a letter prolonging the truce with the barons until the morning of 15 June.[6] This suggests a confidence that a settlement was now possible, although also that some days might still be needed to reach it, as indeed was the case. Holt has suggested, very reasonably, that behind this confidence lay the reaching of some preliminary agreement.[7] In other words, it was on 10 June that John sealed the Articles of the Barons. He had probably agreed them orally earlier as a basis for negotiations, but the baronial negotiators whom he met on 10 June needed something more. If they were to hold their own party to the truce, they had to show some evidence of John's good faith. That was now provided by John's seal appearing on the Articles. It seemed to show that he had indeed conceded those 'chapters which the Barons seek', as the heading in the Articles put it. John, for his part, thus hoped to draw the barons into negotiations and end the civil war. He was not, he would think, actually committed to anything, for even with the seal the Articles, lacking address, witness and dating clauses, had no legal force. John could still hope to secure concessions. He might renege on the whole deal. The next few days would tell.

The Articles of the Barons were the foundation for the Charter. Fifty-six of Magna Carta's sixty-three chapters (including here the security clause) were founded on chapters in them. Many retained the same phraseology. Whole runs of chapters in the Charter also follow the same order as that in the Articles, especially between chapters 2 and 6, and again, with little interruption, between chapters 15 and 42. Only five of the Charter's chapters, along with its preamble and dating clause, were entirely new. Yet there was still much to argue over. Four of the five new chapters were highly significant, while many others were modified in important ways, sometimes in favour of the king, sometimes against him. Thought also went into improving the coherence of the document, hence some of the changes in chapter order. In the end Magna Carta runs to some 3,550 words as against the circa 1,945 of the Articles of the Barons.

GIVE AND TAKE IN THE NEGOTIATIONS

John had some successes in the negotiations. The stipulation in the Articles of the Barons that heirs should be married 'by the counsel of the nearest kin' was watered down to the need just to inform the nearest kin, which gave the king much more freedom to bestow marriages on whom he wished. John retaliated against the Londoners (whom he must have regarded with intense hostility) by removing the stipulation, found in the Articles, that tallages imposed on the city, and other privileged towns, needed the consent of the kingdom.[8] It was now only aids, and those just from London, that were so covered. John had thus preserved his lucrative right to tallage towns at will as part of the royal demesne. The towns, in return, simply got an innocuous new chapter (although it is not made separate in modern numbering), which said that cities, boroughs, vills and ports should enjoy all their liberties and customs. There were other gains, partly helped by Archbishop Langton's attitude (examined in more detail later). Thus judgements on the disseisins committed by Henry II and Richard were now to be left until John abandoned or returned from his prospective crusade.

On the other side, the barons pushed very hard to improve the offer. They scored a major victory in the area of reliefs. The Articles of the Barons here had left the size of these to be decided in the Charter, so there was everything to play for. In the event, the Charter laid down that the heirs of earls and barons should both pay a relief of £100, while the heirs of knights holding from the king should pay £5 for each fee. John, by contrast, had charged baronial reliefs of hundreds, sometimes thousands, of pounds and would have fiercely denied that there was anything 'ancient' about the £100 relief he was now pinned back to. The barons also gained in a more minor way through the tightening up of various chapters. The Articles of the Barons had retreated from the demand of the Unknown Charter that wardships be run by four knights of the fee. Now something like that came back in, if in reduced fashion, through the stipulation that, if the guardian misbehaved, then the wardship should be entrusted to two of the fee's law-worthy men. This was to be true whether the king had entrusted the custody to a sheriff, or had sold it to someone. John's only compensation was that, in both cases, the men were to answer to him for the issues, so at least he would not lose the revenues which were reasonably due. Tenants-in-chief also gained in chapter 26 by a tightening up of the procedure for the payment of debts during minorities, whereby the sheriff had now to prove what was owed by reference to letters patent of summons.[9]

When it came to the contentious issue of the royal forest, John's opponents were able at Runnymede to improve on the Articles of the Barons. Unlike the Unknown Charter, the Articles had said nothing about deforesting the large areas made forest by Henry II. They had focused simply on the afforestations of John. Now, in chapter 53 of Magna Carta, the afforestations of Henry and Richard came back in. True, it was only through making John promise to give justice on the issue when he returned from or abandoned his prospective crusade, but still that was better than nothing. In the same chapter John also promised, when the crusade was over, to give justice in two other contentious areas, one where lords were claiming rights over abbeys founded in their fees, and the other where the king had taken the wardship of an estate although only a small part of it was held from him by knight service.

THE LIGHT THROWN BY THE DRAFTS

In throwing light on the negotiations, the copies of the Charter made later in the thirteenth century come into play, since in some places almost certainly, in others quite possibly, they preserve elements of drafts made at Runnymede.[10] The chapter on relief, as we have said, was a great baronial victory, yet there are signs that the barons wanted more. The odd phraseology of the chapter has often been pointed out, with earls and barons being treated separately although their reliefs are the same. Was this because there had been the intention of giving them different amounts? The answer, it would seem, is yes, because in a copy of the Charter in a statute book preserved in the Huntington Library in California, which Galbraith argued was derived from a late draft of the Charter, the relief of a baron is put at 100 marks, not at £100.[11]

John had at least resisted that successfully, and he may have resisted something else as well, namely any suggestion that earldoms themselves were hereditary; hence the curious statement that an earl succeeded simply to the 'barony of an earl', so not actually to an earldom at all. That this too was an area of dispute is suggested by one copy of the Charter in which heirs of earls are indeed to give a £100 relief 'for a whole earldom' – 'de comitatu integro'.[12] If this was pressed at Runnymede, it failed to gain purchase, but at least the earls were given separate treatment in the Charter and avoided being lumped in with the barons. That may have been what John wanted, for in several copies of the Charter the chapter does run them together, simply stating that heirs of earls and barons are both to give a £100 relief 'for a whole barony', so there was here no reference to the separate 'barony of an earl'.

The most striking of all the new chapters in Magna Carta was chapter 14, which laid down in detail the constitution for the assembly that could give the common consent of the kingdom to taxation: the archbishops, bishops, abbots, earls and greater barons were thus to be summoned individually and the other tenants-in-chief severally through the sheriffs. The background here was, of course, John's great tax of 1207. He had claimed that it had been agreed by 'his council', but that, of course, might be no more than his own ministers. In direct response, the Articles of the Barons had laid down that taxes should be imposed not by the king's council but by 'the common counsel of the kingdom'. But why did Magna Carta, in an entirely new chapter, feel the need to go further, in the process setting out what was in effect the first written constitution of parliament? Copies of the Charter which preserve elements of drafts may provide some explanation. They suggest that at Runnymede the idea that the king's council should have a role in agreeing taxation was resurfacing and needed to be knocked on the head. In a copy of the Charter found in a late thirteenth-century cartulary of Peterborough abbey, now in the possession of the Society of Antiquaries, chapter 12 reads 'No scutage or aid is to be levied in our kingdom save by our council and by the common counsel of our kingdom' – '*per consilium nostrum et per consilium commune regni nostri*'. Now it may be that this is no more than an inadvertent scribal addition made in the process of transmission. On the other hand, it occurs in a chapter clearly much discussed at Runnymede, hence the way the new chapter 14 was added to it. This Peterborough copy of the Charter, moreover, like some others, as we will see, certainly has a draft version of the chapter on fines, since the phraseology there is far closer to the text of the Articles than to that of the eventual Charter.[13] The king's council also appears in what is probably one of the earliest copies of the Charter. This is found not in a cartulary or statute book but on a single sheet of parchment now preserved in the Bodleian Library in Oxford. It is unique in having John sometimes speak in the first person. It also in chapter 48 has wording that seems to come from a draft, since in one place it is closer to the Articles than to the Charter. In chapter 12 of this Bodleian copy, the reading is 'No scutage or aid is to be levied in my kingdom save by our council' – '*per consilium nostrum*'.[14] It seems likely that 'and by the common counsel of our kingdom' has been omitted here, for the copy still has chapter 14 on how the common counsel of the kingdom should be obtained. Perhaps the copy derived from a draft made difficult to follow from the number of changes to the chapter. At the very least, these variants raise the possibility that John put up a rear-guard action at Runnymede and tried to give a role to 'his council' in the levying of taxation. If so, one can understand why the eventual Charter, having affirmed that taxes must be levied by the common consent of the kingdom, went on to make crystal clear the nature of the assembly from which that consent must come.[15] At least John would have welcomed there the presence of lesser tenants-in-chief. He may also have inserted the proviso that the business was to go ahead even if not everyone summoned turned up.

Another significant change to the Articles came in chapter 55 on putting right fines made unjustly and against the law of the land. In chapter 37 of the Articles, these were fines made for dowers, 'maritagia' (marriage portions and marriages) and inheritances. Since no individual king was mentioned, the chapter apparently covered the fines made with Henry II and Richard as well as John. This would explain, the issue being the more contentious, why Archbishop Langton was called in to assist the twenty-five, if they had to judge any disputes, whereas when it came simply to John's disseisins, in chapter 25 of the Articles, the twenty-five had felt able to act alone.[16] In some copies of Magna Carta, the chapter on fines retains its Articles form, save the fines are those made simply with John, so not with Henry and Richard. The chapter thus reads: 'All fines which have been made with us for dowers, maritagia and inheritances . . . unjustly and against the law of the land are to be wholly remitted.'[17] In the final version of the Charter, however, the barons hit back and effected a dramatic widening of the chapter. As it stood in the Articles and the drafts, it certainly addressed major grievances, but it also left untouched a whole range of fines, most notably those made to recover the king's benevolence and secure the return of confiscated land.[18] When we get to the final text in the Charter, therefore, the whole scope of the chapter has been expanded. 'Dowers, maritagia and inheritances' disappear, and the chapter covers 'all fines' made with John 'unjustly and against the law of the land'. The clause now got to the heart of his arbitrary rule.

ARCHBISHOP LANGTON'S INTERVENTION

Archbishop Langton, as we have seen, had not engaged with the development of the baronial demands in 1214 and 1215. To do so would have been tantamount to joining the rebellion, which he was absolutely not prepared to do. It was only at Runnymede that the situation changed in a definitive way. John sealed the Articles of the Barons and thus accepted them as a basis for the settlement. Langton could step in without being accused of treason. As a proof of John's acceptance, the archbishop took away from Runnymede a copy of the Articles with John's seal attached, and deposited it in his archives. It was in effect his cover note, his licence to take part, which he could cite to king and pope if they later questioned his involvement.[19]

With this sanction, Langton turned to the roles assigned him in the Articles and modified them, or agreed to their modification, in every single place. Most important of all, as we saw in the last chapter, he removed the demand that he and his fellow bishops should guarantee John's undertaking not to appeal to the pope. Reference to the pope disappeared, and John simply said he would not seek from anyone anything by which his concessions might be revoked. The only thing Langton was now asked to guarantee was the Charter's final text. Langton also intervened when it came to the disseisins committed by Henry II and Richard. Under chapter 25 of the Articles, those thus disseised were to have 'right' determined without delay by judgement of their peers in the king's court. If, however, John was to have the 'term' enjoyed by other crusaders, then the archbishop and his fellow bishops were to give the judgement without appeal. The 'term' here meant the period during which John as crusader could enjoy various protections. He was still, before his departure, expected to right his own wrongs, indeed, he was under an obligation to do so. But the barons clearly feared that he might be exempt from having to deal with the wrongs of his father and brother. In that case, the barons hoped that consideration of the disseisins committed by Henry and Richard might move from the secular to the ecclesiastical jurisdiction, with Langton and the bishops giving judgement on them. The Articles did not say who was to decide whether John got the crusader's 'term', but almost certainly the task fell to Langton.[20] The decision was very favourable to John. Thus Langton both gave him the 'term' and decided it should last for the fullest possible period, namely for as long as the prospective crusade continued.[21] That is why John, in chapters 52, 53 and 57 of the Charter, was to deal with various issues only when he returned from or abandoned his crusade. Having given John the crusader's 'term', Langton then refused to have anything to do with the substitute judgement the Articles had asked of him. Instead, John was to give justice to those complaining of disseisin by Henry or Richard only when his crusade, in one way or another, was over.

Langton's decision over the crusader's 'term' affected the Welsh. The disseisins that they had suffered at the hands of Henry and Richard were now, like those suffered by the English, to be dealt with only once John had ended his prospective crusade. Langton also stood down from his role in judging whether John's charters allowed Llywelyn's son and the other Welsh hostages to be retained. In Magna Carta, the son and the hostages were simply to be returned 'immediately', and there was no mention of Langton or the charters. It has been suggested that this was because the archbishop, at Runnymede, had indeed sat in judgement on the charters and decided the issue against the king.[22] This seems most unlikely. Such a judgement would have required formal proceedings, and the production and careful inspections of charters, for which there can have been no time at Runnymede. Indeed, it was not until July that Langton and various loyalist magnates issued a letter testifying to the terms of the 1211 charter which John had extracted from Llywelyn.[23] It seems far more likely that Langton had declined to play his allotted role, and this had enabled Llywelyn's allies to insist on the immediate return of the hostages.

Langton also stood down when it came to chapter 59 on the treatment of the king of Scots. Instead of Langton deciding whether John's charters meant Alexander should be treated differently from the barons of England when it came to restoration of liberties and rights, the decision was now passed to a judgement of Alexander's peers in the king's court. Again, it is difficult to see how this amounted to Langton deciding the issue in John's favour, as has been suggested. He had simply passed the buck and left it for others to decide.[24] These changes left only one instance in the Charter where Langton's judgement still appeared, and even here his role was qualified. This was in chapter 55. Here Langton was to sit with the twenty-five in judging the unjust fines and amercements imposed by John. The archbishop was, however, to be involved only 'if he will be able to attend'. If he could not attend, the business was to go ahead without him. This cautionary note about his availability one suspects came from Langton himself.

Langton, therefore, might seem to have engaged with the Charter at Runnymede only to distance himself from it. Yet this is far from the whole story. He was, after all, prepared to guarantee the terms of the Charter, and, if in a qualified way, take part in the work of the twenty-five barons of the security clause. Indeed, he remained in the chapter on fines even though the original reason for his inclusion (that it covered Henry and Richard) no longer applied. In associating himself with the twenty-five, he thus condoned the most revolutionary feature of the Charter. If, moreover, Langton removed the pope from the firing line, that might increase rather than reduce the chances of the Charter's survival. There was also one other positive thing that Langton did for the Charter at Runnymede. It was far and away the most important addition made there, and was of overwhelming importance for the Charter's future. This was that Langton put the church into Charter. In other words it was Langton who crafted and inserted what now became the first clause, on the liberties of the church.

Historians have usually ascribed this clause to Langton, yet have regarded its presence as almost routine and unimportant. It was neither. The clause might easily have been left out of Magna Carta. For all John's sealing of the Articles, it remained obvious that the Charter was being forced upon him. Here the contrast with Henry I's Coronation Charter was very clear. It had a first clause on the church, but then it was a freely given grant. Magna Carta, on the other hand, Langton must have known, was always liable to be quashed by the pope for having been extracted 'by violence and fear', as Innocent indeed later put it.[25] The violent threats that forced Thomas Becket to accept the iniquitous Constitutions of Clarendon would have been another point of reference.[26] Langton, therefore, had good grounds for keeping the church out of the Charter, and preventing its liberties being stained by the doubtful origins of the secular concessions. The church had already secured its gains in the charter of November 1214, which guaranteed it free elections. Why not leave it at that? Langton then would have been anticipating his successors, the bishops of 1258, who withdrew from the revolutionary Westminster parliament before the coercion of the king, and never afterwards included the church in the reforms.[27] Langton might well have done the same in 1215.

Yet, on the other hand, Langton had powerful reasons for bringing in the church. His biblical commentaries show that he believed in pinning the king down to written rules. He must have thought that, for all the dangers, the 1215 Charter might succeed and become the fundamental text for English government. The church needed to be in the Charter as it had been in 1100. How then could Langton square this circle? He did so by a brilliantly devised chapter which put the church into the Charter right at the start while at the same time decoupling and distancing its concessions from those made to the rest of the kingdom. In the process, it was made quite clear that the concessions to the church were freely given and were quite unrelated to any coercion.

In the chapter, therefore, the freedom of the church was given as a concession to God, not to the kingdom:

> In the first place, [we] have granted to God and by this our present charter have confirmed, for us and our heirs in perpetuity, that the English church is to be free . . .

After this concession to God, the Charter then started all over again and announced 'We have also granted to all the free men of our kingdom . . . all the below written liberties'. In the printed versions of the Charter, this is still part of chapter 1 on the church, although in three of the four engrossments it appears rather as a new chapter. The division here between the concessions made to God and those made to the kingdom had no exact precedent. The 1100 Charter set the church free and then abolished all evil customs that had oppressed the kingdom, but no clear division was made between the two, for the concessions were not actually given to anyone at all. In the Coronation Charter of Henry II, the concessions were made to 'God, holy church, and all my earls and barons and all my men', which meant there was no separation, as there was in 1215, between church and realm, or realm and God. The same was true in the charter that King Pedro granted to Catalonia in 1205.[28]

Langton did not merely separate the concessions made to church and realm. He also inserted a remarkable passage which showed that, when it came to the former, John had acted completely willingly. The English church, John says, 'is to be free':

> ... and we wish it so to be observed; which is manifest from this, namely that the liberty of elections, which is deemed to be of the greatest importance and most necessary for the English church, by our free and spontaneous will, before the discord moved between us and our barons, we granted and confirmed by our charter, and obtained its confirmation from the lord pope, Innocent the third ...

John's good faith when it came to the church was thus clear, for he had made the concession over elections 'before the discord moved between us and our barons'. There was, therefore, a clear qualitative difference between the liberties conferred on the church and those conferred on the rest of the kingdom. John had granted the former freely, before 'the discord'. The implication, inevitably, was that in granting the latter, he had not been acting spontaneously. Langton might regret the implication, but he had first and foremost to protect the liberty of the church. He had done this too by referring to Innocent's confirmation, which cloaked the church's liberty in a kind of papal imprimatur. He could not do the same for the Charter as a whole, but at least he had removed the clause that positively invited Innocent to quash it.

Having introduced the church, and modified the role assigned him in the Articles, Langton left the Charter alone. Despite his veneration for Becket, he did nothing to reaffirm Henry II's concession freeing clerks accused of crime from secular jurisdiction. He ignored John's promise of 1213 not to outlaw clerks, although it would have sat well with chapter 39.[29] He did not insist that chapter 4 on the running of wardships should also apply to ecclesiastical vacancies, unlike the Charter of 1216, where a clause to that effect was introduced. Langton also failed to support the Charter in one highly practical and deeply symbolic way. However much they might have wished to do so, he and his fellow bishops issued no sentence of excommunication against contraveners of the Charter of 1215. That had to wait until 1225, when all taint of coercion was at last removed. Yet what Langton had done in 1215 was enough. Privileged in its first chapter, he had provided the church with an impelling reason for giving Magna Carta its full support. That was to be a major factor in its survival and the central place it attained in public life. Once, moreover, the Charter had been conceded, the archbishop did all he could to preserve it and the peace it was supposed to bring.

THE WELSH AND THE KING OF SCOTS

How did the Welsh and the Scots fare generally at Runnymede? The answer is with mixed fortunes, for again there was considerable give and take. The Welsh gained, as we have seen, in their hostages, including the son of Llywelyn, being now returned 'immediately', without reference to any charters that might make it otherwise. The obnoxious treaty of 1211, under which the son and hostages had been surrendered, was apparently no more. On the other hand, the Welsh lost out, like their English counterparts, over the disseisins committed by Henry II and Richard, with any redress being postponed until the end of John's prospective crusade. They also lost out in another way. Whereas, in the Articles, Welshmen disseised by John in England or in Wales were to be restored 'without plea' (chapter 44), in the Charter (chapter 56) the possibility of a plea, which of course meant John's plea, was entertained. If there was 'contention', the case was to be tried 'by judgement of peers', in the March, according to the laws of England, Wales or the March, depending on where the land was situated. The reference to the various laws came from chapter 44 of the Articles, where the context had been slightly different.[30] The reference to 'in the March' was new and advantaged the Welsh, since it prevented such cases having to follow the king and the court *coram rege*.

In all this, the Welsh rulers had won more than had King Alexander, in part perhaps because the latter was not yet in arms against the king. The charters that John had extracted from Alexander's father, William the Lion, in 1209, recording the Treaty of

Norham, were still on the agenda, for here another form of judgement was found after Archbishop Langton's withdrawal. It was
now Alexander's peers in the king's court who were to decide
whether the charters meant he could be treated differently from
the other barons of England, this when it came to his liberties and
rights and the return of his hostages and his sisters (chapter 59). If
his peers, as seemed likely, decided against the charters, then, the
implication was, the hostages would be returned under the terms
of Magna Carta's chapter 49. The assumption obviously was that
the sisters too would be released. On this point, Alexander's
friends had done well, for the return of the sisters was included at
Runnymede itself, having not been in the Articles of the Barons.
The sisters, Margaret and Isabella, had been handed over to King
John under the treaty of 1209. According to its terms, he had until
October 1217, when his eldest son would be ten, to begin marrying them off. In 1215, therefore, he was not in breach of the treaty.
That Alexander and his allies still demanded the return of the sisters showed very clearly that they regarded the treaty as invalid.
When it came to Alexander's claims to the northern counties, on
the other hand, John might hope the changes at Runnymede had
brought him an advantage. Since the counties had been lost to the
king of Scots under Henry II, the claim should now wait until the
end of John's prospective crusade. Whether the English barons
would bother with such distinctions was, however, another matter.

WOMEN, PEASANTS, TOWNS, BARONS, KNIGHTS AND FREE TENANTS

One of the most striking new chapters introduced at Runnymede
was chapter 54, the only one in which the word 'woman' –
'femina' – appeared. This chapter directed that no one was to be
arrested or imprisoned on the appeal, that is accusation, of a woman
for the death of anyone other than her husband.[31] How on earth
did chapter 54 appear at Runnymede? The answer may be that it
was through the intervention of those who had worked for the
king as judges, not all of whom, as we have seen, were necessarily
any longer on his side.[32] The judges knew that female appeals were
very frequent. They also knew that in practice, as the chapter itself

implies, the legal rule restricting such appeals to the death of the husband had not always been enforced in cases of homicide. Men, therefore, accused by women of other homicides, had found themselves imprisoned pre-trial. Now that would no longer happen, those accused being able to give sureties for their appearance in court.[33]

At Runnymede, lords also gave less than friendly thought to their unfree peasants. It was now that the remarkable clause was inserted into chapter 20 which showed that villeins were protected only from amercements imposed by the king. In other words, as far as the Charter was concerned, lords could impose on their unfree peasants whatever amercements they liked.[34] The Charter, like the Articles, also failed to deal with an issue of major concern to peasants, although curiously enough it had been covered in the Unknown Charter. Its last clause, almost as an afterthought, demanded that 'no man should lose life or limb' for an offence against the beasts of the forest. The Unknown Charter was very much a baronial document, yet this was not an issue that had direct relevance to barons or knights. It was peasants, unable to pay heavy amercements, who would lose life or limb for forest offences.[35] The Anonymous of Béthune thought there was a clause in Magna Carta on the subject.[36] In fact, it had to wait until the Forest Charter of 1217. At Runnymede, the barons, with much else to think about, just could not take the trouble to include it.

The earls and barons did take trouble in issues that concerned themselves. They realized that in the Articles, when it came to amercements, they had no special treatment and were at best lumped in with the free men who were to be amerced by 'upright men of the neighbourhood'. The Charter put this right in a new chapter (21), which stated that earls and barons were to be amerced by their peers. The tenants-in-chief also took pains to show that some concessions related just to themselves. Thus the early chapters of the Charter on relief and wardships were now drafted to demonstrate that. The barons were not told to pass on these concessions to their men, as in the Charter of 1100. Instead, under-tenants had to rely on just the blanket injunction in chapter 60. The barons also looked after themselves, and did down a class of under-tenants, in another area. Under chapter 27 of the Articles, free men were not to lose the privileges of knighthood because they held tenements from the king in return for providing arrows or other weapons. In the Charter, this was scrapped and replaced by an entirely new chapter (although it is never printed as such), which protected a lord's right to have the wardship of such men, if they also held from him by knight service.[37] Under-tenants also lost out, perhaps inadvertently, perhaps not, by a reorganization of the Charter. Thus the clause which ordered guardians to return lands fully stocked to heirs when they came of age was moved from chapter 35 in the Articles to chapter 5 in the Charter. In the Articles it had been tacked onto the chapter about the payment of Jewish debts during a minority, and clearly applied to under-tenants as well as to tenants-in-chief. In Magna Carta it followed chapter 4 on wardships, which was clearly about those in the hands of the king, and thus only for tenants-in-chief. There were also implications, perhaps again inadvertent, perhaps not, in the way some other chapters were redrafted. Thus the constables and bailiffs prevented from seizing corn and chattels now became (in chapter 28) those of the king. Whereas chapter 30 of the Articles had said that right was not to be denied, deferred or sold, so applying to the conduct of everyone, in the Charter the equivalent chapter, the famous chapter 40, simply applied to the king.

The self-regard of the barons was also shown in one of the most striking chapters introduced at Runnymede, namely chapter 14 defining the assembly that was to give the kingdom's common consent to taxation. It was, of course, to be entirely an assembly of tenants-in-chief, dominated by the greater barons. Despite all the reasons why they might have been included, there was to be no formal place for 'magnates' who did not hold in chief. And there was to be no place for knights representing the counties or burgesses the towns. The exclusion of London seems especially remarkable, given the importance of the city in the rebel coalition. The mayor was one of the twenty-five barons. After the collapse of the Magna Carta peace, the barons and the citizens of London wrote jointly to King Alexander 'against' King John. There were also feelings in the city that it should be represented at national assemblies when taxation was discussed.[38] Something of the paradox was revealed in the Charter itself, which, on the one hand, said that aids could only be levied on London by the common counsel of the kingdom, and then denied London any place in the assembly from which that common counsel came. The baronial leaders at Runnymede also failed to protect London and other privileged towns from John's determination to get tallage out of the Charter. Not surprisingly perhaps, since if the king was prevented from tallaging his towns at will, then lords might find themselves similarly restricted when it came to tallaging the boroughs subject to their own jurisdictions. Had the negotiations been taking place in London, perhaps the city would have done better. As it was, although Robert fitzWalter was hereditarily the leader of London's militia, no chronicler mentions the presence of London forces at Runnymede.[39]

Knights and free tenants did make some gains at Runnymede. If the chapters on relief and wardships were now specifically for tenants-in-chief, the section on the marriage of heirs was separated from them, and made a chapter on its own, namely chapter 6, which suggested it had a general relevance. There followed chapters 7 and 8 on widows, the second having been restored to what was probably its original place, having dropped down to chapter 17 in the Articles. Chapter 8 (in stating that a widow must get the consent of her lord if she wished to remarry) clearly applied to under-tenants, and therefore strengthened the assumption that this was also to be true of the preceding chapter, giving widows free entrance into their property. Most striking of all, however, was chapter 16. Here, the stipulation that no one should be forced to do more than due service for a knight's fee was expanded to include other free tenements as well. This meant it had a vastly greater social range, since it now protected all those who held by rent.

When it came to local government, knights and free tenants cannot have welcomed the dilution of chapter 45, in which the king's officials were now required to know not the 'law of the land' but the less local 'law of the kingdom'. The contemporary French translation of the Charter retains here 'la lei de la terre', which suggests that 'law of the land' may have survived in some engrossments.[40] Knights had also reason to question the changing treatment of the office of coroner, an office, of course, which they held. In chapter 14 of the Articles, the sheriffs were not to interfere with the pleas of the crown without the coroners. In chapter 24 of Magna Carta neither sheriffs nor coroners were to hold the pleas of the crown. Local society would have been as happy as the king with the implication that crown pleas were only to be heard by the king's judges, but, in the process, the chapter had been changed from one trusting the coroners to one distrusting them. Against these setbacks, however, if such they were, there was a major gain.

The twelve knights, elected in each county to reform evil practices, now got their own separate chapter, namely chapter 48, instead of being tacked on to the end of the Articles' chapter 39. The whole process was also given much more bite. In the Articles, the malpractices were to be 'corrected' by the knights, and it was not said when. In the Charter, by contrast, the abuses were to be 'wholly abolished' by the knights within forty days, and 'never revived'. The threatening nature of the power thus conferred is shown by the way in which John managed to insert one brake on the process. The abolitions were to take place only once he had been informed of what was proposed. Doubtless the king hoped at that stage to make objections and ask for delays. In several copies of the Charter which preserve elements of earlier drafts, this saving clause does not appear at all.[41] This strongly suggests that John got it inserted at a late stage in the negotiations, the copies preserving a text from before the addition was made. This fits exactly with the two original engrossments now in the British Library, the one that went to Canterbury and Cii, in both of which the saving clause appears in an extra line below the text of the Charter with an indication of where it should go. It looks as though in the draft from which the engrossments were being copied, the saving clause had in some way been arrowed in as a late addition, and been missed by the clerks first time round. Arguments over chapter 48 are also revealed by the single-sheet copy of the Charter in the Bodleian Library referred to above. There the malpractices are still 'to be corrected' – 'emendentur' – as in the Articles, not 'abolished' – 'deleantur' – as in the final text of Magna Carta. The toughening up of this chapter was a great victory for the knights.

Knights must also have been very much concerned and presumably involved, along with the king's judges, when it came to changes related to the hearing of the common-law legal procedures. Chapter 18 now made clear that the forum for the assizes must be the county court. A new addition to the chapter (made wrongly by Blackstone as a separate chapter 19) answered the plea in the Articles for the hearing of the assizes of novel disseisin and mort d'ancestor to be speeded up. If the cases could not be heard on the day of the county court, then sufficient knights and free tenants who attended the court should remain behind so that judgements could be made. Strictly speaking, all that was needed for judgements were the jurors and the judges, as the Articles had recognized. What

Magna Carta wanted was a wider body of knights and free tenants to witness and guarantee the judgements – a notable testimony to the importance of the court and the place of the knights and free tenants within it. It may be that knightly opinion defeated further modifications to the assize procedures laid down in chapters 18 and 19. Some later copies of the Charter thus have the judges visiting three times a year, not four, and in the Charter of 1217 their visitations were reduced to just one. In 1217 the idea of the judges staying on to hear left-over pleas was abandoned. Instead they were to hear them later on in their circuit. The 1217 Charter also dispensed with the four knights elected in the county court and just said vaguely that the judges were to hear cases with the knights of the county. If this change, which clearly reduced knightly control of the assizes, was pressed at Runnymede, the knights had successfully resisted it.

EXPANSION, CLARIFICATION
AND REORGANIZATION

A great deal of thought at Runnymede went into the clarification and reorganization of the chapters in the Articles of the Barons, with the result that the Charter was a clearer and more coherent document. Much of this work was presumably done by the clerical staffs, and perhaps again by those with judicial experience. The main effort presumably came from the baronial side. If the king's men had got involved, John would not have thanked them. He was surely in the business of making the Charter as incomprehensible as possible!

Sometimes Magna Carta simply spelled out in more detail what the Articles had intended. Chapter 9 is a good example of this; here it is, with the passages added to chapter 5 of the Articles of the Barons in italics:

Neither we nor our bailiffs are to seize any land *or rent* for *any* debt, for as long as the chattels of the debtor suffice *to pay the debt*; nor are the sureties of that debtor to be distrained for as long as the chief debtor himself has sufficient for payment *of the debt*. And if the chief debtor fails in the payment *of the debt, not having the wherewithal to pay, the sureties are to answer for the debt*. And if they wish, they are to have the lands *and the rents* of the debtor *until satisfaction is given to them for the debt which before they paid for him* . . .

Here the section from '*until*' replaces the ambiguous 'until that debt is fully paid'. It may be that further clarifications to the chapter were intended but dropped through inadvertence or lack of time. Thus the 1216 Charter after the debtor 'not having the wherewithal to pay' added 'or not wishing to pay when he is able'.[42] Since this phrase is found in several later copies of the 1215 Charter, it may well have been in drafts made at Runnymede. Indeed, perhaps the clerks in 1216 had such drafts to hand.

Considerable efforts were made to tighten up the drafting of the crucial chapters 39 and 40 on justice. Chapter 39 now began 'No freeman', rather than 'The body of a freeman', as in the Articles, probably because it sounded odd to have the body of a freeman disseised.[43] The chapter broadened the ways in which the king might go or send against someone by omitting the Articles' 'by force', while it inserted 'lawful' before 'judgement of his peers'. Chapter 40, apart from making the king the subject of the sentence, now spoke of 'right and justice' – '*rectum aut justitiam*' – rather than simply 'right'. It was through 'justice', of course, that one obtained 'right', and it strengthened the chapter to include both.[44] Similar expertise went into improving the order of the Charter's chapters. The two on debts to the Jews were advanced to chapters 10 and 11 from 34 and 35, thus coming after the chapter on distraint for debt. What became chapter 12 on scutages and aids came up to join them from chapter 32, taking matters about London and the towns with them. As a result of these changes, the first part of the Charter gained a more coherent focus, aimed at the financial operations of royal government. Another improvement was in linking together the two chapters on the assizes, chapters 18 and 19, rather than having them separated as chapters 8 and 13. A rather different fate attended some of the chapters which were most subject to change, for these often dropped right down the order, usually for no particular reason other than that, as we may suspect, they had got shuffled out of their previous positions in the course of their redrafting. Thus the chapter on measures, where a large new section was added on standards, fell from chapter 12 in the Articles of the Barons to chapter 35 in the Charter, where it took the place of the chapter on the king's disseisins. The latter, much altered and argued over when it came to the disseisins of Henry II and Richard, dropped down from chapter 25 in the Articles to near the end of the Charter, becoming chapter 52. There it joined up with two new chapters, chapter 53 about the afforestations of Richard and Henry, and chapter 54 on accusations by women. Chapter 55 was the remodelled chapter on fines, which itself had fallen from chapter 37 in the Articles. In the copies of the Charter where the chapter on fines preserves its Articles form, it actually also preserves its Articles order, pretty clear proof that it was the renegotiation that caused the loss of place. We can imagine remodelled chapters being crossed out in a draft, rewritten on a separate piece of parchment and then being added back in at any convenient point, often near the end. Interestingly, however, there is one copy of the Charter where the remodelled chapter on fines is still in its Articles place, so presumably it derived from a draft where the clerk had put it back there.

Partly as a result of these changes, the order of the Charter remained far from perfect. Indeed an interesting exercise (which I sometimes set MA students) is to attempt a better job. If, for example, the expanded chapter on measures had been placed after that on fish weirs, and the chapter on disseisins had been kept in this area, rather than dropping down to the end of the Charter, it could have created coherent sections on trade and merchants and then on justice. So, for example, the Charter might have run:

32 fish weirs
33 measures
34 merchants
35 entry to kingdom
36 convictions for felony
37 writ precipe
38 writ of life and limbs
39 accusations by bailiffs
40 no one to be proceeded against save by judgement of peers, etc.
41 denial of justice
42 disseisins by John, Richard and Henry

But enough of such games! Time was limited at Runnymede. The negotiators were surrounded by piles of much-worked-over drafts.

Even the drafts from which the final engrossments were copied out were not altogether clear, hence the way the scribes of the Canterbury Charter and Cii made mistakes and had to add text in at the bottom.

THE DATE OF MAGNA CARTA

The negotiations at Runnymede were interrupted and invigorated by one great ecclesiastical festival. Sunday, 14 June was Trinity Sunday. Presumably Archbishop Langton himself conducted the service before King John at Windsor, after which there would have been a feast. The lesson for the day was Revelation 4:1–10, where the twenty-four elders bow down before the throne of God in heaven. At least the number here, twenty-four, saved the rebels from any blasphemous comparisons with the twenty-five barons of the security clause! The day's Gospel, on the other hand, might seem more relevant. It was John 3:1–15, where Christ tells Nicodemus that 'unless a man be born again he cannot see the kingdom of God'. Mere baptism by water, moreover, was not enough. A man must be born again in spirit. Fortunately a sermon that Langton preached on a Trinity Sunday survives. While it probably comes from earlier in his career, it may give some clue to his themes on this occasion. The sermon is mercifully short, taking little more than fifteen minutes to read out, so John would have had no need to ask his archbishop to hurry up, as he had at the start of the reign with Bishop Hugh of Lincoln. If he listened, John would have received some clear lessons as to his behaviour in the future, for Langton urged his listeners to pray to the Father for 'good power', to the Son for 'good wisdom' and to the Holy Spirit for 'good will'.[45] Such injunctions, if given on Trinity Sunday 1215, were well timed, for the negotiations were nearly at an end.

Historians have long debated the true date of Magna Carta.[46] The four original engrossments, as well as the copy in the bishops' letters testimonial, all end with John's statement that it was 'Given by our hand [*Data per manum nostram*] in the meadow which is called Runnymede, between Windsor and Staines, on the fifteenth day of June, in the seventeenth year of our reign.' The natural assumption is that 15 June 1215 is the date of Magna Carta. It is therefore astonishing to find that many leading Magna Carta historians, Holt included, have regarded the 15 June date as noth-ing more or less than 'fictitious'.[47] Instead, they have argued that the terms of the Charter were not agreed until 19 June, and it was only then, or even later, that it was actually issued. The question of the date of the Charter is about more than a few days either way. It is of crucial importance for understanding what happened at Runnymede. The correct date, it will be argued, is indeed 15 June. Only when this is appreciated can one see both the cleverness of John's manoeuvring and the dissatisfaction with the Charter that quickly forced him into further concessions.

The starting point for any discussion of the date of Magna Carta must be the dating clause that we have already quoted: 'Given by our hand in the meadow which is called Runnymede . . . on the fifteenth day of June.' It is remarkable how lightly this tes-timony has been set aside. The dating clause here was absolutely typical of that found in royal charters from the start of the reign of Richard I, when it was first introduced. It was certainly more than formulaic. The place and date change constantly and can be shown in John's reign to correspond with the king's known itinerary. There are also frequent changes in the name of the giver, who might be the chancellor, a chancery official or occasionally the king him-self. In 1215, in the period before Runnymede, the charters were given both by the chancellor, Richard Marsh, and his deputy, Ralph de Neville, at ten different locations.[48] The precise meaning of the clause is also pretty plain. To 'give' the charter 'by the hand' was to authorize its engrossment from the final draft and by extension to authorize its sealing. The natural assumption, therefore, is that John himself authorized the engrossment and sealing of Magna Carta at Runnymede on 15 June. He gave the Charter himself (the only charter he did give in 1215) because the barons, not surpris-ingly, insisted that he take personal responsibility for it, rather than hiving that off to his chancellor.

What on earth, therefore, has led historians (Galbraith being an exception) to reject the 15 June date?[49] One factor was that the 15 June date seemed to leave an inexplicable 'hiatus' between this date for the Charter and the eventual peace that is firmly fixed by documentary evidence for 19 June. Another factor is that it seemed inconceivable John would issue the Charter *before* the peace on 19 June, thus making concessions to people who were still in rebellion against him. Since the 15 June date on the Charter indicated that something had happened on that day, Holt suggested that there was then a solemn and general agreement to accept the Articles as the basis for the Charter.[50] This was taken as 'the authorization' for the Charter, and the date was thus retained in the subsequent drafts during the negotiations between 15 and 19 June, until it finally appeared in the Charter itself.

These arguments can all be challenged. They are for a start inconsistent. They worry about the hiatus between 15 and 19 June while also having to live with a far less explicable one between 10 and 15 June. After all, if John sealed the Articles of the Barons on 10 June, as Holt very reasonably argued, virtually nothing had then happened between 10 and 15 June, if all that occurred on that day was a general agreement to accept them. Much more serious is the fact that an agreement to the Articles, whenever that happened, could not possibly have been the authorization for the Charter itself. The Charter was certainly founded on the Articles, but also differed greatly from them. When a final text was agreed, John must have authorized afresh its engrossment and sealing. If that took place on 19 June, why does the Charter not say so? As we have seen, the 'giving' clause in royal charters was far from frozen and formulaic. Indeed, there is evidence that it *was* changed during the negotiations for Magna Carta, since Galbraith's copy in the Huntington Library was given on 15 June not at Runnymede but at Windsor.

What then of the argument that John would not have granted the Charter to those in rebellion? John would have quite agreed, but, then, by issuing the Charter on 15 June before the peace, he was doing nothing of the kind. The nearest parallel is with November 1216, when Henry III issued a new version of Magna Carta although half the realm was in rebellion against him. The fact of the rebellion limited not the king's actions but the circle of those who benefited from them. It is true that the Charter was granted 'to all the free men of our kingdom', but it went without saying that such free men were within the king's allegiance. The fact that John announced the Charter to all his 'faithful men' made that clear. The liberties in the Charter were thus the exclusive concern of the king's 'fideles'. Rebels, of course, could look enviously at these liberties, but would only enjoy them once they too had become faithful men and had made peace. Indeed, from John's perspective, that was the whole point.

There was nothing, therefore, to stop John authorizing the Charter before the peace, as the dating clause shows that he did. There are also clear indications within the Charter itself that, when it was finalized, the peace was still in the future. Thus, in chapter 51, John promised that 'immediately after the restoration of peace', he would remove all foreign soldiers from the kingdom. Significantly, this passage was added at Runnymede, for it does not appear in the Articles. The 'immediately' was a sop to the barons, but, for the rest, it was John who was behind this clause. He knew there might be a considerable delay between the issuing of the Charter on 15 June and the conclusion of peace, if indeed there was peace at all. It was thus vital to make clear that until and unless there was peace, he would not disarm by dismissing his mercenary soldiers. That was both a safeguard for his own position and a threat of what would happen if the settlement were not accepted. The issuing of the Charter before the peace also explains why, in the preamble, not a single rebel appears among those on whose advice John said he was acting. It was this same group, although their names were not repeated, who witnessed the Charter. If the Charter had been issued after the peace, then it would have been quite possible for ex-rebels, now once more within the king's allegiance, to have been named within it. Indeed, at Runnymede, on 20 June, six of the greatest rebels, now restored to the king's faith, did indeed witness a royal charter. If Magna Carta itself had been finalized on 19 or 20 June, they could have appeared there too, thus giving it a far more consensual nature.[51]

What then was the sequence of events on 15 June? Galbraith thought the Huntington copy of the Charter represented its final draft, hence John was put down as authorizing it at Windsor on 15 June, before he moved to Runnymede for the last negotiations later in the day. That is not impossible, but it is equally likely that the copy had no official status and was simply one view of the situation early on 15 June. Either way, the contrast between the Huntington copy and the final Charter suggests there was still a lot to play for in the final hours. The rebels succeeded in widening the scope of the chapter on fines, while John fought off the idea that the baronial relief should be 100 marks. Archbishop Langton, meanwhile, finally prevented any ban on John appealing to the pope, for it is still there in the Huntington copy. These matters having been settled, John brought the negotiations to an end and said in effect to the baronial envoys 'That's your lot. Take it or leave it.' The baronial envoys took it. If they pressed for more, John might break off the whole business and return to war. There was equally the danger that if the negotiations were continued, radicals in the baronial camp would destroy the Charter by making impossible demands. The barons had achieved a tremendous amount. It was best now to secure it. Both sides thus swore to the terms that had been agreed. It is sometimes said that John and the barons took an oath to the Charter in some great ceremony at the time of the declaration of the peace on 19 June. But the Charter itself lends no support to this idea. Instead, it says that '[an oath] has been sworn both on our part and on the part of the barons'. The Latin here for 'on the part' is 'ex parte', which was precisely how the negotiators acting on behalf of the sides were described in 1215. The implication is that it was these negotiators, acting on behalf of the king, and on behalf of the barons, who swore to the Charter. Since the oath is described as being in the past in the Charter, it must have taken place before John gave the Charter on 15 June.

Once John had authorized the drawing up of the Charter, he proceeded at once to have it engrossed and sealed. Legally there may have been no need for this, since the oaths themselves were a commitment to the Charter. Politically, however, there was every need. The baronial negotiators had now to approach the barons assembled at Runnymede and essentially sell them the settlement. One can imagine the howls of derision and disbelief that would have greeted their efforts without even a proper charter to demonstrate their achievements. On 10 June they had needed John to seal the Articles of the Barons to prove his good faith. How much more was that the case now with Magna Carta!

John came to the same conclusion about the need to issue the Charter, but for different reasons. His aim was to show absolutely and definitively that the negotiations were over. He also made one sovereign gain, for he kept the names of the twenty-five barons of the security clause out of the Charter. As a result, he hoped to reduce the chances of its ever being enforced. At the time John 'gave the Charter', the barons had yet to decide whom the twenty-five were to be. As the Charter puts it, 'the barons shall choose twenty-five barons of the kingdom, whom they wish'. In other words, the choice was still in the future. The negotiators had evidently felt unable to name the twenty-five on the spot on

15 June. Yet they dared not postpone the settlement until they were chosen, for the reasons we have seen. So the baronial negotiators settled and left the names of the twenty-five out of the Charter. John must have been pleased. After all, without knowing the names of the twenty-five, how was the noxious security clause to work? It was now left to the barons to broadcast the names as best they could. The king's hope, of course, was that they would not be very good at it. John's attitude to the Charter thus stands out crystal clear. He hoped it would bring peace and make everyone disarm and go home. Thereafter it could remain as a vague symbol of good government, a testimony to his love for holy church and his desire to reform the realm. But as for its actually being enforced, no way!

JOHN'S FURTHER CONCESSIONS AND THE DECLARATION OF PEACE

John was quickly to be disabused of such hopes. The barons assembled at Runnymede did not make peace and quietly go home. Instead they made clear their dissatisfaction with the deal struck by their negotiators. In the process, they forced John, for all his 'that is that' bluster, into further concessions, although, thanks to the confusion over the chronology, historians have never quite appreciated the fact. It was four days before peace could finally be proclaimed, which of course is the explanation for the 'hiatus' between 15 and 19 June.

There were reasons for dissatisfaction. The key issue of Henry II's afforestations had been ducked. The baronial relief had not gone down to 100 marks. And then there was the inadequacy of the security clause. It had been weakened by the removal of John's promise not to appeal to the pope, which more or less flagged up that he would do so. The fact that the promise was still there in three copies of the Charter (including the Huntington one) shows how hard it died.[52] There were also attempts to sharpen the phraseology of the clause. Whereas, in the Charter, the twenty-five barons, with 'the commune of all the land', were to 'distrain and distress' the king if he offended, several copies of the Charter all say that they were to 'distrain and go against' him. The Latin here is 'contra nos ibunt', which has a very martial ring. It is reminiscent of John's promise on 10 May, when he said that during the negotiations with the barons he would not 'go against them by force or by arms' – 'nec super eos per vim vel per arma ibimus'. It was such open warfare that was envisaged in the rejected draft of the Charter. Another draft of the security clause, one preserved by Roger of Wendover, envisaged a way of controlling the king by getting hold of key castles. Thus the castellans of Northampton, Kenilworth, Nottingham and Scarborough were to take an oath to obey the orders of the twenty-five. The Anonymous of Béthune even believed that no royal bailiff was to be appointed save through the twenty-five, which would have given them total control over the administration of the country.[53] But, of course, there was nothing like that in Magna Carta. John's castellans, sheriffs and other officials were all left in place, apart from the relations of Gerard d'Athée. The reformers in 1258 did not make the same mistake, or rather were in a better position in terms of power to avoid it. Almost the first thing they did was to get control of the king's castles.[54]

If, however, the barons could not alter the Charter, they could demand further concessions outside it. It was that which happened. John had hoped that the Charter would be an end. It was not. The barons made it absolutely clear that if he wanted peace he must give more, and John complied. He thus removed the hated Peter des Roches from the justiciarship, and replaced him with Hubert de Burgh. Hubert was English and a younger son from a Norfolk knightly family. He had gallantly defended Chinon in 1205, and, good at self-publicity, had (so he said) once saved John's nephew, Arthur, from blinding and emasculation – a scene of course made famous by Shakespeare.[55] Hubert was cautious, flexible and, like Geoffrey fitzPeter, very keen to be accepted into the ranks of the high nobility. He eventually became earl of Kent. He was the antithesis of Peter des Roches and the two were to become deadly enemies. According to Hubert's later recollection, which must have been burnt into his mind, John made him justiciar at Runnymede. That, however, was certainly after Magna Carta, for there he is still 'seneschal of Poitou' rather than 'our justiciar', the title he bore in the Charter of 1216. To be sure, des Roches himself, in the 1215 Charter, appears simply as bishop of Winchester, but that does not show he had ceased to be justiciar, because he rarely used the title.[56] His removal was clearly a concession made by John in an effort to contain the discontent swirling around Runnymede. Langton himself, anxious to see peace established, had something to do with it, for, as Hubert also remembered, he was present at the appointment.[57]

Much more serious for John than the making of a new justiciar was his concession over London. It was the fall of London in May 1215 that had forced the king into serious negotiations. Having now issued the Charter, he must have hoped that the barons would vacate the city, and everything would return to normal. There was nothing in the Charter to say anything to the contrary. How wrong John was! He was now forced into a thoroughly disagreeable agreement over the city. The official text of this survives but is undated, and some historians have placed it in late July. It seems almost certain, however, that the agreement was struck at Runnymede shortly before the peace on 19 June. Indeed, in effect, it was a condition of the peace. In the agreement, Robert fitzWalter is described as 'marshal of the army of God and of holy church in England'. This is a title that could not possibly have been countenanced by the king in an official document after the peace on 19 June, when the rebellion was supposed to be over and the baronial army disbanded. This date is confirmed by a newly discovered letter discussed in the next chapter that almost certainly dates from around 19 June. It was issued in the name of five barons who are identical with, and appear in the same order as, the first five barons listed in the treaty over London.[58]

The agreement over London (which carefully respected the city's liberties) was made between John, on the one hand, and, on the other, Robert fitzWalter, heading twelve named earls and barons, and 'other earls, barons and free men of all the kingdom'. All those named were rebels and all were to be members of the twenty-five. Under the terms of the agreement, the barons, far from vacating the city, were to hold it until 15 August. Even worse, Archbishop Langton was to hold the Tower of London until the same date. So instead of the barons having to get out of London, it was John who had to vacate the Tower. The point of all this was to give the barons the coercive power to enforce key aspects of the Charter. Thus if, by 15 August, the oaths to the twenty-five had been taken, and the redress of grievances demanded under chapters 52 and 55 had been made by the king, either voluntarily or by judgement of the twenty-five, then John could recover the city and the Tower. If not, the city was to remain in the hands of the barons, and the archbishop was to maintain hold of the Tower. The treaty over London thus sought to make up for the weakness of the security clause. As Holt remarked, it 'applied the screw'.[59]

The London agreement refers to, and is coterminous with, John's letters of 19 June that set in motion the taking of the oaths and the work of the twelve knights in each county.[60] These can likewise be seen as a new concession forced out of John as a condition of the peace. Chapter 48 had said that local abuses were immediately to be inquired into by elected knights and abolished within forty days, provided the king or the justiciar was informed first, but gave no indication as to how and when the elections were to take place. Doubtless John hoped that the inquiry might be long delayed, if it ever took place at all. In the same way, in the security clause, there was no indication as to how and when 'the commune of all the land' would take its oath to support the twenty-five. Might this too be stillborn? And there was another point. The Charter itself gave no indication as to how it was to be distributed and publicized, unlike the Golden Bull issued by the king of Hungary in 1222. John certainly wanted everyone to know that he had graciously granted a charter and that it had led to peace, but as for letting anyone know of its poisonous contents, that was another matter. He would give no help to making these widely known; indeed the Charter did not require him to do so.

Again John was disabused. In his writ of 19 June, he informed the sheriffs that peace had been made, as they could see from the Charter, which was to be read publicly and adhered to. So it *was* to be publicized. The sheriffs were then told to ensure that everyone took the oath to the twenty-five barons, at the twenty-five's 'order', on a day and at a place the twenty-five fixed. So John here, in an extraordinary abdication of royal authority, was subjecting the sheriffs to the orders of the twenty-five. And if this was not bad enough, a very definite timescale was to be given for the work of the twelve knights. They were now to be elected in the first county court to be held after the receipt of the letters in each county. This provision shows that it was not just the great barons who were discontented with the Charter. Clearly there was also pressure from knights and local society. They were determined to ensure that the abolition of malpractices in the localities actually took place.

John had been outmanoeuvred. By issuing the Charter on
15 June, he had indicated that he would give no more. The barons
had called his bluff and more he had indeed given. He had dismissed Peter des Roches, made the agreement over London and set
in motion the oath to the twenty-five and the work of the knights.
In return, John extracted, on his part, some minimal returns. In
the presence of Archbishop Langton and fellow bishops, the barons promised that they would give him whatever security he
wished (other than surrendering castles and hostages) for the
observation of the peace.[61] The fact that this was an oral promise,
of which no record was made, shows the weakness of John's position. He also failed to get anything more than oral undertakings in
another crucial area. Later he was to claim that, according to the
'reformation of peace', all castles and lands seized during the war
were to be returned by 15 August, so by the date laid down in the
London treaty. In addition, all prisoners held at the time of the
peace were to be released and outstanding ransoms pardoned.[62]
These stipulations were clearly important for John's supporters,
who had suffered during the war, yet they appear in neither the
Charter nor the London treaty. Some echo of John's demands
may have reached the Anonymous of Béthune, who believed that
the twenty-five were to redress the wrongs that John himself
had suffered, but again there was nothing about this in the actual
Charter.[63]

Even with John's further concessions, not all were satisfied. The
Crowland chronicler states that some of the northerners, 'the magnates across the Humber', left Runnymede and, claiming that they
had not been there (and thus not included in the peace), resumed
hostilities.[64] The failure to deal with the afforestations of Henry II
must have been a particular grievance. Nonetheless, the majority
of the barons decided to accept the improved offer and return to
the king's peace. Once John was certain of that, which seems to
have been by the evening of 18 June, he was determined to ensure
that the peace went through. It was thus on 18 June itself that he
wrote to one of his captains, Stephen Harengod, announcing the
making of peace 'on Friday next after the feast of St Trinity at
Runnymede' (so on 19 June), which would have been true by the
time the letter arrived. Haringod was then warned to do nothing to
disturb the peace 'as you love us and our honour and your body'.[65]

In the negotiations at Runnymede, John had done something to modify the baronial demands in the Articles. He had managed to postpone, for the duration of his prospective crusade, the giving of justice on the disseisins committed by Henry II and Richard. He had got rid of any suggestion that tallage needed consent. He had gained greater freedom when it came to marrying off heirs and heiresses. On the other hand, he had been pinned down to pathetically small amounts for comital, baronial and knightly reliefs. He could no longer pretend that taxation commanded consent when it had only been sanctioned by his immediate entourage. In general, the provisions on relief, the marriages of widows, debts to the Jews, aids and scutages, and the county farms, all threatened major reductions in royal revenue and power. However much John protested to the contrary, the chapters forbidding arbitrary disseisins and the denial, delay and sale of justice ran clean counter to his style of kingship. The security clause, if properly enforced, would make him no more than half a king. The treaties that had brought him much of North Wales and promised the subjection of Scotland were dead letters.

For all this, John had accepted the Charter and then made further concessions. His immediate aim was simply to end the civil war. He saw Magna Carta as a peace treaty, hence the way that 'peace and liberties' were linked together in the security clause. The first was to be paid for by the second. John's hope was that everyone, having achieved the Charter, would lay down their arms and go home. Whether they would then manage to implement the concessions remained to be seen. John, after all, still retained control of his castles (other than the Tower) and was still able to appoint whom he liked to local office. There were also elements in Magna Carta to exploit. John could insist that magnates obey the Charter in their dealings with their men, as chapter 60 said they should.[66] He might give justice to everyone, or at least everyone who was free, by developing the common law. The Charter also left significant royal powers intact. John could tallage the towns and tax the Jews at will. He retained the royal forest as it had been under Henry II. He could appoint whomever he liked as his ministers, both at the centre and in the localities, providing that they knew the law of the kingdom, whatever that meant. He could also still give patronage, and reward his servants, as he liked. In terms of what he had to give, he retained his rights over wardships (even if they were not to be pillaged) and over the marriages of heirs (even if they were not to be disparaged). He could still expect a flow of land into his hands through forfeitures and escheats. Provided the Charter was not rigorously enforced, it was not impossible that he could live with it over the longer term.

Both John and his opponents, therefore, decided to make peace. Friday, 19 June was the day of the ceremony. In what perhaps was a procession, like that at a coronation, the barons did homage to the king, renewed their oaths of fealty and received a kiss of peace – something Henry II had conspicuously denied Becket at their last meeting. John then sealed the reconciliation with a great feast, just as he had done on his papal absolution in 1213. His demeanour was calm and jovial.[67] On 20 June, at Runnymede, four members of the twenty-five – the earl of Clare, William de Mowbray, Eustace de Vesci and Roger de Montbegon – and another major rebel, Gilbert de Gant, witnessed a royal charter alongside loyalist barons.[68] John had welcomed them back into the circle of the court. Whatever his real intentions, the king had every reason for pretending he was born again in spirit. This would make it all the more likely that the rebellion would end and less likely that the Charter would be enforced.

12

The Enforcement and Failure
of the Charter

As John feasted with the barons on 19 June, both sides knew that a contest over the Charter was about to begin. John wanted it to bring peace, which meant the disbanding of rebel armies and the restoration of royal authority in the localities. In his mind, the precise details of the Charter were best forgotten, if indeed they ever became known. John's opponents, on the other hand, wanted the Charter rigorously enforced. Some wanted to go beyond it. That these divergent ambitions would lead to the failure of the Charter and the renewal of civil war was always likely, but not inevitable, or at least it did not seem so at the time. Sometime in the month following Magna Carta, Alan Basset took out a nine-month lease that was to run from 20 July 'next after the concord made between the king and his barons at Runnymede'.[1] Alan was one of the counsellors on whose advice John had granted the Charter. He was a man in the know. Yet he evidently did not think the concord was about to collapse. In the cause of peace, John himself was prepared to implement certain aspects of the Charter. Thus at Runnymede on 23 June, he issued orders sending home the foreign knights and serjeants who had arrived at Dover.[2] This was to fulfil the Charter's chapter 51, under which immediately after the peace he was to remove the foreign soldiers who had come 'to the harm of the kingdom'. John doubtless hoped that in return the barons would disarm too.

THE DISTRIBUTION AND PUBLICATION
OF THE CHARTER

If the Charter was to be enforced, its contents had obviously to be made known. In Hungary, the Golden Bull itself declared that there were to be seven engrossments, and went on to stipulate who should receive them. One was to go to the pope to be copied into his Register.[3] Magna Carta, by contrast, gave no clue as to the destination of its engrossments. John's letters of 19 June seem to be more informative, although, as we will see, misleadingly so. In the letters, issued to the sheriffs in each county, John informed them of the peace 'as you can hear and see from our charter, which we have caused to be made, which also we have ordered to be publicly read through all your bailiwick and firmly held'.[4] The sheriffs were also instructed to obey and enforce the Charter. Not unnaturally, this has led many historians to assume that the Charter was sent to the sheriffs and thus there was one for each county. Indeed, Ralph of Coggeshall states that 'the form of peace was set out in a charter, in such manner that each county had its own charter authenticated by the royal seal'.[5] There are good reasons, however, for thinking this was not exactly the case. Coggeshall's own statement may be no more than a deduction from the 19 June letters, of which he evidently had knowledge. The letters of 19 June said the sheriffs were to hear and obey the Charter, certainly, but not that they would receive it or should themselves proclaim it. Indeed, the letters gave no indication at all about the mechanics of distribution and proclamation. All this was strikingly different from the procedure in February 1218 when the sheriffs were sent the new version of the Charter and told to have it read in their fully attended county courts.[6] Nothing like that happened in 1215. In part, this was by John's deliberate design. The last thing he wanted was for everyone to know the precise details of the Charter. He was damned if he would tell the sheriffs to proclaim it.

In being reluctant to send the Charter to the sheriffs, John was, however, of one mind with the barons, although for different reasons. The last thing the barons wanted was to rely on the sheriffs for the Charter's preservation and proclamation, given that the sheriffs were the very people under the Charter's attack. The baronial problem here lay in their failure to assert control over local appointments. John remained free to choose whom he liked as his sheriffs and castellans. Indeed he staged a reshuffle in the week after the peace.[7] The only local officials the Charter sought to remove were the relations of Gerard d'Athée. Here slowly and grudgingly between 2 and 20 July, John complied, moving Geoffrey de Martigny, Engelard de Cigogné, and Andrew and Peter de

Chanceaux out of their castles and counties. But if their replacements were more acceptable (one was Hubert de Burgh), they were just as loyal to King John.[8] John never obeyed the Charter when it came to removing Philip Marc from Nottingham castle and the sheriffdom of Nottinghamshire and Derbyshire.

The barons, therefore, had to make their own arrangements for the publication of the Charter. They had doubtless acquired some engrossments at Runnymede itself, but they needed many more for distribution around the country. The trouble was that only John and his chancery could issue authentic engrossments validated by the royal seal. Here, then, the barons were completely in John's hands. They were not easy hands to be in. There was firstly the practical problem that each Charter took hours to write out.[9] After that, it needed to be sealed, which could produce more delay. A big effort was needed to produce large numbers of Charters in one go, and John had no intention of galvanizing the chancery into making it. The process of extracting engrossments from him became like extracting teeth.

What happened we know from documentary evidence. Precisely because neither the Charters nor the 19 June letters (to which we will return) were sent to the sheriffs in a routine way, the chancery thought it wise to draw up a distribution list, setting out who they were sent to, and this was enrolled on the dorse (reverse side) of the patent rolls.[10] The list states that the bishop of Lincoln received two Charters, the bishop of Worcester one Charter and Master Elyas of Dereham four Charters. Since this information follows the statement that on 24 June the bishop of Lincoln received two of the 19 June letters, the implication is that these Charters were handed over on or after 24 June. There is some indication that Elyas of Dereham may have got his four on 27 June.[11] The list closes with the statement that the Master of Dereham had received a further six Charters on 22 July. Doubtless Elyas would have liked all his ten at his first take, but he was evidently unable to secure them.

Adding up, we have here thirteen Charters in all. What were the two bishops and Elyas of Dereham to do with them? Here the distribution list is of no help. Whereas, with the 19 June letters, it both cites the recipients and then the counties for which the letters were destined, with the Charters it just cites the recipients. The reason for that is clear. Since the letters were addressed to the king's

ministers in each county, they each had a county destination indicated at their start. The Charters, with their general address, did
not have a county destination and so could go anywhere. They
could, of course, have gone to the counties but we may be fairly
sure that did not happen, at least not immediately. Their destination instead was the bishop and the diocese. It was Ivor Rowlands
who first came up with this idea, pointing out that the thirteen
Charters in the list corresponded exactly to the number of dioceses
with bishops in post in 1215. The annals of Dunstable, moreover,
state specifically that the Charters were 'deposited through each
bishopric in safe places'.[12] The safe places almost certainly were the
cathedral churches, where the Charters would be accessible to anyone who wanted to inspect them. Three Charters, the list shows,
went specifically to bishops, one to the bishop of Worcester and
two to the bishop of Lincoln. The fact that the bishop of Lincoln
also received the letters of 19 June for Oxfordshire and Bedfordshire has led to the suggestion that his two Charters were intended
for those counties, both of which were within his diocese. But the
two entries, although consecutive, are clearly separated, that about
the Charters being a new 'item'. A perfectly plausible hypothesis is
that one Charter was for the diocese of Lincoln while the other
was for the diocese of Bath and Glastonbury, where the bishop,
Jocelyn of Wells, was the brother of the bishop of Lincoln, Hugh
of Wells. The Lincoln diocesan destination fits perfectly with Lincoln cathedral's having been the home of one of the engrossments
apparently from the start. The Lincoln engrossment has 'LIN-
COLNIA' written twice in capital letters on the back, almost
certainly by the scribe of the Charter itself. Evidently, he knew its
destination, which could easily have been the case if it was one of
the two taken by the bishop.

What then of the ten Charters received by Elyas of Dereham?
Elyas was the steward of Archbishop Langton, and was close to
other bishops.[13] It would seem, then, highly likely that he passed
to the bishops the Charters which he had obtained. This would
explain again how two more of the surviving originals were both
preserved, probably from the start, at cathedrals, namely Salisbury
and Canterbury. The Salisbury Magna Carta is written in a much
more formal hand than the other three originals, which seem typical chancery products, and it may be that Dereham, importuning
for Charters, persuaded the chancery to accept outside help in

writing them. As for the engrossment now shown to have been kept at Canterbury cathedral, Dereham, with Archbishop Langton's approval, probably sent it there direct. That it was the Charter intended for the diocese and not for Langton personally is shown by the fact that it was kept at the cathedral as opposed to Lambeth palace or the archbishop's treasury at the priory of St Gregory at Canterbury.[14]

For the baronial party, the bishops and their cathedrals were far safer custodians of the Charter than were the sheriffs and their castles, from which the Charter might never again emerge. The brothers Hugh and Jocelyn of Wells, the bishops of Lincoln and Bath and Glastonbury, were former chancery clerks of King John, but they had defied him during the Interdict and gone into exile. Hugh's views on Gerard d'Athée's kin must have paralleled Langton's. In his will, drawn up in 1212 while in exile, Hugh left 40 marks to an unnamed Nottinghamshire knight whose daughter Gerard 'wished to have' for his son. One suspects this was the amount the knight handed over to rescue his daughter from the marriage.[15] Later, in 1219, heading the judges on eyre in Lincolnshire, Hugh and his colleagues wrote a magisterial letter setting out their duty to give justice to all, rich and poor alike, and explaining how the whole county court had rallied behind Gilbert de Gant in support of the 'common liberty of all the kingdom conceded and sworn', a clear reference to the Charter.[16] The bishop of Worcester, Walter de Grey, had been John's chancellor, but he had bought the position for its profits and played little part in day-to-day government. The bishop's positive attitude to the Charter can be judged from the way he took possession both of an engrossment and the 19 June letter for Worcestershire. Perhaps the only bishop who might be suspected of evil designs on the Charter was Peter des Roches of Winchester. Indeed, the Charter had effectively cost him his job as justiciar. Perhaps, in this case, Elyas of Dereham sent the Charter for the Winchester diocese direct to the monks of Winchester cathedral, with whom des Roches was frequently at odds.

Once the Charters of the Charter were safely housed at the cathedrals, the intention was not for them to remain there treasured in magnificent obscurity. Rather they were to be inspected and copied.[17] Both engrossments and copies could also be circulated in the surrounding country. That, of course, was the more necessary since dioceses usually embraced several counties. Lincoln's indeed embraced eight. Thus the Crowland chronicler speaks of 'an exemplar' of the Charter being borne 'through cities and villages'.[18] There may be a clue to what happened with copies of the Charters in the procedures adopted in 1254. In that year the dean of Lincoln sent out transcripts of the 1225 Magna Carta (which he wanted back) so that they could be copied.[19] Was this an echo of a procedure in 1215? The eagerness to get the content of the 1215 Charter across is also seen in the way that it was translated, almost at once, into French.[20] Here again there was a parallel with 1254, when the dean of Lincoln ordered the papal letters confirming the excommunication launched against violators of Magna Carta to be published and proclaimed in both French and English. There is no sign, however, that in 1215 Magna Carta was put across in English either in a written text or (more useful for English-speaking illiterates) verbal proclamation, although to have done so would have helped rally free tenants to the cause.[21]

All this is not to say that the diocesan Charters were the only ones in the localities. There were no bishops of Carlisle, Durham and Norwich, and no archbishop of York, in post at the time of Runnymede, and it is inconceivable that Charters did not reach those areas. We know that a Charter was entrusted to Byland abbey in Yorkshire, where William de Mowbray was patron. Quite probably, the need was supplied by some of the engrossments made at Runnymede itself. There was also another source of information about the Charter, although one hitherto unrecognized. This was through the unofficial copies of the Charter made from drafts which had circulated at Runnymede. Evidently, those involved in the negotiations took such drafts away, and copied them up as authentic 1215 Charters. There is a parallel here with 1258, when drafts of the reforms proposed at the Oxford parliament were likewise taken away and copied into chronicles and collections of documents.[22] Since some of the copies of the 1215 Charter found their way into collections of legislation, they may well have descended from legal circles involved in the negotiations at Runnymede. That some of the copies, quite independently, give the date of 16 June to the Charter, rather than 15 June, may indicate that this was the date on which they were copied.[23] Drafts were copied because, initially at least, originals were not plentiful, while thirst for knowledge of the Charter was great. These later copies seem to derive from no fewer than five versions of the Charter, all in some way independent of one another. The implication is that there were at least five different routes through which drafts of the Charter circulated. Here then was an important channel of information alongside that being opened up by the authorized version itself.

Who then had won the battle over the distribution of Magna Carta? Surely the opposition barons and knights. The fact of the Charter itself was well known. The Crowland chronicler, as we have said, wrote of 'an exemplar' being borne 'through cities and villages'. Ralph of Coggeshall believed that every county had its own engrossment. The Anonymous of Béthune said something about the Charter's contents, some of it accurate, some not.[24] Copies were made, or possessed by, the Londoners, and by the religious houses of Peterborough, Luffield Reading, Stanley, Llanthony Gloucester, Montacute, Exeter and St Augustine's and Christ Church, Canterbury, the two last from different texts. St Albans' versions travelled to Tynemouth, Wymondham and Norwich. One copy of a draft version, found in a legal collection, is in French.[25] Some of this transmission took place considerably after 1215, but it probably reflects the pattern then. John had lost the battle to bury the Charter. Could he win the battle to prevent its execution?

THE TWENTY-FIVE

The execution of the Charter depended on the work of the twenty-five barons. They were to sit in judgement on disseisins and fines, if John refused immediate redress. They were to hear the complaints about breaches of the Charter and indeed any other abuse. If the king failed to put matters right, they were to force him to do so with 'the commune of all the land'. They were also to issue the instructions to the sheriffs for the taking of the oath that would form the commune. The oath itself was to obey the orders of the twenty-five in coercing the king. On 15 June, when John authorized the Charter, the barons had not yet chosen the twenty-five. That was not surprising, for it must have been a difficult and contentious business. Some barons probably refused to become members. Many others may have coveted the position, thinking they would gain status and power. No earl could have been denied membership, but lower down the hierarchy there was much to play for. Presumably the decisions were made in the period between 15 and 19 June. Three independent lists of the twenty-five are known, one copied thrice over from a common source at St Albans abbey, one copied at Reading abbey and one found in a volume of legal texts along with a copy of the Charter itself.[26] In these copies, the first eleven names (as C. R. Cheney noted) appear in the same order, seven earls first, and then William Marshal junior, Robert fitzWalter, Gilbert de Clare (eldest son of the earl of Clare) and Eustace de Vescy.[27] Perhaps at a meeting of the twenty-five, the clerks already had a list of the first eleven, and then, with the members milling around, jotted down the names of the rest in different orders. The twenty-five seem to have been chosen by the time of the treaty over London around 19 June, for although they do not appear in that treaty in a body, all thirteen of the named barons were members.

The twenty-five were hardly a representative baronial group. The first and most striking point was that they were made up entirely of former rebels. There was thus no common ground in support of the Charter. Eight of the twenty-five could be described as northerners, but the majority had their main interests in East Anglia, Essex and the home counties. Only John fitzRobert really linked both north and east. Only William Malet, lord of Curry Malett in Somerset, and a former sheriff of the county, was a West Country baron, despite that region being a centre of discontent. Only Geoffrey de Mandeville, having gained Glamorgan through his marriage, held a major Welsh lordship. Only William of Huntingfield represented tenants-in-chief who held knights' fees rather than baronies, although that was probably not the reason for his inclusion. The northern barons Nicholas de Stuteville, Peter de Brus and Gilbert de Gant did not feature in the group, yet room was found for the eldest sons of three earls, the father of one being the loyalist William Marshal.[28]

Despite these inadequacies, the twenty-five showed at once that they meant business. Robert fitzWalter retained his title of 'marshal of the army of God' and probably neither he nor his colleagues ever disarmed. In one list of the twenty-five, each member is made responsible for raising a military force. These range from the 200 knights promised by Geoffrey de Mandeville and William Marshal junior down to the ten knights of William Malet and some others. The total given was 1,083 knights, a formidable force.[29]

THE EXECUTION AND ENFORCEMENT OF
THE CHARTER IN THE LOCALITIES

The business of taking the oath to the twenty-five had begun at Runnymede, where no fewer than thirty-eight loyalists had been obliged to swear it.[30] The swearing in of the localities was set off by John's letter of 19 June sent to all the sheriffs. Under its terms, the sheriffs were to obey the orders of the twenty-five when it came to arranging the taking of the oath. The sheriffs were also informed that twelve knights, elected at the next county court, were to investigate and then abolish the 'evil customs' of the sheriffs 'as is contained in the charter'. The sheriffs were not, however, actually instructed to do anything about the election. Indeed, the only thing they were told to do directly by the king, apart from obey the twenty-five, was to uphold both the Charter and the peace. John can have had little interest in distributing this letter, any more than he had an interest in distributing the Charter. He certainly wanted people to know there was peace, and that his Charter, graciously conceded, had brought it about. But he may well have informed the sheriffs of the forthcoming peace and warned them to keep it in letters witnessed already on 18 June, if the writ sent to one of his captains, Stephen Haringod, is anything to go by.[31] Beyond that, the king's aim was surely to obstruct rather than accelerate the taking of the oath and the inquiry by the knights.

What happened over the 19 June letters, therefore, paralleled what happened over the Charters, which is why the distribution list dealt with both. John did not have the letters carried to the sheriffs by royal messengers in the usual routine way. Indeed, that is implied in the letters themselves, which tell the sheriffs not that they are being sent the letters but that the letters will simply arrive in their 'parts'. With this the baronial leaders were content. They wanted the letters to be as well known as possible, not sent to sheriffs, who might then keep quiet about them. In the case of the one letter that did go direct to a sheriff, John's aim was probably just that, since the sheriff in question, Engelard de Cigogné, was marked down for dismissal by the Charter.[32] For the rest of the letters, the distribution list shows that they were received for the most part by trusty agents of the barons, or indeed by the barons themselves.

Thus the first letter on the list, significantly for Yorkshire, was received by Philip fitzJohn. He was a tenant of William de Mowbray and the beneficiary of a charter that John issued on 20 June at Runnymede, which was witnessed by many former rebels, including Mowbray himself.[33] Of the following letters, Worcester's was received by its bishop, those for Somerset and Dorset by a clerk of the bishop of Bath, London's by the mayor and sheriffs, those for Leicestershire and Warwickshire by Saer de Quincy, Northumberland's by Eustace de Vescy, and those for twelve counties, including Lincolnshire, by another clerk, Henry de Vere. Vere (like many rebels) had been active in royal service, but he was also a brother of one of the leading rebels, Robert de Vere, earl of Oxford. Next on the list are the letters for Oxfordshire and Bedfordshire, which were received by the bishop of Lincoln. Since this last 'take' is dated to 24 June, one may assume the other letters were received before that date. That none of the recipients took away Charters as well, until the bishop of Lincoln on or after 24 June, is another indication that engrossments were unavailable. The remaining twelve letters, along with his first four Charters, were all received by Elyas of Dereham on what may possibly have been 27 June.[34] Where the letters were then sent by their immediate recipients we will discuss in due course.

Having extracted the letters, the baronial leaders had now to enforce the taking of the oath. This was to be sworn either before them in person, or before those whom they appointed. John, of course, must have hoped that the twenty-five would never make this work. 'How they tried to do so, we do not know. It may well be that they, or groups among them, sent letters to the sheriffs giving them instructions, just as later they sent letters enforcing their judgements. They may also have worked through officials they themselves appointed.' What I have placed here between inverted commas comes from the first draft of this book! Since then a superb discovery by Nicholas Vincent has turned speculation into fact, and in a detail I had not imagined. In a cartulary of St Augustine's abbey, Canterbury, preserved in the Lambeth Palace Library, Vincent has found a copy of the very letter implementing the taking of the oath.[35] This is in a fourteenth-century hand, and comes between a copy of the 1215 Charter and a royal letter (discussed below) of 27 June. Although the copy has some obvious mistakes, the letter itself is clearly genuine. Addressed to the sheriff of Kent and the other royal ministers in the county, it was written in the names of Robert fitzWalter, 'marshal of the army of God and the church', and the earls of Clare, Essex and Gloucester, Norfolk and Winchester, and 'their other colleagues to whom the common oath ought to be sworn throughout England'. The sheriff was informed that he was being sent four knights (their names are given), who were also the bearers of the letter. The knights were to receive on behalf of the four earls and their colleagues the oaths due to be sworn according to the king's letters (evidently those of 19 June). The sheriff was to see this was done on the day and at the place the four knights assigned him. The letter concluded by saying that the four knights were also to be present when the twelve knights were elected in the county court to inquire into the evil customs as 'contained in the charter of the lord king'. This of course referred to the inquiry commissioned by the Charter's chapter 48, the letter of 19 June having stipulated that the twelve knights were to be elected at the next meeting of the county court.

The letter was thus issued in the names of fitzWalter, Richard de Clare, Geoffrey de Mandeville, Roger Bigod and Saer de Quincy. (Evidently Mandeville was now styling himself both earl of Essex and earl of Gloucester, titles John had denied him.) The 'colleagues' – 'socii' – referred to were clearly the rest of the twenty-five barons of Magna Carta's security clause. Although the letter is addressed to the king's officials in Kent, we can be confident that similar missives, setting up four knights, went to the other counties. In the St Augustine's copy, the letter is undated but was probably drawn up around 19 June, in parallel with the king's own letter. As we have seen, all the five named barons appear in the same order in the treaty over London, which can be independently dated to shortly before the peace on 19 June.

Each group of four knights had thus been assigned major tasks, and there were probably other duties. The letter of the four earls and their colleagues did not say the knights would be bringing the king's letters of 19 June, let alone the Charter itself, but it was, one may suspect, to these groups of knights that the 19 June letters were sent by Elyas of Dereham and the other recipients named on the distribution list. When, therefore, the sheriffs were told that the letters would be arriving in their areas, it was the knights who brought them. Likewise it was the knights, once the engrossments of the Charter had reached the cathedrals, who took them on the tours mentioned by

Coggeshall and ensured that they were 'publicly read' and made known to the sheriffs in the way described in the 19 June letter. In some counties, of course, where the king's sheriffs still had power, the knights had a difficult task. In others, subject to baronial sheriffs, they were pushing at an open door.

A heavy burden, therefore, rested on each group of four knights, but they could shoulder it. Assuming they were appointed in all the counties, there must have been approaching 150 of them. All presumably were present at Runnymede, and involved in the rebellion. Indeed, on 22 June, one of the Kentish knights, William of Eynsford, recovered a wardship of which he had been deprived during the war.[36] The Kentish four were Eynsford, William de Ros, Thomas de Canville and Richard of Graveney. All had major holdings in Kent, as well as lands in other counties. All save Canville were tenants of the archbishop of Canterbury, and closely associated with Langton.[37] They would certainly have had access to the engrossment of the Charter sent to Canterbury cathedral. All four had direct experience of John's lordship, the three Canterbury tenants when John held the archbishopric during the Interdict, and Canville as a tenant of the honour of Boulogne, one of the honours which, as the Charter indicated, was in the hands of the king. John was able to pressurize all four to join his Irish expedition of 1210, lending them money, as he did other knights, to keep them going.[38] Richard of Graveney (near Faversham) appeared on many grand-assize juries in John's reign, although these were actually for adjoining Surrey, where he held Tooting Graveney from the abbot of Chertsey. Thomas de Canville held at Westerham in Kent and Fobbing in Essex, and does appear as a Kentish grand-assize knight.[39] William of Eynsford and William de Ros, who head the list, were higher in status, too high to appear on juries. Ros, lord of Lullingstone in Kent, would have been a tenant-in-chief had not John conceded his overlordship to Archbishop Hubert Walter, Langton's predecessor at Canterbury.[40] At Eynsford, in Kent's Darent valley, not far from Lullingstone, William boasted a substantial castle. He was clearly as wealthy as a major baron and in 1212 had offered John 1,200 marks for a wardship.[41] His ancestor's excommunication by Becket, in a dispute over the advowson of Eynsford church, had been one of the early ingredients in the quarrel with Henry II.[42] All four knights rebelled after the failure of the Charter, William of Eynsford being part of the garrison at Rochester castle.[43]

The Kentish four were far from a completely homogeneous group. There were big differences in wealth between William of Eynsford, at the top of the list, and Richard of Graveney at the bottom. Yet all must have taken independent decisions in 1215, and were far from being controlled by their lords. Thomas de Canville's lord was the king. Langton believed in the Charter, but did not condone the rebellion. In other counties, some in each group of four knights would surely have been tenants of the baronial leaders, although that did not mean they lacked an independent voice. The four knights would have been very willing agents when it came to the work assigned them in implementing the oath. That the twenty-five barons were able, throughout England, to appoint men of such local stature shows the power of their position and what John was up against.

Apart from receiving the oath, the four knights in each county were also to preside over the election of the twelve knights empowered to abolish abuses. According to the letter of 19 June, the elections were to take place at the next county court after the receipt of the letters in the sheriff's area.[44] The sheriff was informed of this but given no specific function, although, as he presided at the county court, he might certainly have assumed one. It was thus to guard against his interference, and also to monitor the whole process, that the election was to take place in the presence of the four knights. The expectation was probably that the four would themselves be among the twelve, just as the four knightly electors usually featured in the panels of twelve knights which they elected to hear grand assizes. Since the county court met once a month, all the elections, even allowing for the halting distribution of the letters, could have taken place at the July sessions.

Having arranged for each group of four knights to receive the oath and preside over the election of the twelve knights, the twenty-five did not leave it there. Instead, on 27 June, when the king was at Odiham, they forced John to issue another letter about the oath. It was an amazing missive because it showed that the twelve knights were now intended to become a parallel executive in the counties, alongside and undermining the sheriffs. This was laid bare at the very start of the letter, which was addressed to the sheriff and 'the twelve knights elected' in each county to 'abolish the evil customs' of the sheriff! John now ordered the sheriff and the twelve to seize the lands and chattels of those who refused to take the oath to the twenty-five. If they still did not swear within fifteen days, their chattels were to be sold in aid of the Holy Land, and their lands were to be retained in the hands of the king. Given the likely reluctance of John's sheriffs to do any such thing, one can quite see why the order went to the knights as well. They now had the power to bypass the sheriff and the right to attack their enemies. The order thus threatened to accelerate John's loss of local control. It also showed he had lost control at the centre, for the injunctions were 'provided by judgement of the archbishop of Canterbury and the barons of our kingdom', so not by the king at all. Pains were taken to ensure that the letter reached a wide audience, with that for Hampshire and perhaps for other counties being translated into French.[45]

In default of further discoveries, we have no detailed knowledge of how and how far the oath was taken. The baronial letter simply said that it was to be sworn before each group of four knights at the time and place they assigned the sheriff. This gave the knights considerable leeway, and did not pin them down to the next meeting of the county court, which was the venue stipulated for the election of the twelve. Perhaps special meetings of the county and hundred courts were envisaged. That something did happen is clear from the chroniclers. The Crowland chronicler says that 'an oath was sworn by everyone that they should observe [the Charter] at the king's order'. Ralph of Coggeshall wrote of a 'general oath' being made 'by everyone, both knights and free men, through all the counties of England'. Both Coggeshall and Wendover recognized that the oath involved the coercion of the king. All three chroniclers knew of the 19 June letter that set the process in motion.[46]

Another aspect of the work of the twenty-five was to deal with complaints about breaches of the Charter and other abuses, with those complaining having to bring their cases before four members of the twenty-five. Clearly for this to work knowledge of the membership was vital. In the event, the Magna Carta settlement collapsed before the scheme could be put to any kind of test. The twenty-five's regional imbalance would never have helped the process. Had there been a real will to open up redress to lower sections of society, quite different procedures might have been adopted.[47] But at least the swearing of the oath to the twenty-five must have made their names known. Perhaps indeed the groups of four knights read out the names at the swearing ceremonies.

The principal work of the twelve knights, as laid down in the security clause, was to investigate and abolish, within forty days, the malpractices of the king's local officials, although John or his justiciar was to be informed of what was proposed first. That the knights, officially or not, got going very soon after Runnymede is shown by a remarkable letter issued by Archbishop Langton and the bishops, probably in the second half of July. The letter stated that, in the negotiations over the chapter (48) commissioning the work of the twelve knights, both sides had understood that the customs necessary for the running of the royal forest should remain in place.[48] Had some effort been made to inform John of what the knights were proposing, as the Charter laid down? Probably not. Rather, John was hearing from his local agents what was going on. The exclusive focus on the royal forest in Langton's letter is not surprising. Other abuses, such as exactions at local courts, could be resisted certainly but could only really be abolished by future legislation, as indeed happened in the Charter of 1217. The royal forest was different. Here the knights could take direct action by simply declaring Henry II's afforestations invalid, and thus allowing everyone to cut the trees and hunt the animals within them. The Crowland chronicler gives a vivid picture of the magnates, especially in the north, careering through the land, selling the king's woods and killing his beasts, as well as pillaging his houses and manors. This was part of a more general breakdown. After Magna Carta, the Crowland chronicler told how John sent his sheriffs through the provinces to provide for peace 'in the accustomed manner' and 'procure what was due to the fisc'. In the areas controlled by the barons, however, the sheriffs were either seized or driven out. In Norfolk and Suffolk, the counties continued to be run by the rebel pair Roger de Cressy and William fitzRoscelin.[49]

John's hopes when he agreed the Charter had been utterly dashed. It had not been left as a vague and, in terms of its details, a little-known symbol of his benevolence. Instead the Charter was being preserved in cathedrals, paraded through the counties, copied from unofficial drafts, and vigorously and perversely enforced. The king's officials, instead of recovering their authority, were being abused and defied. And this was not all that John had to stomach.

THE PROCESS OF RESTORATION

Under the terms of the Charter, the king was obliged to restore immediately the lands, castles, liberties and rights that he had taken from people 'without lawful judgement of their peers'. Any dispute was to be decided by judgement of the twenty-five barons. These were no idle words. In the ten days from 19 June, John was forced to make some fifty acts of restoration, twelve of the twenty-five barons being among the beneficiaries.[50]

Save in the few cases where he was simply restoring what he had seized during the war, John was here redressing his own arbitrary disseisins, or what were alleged to be arbitrary disseisins. Sometimes he openly confessed as much. On 19 June itself, he acknowledged that he had disseised the earl of Hereford of his Trowbridge lands unjustly, and he instructed the earl of Salisbury, under the terms of the Charter, to restore them.[51] Ten days later he admitted that Clemencia, wife of Henry de Braibeuf, had been disseised of her dower (in Headington, adjoining Oxford) 'by our order without judgement'.[52] Likewise, on 24 June, he restored the son of Earl David to Godmanchester, of which he had been disseised 'by our will and without judgement'. Three days before, Earl David himself had been restored to 'his' castle of Fotheringhay, seized after the plot of 1212.[53] Two of the ringleaders of the 1212 plot and the 1215 rebellion likewise secured redress. Robert fitzWalter recovered 'as his right' Hertford castle.[54] Eustace de Vescy regained the privilege of running his dogs in the forest of Northumberland 'as he ought to have this and is accustomed'.[55]

Among other members of the twenty-five, William de Lanvallei recovered his 'right' in the manor of Kingston in Somerset; Richard de Munfichet his 'right' to be custodian of the Essex forest; Geoffrey de Say the wardship of the heir of one of his tenants; and Earl Richard de Clare the vill of Buckingham, this the marriage portion of his daughter, widowed when John starved to death her husband, William de Briouze junior. Another leading rebel, Robert de Brus, recovered his fair at Hartlepool as conceded in John's charter to his father. In some cases it was not so much that John had disseised individuals as that he had refused to acknowledge rights, or alleged rights, in the first place. Two important concessions came very much into that category. Robert de Vere was at last recognized as earl of

Oxford and conceded the earl's third penny of the county, while Saer de Quincy, earl of Winchester, gained the castle of Mountsorrel that he had claimed vainly since 1204 as his wife's inheritance.

As the dam began to break, and the waters of redress poured over him, John made desperate efforts to patch the leaks and stem the flood. One tactic, employed against Eustace de Vescy and Gilbert de Gant, was to order restoration 'if' what was said was true, which left it open to the recipient of the writ (the sheriff or current holder) to say that it wasn't true. This did not always work. Having told the sheriff of Oxfordshire to restore William fitzEllis, 'if' he had been disseised unjustly, John next day substituted an order that simply gave William possession as it had been 'adjudged'.[56] In a much more important case, John's efforts were similarly in vain. He asked for a delay in returning to the earl of Hereford the honour of Trowbridge. The earl accepted a short postponement for the return of the castle but none at all for the lands. John had thus to write to the earl of Salisbury telling him to put Hereford in possession 'without delay'. That this letter was issued on 19 June, and explained that the immediate restoration of lands, castles and rights taken by the king 'unjustly and without judgement' was a condition of the peace, shows the pressure John was under.[57] The king was similarly unsuccessful in trying to resist some of the demands of Geoffrey de Mandeville. Here he ordered a local inquiry into rights that Geoffrey claimed only then to cancel it and simply to concede the rights as they had been held by Geoffrey's father-in-law.[58] John resisted more successfully in the case of Geoffrey's claim to the Tower of London, although the wonder is that he had to resist at all. After all, the claim presumably went back to charters that the Mandevilles had obtained during King Stephen's reign, and it was not John but Henry II who, in the first instance, had ignored them. This was surely a case that should, under the Charter, have waited until John returned from or abandoned his prospective crusade. Geoffrey nonetheless put it on the agenda and when the Tower was entrusted, under the treaty over London made at Runnymede, to Archbishop Langton, it was 'saving to anyone his right in the custody'.[59] John likewise strove to fend off William de Mowbray's claim to hold in hereditary right both York castle and the Yorkshire forest. This too had been denied in the first instance not by John but by his predecessors. Yet on 19 June, John was forced to entrust York castle to Mowbray until 'we have inquired whether the castle belongs to him in hereditary right or not'. When Mow-bray followed this up by saying that an inquiry had already been held, John expressed astonishment, and ordered the sheriff of Yorkshire to discover when it had been held and on whose author-ity. Evidently he thought, probably rightly, that Mowbray had simply staged an inquiry of his own.[60]

There is no sign that judgements of the twenty-five played a formal part in these restorations, or at least none are mentioned in the implementing writs. The judgement referred to in connection with William fitzEllis was probably one in an earlier lawsuit.[61] We know that the twenty-five did issue their own writs, announcing their judgements, but the only example comes from much later, and after relations with John had completely broken down.[62] Probably, at this stage, the emphasis was on getting John to confess and imme-diately reverse his disseisins. More contentious issues were postponed to another council, which was scheduled to meet at Oxford on 16 July. When agreement was reached over this meeting, proceedings at Runnymede came to an end, and the barons returned to London.[63] The date of 16 July was well before the 15 August deadline in the London treaty, when it would be judged whether John had complied with the settlement and could recover London from the barons and the Tower from Archbishop Langton.

One tailpiece. There was just one unmarried woman (a widow) who was able to profit from the restorations at Runnymede. This was Matilda de Courtenay. On 19 June itself she secured a writ returning her dower in Waddesdon, Buckinghamshire. Matilda had lost her dower and other lands in England as a result of taking the French allegiance in 1204. Seeking their recovery, in November 1213 she obtained a safe conduct, at the petition of the papal leg-ate, to come to England to speak with King John. There may well have been other noblewomen at Runnymede, but Matilda is the only one for whom we have some evidence.[64]

THE OXFORD COUNCIL, 16–23 JULY

For the moment John was still able, with his 'ifs' and inquiries, to fashion a little wriggle room when faced with all the demands for redress. Nonetheless, in the great wave of restorations after the peace on 19 June, he must have felt he was near to drowning.

In these circumstances, the wonder is that John went along with the Charter for as long as he did. But there remained powerful reasons for at least giving it a try. The barons remained in arms and held London fast. In a letter written in late June, Robert fitz-Walter, still styling himself 'marshal of the army of God', reminded another member of the twenty-five, William d'Aubigné, Lord of Belvoir, of how vital was possession of the city, 'our refuge', and how disastrous would be its loss to the king. Accordingly, a tournament, planned for Stamford in Lincolnshire, was now to be held near London, and there d'Aubigné was summoned to come with horses and arms. The prize would be a bear given by 'a certain lady'. John also faced the destruction of his ordinary revenues as the barons and knights swept through the counties, pinning the king's men back to their castles. At the Oxford council itself, still struggling to pay the 1,100 marks he owed the Templars, John told the exchequer to give them the money in instalments, 'great or small', as it came in.[65] Evidently the exchequer had no reserves of cash. Nor in reality was any money coming in, as John well knew, judging from the dearth of orders even of this kind. Indeed, where was the exchequer? Some of its rolls remained in London, where next year they fell into the hands of Prince Louis. Other rolls were moved to Reading abbey and then to Odiham.[66]

John, therefore, still clung to his policy, hoping that the Charter would bring a restoration of peace and order. He was also developing an excellent public line to justify his conduct and damn that of his opponents. *He* was doing all he could to observe the terms of the peace, by fulfilling everything that was asked of him. Yet his enemies were doing nothing to fulfil their side of the bargain, and were doing him injury everywhere. That this argument is recited in the Crowland chronicle shows John's success in getting it across.[67]

Having left Windsor on 26 June, John went first to Winchester and then to his castles at Marlborough, Devizes and Corfe. He left Corfe on 13 July. He *would* go to the Oxford council due to start on 16 July and make the best of it. On 15 July, realizing he would be late, the king stopped on the road between Newbury and Abingdon, wrote to Archbishop Langton and the 'barons of England' explaining the delay, and gave them the names of an impressive delegation who were coming on ahead.[68] In fact, John did reach the Oxford area on 16 July, but decided to spend the night at Woodstock. He arrived at Oxford next day. He was to stay there until 23 July.

The Oxford council is of great importance, something first grasped by H. G. Richardson, however much he was wrong about certain details.[69] It was the last time that John met the barons face to face before the renewal of the civil war, for he refused to attend any later gatherings. In 1218 the exchequer could still date events by reference to 'when the council was at Oxford'.[70] John came to it determined to get his due. The envoys sent ahead on 15 July were to receive what was due to him as well as to give what was owed.[71] What John felt he was owed is very clear: a laying down of arms and a restoration of order so that the sheriffs could once again maintain peace and collect revenue. He also expected to have what was due from London. He could not hope to recover the city itself from the barons before 15 August, but meanwhile, as the treaty said, he should receive his due farms and debts. He had received not a penny. At Oxford itself, John acknowledged, in a letter to the king of France, that the Londoners were likely to disobey his orders. A few days later, when he tried to arrange for a debt to be paid from money owed by the city, he accepted that the mayor might not 'wish' to obey him.[72] What a situation for a king to be in!

The barons were equally clear what they wanted from the king. He should now settle all the claims delayed because they were contentious, the most spectacular being Geoffrey de Mandeville's claim to the Tower of London, and William de Mowbray's to York castle and the Yorkshire forest. There was also the question of the unjust fines and amercements which, under chapter 55 of the Charter, were either to be forgiven by John or adjudged by the twenty-five and (if he could be there) Archbishop Langton. The king had promised as early as 10 May that two of these fines – the ones made by Geoffrey de Mandeville and Giles de Briouze, bishop of Hereford – should be referred to the judgement of his court.[73] And then there was the fine of Nicholas de Stuteville which, because it was unpaid, allowed John to retain his castle of Knaresborough. The king had certainly made many restorations of land, but he had done nothing about these or any other fines, presumably because he argued that they were not unjust. It was, of course, perfectly possible for the twenty-five to press ahead and give judgements of their own on these matters, as indeed they did later. There was nothing in the Charter which said that John had to be involved. Yet clearly those judgements would have far more weight if John accepted them, and announced them in parallel letters. Indeed, unless the exchequer started to obey the twenty-five, it was only letters of John that could get fines removed from the pipe rolls.

At the Oxford council John made some last concessions. Thus, on 22 July, Elyas of Dereham obtained six engrossments of Magna Carta from the chancery. If, as seems likely, Elyas distributed these to the bishops, he had an easy task since as many as eight of them (including Archbishop Langton) were present at the council. It was also during the council that, in accordance with the terms of the Charter, the king moved Peter de Chanceaux from Bristol and Andrew de Chanceaux from the county and castle of Hereford.[74] It may also have been following a decision at the council that John, a few days later, gave the castle of Colchester to one of the twenty-five, William de Lanvallei, William claiming it in hereditary right.[75] This was the last significant restoration the king was to make.

At the same time, John gained some successes of his own. With Llywelyn and the other Welsh rulers being given safe conducts through Langton to come to court, the king seems to have pushed back onto the agenda Llywelyn's 1211 charter of submission, although this had been removed from consideration at Runnymede. At any rate, it was probably at the Oxford council that Langton and a group of loyalist magnates issued a letter testifying to its terms.[76] It was probably also at Oxford that John persuaded Langton and the bishops to make two important declarations. In one, that already referred to, they explained how the terms of the inquiry by the knights should be understood.[77] In the other, they affirmed that in their hearing, when the peace was made, the barons had promised to give whatever security the king wished for its keeping, save for the surrender of castles and hostages. The declaration then explained how the barons had reneged on their undertaking, for, when John demanded charters, guaranteeing their faithful service, they refused to give them. The king's demand had been a crucial test of baronial loyalty, and one they had failed. This did not quite amount to a declaration of war, but it came close to it.

Not surprisingly, during the council the two sides seemed totally apart. Gone was that moment at Runnymede when John feasted with the baronial leaders and allowed them to attest a royal charter alongside loyalist magnates and ministers. The king issued no fewer than six charters at Oxford. The long witness lists featured the name of not a single former rebel.[78] An anecdote preserved by the Anonymous of Béthune which almost certainly belongs to this time adds vividly to the picture. One day the twenty-five barons came to the king's court to make a judgement. The king was ill in bed, with his feet so painful that he was unable to walk, presumably due to gout. He asked the twenty-five to come to him in his chamber. They refused. It would, they said, be against their rights. So John was carried to the twenty-five, who refused to rise to greet him. The Anonymous observed that such examples of pride and outrageous behaviour were frequent.[79] They showed all too clearly that the twenty-five regarded their status as quite equal to the king's, as did the oath taken to obey them by the commune of the land, and the refusal to give John charters of faithful service. John's own mercenaries, according to Matthew Paris, declared that it was the twenty-five who were now the king of England. That must have been how John felt.

John remained equally alarmed about what was going on in the localities. On 23 July, at the end of the council, he sent a furious letter to the earls, barons, knights, free tenants and everyone else in Yorkshire. 'As they loved themselves and all they had', they were to return the lands and castles that they had seized during and 'after the war'. They were to do this by the 15 August deadline contained in the 'reformation of peace'. They were also to return the chattels and prisoners likewise seized 'after the peace'. Evidently there had been no peace.[80]

The anecdote of the Anonymous of Béthune shows the twenty-five at work, although at work still in the king's court and in his presence. Perhaps John's perfunctory order restoring William de Lanvallei to Colchester was a grudging fulfilment of a judgement by the twenty-five. But if there were other judgements, the twenty-five had to go it alone, for there is no sign of John implementing them. Nothing seems to have been done about the fines, and it was not until September that the twenty-five issued their judgement returning Knaresborough castle to Nicholas de Stuteville.[81] It was not just John who was angry. According to the Melrose chronicler, his opponents, feeling that he had violated the articles of the peace, left the Oxford council 'with great rancour'.[82]

THE ABANDONMENT OF THE CHARTER

It was John, however, who drew the conclusions. In his letter to those in Yorkshire, he still indicated he was trying for peace. 'We do not wish,' he said, 'that by the detention of any of the foresaid things against the form of the peace, that the peace in anything should be disturbed or violated.'[83] But this was merely a cover for his real intentions.

The events at the Oxford council had made up John's mind. He decided to ask the pope to quash the Charter. The papal letter doing just that was issued on 24 August.[84] The fit with the end of the Oxford council on 23 July is tight but exact. The messengers had to travel from Oxford and reach Anagni, some forty-four miles south-east of Rome, where the letter was issued. From Oxford to Anagni is 1,250 miles. Supposing the messengers left on 24 July, and arrived on 22 August, thus allowing a day or so for Pope Innocent's response, they would have averaged forty-two miles a day, or a little more if one day was taken up by the Channel crossing. There is nothing impossible about that, given the supreme urgency of the journey. Innocent's decision would have been immediate, and he could draw, for the phraseology of his letter, on his previous missives.[85] In any case, the messengers may well have left before the end of the council. The king's furious letter to the Yorkshiremen on 23 July was thus in effect a farewell to the Charter.

John's decision was momentous, and must have been taken after deep discussions with his leading counsellors – with Peter des Roches, Hubert de Burgh, and the earls of Pembroke, Chester and Derby, who were all at Oxford. These men met in the king's chamber, sitting on his bed, as he lay there tortured by his gouty feet. The discussions were, of course, deeply private because the last thing John wanted was to let his enemies know what was on his mind. The Anonymous says the envoys were sent 'most secretly'.[86] John's public position remained the same: he was doing what was required of him under the peace; it was the opposition who were the violators.

For John, abandoning the Charter was a high-risk course. It meant fighting a war, which he might lose, given that his opponents were bound to call in aid from France. But John's acceptance of the

Charter had always been posited on two things. The first was that, whatever the Charter said, the twenty-five barons of the security clause would not develop into some parallel power in the land, challenging royal authority in an impossible fashion. The second was that the Charter would lead to peace and the restoration of royal government in the shires. When neither of these premises proved correct, John decided to abandon the Charter. Did some of the baronial leaders realize that things were heading towards a smash, and that a stop needed to be put to the local anarchy and the arrogance of the twenty-five? Then perhaps both sides, in a plethora of complaints and inquiries, could have tussled over what the Charter meant under the umbrella of its peace. Something along those lines happened, when it came to implementing the Forest Charter, during the minority of Henry III. John might have been willing for a while at least to go down such a path. But the pent-up feeling in the localities, and the anger and suspicion of the baronial leaders, blocked off that possibility. If there were voices of caution, they fell on deaf ears.

Although it was the events at the Oxford council that persuaded John to abandon the Charter, he was not unprepared. For some time, he had been building up funds. On 6 July, when at Devizes, he received 9,900 marks, contained in sixty-six sacks, from the treasury at Corfe castle. Two days before, the king had taken a great mass of treasure (simply in weight of silver it was around 440 marks) out of the tower at Marlborough and had it carried to his chamber.[87] This was part of a more general policy of calling in his silver and jewels, deposited at religious houses around the country. On 24 June letters went out to sixteen of them to that effect. The result was that in the next few weeks, as his position in the country deteriorated, John became surrounded by a fantastic accumulation of silver cups, jugs, basins, dishes, candelabras, staffs and belts, many of them encrusted with pearls and jewels.[88] While, moreover, John had removed the Athée clan from some of the castles and counties, he still retained them in his service. Indeed, on 2 July, John ordered Geoffrey de Martigny, having vacated Northampton castle, to join him with all the knights and serjeants from the garrison.[89]

After the Oxford council, John's new direction was revealed not by his words but by his actions. He never again met the assembled barons. In late July and early August, he made a quick visit to the Welsh marches and then headed for the Channel coast. From

9 August, all the way through until 9 October, he hardly moved from there, spending his time at Wareham, Sandwich, Dover and Canterbury. His aim was to secure the ports, and arrange for the import of foreign mercenaries. On 12 August, with a fair promise to the duke of Brittany of restoring his lands in England, John asked him to come with as many knights as he could muster. On 28 August, the king was arranging for a loan of 1,000 marks to pay the wages of the knights coming to England.[90] He was preparing for war.

Archbishop Langton, however, was still making valiant efforts to save the peace. Under the London treaty, John had until 15 August to implement the Charter and thus recover the city from the barons and the Tower from the archbishop. Naturally, there was no question of such a recovery now, but Langton still strove to bring the sides together. He and his fellow bishops met at Oxford on 16 August, hoping that the king would join them there for negotiations with the barons at Brackley. It nearly worked. John did indeed leave Wareham and get as far as Marlborough, only then to turn back. He sent envoys instead who declared that, having fulfilled his side of the bargain, the king had received only injury in return. He would not come now since the barons were in arms. This was all too true, for the barons, instead of staying at Brackley, had progressed to Oxford 'in armed array'. The crisis was further ratcheted up by the unveiling at Oxford of papal letters issued on 7 July.[91] These were written in reply to John's letter of 29 May, so in ignorance of the Magna Carta settlement, but since that was virtually dead it hardly mattered. The papal letters, from John's point of view, were perfectly suited to the new situation.[92] Innocent thus berated Langton for failing to support the king, and then excommunicated all those disturbing king and kingdom. Langton, on pain of suspension, was commanded to proclaim the sentence of excommunication, while the bishop of Winchester, the papal representative Pandulf and the abbot of Reading were given authority to see all this was carried out. At the Oxford council, Langton was able to postpone taking any action, while he and fellow bishops went to see John in one final bid to bring him to a meeting. They failed in the attempt, but the meeting went ahead anyway, at Staines between 26 and 28 August. Here Langton promulgated the sentence of excommunication, although only in general terms, without pointing the finger at any individual baron. It was possible indeed to interpret the sentence as aimed as much at John as his opponents.[93]

When the barons returned to London, after the Staines meeting, they made more formal arrangements for taking over the government of the country, groups of shires being placed under individual members of the twenty-five. John's own reaction came in a letter of 5 September, issued by the bishop of Winchester, Pandulf and the abbot of Reading. Doing what Langton had refused to do, they now implemented the papal orders of 7 July, and excommunicated the baronial leaders by name, together with the city of London. The letter was cleverly drafted. It did not actually condemn the Charter. Indeed it still took the old line that it was the barons who were violating it, violating 'what had been ordained by the lord king by the counsel of the magnates who were then his familiars'. It then went on to stigmatize the gifts of land and the making of judgements without authority of the king, clearly referring to how the twenty-five were plunging ahead on their own.[94] When the barons heard of their excommunication, they brushed it aside and appealed to the general council that was soon to meet in Rome. If the sentence had any effect, it confirmed them in the decision they were now taking. This was to set in train the process of deposing King John and electing another king in his place, electing none other than Prince Louis, the eldest son of King Philip Augustus of France.

In the narrative of the Crowland chronicler, the decision to summon a council to bring this about is placed between the barons' return to London after the Staines meeting in late August and the issue of the 5 September letter. Perhaps John knew what was happening by 9 September, when he made various concessions on trading matters to King Philip, and then sent him envoys.[95] The opposition had got far more from Magna Carta than had John, but now recognized its failure. John was reneging on the Charter and resorting to war. Although no papal missive condemning the Charter had arrived, everyone knew it was on its way. The barons, in these circumstances, could simply have waged war under the sanction of the Charter, supported by 'the commune of all the land'. But there was no point trying to force the king to keep the Charter when he was bent on rejecting it altogether. John could not be restrained, he could only be replaced. In 1212 the king's removal had seemed justified by papal threats of deposition. These could no longer be pleaded in 1215, but his removal still seemed unproblematic. John had become king, so he proclaimed in 1199, 'by the unanimous consent and favour of the clergy and people'.[96] Given that he had ruled so badly, what was to stop clergy and people withdrawing their consent and choosing another king? Both the Crowland and Coggeshall chroniclers thus narrate the process without turning a hair. According to the former, the barons realized that the business needed 'the common consent of all the kingdom'. They thus summoned 'all the chief men' to meet at a designated time and place. When the assembly met, voices were still raised in the king's favour, but the majority opinion was decisively against him. He was deposed, and the throne offered to Prince Louis. Louis' own manifesto, when he arrived in England in 1216, explained events in the same terms. The barons 'chose us as king and lord', John 'having been judged unworthy of the kingdom by the common counsel and approval of the kingdom'.[97]

The choice of Louis was not without drawbacks. Philip Augustus had intended to make him king at the time of the abortive invasion in 1213, but had forbidden promises about the return of Norman lands to those disinherited in 1204.[98] Probably the same was true in 1215, so that was disappointing. The barons had also to reckon with John conjuring up national feeling against a French threat. Although, moreover, Louis had a hereditary claim, which he set out in his manifesto, it was almost laughably tenuous: since John had been convicted of treason for betraying his brother Richard, he should not have succeeded in 1199. Instead, the true heir to the throne was the only other surviving child of Henry II, his daughter Eleanor, married to the king of Castile, and Eleanor had generously passed her rights to her daughter Blanche and Louis on their marriage.

There were, however, good reasons for choosing Louis. How far his character was known is unclear, but it certainly turned out to be the total reverse of King John's, for Louis was uxorious, pious and honourable. He also came from a ruling dynasty very different from the Angevins. This was an age in which, as R. W. Southern wrote, 'the French kings alone among the kings of Europe enjoyed the help of a constantly favourable public opinion.' With a great landed base, 'they grew rich without becoming unpopular'. There was no French Magna Carta.[99] England could now bask in the same sunlight, all the more so with the end of the financial demands needed to support wars in France. These considerations were,

however, the icing on the cake. The main reasons for choosing
Louis resided in the facts of power. The barons were involved in a
life and death struggle. Victory at all costs was the aim. It was the
French monarchy that could bring it. As the Crowland chronicler
observed, the barons, lacking confidence in themselves, appealed
to Louis to come in strength to rescue them from 'the hands of the
tyrant'. Backed by his father, Louis could draw on all the resources
of the French monarchy. That surely should guarantee victory. The
same could not be said of King Alexander of Scotland, who might
otherwise have been a candidate. It was the Capetian prince who
could rescue England from the Angevin tyrant.

We do not know exactly when the assembly deposing John and
electing Louis met. After the magnates had been 'cited' to appear at
it, John's supporters, according to the Crowland chronicler, argued
that he was still prepared to maintain the 'peace' and so should not
be deposed. This suggests the meeting was before the arrival, in late
September, of the papal bull condemning the Charter. It may be,
however, that the chronicler is here simply painting a general picture
of the attitudes of John's supporters. Given the formal summonses
of which he speaks, and the forty days' interval mentioned in the
Charter, October would seem the most likely time for the assembly.
It thus took place in the full knowledge of the papal bull.

Dated 24 August, the papal bull would have taken a month to
arrive in England and so was presumably received towards the end
of September. Preserved in the British Library, and a star exhibit in
the 2015 exhibition, it measures some 50 by 46 centimetres, and
is finely written in a large, clear hand. It is an impressive-looking
document. The bull narrated the whole course of the quarrel and
declared that 'by such violence and fear as might affect the most
courageous of men', John had been forced to accept an agreement
shameful, demeaning, illegal, unjust, and harmful to royal rights and
the English people. Pope Innocent thus declared the Charter 'null,
and void of all validity for ever'.[100] After the bull's arrival, John
could proclaim the end of the Charter, supported by the full panoply
of papal authority. His enemies were confirmed in their decision to
depose him. The die was cast. In the second week of October, the
barons gained control of Rochester. On 13 October John began
his long siege of the castle.[101] The civil war had begun.

If anyone had struggled to save the Charter, it was Archbishop
Langton. His efforts to take a middle ground and give each side its

due seem altogether admirable. On the one hand, he and his fellow bishops were ready to help the king. They issued proclamations exposing the baronial refusal to give John guarantees of loyal service. They also set out the correct interpretation of chapter 48 empowering the twelve knights. On the other hand, through his steward Elyas of Dereham, Langton played a central role in the distribution of the Charter, and the letters of 19 June. His own knights were implementing the oath to the twenty-five in Kent. Langton himself took part in the judgement by which those who refused the oath were to have their property seized. Indeed, it was surely the archbishop who decided that their chattels should be sold in aid of the Holy Land. In thus supporting the oath, Langton was associating himself with the most radical part of the Charter. There were practical reasons for doing so, for if the oath was obstructed, a renewal of civil war was bound to result. There were also, one may suspect, ideological reasons. The archbishop saw a parallel between the 'community of all the land', formed by the oath, and the church as the congregation of clergy and people from which, he believed, secular authority derived.[102] Taking the oath was thus a condition for being part of the community of the land and congregation of the faithful. Indeed, the secular and the religious were linked in the support envisaged for John's prospective crusade.

Langton had struggled until the last moment to bring the sides together, but, after the failure of the Staines meeting, his role as a peacemaker was over. He was being ordered, in the 5 September letter, to publish the sentences of excommunication. If he obeyed, he would have definitively sided against the barons. If he refused, he would have sided against the king. Langton evaded the issue and, within a few days of the 5 September mandate, left England for the papal court. Pandulf and his colleagues duly suspended him from office.

There was a subtext to Langton's role in the great crisis of 1215. This concerned the castle of Rochester.[103] After his absolution by Langton in 1213, in an effort to appease the archbishop, John had accepted Canterbury's long-standing claims to possession of the castle. Given its strength and strategic importance, however, Langton, at John's request, had allowed the sheriff of Kent, Reginald of Cornhill, to continue as castellan. In 1215, however, John began, rightly, to suspect Cornhill's loyalty. As a result, both on 25 May and 15 August 1215, he tried to persuade Langton to hand the castle over to more trusted royal agents. The archbishop never complied. The request in May came at the very moment when peace negotiations were beginning in earnest, which was not a good time, Langton may have felt, for a shift in the strategic balance. Once peace was established, as it was at Runnymede in June, Langton was entitled, under his earlier agreement with John, to recover the castle of Rochester, and the king seems to have accepted the point. According to Wendover, he restored the castle to the archbishop, although in practice this made no difference to Cornhill's tenure. When John, in August, renewed his pressure to surrender the castle, Langton was still hoping to act as a mediator and bring the parties together. According to Coggeshall, he refused to resign either Rochester castle or the Tower of London, 'without judgement'. If this was to be a judgement of the twenty-five, then Langton was still recognizing their authority. Yet there are signs that the barons too were worried about his attitude. Coggeshall has the story of Robert fitzWalter briefly occupying Rochester castle, fearful that Langton would hand it over to the king. This took place, Coggeshall says, while John was at Canterbury and Dover, which would fit exactly with the seizure of fitzWalter's lands ordered at Dover on 17 September.[104] The archbishop's relations with John had certainly not broken down at this point. On 10 September the king issued a full and fulsome letter placing Langton's possessions, during his absence, under royal protection.[105] Things looked different in October when Reginald of Cornhill handed Rochester castle over to the barons. It was only then that John branded Langton 'a notorious and barefaced traitor' for failing to surrender it.[106]

Holt has argued that, in the run up to the hostilities, John 'had won the war of nerves and propaganda'. The king had done so by sticking to the line that *he* was ready to observe the peace; hence the argument of his supporters when they refused to countenance his deposition. By asking the pope to quash the Charter, however, John necessarily abandoned his virtuous stance. His hypocrisy had been exposed. Had he really issued the Charter for 'the honour of God and the exaltation of holy church, and the reform of our kingdom', he should have stuck to it, or at the very least, like his son, have reissued it with the more doubtful parts left out. But John's commitment to the Charter was always skin deep. He wanted its peace, not its implementation. The position of John's opponents was no more reputable. They had taken far more than was justified in the localities. They had never disarmed. Both sides got what they deserved, a renewal of civil war.

In 1216 John made those submitting to him forswear the Charter.[107] If he won the civil war, he was not going to have that again. On the baronial side, the twenty-five were still wielding authority in the autumn of 1215. On 30 September letters issued in the names of Geoffrey de Mandeville, Saer de Quincy and Richard de Clare, and attested by Robert de Vere, earl of Oxford, sought to implement the twenty-five's judgement returning Knaresborough castle to Nicholas de Stuteville.[108] Probably it was the twenty-five who convoked the assembly that deposed the king. Louis' own commitment to Magna Carta, however, is hard to gauge. He certainly had a good knowledge of the Charter, for when he finally left England the prince surrendered, among other documents, 'the charters concerning the liberties made in the time of King John at the meadow of Runnymede'.[109] In the archives of the king of Scotland, there was found, at the end of the thirteenth century, a 'letter of Louis, son of the king of France, concerning the confirmation of the charter of the barons of England'. This has been interpreted as a letter confirming Magna Carta, but one wonders whether that was the case.[110] It seems odd for such a letter to be sent to the king of Scotland. Much more likely, Louis' letter was a confirmation of a charter in which the barons of England offered him the throne. The Crowland chronicler states that the agreement with Louis was affirmed with 'conventions and securities'.[111] It is surely inconceivable, in such an agreement, that Louis would have accepted all the restrictions in the Charter, let alone the security clause. The long manifesto which he issued on his arrival in England said nothing about the Charter and merely opined that he had come to restore both church and kingdom to their 'ancient and due liberty'.[112] No chronicler has anything to say about Louis' attitude either. Had he become king, he would probably have done no more than issue a Coronation Charter confirming ancient liberties and offering law and justice in the future.

In the autumn of 1215, therefore, on the one side was King John, now determined to crush the Charter. On the other, the prospect of a new king with no commitment to it. Magna Carta seemed a failure without a future.

13

The Revival of the Charter, 1216–1225

Prince Louis had landed at Thanet in Kent on 21 May 1216, with a large French force. John felt unable to resist him and beat a hasty retreat.[1] He thus avoided risking everything in a single battle, as King Harold had done so fatally in 1066, but signalled his weakness in humiliating fashion. With Louis receiving a triumphant welcome in London, many of John's leading men deserted. Of the sixteen lay counsellors whom he had named at the start of Magna Carta, Alan of Galloway and Robert of Ropsley had already done so. They were followed, after Louis' arrival, by Hugh de Neville, John fitzHugh, and the earls of Salisbury, Warenne and Arundel. Of the earls that the king had named, only William Marshal remained loyal. At some point, at least seventeen of John's household knights joined the rebels, including such trusted figures as John of Bassingbourn. Some of these men harboured material grievances and personal grudges against the king. Some were under pressure locally with powerful neighbours in the rebel camp.[2] Above all, especially after Louis' arrival, they calculated that John was finished.

King Alexander made the same calculation. Back in October 1215, with John occupied investing Rochester castle, he had laid siege to Norham castle on the Anglo-Scottish border. His alliance with the rebels had been sealed by 'the barons of England', which probably meant the twenty-five, conceding his claims to the three northern counties. Eustace de Vesci came to Norham and personally invested Alexander with Northumberland. Having taken the castle at Rochester at the end of November, however, John gained revenge. He marched north, reached Berwick in mid-January 1216, and then sent troops to ravage the country as far north as the Forth. 'We will chase the red Scottish fox from his lair,' he allegedly remarked, alluding to the colour of Alexander's hair. With Louis' arrival Alexander took fresh courage. In August 1216 he seized Carlisle and then came south himself to meet Louis at Dover, and do homage for the northern counties.[3] Meanwhile Llywelyn, at the head of a confederation of Welsh rulers, had conquered Cardigan and Carmarthen and driven Gwenwynwyn (lured back to John's side) from southern Powys. John, however, was defiant. Having spent much of the summer gathering his forces at Corfe castle, in July he set off on a ravaging campaign that took him to the Welsh marches and then across to the eastern counties.

By the end of September 1216, John was at Lincoln. He broke up the baronial siege of the castle, and then headed south to King's Lynn. On 12 October part of his baggage train was lost, including the relics of his chapel, when it was sucked into the sands of the Wellstream while attempting a short cut across this inlet of the Wash before the tide had properly receded.[4] The loss of the relics was the more grievous because John was now desperately sick with dysentery. On 15 October, in a moving letter from Sleaford, he informed the pope that his life was wholly despaired of, and begged for spiritual aid:

> Since grace is not denied those asking for mercy, we beg you father that you will stretch out to us the hands of absolution in remission of our sins, that supported by the work of your mercy, He who punishes beyond deserts and rewards beyond deserts, will look on us with the eye of his mercy, and deem us worthy to be placed in the number of the elect.[5]

Some hope, one might think, but at least John had already taken steps to expiate his greatest crime. On 10 October, at King's Lynn, the king had granted land for the site of a religious house to be founded at Aconbury in Herefordshire – for the souls of the murdered Matilda de Briouze and her son.[6] John was also thinking of how to secure what he called the 'perpetual hereditary succession' of his dynasty. In his letter of 15 October, he thus placed the kingdom and Henry, his heir, under papal protection. He also begged his entourage to ensure that William Marshal became regent. Yet still John was on the move. On 15 or 16 October he was carried on a litter the twenty miles from Sleaford to Newark. There in the castle, in the middle of the night of 17–18 October, he died, as a great storm howled around the town and made the citizens fear for the safety of their houses. When John de Savigny (Ralph of Cogges-hall's informant from whom this comes) entered Newark early next morning, he found the king's servants unwilling to tell him what had happened. Indeed, so Savigny alleged, they had fled, leaving the king's body naked, until the constable of the castle found something to cover it. Savigny himself, allowed in to see the corpse, remained with it for about an hour and celebrated Mass for the king's soul.[7]

John had originally intended to lie in the Cistercian abbey that he had founded at Beaulieu, but this was in an area controlled by the rebels. In his will, drawn up in his last days, John thus asked instead to be buried in Worcester cathedral, 'in the church of Saint Mary and Saint Wulfstan'. There was also a spiritual reason for this. Beaulieu abbey had no saint. Worcester, on the other hand, had Wulfstan, bishop of Worcester from 1062 to 1095. Wulfstan's canonization had taken place in 1203, after numerous miracles at his tomb: in 1201 more than a dozen people had been cured in one day. In 1207 John himself prayed 'for some time' beside the tomb, and conferred benefits on Worcester cathedral. In a reign full of spiritual darkness, Wulfstan's canonization was one bright light. Surely he would now intercede, and secure John's inclusion among the number of the elect.[8] At Worcester, accordingly, John was buried. When his tomb was opened in 1797, he was found to be wearing on his head what was taken at the time to be a monk's cowl. Much more likely, it was John's cap of unction, the cap that was placed on the king's head at the coronation in order to absorb and retain for a period the holy oil of the anointing.[9] John had evidently kept this most holy object with him. It had not done him much good in this life. Perhaps now it would help him in the life hereafter.

MAGNA CARTA 1216[10]

With John's death, would his remaining supporters go over to Louis and bring the war to an end? After all, John's son Henry was only nine and Louis controlled well over half the kingdom. Nothing like that happened. Instead John's supporters proceeded at once to Henry's coronation (at Gloucester, for Louis controlled London and Westminster abbey), and pressed the Marshal to assume the regency. After some hesitation, for he was around seventy, he accepted.

Not to be underestimated in explaining this conduct are ideas of loyalty and honour. They run through the account in the *History of William Marshal* and the papal and royal letters of the time. 'Let your fidelity and constancy be commended for all time to the praise and glory of your name', ran one missive to the garrisons of Bedford and Northampton.[11] There were also hard material reasons. Many of John's captains and castellans could hope for no equivalent employment on the other side. Some of his great baronial supporters had private disputes with Louis' partisans. Thus the earl of Chester's claims to the earldom of Lincoln and the castle of Mountsorrel put him at odds with Gilbert de Gant and Saer de Quincy.

There were also reasons to hope that Louis' supporters might think again, now that they were faced not by the hated John but by his young innocent son. 'The candle of the child called back the stars which had been scared by the father's thunder,' wrote one poet.[12] Louis' English followers also found themselves in conflict with his French entourage over place and patronage. Their cause was further damaged by the arrogant and brutal conduct of the French soldiery. Thus a war being fought, so Louis said, to save the English from a tyrannical king, could now be portrayed by his opponents as one fought 'to deliver England from the French'.[13] There was one other cardinal factor sapping Louis' strength, namely the attitude of the pope. On his orders, Louis and his followers had all been excommunicated. As a result, they could have no overt support from the English bishops, nor any other high ecclesiastic. Louis could not be crowned, for all his possession of Westminster abbey. There was no one to crown him. In giving papal support to John and his son, one person stood out. This was the papal legate, Guala Bicchieri, who had arrived in England in the spring of 1216. He displayed stupendous energy in the royal cause and eventually turned it into a crusade. Thus, as the Crowland chronicler shrewdly observed, 'those who once called themselves the army of God and boasted that they fought for the liberties of the church and the kingdom, were reputed to be the sons of Belial and compared to infidels'.[14]

The situation of the minority government was thus not hopeless, yet it remained bleak. Henry's very coronation banquet at

Gloucester was disturbed by news that the Marshal's castle at nearby Goodrich was under attack. Total defeat was a very real prospect. The result was a momentous decision, which changed the course of history. The minority government now accepted what John had rejected: it accepted Magna Carta, thus laying the foundations for its survival. The aim, of course, was to tempt rebels back into the young king's camp, by conceding what they had initially been fighting for. Clearly the Charter, although rejected by John and sidelined by Louis, was still thought to retain its attractive power.

For the great barons on Henry's side the decision to accept the Charter was easy. They, just as much as any rebel, would benefit from its 'baronial' clauses. For Guala, who with the Marshal authorized and sealed the document, the decision required courage and imagination. After all, papal policy was now stood on its head, and without any opportunity of consulting Honorius III, who had been elected pope on Innocent III's death earlier in 1216. But the pope was always good at adjusting to new realities, and Guala doubtless saw and explained the political imperatives, which justified his action. He would also have explained that Henry's Charter was different from John's in omitting its most obnoxious inroads into royal power. In effecting that omission, Guala was doubtless at one with some of John's most ruthless administrators, notably Peter des Roches and William Brewer, who were among the advisers mentioned by the king at the start of the new Charter. But probably everyone agreed that some of the most radical demands were impractical, especially in a war situation. None of the omissions were reversed and so the decisions taken now were of fundamental importance for the shape of the final, definitive Charter of 1225.

The new Charter was written in Henry's name, and was authorized by, that is 'given by the hands' of, Guala and William Marshal (the latter with his title as regent) at Bristol on 12 November in the first year of the reign, so 12 November 1216. Guala and the Marshal also sealed the Charter, since, as it explained, the king had no seal. The Charter provided a new list of counsellors on whose advice the king had acted, in part of course because some of the old ones had joined the rebels. After Guala, there were eleven bishops, headed by Peter des Roches of Winchester, although those of St David's and Bangor were so obscure that one of the clerks, writing out an engrossment, did not know their names. The twenty-four laymen were headed by William Marshal and only six names were part of the 1215 list.[15] The earls, apart from the Marshal himself, were those of Chester, Derby and Aumale, the last a former rebel and indeed member of the twenty-five. The list was supposed to impress the rebels with the scale of the young king's support, and it certainly included, as the 1215 Charter did not, a powerful group of Welsh marcher barons. In a war-torn situation, they could leave their lordships briefly to come to Bristol. Runnymede had been a different matter.

The first conspicuous change to the 1215 Charter came right at the start. Chapter 1 still gave freedom to the church, but omitted 1215's confirmation of John's charter guaranteeing free elections. Archbishop Langton would have hated that but he was an absentee. After his departure for the papal court in October 1215, he did not return to England until 1218. The decision now was Guala's. He must have judged, not unreasonably, that freedom of elections during the war might mean freedom to elect supporters of Louis. The only compensation was that vacant bishoprics and abbeys were now given the same protection from exploitation as secular wardships. The Charter also omitted 1215's chapter on wills (27), perhaps because they were considered entirely a matter for church regulation.

The most important change in the Charter came, however, at the end. There the security clause with its twenty-five barons, and the oath taken by the community of all the land, disappeared altogether. Also omitted was the chapter that had sought to remedy John's unjust disseisins, if necessary after judgements by the twenty-five, the chapter, that is, which had forced him to make so many restorations in the period after Runnymede. The chapter on remedying unjust fines went too, as did that on the grievances of King Alexander. Doubtless he was considered a hopeless case. The only chapter redressing the wrongs of the past which remained was that on the Welshmen disseised by John, probably because some were on the king's side, or were hoped to be.

In the field of local government, the 1216 Charter also excised another chapter of the 1215 Charter which had stripped John of so much power and caused so much disruption, namely that which set up the twelve elected knights in each county with authority to investigate and abolish the malpractices of the king's local officials. Out too went the stipulation that royal officials needed to know the law of the kingdom, and the chapter dismissing the kinsmen of Gerard d'Athée. They indeed were now performing sterling service in the war, with Engelard de Cigogné as castellan of Windsor. A person of comparable status, soon to rise to almost comital power, the Norman, Falkes de Bréauté, actually featured as one of the advisers of the 1216 Charter.

Alongside these changes, there were some others made, in part at least, to defend the rights and revenues of the crown. Thus the 1216 Charter omitted the stipulation that information about marriages proposed for heirs needed to be given to the next of kin; this itself was a retreat from the Articles of the Barons, which had asked for such marriages to take place with the kin's 'counsel'. The 1216 Charter also omitted altogether chapters in the 1215 Charter on scutages and aids, debts owed to the Jews, and the increments and (by implication) profits exacted from the counties. So there was nothing on taxation needing the common consent of the kingdom, and nothing correspondingly on the constitution of the assembly that might give it. Out as well went 1215's chapter 42, giving free entry to and exit from the kingdom, not surprisingly in this time of war. The Charter was quite open about some of these omissions. At the end, it observed that, since some of the chapters 'in the earlier charter' seemed 'weighty and doubtful', they had been put in abeyance until the king could have further counsel about them. He would then do whatever was for 'the common utility of all'. The security clause and the twenty-five were not mentioned here. Nor were the missing chapters, the source of so much contention, on the redress of past fines and disseisins. Evidently their removal was non-negotiable. But flagged up were the issues of scutages and aids, debts to the Jews, and, referring here to the investigation of the twelve knights, the issues of forests and foresters, and the customs of the counties. In part the new Charter was thus an offer to the rebels and an attempt to draw them into negotiation. It also rewarded the men of the Cinque Ports, 'the barons' as they were called, who were giving vital support to the crown. They were now included in the chapter that confirmed the liberties of London and other (unnamed) towns and ports.

The Charter was drawn up in a spirit of surprising confidence, given the general situation. That is seen in the beautiful writing of the only surviving original, preserved at Durham cathedral. It can be seen too in the trouble taken to make a whole series of small changes. Thus widows were not to remain in castles; sureties were to answer if the debtor could pay but refused to do so; constables could take corn from the vills in which their castles were situated but must pay for it in three weeks; the sheriffs and bailiffs, if they took horses and other chattels, were to pay for them at stipulated rates. The provision in 1215 that a guardian was to return land stocked 'according to ... the time of the wainage', which meant the agricultural season, was altered to 'at least according to how he received it'.[16] Evidently the drafters thought the Charter was worth the effort of these detailed changes and might last.

The 1216 Charter certainly reached the north, for the one original is in the Durham cathedral archives, while copies are found in later York Minster cartularies.[17] Two single sheet copies in the French royal archives probably came from material that Louis took with him from England.[18] Although seriously weakened when it came to enforcement, redress of past grievances and the reform of local government, the essence of the 1215 Charter and much of its detail remained intact. The 1216 Charter might be measured against what Louis had to offer. There is no evidence that he responded by issuing a charter of his own. That failure may have seemed the more important as his French entourage and soldiery became increasingly unpopular. The fact of the new Charter, together with John's death, may well explain why the English rebel barons did not fight harder when the decisive confrontation came at the battle of Lincoln on 20 May 1217. In that conflict Louis' Anglo-French forces were shattered by William Marshal. Not a single English rebel of any status was killed, while forty-six were captured along with three hundred unnamed knights. The captives included the earls of Winchester and Hereford (Saer de Quincy and Henry de Bohun), Robert fitzWalter, Gilbert de Clare (the eldest son of Earl Richard, who died later in the year), William de Mowbray, Gilbert de Gant, Robert de Ros, Nicholas de Stuteville, Roger de Cressy and Henry, son of Earl David.[19] Geoffrey de Mandeville and Eustace de Vesci had both died the previous year, the one killed in a tournament, the other shot through the head by an arrow during a siege of Barnard castle. The heart had been ripped from the baronial party. Louis himself missed the battle of Lincoln since he was besieging Dover castle. Its long and gallant defence by Hubert de Burgh had been a major reason for his difficulties. His last hope resided in a great fleet bringing him reinforcements from France. The hope evaporated when, on 24 August 1217, the fleet was destroyed by de Burgh in a sea battle off Sandwich in Kent.

MAGNA CARTA 1217 AND THE
CHARTER OF THE FOREST

Louis now realized he must give up. In September 1217, under the Treaty of Kingston/Lambeth, he resigned his claims to the English throne, but loyally obtained the best terms that he could for his followers. Everyone was to recover freely the lands that they had held at the start of the war. The rebels thus did far better than their Montfortian successors in 1266, who had to buy back their lands. Magna Carta was also part of the settlement. Louis' supporters certainly needed it now that he was not to be their king. Accordingly, in November 1217, Henry III issued a new version of the Charter, this time accompanied by a quite separate Charter regulating the running of the royal forest.

I say November 1217 but, in fact, the four surviving engrossments of the 1217 Charter completely lack the 'given by the hand' clause normal at the end of royal charters, and thus provide no indication of their place and date of issue. Instead they simply end with the statement that, since the king has no seal, they are being sealed by Guala and the Marshal.[20] One of the two surviving engrossments of the Forest Charter, that at Lincoln, ends in the same way.[21] The most likely explanation for the absence of the 'giving' clause and thus of the date is that all five of these engrossments were drawn up for distributions of the Charters arranged in 1218, and it was thought confusing to include the earlier date of the original issue. The November date is derived first and foremost from the other surviving engrossment of the Forest Charter, which has always been in the episcopal archives at Durham. Although now damaged, enough remains to deduce that it was 'given by the hands' – 'data per manus' – of the Marshal and Guala at St Paul's, London, on a day in November in the second year of the king's reign, so November 1217.[22] The new Magna Carta was clearly drafted with the Forest Charter in mind, for the two forest chapters remaining in 1216 were moved across to it. The preambles to the two Charters also have identical wording. One can be fairly sure, therefore, that they share the same date and that Henry's second Magna Carta belongs to November 1217.

Just what the date was in November is more problematic.

Virtually all modern authorities give it as 6 November. Yet the Durham Forest Charter, the only engrossment to have a date at all, while it certainly indicates November, equally certainly does not mention the sixth. Instead, the first letter of the date seems, if anything, to be a 'Q'. The rest of the number is then lost but, judging from the space it occupied, it was most likely 'Quartodecimo' or 'Quintodecimo'.[23] This, however, is an impossible date for a document given at St Paul's, since, by 14–15 November, the Marshal had left London and was on his way to Gloucester. One explanation might be that 14 or 15 November was the day on which the clerk actually wrote out the Durham Charter, although that was not chancery practice for the Charters of 1215. Whatever the case, the chancellor, Richard Marsh (of whom more shortly), must have been satisfied, since he presumably received this engrossment as bishop of Durham. Where then does the 6 November date come from? The answer is not from engrossments but from copies of Magna Carta and the Charter of the Forest, which end with the statement that they have been 'given' at St Paul's on 6 November.[24] This provides a believable date for the Charters since the government certainly was in London on the sixth. These copies, however, are all given not by the legate and the regent but by the chancellor, Richard Marsh, bishop of Durham.[25] No copyist could have made up this giving clause, and it must be contemporary. What is going on? Marsh had a high opinion of his status as chancellor, and once upbraided his deputy, Ralph de Neville, with forgetting his title.[26] He would surely have wished to 'give' the 1217 Charters. The copies in which his name appears may possibly derive from engrossments in which he did so. More likely, however, is that they descend from rejected drafts. Just as Marsh was passed over in 1215 as 'giver', in favour of the king, so, in 1217, he was passed over in favour of the legate and the regent. They had already given the Charter of 1216, thus imbuing it with the maximum possible authority. They decided to do the same with the Charters of 1217. That is a measure of their importance.[27]

The 1217 Charter differed in significant ways from its predecessor, largely in making further concessions to the kingdom. There was every need to do so. The minority government, headed by the Marshal, had won the war but still needed to affirm the peace. Former rebels, having recovered their estates, could very well make trouble if they were dissatisfied with the new conditions.

The fragile political situation is reflected in the prologue to the Charter, which, in contrast to those of both 1215 and 1216, had no lengthy list of royal counsellors. The only people mentioned by name were Guala, the archbishop of York, the bishop of London and William Marshal. Evidently, the drafters shied away from simply listing, as before, the king's own supporters. That would have seemed all too partisan. Equally, it was not yet possible for loyalists and former rebels to join together as counsellors or witnesses. The unstable situation was also shown at the end of the Charter, where a new chapter said that, by 'the common counsel of all our kingdom', the unauthorized castles built during the war were to be destroyed.

The 1217 Charter also did something about one of the issues flagged up in 1216, namely scutages and aids. It was not much, but at least chapter 44 directed that scutages should be taken henceforth as under Henry II, which implied less frequently and at lower rates than under John. More important was a new concession in the area of local government, one that fulfilled the offer in the Charter of 1216 to look again at the 'customs of the counties'. Quite probably the concession was also responding to an issue raised by the twelve knights during their investigations and abolitions in 1215. Thus chapter 42 in the Charter of 1217 laid down that county courts were only to be held once a month, or at longer intervals if those were customary. The sheriffs were only to hold their tourns, the especially well-attended sessions of the hundred courts, twice a year, at Easter and Michaelmas. The view of frankpledge was only to be held at Michaelmas, and no more was to be taken by the sheriff than had been customary under Henry II.[28] The chapter was a great victory for local society, burdened as it was by frequent attendance at courts and by amercements for failing to turn up. Indeed, chapter 42 covered the same issues as the charter purchased by the men of Devon in 1204.[29]

These victories paled before the triumph of the entirely new Charter governing the royal forest, a charter with which Magna Carta would thereafter always be linked. The king most blamed for the vast extension to the royal forest was Henry II. John and Richard had, if anything, reduced its area – of course in return for money. In 1215 the Unknown Charter had called for Henry's afforestations to be reversed. The Articles of the Barons had backed down on the issue and had only targeted the minimal afforesations of John. Magna Carta had reintroduced the issue of Henry's and Richard's afforestations, but only as matters for attention once John ended his prospective crusade. The 1216 Charter left out the afforestations of Henry and Richard altogether and kept in just those of John, although raising at the end the issue of 'forests and foresters' as a matter for later discussion. Now, the Forest Charter of 1217 came back to Henry II with seeming vengeance. 'First of all', it declared, all the forests that Henry II had afforested were to be surveyed by good and law-worthy men, and then deforested. Also to go, although here no investigations were necessary, were the afforestations of John and Richard.

These stipulations were part of a Charter – running to seventeen chapters, so smaller than Magna Carta, but still a substantial document – that must have required a great deal of work. The Forest Charter of 1217 brought back (as chapter 2) the 1215 chapter from Magna Carta, omitted in 1216, which exempted men living outside the forest from coming before the forest justices. Chapter 10 of the Forest Charter also averred that 'no one' was to lose life or limb for an offence against the protected beasts of the forest, thus meeting a demand of the Unknown Charter, one indeed which the Anonymous thought had featured in the Charter of King John. The range of forest offences was also reduced by allowing free men, having woods within the forest, to erect mills, make ponds and ditches, and create new arable land. The Charter limited the number of forest officials, and regulated their activities, as far as stipulating how much should be charged for carts going through the forest, and how many claws should be cut from the paws of dogs so as to render them harmless to the beasts of the forest.

This attention to detail was seen in changes to the 1217 Magna Carta. What was largely a new chapter, preventing riverbanks being enclosed other than they were in the time of Henry II, was brought in very logically after that on the building of bridges over rivers. In some of the changes one can sense the hand of the king's judges who were gathering for the reopening of the bench at Westminster. Thus a widow's dower was defined as a third of the land her husband had held in his lifetime unless less had been agreed at the time of the marriage. The burdens on the judges themselves were reduced, and their authority was increased, in the chapters about the common-law legal actions. The judges had now to visit each county only once a year. They no longer had to hold the assizes on the day of the county court and with four knights of the county, elected by the court. They were simply to act 'with the knights of the county'. If they could not finish the business, they were to hear the cases later on their eyre, instead of remaining on to hear them with sufficient knights and free tenants; more convenient for the judges, less convenient for jurors and litigants or at least those of the county concerned. Difficult cases were to be referred to the justices of the bench. All this applied to the assizes of novel disseisin and mort d'ancestor. Those of darrein presentment (about appointments to church livings) were to be heard exclusively at the bench, so not locally at all.

THE SETTLEMENT WITH WALES AND THE INDEPENDENCE OF SCOTLAND

The 1217 Charter omitted the 1216 chapter about the Welsh, so Magna Carta ended up with no reference to the law of Wales. This was because the minority government realized it would have to make a separate peace with Llywelyn, which it did, much to Llywelyn's advantage, at Worcester in March 1218. There was also a separate peace with King Alexander, so, unlike the Charter of 1215, the 1217 Charter and its successor in 1225 had nothing on Scotland. Alexander vacated Carlisle (his one concrete gain from the war) and came south to King Henry's 1217 Christmas court at Northampton. There, according to the chronicle of Melrose (the only source), he did homage for the earldom of Huntingdon (held from him by Earl David) and for the other lands that his predecessors had held from the king of England.[30] Doubtless Henry reserved his rights over the kingdom, while Alexander reserved his to the northern counties, but the key point of settlement was this: Alexander had not done homage as he had to John in 1209, homage, that is, 'as William, king of Scotland, did homage' to Henry II. In other words, Alexander had not done homage for the kingdom of Scotland. He had escaped the noose that John had prepared for him. The civil war of 1215–17 and the consequent collapse of English royal authority thus had momentous consequences for the political shape of Britain. It had ensured the continuation of Scottish independence.

THE FINAL AND DEFINITIVE
MAGNA CARTA OF 1225

Struggling to restore peace and order to the kingdom, the minority government gave wide publicity to the 1217 Charters. In February 1218 it thus sent engrossments to all the sheriffs with orders that they be read in the county court, 'having gathered together the barons, knights and all the free tenants of the county'. This was the letter in which the first reference to 'magna carta' itself appeared.[31] The sheriffs were also to see that the chapters of the Charter were 'in all things sworn to and observed'. This echoed the oath taken by 'the community of all the land' to support the Charter of 1215. But whereas then the oath had been to fight with the twenty-five against the king, now it was linked to a second oath in which the assembled barons, knights and free tenants were to swear fealty to him. That there was to be a new monarchy whereby allegiance to the king was inextricably linked with allegiance to the Charter could not have been more clearly demonstrated.

Not surprisingly, the 1217 Charter became far better known than its 1216 precursor. There are four surviving engrossments, probably all from the circulation of 1218, as opposed to only one engrossment surviving from 1216. There are also a good number of copies, although often in a form in which the 1217 charter is conflated with that of 1225. The Forest Charter was itself circulated again in April 1218.[32] This did not mean that either Charter would be enforced. There was an immediate struggle over the Forest Charter. This, as we have seen, laid down that the afforestations of Henry II were to be abolished, once they had been established by 'good and law-worthy men'. Sensing danger here, the government did nothing to set the work of the men in motion. The result was that some counties pressed ahead on their own, until (in July 1218) the government at last sanctioned official surveys of Henry II's afforestations by 'twelve law-worthy and prudent knights'. When, however, the surveys indicated the vast extent of Henry's afforestations, so that if removed the king would be left with little more than his demesne woods, the minority government refused to implement them. Instead, it developed the argument that the afforestations of Henry II meant only those which he had made after having restored the losses under King Stephen. The result was a stalemate, although one that gave the Forest Charter all the more publicity.

There could also be anxiety over the validity of the Charters themselves. The young king's seal had been inaugurated in 1218, which left a question mark over Charters authenticated merely with the seals of the regent and the papal legate. The fact that the Charters had their origins in the coercion of King John also cast a shadow. A dramatic exchange during a great council in January 1223 shows that this had not been forgotten. On that occasion, in response to a proposed inquiry into royal rights, Archbishop Langton and other magnates demanded that the king confirm Magna Carta. At this, William Brewer, doyen of John's exchequer, barked out 'the liberties which you seek, since they were violently extorted, ought not rightfully to be observed'. Langton rebuked him: 'William, if you loved the king, you would not disturb the peace of the kingdom.' Henry himself, now fifteen, then stood forward and declared that he would indeed observe 'all the liberties to which we have sworn'.[33] Brewer, however, had made a powerful point.

The king's oral confirmation of the Charters in 1223 set the stage and also showed the need for the final and definitive Charters that he issued two years later. In bringing that about, a central role was played by two men, Langton himself and the justiciar, Hubert de Burgh. De Burgh had taken over the government just before the Marshal's death in 1219, gradually sidelining his deadly rival, the king's tutor, Peter des Roches. A man on the make, de Burgh was eager to ascend into the ranks of the high nobility. He also believed in doing his job as justiciar, which was to dispense justice and restore and maintain the rights of the crown. Such a restoration, he recognized, must take place within the context of Magna Carta. This was not just because of the fear of renewed rebellion. De Burgh also needed the support of former rebels to stabilize his regime and restore royal authority. Here, through a remarkable turn-around, his enemies were the very loyalists who had helped win the war. John's old sheriffs and castellans now claimed that they could not be removed until the king came of age, which, if that meant twenty-one, would not be until 1228. They also aspired to retain all the revenues from their local offices and govern them almost as they wished. Some of the chief culprits came from the ranks of John's foreign agents, and were closely allied to Peter des Roches. Hence the way the politics of the minority came to be portrayed as a struggle between the English and the aliens, giving a great boost to English national feeling. Most conspicuous among the 'evil' foreigners was Falkes de Bréauté, the illegitimate son of a Norman knight. (The name Falkes, according to one tale, derived from the scythe – 'faux' in French – with which he had killed someone in his father's meadow in Normandy.) He had begun his career, called simply 'Falkes', as a 'poor serjeant' of King John. From there, articulate and clever, 'small of body but most valiant', as the Anonymous put it, he had risen fast. He now controlled the earldom of Devon and was sheriff of six counties across the Midlands.[34] If royal authority was to be restored, and de Burgh was to be secure, it was vital to break the power of such men.

Having spent the years 1216-17 in northern Italy, France and Flanders, in May 1218, with his suspension from office lifted by the pope, Langton had returned to England to take up his duties as archbishop of Canterbury. He was passionately committed to the Charter, and wished to place it on a firm and unimpeachable footing, free from Brewer's imputations. Yet he also saw the need to recover royal power. Without that, the king could never maintain peace and protect church and people. Langton agreed with de Burgh in seeing the foreign sheriffs and castellans as the source of much of the trouble. At the end of 1223, he helped de Burgh bring about their dismissal as part of a general redistribution of local offices. Next year, he and his episcopal allies stood shoulder to shoulder with de Burgh in putting down the revolt of Falkes de Bréauté. While that was happening, however, disaster took place abroad. King Philip Augustus, scourge of the Angevin dynasty, had died in 1223. His successor was his son Louis, the very person who had tried to make himself king of England. Louis now took revenge for his defeat by invading what remained of Henry III's continental dominions. He conquered Poitou with ease, and went on to threaten Gascony. Only a major effort from England could save the situation, and to finance that a great tax was a necessity. This was the catalyst behind the final and definitive version of Magna Carta, which King Henry issued, along with a new Charter of the Forest, at Westminster on 11 February 1225. Just as the financial demands of the continental empire generated the grievances that produced the first Magna Carta of

1215, so those demands necessitated the tax that produced the final Magna Carta of 1225. Without England's involvement on the continent, there would have been no Magna Carta.

The Magna Carta of 1225 had a status from the start far above that enjoyed by its predecessors, one which placed it on a secure and inviolable footing. *This* Charter had not been forced upon the king, as the Charter itself made very clear. Thus, in the preamble, Henry stated that he was making the concessions by his 'spontaneous and good will'. The king could say that, as he could not in 1216 and 1217, because he was now seventeen. Already at the end of 1223 he had started to witness royal letters, and thus take responsibility for government orders. As early as 1218, his seal had been inaugurated and it was this that authenticated the Charter of 1225, as can be seen from the splendid example which hangs beneath the engrossment preserved at Durham. Yet it was not simply the king's age that made the difference to the 1225 Charter. Indeed, there remained a view that Henry would not attain his majority until he was twenty-one in 1228. In 1225 he was still prevented from issuing his own charters and making grants in perpetuity.[35] The 1225 Magna Carta was thus an exception to this continuing restriction of the minority. The key factor that elevated the 1225 Charter, removed the taint of coercion and proved Henry's spontaneity was different. It was that the Charter was purchased from the king in return for a grant of taxation, the taxation, of course, which was needed to rescue Gascony from the French. The Charter itself made the point explicitly. As Henry declared in the final chapter:

> For the concession and gift of these liberties and the other liberties contained in our charter of liberties of the forest, the archbishops, bishops, abbots, priors, earls, barons, knights, free tenants, and all of our kingdom, have given us a fifteenth part of all their movables.

This link between the Charter and the tax was always remembered.[36] It meant Magna Carta had escaped its doubtful origins in the wars of 1215–17. The Charter of 1225 was new and pure, produced not by coercion but by a freely struck bargain between king and kingdom.

Archbishop Langton was the first witness to the new Charter. Judging from a later remark, he had hoped in 1225 to secure more liberties for the church. These might have included a confirmation of John's charter granting free elections.[37] Here the archbishop was unsuccessful. Langton, nonetheless, gave every possible support to the 1225 Magna Carta. It was he, one suspects, who ensured that the bargain from which it sprung was described in the Charter, so that it carried for all time the proof of its consensual origins. Precisely because of those origins, Langton was able to do something else, namely bring church and realm together in the Charter, instead of keeping them separate, as they had been in 1215. In the 1215 Charter, the freedom of the church had been granted to God, and was made quite distinct from the concessions made to the kingdom. The point was to avoid any suggestion that the church's freedom was the product of coercion, whatever might be the case with the liberties granted to everyone else. Indeed, it was only in respect of the liberties of the church that the Charter mentioned John's 'free and spontaneous will'.[38] In Henry III's Charters, the division between church and kingdom remained, but, in 1225, Langton nullified the effect by introducing a new preamble that brought churchmen and laymen together as beneficiaries of the king's concessions.

As Henry said:

> By our spontaneous and good will, we have given and conceded to archbishops, bishops, abbots, priors, earls, barons, and all of our kingdom, these below written liberties to be held in our kingdom of England in perpetuity.

So churchmen and laymen, separate when it came to the concessions in 1215, were now together. The king's free will, only proclaimed when granting the church's liberties in 1215, was now proclaimed for the liberties of everyone. The new preamble and conclusion to the Charter showed something else as well in which we may detect Langton's ideology and influence. This was a new inclusivity. The 1215 Charter had been granted just to the free men of the kingdom. The 1225 Charter was granted to 'everyone' – 'omnes' – which meant to everyone, free and unfree alike. By the same token, it was 'everyone' who was said to have granted the tax that secured the concessions. That unfree peasants had consented to the tax was, of course, a fiction, but they certainly had to pay it and thus could feel a stake in the Charter.

The Charter of 1225 was also validated in a new way at its end. With any suggestion of coercion removed, it was possible to restore the king's promise, omitted in 1216, not to seek anything to invalidate the Charter. If he did, it was to be held 'as nothing'. The Charter was also witnessed by all the kingdom's great and good, whatever side they had taken in the war. The Charters of 1215 and 1216 had merely listed the king's partisans as his advisers. The Charter of 1217 had hardly listed any advisers at all. None of these Charters had witness lists. The 1225 Charter was quite different. It made no reference to the king's advisers at the start, but had a great list of witnesses at the end. Sensing the importance and novelty of this, the copy of the Charter made soon afterwards at Cerne abbey in Dorset set out the witness list in beautifully elaborate fashion, and then wrote out the place and date of issue in capital letters.[39] The witness list was headed by Langton, eleven bishops and twenty abbots. Hubert de Burgh, as justiciar, headed the laymen, followed by nine earls and twenty-three other magnates. Eight members of the twenty-five barons from the Charter of 1215 – including Robert fitzWalter, John de Lacy and Robert de Ros – together with many other former rebels, including Reginald de Briouze, brother of the murdered William – now rubbed shoulders with such loyalists as the earls of Chester and Derby, William Brewer, Peter and Matthew fitzHerbert, Brian de Lisle and Peter de Maulay. Doubtless Saer de Quincy would have been there too, but he had died on crusade in 1219. The Charter was no longer a party document.

The church's support for the Charter was very clearly seen in the large number of ecclesiastical witnesses. It was also seen in something else of vital importance for the Charter's future. In 1215 Langton had felt unable to support John's Charter by launching sentences of excommunication against those who transgressed it. There had been no sentences in either 1216 or 1217. But 1225 was different. Because of its new validity, Langton and his fellow bishops now pronounced a sentence against all who contravened the Charter.[40] This became the precursor of further sentences promulgated in 1237 and 1253, the second with great passion and publicity. The church was fully mobilized behind Magna Carta. That was an important reason for the central place it obtained in public life.

There is just one curious addendum to all this. The 1215 Charter had been given by the hand of the king. Those of 1216 and 1217 had been given by the hands of the papal legate and the regent. The 1225 Charter was given by no one at all. It just ends by saying it has been 'given at Westminster'. Why was it not given by Richard Marsh as chancellor? After all, there was no legate or regent any more, and no tradition of charters being given by the justiciar. Why, even more, was it not given, like the Charter of 1215, by the king? Surely that would have befitted its new status. I have no ready explanation for this. It is possible that Marsh was absent, for he does not appear among the episcopal witnesses of the Charter. Perhaps the failure to name the giver was connected in some way to his claims and sensitivities.

There is one other feature of the 1225 Charter that owes more to later editors than to anything in the contemporary record. This is its division into chapters and numbering. The Charters of 1217 and 1225 are for the most part identical apart from their prefaces and conclusions. Yet the former is conventionally given forty-seven chapters and the latter only thirty-seven. The reason is that several chapters that appear on their own in 1217 are amalgamated in 1225. Thus the famous chapters 39 and 40 in the 1215 Charter appear as chapters 35 and 36 in 1217 and as chapter 29 in 1225. The conventional numbering of the 1216 and 1217 Charters is actually that of Blackstone's of 1759. He was guided by the numbering that he had already given to the Charter of 1215. When he came to the Charter of 1225, however, he was presented with a difficulty, for this had been printed with numbered chapters in the early sixteenth century. The number of chapters was thirty-seven, which went back to the numeration found in copies of the Charter made in the late thirteenth and early fourteenth centuries. Other copies of that date, however, have numbers both higher and lower. Such variations were hardly surprising. Since the engrossments had now lost touch with any chapter-by-chapter negotiations, the capitals that began new chapters no longer had the same emphasis as found in 1215. This allowed copyists to make their own judgements about the divisions. Thus sometimes '29' is a single chapter, sometimes it consists of two chapters. Blackstone, however, when numbering the 1225 Charter, decided to stick with the first printed edition and its thirty-seven chapters. It has been thirty-seven ever since, thus bringing about the disjunction with the numbering of the charter of 1217.[41]

THE NATURE OF THE 1225 CHARTER

The Charter of 1225, apart from its new preamble and conclusion, was virtually identical to the Charter of 1217. Roger of Wendover went further and declared that it was identical to the Charter of King John in 1215. Here he was wrong. There were many differences between the 1215 and 1225 Charters. Did these differences end up by making the final Charter, assuming it was obeyed, more or less restrictive on kingship? The question cannot be answered in any clear-cut fashion.

The greatest difference between the 1215 and 1225 Charters was the absence of the security clause in the latter, which meant the 1225 Charter itself contained no constitutional means for its enforcement. In that sense it was far weaker than its 1215 counterpart. Since, however, such a clause, if implemented, might have destroyed the 1225 Charter altogether in a new civil war, it was arguably better off without it. Something, moreover, had been introduced in its place – the threat of excommunication. The same change was made to Hungary's Golden Bull in 1231.[42] It remained to be seen, however, whether excommunication would be in any way effective. If it was, it had one significant advantage over the arrangements in the security clause of 1215. They had been directed simply at the king and his ministers. The penalty of excommunication, on the other hand, would be incurred by any violators of the 1225 Charter, and so equally threatened magnates and their officials. Out with the security clause also went the chapters from the 1215 Charter dealing with John's unjust fines and disseisins. Had some means to redress these been provided, they would certainly have been exploited by barons and baronial widows under Henry III. The reason nothing was done was almost certainly due to the government's fear of stirring up dispute. Those with grievances were thus left to pursue them, without help and encouragement from the Charter, through a petition to the king or legal actions in the courts.

For the localities, the omission in the 1225 Charter of chapter 25 from 1215, banning the increments and profits that John had demanded from the counties, was a major loss, and one the government was to exploit. On the other hand, the Charter's new chapter on the running of the county and hundred courts (chapter

35 in 1225 and chapter 42 in 1217) offered some compensation, and was vigorously defended and exploited by county knights.[43] Despite the offer in the Charter of 1216, nothing had come back in on debts to the Jews. Consequently the king could still demand the interest as well as capital when they came into his hands. He did, however, later reaffirm the 1215 Charter's ban on interest accruing during minorities.[44] On the face of it, there was also a very serious omission in the field of taxation for it no longer required the kingdom's common consent. The 1225 Magna Carta said that everyone had given the tax in return for the Charter, but failed to lay down such consent as a pattern for the future. As far as the Charter was concerned, the king could levy taxation at will. Against these omissions, contemporaries might weigh the introduction of the Forest Charter. Of this, too, Henry III provided a new version in 1225, now embellished with a preamble and conclusion the same as Magna Carta's. If the Forest Charter could be enforced, especially in the area of Henry II's afforestations, it promised a very major diminution of royal power.

In terms of the social balance within the Charter, the changes since 1215 had, in some ways, strengthened the authority of lords over their tenants. That is not surprising. The great men of the realm, during the minority of Henry III, were essentially in control of government. The earl of Chester had already been obliged to issue a charter passing down to his tenants concessions such as those in the 1215 Charter. He and his fellows now wished to safeguard their positions. The new Charters thus continued the work of Magna Carta in protecting the interests of 'the lord of the fee'.[45] In two chapters introduced in 1217, no free man was to alienate land if it prevented him performing the service that he owed to the lord of the fee; and, if anyone gave land to a religious house in such a way as to deprive the lord of his due service, the lord of the fee could take possession of it.[46] The general run of free tenants was discriminated against when only the demesne carts of knights (which would here include barons), ladies and ecclesiastical persons were protected from seizure by sheriffs and bailiffs.[47] At the end of the 1217 Charter, the stipulation in 1215 that everyone should pass the concessions down to their own men was retained, but now seemed qualified by a new passage, which immediately followed: 'saving archbishops, bishops, abbots, priors, Templars, Hospitallers, earls, barons, and all other persons, ecclesiastical

and secular, the liberties and free customs which they had before'.
One wonders whether there was any debate about this, because in
the Forest Charter the saving clause comes before rather than after
the passage about the passing down of the concessions, so no longer
qualifying it. In 1225, moreover, the Charter itself adopted the
Forest Charter's order. Does one detect here Langton's influence?

Magnates also gained by what was left out of the 1225 Charter.
Nothing specific in the new regulations about the hundred courts
showed that they applied to the hundreds, rapidly increasing in
number, which were in private hands.[48] It was the sheriff or his
bailiff who was to hold the tourn only twice a year.[49] It was the
sheriff who was to be content with what had been taken at the
view of frankpledge during the reign of Henry II. This was no
innocent and unnoticed omission, for, in 1234, Henry III sought
to correct it. In August of that year he drew attention to the
clause at the end of Magna Carta, and went on to say that, as a
consequence, 'archbishops, bishops, earls, barons and our other
magnates', should observe the Charter towards their own men.
The king then got to the point, which was that the chapter in
Magna Carta limiting meetings of the hundred court to two a year
should be observed in private hundreds as well as in royal ones.
Although the king soon issued another proclamation, explaining
that it was only the tourn which was to be twice a year, and that
routine meetings of the hundred should be every three weeks, he
again made clear that this was to apply in 'the courts of magnates'
as well as those of the king.[50]

Great lords were also behind the omission from the Henry III
Charters of anything about the common consent to taxation. The
1215 Charter, of course, had said that consent was necessary
for the levying of both scutages and aids (other than aids due on
the three customary occasions). The king had good reason to
object to this when it came to scutages, since he could see the duty
to pay them, in place of military service, as integral to the tenurial
obligations of his tenants-in-chief. But the removal of the demand
for consent to scutages, in favour of just saying that they should be
levied as under Henry II, made it all the more possible to retain
something on consent to aids. One can see why great lords might
think that was both unnecessary and objectionable; unnecessary
because, especially in current conditions, they knew that it was
simply impossible for a king to raise a tax without consent;

objectionable, because if aids levied by the king were restricted and needed consent, so might the aids that magnates sought to levy on their own tenants. A change to the 1216 Charter shows just that thinking, and reveals the baronial reason for leaving out the chapter on consent. For out with it, as a natural corollary, went the chapter that prevented lords taking more than the three customary aids from their free men. Magna Carta thus came to lack the chapter that had most explicitly favoured under-tenants in the Charter of 1215.

Offsetting this balance tipping against them, under-tenants made one significant gain. In its chapter 3, the 1215 Charter had been concerned with the 'heir of any such one', referring here to the heir of the tenant-in-chief whose relief was regulated in chapter 2. It had laid down that such heirs, when coming of age, having been in wardship, should succeed to their estates without payment of a relief or fine. To this chapter the Charter of 1216 made a significant addition, widening the chapter's scope in such a way as to protect under-tenants from their lords. Thus it now laid down that the 'lord' of 'any such one' was not to have his wardship before taking his homage. The use of 'lord' here instead of 'we', that is the king, was deliberate and showed that the chapter, despite the retention of 'any such one', was meant to apply to lord—tenant relations as well as relations between the king and his tenants-in-chief. In insisting that heirs should do homage before being taken into wardship, the aim was to protect their rights and ensure that they did indeed succeed when they came of age. That this was done in 1216, in the middle of the war, shows how important the issue was for knightly under-tenants. It was an issue of long standing, for the Assize of Northampton of 1176 had asserted that the lords should take the homage of underage heirs. That lords were uneasy about the new provision in 1216 is shown by the way they inserted a saving clause. They were not to lose the wardship if the heir, while still underage, became a knight. This again suggests the knightly audience to which the new clause was meant to appeal.[51]

When it came to local affairs, it was panels of knights who acted as the 'good men' in each county empowered by the Forest Charter to establish the afforestations of Henry II. Here the knights gained great local power, which they used with a will.[52] The knights, however, bulked less large in the 1225 Charter than in that of 1215. The stipulation that the king's judges should hear the assizes with four knights of the county was a poor substitute for the judges having to sit with four knights elected in the county court. There were also no longer the twelve knights elected in each county to abolish the malpractices of the king's officials. Nothing was done to revive these groups in a different form by giving them a standing commission to hear complaints about breaches of the Charter.

In Henry III's Charters, improvements were made to the benefit of widows. If the Charter of 1216 prevented them staying in castles while their dowers were assigned, they were to have a suitable house in its place and (by an addition in 1217) a reasonable share of the common goods for their maintenance. The 1217 Charter also defined dower itself in terms very much to their benefit (and also, of course, to the benefit of any second husband). It was to be a third of 'all the land' that the husband had held in his lifetime (which meant during the lifetime of his marriage), unless less had been agreed at the time of the wedding. This meant that widows were entitled to a third of the property that their husbands had taken into the marriage and also a third of any subsequent acquisitions. Although this may have recognized the law as increasingly practised before 1215, it was still valuable to have it defined in the 1225 Charter, for both *Glanvill* and *Bracton* confined dower to what the husband held at the point of marriage.[53] This was some compensation for widows no longer able to complain about the unjust fines exacted from them by King John. So was the inclusion of 'ladies' in the chapter (21 in 1225) protecting the demesne carts of knights and ecclesiastics from seizure.

Small but significant alterations in the new Charters were made to do down the unfree peasants.[54] Chapter 15 of the 1216 Charter made it clear that villeins were only protected from excessive amercements when imposed by the king, so not, therefore, when imposed by their lords. The 1217 Charter, in a further change to the same chapter, deprived the king's own villeins of any protection under its terms. As far as the Charter was concerned, the king was thus able, just like any lord, to amerce his villeins as he wished. There was also a telling change to chapter 39 of the 1215 Charter. That had protected free men from unjust disseisin without specifying the nature of the property involved. It could thus be argued that it protected a free man who held land in villeinage. The 1217 Charter made clear this was not the case by now stating that a free man was not to be disseised of his 'free tenement'.[55] In other words, he could be disseised of any land owing villein customs and services. More positively, unfree peasants might certainly hope to gain from the new chapter which limited the sheriff's exactions at the view of frankpledge when he inspected the tithing groups (chapter 42 in 1217, chapter 35 in 1225). However, the chapter failed, as we have seen, to make clear that it applied to private hundreds. The Forest Charter itself did something for the unfree in directing that 'no one' was to suffer death or mutilation as punishments for offences against the beasts of the forest. That this was deliberately designed to include the unfree is shown by its use of 'no one', for elsewhere, with one exception, the beneficiaries of the Forest Charter were free men. The fact that the chapter went on to specify imprisonment as the punishment, when the offenders had not the resources to pay amercements, shows how poor they were expected to be. The Forest Charter had one other chapter of broad social appeal, when it took over from the 1215 Charter the stipulation that 'men' outside the forest need not come before the forest justices. For the rest, the beneficiaries in chapter after chapter of the Forest Charter went no lower than free tenants or free men. It was thus archbishops, bishops, abbots, priors, earls, barons, knights and free tenants who were to enjoy their woods as they had existed at the time of Henry II's coronation. It was, however, a more exclusive group, just archbishops, bishops, earls and barons, who had the privilege of taking one or two beasts as they rode through the royal forest, provided they blew their horns first lest they 'seem to be doing it furtively'.

The texts of the 1225 Magna Carta and Charter of the Forest became definitive. Henry III, Edward I and their successors never issued new versions of the Charters. They simply confirmed those of 1225. It is thus the 1225 Charters, or what is left of them after various repeals, which are on the statute book today.[56] The mere existence of the Charters did not, however, ensure either their enforcement or their continued relevance. Did they make a difference? The final chapter addresses that question.

14
Did Magna Carta Make a Difference?

If the Charters were to make a difference, it was vital that they should be well known, both in their general principles and in their detail.[1] Here they were helped by the confirmation of the 1225 Charters at intervals throughout the century. In 1237, in return for a grant of taxation, Henry III confirmed the liberties 'both in our magna carta and in our charter of the forest, notwithstanding that the foresaid charters were made when we were of minor age'.[2] This removed any last doubt about the Charters, because Henry had granted them in 1225 while he was still under twenty-one. The witnesses in 1237 included three of John's advisers in the 1215 Charter, Peter des Roches, William, earl of Warenne, and Hubert de Burgh, as well as the sons of William Marshal, William Longespee and Alan Basset. There were three survivors of the twenty-five barons, John de Lacy, Richard de Percy and Richard de Munfichet, together with the sons of Eustace de Vesci and Robert de Ros. As Holt remarked, 'Magna Carta was secured within a generation but only just'.[3] After 1237, Henry III confirmed the Charters, with great solemnity, in 1253 and 1265, as did Edward I in 1297 and 1300.

PROCLAMATION AND COPYING

Both the new versions of the Charter and the subsequent confirmations were linked to proclamations of the contents and distributions of the texts.[4] A start here had been made in 1218, when the sheriffs were sent engrossments of the Charters of 1217, and told to read them in their county courts, 'having gathered together the barons, knights and all free tenants of the county'. Then, in 1225, the Charters were again sent to the counties, where the sheriffs were ordered to read and proclaim them.[5] In 1255, following his confirmation of two years before, Henry III ordered further proclamations in 'full county court'. Ten years later, the short-lived Montfortian government sent the 1225 Charters to the counties, where they were to be kept by 'trustworthy men elected for the purpose' and read twice a year in the county court.[6] In 1297, echoing what had happened in 1215, the 1225 Charters were sent to every cathedral, with orders that they be read twice a year 'before the people'. They were also sent to judges, sheriffs and town officials, with orders for their publication. In 1300 the sheriffs were to read the Charters four times a year 'before the people in full county court'.[7] We do not know the language of these readings, but they were probably in French as well as Latin. The 1215 Charter had been translated at once into French, and later in the century it was translated again. Equally translated were the Charters of 1217 and 1225.[8] There was also some move to put the Charter across in English. The 1253 sentence of excommunication against violators of the Charter, as confirmed by the pope, was ordered to be published in French and English. In 1300 Edward I, according to a St Albans chronicle, ordered 'Magna Carta' itself to be declaimed in Westminster Hall, both 'literally', so presumably in Latin, and then 'in the language of the country [*lingua patria*]'.[9]

Of course, whatever the language, these readings can only have gone so far. They were probably one-off rather than regular events, since the schemes of 1265, 1297 and 1300 for several readings a year almost certainly came to nothing. Simon de Montfort's regime collapsed within five months of confirming Magna Carta and Edward I went back on his promises. The proclamations helped raise awareness of the Charters, but can scarcely have got across their complex details. It took me thirty-nine minutes to read out the 1225 Charters, so if they were proclaimed in more than one language, the exercise took well over an hour. Some in the county court may have listened with rapt attention. Others probably went out to the ale house. For getting the detail across, the important things were the actual texts. These were available in cathedrals and elsewhere in the engrossments of 1215, 1216, 1217 and 1225, and in the confirmations of 1265, 1297 and 1300, all of which contained the full 1225 texts. Judging from what survives, these texts were not circulated in equal measure. There is only one known engrossment of the 1216 Charter, that at Durham cathedral. No original confirmations from 1265 survive and one suspects they were not widely distributed, given the political situation. By contrast, there are four engrossments surviving from 1215, 1217 and 1225, together with four of the 1297 confirmation and five or six of the 1300 confirmation.[10]

Alongside these governmental efforts to publicize the Charters, there were also the unofficial efforts of the church. In 1254 each diocese was sent transcripts of the 1225 Charters so that they could be copied out. In 1279 Archbishop Pecham ordered copies of Magna Carta to be put up in cathedral and collegiate churches 'so that everyone entering the church can plainly see it with their eyes'. As a safeguard against wear and tear, he even laid down that the texts were to be renewed each year. In fact, the copies were soon taken down from the church doors, Edward I objecting to this independent initiative, but people now knew where to find them.[11]

From these various texts numerous copies of the Charters were made, and these in turn spawned further copies. The search is ongoing but I have, at present, records of well over a hundred copies of the John or Henry III Magna Carta made in the century after Runnymede.[12] Over thirty of these are of the 1215 Charter. Of the remainder, four come from the 1216 Charter (including the two in the French royal archives), ten from the 1217 Charter, thirty from the Charter of 1225, twenty from various conflations of 1217 and 1225 (of which more shortly) and over thirty from the confirmations of Edward I.[13] This shows the success of Edward I's proclamations, but also that the Charter was well known in some form before then. The greatest repositories were the unofficial legal collections called by modern historians 'statute books', followed by monastic cartularies and chronicles. That knights made their own records is shown by both the 1217 Forest Charter and the 1225 Magna Carta appearing in the cartulary of the Northamptonshire Hotot family.[14]

This plethora of material created some confusion. Many copies of the 1215 Charter, even in statute books, were not of the final, authorized text. Here lay the origin of the belief that the baronial relief was only 100 marks, a sum that was eventually made official when it featured in the 1225 text issued in 1297.[15] There was even more confusion over Henry III's Charters, for frequently copied texts were ones that conflated the versions of 1217 and 1225. The conflations took various forms, but often had the Charter being issued on the advice of Guala and the Marshal, as in 1217, while including Henry acting spontaneously and of his good will in return for a tax, as in 1225. Many conflations also have the Charter being given by the hand of the chancellor, Richard Marsh, thus containing material apparently from drafts.[16] In origin, these conflations, arising from misguided attempts to combine the texts of 1217 and 1225 into a single Charter, were the product of considerable editorial work. They show interest in Magna Carta's detail and actually became better known than straight copies of the 1217 Charter. Interest in the detail is also shown in the way the chapters were numbered and occasionally annotated with marginal comments indicating the subject matter. At Cerne abbey in Dorset interest was shown in another way. A clerk, writing out the 1225 Magna Carta and Forest Charter, had the clever idea of combining them into one. The text was then doctored further by a colleague adding in passages found in the 1217 Charter omitted in 1225.[17] At St Albans, when Matthew Paris finally obtained an authentic copy of the 1215 Charter, he made determined efforts to correct Roger of Wendover's version, which was a wondrous conflation of the texts of 1215, 1217 and 1225.[18] There were also attempts to bring the Charter up to date, the most conspicuous being a single-sheet copy that combined the Charters of 1217 and 1225, and then supplied the date of 11 February 1252, as opposed to 1225, together with a first witness to suit, namely the archbishop of Canterbury, Boniface of Savoy.[19]

Many contemporaries, however, were quite aware, as Paris came to be, that the Charters of John and Henry III were different animals. Thus, in statute books and cartularies, John's Charter sometimes preceded Henry's, and was called the charter, provisions or statute of Runnymede, as against Henry's Magna Carta. Copyists give no sign that the 1215 Charter might be invalid, and superseded by the Charter of Henry III. Pope Innocent III's condemnation of John's Charter was rarely copied.[20] There are likewise few copies of the Charter of 1216, with its observation that some parts of the earlier Charter had been omitted as 'doubtful'. Contemporaries clearly thought the 1215 Charter was still operative. At the parliament of October 1255, the magnates complained that they had not been summoned according to the terms of Magna Carta. This must have been a reference to the Charter of 1215, since the chapter on the form of summons was dropped from the later versions.[21] On a more detailed point, a defendant in a legal action under Edward I claimed that his case should be decided by the 'law of the March' in accordance with the 'statute of Runnymede'. This chapter had been present in the Charter of 1216, but was omitted thereafter.[22]

The abundance of material, whatever its accuracy and validity, all made the detail of the Charter known. It became far more than a vague symbol of good government. In 1219 the whole county court of Lincoln, defending 'the common liberty of all the kingdom conceded and sworn', backed the former rebel Gilbert de Gant when he complained of disseisin 'without judgement'. This seems a clear reference to what had been chapter 39 in the 1215 Charter.[23] Next year, the stewards of the 'magnates' of Yorkshire refused to pay a tax on grounds that echoed the chapters on consent to taxation in the 1215 Charter.[24] As early as 1221, a defendant in an Essex case over the succession to a mere twenty-seven acres of land, one Thomas Crowe, was able to move the litigation from the bench to the justices in eyre on the grounds that 'the king by his charter has conceded that assizes of this kind should be taken in the counties and not outside', a reference to chapter 13 of the 1217 Charter.[25] This appears to be the first successful appeal to Magna Carta in the courts. In 1226 knights in Lincolnshire stoutly defended their interpretation of the chapter on the holding of the county and hundred courts against the activity of the sheriff. It was probably contentions over this chapter that led the king, in the same year, to summon before him four knights from eight counties to settle disputes with the sheriffs over articles in the Charter. Next year, four knights from each county, elected in full county court, were ordered to bring forward complaints against the sheriff 'on articles contained in the charter of liberties'.[26]

These individual examples can be put in a wider context. In pioneering work, Faith Thompson found specific references to twenty-four of the thirty-seven chapters of the 1225 Charter in thirty different years between 1221 and 1306. The social range of those appealing was broad. It included earls, barons, county knights, free tenants, townsmen and churchmen. Thompson compiled this list in the 1920s from the very limited material then in print. A comprehensive trawl through all the sources (especially the plea rolls) would probably increase the references many times over.[27] The Charter was known and valued from top to bottom of society. When the king's council and 'the magnates of England' in 1237 had to decide an unprecedented case about the succession to the earldom of Chester, they turned to 'the charter of liberties' for guidance.[28] The knights of Wiltshire deposited the 1225 engrossment of the Charter sent to their county for safekeeping in Lacock abbey. (It is now in the British Library.) Around 1300 the peasants of Bocking in Essex appealed to Magna Carta in their complaints against the malpractices of their lord's bailiff in the manorial court.[29]

THE IRRELEVANCE OF THE CHARTER

It was one thing for the Charters to be known, another for them actually to impact on the operations of government. On the extent of the impact, contemporaries gave a depressing verdict. They complained over and over again that the Charters were not being enforced. Yet rather than find effective ways to enforce them, they turned to more radical and detailed schemes of reform which suggested that the Charters were at best in need of fundamental strengthening, at worst were becoming out of date. Indeed, the politics of England in the hundred years after 1215 could be seen as a commentary on the inadequacy of Magna Carta.[30]

One immediate problem was that the new versions of the Charter provided no mechanism for reversing the unjust disseisins of King John, something made worse by the fact that the restorations made in 1215 had no validity. The 1225 Charter, by a small addition, indicated that the chapter forbidding unjust disseisin was in no way retrospective: no free man was to be disseised 'henceforth'.[31] The best those with grievances could do was to bring legal actions against the current incumbents, alleging arbitrary disseisin by King John. In this way Humphrey de Bohun, earl of Hereford (son of the Henry de Bohun of John's reign), eventually forced the earl of Salisbury's widow into a compromise over Trowbridge.[32] Such actions, however, were rare. Nothing more was heard of the Quincy claim to Mountsorrel or the fitzWalter claim to Hertford. The new Charters equally provided no mechanism for overthrowing John's unjust fines and amercements. These all remained on the pipe rolls. Few had imitated John de Lacy's nimble footwork in 1215 when he secured a pardon and then two months later joined the rebellion. The abbot of St Albans, in return for four palfreys worth 20 marks, did manage to get the 300-mark forest amercement imposed under John 'by will rather than reason' pardoned.[33] On the other hand, the unpaid Stuteville fine of 10,000 marks provided the means by which Hubert de Burgh secured hold of Knaresborough and Boroughbridge. The Mandevilles and their Bohun heirs remained saddled with Geoffrey de Mandeville's fine to marry the countess of Gloucester, although they had reaped absolutely no benefit from it. At least the king was less energetic in exacting his half of the fine than were Archbishop Langton and his successors when it came to the half granted to Canterbury.[34] Widows likewise were left owing the sums they had promised to remain single and secure their dowers, marriage portions and inheritances. Under John, Margaret, widow of Robert fitzRoger, had not begun to pay off her fine of £1000 to have her inheritance and be allowed to stay single. In the minority of Henry III she was made to pay it off at 100 marks a year.[35]

For immediate political reasons, Henry III entered full power in January 1227, when still only nineteen, but it was not until 1234 that he finally rid himself of Hubert de Burgh and Peter des Roches, the overweening ministers whom he had inherited from his father. Henry's personal rule thereafter, down to its collapse in 1258, seemed in some ways very different from John's. Henry was uxorious and pious. He rebuilt Westminster abbey in honour of his patron saint, Edward the Confessor. He was physically lazy and liked to linger and luxuriate at his favourite palaces in the south. If he had to go north, he hurried back to 'the delight and rest' of Westminster.[36] At heart, Henry wished to be a just and consensual king, giving peace to his people, in the supposed mould of the Confessor. In this respect he was perfectly fitted to a post-Magna Carta age. Yet Henry's rule also raised problems with which the Charter did not deal. Henry was, as contemporaries said again and again, 'simplex', meaning essentially naive, not something that could ever have been said about King John – as Holt once remarked to me with a laugh! This would have mattered less had Henry, here departing from his Confessorian model, not also been ambitious, if in an armchair kind of way. The result was a series of ill-conceived policy initiatives, decided often in private, which culminated in the 1250s in an absurd scheme, concocted by the pope, to place Henry's second son on the throne of Sicily. This project totally alienated the church, which had to find the funds. There was nothing at

all in the Charter that prevented the king signing up to such enter-
prises or pursuing whatever foreign policies he liked.

The Charter also placed no restrictions on the king's ability to
appoint counsellors and give patronage. This too became a major
issue as Henry, warm hearted, open handed and family orientated,
established in England both the Savoyard uncles of his wife, Eleanor of Provence, and his own Poitevin half-brothers, the offspring of
his mother's second marriage after she returned to Angoulême in
1218. The results were factional struggles at court between the
two groups, in which native magnates became involved.[37] Since the
Charter afforded no help in any of these areas, new schemes of
reform emerged that sought to give to parliaments (as great assemblies of the kingdom were increasingly being called) the right to
choose the king's ministers; these ministers would then exercise a
proper control over patronage, expenditure and the dispensation
of justice. Such a programme was already apparent in the 'Paper
Constitution' of 1244. It was finally realized in the great political
revolution of 1258 when the Provisions of Oxford reduced the
king to a cipher and placed government in the hands of a magnate
council of fifteen, responsible to three annual parliaments. The
Charter seemed left far behind.[38]

It seemed left behind too when it came to the growing national-
ism of the period between 1258 and 1265, in which hostility to
the king's foreign relatives played a major part. The 1215 Charter
certainly expelled the foreign mercenaries, who had 'harmed the
kingdom', and dismissed some of John's foreign servants from
office. But it was the reformers of 1258 who demanded that the
king's castles be entrusted to men 'born of the kingdom of England', and defined 'disparagement' as marriage 'to men who are
not of the nation of England'. In 1263 Simon de Montfort added
to the Provisions of Oxford a new 'statute' which confined office
to Englishmen, and, with certain qualifications, expelled foreigners from the kingdom 'never to return'.[39]

Churchmen had their own reasons to deem the Charter inadequate. True, they appealed to chapter 1, which set the church free.
They made great efforts to enforce the Charter generally. But they
also drew up long schedules of complaint about issues on which the
Charter was silent. In two of these schedules from the 1250s, the
Charter only appears in six of the sixty-seven clauses.[40] It was no
specific help when, for example, the government challenged the

jurisdiction of church courts, the immunity of clerks from criminal prosecution, and the claims of various bishops and monastic houses to have the amercements that were imposed on their men by the king's judges.

The Charter seemed equally inadequate when it came to Henry's rule in the shires. Here changes at the centre of government had a malign impact locally. After 1234, as he could perfectly well do under the Charter, Henry left the office of chief justiciar unfilled. After 1238 he no longer had a chancellor in day-to-day charge of the seal. The suspension of these offices impacted locally because there were no longer great, identifiable ministers at the centre to whom those suffering from local officials could go with their complaints. Indeed, it was often unclear who actually held the seal. This did not matter to great men, native and foreign, within the circle of the court. It mattered a lot to the magnates, knights, free tenants, and churchmen and townsmen outside it. The 'Paper Constitution' in 1244 was aware of this problem. The four counsellors it imposed on the king were to hear complaints and help those suffering injustices. In 1258 the Provisions of Oxford restored the office of justiciar with a specific brief 'to uphold right to all persons'.

These changes at the centre became all the more serious as Henry's government began to press down harder on local society. With his income reduced by Magna Carta, and failing to get general taxation from parliament after 1237 (for who would give money to such a king?), Henry had no alternative but to make money in other ways. While his total revenues were far smaller than those of his father, he hit hard at certain targets. He thus exploited the dropping of chapter 25 of the 1215 Charter. This had banned the exaction of increments by name and profits by implication from the counties, thus gravely restricting the money which could be made from the revenues that went towards the county farm.[41] In the process, it had hoped to make the sheriffs, who had to raise the extra sums, less oppressive. Unrestricted by this chapter, between 1241 and 1258 the increments imposed on the counties steadily rose in size. Again it was left to the reformers of 1258 to deal with the issue. Their plan was to get the sheriffs to account for all their revenues, and to give them salaries, which was to attempt the same result as chapter 25 but in another way.[42]

Magna Carta was equally no specific help when it came to the kind of people who were sheriffs. Even the stipulation that officials should know the law of the kingdom had been left out of the post-1215 Charters. Henry took advantage. His sheriffs, according to one schedule of complaint, were 'men coming from far away and utter strangers in their counties'.[43] The reforms of 1258-9, therefore, laid down that the sheriffs should be senior local knights, partly elected in the county court.[44] Henry's government also became more oppressive through the amercements imposed by the justices in eyre. Magna Carta, if obeyed, regulated the level of amercements and said their amounts must be determined by men of the neighbourhood, but it was silent about the range of offences for which amercements might be imposed. Henry's judges, therefore, dreamed up new offences, amercing vills, for example, because not all over the age of twelve had come to coroner's inquests. This was a practice that had to be banned by the reforming legislation of 1259.[45]

There was another great area where Magna Carta's inadequacy was apparent, as indeed it had been from the start. This was its failure to protect men from oppression by their lords.[46] One area of particular concern in Henry's reign was the running of private courts, of both the hundred and the honour.[47] With the growth of the common law, magnates could not compel tenants to litigate in their courts, but they could try to enforce a duty to attend, imposing heavy amercements on tenants when they failed to turn up.[48] In 1234 Henry had tried to make the Charter more relevant to private courts, but it was left to the legislation of 1259 really to tackle the issue of attendance. The Provisions of Westminster, in three lengthy chapters at the start, thus limited the obligation to attend 'the courts of magnates' and provided a remedy for those forced to attend them contrary to its terms. It also abolished in royal courts and 'courts of barons' the fine 'beaupleder', a fine offered before proceedings started, by those attending the court, to escape being penalized for omissions and mistakes in giving evidence. The contrast with the 1217/1225 Magna Carta's regulations on the frequency of courts, which made no specific reference to those of magnates, is striking.[49]

The 1259 legislation also did more than Magna Carta in protecting tenants at the critical moment of succession, when there was always the danger that a lord might seek to deny a new tenant entry into his inheritance. The 1216 Charter had done something about this issue, laying down that a lord must receive a tenant's homage before taking him and his lands into wardship. Now the legislation of 1259 made it possible for tenants to gain damages from their lords if they recovered their inheritances only after litigation.[50]

The contrast between the 1215 Magna Carta and the reforms of 1258–9 in how relations between lords and men were treated was strikingly apparent in the inquiries they both commissioned into local abuses. The inquiry by the knights commissioned by chapter 48 of the 1215 Charter had been entirely into the abuses of the king's local officials. In 1258 the equivalent inquiry, by four knights in each county, was into the malpractices of 'all persons whatsoever'. It was linked to a visitation of the justiciar and other judges, who were to hear complaints against both royal and magnate officials. Many complaints against the latter were indeed brought forward on these eyres. Both royal and magnate officials were also to take the same oath to act justly. The leading reformers even issued a special charter promising to submit themselves and their bailiffs to investigation and correction.[51]

There were several reasons why the grievances of knights and under-tenants bulked larger in 1258–9 than in 1215, thus moving the agenda on beyond Magna Carta. Such grievances had always been there but they were sharpened by the conditions of Henry III's personal rule. His laxness and indulgence had made it possible for both his foreign relatives and English magnates to expand their local rule. The growing army of professional administrators gave them the means to do so.[52] At the same time, the gradual weakening of the tenurial bond, the opportunities offered by the common law, and the increasing role they played in the running of local government gave knights and free tenants more independence and a louder voice.[53] If knights in 1215 protested, as they may well have done, against narrowly baronial schemes of reform like the Unknown Charter, thus helping to move the agenda onto the Articles of the Barons, they protested far more visibly in 1259. At the October parliament a body of knights, described as 'the community of the bachelry of England', protested that 'the barons' had got all they wanted and had done nothing for 'the utility of the republic'. The protest had a result, for it pushed through the Provisions of Westminster with its chapters about attendance at magnate courts and the succession of under-tenants.[54]

There were also ideological developments. The friars, who arrived in England in the 1220s, taught concern for the oppressed. Very much in that spirit, Simon de Montfort, in his will drawn up in 1259, sought to compensate 'the poor people of my land . . . namely the cultivators', whom he might have oppressed.[55] Such sentiments help to explain another respect in which the reforms of 1258–9 contrasted with Magna Carta, namely the way they seemed to reach out to peasants, free and unfree. There was none of the blatant discrimination against the unfree found in Magna Carta. Investigations after the fall of the Montfortian regime show peasants in the armies, raiding bands and garrisons of the period. In 1265 itself, in a famous incident just after the battle of Evesham, the peasants of Peatling Magna in Leicestershire obstructed royalists going through the village, on the grounds that they were acting 'against the welfare of the community of the realm and the barons'. Evidently, the peasants felt part of the community of the realm, and believed that the barons were acting in its interests.[56] The rhetoric of the period was far more inclusive than it had been in 1215.[57] The leading reformers in 1259 swore that their officials would take nothing unjustly from 'free man or villein'. Likewise the justiciar set up by the reforms swore to give justice to 'rich and poor, serf and free'.[58] There was also some reality behind these sentiments. The legislation of 1258–9 benefited peasants, free and unfree alike, by limiting the numbers who had to come to coroners' inquests, restricting the incidence of the 'murdrum' fine and abolishing the beaupleder fine in private courts.[59] It was to the legislation of beaupleder, in a later form, that the peasants of Swaffham Prior in Cambridgeshire appealed when resisting the exactions of the prior of Ely.[60] In striking contrast to what seems to have happened in 1215, key reforms in 1258 were proclaimed in English as well as French and Latin.[61]

Another contrast between 1215 and 1258–65 lay in the quality of leadership. There was no equivalent in the earlier period to Simon de Montfort.[62] At the start in 1258 he was the most passionate and committed of the reformers. He upbraided backsliders and harped again and again on the oath everyone had taken to support the Provisions of Oxford. He was the only magnate who refused to accept the king's recovery of power in 1261, instead retiring to France. He returned to England in 1263 to place himself at the head of a movement calling for the revival of the

Provisions of Oxford. He was now the sole leader of the opposition. Between his victory at Lewes in May 1264 and his death at the battle of Evesham in August 1265, he was the effective ruler of England. No one had achieved such prominence in 1215. Equally no one was driven, as far as we know, by such a sense of idealistic purpose. At first sight, Montfort should have been the last person to lead a movement against the king, especially one with hostility to foreigners at its heart. He was a younger son of the great French noble, also called Simon de Montfort (of Montfort l'Amaury just outside Paris), who had led the Albigensian crusade and been canvassed as John's successor during the plot of 1212. Montfort junior had come to England in 1230. He had made good the family claim to the earldom of Leicester and married Eleanor, Henry III's sister.[63] Surely he would now be a mainstay of the king's regime. Not a bit of it. Montfort was driven into opposition by material grievances and personal slights. Surrounded by idealistic churchmen, and remembering the heroism of his father, he also came to see the cause of reform as a crusade. He believed that 'the common enterprise' must be about more than the selfish interests of the great barons. Had there been a leader like that in 1215, Magna Carta might have looked rather different.

Montfort certainly believed Magna Carta was important. Indeed, during the great parliament which he held between January and March 1265, he made Henry III confirm it, and ordered that its violators be severely punished.[64] When, moreover, Montfort devised a writ allowing legal actions against the levying of the beaupleder fine in private courts, he cloaked it in the authority of the Charter, rather than in that of the 1259 legislation where in fact it appears.[65] Yet Montfort's regime depended, of course, not on Magna Carta but on the far more radical Provisions of Oxford. To them he added in 1263 the 'statute' against the aliens. The extent to which he had gone beyond the Charter was clear when it came to the composition of his parliaments. Parliament, as envisaged in the Charter of 1215, was an assembly composed entirely of tenants-in-chief. Although there was a move to include knights from the shires in 1254, this had only been for the purposes of getting a tax and in unusual circumstances. There were no county representatives called for in parliament as envisaged in the reforms of 1258. All this changed in the revolutionary period that followed, in large part thanks to Montfort's drive and vision.[66] With

his allies, he summoned three knights from each county to a baronial assembly in 1261. In June 1264, after his victory at Lewes,
he summoned from each shire four elected knights to parliament
to discuss the affairs of the realm. And then, for his parliament of
1265 he summoned two knights from each county and two burgesses from each of the towns. This was the first time that knights
and burgesses had been summoned together to parliament, the
House of Commons in embryo.[67] Here too Montfort had left the
Charter far behind.

The inadequacy of the Charter was, therefore, very apparent by
the end of Henry's reign in 1272. The reign of his son, Edward I
(r. 1272–1307), posed a set of new problems for which once again
the Charter was of limited help. From 1294, Edward placed burdens on his kingdom as heavy as King John's in order to support
his wars in France, Wales and Scotland. He was made to confirm
the Charters but he also, in 1297 and 1300, made a series of new
concessions that brought them up to date. One key issue concerned the king's right of prise or compulsory purchase. The
Charter had something on this, insisting on prompt payment for
the taking of corn and other chattels, and horses and carts.[68] But it
said nothing about the scale of such takings, and these Edward
expanded way beyond what was customary. One of the new articles
in 1300, therefore, regulated prise in detail, trying to make sure
goods were only taken by authorized officials to support the king's
household.[69]

BREACHES OF MAGNA CARTA

If one problem with the Charter was its irrelevance, another was
that even when it was relevant, it was not obeyed. A lengthy schedule from 1264, criticizing Henry III's rule, thus started with all the
ways in which he had breached the Charter.[70] First up was Henry's
ruthless exploitation of ecclesiastical vacancies and his manipulation of elections, grievous breaches of his promise in the Charter
to set the church free.[71] A great deal of space was also devoted to
Henry's denial of justice, thus breaching chapter 40 of the 1215 Charter, which became part of chapter 29 in 1225. Such abuse did not
affect the general run of people in their litigation against each other
according to the forms of the common law. It very much affected

them when up against Henry's favourites and their followers. The
latter were protected from legal actions and placed, so it seemed,
above the law. As a result, their local officials felt they had a free rein.
'If I do you wrong, who is there to do you right?', asked William
de Bussey, steward of the king's half-brothers.[72] The beneficiaries
were not just the king's foreign relatives. They also included great
English nobles such as the king's brother, Richard, earl of Cornwall, and Richard de Clare, earl of Gloucester. The victims were
magnates outside the charmed circle of the court, together with
knights, free tenants and local communities, many of whom finally
made their complaints in 1258–9.[73]

The complaint that the Charters were not being enforced locally
was put to Henry himself very clearly in 1254 in a letter from the
regents, the king then being in Gascony. 'Many complain that the
Charters are not kept by the sheriffs and your other bailiffs.' If,
therefore, Henry wanted a tax, he must order the Charters to be
upheld by the sheriffs and have this publicly proclaimed.[74] Contemporaries were quite able to allege violations of specific chapters. In
defiance of chapter 4 of the 1225 Magna Carta, wardships were
being pillaged – there is no evidence in that case of their being
entrusted to two men of the fee, as the Charter required. In defiance of chapter 18, chattels were being seized on the death of
tenants-in-chief on the pretext of debts owed the crown – there is
no evidence of the procedure being used by which letters patent
were first to prove the existence of a debt. The king's power over
wardships was increased by the development of the office of escheator, unmentioned in the Charter, whose brief was to deal with
land coming into the hands of the crown.[75] Other alleged breaches
of the Charter included amercements being imposed by justices,
sheriffs, bailiffs and stewards at their will and pleasure, this instead
of being assessed by local men according to the nature of the
offence. According to a legal tract, called *The Mirror of Justices*,
written in London in the late thirteenth century, if assessors were
employed, then they sometimes had to act in the houses of magnates rather than in a public place.[76] As the complaint here shows,
this was another grievance against private as well as royal courts.
Indeed, when in the 1260s, probably during the Montfortian regime,
a writ was drawn up making possible legal actions against breaches
of the amercements chapter in the Charter, it was directed against the
lords of private courts. In the 1270s the bishop of Worcester was

accused directly of breaching the Charter when imposing amercements in his hundred court of Henbury in Gloucestershire.[77]

Another area of local discontent concerned the forest. In 1225 the government at last accepted the counties' interpretation of chapter 1 of the Forest Charter, and the result was extensive deforestation. Then, however, when Henry III assumed full power in 1227, some of the deforestations were reversed, on the grounds that chapter 1 only meant to deforest what Henry II had added to the forest, having restored the losses in Stephen's reign. This was another grievance raised in 1258. It was raised again under Edward I. Between 1301 and 1305 he was forced to accept extensive deforestations under the Charter's terms, only then in 1306, like Henry III, to reverse them.[78]

There was also debate and discontent over the government's treatment of the new chapter introduced in 1217 (chapter 35 in 1225) on the running of the local courts. In 1234 the king had seemed to accept that, under its terms, the hundred and wapentake courts should be held by the sheriff only twice a year. This view lay behind the protests of the Lincolnshire knights in 1226 against the activities of their sheriff. Then, however, a couple of months later in 1234, the king changed his mind. He had some reason for doing so, because the chapter actually said that it was the tourn, the especially well-attended session of the hundred and wapentake courts, which was to be held twice a year. On other sessions the chapter was silent. The king now explained that the relevant chapter of the Charter had been read before the great and good of the kingdom. They had decided that just two tourns a year were insufficient for keeping the peace. Between such sessions, the courts of hundred and wapentake and the courts of magnates should meet once every three weeks. This was presented as a concession, since under Henry II, so the king said, fortnightly meetings had been customary.[79] Local opinion was hardly appeased. In Lincolnshire, in 1237, the Charter was read again, this time in the hundred and wapentake courts, and it was asserted that they should only meet twice a year.[80] Lincolnshire was not alone in straining the meaning of the Charter. In Northumberland, in 1269, 'the community of the county' complained that whereas, 'according to the tenor of Magna Carta', they had been free of the sheriff's tourn, the sheriff, William Heron, had held two tourns a year, and amerced those who did not turn up 'at his will'. Yet the Charter actually said nothing to justify such freedom from the tourn, and Heron could have said he was merely enforcing the two yearly tourns that it allowed.[81]

In the examples mentioned above at least the Charter was appealed to. Yet there are many cases where it was breached in silence, either because it was unknown or because it was thought to be irrelevant. When the justiciar, Hugh Bigod, visited Kent and Surrey in 1258–9, he heard complaints about the forest, the tourn, amercements, imprisonment and wardships, all of which could be seen as breaches of the Charter, yet the Charter was not once mentioned. While in the hands of one of the king's Poitevin half-brothers, the woods and fish ponds of Geoffrey de Lucy had been destroyed and the buildings allowed to go to ruin – clear breaches of the Charter, but Lucy did not say so.[82]

ENFORCEMENT

If Magna Carta was being breached, what could one do about it? The answer was not nothing, but still not enough. By far the most striking attempts at enforcement lay in the ecclesiastical sentences of excommunication. These had begun in 1225 with that of Archbishop Langton. They continued in 1237, when Henry's confirmation of the Charters was linked to a sentence promulgated by the archbishop of Canterbury, Edmund of Abingdon, one of Langton's former pupils. Thereafter excommunications were pronounced at the time of all the confirmations. Easily the best known was that fulminated in 1253 by Archbishop Boniface of Savoy and thirteen bishops before a great audience in Westminster Hall. This sentence was given massive publicity by the church, and was copied into numerous cartularies and statute books, often alongside the Charters.[83] Unfortunately, complaints that the sentences were ignored went hand in hand with complaints about breaches of the Charter.[84] The sentences were supposed first and foremost to have a deterrent effect. The king and everyone else, it was hoped, would live in their fear, and act accordingly. Those who had incurred the sentence should seek absolution, and, of course, behave better in the future. In 1237 Henry III and his barons, 'fearful' that they had indeed fallen under the sentence, asked for absolution from Archbishop Edmund. They were given it with the warning not to violate the Charter again or they would relapse into their previous excommunicated state.[85] The episode highlighted the value of excommunication, as opposed to the old security clause, in that it applied to everyone breaching the Charter, not just the king and his ministers. The trouble was that all this depended on the transgressors recognizing their faults and acting accordingly. If, on the other hand, they denied any misconduct, nothing happened. In 1253 there was an attempt to make the procedure more pointed. Anyone who did not acknowledge the violation was to incur the sentence of excommunication if, once warned, matters were not put right within fifteen days, this by the judgement of the ordinary, that is the bishop or the archdeacon. The king, however, refused to accept this entirely ecclesiastical procedure and said the cases were to be referred to the judgement of his court. Either way, these schemes seem to have had no practical effect.[86]

There were also various secular avenues for enforcing the Charter. An appeal to it was very likely to be upheld in the courts, as we see from Thomas Crowe's case as early as 1221.[87] When Edward I, in 1297, enjoined his judges to allow the Charters in all their points in the cases before them, he was affirming what had long been practice.[88] In Crowe's case, the violation of the Charter came up in the course of the proceedings, and was not the actual origin of the action. But it was also possible to begin a legal action by writ in cases where the Charter had been breached. One of the most significant and popular of such writs was that available to a widow seeking her 'reasonable dower'. The writ did not mention Magna Carta's provisions on dower, but in effect the litigation was a way of enforcing them.[89] Other writs made specific mention of the Charter, most notably the one founded on the chapter about the levying of amercements. This, however, only appears in the 1260s, and hardly led to a flow of litigation, important though the issue was.[90] The *Mirror of Justices*, trying to solve the problem of enforcement, suggested that those deprived of liberties in the Charter should recover them with damages by an action of novel disseisin. That may have been impractical, but it suggests something more was required.[91]

Another avenue for those seeking redress was through the evidence given by the twelve jurors representing each hundred during visitations of the justices in eyre. Several of the questions put to the juries by the judges, without mentioning the Charter, covered issues it dealt with, as for example prises and the holding of pleas of the crown. Breaches of the Charter could also be raised under questions about the introduction of new customs and the excesses of the sheriffs.[92] Given the personnel of the juries on hundreds, this was a way in which free tenants, including those from the peasantry, could ventilate their grievances. They could do so, moreover, without the time and expense involved in litigation by writ.[93] There is, however, very little evidence that this was a route much followed. General eyres were only held once every seven years or so. The judges hardly encouraged appeals to the Charter, for, in their articles of inquiry, there was no question explicitly on the subject of Magna Carta. The only time a question relating to the Charter appeared was during the reforming eyre of 1259. It was not until 1280 that questions were introduced relevant to Magna Carta's chapters on amercements and the tourn.[94] It must also have been difficult to complain about sitting sheriffs and powerful magnates. The complaints against the sheriff William Heron only emerged after he had left office. In Heron's case, moreover, the men of Northumberland went not direct to the eyre but to the king. Henry III then ordered the justices in eyre to stage an inquiry.[95] A complaint to the king was thus another way of initiating an action about the Charter, but again this does not seem to have been a popular procedure, perhaps because it was not advertised and encouraged; and because it was not a regular procedure, the king's response remained a matter of grace.

In all this, one obvious way of enforcing Magna Carta in the localities was not adopted, namely that of setting up permanent panels of judges in each county with commissions to hear complaints about breaches of the Charter. This would have made it much easier for lower sections of society to secure speedy redress. The need for such a procedure was perfectly appreciated. When William of Horton, a monk of St Albans and its legal expert, explained in the 1250s why the Charters were not observed, he said it was because 'specific keepers are not appointed to hear the complaints of the community'. In fact, it was not until 1300 that three knights were appointed in each county to hear such cases.[96] They did not last long, since Edward I soon reneged on his concessions. Anyway, the reform came seventy-five years too late. Had such panels been introduced in 1225, they might have had a real effect. The truth is that, while the king was very ready to proclaim the Charters, and say that everyone must obey them, he was never willing to set up proper procedures to see that that actually happened. To have done so would have risked creating rival centres of authority in the shires, a bit like those threatened by the twelve knights of 1215. Not surprisingly, the only occasion before 1300 when such of panels of knights were envisaged was during the short-lived reforms of 1259, and even here there was concern about how their work might affect the sheriffs in the performance of their duties.[97] King John's vision of the Charter as a vague symbol of good government with limited practical consequences seems to have been exactly that of his successors. Both Henry III and Edward I could actually have done more to distribute their actual texts. Apart from the Montfortian confirmation of 1265, there was no official distribution of the texts between 1225 and 1297; hence the need felt to concoct up-to-date versions such as that of 1252, and the importance of the church's independent distributions. To these, as we have noted, King Edward actually objected and in 1279 ordered copies of the Charter to be taken down from the church doors.[98]

In dragging their feet over enforcing the Charter, the kings were, to some extent, at one with the great magnates. The latter might appeal to the Charter if they felt they were being denied justice, but as for having it enforced against themselves, that was quite a different matter. The last thing they wanted to see was a panel of knights in each county who might, like those envisaged in 1259, 'inquire about the bailiffs of the great men in the land, and about the great men themselves'.[99] Henry III repeatedly demanded that magnates themselves observe the Charter, but it was largely talk, in part designed to deflect the accusation that he was not obeying it himself. In reality, he was not prepared to upset his own officials or the great men of the land by any rigorous policy of enforcement. King and magnates seemed engaged in a conspiracy against everyone else.

THE TRIUMPH OF MAGNA CARTA

We have painted a pretty dismal picture of the Charter in the first years of its history. It is fortunately but a partial one. The Charter's impact in the thirteenth century was actually very great. Its arrival does mark a 'before' and 'after' in English history. For a start, the efforts at publication and enforcement meant that the fact of the Charter was enormously well known. Even for those who knew merely the fact and not the details, the fact was massive, for it embodied the basic principle of the Charter. The king was now subject to the law. This idea had, of course, a long pedigree, but now its truth was proved in a document of unimpeachable authority and overwhelming fame. Many, moreover, did know the detail of the Charter. The 'assertiveness and self-confidence' of local communities 'grew directly from its provisions'.[100] Magna Carta was empowering. Although, moreover, many of the reforms of 1258–9 and the later legislation of Edward I went far beyond Magna Carta, in a real sense they were building on its foundations. One can see that in the way a great schedule of complaint against the rule of Henry III, drawn up in 1264, made its starting point the breaches of the Charter before going on to other abuses.[101]

In some areas, the Charter was arguably at least a little more effective than the complaints made out. Henry himself would have denied that he was in breach of the Charter when it came to the church. He was certainly guiltless of keeping bishoprics empty so that he could take their revenues, in the manner of the twelfth-century kings. The long vacancies in his time arose when he objected to the person elected, as King John's charter acknowledged he could if the grounds were 'reasonable', and Henry would certainly have said they were that. If his officials breached the Charter in their ruthless exploitation of vacancies, Henry did sometimes try to restrain them.[102] Under Edward I, there were no major disputes over episcopal elections. Indeed, in 1279, Edward accepted the papal appointment of the Franciscan scholar John Pecham as archbishop of Canterbury, despite having lobbied hard for his chancellor, Robert Burnel. The king's conduct here contrasted sharply with that of John over Archbishop Langton.[103]

Some of the Charter's most important chapters were obeyed. Nothing for earls and barons was more important than the £100 relief, and by and large that was the sum charged after 1216 for those inheriting when they were of full age.[104] Since John had charged reliefs of hundreds, sometimes thousands of pounds, this was a remarkable change, one that hit both royal revenue and royal power.

The Charter also made a real difference to the widows of tenants-in-chief. The stipulation here, as in 1215, was that no widow should be forced to remarry if she wished to live without a husband, provided she gave security that she would not remarry without the king's consent. The implication was that the marriages of widows were no longer in the king's gift.[105] At first sight, this seems to have had little effect since post-1215 government records frequently talk of such marriages as belonging to the king. In the fine rolls between 1216 and 1234, moreover, fourteen men offered the king money to marry widows. These offers are not, however, all that they seem. In three cases the need for the widow's consent was mentioned, in one it had to be in writing.[106] In others, what was probably being bought was the king's consent to a marriage which had already been agreed by both parties, a consent which remained necessary under the Charter. In others again, the king probably accepted that the widow might refuse the marriage, and he was simply granting any fine she might make to marry whom she wished. In 1243 these were the terms under which Henry III granted the marriage of Margery, countess of Warwick, to his favourite, John de Plessis.[107] Since the Charter acknowledged the need for the king's consent, he was within his rights in demanding money to waive the right. What was no longer allowed was King John's practice of charging money for permission to stay single, and here a real change is apparent. In his sixteen-year reign, there were fifty-nine fines made by widows for, among other things, such permission. In the twenty-six years between 1216 and 1242, the fine rolls reveal only five.[108] The thirteenth century was distinguished by many famous noble women who, profiting from the terms of the Charter, elected to remain single, and enjoyed long years of widowhood. One such widow, Isabella, countess of Arundel, upbraided Henry III to his face about breaches of the Charter.[109] The king was also less than stringent in enforcing his right to consent. As far as can be seen, there was no routine system for taking security from widows.[110] Henry's order in 1243 that Warwick castle be seized as security from Margery, countess of Warwick, was altogether exceptional, as were the pressures that made her in the end marry John de Plessis. Indeed, Henry plaintively observed, in issuing the order over Warwick castle, that 'very many ladies of the kingdom have got themselves married obscurely to whomsoever they wished, without asking our permission, and spurning the security they ought to give'.[111]

Another area in which widows profited was that of entry into their inheritances, dowers and marriage portions. Magna Carta directed that this should be free, and there are few examples of such payments in Henry III's fine rolls. When Alice, widow of Henry de Neville, offered 100 marks in 1227 to marry freely, her marriage portion and dower were given her without charge.[112] Widows, when litigating under the writ of dower we have mentioned, likewise gained from the new section in the 1217 Charter stipulating that the dower should be a third of the land held by a husband during his (married) lifetime, unless a smaller portion had been agreed at the time of the wedding. This helped lay to rest the lingering idea that a dower was only due from the land the husband held on the day of the marriage. The widow was thus entitled to a dower in her husband's acquisitions. The Charter also played a part in making it possible for widows to turn down any nominated dower and have instead the third as defined by Magna Carta.[113]

Magna Carta had acted against women in general by stating that no one was to be arrested or imprisoned on the accusation of a woman for the death of anyone other than her husband. This restriction was not, however, designed to limit the actual occasions on which women could bring appeals. Indeed, in so far as it lessened the pre-trial consequences for a man accused of killing someone other than a husband, it may have helped appeals in such cases to continue. Certainly, a sample of over 1,200 female appeals found in plea rolls between 1194 and 1294, with most of the evidence coming post-1215, shows that the legal rule restricting female appeals to the killing of husbands, rape and other bodily injury was not automatically enforced. Female appeals were also made in large numbers, constituting 36 per cent of the whole. Of the 126 rape accusations, only nineteen resulted in a conviction, but another thirty-five ended in a settlement. In general, the outcomes in female-prosecuted cases were not very different from those prosecuted by men. The women seem to have appeared personally. Women, therefore, mostly of peasant status, were very much public figures in the courts. Their presence, however, diminished in the course of the century as the number of appeals both by men and by women declined, leaving prosecution much more exclusively in the hands of local juries. Women, of course, did not sit on juries. But at least this change was the by-product of the general decline in the appeal rather than the result of any particular animus against women.[114]

When it came to legal actions being brought against his favourites, Henry was certainly prepared to deny justice, as we have said. But he did not sell it. His fine and pipe rolls are quite innocent of the offers of money for 'justice' that feature on those of King John. To that extent, Henry did obey chapter 40 of the 1215 Charter. Henry also, perhaps most important of all, obeyed chapter 39. Unlike his predecessors, he did not disseise men of property without judgement, by acts of will.[115] By the same token, he did not demand large sums of money for the return of such properties and the recovery of his grace. There was just one period of his reign when Henry sought to emulate the actions of his father. This was between 1232 and 1234 when, having dismissed Hubert de Burgh, he came under the spell of Peter des Roches. The result was a civil war, des Roches's dismissal and the solemn reversal of the disseisins that Henry committed. The basic principles of the Charter in this vital area had been vindicated.[116] Henry never attempted such actions again.[117] Hence the total contrast between the revolutions of 1215 and 1258. In 1215 the disseisins committed by John, as indeed by Richard and Henry II, were major issues. Many of John's were reversed in the weeks after Magna Carta. In 1258 the office of justiciar was revived with a brief to give justice to everyone. But his chief business was to deal with local grievances. He heard only one major case in which a disseisin by the king was alleged, and on that he gave no judgement, in part because the claim (Roger de Mortimer's to Lechlade) was far from clear-cut.[118]

Earls and barons also gained from the chapter on amercements, which, the Charter said, were to be assessed by their peers in accordance with the scale of the offence. This was designed to prevent amercements being imposed arbitrarily either by the exchequer or by will of the king. It has been said the chapter was a failure, but that is far from the case.[119] *Bracton*, it is true, said that judgement by peers could mean either judgement by the barons of the exchequer or judgement before the king himself.[120] There is good evidence, however, that in Henry's reign the latter was the norm. There survives from the 1250s a record sent to the exchequer of amercements imposed on barons and others of equivalent status 'before the king' – '*coram rege*'. The amercements in question had arisen from convictions before the justices in eyre, so it looks as though it was routine for such cases to go to the court *coram rege* for the amercements to be imposed.[121] Likewise, in 1241, it was stated that barons who had committed forest offences were amerced 'before the lord king'. In the majority of cases we have no information as to what amercement *coram rege* involved, but it is very unlikely that it was simply by will of the king. Instead, the armercements were probably assessed by the court *coram rege*, which was presided over by professional judges and could be strengthened by the attendance of a baron's peers if necessary. In routine cases, this may or may not have happened, but there are some very clear examples of a baron's peers intervening and restraining the king in cases of great moment. In 1241 a court composed of twenty earls, barons, magnates and ministers dismissed out of hand Henry's claim that he had suffered damage to the tune of 10,000 marks at the hands of Gilbert Marshal, earl of Pembroke (the former regent's son). Again, in 1256, when Henry by his own will slapped a £100 amercement on the bishop of Bath, it was then reduced to 50 marks 'by consideration of the peers of the bishop in the presence of the king'.[122] There are also reasons for thinking that, in the same year, the astronomical amercement of 100,000 marks, which an emotional Henry in a wholly exceptional case wished to impose on Robert de Ros, was reduced by a court, including Ros's peers, to 1,000 marks. (Ros was a son of the baron of 1215. His offence was mistreating the king's young daughter, wife of Alexander III of Scotland, while the pair were in his care in Edinburgh castle.)

Apart from saying that amercements of earls and barons should be assessed by their peers, the Charter also stipulated that their size should match the offence. Under Henry III, it was not uncommon for lay and ecclesiastical barons to be amerced £100 for offences that came under the broad heading of contempt of court. These sums seem large, but they were probably considered commensurate with baronial status. The amounts were often left unpaid or pardoned.[123] The scale of amercements imposed *coram rege*, found on the record mentioned above, were far more modest. In the twenty-three cases recorded, they ranged from 5 marks to £20. The amercement of earls and barons in 1258 was a dog that did not bark. Evidently it was no longer an issue. Magna Carta had done its work. That had another important consequence and one intended by the framers of the Charter. Because earls and barons were confident that amercements would be reasonable in size, they no longer felt the need to offer large sums of money for the king's benevolence.[124]

Earls and barons, then, profited from the Charter. So did the king's knightly tenants-in-chief, since the £5 relief for a knight's fee was observed just as much as the £100 relief. The lack of protest on the issues suggests that lords themselves obeyed the Charter when it came to assessing the reliefs and treating the widows of their under-tenants. Knights and under-tenants also gained from continued expansion of the common law, which the Charter sought to facilitate. The stipulation that common pleas were to be held in a fixed place, which meant either the eyres or the bench at Westminster, was completely obeyed. Indeed, the expansion over the century of litigation at the bench was absolutely phenomenal.[125] As for the common pleas in the localities, the watered-down chapter in the 1217 Charter by which judges were to travel once a year through the counties to hear the assizes, with knights of the county, was never implemented. Instead, groups of four local knights, and later individual judges who probably co-opted knights to sit with them, were commissioned, on demand, to hear individual assizes. These commissions usually cost half a mark or so, and were thus not as cheap as the 6d writs 'of course', which could begin actions at the general eyre. Essentially they were for speeding up the judicial process, at a cost that seemed reasonable and was not regarded as the selling of justice. The commissions were bought in increasing numbers. In the fine roll for the regnal year 1256–7, some 270 were purchased. Henry was making the common law available in a way that John had failed to do. Indeed, the fine roll of 1256–7, in total, had around 500 offers of money to buy writs that would initiate or further common-law legal actions. In the fine roll of 1207–8, there were seventy of them.[126] The rolls, moreover, do not record at all the purchase of the 6d writs 'of course', which were still perfectly available and were bought in large numbers when eyres were imminent. Magnates certainly got their way in respect of the writ 'precipe'. Here the chapter (24 in the 1225 Charter) banning its issue if it undermined private courts was obeyed. Indeed the writ disappeared, but it was a victory of little significance. As *The Mirror of Justices* observed, there were many other writs by which 'lords lose the cognizance of matters concerning their fees and the profits of their courts'.[127]

In the area of the forest, Henry had been less dismissive of the Forest Charter than his critics claimed. Although some of the deforestations implemented in 1225 were reversed, others stood, and the result was a substantial reduction in the area of the royal forest. In effect a working compromise was achieved with the counties, which was not altered, despite the grumbles, in 1258. Equally, given all the controversy over chapter 35 (in the 1225 Charter) on the running of the county and hundred courts, it is difficult to believe that the sheriffs did not tread more carefully. Conceivably more research into their financial returns may provide some detail here. Much more significant was the victory of local society when it came to the type of person who should be sheriff. The desire of the counties to have a local man in the office had been behind the stipulation in chapter 45 of the 1215 Charter that sheriffs and other officials should know and wish to obey 'the law of the kingdom' or, as the Articles of the Barons put it, 'the law of the land'. The chapter had been omitted after 1215, as we have seen. The reforms of 1258–9, insisting that the sheriff should be a local knight, had not outlasted the king's recovery of power. But then in 1278, Edward I, in an act of conciliation, removed all the sheriffs and replaced them with knights from their own counties. It was county knights who were the usual sheriffs thereafter.[128] With the introduction in the next century of the justice of the peace, local society had won its struggle to provide local government with its personnel. The 1215 Charter, in its chapter 45, and in the role it assigned to elected knights in each county as judges and as reformers of abuse, had pointed the way to that victory.

The Londoners knew Magna Carta well, and made copies of both John's and Henry's Charter. They may have gained little from its confirmation of their liberties, which were suspended many times in the thirteenth century.[129] At least, however, the chapter removing fish weirs from the rivers had some effect, in part through their own efforts.[130]

What of the unfree? Was the change in 1225 that saw the king granting the Charter to 'all men', as opposed to 'all free men', just Langtonian rhetoric? Perhaps not quite. Death and mutilation seem to have been abolished as penalties for forest offences, so peasants gained there. If exactions at the view of frankpledge were modified, then they gained there too. They may also have profited from the chapter (14 in 1225) on amercements, which said that for villeins, as for everyone else, these should be assessed by men of the neighbourhood. On the visitations of the king's judges, or eyres, amercements were generally assessed by knights and leading men of the hundreds, so by good men of the neighbourhood in accordance with the Charter.[131] This was probably the usual procedure before 1215, but the Charter at least made it harder to breach. The villeins were, of course, under the terms of the Charter, only protected from excessive amercements imposed by the king, not by their lords (and the king's villeins, from 1217, not at all).[132] But both the principle and practice of the chapter spilled over into manorial courts. It was in the spirit of the Charter that Walter of Henley's book on the running of manors, written in the second half of the thirteenth century, urged lords to see that those 'falling into danger of their courts' were amerced by their peers. This was not just a pious aspiration. In 1229, on the manors of the bishopric of Durham, amercements were assessed by local men, according to the scale of the offence ('delictum'), and saving a free man his means of livelihood ('contenementum'), a merchant his merchandise, and a rustic his wainage, which was almost a direct quote from Magna Carta. Perhaps a growth in such procedures helps explain the evidence that amercements in manorial courts declined in size in the later thirteenth century.[133]

There was also an idea that villeins might have some redress against their lords if Magna Carta's chapter on amercements was breached. *Bracton*, in a passage not found in *Glanvill* or other sources, opined that villeins had an action against their lords 'if the wrong is an insufferable one, as where their lords so strip them that their wainage cannot be saved them'.[134] In the 1260s the writ that enabled legal actions to be taken against amercements in private courts in breach of Magna Carta stated that villeins were to be amerced saving their 'wainage'. The implication was that the action was available to them, although under the strict terms of the Charter it should not have been.[135] It was this very chapter in Magna Carta that the peasants of Bocking in Essex appealed to around 1300. Whereas previously their amercements had been assessed by their peers, and in accordance with the offence, now the lord's bailiff was amercing them at will, two or three times as much, 'against the Great Charter which holy church ought to uphold'.[136]

How far the unfree were able to take concrete advantage of these opportunities is another matter. There appear to be no examples of villeins bringing actions against their lords on the issue of amercements. The fact that the peasants of Bocking appealed to the church to uphold the Charter speaks volumes. Nor did *Bracton*'s view on the issue go unchallenged. A later interpolation into the text said that 'whenever the lord pleases he can take away from his villein his wainage and all his goods'.[137] In the Charter, it was only the free tenements that were protected from demands for more than due service. The author of *The Mirror of Justices* observed that if this chapter (10 in 1225) had covered land held in villeinage (as he thought it should), then there would 'hardly be a man in the realm who has tenants and who does not trespass against it by himself or his ministers'.[138]

The benefits of Magna Carta, therefore, were far from spread evenly across society, yet all sections of society (apart from the Jews) had some stake in it. Everyone, moreover, was affected in some way by the momentous change in kingship that the Charter's letter and spirit helped bring about. The kind of arbitrary, indeed tyrannical rule seen under King John had disappeared. In the fine roll of 1207–8 there were twelve offers of money, totalling some £5,580, to escape the king's rancour and recover his benevolence. In Henry III's fine roll for 1256–7, there is only one (of £500), and it was quite untypical. In all the rolls of Henry's personal rule between 1236 and 1258 there are only four more such fines with a total value of £1,673. There was equally no equivalent in the rolls between 1236 and 1258 of the fines so common under John to recover land seized into the king's hands. There are thirteen of these in the fine roll of 1207–8 alone. This was all part of a gigantic decline in royal revenue generally from fines offering money to the king for concessions and favours. In 1207–8 John was offered some £22,000. In 1256–7 the amount offered Henry III was around £4,000. The average promised John in the rolls of 1199–1200, 1204–5, 1207–8 and 1213–4 was £26,500. Under Henry, between 1234 and 1242, it was £4,000.[139] Although these figures are subject to all kinds of qualifications and distortions (in 1241–2 there was one fine for a wardship of £6,666), taken as a whole they illustrate, in graphic fashion, the collapse of the king's ability to extract money by arbitrary means. Of course, as Henry was well aware, there remained ways, within the law of the land, in which he could seize property in order to enforce the payment of debts, but, when it came to his leading magnates, he rarely resorted to them.

He was much more likely to set reasonable terms for repayment. Henry's indulgent personality was a factor in this extraordinary contrast with the reign of his father, but there was more to it than that. Fine income did not recover under the hard-driving Edward I. In the roll of 1304–5 the total offered him was £1,121 with thirty-eight 'reasonable reliefs', which were presumably levied according to the terms of Magna Carta. Kingship seemed totally different from what it had been one hundred years before.[140] It seemed different in another way. During his personal rule, Henry took not a single hostage.

There was one other consequence of the Charter that was felt by all sections of society. This was the emergence of the tax-based parliamentary state. Because the letter and spirit of the Charter, coming on top of the decline in easy money from royal lands, stopped up so many sources of royal income, the post-1215 kings desperately needed general taxation to fill the gap. Yet here the Charter kicked in again, because it laid down that taxation could only be levied with the common consent of the kingdom, which came to mean the consent of parliament. True, the chapter on consent was left out of the post-1215 Charters, but the magnates still believed it was valid. The engrossments of the 1215 Charter, and the numerous copies of it that circulated, helped to confirm this belief. Henry III found it impossible to raise taxation without consent. The episode in 1220, when the stewards of the Yorkshire magnates claimed that their lords had not been consulted over a tax, made the point. The lack of consultation was probably true, although more by the incompetence of the minority government than by design.[141] Henry, in line with the 1215 Charter, later sought consent for scutages, and even for the customary aids that the Charter permitted.[142] The only time that Edward I tried to levy a tax without consent (in 1297) he faced a near revolt. He was forced to agree that he would levy taxation only 'with the common assent of all the kingdom'.[143] In general, Edward gained consent by timely concessions and reform of the realm. He could let the counties have their knightly sheriffs, and accept a minimal income from fines, because this made the granting of taxation by parliament all the more likely. The concession Edward made in 1290, in order to secure the most lucrative tax of the reign, was the expulsion of the Jews from England. Indirectly, therefore, in reinforcing the need for consent, and the consequent need for concessions, Magna Carta contributed to the fate of the one section of society that had gained nothing from its terms.[144]

The parliament of 1290 was attended by knights representing the counties and burgesses the towns. Montfort's parliament of 1265 had set a pattern increasingly followed thereafter. By the end of Edward's reign in 1307 the knights and burgesses were close to being a fixture. Magna Carta in 1215 had envisaged consent to taxation being given by an assembly merely of tenants-in-cheif. Here it looked to the past but gave a pointer to the future since many of the lesser tenants-in-chief summoned generally by the sheriffs would have been of knightly status. The Charter also protected the privileges of London and other towns, and recognized the role of the knights in dispensing justice and reforming abuses in the localities. In 1215 itself Magna Carta hardly seemed to have a future. It was supposed to last for ever, 'in perpetuity', but within little more than a month of the meeting at Runnymede, John had decided to abandon it. His baronial opponents effectively did the same when, later in the year, they offered the throne to Prince Louis, eldest son of the king of France.

Magna Carta, however, survived. It did so because it asserted one fundamental and treasured principle, that of the rule of law. It also, in its individual chapters, responded to real grievances and offered, at least in some cases, what seemed effective solutions. In the thirteenth century the Charter was hardly of equal benefit to all sections of society. Yet society changed while Magna Carta remained, so that in the end the principle of the rule of law shielded everybody. Already by 1300 those from top to bottom of English society saw the Charter as a protection against arbitrary rule. Magna Carta was set on the long journey that would take it around the world. It would indeed last 'in perpetuity'.

Glossary of Terms

This Glossary provides brief definitions of terms found in Magna Carta and elsewhere in this book. It makes no claims to catch all the senses in which the terms could be used.[1] Unless stated, references to the chapters of Magna Carta are to those in the Charter of 1215.

advowson The right of nominating a cleric to an ecclesiastical benefice, most frequently a parish. The right was possessed by many lay lords of manors, as well as bishops, monasteries and cathedral chapters.

afforestation The bringing of an area within the bounds of the royal forest, thus subjecting it to royal forest law. See *assart, purpresture, waste.*

aid (i) A payment demanded by a lord (including the king) from his tenants by knight service. Magna Carta sought to limit such aids to three customary occasions. (ii) A tax levied by the king on the kingdom. See *knight service.*

amercement A financial penalty for falling into the mercy of the king or a lord through the committal of some offence. Usually the result of conviction before a court. What would now be called a 'fine'.

Angevin empire The totality of the territory under the Angevin kings. Greatly reduced by John's loss of Normandy and Anjou in 1204.

Angevins A term used by historians to cover kings Henry II (r. 1154–89), Richard I (r. 1189–99) and John (r. 1199–1216). Derived from Henry II being the son of Geoffrey of Anjou ('Angevin' meaning 'relating to Anjou').

appeal An accusation brought in court by one individual against another, usually of violence or theft.

assart The clearing of an area within the royal forest and thus subject to royal forest law so as to create new arable land. It was a punishable offence to create an assart without the king's licence.

assize (i) Legislation, so 'the Assize of Northampton'. (ii) A legal action like those named in chapter 18 of Magna Carta. See *darrein presentment, grand assize, mort d'ancestor, novel disseisin* and *recognition.*

bailiff A local official.

bailiwick A local area subject to the authority of an official, so a county or hundred.

baron In Magna Carta a lord who holds a barony from the king and owes a relief of £100. See *relief*. Can also be used more loosely to mean a great man.

barony The estate held by a baron from the king and for which he owes, in Magna Carta a relief of £100. The 'barony of an earl' had the same structure (see *fee*) as the barony of a baron.

beaupleder A fine levied at the start of a session of a court by the presiding officials on those attending, in order for the latter to escape penalization for mistakes in giving evidence and other procedural errors.

bench The central court held by the king's judges, usually at Westminster. It heard mostly civil pleas according to the procedures of the common law. Later called the court of common pleas or the common bench.

Bracton The short title for a great book on the laws and customs of England. Thought once to have been written in the 1250s by the judge Henry de Bracton. Now largely accepted that it was written in the 1220s and 1230s by the legal circle around the judge William of Raleigh, Bracton himself simply making later additions to the text.

burgage A form of tenure for town property in return for rent, with freedom of alienation.

chamber An office travelling with the king whose officials received, stored and disbursed his money.

chancery An office, mostly travelling with the king, whose clerks wrote and sealed the king's charters, letters and writs. The head was the chancellor, although he could be an absentee. The chancery rolls were the rolls on which the chancery recorded its output, with each roll covering one regnal year. See also *letters close*, *letters patent* and *writ*.

chattels Movable property, especially corn and animals.

chief justiciar The king's chief minister; in charge of government during the king's absence from the kingdom. Sometimes just called 'the justiciar'. There was also a chief justiciar in Ireland.

clerks Clerks were both those ordained as bishops, priests and deacons, and those who were tonsured but remained in minor orders, often with little immediate intention of proceeding to the priesthood. Many of the clerks working for the king fell into the latter category.

common law, common-law litigation See the next entry.

common pleas Civil litigation in the king's courts that followed standard procedures common to the whole kingdom. Such litigation formed a central element in the common law. 'Common pleas' and 'common-law litigation' are largely synonymous terms. See *darrein presentment*, *grand assize*, *mort d'ancestor* and *novel disseisin*.

common term of crusaders The period within which a crusader enjoyed various privileges and protections.

coram rege This translates literally as 'in the presence of the king'. The term for the judicial court that travelled with the king, later called the court of king's bench.

cottar An unfree peasant smallholder.

county The chief local government division of the kingdom. The boundaries of the medieval counties remained largely unchanged until 1974. There were thirty-eight counties in 1215. In Latin, 'comitatus' is both the word for county and county court. In chapter 18 of Magna Carta 'comitatus' is used in both senses.

county farm The fixed annual payment for which the sheriff of a county answered each year at the exchequer. The farms by John's reign had remained much the same for many years and hence in Magna Carta's chapter 25 are described as 'ancient'. The farm was derived from amercements imposed in the county and hundred courts, from traditional payments (such as 'sheriff's aid'), from the demesne manors of the king in the sheriff's hands, and from any subsidiary farms of hundreds, wapentakes and ridings. See also *demesne manor, increment* and *profit*.

darrein presentment A common-law legal action, or 'assize', to determine who had the right to nominate to a church living, the living being usually a parish. The verdict was given by a jury of free men from the neighbourhood of the property in dispute. See *advowson* and *recognition*.

deforestation The taking of areas out of the royal forest and freeing them from royal forest law.

demesne manor A manor in a lord's hands, rather than held from him by a tenant. The king's demesne manors referred to in chapter 25 of Magna Carta had often been in his hands since Domesday Book.

Dialogus de Scaccario The great book written on the workings of the exchequer by Henry II's treasurer, Richard fitzNigel. It was begun in 1177 and finished sometime in the 1180s.

diffidatio The formal act in which allegiance to a lord is renounced and the lord defied.

disparagement The offence given when an individual was married to someone of lower social status.

disseisin Dispossession, usually applied to dispossession of land, but could also be of rights.

distrain To force someone to do something, usually by the seizure of chattels and land. The corresponding noun is 'distraint'.

distress To compel and constrain someone to do something by force. Has much the same meaning as 'to distrain'.

dower The portion of her husband's lands that a widow is entitled to after his death. On the widow's death the dower reverts to her husband's heir.

earl The English term for the Latin 'comes' and the French 'count'. A largely honorary title of high status, often but not always attached to a county.

ell A unit of measurement of 45 inches.

engrossment An authorized original of a document as opposed to a later copy. To engross is to write out such a document.

escheat Land that has come into the king's hands, often through the failure of heirs or forfeiture.

escheator The royal official who administered land that had come into the king's hands via an escheat or wardship. See *wardship*.

exchequer The central institution of royal government, usually sitting at Westminster, which exacted and audited the king's annual revenue. See also *pipe roll* and *Dialogus de Scaccario*.

eyre A visitation of the king's justices in the localities, hence 'justices in eyre'. See also *itinerant justices*. A 'general eyre' is a term given by historians for a visitation in which panels of judges, empowered to hear 'all pleas' (so both criminal and civil) and investigate royal rights and local abuses, were sent through the whole country.

fair A large annual gathering for trade held at a fixed date each year, as opposed to a market, which was usually weekly. New markets and fairs needed to be licensed by the king.

faithful man In Magna Carta, a man who has sworn an oath of fealty, that is loyalty, to the king. All adult males, free and unfree, were obliged to take such an oath.

farm A fixed annual payment owed for a county, hundred, wapentake, town, manor, forest or other bailiwick. See *county farm*.

fee An estate that was held by knight service from the king or other lord. The fee of an earl or a baron comprised both his demesne manors and the lands held from him by his own tenants. It might equally be called his 'barony' or 'honour'. A single knight's fee was an estate for which the service of one knight was owed. See *holding land from a lord*, *honour* and *knight service*.

fee farm A form of land tenure in return for rent.

felony A serious crime.

fine An offer of money accepted by the king in return for a concession or favour. 'Offer' has the same meaning

fine roll A roll, one for each regnal year, on which the chancery recorded the fines made with the king. A copy was sent to the exchequer so that it knew what money to collect.

forest The royal forest was the area subject to the king's forest law.

frankpledge The 'frankpledge' or 'tithing' was a group of adult males (so aged twelve and over), often ten or twelve strong, who were sworn to keep the king's peace and guarantee the good conduct of their fellows. All adult males of unfree status south of the Humber were supposed to be in such groups. The 'view of frankpledge' was the inspection made by the sheriff or bailiff at the hundred or wapentake court to check that the unfree were in their groups. The financial exactions imposed at the view were very unpopular. Chapter 42 of the 1217 Charter (chapter 35 in the Charter of 1225) stipulated that the view should only be held once a year, at the Michaelmas tourn. See *tourn*.

free man Any man who was not legally unfree. See *villein*.

free tenant A free man who held a free tenement.

free tenement Land held freely from a lord, so in return for knight service or rent, as opposed to being held by unfree services. See *knight service* and *labour services*.

given by the hand Words that appear at the end of royal charters and mean 'authorized by'. The 'giver' was the person who had authorized the charter's writing out (engrossment) and sealing.

Glanvill The short title for the great book on the laws and customs of England that explained the forms of the early common-law legal actions. It was probably written between 1187 and 1189. Although it goes by the name of Henry II's chief justiciar, Ranulf de Glanvill, he is not thought to have been the author, although the work was probably produced in his legal circle.

grand assize A common-law legal action to determine the ultimate right to property. The verdict was given by twelve knights chosen by four of their fellows.

hauberget A type of cloth.

heriot A payment (usually of horses and military equipment) due to a lord on the death of one of his men.

holding land from a lord An individual who 'held' land from a lord was in possession of the land as the lord's tenant, and owed him services according to the terms of the tenure. See *knight service*, *tenant-in-chief* and *under-tenant*.

homage The ceremony in which a new tenant by knight service became the man of his lord, creating a mutual bond of loyalty. See *knight service*.

honour A baron's estate comprising both his demesne manors and the lands held from him by his tenants. See *fee*.

honorial court A court held by a baron or other lord for his tenants by knight service. It had jurisdiction over possession of the fees held by the tenants and over services owed the lord.

hundred An administrative subdivision of a county, with its own court that met fortnightly under Henry II. In some parts of the country, notably Yorkshire, Lincolnshire, Nottinghamshire and Derbyshire, the subdivisions were called wapentakes rather than hundreds. There were around 630 hundreds and wapentakes in the thirteenth century. A good proportion of them were in private hands and thus run by a lord, and his bailiffs rather than by the sheriff. See *jury of presentment*.

hundred jurors Twelve men, drawn from the leading free men of the hundred or wapentake, who sat on the jury of presentment that gave evidence to the justices in eyre. Similar juries also gave evidence before numerous other government inquiries. See *jury of presentment*.

increment A fixed annual payment made additional to a farm. In Magna Carta's chapter 25 the increment is that owed by the sheriff over and above the 'ancient' farm of his county. See *county farm*.

itinerant justices Justices of the king on a visitation to hear pleas in the counties. The same as justices in eyre. See *eyre*.

jury of presentment A jury of twelve free men representing the hundred or wapentake, which came before the justices of the general eyre and answered a series of questions about crime and royal rights since the last visitation. In effect a jury of accusation when it came to those who had committed a crime. See *eyre*.

justices in eyre See *eyre* and *itinerant justices*.

justiciar See *chief justiciar*.

knight (i) Someone who has gone through a formal ceremony making him a knight by being girded with the sword of knighthood. The girding could be performed by the king or a great lord. Knighthood was not hereditary. (ii) Someone who, without necessarily having gone through the ceremony, is regarded and described as a knight for the purposes of sitting on juries and performing other judicial tasks. Kings, earls and barons were girded with the sword of knighthood. However, the very great majority of knights in both the above categories were men of lesser wealth and status, and were under-tenants, holding their land from earls and barons in return for knight service, although some were tenants-in-chief holding directly from the king. See *knight service*.

knight service A form of tenure in which a tenant does homage to his lord for the land he holds from him and has to provide in return the service of a number of knights. The lord also expects counsel, money payments in the form relief and aid, and has rights over wardships and the marriages of heirs and widows. Tenants-in-chief – earls, barons and knights – held from the king by knight service and thus had the obligation to provide knights for the king's army. Knightly under-tenants had an obligation to provide knights for their overlords when the king summoned an army, and also, more arguably, when their overlords were in rebellion. In practice, however, such military obligations were often discharged by a money payment. See *scutage*. For the lord, it was often his right to relief, and his control over wardships and marriages, that were the most valued aspects of tenure by knight service. See *aid*, *relief* and *wardship*.

labour services The services owed by an unfree peasant to his lord in return for his land. They involved providing agricultural labour to the lord, often on a weekly basis. The obligation to perform such services was itself a proof of unfreedom. See also *merchet*.

lay fee Land that owes secular services, so knight service or rent.

letters close Letters of the king, issued by the chancery, and closed by being folded and tied up, with a dab of wax from the seal across the fold. The usual vehicle for administrative orders. Recorded by the chancery on the close rolls. See also *chancery* and *writ*.

letters patent Letters of the king, issued by the chancery, that were left open or 'patent' with the seal hanging down beneath. Used for proclamations and the making of appointments. Recorded by the chancery on the patent rolls.

liberty (i) A privilege conferred by the king. (ii) An exempt area of jurisdiction such as a private hundred. See *hundred*.

liberty of elections The church's right freely to elect bishops and heads of religious houses.

magnate A general term for great lord.

March of Wales The border area between England and Wales proper.

mark A term of financial account: two thirds of a pound; 160 pennies.

marriage portion In Latin *maritagium*. The property assigned to a woman by her natal family on her marriage. It was controlled by the husband during marriage. After the wife's death it would usually pass to her heir, although this would depend on the terms of the initial gift.

merchet A payment made by an unfree peasant to his lord for permission to give his daughter in marriage. The making of such a payment was evidence of unfreedom.

mort d'ancestor A common-law legal action, or 'assize', by which free tenants could obtain their inheritances on the death of ancestors of whom they are the heirs. The verdict was given by a jury of twelve free men from the neighbourhood of the property in dispute. See *recognition*.

murdrum fine A fine paid by local communities when they could not prove the villein status of someone dead by other than natural causes.

novel disseisin A common-law legal action, or 'assize', by which free tenants could recover property of which they had recently been disseised (dispossessed) unjustly and without judgement. The verdict was given by a jury of twelve free men from the neighbourhood of the property in dispute. See *recognition*.

offer See *fine*.

ordinary An ecclesiastical official. The deputy of a bishop or a bishop himself.

peers Social equals.

penny The silver penny (in Latin 'denarius') was the only coin in circulation. There were 12 in a shilling, 160 in a mark and 240 in a pound.

pilgrimage In Magna Carta 'pilgrimage' means 'crusade'. There was no word for 'crusade' as such. However, those who had taken the cross were described as 'crucesignati', meaning 'men signed by the cross'.

pipe roll The annual roll on which the exchequer recorded its annual audit of the revenue due the crown. It was organized in county sections.

pleas of the crown Serious crimes that only the king can try and punish. They comprised treason, homicide, affray, premeditated assault, burglary, rape, serious theft and arson.

pound A term of financial account; 240 pennies in a pound; 20 shillings in a pound. A mark is a two thirds of a pound.

precipe See *writ of precipe*.

prise The king's right to take goods by compulsory purchase. Payment might in fact be delayed, if made at all. Also called 'purveyance'.

profit The term for the variable revenue accounted for each year at the exchequer by a sheriff over and above the county farm and any increment. A sheriff responsible for 'profit' was described as a 'custodian', and was in effect accounting for all the revenue he received. See *county farm* and *increment*.

purpresture An encroachment on an area subject to royal forest law by the making of an enclosure, erecting a building, or doing any other work. A punishable offence.

purveyance See *prise*.

put to law To subject a person to a legal procedure leading to trial, and also the procedures of the trial itself.

quarter A measure of capacity, sometimes the equivalent of 36 litres.

recognition A common legal action, or assize, like those mentioned in Magna Carta's chapter 18, culminating in a verdict given by a jury from the neighbourhood of the property in dispute. The men of the jury are 'recognitors'.

relief A payment made by a tenant-in-chief to the king or by an under-tenant, holding by knight service, to a tenant-in-chief in order to gain possession of his landed inheritance.

riding A local government division in Yorkshire and Lincolnshire.

russet A type of cloth.

scutage A money payment owed by a tenant-in-chief in place of sending his quota of knights to the king, assessed on the number of knights he owed. A tenant-in-chief would endeavour to recoup the scutage he owed the king from his own tenants by knight service.

seisin Possession, usually of land. To put someone 'in seisin' is to put them in possession.

serjeant A professional soldier or militarily active landholder below the rank of knight; later sometimes synonymous with 'esquire'.

serjeanty A form of tenure in return for performing duties to the king (such as providing a serjeant for his army) or giving him objects. The objects, in the example of a 'small serjeanty' given in chapter 37 of Magna Carta, are knives and arrows.

sheriff The king's chief local government agent; in charge of a county; appointed and dismissed by the king.

shilling A term of financial account. There were 12 pennies in a shilling and 20 shillings in a pound.

socage A form of free tenure in return for rent. The lord had no rights of wardship over land held in socage. See *wardship*.

sokeman A peasant who holds his land largely or exclusively in return for a money rent. If he owes labour services, they are relatively light. Many but far from all sokemen were considered free men.

statute book An unofficial collection of legislation and legal texts, common from the second half of the thirteenth century.

surety A person who guarantees the payment of a debt owed by another person.

take the cross The act of undertaking to go on a crusade.

tallage A tax levied at the king's pleasure on his towns and demesne manors. See *demesne manor*.

tenant-in-chief A tenant who holds his land directly, so 'in chief', from the king in return for knight service. He might be an earl, a baron or a knight. See *knight service*.

tenement A land-holding.

tithing See *frankpledge*.

tourn A session of the hundred or wapentake court at which the fullest possible attendance was demanded by the sheriff or bailiff. The tourn was limited to sessions at Easter and Michaelmas by chapter 42 of the 1217 Charter (chapter 35 in the 1225 Charter). See also *frankpledge*.

under-tenant A tenant who holds his land from a tenant-in-chief as opposed to the king. An under-tenant could hold by rent or by knight service. Tenants could also hold land from under-tenants, thus creating a chain of tenure. See *knight service* and *tenant-in-chief*.

vacant abbey The state of an abbey between the death of one abbot and the appointment of another. During this period the king was entitled to the revenues of the abbot. He was also entitled to the revenues of a bishopric during the equivalent interval.

view of frankpledge See *frankpledge*.

vill A village or small town.

villein A peasant who was legally unfree. Land held in villeinage was land for which customs and services characteristic of unfree tenure were owed. See *labour services* and *merchet*.

virgate An area of land, often between 24 and 30 acres, but could be smaller.

wainage (i) In Magna Carta's chapter 20 a villein's means of livelihood, so his crops under cultivation (tillage), seed corn, ploughs and plough teams. (ii) In chapter 5 (a) the same items as above but this time belonging to the person in wardship, and (b) the time of the agricultural season.

wapentake The subdivision of a county, equivalent to a hundred, found in Yorkshire, Lincolnshire, Nottinghamshire, Derbyshire and Leicestershire. See *hundred*.

wardrobe The wardrobe, which travelled with the king, was where he stored goods, cash and precious objects. The chamber often stored the money it received in the wardrobe. See *chamber*.

wardship When a tenant-in-chief died, the king had the custody, or wardship, of his estate during the minority of the heir. He also had the right to marry off the heir. A tenant-in-chief had the same rights of wardship and marriage over his own tenants by knight service. See *knight service*.

warrant The king's obligation to warrant land held by another, referred to in chapters 52 and 57 of Magna Carta, meant his obligation to defend the holder's right to the land in any lawsuit. It arose because the land was held by grant of the king.

warrens Areas where the hunting of foxes and hares was forbidden, so not just the deer and boar protected by royal forest law.

waste The felling of trees and other destruction in areas subject to royal forest law. A punishable offence.

writ In its form a writ was a letter close. The term 'writ' was used to describe letters close that dealt with matters connected with the judicial process. See *letters close*.

writ 'of course' A standard form writ automatically available at small cost (probably 6d) to initiate common-law legal actions such as the grand assize, novel disseisin and mort d'ancestor. See *grand assize, mort d'ancestor* and *novel disseisin*.

writ of inquisition concerning life or limbs A writ securing a trial by jury for someone accused of a crime for which the penalty might be loss of life or limbs.

writ of liberate In this case not a letter close connected with the law, but one addressed to the exchequer ordering it to disburse money.

writ of precipe 'Precipe' means 'command'. The writ, referred to in chapter 34 of Magna Carta, commanded the restoration of land on pain of the case being transferred to the king's court.

Map of the English Counties

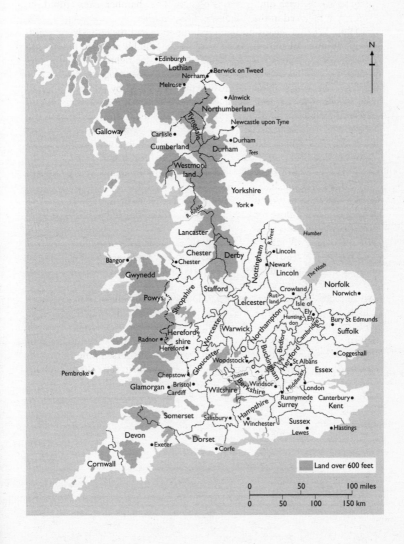

Appendix I
King John's letter announcing the terms of the 1209 Treaty of Norham

In 1209 King John forced what historians call the Treaty of Norham on William the Lion, king of Scots. Hitherto the content of the treaty has only been known from the accounts of chroniclers. There survives, however, in a cartulary of St Augustine's abbey, Canterbury, a copy of King John's letter announcing what are evidently the terms of the treaty. I have discussed the significance of the letter between pp. 238 and 241 above. I hope also to comment on it in a forthcoming article. Here I simply provide a transcription of the Latin text accompanied by a translation.

The St Augustine's cartulary containing John's letter is now preserved at The National Archives: TNA E 164/27. The letter is between folios 137 and 137v. The cartulary has material arranged roughly chronologically down to 1323. It also contains a chronicle covering the years AD 1 to 1324, while a continuation down to 1332 is clearly an addition. It would seem, therefore, that the cartulary is a work of the mid-1320s.* The hand in which the letter is written is compatible with that date.† Alongside charters bearing on the properties and rights of the abbey, the cartulary also has some documents of a public nature. The 1209 letter is preceded by a letter of King John about the lifting of the Interdict.‡ It is followed by a copy of the manifesto that Prince Louis issued on his arrival in England in 1216. This is also found in other St Augustine's cartularies.§

The text of John's letter is as follows. I have retained the capitalization of the original, but not the punctuation. The division into paragraphs is my own, the original text being continuous.¶

---

* For the cartulary, see Davis, Breay, Harrison and Smith, *Medieval Cartularies*, p. 41, no. 195.
† I am grateful to Teresa Webber for advice about the hand.
‡ I hope to comment on this on a later occasion.
§ It is printed in *F*, p. 140, from the St Augustine's cartulary BL Cotton Julius D ii.
¶ I am grateful to Henry Summerson for help with both the transcription and the translation of the letter.

Omnibus dei fidelibus ad quos littere iste pervenerint, J. dei gratia etc. salutem.

Sciatis quod ita convenit inter nos et Dominum Willelmum regem Scocie, scilicet quod Alexander filius eius fecit nobis homagium sicut idem W. rex Scocie fecit homagium Domino H. regi Anglie patri nostro nec tunc recedet prefatus W. rex Scocie de homagio quod nobis fecit quamdiu vixerit.

Preterea idem W. rex Scocie tradidit nobis duas filias suas, scilicet Margaretam primogenitam filiam suam et aliam Ysabellam ita quod Henricus primogenitus noster desponsabit predictam Margaretam quando ipse erit* ix vel x annorum vel antea.

Et ex quo eam desponsaverit nos infra annum vel bienium proximum maritabimus predictam Ysabellam ad gratiam et ad honorem nostram et predicti regis Scocie.

Et si humaniter contigerit de (eadem Margareta)† H. filio nostro antequam ducat in uxorem predictam Margaretam, Ricardus filius noster ipsam desponsabit. Et si humaniter contigerit de eadem Margareta antequam desponsetur, predicta Ysabella predicto modo maritabitur Henrico filio nostro vel Ricardo filio nostro si humaniter contigerit de eodem H. filio nostro antequam ipsam desponsaverit.

Et si humaniter contigerit de W. rege Scocie, nos et filii nostri et nostri erimus auxiliantes predicto Alexandro filio suo tanquam homini nostro ad ipsum tenendum in terra sua et in dignitatibus suis.

Eodem modo erunt idem rex Scocie et filius suus et sui auxiliantes filio nostro tanquam domino suo si de nobis humaniter contigerit.

Et nos et idem rex Scocie et filii nostri iuvabimus nos adinvicem dum vixerimus.

Et salve remanebunt eidem regi Scocie et filio suo omnes libertates et dignitates sui et totum clamium quod idem rex Scocie in Northumberland', Westmerland' et Cumberland' habuit et omnes alie querele et clamia.

Et omnia mala inter nos mota cessabunt in perpetuum per hac conventionem.

* A gap of about four characters has been left between 'erit' and 'ix'.
† The words I have put within brackets are underlined for deletion.

To all God's faithful people, to whom these letters arrive, John by the grace of God etc., greeting.

You are to know that it has been agreed between us and lord William, king of Scotland, in this fashion, namely that Alexander his son has done us homage as William, king of Scotland, did homage to the lord Henry, king of England, our father; nor now will William, king of Scotland, withdraw from the homage which he has done us as long as he lives.

Moreover, William, king of Scotland, has handed us his two daughters, namely Margaret, his first-born daughter, and Isabella, the other, so that Henry, our eldest son, will marry the foresaid Margaret when he will be nine or ten years old or before.

And when he has married her, we, within the next year or two years, will marry off the foresaid Isabella at our pleasure and to our honour and to that of the foresaid king of Scotland.

And if Henry our son dies before he marries the foresaid Margaret, Richard our son will marry her. And if Margaret dies before she is married, the foresaid Isabella is to be married in the same way to Henry our son, or to Richard our son if Henry our son dies before he marries her.

And if William, king of Scotland, dies, we and our sons and our men will aid the foresaid Alexander, his son, as our man, in maintaining him in his land and his dignities.

In the same way, the king of Scotland and his son and his men will aid our son as their lord if we die.

And we and the same king of Scotland and our sons will help each other for as long as we live.

And there will remain saved to the king of Scotland and his son all his liberties and dignities and all claim which the same king of Scotland had in Northumberland, Westmorland and Cumberland and all other suits and claims.

And all ills moved between us will cease in perpetuity by this agreement.

Appendix II
The Canterbury Magna Carta

The engrossment of Magna Carta preserved in the British Library and known as Ci was given to Sir Robert Cotton in 1630 by Sir Edward Dering. It was, at the time of the gift, with Dering at Dover castle, where he was lieutenant. I have said in Chapter 1 that in the late thirteenth century Ci resided in the archives of Canterbury cathedral.* The evidence is as follows. Preserved to this day in the cathedral archives is a great register of Canterbury cathedral priory. It is now labelled Register E. Apart from later additions, Register E was probably finished in the early 1290s. The hand appears much the same down to a document dated 7 August 1291. Another document dated 14 June 1294, by contrast, seems a later addition, as does material from the reign of Edward II.† Register E is chiefly concerned with charters making concessions to the priory, but it also has some public documents, and between folios 46v and 48v there is a copy of the 1215 Magna Carta: 'carta eiusdem [King John] magna De Ronnemed'.‡ A collation of Register E's Magna Carta with Ci, as displayed in John Pine's engraving of 1733, strongly suggests that the one was copied from the other. This is because certain mistakes in the Register E copy of the Charter are readily explicable if the scribe was copying from Ci, one mistake, that explained under item 3 below, being especially telling.

---

† Canterbury Cathedral Archives, Register E, fos. 56–59v. There is the same break in Register A, at fos. 152–153v. What are now Registers A to D began life as a contemporary duplicate of Register E. The duplicate was broken up into separate volumes, after the insertion of a large amount of later material. Some material was also lost in the process and Registers A to D have no copy of the 1215 Magna Carta. For all the Canterbury registers, see Davis, Breay, Harrison and Smith, *Medieval Cartularies*, pp. 36–40, with E as no. 168 and A to D as nos. 169–72. I am most grateful to Cressida Williams, the Canterbury cathedral and city archivist, for sending me images of the folios in Register E containing the copy of Magna Carta.
‡ 'carta eiusdem' refers to the charter copied next, above which is John's charter conceding the church freedom of elections. I am citing here the pencil numbering of the folios.

1. In his copy of chapter 37 of the Charter, the Register scribe omitted the words in square brackets from the following passage: 'non habebimus custodiam [heredis nec terre sue que est de feodo alterius occasione illius feodifirme vel socagii vel burgagii nec habebimus custodiam] illius feodifirme . . .'. The text of Ci offers an explanation of what happened here, since, if the scribe had paused after the first 'custodiam', his eye could easily have skipped on to 'illius feodifirme' because, in Ci, the 'custodiam' before 'illius feodifirme' – 'custodiam illius feodifirme' – is at the start of the next line.

2. In chapter 52, the Register scribe has written 'catallis' (chattels) rather than the 'castellis' (castles), found correctly in the Lincoln, Salisbury and Cii engrossments. In Ci, however, the 'ca' comes at the end of the line, and the next line continues with 'stallis'. The 's' and 't', moreover, are run together, making it the easier for a copyist to read 'catallis'.

3. In chapter 53, the correct text of the Charter read:

> Eundem autem respectum habebimus et eodem modo de iusticia exhibenda de forestis deafforestandis vel remansuris forestis quas Henricus pater noster vel Ricardus frater noster afforestaverunt . . .

The Register scribe, however, here repeats himself so the text runs:

> Eundem autem respectum habebimus et eodem modo de iusticia exibenda De forestis et afforestandis vel remansuris forestis. Eundem autem respectum habebimus et eodem modo de iusticia exhibenda de forestis deafforestandis quas Henricus pater noster . . .*

What has happened here seems clear by reference to Ci. There the text just runs:

> Eundem autem respectum habebimus [*] de forestis deafforestandis [*] quas Henricus Pater noster . . .

However, a small sign just above and before the 'Eundem', in the shape of a line with a diamond-like shaped head, indicates that two passages need to be inserted into the text. I have indicated the places where they belonged by [*] in the above quotation. The two missing passages are found at the bottom of Ci, where the sign reappears:

* The 'exibenda' and 'exhibenda' is as per the scribe.

Eundem autem Respectum habebimus et eodem modo de Justicia exhibenda
De forestis deafforestandis vel remansuris forestis.

Here only the non-underlined words were meant to be inserted. The
underlined ones were those in the text preceding the places where the
insertions were to go, and were thus included as finding aids. When
the Register scribe got to this section of Ci, he correctly noted that, after
'habebimus', he needed to bring up into his main text what was at the
bottom of Ci, but instead of stopping at 'exhibenda' he went on to copy
the whole of what followed – 'De forestis deafforestandis vel remansuris
forestis' – leaving out the underlining but including the capital 'D' in 'De'.
In the process he managed to write 'et afforestandis' rather than 'deafforestandis'.* The scribe had, therefore, been alerted, by neither the
underlining nor the capital in 'De', to the fact that 'De forestis deafforestandis vel remansuris forestis' was separate from 'Eundem autem
respectum habebimus et eodem modo de iusticia exhibenda', and was
there to deal with the second omission. The scribe's only excuse was that
at the bottom of Ci the 'de iusticia exhibenda' and 'De forestis deafforestandis . . .' did run on with only a single letter gap between them. Having
made his mistake, at least the scribe immediately recognized it as such,
and sought to put matters right. In actual fact, had he been more astute,
he would have seen that he could have left well alone and gone straight on
to 'quas Henricus . . .' Apart from the capital 'D' in the 'De', the passage
at the bottom of Ci – 'De forestis deafforestandis vel remansuris forestis' –
with the 'De forestis deafforestandis' indicating where 'vel remansuris
forestis' should go, was exactly how the Charter *did* continue, with 'de
forestis deafforestandis' following on immediately from 'de iusticia exhibenda'. Failing to appreciate this, the scribe decided his mistake needed
remedy. However, perhaps unwilling to spoil the look of his text, or perhaps just not bothered, he did not cross out what he had written, or write
a new version over an erasure. Instead, he left the passage in place, and
started the chapter all over again – 'Eundem autem respectum . . .', thus
creating the curious repetition we have mentioned. Even then, the scribe

---

* In the passage '[De forestis deaffore]standis vel remansuris forestis' at the bottom
of Ci, the section I have put between square brackets was damaged by the fire of
1731, and was supplied in the Pine engraving by reference to Cii, the other engrossment possessed by the British Museum, where the same omission in the text was
corrected in the same way with 'De forestis deafforestandis vel remansuris forestis'
appearing at the bottom of the document. (BL Cotton Charter XIII 31b records the
damage in the fire and the number of letters that had to be supplied by reference to
Cii. See also above, p. 15–16 and note 40.) If I am right in thinking that E was
indeed copied from Ci, then E confirms that the section at Ci's foot did indeed start
'De forestis'. E's 'et afforestandis', rather than 'deafforestandis', a variant that
makes no sense, would seem simply to be a careless mistake.

480APPENDIX II

did not get the text quite right, because this time he failed to include the 'vel remansuris forestis' of the second insertion.

4. One small final point relates not to any mistake but to the spelling of 'Runnymede' at the end of the Charter. In the Register copy it appears as 'Runingmed', just as in Ci, and also as in the Salisbury engrossment. Cii, on the other hand, has 'Ronimed' and Lincoln 'Runimed'.*

There are, therefore, good grounds for thinking that Ci was in the archives of Canterbury cathedral in the late thirteenth century, when the copy in Register E was made from it.† Its appearance in 1630 with Dering at Dover castle is easily explained, given the documents he is known to have purloined from Canterbury cathedral. Ci's presence at Dover has accordingly nothing to do with any connection with the Cinque Ports, as is sometimes supposed. Chapter 12 sets out the reasons for thinking that Ci was, in fact, the Charter sent to the Canterbury diocese in 1215.‡ Probably it was kept from the start at the cathedral. It can henceforth be known as 'the Canterbury Magna Carta'.

* Cii is also separated from Ci and the Register copy by having the people in chapter 50 listed in a different order, with 'Andream [de Cancellis]' coming fourth rather than second. E does not repeat Canterbury's mistaken 'concessissimus' in chapter 60, having correctly 'concessimus'.
† There is an earlier copy of the 1215 Charter made at Canterbury cathedral priory. This is found among a miscellaneous collection of material, related to the priory, which was written up during the archbishopric of Robert Kilwardby (1273–8). The folios were subsequently bound up with later material to form what is now BL Galba E iii. (See Davis, Breay, Harrison and Smith, *Medieval Cartularies*, no. 182.) The copy of the Charter is found between fos. 72v and 80. It seems likely that it too was copied from Ci, but since the scribe avoided the same telling mistakes, there is no means of proof. It is worth noting, however, that the Galba copy, like Ci and Register E, has 'Runingmed'.
‡ See above, pp. 373–9.

Bibliography

This Bibliography is largely but not exclusively confined to primary and secondary sources cited in the endnotes. Its relationship to the form of citation in the endnotes is explained in the Note on the Text on p. 15. I am grateful to Christopher Tilley for a great deal of help with the Bibliography's construction.

UNPRINTED PRIMARY SOURCES

Full references to unprinted primary sources are given in the endnotes, where BL stands for the British Library and TNA for The National Archives at Kew.

PRINTED PRIMARY SOURCES

Abingdon	*Two Cartularies of Abingdon Abbey*, ed. C. F. Slade and G. Lambrick, 2 vols. (Oxford Historical Society, new series, 32–3, 1990–91).
AC	*Annales Cambriae*, ed. J. Williams ab Ithel (Rolls Series, London, 1860).
Acta Hugh of Wells	*The Acta of Hugh of Wells, Bishop of Lincoln 1209–1235*, ed. D. M. Smith (Lincoln Record Society, 88, 2000).
Adam of Eynsham	*The Life of St Hugh of Lincoln*, ed. D. L. Douie and H. Farmer, 2 vols. (London, 1962). All references are to volume 2.
Anonymous	*Histoire des Ducs de Normandie et des Rois d'Angleterre*, ed. F. Michel (Paris, 1840). This volume contains the chronicle of the Anonymous of Béthune.

APS   *Acts of the Parliaments of Scotland. Volume 1: AD*
                               MCXXIV–MCCCCXXIII, ed. T. Thomson
                               and C. N. Innes (Edinburgh, 1814).

Articles of   Latin text and English translation in, respectively,
the Barons   Holt, *Magna Carta*, pp. 432–440 and *EHD*
                               1189–1326, pp. 311–6, as cited below.

ASL   *Acta Stephani Langton Cantuariensis Archiepiscopi*
                               1207–1228, ed. K. Major (Canterbury and York
                               Society, 50, 1950).

ASR   *Anglo-Scottish Relations 1174–1328*, ed. E. L. G.
                               Stones (Oxford, 1965).

AWR   *The Acts of Welsh Rulers, 1120–1283*, ed. H. Pryce
                               with the assistance of C. Insley (Cardiff, 2005).

Basset Charters   *The Basset Charters, c. 1120 to 1250*, ed. W. T. Reedy
                               (Pipe Roll Society, new series, 50, 1989–91).

BF   *Liber Feodorum: The Book of Fees commonly called*
                               Testa de Nevill, 3 vols., with continuous pagination
                               (London, 1920–31).

BNB   *Bracton's Note Book*, ed. F. W. Maitland, 3 vols.
                               (London, 1887).

Bower   *Scotichronicon by Walter Bower in Latin and*
                               English, vol. 4, ed. D. J. Corner, A. B. Scott,
                               W. W. Scott and D. E. R. Watt (Aberdeen, 1989).

Bracton   *Bracton de Legibus et Consuetudinibus Angliae:*
                               Bracton on the Laws and Customs of England,
                               ed. G. E. Woodbine, translated with revisions and
                               notes by S. E. Thorne, 4 vols. (Cambridge, Mass.,
                               1968–77).

Brut   *Brut Y Tywysogyon or The Chronicle of the Princes:*
                               Red Book of Hergest Version, ed. T. Jones (Cardiff,
                               1955).

Building   *Building Accounts of King Henry III*, ed. H. M.
Accounts   Colvin (Oxford, 1971).

Burton   'Annales de Burton', in *Annales Monastici*, ed. H. R.
                               Luard, 5 vols. (Rolls Series, London, 1864–9), vol. 1.

CACW   *Calendar of Ancient Correspondence concerning*
                               Wales, ed. J. G. Edwards (Cardiff, 1935).

Calendar of   *A Calendar of the Inner Temple Records*, ed. F. A.
Inner Temple   Inderwick and R. A. Roberts, 5 vols. (London,
Records   1896–1937).

Cartularies of   *The Cartularies and Registers of Peterborough*
Peterborough   *Abbey*, ed. J. D. Martin (Northamptonshire
Abbey   Record Society, 28, 1978).

CCR 1272–9   *Calendar of Close Rolls, 1272–1279* (London, 1990).

CChR	*Calendar of Charter Rolls Preserved in the Public Record Office. Volume I: Henry III 1226–1257* (London, 1903).
Cerne Cartulary	'The Cartulary of Cerne Abbey', *Proceedings of the Dorset Natural History and Antiquarian Field Club*, 29 (1908), pp. 195–207.
CFR	*Calendar of the Fine Rolls of the Reign of Henry III*, available both on the Henry III Fine Rolls Project's website (http://www.finerollshenry3.org.uk) and within *Calendar of the Fine Rolls of the Reign of Henry III, 1216–1242*, 3 vols., ed. P. Dryburgh and B. Hartland, technical editors A. Ciula, J. M. Vieira and T. Lopez (Woodbridge, 2007–9).
Church, Constitutio	*Constitutio Domus Regis, Disposition of the King's Household*, ed. S. D. Church (Oxford, 2007), published with *Richard FitzNigel, Dialogus de Scaccario, The Dialogue of the Exchequer*, ed. E. Amt
CIM	*Calendar of Inquisitions Miscellaneous Preserved in the Public Record Office*, vol. 1 (London, 1916).
CMS	*De Antiquis Legibus Liber: Cronica Maiorum et Vicecomitum Londoniarum*, ed. T. Stapleton (Camden Society, 1846).
Codex Justinianus	http://www.thelatinlibrary.com/justinian/codex8.html
Coggeshall	*Raduphi de Coggeshall Chronicon Anglicanum*, ed. J. Stevenson (Rolls Series, London, 1875).
Coronation Charter of Henry I	Latin text and English translations in R. Sharpe, 'Charters of Liberties and Royal Proclamations': http://actswilliam2henry1.files.wordpress.com/2013/10/h1-a-liberties-2013-1.pdf, pp.60–6.
Correspondance Administrative	*Correspondance Administrative d'Alfonse de Poitiers*, ed. A. Molinier (Paris, 1894).
CPR	*Calendar of Patent Rolls preserved in the Public Record Office: Henry III 1232–1272*, 4 vols. (London, 1906–13).
CPREJ	*Calendar of the Plea Rolls of the Exchequer of the Jews preserved in the Public Record Office*, ed. J. M. Rigg (Jewish Historical Society, 1, 1905).
CR	*Close Rolls of the Reign of Henry III preserved in the Public Record Office: 1227–1272*, 14 vols. (London, 1902–38).
Crouch,	D. Crouch, ed., 'The complaint of King John against

'Complaint'   William de Briouze (*c.* September 1210)', in J. S.
                     Loengard, ed., *Magna Carta and the England of
                     King John* (Woodbridge, 2010), pp. 168–79.

Crowland   *Memoriale fratris Walteri de Coventria*, ed. W.
                     Stubbs, 2 vols. (Rolls Series, London, 1872–3). All
                     references are to volume 2.

Crowland,   D. M. Stenton, *English Justice between the Norman
Spalding   Conquest and the Great Charter* (London, 1965),
                     pp. 154–215, where Crowland abbey's account of
                     its dispute with Spalding priory is translated.

CRR   *Curia Regis Rolls preserved in the Public Record
                     Office: Richard I–1250*, 20 vols. (London,
                     1922–2007).

C&S   *Councils & Synods with other documents relating
                     to the English Church. Volume II: 1205–1313*,
                     2 vols. with continuous pagination, ed. F. M.
                     Powicke and C. R. Cheney (Oxford, 1964).

CWR   *Calendar of Various Chancery Rolls . . . Welsh
                     Rolls, 1277–1326* (London, 1912).

DBM   *Documents of the Baronial Movement of Reform
                     and Rebellion, 1258–1267*, ed. R. F. Treharne
                     and I. J. Sanders (Oxford, 1973).

DD   *Diplomatic Documents preserved in the Public
                     Record Office, 1101–1272*, ed. P. Chaplais
                     (London, 1964).

DI   *Documents Illustrative of English History in the
                     Thirteenth and Fourteenth Centuries*, ed. H. Cole
                     (London, 1844).

Dialogus   *Richard fitzNigel, Dialogus de Scaccario, The
                     Dialogue of the Exchequer*, ed. E. Amt (Oxford,
                     2007).

Dunstable   'Annales Prioratus de Dunstaplia AD 1–1297', in
                     Annales Monastici, 5 vols., ed. H. R. Luard (Rolls
                     Series, London, 1864–9), vol. 3.

Early Yorkshire   *Early Yorkshire Charters*, vols. 1–3, ed. W. Farrer
Charters   (Edinburgh, 1914–16); vols. 4–12, ed. C. T. Clay
                     (Yorkshire Archaeological Society, Record Series,
                     extra series, 1–10, 1935–65).

EHD 500–1042   *English Historical Documents, 500–1042*, ed. D.
                     Whitelock (London, 1968).

EHD 1042–1189   *English Historical Documents, 1042–1189*,
                     ed. D. C. Douglas and G. W. Greenaway (London,
                     1953).

EHD 1189–1327   *English Historical Documents, 1189–1327,* ed. H.
                       Rothwell (London, 1975).

Election of   *The Chronicle of the Election of Hugh, Abbot of*
Abbot Hugh   *Bury St Edmunds and Later Bishop of Ely,*
                       ed. R. M. Thomson (Oxford, 1974).

Enchiridion   *Enchiridion Fontium Historiae Hungarorum,*
                       ed. M. Henrik (Budapest, 1902), with the texts of
                       Hungary's Golden Bull between pp. 134 and 143.

English Lawsuits   *English Lawsuits from William I to Richard I,*
                       ed. R. C. van Caenegem, 2 vols. (Selden Society
                       106–7, 1990–91).

ERW   *Early Registers of Writs,* ed. E. de Haas
                       and G. D. G. Hall (Selden Society, 87, 1970).

F   *Foedera, Conventiones, Litterae et cujuscumque*
                       generis Acta Publica, ed. T. Rymer, new edn, vol. 1,
                       pt. i, ed. A. Clark and F. Holbrooke (London, 1816).

FH   *Flores Historiarum,* ed. H. R. Luard, 3 vols (Rolls
                       Series, London, 1890).

Fleta   *Fleta,* vol. 2, ed. H. G. Richardson and G. O.
                       Sayles (Selden Society, 72, 1953).

Forest Charter of,   Latin text and English translation in respectively *SR,*
1217 and 1225   pp. 20–2, 26–7, and *EHD 1189–1327,* pp.
                       337–40, 347–9, as cited below; Latin text of 1225
                       Charter also in Holt, *Magna Carta,* pp. 512–7.

Fulbert of   *The Letters and Poems of Fulbert of Chartres,*
Chartres   ed. F. Behrends (Oxford, 1976).

Furness   *Chronicles of the Reigns of Stephen, Henry II and*
                       Richard I, ed. R. Howlett, 2 vols. with continuous
                       pagination (Rolls Series, London, 1884–5).
                       Volume 2 contains the continuation of William of
                       Newburgh made at Stanley and Furness abbeys.

Geoffrey of   Geoffrey of Monmouth, *History of the Kings*
Monmouth   *of Britain,* translated by L. Thorpe (Harmonds-
                       worth, 1966).

Gerald of Wales   *Expugnatio Hibernica, The Conquest of Ireland,*
                       by Giraldus Cambrensis, ed. A. B. Scott and F. X.
                       Martin (Dublin, 1978).

Gervase   *The Historical Works of Gervase of Canterbury,*
                       ed. W. Stubbs, 2 vols. (Rolls Series, London,
                       1879–80).

Gesetze   *Die Gesetze der Angelsachsen,* vol. I, ed. F.
                       Liebermann (Halle, 1903).

Gesta Annalia   *Johannis de Fordun, Chronica Gentis Scotorum,*
                       ed. W. F. Skene (Edinburgh, 1871).

Gesta Stephani   *Gesta Stephani*, ed. K. R Potter (London, 1955).

Glanvill   *Tractatus de Legibus et Consuetudinibus Regni*
                     Anglie qui Glanvilla vocatur, ed. G. D. G. Hall
                     (London, 1965).

Guala   *The Letters and Charters of Cardinal Guala*
                     Bicchieri, Papal Legate in England, 1216–1218,
                     ed. N. Vincent (Canterbury and York Society, 83,
                     1996).

Guisborough   *The Chronicle of Walter of Guisborough*, ed. H.
                     Rothwell (Camden Society, 89, 1957).

Holt,   J. C. Holt, 'A Vernacular-French text of Magna Carta
'Vernacular-   1215', *English Historical Review*, 89 (1974),
French Text'   pp. 346–64, reprinted in his *Magna Carta and*
                     Medieval Government (Woodbridge, 1985), pp.
                     239–58.

Hotot Estate   *Estate Records of the Hotot Family*, ed. E. King, in
Records   *A Northamptonshire Miscellany* (Northampton-
                     shire Record Society, 32, 1982).

Howden   *Chronica Magistri Rogeri de Houedene*, ed. W.
                     Stubbs, 4 vols. (Rolls Series, London, 1868–71).

Howden, *GR*   *Gesta Regis Henrici Secundi et Gesta Regis Ricardi*
                     Benedicti abbatis, ed. W. Stubbs, 2 vols. (Rolls
                     Series, London, 1867).

James of Aragon   *The Book of Deeds of James of Aragon: A*
                     Translation of the Medieval Catalan 'Llibre dels
                     Fets', ed. D. Smith and H. Buffery (Aldershot, 2003).

Jocelin of   *The Chronicle of Jocelin of Brakelond*, ed. H. E.
Brakelond   Butler (London, 1951).

John of Salisbury   John of Salisbury, *Policraticus: of the Frivolities of*
                     Courtiers and the Footprints of Philosophers, ed. and
                     translated by C. J. Nederman (Cambridge, 1990).

John of   *Bartholomaei de Cotton, Historia, Anglicana*, ed.
Wallingford   H. R. Luard (Rolls Series, London, 1859).

LAR   *The Earliest Lincolnshire Assize Rolls 1202–1209*,
                     ed. D. M. Stenton Lincoln Record Society, 22, 1926)

Lawman   *Lawman – Brut*, ed. R. Allen (London, 1992).

Layettes   *Layettes du Trésor des Chartres*, ed. A. Teulet, H.-F.
                     Delaborde and E. Berger, 5 vols. (Paris,
                     1863–1909).

LHP   *Leges Henrici Primi*, ed. L. J. Downer (Oxford,
                     1972).

Letters of   *The Letters of Robert Grosseteste, Bishop of*
Grosseteste   *Lincoln*, ed. F. A. C. Mantello and J. Goering
                     (Toronto, 2010).

Lincs. Worcs. Eyre	*Rolls of the Justices in Eyre for Lincolnshire, 1218–19, and Worcestershire, 1221*, ed. D. M. Stenton (Selden Society, 53, 1934).
'London municipal collection'	'A London municipal collection from the reign of John', ed. M. Bateson, *English Historical Review*, 67 (1902), pp. 480–511, 707–30.
Lost Letters	*Lost Letters of Medieval Life: English Society, 1200–1250*, ed. M. Carlin and D. Crouch (Philadelphia, 2013).
Magna Carta 1216, 1217 and 1225	Latin texts and English translation in respectively *SR*, pp. 14–19, 22–5, and *EHD 1189–1327*, pp. 327–46, as cited below; Latin text of the 1225 Charter also in Holt, *Magna Carta*, pp. 501–7.
Magna Carta of Cheshire	*The Chartulary or Register of the Abbey of St Werburgh Chester*, ed. J. Tait, part 1 (Chetham Society, new series, 79, 1920), pp. 101–9.
Margam	'Annales de Margam (AD 1066–1232)', in *Annales Monastici*, 5 vols., ed. H. R. Luard (Rolls Series, London, 1864–9), vol. 1.
Marshal	*History of William Marshal*, ed. A. J. Holden, S. Gregory and D. Crouch, 3 vols. (Anglo-Norman Text Society, Occasional Publication Series, 4–6, 2002–6).
Missala Ecclesie Westmonasteriensis	*Missala ad Usum Ecclesie Westmonasteriensis*, ed. J. Wickham Legg, 3 vols. (Henry Bradshaw Society, 1, 5, 12, 1891, 1897, 1913).
Mirror	*The Mirror of Justices*, ed. W. J. Whittaker, with an introduction by F. W. Maitland (Selden Society, 7, 1893).
Melrose	D. Broun and J. Harrison, *The Chronicle of Melrose Abbey. A Stratigraphic Edition. Volume I: Introduction and Facsimile Edition* (Scottish History Society, 2007). Citations are to the folios of the facsimile edition provided as a CD with this volume.
MGL	*Munimenta Gildhallae Londoniensis*, ed. H. T. Riley, 3 vols. (Rolls Series, London, 1859–62).
MR 1199	*The Memoranda Roll for the Michaelmas term of the first year of the reign of King John, 1199–1200*, ed. H. G. Richardson (Pipe Roll Society, new series, 59, 1943).

MR 1208	*The Memoranda Roll for the tenth year of the reign of King John, 1207–8,* ed. R. Allen Brown (Pipe Roll Society, new series, 69, 1956).
Newburgh	The chronicle of William of Newburgh in *Chronicles of the Reigns of Stephen, Henry II and Richard I,* ed. R. Howlett, 2 vols., continuous pagination (Rolls Series, London, 1884–9).
Northumberland Assize Rolls	*Three Early Assize Rolls for Northumberland,* ed. W. Page (Surtees Society, 88, 1891).
O'Brien, *God's Peace*	B. R. O'Brien, *God's Peace and King's Peace: The Laws of Edward the Confessor* (Philadelphia, 1999), with the text of the *Leges Edwardi Confessoris,* between pp. 156 and 203.
Osney	'Annales Monasterii de Oseneia', in *Annales Monastici,* 5 vols., ed. H. R. Luard (Rolls Series, London, 1864–9), vol. 4.
Paris	*Matthaei Parisiensis, monachi Sancti Albani Chronica Majora,* ed. H. R. Luard, 7 vols. (Rolls Series, London, 1872–83). Unless stated, all references are to volume 2.
Paris, *GA*	*Gesta Abbatum Monasterii Sancti Albani,* ed. H. T. Riley, 3 vols. (Rolls Series, London, 1867–9). All references are to volume 1, where the section on John's reign is by Matthew Paris.
Paris, *HA*	*Matthaei Parisiensis, monachi Sancti Albani, Historia Anglorum,* ed. F. Madden, 3 vols. (Rolls Series, London, 1866–9).
Patent Rolls	*Patent Rolls of Henry III preserved in the Public Record Office, 1216–1232,* 2 vols. (London, 1901–3).
PCCG	*Pleas of the Crown for the County of Gloucester, before the Abbot of Reading and his Fellows Justices Itinerant, in the Fifth Year of the Reign of King Henry the Third and in the Year of Grace 1221,* ed. F. W. Maitland (London, 1884).
Peter de Brus Charter	*Cartularium Prioratus de Gyseburn volumen primum,* ed. W. Brown (Surtees Society, 86, 1889), pp. 92–4.
Pipe Roll 31 Henry I	*The Great Roll of the Pipe for the Thirty First Year of the Reign of King Henry I Michaelmas 1130,* ed. J.A. Green (Pipe Roll Society, new series 57, 2012).
Political Songs	*The Political Songs of England, from the reign of John to that of Edward II,* ed. T. Wright (Camden Society, 1839), with a new edition edited by P. Coss (Camden Society Classic reprints, 1996).

PR   *Pipe Roll*. Citations to pipe rolls are to volumes
                published by the Pipe Roll Society. The year in the
                citation is that which appears on the cover of each
                volume.

PR 1215   *Pipe Roll 17 John*, ed. R. A. Brown, and *Praestita Roll
                14–18 John*, ed. J. C. Holt (Pipe Roll Society, new
                series, 37, 1961).

RA   *The Registrum Antiquissimum of the Cathedral Church
                of Lincoln*, vol. 1, ed. C. W. Foster (Lincoln Record
                Society, 27, 1931).

RBE   *The Red Book of the Exchequer*, ed. H. Hall, 3 vols.
                (Rolls Series, London, 1896).

RCh   *Rotuli Chartarum in Turri Londinensi asservati*, ed. T.
                Duffus Hardy (Record Commission, London, 1837). This
                volume prints the charter rolls of John's reign.

Regesta   *Regesta Regum Anglo-Normannorum, 1066–1154.
                Volume III: 1135–54*, ed. H. A. Cronne and R. H. C.
                Davis (Oxford, 1968).

RF   *Rotuli de Oblatis et Finibus in Turri Londinensi
                asservati, Tempore Regis Johannis*, ed. T. Duffus Hardy
                (Record Commission, London, 1835). This volume
                prints the fine rolls of John's reign.

RH   *Rotuli Hundredorum*, 2 vols. (Record Commission,
                London, 1812, 1818).

Rishanger   *Willelmi Rishanger Chronica et Annales*, ed. H. T. Riley
                (Rolls Series, London, 1865).

RL   *Royal and other Historical Letters illustrative of the
                Reign of Henry III*, ed. W. W. Shirley, 2 vols. (Rolls
                Series, London, 1862, 1866). All references are to
                volume 1, unless stated.

RLC   *Rotuli Litterarum Clausarum in Turri Londinensi
                asservati*, ed. T. Duffus Hardy, 2 vols. (Record Commis-
                sion, London, 1833–4). All references, unless stated, are
                to volume 1, which prints the close rolls for John's reign.

RLJ   *Rotuli de Liberate ac de Misis et Praestitis, Regnante
                Johanne*, ed. T. Duffus Hardy (Record Commission,
                London, 1844).

RLP   *Rotuli Litterarum Patentium in Turri Londinensi
                asservati*, ed. T. Duffus Hardy (Record Commission,
                London, 1835). This volume prints the patent rolls of
                King John.

Rolls of the   *Rolls of the King's Court in the Reign of King
King's Court   Richard the First, 1194–1195*, ed. F. W. Maitland
                (Pipe Roll Society, 14, 1891).

Rolls War.   *Rolls of the Justices in Eyre being the rolls of pleas
                    and assizes for Gloucestershire, Warwickshire and
                    Staffordshire, 1221–1222*, ed. D. M. Stenton (Selden
                    Society, 59, 1940).

RRS   *Regesta Regum Scottorum. Volume II: The Acts of
                    William I, King of Scots, 1165–1214*, ed. G. W. S.
                    Barrow with the collaboration of W. W. Scott
                    (Edinburgh, 1971).

SAEC   *Scottish Annals from English Chroniclers* AD *500 to
                    1286*, ed. A. O. Anderson, 2nd edn (Stamford, 1991).

Sarum Missal   *The Sarum Missal in English* (London, 1868).

SC   *Select Charters and Other Illustrations of English
                    Constitutional History from the Earliest Times to the
                    Reign of Edward the First*, ed. W. Stubbs, 9th edn,
                    revised throughout by H. W. C. Davis (Oxford,
                    1921).

SCWR   *Select Cases of Procedure without Writ*, ed.
                    H. G. Richardson and G. O. Sayles (Selden
                    Society, 60, 1941).

SLI   *Selected Letters of Pope Innocent III concerning
                    England (1198–1216)*, ed. C. R. Cheney and W. H.
                    Semple (London, 1953).

Southwark and   'The Annals of Southwark and Merton', ed. M.
Merton   Tyson (Sussex Archaeological Collections 36, 1925),
                    pp. 24–57.

Special Eyre   *The 1258–9 Special Eyre of Surrey and Kent*, ed. A. H.
                    Hershey (Surrey Record Society, 38, 2004).

SPF   *Select Pleas of the Forest*, ed. G. J. Turner (Selden
                    Society 13, 1899).

SPMC   *Select Pleas in Manorial and other Seignorial Courts*,
                    ed. F. W. Maitland (Selden Society, 2, 1888).

SR   *The Statutes of the Realm. Printed by command of
                    his Majesty George the Third in pursuance of an
                    address of the House of Commons of Great Britain;
                    volume the first* (London, 1810).

St Augustine's   *William Thorne's Chronicle of Saint Augustine's
Canterbury   Abbey Canterbury*, trans. A. H. Davis (Oxford,
                    1934). This English translation is collated with the
                    Latin text printed in *Historiae Anglicanae Scriptores
                    X*, ed. R. Twysden (London, 1652).

Statute of   *Histoire Générale de Languedoc, avec des notes
Pamiers   et les pièces justificatives*, vol. XVIII, ed. C. Devic
                    and J. Vaissete (Toulouse, 1879), columns 625–35.

BIBLIOGRAPHY   491

Tewkesbury   'Annales Monasterii de Theokesberia', in *Annales
                      Monastici*, ed. H. R. Luard, 5 vols. (London,
                      1864–69), vol. 1.
The bull   F. M. Powicke, 'The bull "Miramur plurimum"
'Miramur   and a letter to Archbishop Stephen Langton,
plurimum'   5 September 1215', *English Historical Review*,
                      44 (1929), pp. 87–93.
Thomas of   *Thomas of Marlborough, History of the Abbey
Marlborough   of Evesham*, ed. J. Sayers and L. Watkiss (Oxford,
                      2003).
                      Liber Pauperum of Vacarius, ed. F. du Zulueta
                      (Selden Society, 43,
Walter of Henley   *Walter of Henley and Other Treatises of Estate
                      Management and Accounting*, ed. D. Oschinsky
                      (Oxford, 1971).
Walter Map   *Walter Map, De Nugis Curialium, Courtiers'
                      Trifles*, ed. M. R. James, revised by C. N. L.
                      Brooke and R. A. B. Mynors (Oxford, 1983).
Waverley   'Annales Monasterii de Waverleia, AD 1–1291', in
                      Annales Monastici, ed. H. R. Luard 5 vols. (Rolls
                      Series, London, 1864–69), vol. 2.
Wendover   Wendover's chronicle (his 'Flowers of History') is
                      usually cited here from the earliest surviving text,
                      which is that found, with Paris's additions, in
                      Matthew Paris's *Chronica Majora: Matthaei
                      Parisiensis, monachi Sancti Albani Chronica
                      Majora*, ed. H. R. Luard, 7 vols. (Rolls Series,
                      London, 1872–83). Unless stated, all references are
                      to volume 2.
Wendover *Flores*   *The Flowers of History by Roger de Wendover*,
                      ed. H. G. Hewlett, 3 vols. (Rolls Series, London,
                      1886–9).
William le   *Gesta Philippi Augusti Francorum Regis auctore
Breton   Guillelmo Armorico, ipsius Regis Capellano*, in
                      *Recueil des Historiens des Gaules et de la France
                      Tome Dix-Septième*, nouvelle édition, ed. L.
                      Delisle (Paris, 1878), pp. 62–116.
Winchester   'Annales de Monasterii de Wintonia, 519–1277', in
                      Annales Monastici, ed. H. R. Luard, 5 vols. (Rolls
                      Series, London, 1864–9), vol. 1.
Worcester   'Annales Prioratus de Wigornia, AD 1–1377', in
                      Annales Monastici, ed. H. R. Luard, 5 vols. (Rolls
                      Series, London, 1864–9), vol. 4.

SECONDARY SOURCES

Alexander, J. and Binski, P., eds., *Age of Chivalry: Art in Plantagenet England, 1200–1400* (London, 1988).

Allen, M., *Mints and Money in Medieval England* (Cambridge, 2012).

Allen, M., 'The volume of the English currency, 1158–1470', *New Economic History Review*, 54 (2001), pp. 595–611.

Allen, R., 'Eorles and Beornes: contextualising Lawman's "Brut"', *Arthuriana*, 8 (1998), pp. 4–22.

Altamira, R., 'Magna Carta and Spanish medieval jurisprudence', in H. E. Malden, ed., *Magna Carta Commemoration Essays* (London, 1917), pp. 227–43.

Ambler, S., 'The Montfortian bishops and the justification of conciliar government in 1264', *Historical Research*, 85 (2012), pp. 193–209.

Ambler, S., 'Peacemakers and partisans: bishops and political reform in England 1213–1268' (University of London, doctoral thesis, 2012).

Ambler, S., 'Christmas at the court of King John', Magna Carta Project, blog posted on 9 December 2013: http://magnacartaresearch.blogspot.co.uk/2013/12/christmas-at-court-of-king-john.html.

Ambler, S., 'On kingship and tyranny: Grosseteste's memorandum and its place in the Baronial Reform Movement', *Thirteenth-Century England*, 14 (2013), pp. 115–28.

Ambler, S., 'Magna Carta: its confirmation at Simon de Montfort's parliament of 1265', forthcoming.

Annesley, S., 'The impact of Magna Carta on widows: evidence from the fine rolls, 1216–1225', Henry III Fine Rolls Project, Fine of the Month for November 2007: http://www.finerollshenry3.org.uk/content/month/fm-11-2007.html.

Annesley, S., 'Isabella countess of Arundel's confrontation with King Henry III', Henry III Fine Rolls Project, Fine of the Month for August 2009:http://www.finerollshenry3.org.uk/content/month/fm-08-2009.html.

Annesley, S., 'Countesses in the age of Magna Carta' (University of London, doctoral thesis, 2011)

Asaji, K., *The Angevin Empire and the Community of the Realm in England* (Osaka, 2010).

Ashbee, J., '"Gloriette" in Corte castle, 1260', Henry III Fine Rolls Project, Fine of the Month for July 2011, Henry III Fine Rolls Project: http://www.finerollshenry3.org.uk/content/month/fm-07-2011.html.

Ashe, L., 'William Marshal, Lancelot and Arthur: Chivalry and Kingship', in *Anglo-Norman Studies*, 30 (2008), pp. 19–40.

Aurell, M., *The Plantagenet Empire, 1154–1224*, translated from the French by David Crouch (Harlow, 2007).

Bailey, M., *The English Manor c.1200–c.1500* (Manchester, 2002).

Bailey, M., *Medieval Suffolk: An Economic and Social History, 1200–1500* (Woodbridge, 2007).

Baldwin, J. W., *Masters, Princes and Merchants: The Social Views of Peter the Chanter and His Circle*, 2 vols. (Princeton, 1970).

Baldwin, J. W., *The Government of Philip Augustus: Foundations of French Royal Power in the Middle Ages* (Berkeley, 1986).

Baldwin, J. W., 'Master Stephen Langton, future archbishop of Canterbury: the Paris schools and Magna Carta', *English Historical Review*, 123 (2008), pp. 811–46.

Ballard, A., *British Borough Charters, 1042–1216* (Cambridge, 1913).

Barlow, F., *Thomas Becket* (London, 1987).

Barratt, N., 'The revenue of King John', *English Historical Review*, 111 (1996), pp. 835–55.

Barratt, N., 'The revenues of John and Philip Augustus', in S. D. Church, ed., *King John: New Interpretations* (Woodbridge, 1999), pp. 75–99.

Barratt, N., 'The English revenue of Richard I', *English Historical Review*, 116 (2001), pp. 635–56.

Barratt, N., 'The 1213 pipe roll and exchequer authority at the end of John's reign', *Thirteenth Century England*, 12 (2009), pp. 31–44.

Barron, C., *London in the Later Middle Ages: Government and People, 1200–1500* (Oxford, 2004).

Barrow, J., ed., *English Episcopal Acta 35: Hereford 1234–1275* (Oxford, 2009).

Bartlett, R., *Gerald of Wales: 1146–1223* (Oxford, 1982).

Bartlett, R., *Trial by Fire and Water: The Medieval Judicial Ordeal* (Oxford, 1986).

Bartlett, R., *England under the Norman and Angevin Kings, 1075–1225* (Oxford, 2000).

Bazeley, M., 'The extent of the English forest in the thirteenth century', *Transactions of the Royal Historical Society*, 4th series, 4 (1921), pp. 140–72.

Bémont, C., *Simon de Montfort, Comte de Leicester* (Paris, 1884).

Biancalana, J., 'Widows at common law: the development of common law dower', *The Irish Jurist*, new series, 23 (1988), pp. 255–329.

Binski, P., *Becket's Crown: Art and Imagination in Gothic England, 1170–1350* (New Haven, 2004).

Bisson, T. N., *The Crisis of the Twelfth Century: Power, Lordship and the Origins of European Government* (Princeton, 2009).

Bisson, T. N., 'An "Unknown Charter" for Catalonia (A. D. 1205)', in his *Medieval France and her Neighbours: Studies in Early Institutional History* (London, 1989), pp. 199–212.

Blackstone, W., *The Great Charter and the Charter of the Forest, with other authentic instruments* (Oxford, 1759).

Bolton, J. L., *The Medieval English Economy, 1150–1300* (London, 1980), with a second edition (1985).

Bolton, J. L., *Money in the Medieval English Economy, 973–1489* (Manchester, 2012).

Bolton, J. L., 'The English economy in the early thirteenth century', in S. D. Church, ed., *King John: New Interpretations* (Woodbridge, 2009), pp. 27–40.

Borrie, M., 'What became of Magna Carta?', *British Library Journal*, 2 (1976), pp. 1–7.

Brand, P., *The Making of the Common Law* (London, 1992).

Brand, P., *The Origins of the English Legal Profession* (Oxford, 1992).

Brand, P., *Kings, Barons and Justices: The Making and Enforcement of Legislation in Thirteenth-Century England* (Cambridge, 2003).

Brand, P., 'The date and authorship of *Bracton*: a response', *Journal of Legal History*, 31 (2010), pp. 217–44.

Britnell, R. H., *The Commercialisation of English Society, 1000–1500* (Cambridge, 1993).

Brooke, C. N. L., assisted by G. Keir, *London 800–1216: The Shaping of a City* (London, 1975).

Broun, D., 'A new look at *Gesta Annalia* attributed to John of Fordun', in B. E. Crawford, ed., *Church, Chronicle and Learning in Medieval and Early Renaissance Scotland* (Edinburgh 1999), pp. 9–30.

Broun, D., and J. Harrison, *The Chronicle of Melrose Abbey. A Stratigraphic Edition. Volume I: Introduction and Facsimile Edition* (Scottish History Society, 2007).

Brown, P., *Sibton Abbey Cartularies and Charters, part I* (Suffolk Records Society, 1985).

Brown, R. A., 'Royal castle-building in England, 1154–1216', in his *Castles, Conquest and Charters: Collected Papers* (Woodbridge, 1989), pp. 19–64, reprinted from *English Historical Review*, 70 (1955), pp. 353–98.

Brown, R. A., 'A list of castles, 1154–1216', in his *Castles, Conquest and Charters: Collected Papers* (Woodbridge, 1989), pp. 90–121, reprinted from *English Historical Review*, 74 (1959), pp. 249–80.

Brundage, J. A., *Medieval Canon Law and the Crusader* (Madison, 1969).

Brunner, O., *Land and Lordship: Structures of Governance in Medieval Austria*, trans. from 4th edn by H. Kaminsky and J. Van Horn Melton (Philadelphia, 1992).

Buc, P., *L'Ambiguïté du Livre: Prince, pouvoir, et peuple dans les commentaires de la Bible au moyen âge* (Paris, 1994).

Burt, C., 'Political ideas and dialogue in England in the twelfth and thirteenth centuries', *Thirteenth Century England*, 13 (2011), pp. 1–10.

Cam, H. M., *Studies in the Hundred Rolls: Some Aspects of Thirteenth-Century Administration* (Oxford, 1921).

Cam, H. M., *The Hundred and the Hundred Rolls* (London, 1930).

Cam. H. M., 'The king's government as administered by the greater abbots of East Anglia' in her *Liberties and Communities in Medieval England* (Cambridge, 1944), pp. 183–204.

Carpenter, D. A., *The Minority of Henry III* (London, 1990).

Carpenter, D. A., *The Reign of Henry III* (London, 1996).

Carpenter, D. A., *Struggle for Mastery: Britain 1066–1284*, paperback edition (London, 2004).

Carpenter, D. A., 'Sheriffs of Oxfordshire and their subordinates, 1194–1236: a study in politics, patronage and society (University of Oxford, doctoral thesis, 1973).

Carpenter, D. A., 'The decline of the curial sheriff in England, 1194–1258', in his *Reign of Henry III*, pp. 151–82, reprinted from *English Historical Review*, 91 (1976), pp. 1–32.

Carpenter, D. A., 'Was there a crisis of the knightly class in the thirteenth century? The Oxfordshire evidence', in his *Reign of Henry III*, pp. 349–80, reprinted from *English Historical Review*, 95 (1980), pp. 721–52.

Carpenter, D. A., 'From King John to the first English duke', in R. Smith and J. S. Moore, eds., *The House of Lords: A Thousand Years of Tradition* (London, 1994), pp. 28–43.

Carpenter, D. A., 'The dating and making of Magna Carta', in his *Reign of Henry III* (London, 1996), pp. 1–16.

Carpenter, D. A., 'Justice and jurisdiction under King John and King Henry III', in his *Reign of Henry III* (London, 1996), pp. 17–44.

Carpenter, D. A., 'Abbot Ralph of Coggeshall's account of the last years of King Richard and the first years of King John', *English Historical Review*, 113 (1998), pp. 1210–30.

Carpenter, D. A., 'A noble in politics: Roger Mortimer in the period of baronial reform and rebellion, 1258–1265', in ed. A. J. Duggan, *Nobles and Nobility in Medieval Europe* (Woodbridge, 2000), pp. 183–204.

Carpenter, D. A., 'The second century of English feudalism', *Past & Present* 168 (2000), pp. 30–71.

Carpenter, D. A., 'The English royal chancery in the thirteenth century', in ed. A. Jobson, *English Government in the Thirteenth Century* (Woodbridge, 2004), pp. 49–70.

Carpenter, D. A., 'The household rolls of King Henry III of England (1216–72)', *Historical Research*, 80 (2006), pp. 22–46.

Carpenter, D. A., 'The career of Godfrey of Crowcombe: household knight of King John and steward of King Henry III', in eds. C. Given-Wilson, A. J. Kettle and L. Scales, *War, Government and Aristocracy in the British Isles, c.1150–1500: Essays in Honour of Michael Prestwich* (Woodbridge, 2008), pp. 26–54.

Carpenter, D. A., 'Hubert de Burgh, Matilda de Mowbray, and Magna Carta's protection of widows', Henry III Fine Rolls Project, Fine of the

Month for March 2008: http://www.finerollshenry3.org.uk/content/month/fm-03-2008.html.

Carpenter, D. A., 'The struggle to control the Peak: an unknown letter patent from January 1217', in *Foundations of Medieval Scholarship: Records Edited in Honour of David Crook*, eds. P. Brand and S. Cunningham (York, 2008), pp. 35–50.

Carpenter, D. A., '*In testimonium factorum brevium*: the origins of the English chancery rolls', in ed. N. Vincentt, *Records, Administration and Aristocratic Society in the Anglo-Norman Realm* (Woodbridge, 2009), pp. 1–28.

Carpenter, D. A., 'Archbishop Langton and Magna Carta: his contribution, his doubts and his hypocrisy', *English Historical Review*, 126 (2011), pp. 1041–65.

Carpenter, D. A., 'The vis et voluntas of King Henry III: the downfall and punishment of Robert de Ros', Henry III Fine Rolls Project, Fine of the Month for August 2012: http://www.finerollshenry3.org.uk/redist/pdf/fm-08-2012.pdf.

Carpenter, D. A., 'Chronology and truth: Matthew Paris and the *Chronica Majora*', a 'related paper' placed on the website of the Henry III Fine Rolls Project (2013): http://www.finerollshenry3.org.uk/redist/pdf/Chronologyandtruth3.pdf.

Carpenter, D. A., 'Magna Carta 1253: the ambitions of the church and the divisions within the realm', *Historical Research*, 86 (2013), pp. 179–90.

Carpenter, D. A., 'The Cerne abbey Magna Carta', Magna Carta Project, Feature of the Month, April 2014: http://magnacartaresearch.org/read/feature_of_the_month/Apr_2014.

Carpenter, D. A. 'Copies of Magna Carta in the century after 1215' to be found on the website of the Magna Carta Project: http://magnacarta.cmp.uea.ac.uk.

Cassidy, R., 'William Heron, hammer of the poor, persecutor of the religious, 1246–1258', *Northern History*, 50 (2013), pp. 9–19.

Cassidy, R., 'Bad sheriffs, custodial sheriffs, and control of the counties', forthcoming in *Thirteenth Century England*, 15.

Chaplais, P., *English Royal Documents, King John–Henry VI, 1199–1461* (Oxford, 1971).

Cheney, C. R., *Hubert Walter* (London, 1967).

Cheney, C. R., *Pope Innocent III and England* (Stuttgart, 1976).

Cheney, C. R., 'The alleged deposition of King John', in R. W. Hunt, W. A. Pantin and R. W. Southern, eds., *Studies in Medieval History presented to Frederick Maurice Powicke* (Oxford, 1948), pp. 100–116.

Cheney, C. R., 'The eve of Magna Carta', *Bulletin of the John Rylands Library*, 38 (1955–6), pp. 310–41.

Cheney, C. R., 'The twenty-five barons of Magna Carta', *Bulletin of the John Rylands Library*, 50 (1967–8), pp. 280–307.

Church, S. D., *The Household Knights of King John* (Cambridge, 1999).

Church, S. D., ed., *King John: New Interpretations* (Woodbridge, 1999).

Church, S. D., 'A question of numbers: the knights of the household of King John', *Thirteenth Century England*, 4 (1992), pp. 151–65.

Church, S. D., 'The earliest English muster roll, 18/19 December 1215', *Historical Research*, 67 (1994), pp. 1–17.

Church, S. D., 'The rewards of royal service in the household of King John: a dissenting opinion', *English Historical Review*, 110 (1995), pp. 277–302.

Church, S. D., 'The 1210 campaign in Ireland: evidence for a military revolution?', *Anglo-Norman Studies*, 20 (1998), pp. 45–57.

Church, S. D., 'Some aspects of the royal itinerary in the twelfth century', in *Thirteenth Century England*, 11 (2007), pp. 31–45.

Church, S. D., 'King John's testament and the last days of his reign', *English Historical Review*, 125 (2010), pp. 505–28.

Clanchy, M. T., *England and its Rulers, 1066–1272*; second edition with an Epilogue on Edward I (1272–1307) (Oxford, 1998).

Clanchy, M. T., *From Memory to Written Record: England 1066–1307*, 2nd edn (Oxford, 1993). There is now a third edition (2012).

Clanchy, M. T., 'Magna Carta, clause 34', *English Historical Review*, 79 (1964), pp. 542–8.

Clanchy, M. T., 'The franchise of return of writs', *Transactions of the Royal Historical Society*, 5th series, 17 (1967), pp. 59–82.

Clanchy, M. T., 'Magna Carta and the common pleas', in H. Mayr-Harting and R. I. Moore, eds., *Studies in Medieval History presented to R. H. C. Davis* (London, 1985), pp. 219–32.

Clasby, M., 'The abbot of St Albans, the royal will and Magna Carta', Henry III Fine Rolls Project, Fine of the Month for September 2009: http://www.finerollshenry3.org.uk/content/month/fm-09-2009.html.

Cokayne, G. E., *Complete Peerage of England, Scotland, Ireland and Great Britain and the United Kingdom*, ed. V. Gibbs et al., 12 vols. in 13 (London, 1912–59).

Collins, A. J., 'The documents of the Great Charter of 1215', *Proceedings of the British Academy*, 34 (1948), pp. 233–79.

Colvin, H. M., ed., *The History of the King's Works: The Middle Ages*, 2 vols. (London, 1963).

Coss, P. R., *Lordship, knighthood and locality: a study in English society, c. 1180–c. 1280:* (Cambridge, 1991).

Coss, P. R., *The Knight in Medieval England, 1000–1400* (Stroud, 1993).

Coss, P. R., *The Lady in Medieval England* (Stroud, 1998).

Coss, P. R., *The Origins of the English Gentry* (Cambridge, 2003).

Coss, P. R., 'Knighthood and the early thirteenth-century county court', *Thirteenth Century England*, 2 (1988), pp. 45–58.

Crook, D., *Records of the General Eyre* (London, 1982).

Crook, D., 'The sheriff of Nottingham and Robin Hood: the genesis of the legend?', *Thirteenth Century England*, 2 (1988), pp. 59–68.

Crook, D., 'The forest eyre in the reign of King John', in J. S. Loengard, ed., *Magna Carta and the England of King John* (Woodbridge, 2010), pp. 63–82.

Crouch, D., *William Marshal: Court, Career and Chivalry in the Angevin Empire, 1147–1219* (London, 1990). There is a second edition, *William Marshal: Knighthood, War and Chivalry* (London, 2002).

Crouch, D., *The Image of Aristocracy in Britain, 1000–1300* (London, 1992).

Crouch, D., *The Birth of Nobility: Constructing Aristocracy in England and France, 900–1300* (Harlow, 2005).

Crouch, D., *The English Aristocracy, 1070–1272: A Social Transformation* (New Haven, 2011).

Crouch, D., 'Normans and Anglo-Normans: a divided aristocracy?' in D. Bates and A. Curry, eds., *England and Normandy in the Middle Ages* (London, 1994), pp. 51–67.

Crouch, D., 'Baronial paranoia in King John's reign', in J. S. Loengard, ed., *Magna Carta and the England of King John* (Woodbridge, 2010), pp. 45–62.

Danziger, D. and Gillingham, J., *1215: The Year of Magna Carta* (London, 2003).

Davies, R. R., *Conquest, Coexistence and Change: Wales 1063–1415* (Oxford, 1987).

Davis, G. R. C., Breay, C., Harrison, J. and Smith, D. M., *Medieval Cartularies of Great Britain and Ireland* (London, 2010).

Davis, H. W. C., 'An unknown charter of liberties', *English Historical Review*, 20 (1905), pp. 719–26.

D'Avray, D., *Medieval Marriage: Symbolism and Society* (Oxford, 2005).

D'Avray, D., 'Magna Carta: its background in Stephen Langton's academic biblical exegesis and its episcopal reception', *Studi Medievalii*, 3rd series, xxxviii (1997), pp. 425–38.

Delisle, L., 'Mémoire sur une lettre inédite adressée à la reine Blanche', *Bibliothèque de l'École des Chartes*, 17 (1856), pp. 513–55.

De Zulueta, F. and Stein, P., *The Teaching of Roman Law in England around 1200* (Selden Society, supplementary series, 8, 1990).

Draper, P., 'King John and Wulfstan', *Journal of Medieval History*, 10 (1984), pp. 41–50.

Du Boulay, F. R. H., *The Lordship of Canterbury: An Essay on Medieval Society* (London, 1966).

Duby, G., *Le Dimanche de Bouvines 27 Juillet 1214* (Paris, 1985).

Duffy, S., 'John and Ireland: the origins of England's Irish problem', in S. D. Church, ed., *King John: New Interpretations* (Woodbridge, 1999), pp. 221–45.

Duggan, A., *Thomas Becket* (London, 2005).

Duncan, A. A. M., 'John king of England and the king of the Scots', in S. D. Church, ed., *King John: New Interpretations* (Woodbridge, 1999), pp. 247–71.

Duncan, A. A. M., 'Sources and uses of the chronicle of Melrose', in S. Taylor, ed., *Kings, Clerics and Chronicles in Scotland, 500–1297* (Dublin, 2000), pp. 147–85.

Dyer, C., *Standards of Living in the later Middle Ages: Social Change in England, c.1200–1520* (Cambridge, 1989).

Dyer, C., *Making a Living in the Middle Ages: The People of Britain, 850–1520* (London, 2002).

Eaglen, R. J., *The Abbey and Mint of Bury St Edmund's to 1279* (London, 2006).

Edwards, J. B., 'The English royal chamber and chancery in the reign of King John' (University of Cambridge, doctoral thesis, 1974).

Eyton, R. W., *Antiquities of Shropshire*, 12 vols. (London, 1854–60).

Faulkner, K., 'The transformation of knighthood in early thirteenth-century England', *English Historical Review*, 111 (1996), pp. 1–23.

Faulkner, K., 'The knights in the Magna Carta civil war', *Thirteenth Century England*, 8 (2001), pp. 1–12.

Fedorenko, G., 'The thirteenth-century *Chronique de Normandie*', *Anglo-Norman Studies*, 35 (2013), pp. 163–80.

Fox, J. C., 'The originals of the Great Charter', *English Historical Review*, 39 (1924), pp. 321–36.

Fryde, N., *Why Magna Carta? Angevin England Revisited* (London, 2001).

Galbraith, V. H., *Studies in the Public Records* (London, 1948).

Galbraith, V. H., 'The literacy of the medieval English kings', *Proceedings of the British Academy*, 21 (1935), pp. 201–37.

Galbraith, V. H., 'Runnymede revisited', *Proceedings of the American Philosophical Society*, 110 (1966), pp. 307–17.

Galbraith, V. H., 'A draft of Magna Carta (1215)', *Proceedings of the British Academy*, 53 (1967), pp. 345–60.

Gallagher, E. J., ed., *The Civil Pleas of the Suffolk Eyre of 1240* (Suffolk Records Society, 52, 2009).

Garnett, G., *Conquered England: Kingship, Succession, and Tenure, 1066–1166* (Oxford, 2007).

Gillingham, J., *Richard I* (London, 1999).

Garnett, G., 'The origins of the crown', in J. Hudson, ed., *The History of English Law: Centeuary Essays on 'Pollock and Maitland'* (Oxford, 1996), pp. 171–214.

Gillingham, J., *The English in the Twelfth Century: Imperialism, National Identity and Political Values* (Woodbridge, 2000).

Gillingham, J., *The Angevin Empire*, 2nd edn (London, 2001).

Gillingham, J., '1066 and the introduction of chivalry into England', in his *The English in the Twelfth Century*, pp. 209–32, reprinted from G. Garnett and J. Hudson, eds., *Law and Government in Medieval England and Normandy. Essays in Honour of Sir James Holt* (Cambridge, 1994), pp. 31–55.

Gillingham, J., 'Killing and mutilating political enemies in the British Isles from the late twelfth to the early fourteenth century: a comparative study', in B. Smith, ed., *Britain and Ireland, 900–1300* (Cambridge, 1999), pp. 113–34.

Gillingham, J., 'The Anonymous of Béthune, King John and Magna Carta', in J. S. Loengard, ed., *Magna Carta and the England of King John* (Woodbridge, 2010), pp. 27–44.

Gillingham, J., 'Coeur de Lion in captivity', *Quaestiones Medii Aevi Novae*, 18 (2013), pp. 59–83.

Gillingham, J., 'John (1167–1216)', *The Oxford Dictionary of National Biography*: http://dx.doi.org/10.1093/ref:odnb/14841.

Goddard, R., *Lordship and Medieval Urbanisation: Coventry 1043–1355* (Woodbridge, 2004).

Golob, P. E., 'The Ferrers earls of Derby: a study in the Honour of Tutbury 1066–1279' (University of Cambridge, doctoral thesis, 1984).

Gransden, A., *Historical Writing in England, c.550–c.1307* (London, 1974).

Gransden, A., ed., *The Customary of the Abbey of Bury St Edmunds* (Henry Bradshaw Society, 99, 1973).

Gransden, A., 'A democratic movement in the abbey of Bury St Edmunds in the late twelfth and early thirteenth centuries', *Journal of Ecclesiastical History*, 26 (1975), pp. 25–39.

Green, J. A., '"A Lasting Memorial": the charter of liberties of Henry I', in M. T. Flanagan and J. A. Green, eds., *Charters and Charter Scholarship in Britain and Ireland* (Basingstoke, 2005), pp. 53–68.

Green, V., *An Account of the Discovery of the Body of King John* (London and Worcester, 1797).

Hagger, M., 'A pipe roll for 25 Henry I', *English Historical Review*, 122 (2007), pp. 133–40.

Harcourt, L. W., 'The amercement of barons by their peers', *English Historical Review*, 22 (1907), pp. 732–40.

Harper-Bill, C., ed., *Blythburgh Priory Cartulary*, 2 vols. (Suffolk Records Society, 1980–81).

Harris, B. E., 'King John and the sheriffs' farms', *English Historical Review*, 79 (1964), pp. 532–42.

Harrison, D., *The Bridges of Medieval England: Transport and Society, 400–1800* (Oxford, 2004).

Harriss, G. L., *King, Parliament and Public Finance in Medieval England to 1369* (Oxford, 1975).

Hartland, B. and Dryburgh, P., 'The development of the fine rolls', *Thirteenth Century England*, 12 (2009), pp. 193–205.

Harvey, K., *Episcopal Appointments in England, c.1214–1344: From Episcopal Election to Papal Provision* (London, 2014).

Harvey, K., 'An un-christian king? King John and the Lenten fast', Magna Carta Project, blog posted on 12 March 2014: http://magnacartaresearch.blogspot.co.uk/2014/03/an-un-christian-king-king-john-and.html.

Harvey, P. D. A., ed., *The Peasant Land Market in Medieval England* (Oxford, 1984).

Harvey, P. D. A., 'The English inflation of 1180–1220', *Past & Present*, 61 (1973), pp. 3–30.

Hatcher, J., 'English serfdom and villeinage: towards a reassessment', *Past & Present*, 90 (1981), pp. 3–39.

Helmholz, R. H., 'Magna Carta and the *ius commune*', *University of Chicago Law Review*, 66 (1999), pp. 297–371.

Hershey, A. H., 'Justice and bureaucracy: the English royal writ and "1258"', *English Historical Review*, 113 (1998), pp. 829–51.

Hershey, A. H., 'The rise and fall of William de Bussey, a mid thirteenth-century steward', *Nottingham Medieval Studies*, 44 (2000), pp. 104–22.

Hey, J., 'Two oaths of the community in 1258', *Historical Research* (forthcoming).

Hilton, R. H., *A Medieval Society: the West Midlands at the end of the thirteenth century* (Cambridge, 1983).

Holden, B. W., *Lords of the Central Marches: English Aristocracy and Frontier Society, 1087–1265* (Oxford, 2008).

Holden, B. W., 'The balance of patronage: King John and the earl of Salisbury', *Haskins Society Journal*, 8 (1996), pp. 79–89.

Holden, B. W., 'King John, the Braoses and the Celtic fringe, 1207–1216', *Albion*, 33 (2001), pp. 1–23.

Holford, M. L. and Stringer, K. J., eds., *Border Liberties and Loyalties: North-East England, c.1200–c.1400* (Edinburgh, 2010).

Holt, J. C., *The Northerners: A Study in the Reign of King John* (Oxford, 1961).

Holt, J. C., *Magna Carta* (Cambridge, 1965); 2nd edn (Cambridge, 1992). Unless stated, all references are to the second edition. It is cited throughout as Holt, *MC*.

Holt, J. C., *Magna Carta and Medieval Government* (London, 1985).

Holt, J. C., *Colonial England, 1066–1215* (London, 1997). Chapters 11 to 13 of this volume have Holt's Royal Historical Society lectures on feudal society and the family, delivered between 1983 and 1985.

Holt, J. C., 'The making of Magna Carta', in his *Magna Carta and Medieval Government*, pp. 217–38, reprinted from *English Historical Review*, 72 (1957), pp. 401–22.

Holt, J. C., *King John* (Historical Association pamphlet, 1963), reprinted in his *Magna Carta and Medieval Government*, pp. 85–110, from where the page references come.

Holt, J. C., 'The St Albans chroniclers and Magna Carta', in his *Magna Carta and Medieval Government*, pp. 268–88, reprinted from *Transactions of the Royal Historical Society*, 5th series, 14 (1964), pp. 67–88.

Holt., J. C., 'Feudal society and the family IV: the heiress and the alien', *Transactions of the Royal Historical Society*, 5th series, 35 (1985), pp. 1–28, reprinted in his *Colonial England*, pp. 245–70.

Holt, J. C., 'King John's disaster in the Wash', in his *Magna Carta and Medieval Government*, pp. 111–22.

Holt, J. C., 'The Salisbury Magna Carta', in his *Magna Carta and Medieval Government*, pp. 259–64.

Holt, J. C., 'The *Casus Regis*: the law and politics of succession in the Plantagenet dominions, 1185–1247', in his *Colonial England*, pp. 307–26.

Holt, J. C., 'Magna Carta, 1215–1217: the legal and social context', in his *Colonial England*, pp. 291–306.

Howell, M. E., *Regalian Right in Medieval England* (London, 1962).

Hoyt, R. S., *The Royal Demesne in English Constitutional History*: 1066–1272 (Ithaca, NY, 1950).

Hudson, J., *The Formation of the English Common Law: Law and Society from the Norman Conquest to Magna Carta* (London, 1996).

Hudson, J., *The Oxford History of the Laws of England. Volume II: 871–1216* (Oxford, 2012).

Hudson, J., 'Henry I and counsel', in J. R. Maddicott and D. M. Palliser, eds., *The Medieval State: Essays Presented to James Campbell* (London, 2000), pp. 109–26.

Hudson, J., 'Magna Carta, the *ius commune*, and English common law', in J. S. Loengard, ed., *Magna Carta and the England of King John* (Woodbridge, 2010), pp. 99–119.

Hunnisett, R. F., *The Medieval Coroner* (Cambridge, 1961).

Hurnard, N. D., 'Magna Carta, clause 34', in R. W. Hunt, W. A. Pantin and R. W. Southern, eds., *Studies in Medieval History Presented to Frederick Maurice Powicke* (Oxford, 1948), pp. 157–79.

Huscroft, R., *Expulsion: England's Jewish Solution* (Stroud, 2006).

Huscroft, R., 'The political career and personal life of Robert Burnel, chancellor of Edward I' (University of London, doctoral thesis, 2000).

Hyams, P. R., *King, Lords and Peasants in Medieval England: The Common Law of Villeinage in the Twelfth and Thirteenth Centuries* (Oxford, 1980).

Hyams, P. R., *Rancor and Reconciliation in Medieval England: Wrong and its Redress from the Tenth to Thirteenth Centuries* (Ithaca, NY, and London, 2003).

Hyams, P. R., 'The origins of a peasant land market in England', *Journal of Economic History*, 23 (1970), pp. 18–31.

Janken, J. and Sapoznik, A., 'Spade cultivation and the intensification of land use, 1000–1300: written sources, archaeology and images', forthcoming.

Jenkinson, H., 'The jewels lost in the Wash', *History* 8 (1923), pp. 161–8.

Jobson, A., ed., *English Government in the Thirteenth Century* (Woodbridge, 2004).

Jobson, A., *The First English Revolution: Simon de Montfort, Henry III and the Barons' Wars* (London, 2012).

Jobson, A., 'Rebellion in Gloucestershire, 1215–1217: new evidence', forthcoming.

Johns, S., *Noblewomen, Aristocracy and Power in the Twelfth-Century Anglo-Norman Realm* (Manchester, 2003).

Jolliffe, J. E. A., *Angevin Kingship*, 2nd edn (London, 1963).

Jolliffe, J. E. A., 'The chamber and castle treasuries under King John', in R. W. Hunt, W. A. Pantin and R. W. Southern, eds., *Studies in Medieval History Presented to Frederick Maurice Powicke* (Oxford, 1948), pp. 117–42.

Kanter, J., 'The four knights' system and the evidence for its use in the fine rolls', Henry III Fine Rolls Project, Fine of the Month for March 2007: http://www.finerollshenry3.org.uk/content/month/fm-03-2007.html.

Kanter, J., 'Peripatetic and sedentary kingship: the itineraries of John and Henry III', *Thirteenth Century England*, 13 (2011), pp. 11–26.

Kantorowicz, E. H., *Laudes Regiae: A Study in Liturgical Acclamations and Medieval Ruler Worship* (Berkeley and Los Angeles, 1946).

Kaye, H., 'Serving the man that ruled: aspects of the domestic arrangements of the court of King John, 1199–1216' (University of East Anglia, doctoral thesis, 2013).

Keefe, T. K., *Feudal Assessments and the Political Community under Henry II and His Sons* (Berkeley, 1983).

Keefe, T. K., 'King Henry II and the earls: the pipe roll evidence', *Albion*, 13 (1981), pp. 191–222.

Keefe, T. K., 'Proffers for heirs and heiresses in the pipe rolls: some observations on indebtedness in the years before Magna Carta (1180–1212)', *Haskins Society Journal*, 5 (1996), pp. 99–109.

Keene, D., 'Medieval London and its region', *London Journal*, 14 (1989), pp. 99–111.

Keene, D., 'London from the post-Roman period to 1300', in D. M. Palliser, ed., *The Cambridge Urban History of Britain. Volume I: 600–1540* (Cambridge, 2000), pp. 187–216.

Kellett, A., 'King John in Knaresborough: the first known royal Maundy, *Yorkshire Archaeological Journal*, 62 (1990), pp. 69–90.

Ker, N. R., 'Liber custumarum and other manuscripts formerly at Guildhall', *Guildhall Miscellany*, vol. 1, no. 3 (London, 1954).

King, E., *England 1175–1425* (London, 1979).

Kitchen, C., 'Authentic images or manipulations? Printed facsimiles of archival documents in England to 1885', *Archives et Bibliothèques de Belgique* (numéro spécial 91, 2 vols., Brussels, 2010), ii, pp. 365–96.

Klerman, D., 'Settlement and decline of private prosecution in thirteenth-century England', *Law and History Review*, 19 (2001), pp. 1–65.

Klerman, D., 'Women prosecutors in thirteenth-century England', *Yale Journal of Law & the Humanities*, 14 (2002), pp. 271–318.

Kosminsky, E. A., *Studies in the Agrarian History of England in the Thirteenth Century* (Oxford, 1956).

La Monte, J. L., *Feudal Monarchy in the Latin Kingdom of Jerusalem, 1100–1291* (Cambridge, 1932).

Landon, L., *Itinerary of King Richard I* (Pipe Roll Society, new series, 13, 1935).

Lapsley, G. T., 'Buzones', in his *Crown, Community and Parliament* (Oxford, 1951), pp. 63–110, reprinted from *English Historical Review*, 47 (1932), pp. 177–93.

Latimer, P., 'Early thirteenth-century prices', in S. D. Church, ed., *King John: New Interpretations* (Woodbridge, 1999), pp. 41–73.

Latimer, P., 'The English inflation of 1180–1220 reconsidered', *Past & Present*, 171 (2001), pp. 3–29.

Latimer, P., 'Rebellion in south-western England and the Welsh marches', *Historical Research*, 80 (2007), pp. 185–224.

Lawlor, H. J., 'An unnoticed Charter of Henry III, 1217', *English Historical Review*, 22 (1907), pp. 514–18.

Legge, M. D., 'William the Marshal and Arthur of Brittany', *Historical Research*, 55 (1982), pp. 18–24.

Letters, S., with M. Fernandes, D. Keene and O. Myhill, *Gazetteer of Markets and Fairs in England and Wales to 1516*, 2 vols. (List and Index Society, special series, 32, 33, 2003), online at http://www.history.ac.uk/cmh/gaz/gazweb2.html.

Lloyd, J. E., *A History of Wales from the Earliest Times to the Edwardian Conquest*, 2 vols. (London, 1911).

Lloyd, S., *English Society and the Crusade, 1216–1307* (Oxford, 1988).

Loengard, J. S., ed., *Magna Carta and the England of King John* (Woodbridge, 2010).

Loengard, J. S., '*Rationabilis Dos* and the widow's "fair share" in the earlier thirteenth century', in S. S. Walker, ed., *Wife and Widow in Medieval England* (Ann Arbor, 1993), pp. 59–80.

Loengard, J. S., 'What did Magna Carta mean to widows?', in J. S. Loengard, ed., *Magna Carta and the England of King John*, pp. 134–50.

McGlynn, S., *Blood Cries Afar: The Forgotten Invasion of England, 1216* (Stroud, 2011).

McKechnie W. S., *Magna Carta: a Commentary on the Great Charter of King John* (Glasgow, 1905); second edition (1914).

McKenna, C., 'The de Beckerings of Lincolnshire: a case study of knights in the late twelfth and early thirteenth centuries' (King's College London, MA dissertation, 2013).

Maddicott, J. R., *Simon de Montfort* (Cambridge, 1994).

Maddicott, J. R., *The Origins of the English Parliament* (Oxford, 2010).

Maddicott, J. R., 'Magna Carta and the local community, 1215–1259', *Past & Present*, 102 (1984), pp. 25–65.

Maddicott, J. R., 'Edward I and the lessons of baronial reform: local government 1258–80', in *Thirteenth Century England*, 1 (1986), pp. 1–30.

Maddicott, J. R., ' "An infinite multitude of nobles": quality, quantity and politics in the pre-reform parliaments of Henry III', in *Thirteenth Century England*, 7 (1999), pp. 17–46.

Maddicott, J. R., 'The oath of Marlborough, 1209: fear, government and popular allegiance in the reign of King John', *English Historical Review*, 126 (2011), pp. 281–318.

Maddicott, J. R., 'Politics and the people in thirteenth-century England', *Thirteenth Century England*, 14 (2013), pp. 1–14.

'Magna Carta repeals': http://www.legislation.gov.uk/aep/Edw1cc1929/25/9/contents.

Malden, H. E., ed., *Magna Carta Commemoration Essays* (Royal Historical Society, London, 1917).

Mason, E., 'St Wulfstan's staff and its uses', *Medium Ævum*, 53 (1984), pp. 157–79.

Mason, E., 'The hero's invincible weapon: an aspect of Angevin propaganda', in C. Harper-Bill and R. Harvey, eds., *The Ideals and Practice of Medieval Knighthood III* (Woodbridge, 1990), pp. 121–37.

Masschaele, J., *Jury, State and Society in Medieval England* (Basingstoke, 2008).

Masschaele, J., 'The English economy in the age of Magna Carta', in J. S. Loengard, ed., *Magna Carta and the England of King John* (Woodbridge, 2010), pp. 151–67.

Meekings, C. A. F., *Crown Pleas of the Wiltshire Eyre, 1249* (Wiltshire Archaeological and Natural History Society, Records Branch, 16, 1960).

Meekings, C. A. F., *The 1235 Surrey Eyre. Volume I: Introduction* (Surrey Record Society, 31, 1979).

Miller, E. and Hatcher, J., *Medieval England: Rural Society and Economic Change, 1086–1348* (London, 1978).

Miller, E. and Hatcher, J., *Medieval England: Towns, Commerce and Crafts, 1086–1348* (London, 1995).

Milsom, S. F. C., *The Legal Framework of English Feudalism: The Maitland Lectures given in 1972* (Cambridge, 1976).

Mitchell, S. K., *Studies in Taxation under John and Henry III* (New Haven, 1914).

Moore, A. K., 'The loss of Normandy and the invention of *Terre Normannorum*, 1204', *English Historical Review*, 125 (2010), pp. 1,071–1,109.

Moore, A. K., 'The Thorrington dispute: a case study in Henry III's intervention with judicial process', Henry III Fine Rolls Project, Fine of the Month for July 2009: http://www.finerollshenry3.org.uk/content/month/fm-07-2009.html.

Morris, J. E., *The Welsh Wars of Edward the First* (Oxford, 1901).

Morris, M., *The Bigod Earls of Norfolk in the Thirteenth Century* (Woodbridge, 2005).

Mundill, R., *England's Jewish Solution: Experiment and Expulsion, 1262–1290* (Cambridge, 1998).

Musson, A., 'The local administration of justice: a re-appraisal of the "four knights" system', in A. Jobson, ed., *English Government in the Thirteenth Century* (Woodbridge, 2004), pp. 97–110.

Nelson, J. L., *Politics and Ritual in Early Medieval Europe* (London, 1986).

Nelson, J. L., 'Bad kingship in the earlier Middle Ages', *Haskins Society Journal*, 8 (1999), pp. 1–26.

Nichols, J. F., 'An early fourteenth-century petition from the tenants of Bocking to their manorial lord', *Economic History Review*, 2 (1930) pp. 300–7).

Norgate, K., *John Lackland* (London, 1902).

Norgate, K., *The Minority of Henry the Third* (London, 1912).

O'Brien, B. R., *God's Peace and King's Peace: the Laws of Edward the Confessor* (Philadelphia, 1999).

ODNB: H. C. G. Matthew and B. Harrison, eds., *The Oxford Dictionary of National Biography*, 60 vols. (Oxford, 2004), with the online edition at http://www.oxforddnb.com. Biographies of all the leading actors in 1215 may be found here.

Painter, S., *Studies in the History of the English Feudal Barony* (Baltimore, 1943).

Painter, S., *The Reign of King John* (Baltimore, 1949).

Palliser, D. M., ed., *The Cambridge Urban History of Britain. Volume I: 600–1540* (Cambridge, 2000).

Pallister, A., *Magna Carta: The Heritage of Liberty* (Oxford, 1971).

Palmer, R. C., *The County Courts of Medieval England* (Princeton, 1982).

Petit-Dutaillis, C., *Étude sur la vie et le règne de Louis VIII, 1187–1226* (Paris, 1894).

Pollock, F. and Maitland, F. W., *The History of English Law*, 2nd edn, 2 vols. (Cambridge, 1968).

Poole, A. L., *From Domesday Book to Magna Carta, 1087–1216* (Oxford, 1951).

Poole, R. L., 'The publication of Great Charters by the English Kings', *English Historical Review*, 28 (1913), pp. 444–53.

Post, G., *Studies in Medieval Legal Thought: Public Law and the State, 1100–1322* (Princeton, 1964).

Power, D. J., *The Norman Frontier in the Twelfth and Early Thirteenth Centuries* (Cambridge, 2004).

Power, D. J., 'King John and the Norman aristocracy', in S. D. Church, ed., *King John: New Interpretations* (Woodbridge, 1999), pp. 117–36.

Powicke, F. M., *Stephen Langton* (Oxford, 1928).

Powicke, F. M., *The Loss of Normandy (1189–1204): Studies in the History of the Angevin Empire*, 2nd edn (Manchester, 1961).

Powicke, F. M., 'Per judicum parium vel per legem terrae', in H. E. Malden, ed., *Magna Carta Commemoration Essays* (London, 1917), pp. 96–121.

Prescott, A. ' "Their present miserable state of cremation": the restoration of the Cotton library', http://www.uky.edu/~kiernan/eBeo_archives/articles90s/ajp-pms.htm.

Prestwich, M., *Edward I* (London, 1988).

Prestwich, M., *Armies and Warfare in the Middle Ages: The English Experience* (New Haven and London, 1996).

Raban, S., *A Second Domesday? The Hundred Rolls of 1279–80* (Oxford, 2004).

Rady, M., 'The right of resistance in Hungary', http://www.academia.edu/3683922/The_Right_of_Resistance_in_Hungary._A_Lecture (2013).

Ramsay, J. H., *The Angevin Empire* (London, 1903).

Ramsay, J. H., *A History of the Revenues of the Kings of England* (Oxford, 1925).

Ray, M., 'The lady is not for turning: Margaret de Redvers' fine not to be compelled to marry', Henry III Fine Rolls Project, Fine of the Month for December 2006: http://www.finerollshenry3.org.uk/content/month/fm-12-2006.html.

Razi, Z. and Smith, R., eds., *Medieval Society and the Manor Court* (Oxford, 1996).

Reynolds, S., *An Introduction to the History of English Medieval Towns* (Oxford, 1977).

Reynolds, S., *Kingdoms and Communities in Western Europe, 900–1300* (Oxford, 1984).

Reynolds, S., *Fiefs and Vassals: The Medieval Evidence Reinterpreted* (Oxford, 1994).

Reynolds, S., 'The rulers of London in the twelfth century', *History*, 57 (1972), pp. 337–57.

Reynolds, S., 'Magna Carta 1297 and the legal use of literacy', *Bulletin of the Institute of Historical Research*, 62 (1989), pp. 233–44.

Richardson, H. G., *The English Jewry under Angevin Kings* (London, 1960).

Richardson, H. G., 'The morrow of the Great Charter', *Bulletin of the John Rylands Library*, 28 (1944), pp. 422–43.

Richardson, H. G., 'The morrow of the Great Charter: an addendum', *Bulletin of the John Rylands Library*, 29 (1945), pp. 184–200.

Richardson, H. G., 'The coronation in medieval England', *Traditio*, 16 (1960), pp. 111–202.

Richardson, H. G. and G. O. Sayles, *The Governance of Medieval England from the Conquest to Magna Carta* (Edinburgh, 1964).

Richardson, H. G. and G. O. Sayles, *Law and Legislation from Aethelberht to Magna Carta* (Edinburgh, 1966).

Ridgeway, H. W., 'The Lord Edward and the Provisions of Oxford (1258): a study in faction', *Thirteenth Century England*, 1 (1986), pp. 89–99.

Ridgeway, H. W., 'King Henry III and the "aliens" 1236–1272', *Thirteenth Century England*, 2 (1988), pp. 81–92.

Ridgeway, H. W., 'Foreign favourites and Henry III's problems of patronage, 1247–1258', *English Historical Review*, 109 (1989), pp. 590–610.

Ridgeway, H., 'Mid thirteenth-century reformers and the localities: the sheriffs of the baronial regime', in P. Fleming, A. Gross and J. R. Lander, eds. *Regionalism and Revision: The Crown and its Provinces in England 1250–1650*, (London, 1998), pp. 59–86.

Riley-Smith, J., *The Feudal Nobility of the Kingdom of Jerusalem, 1174–1277* (London, 1973).

Roberts, P. B., *Studies in the Sermons of Stephen Langton* (Toronto, 1968).

Round, J. H., *The Commune of London, and Other Studies* (Westminster, 1899).

Rowlands, I. W., 'King John, Stephen Langton and Rochester castle, 1213–1215', in *Studies in Medieval History Presented to R. A. Brown*, ed. C. Harper-Bill, C. J. Holdsworth and J. L. Nelson (Woodbridge, 1989), pp. 267–80.

Rowlands, I. W., 'The text and distribution of the writ for the publication of Magna Carta, 1215', *English Historical Review*, 124 (2009), pp. 1422–31.

Sanders, I. J., *Feudal Military Service in England: A Study of the Constitutional and Military Powers of the 'Barones' in Mediaeval England* (London, 1956).

Sanders, I. J., *English Baronies: A Study of their Origin and Descent, 1086–1327* (Oxford, 1960).

Saul, N., 'Magna Carta and British values', *History Today: The Blog*, posted 16 June 2014: http://www.historytoday.com/blog/2014/06/magna-Carta-and-british-values.

Sharpe, R., 'Charters of liberties and royal proclamations', http://acts william2henry1.files.wordpress.com/2013/10/h1-a-liberties-2013-1.pdf.

Smith, J. B., 'The Treaty of Lambeth, 1217', *English Historical Review*, 94 (1979), pp. 562–79.

Smith, J. B., 'Magna Carta and the charters of the Welsh Princes', *English Historical Review*, 99 (1984), pp. 344–362.

Southern, R. W., 'England's first entry into Europe', in his *Medieval Humanism and Other Studies* (Oxford, 1970).

Stacey, R. C., *Politics, Policy and Finance under Henry III, 1216–1245* (Oxford, 1987).

Stacey, R. C., '1240–1260: a watershed in Anglo-Jewish relations', *Historical Research*, 61 (1988), pp. 135–50.

Stacey, R. C., 'Crusades, crusaders and the baronial *gravamina* of 1263–1264', *Thirteenth Century England*, 3 (1991), pp. 137–50.

Stacey, R. C., 'Parliamentary negotiation and the expulsion of the Jews from England', *Thirteenth Century England*, 6 (1997), pp. 77–102.

Stacey, R. C., 'The English Jews under Henry III', ch. 2 of *Jews in Medieval Britain*, ed. P. Skinner (Woodbridge, 2003).

Stafford, P., 'The laws of Cnut and the history of Anglo-Saxon royal promises', *Anglo-Saxon England*, 10 (1982), pp. 173–90.

Stenton, D. M., 'King John and the courts of justice', ch. 4 of her *English Justice between the Norman Conquest and the Great Charter* (London, 1965).

Stenton, F. M., *The First Century of English Feudalism, 1066–1166*, 2nd edn (Oxford, 1961).

Stevenson, A., 'From Domesday Book to the Hundred Rolls: lordship, landholding and local society in England, 1066–1280' (University of London, doctoral thesis, 2014).

Stevenson, W. B., 'England and Normandy, 1204–59', 2 vols. (University of Leeds, doctoral thesis, 1976).

Stewart, S., ed., *The 1263 Surrey Eyre* (Surrey Record Society, 40, 2006).

Stewart-Parker, W. J., 'The Bassets of High Wycombe: politics, lordship, locality and culture in the thirteenth century' (University of London, doctoral thesis, 2013).

Strickland, M., *War and Chivalry: The Conduct and Perception of War in England and Normandy, 1066–1217* (Cambridge, 1996).

Strickland, M., '*In coronam regiam iniuriam*: the barons' war and the legal status of rebellion, 1264–1266', in P. Andersen, M. Münster-Swendsen and H. Vogt, eds., *Law and Power in the Middle Ages* (Copenhagen, 2008), pp. 171–98.

Strickland, M. 'The enforcers of Magna Carta (act. 1215–1216)', *The Oxford Dictionary of National Biography*: http://www.oxforddnb.com/view/theme/93691.

Strickland, M., 'Fitzwalter, Robert (d. 1235)', *The Oxford Dictionary of National Biography*: http://dx.doi.org/10.1093/ref:odnb/9648.

Stringer, K. J., *Earl David of Huntingdon, 1152–1219: A Study in Anglo-Scottish History* (Edinburgh, 1985).

Stringer, K. J., 'Periphery and core in thirteenth-century Scotland: Alan, son of Roland, lord of Galloway and constable of Scotland', in *Medieval Scotland:*

Crown, Lordship and Community: Essays Presented to G. W. S. Barrow, ed. A. Grant and K. J. Stringer, eds., (Edinburgh, 1993), pp. 82–113.

Stringer, K. J, 'Kingship, conflict and state making in the reign of Alexander II: the war of 1215–1217 and its context', in R. D. Oram, ed., *The Reign of Alexander II 1214–1249* (Leiden and Boston, 2005), pp. 99–156.

Stringer, K. J., 'States, liberties and communities in medieval Britain and Ireland (*c*. 1100–1400)', in M. Prestwich, ed., *Liberties and Identities in the Medieval British Isles* (Woodbridge, 2008), pp. 5–36.

Summerson, H., commentaries on the chapters of the 1215 Magna Carta to be found on the website of the Magna Carta Project: http://magna cArta.cmp.uea.ac.uk.

Sutherland, D. W., *Quo Warranto Proceedings in the Reign of Edward I (1278–1294)* (Oxford, 1963).

Swanson, J., *John of Wales: A Study of the Works and Ideas of a Thirteenth-Century Friar* (Cambridge, 1989).

Tait, J., 'Studies in Magna Carta: waynagium and contenementum', *English Historical Review*, 27 (1912), pp. 720–28.

Taylor, A., 'Robert de Londres, illegitimate son of William, king of Scots', *Haskins Society Journal*, 19 (2008), pp. 99–119.

'The Lands of the Normans in England (1204–1244)', project website: http://www.hrionline.ac.uk/normans/.

Thomas, H. M., *Vassals, Heiresses, Crusaders, and Thugs: The Gentry of Angevin Yorkshire, 1154–1216* (Philadelphia, 1993).

Thomas, H. M., *The English and the Normans: Ethnic Hostility, Assimilation and Identity 1066–c.1220* (Oxford, 2003).

Thompson, F., *The First Century of Magna Carta: Why it Persisted as a Document* (Minneapolis, 1925).

Thompson, F., *Magna Carta: Its Role in the Making of the English Constitution, 1300–1629* (Minneapolis, 1948).

Tilley, C. D., 'The honour of Wallingford, 1066–1300' (University of London, doctoral thesis, 2012).

Tilley, C. D., 'Magna Carta and the honour of Wallingford', *Historical Research*, forthcoming.

Titow, J. Z., *English Rural Society, 1200–1350* (London, 1969).

Tout, T. F., *Chapters in the Administrative History of Mediaeval England: The Wardrobe, the Chamber, and the Small Seals*, 6 vols. (Manchester, 1920–33).

Turner, R. V., *The King and his Courts: The Role of John and Henry III in the Administration of Justice, 1199–1240* (Ithaca, NY, 1968).

Turner, R. V., *The English Judiciary in the Age of Glanvill and Bracton, c. 1176–1239* (Cambridge, 1985).

Turner, R. V., *Men Raised from the Dust: Administrative Service and Upward Mobility in Angevin England* (Philadelphia, 1988).

Turner, R. V., *Judges, Administrators and the Common Law in Angevin England* (London, 1994).

Turner, R. V., *King John* (London, 1994).

Turner, R. V., *Magna Carta through the Ages* (Harlow, 2003).

Turner, R. V., 'The exercise of the king's will in inheritance of baronies: the example of King John and William Briwerre', in his *Judges, Administrators and the Common Law*, pp. 269–88.

Turner, R. V., 'The Mandeville inheritance, 1189–1236', in his *Judges, Administrators and the Common Law*, pp. 289–306.

Turner, R. V., 'Simon of Pattishall, early common law judge from Northamptonshire', in his *Judges, Administrators and the Common Law*, pp. 199–214.

Turner, R. V., 'Richard Lionheart and English episcopal elections', *Albion*, 29 (1997), pp. 1–13.

Tyerman, C., *England and the Crusades, 1095–1588* (Chicago, 1988).

Ullmann, W., *Principles of Government and Politics in the Middle Ages* (London, 1961).

Van Caenegem, R. C., *Royal Writs in England from the Conquest to Glanvill: Studies in the Early History of the Common Law* (Selden Society, 77, 1959).

Van Laarhoven, J., 'Thou shalt *not* slay a tyrant! The so-called theory of John of Salisbury', in M. Wilks, ed., *The World of John of Salisbury* (Oxford, 1984), pp. 319–41.

Valente, C., *The Theory and Practice of Revolt in Medieval England* (Farnham, 2003).

Veach, C., *Lordship in Four Realms: The Lacy Family, 1166–1241* (Manchester, 2014).

Veach, C., 'King John and royal control in Ireland', forthcoming in *English Historical Review*.

Vincent, N., *Peter des Roches: An Alien in English Politics, 1205–1238* (Cambridge, 1996).

Vincent, N., *The Magna Carta* (Sotheby's, NY, 2007).

Vincent, N., *A Brief History of Britain, 1066–1485* (London, 2011).

Vincent, N., *Magna Carta: A Very Short Introduction* (Oxford 2012).

Vincent, N., ed., *English Episcopal Acta 9: Winchester 1205–1238* (Oxford, 1994).

Vincent, N., 'Hugh de Neville and his prisoners', *Archives*, 88 (1992), pp. 190–7.

Vincent, N., ed., *Records, Administration and Aristocratic Society in the Anglo-Norman Realm* (Woodbridge, 2009).

Vincent, N., ed., *Norman Charters from English Sources: Antiquaries, Archives and the Rediscovery of the Anglo-Norman Past* (Pipe Roll Society, new series, 59, 2013).

Vincent, N., 'A roll of knights summoned to campaign in 1213', *Historical Research*, 66 (1993), pp. 89–97.

Vincent, N., 'The borough of Chipping Sodbury and the fat men of France (1130–1270)', *Transactions of the Bristol and Gloucestershire Archaeological Society*, 116 (1998), pp. 141–59.

Vincent, N., 'Isabella of Angoulême: John's Jezebel', in *King John: New Interpretations*, ed. S. D. Church (Woodbridge, 1999), pp. 165–219.

Vincent, N., 'Warin and Henry fitzGerald, the king's chamberlains: the origins of the fitzGeralds revisited', *Anglo-Norman Studies*, 21 (1999), pp. 233–60.

Vincent, N., 'Master Elyas of Dereham (d. 1245): a reassessment', in C. M. Barron and J. M. Stratford, eds., *The Church and Learning in Later Medieval Society: Essays in Honour of R. B. Dobson* (Stamford, 2002), pp. 128–59.

Vincent, N., 'Who's who in Magna carta clause 50?', in *Le Médiéviste et la Monographie Familiale: sources, méthodes et problématiques*, ed. M. Aurell (Turnhout, 2004), pp. 235–64.

Vincent, N., ' "Why 1199?" Bureaucracy and enrolment under John and his contemporaries', in A. Jobson, ed., *English Government in the Thirteenth Century* (Woodbridge, 2004), pp. 17–48.

Vincent, N., 'Did Henry II have a policy towards the earls?', in *War, Government and Aristocracy in the British Isles, c.1150–1500: Essays in Honour of Michael Prestwich*, ed. C. Given-Wilson, A. Kettle and L. Scales (Woodbridge, 2008), pp. 1–25.

Vincent, N., 'Stephen Langton, archbishop of Canterbury', in ed. L.-J. Bataillon, N. Bériou, G. Dahan and R. Quinto, *Étienne Langton, Prédicateur, Bibliste, Théologien* (Turnhout, 2010), pp. 51–123.

Vincent, N., 'English liberties, Magna Carta (1215) and the Spanish connection', in *1212–1214: El trienio que hizo a Europa. Actas de la XXXVII Semana de Estudios Medievales de Estella, 19 al 23 de Julio de 2010* (Pamplona, 2011), pp. 243–61.

Vincent, N., 'The twenty-five barons of Magna Carta: an Augustinian echo?', in ed. P. Dalton and D. Luscombe, *Rulership and Rebellion in the Anglo-Norman World, c.1066–c.1216: Essays in Honour of Professor Edmund King* (Farnham, 2014).

Warren, W. L., *King John* (London, 1961).

Warren, W. L., *Henry II* (Berkeley and Los Angeles, 1973).

Warren, W. L., 'Painter's King John – forty years on', *Haskins Society Journal*, 1 (1989), pp. 1–10.

Waugh, S. L., *The Lordship of England: Royal Wardships and Marriages in English Society and Politics, 1217–1327* (Princeton, 1988).

Waugh, S. L., 'Tenure to contract: lordship and clientage in thirteenth-century England', *English Historical Review*, 101 (1986), pp. 811–39.

Waugh, S. L., 'The origins and early development of the articles of the escheator', *Thirteenth Century England*, 5 (1995), pp. 89–114.

Webster, P., 'King John's piety' (University of Cambridge, doctoral thesis, 2007).

Weiler, B., 'Symbolism and politics in the reign of Henry III', *Thirteenth Century England*, 9(2003), pp. 15–42.

West, F. J., *The Justiciarship in England, 1066–1232* (Cambridge, 1966).

White, A. B., *Self-Government at the King's Command* (Minneapolis, 1933).

White, A. B., 'The name Magna Carta', *English Historical Review*, 30 (1915), pp. 472–5, and 32 (1917), pp. 554–5.

Wild, B. L., ed., *The Wardrobe Accounts of Henry III* (Pipe Roll Society, new series, 68, 2012).

Wilkinson, L. J., *Women in Thirteenth-Century Lincolnshire* (Woodbridge, 2007).

Wilkinson, L. J., *Eleanor de Montfort: A Rebel Countess in Medieval England* (London, 2012).

Wilkinson, L. J., 'Women as sheriffs in early thirteenth-century England', in A. Jobson, ed., *English Government in the Thirteenth Century* (Woodbridge, 2004), pp. 111–24.

Williams, G. A., *Medieval London: From Commune to Capital* (London, 1963).

Young, C. R., *The Royal Forests of Medieval England* (Philadelphia, 1979).

Young, C. R., *The making of the Neville family in England, 1166–1400* (Woodbridge, 1996).

Notes

1 Magna Carta: The Documents

1. The four originals of the Charter vary slightly in their word length, as will be evident from the notes to the Latin text in chapter 2.

2. For languages in this period, see ch. 6 of Clanchy, *Memory to Written Record*.

3. Holt, 'Vernacular-French text'; BL Harley MS 409, fo. 48v, referring here to the Charter of Henry III.

4. See below, pp. 78–86.

5. Anonymous, pp. 129, 158; Gillingham, 'Anonymous', pp. 34–6; Marshal, line 13,159.

6. Walter Map, pp. 476–7; Galbraith, 'Literacy', pp. 213–15.

7. *Rishanger*, p. 405; Thompson, *Magna Carta*, pp. 147–50; for the view that the Charter was proclaimed earlier in English, see Clanchy, *Memory to Written Record*, pp. 220–21, and see below, pp. 136–7.

8. *F*, p. 137.

9. Crowland, p. 221; Coggeshall, p. 172; Dunstable, p. 43; Wendover, p. 589.

10. The printed text of the letter is *RLC*, pp. 377–8, from TNA C 54, 19, m. 11d. See White, 'The name Magna Carta'. A second copy of the order on the duplicate chancery close roll follows the corrected version. The order was addressed to the sheriff of Yorkshire but probably went to all the sheriffs.

11. *RLC*, p. 73b.

12. Wendover, iii, pp. 91–2.

13. *RLC*, ii, p. 73.

14. *CChR*, pp. 225–5; *SR*, p. 28.

15. Paris, iii, p. 382.

16. *CR 1251–3*, p. 482; Paris, vi, pp. 249–50; Paris, v, p. 375; Dunstable, p. 189.

17. Burton, p. 321; *DBM*, pp. 320–21.

18. Illustrated in Prestwich, *Edward I*, plate 20.

19. Wendover, *Flores*, ii, pp. 119–34; Paris, pp. 589–694. For all this see Holt, 'The St Albans choniclers'.

20. Paris, vi, p. 523.

21. Collins, 'Documents', pp. 235, 237–8. A copy of the 1215 Charter in a register of Canterbury cathedral was described as 'carta [of King John] magna De Ronnemed': Canterbury Cathedral Archives, Register E, fo. 46v.

22. *FH*, ii, pp. 153, 182, 220, 384–5, 409.

23. Thompson, *Magna Carta*, pp. 166, 182, 187, 197.

24. TNA E 164/2, fos. ccxxxiiii–ccxxxvii.

25. Collins, 'Documents', pp. 249–52 and plate 13; Holt, *MC*, pp. 491–2.

26. This was noticed by Blackstone, *Great Charter*, p. 22 note i.

27. For a much fuller discussion of the date of Magna Carta, see below, pp. 361–6.

28. Coggeshall, p. 172.

29. For measurements see Collins, 'Documents', p. 267, and Vincent, *The Magna Carta*, pp. 56–9.

30. Fox, 'Originals', p. 323.

31. Fox, 'Originals', p. 333 and note 2.

32. For the debate, see Holt, 'Salisbury Magna Carta', and Holt, *MC*, p. 442. I am grateful to Teresa Webber for confirming that the hand of the Salisbury Charter is perfectly compatible with 1215. It is hard to interpret the passage in which '*dupplicata*' appears on the back of the Salisbury Charter. I do not think it is significant.

33. See Fox, 'Originals', p. 330, for his comments, having collated the four originals.

34. See Collins, 'Documents', pp. 270–73.

35. Collins, 'Documents', p. 272.

36. Fox, 'Originals', p. 334; Collins, 'Documents', p. 272.

37. Collins, 'Documents', pp. 264–5; *RA*, p. 137.

38. For Wyems, see *Calendar of Inner Temple Records*, ii, pp. 30, 96, 121, 136, references that come from Paul Brand.

39. Collins, 'Documents', p. 260.

40. BL Cotton Charter XIII 31b, which has a transcription of the Charter made in 1731 after the fire with the letters supplied from Cii indicated in red. Fox, 'Originals', p. 323, says that twenty-seven letters had to be supplied, but eighteen of these come in a correction at the foot of the Charter, where they repeat the main text so as to indicate where the correction should go. See below, p. 58n.

41. Prescott, 'Restoration of the Cotton library', at note 134.

42. For Dering and the Canterbury archives, see Vincent, ed., *Norman Charters*, pp. 101–2.

43. Canterbury Cathedral Archives, Register E, fos. 46v–49v.

44. See Sharpe, 'Charters of liberties', pp. 37–8.
45. Baldwin, 'Master Stephen, Langton', pp. 838–46.
46. For the Articles and what follows, see Collins, 'Documents', pp. 234–43.
47. Holt, *MC*, pp. 242–7, 429–32; F, p. 129.
48. Holt, 'Vernacular-French text'.
49. Galbraith, 'A draft of Magna Carta'.
50. See below, pp. 345–7. I have set out the evidence in full in 'Copies of Magna Carta' on the website of the Magna Carta Project: http://magnacarta.cmp.uea.ac.uk.
51. Holt, *MC*, pp. 445–6.
52. Society of Antiquaries of London, MS 60, fos. 225v–228v.
53. These are listed and discussed, I hope with others found after going to press, in 'Copies of Magna Carta', on the website of the Magna Carta Project.

2 The Chapters, Contents and Text of Magna Carta

1. Cambridge University Library Ee. 2. 19, fos. 1–5. This volume is a statute book.
2. *SC*, pp. 300–302.
3. *RLP*, p. 148.
4. See Helmholz, 'Magna Carta', pp. 323–4.
5. Blackstone, *Great Charter*, pp. 10–24.
6. *SR*, pp. 9–13. J. C. Fox's unpublished collation in BL Add. MSS 41178, pp. 10–18, against which I have checked my own, uses all the engrossments but not the copy in the bishops' letter.
7. *SR*, pp. 9–13.
8. In many medieval hands it is hard to distinguish between 'c' and 't'. When they can be distinguished, the letters often appear to be interchangeable. The *Statutes of the Realm* text of the Lincoln Charter has 't' much more frequently that 'c'. It is sometimes hard to be sure, but I think this is correct, and my text largely follows that of the *Statues*, and so has '*iuditium*' and '*iustitia*', but also '*justiciarius*'. The other engrossments seem to use 'c' more often. Scribes were also inconsistent in their use of 'i' and 'j', and here I have followed what is in the text. I am grateful to Julia Crick for help with the Charter's paleography.
9. *F*, between pp. 128 and 129. I am grateful to Simon Luterbacher of Bloomsbury and Suzanne Irvine of Bonhams for sending me photographs of prints of the Pine engraving that came up for sale at their auction houses. Both fetched thousands of pounds.
10. TNA E 164/2, fos. ccxxxiiii–ccxxxvii.
11. Holt, *MC*, pp. 448–73.

3 King John and the Sources for His Reign

1. The 'movability' of conflicts across the Angevin dominions is a major theme in Veach, *Lordship in Four Realms*.
2. Power, *Norman Frontier*, pp. 414–15.
3. I take these details from Gillingham, *Richard I*, p. 324, a splendid biography.
4. Tewkesbury, p. 84.
5. V. Green, *Body of King John*, p. 4. A less authoritative account gives the height as five feet five inches: Poole, *Domesday Book to Magna Carta*, p. 486 note 2.
6. Gervase, ii, p. 92; Paris, p. 561.
7. For Gerald, see Bartlett, *Gerald of Wales*.
8. Gerald of Wales, pp. 202–5, 236–7.
9. Howden, iii, p. 198.
10. Howden, iv, pp. 5, 16, 60, 81.
11. For the Interdict, see below, pp. 198–9. For the contemporary historians of John's reign, see Gransden, *Historical Writing in England*, ch. 15.
12. Coggeshall, pp. 102–10; Carpenter, 'Coggeshall'.
13. *St Augustine's Canterbury*, pp. 137–57. Cheney, *Hubert Walter*, pp. 85–6. The St Augustine's account (pp. 155–6) says that John only took a palfrey for the settlement, not the rest of the 200 marks on offer. But the pipe roll shows he did take the money: *PR 1203*, pp. 103–4; *PR 1207*, p. 33.
14. Coggeshall, pp. 101, 93.
15. Gervase, ii, pp. 92–3. Gervase added that any reputation for softness was soon belied by John's later conduct, thinking here of his attack on the church.
16. See below, pp. 198–9.
17. For what follows, see Adam of Eynsham, pp. 137–44, 188.
18. Jocelin of Brakelond, p. 116.
19. For the chronicle of which the Anonymous's account is part, see Fedorenko, 'The thirteenth-century *Chronique de Normandie*'.
20. *RLC*, p. 208b.
21. Anonymous, p. 105. I am using the translation in Gillingham, 'Anonymous', pp. 37–8.
22. Anonymous, pp. 114–15, 119.
23. For discussions, see Powicke, *Loss of Normandy*, pp. 315–22; Legge, 'William the Marshal and Arthur of Brittany'.
24. Margam, p. 27.
25. Coggeshall, pp. 139–41, 145. The Briouzes were patrons of Margam.
26. *F*, p. 140.
27. Wendover, pp. 523–4.

28. Anonymous, pp. 114–15. I owe the translation to Cristian Ispir. Wendover, p. 531, Waverley, p. 265, and Margam, p. 30 (less explicitly), place the murder at Windsor.

29. These episodes are discussed in Gillingham, 'Anonymous', pp. 34–6.

30. The Anonymous places the scene at Windsor, but John's itinerary shows it must have been at the Tower.

31. Anonymous, pp. 139–41.

32. Anonymous, pp. 143–4.

33. As observed by Gillingham, 'Anonymous', p. 35.

34. Crouch, *William Marshal*, is another splendid biography.

35. Marshal, lines 13,267–70.

36. Marshal, lines 13,927–35, 14,473–84.

37. For the context here, see below, p. 203.

38. Marshal, lines 12,507–12; Legge, 'William the Marshal and Arthur of Brittany'.

39. Margam, p. 26.

40. Marshal, lines 13,801–8.

41. Marshal, lines 13,787–800.

42. Marshal, lines 13,191–214.

43. When in 1207 Geoffrey, archbishop of York, fell at the king's feet begging for his grace, John grovelled in his turn: 'look, I am doing as much for you as you are for me'. Here, however, John had picked his target well, since if anyone deserved ridicule it was his half-brother Geoffrey. See Gervase, ii, pp. lix–lx.

44. Marshal, lines 13,188, 13,227–32. There are many references to Bassingbourn in Church, *Household Knights*.

45. Marshal, lines 12,437–530.

46. Marshal, lines 12,580–84.

47. Coggeshall, p. 144.

48. Coggeshall, pp. 165, 170, 175, 181–2.

49. Coggeshall, p. 184.

50. Cristian Ispir is preparing a new edition of the chronicle as part of a doctoral thesis.

51. Crowland, pp. 203, 207, 210, 215, 232. I owe to Nicholas Vincent the suggestion that Crowland's source for Marius was Lucan's *Pharsalia* (Book II).

52. Crowland, Spalding, pp. 196–211.

53. Wendover, p. 527; Dunstable, p. 34; Lambeth Palace Library MS 371, fo. 56. Wendover was probably right in saying that Geoffrey was arrested by the knight William Talbot. Dunstable has the arrest being made by the earl of Salisbury, and Talbot was in his service; see Church, *Household Knights*, pp. 33–4.

54. Paris, pp. 667–9.

55. For edited and translated texts of both works, see *Dialogus* and

Glanvill. I have not, in this section on the record sources, discussed the vast corpus of private charters, both printed and unprinted, that are a central source for the social structures of both the twelfth and thirteenth centuries. Holt made extensive use of the twelve-volume *Early Yorkshire Charters*.

56. Marshal, lines 13625–32; *RLC*, p. 111; *RLP*, p. 33; Galbraith, *Studies*, p. 125.
57. *RCh*, pp. 92b–93; *RLC*, pp. 174, 176, 177, 182b; *RLP*, pp. 126b, 127, 133.
58. *PR 1208*, p. 139.
59. Paris, *GA*, p. 228.
60. *RLC*, pp. 99, 179.
61. *RLC*, pp. 175b, 154b; *RLP*, p. 105b.
62. *RLC*, p. 132; Crouch, *William Marshal*, pp. 108–9.
63. D. M. Stenton, 'King John', especially pp. 89–94.
64. D. M. Stenton, 'King John', p. 97.
65. *RLJ*, p. 110.
66. *DI*, pp. 250, 253.
67. *DI*, p. 248.
68. *DI*, pp. 241, 243; *RLJ*, pp. 95–6; *PR 1204*, p. xxxvi.
69. I owe this point to Katherine Harvey, 'An un-christian king?'. More generally, see Webster, 'King John's piety'.
70. See below, pp. 205–6.
71. Church, *Household Knights*, pp. 37–8.
72. *DI*, p. 234.
73. *RF*, p. 275; Holt, *King John*, p. 88.
74. William le Breton, p. 110.
75. *RLC*, p. 105.
76. Norgate, *John Lackland*, p. 2.
77. Marshal, lines 18,078–87.
78. For Isabella, see Vincent, 'John's Jezebel'.
79. Anonymous, pp. 180–81. For Eleanor, see Wilkinson, *Eleanor de Montfort*.
80. Wendover, p. 489.
81. Paris, p. 563.
82. *RLC*, pp. 177, 180b; *RLP*, p. 124b.
83. Delisle, 'Mémoire', pp. 525–6; Vincent, 'John's Jezebel', p. 211.
84. Anonymous, pp. 104–5. I have used the translation in Gillingham, 'Anonymous', pp. 39–40.
85. Vincent, 'John's Jezebel', p. 198.
86. Brown, 'Royal castle-building', p. 60; Colvin, *King's Works*, ii, pp. 617–19.
87. *RLP*, p. 138b.
88. See Ashbee, '"Gloriette" in Corfe castle'.

4 Magna Carta and Society: Women, Peasants, Jews, the Towns and the Church

1. I am grateful to Alexandra Sapoznik for commenting on a draft of this chapter.
2. Dunstable, p. 43.
3. See Masschaele, 'English economy'. For general surveys, see Bolton, *Medieval English Economy*; Miller and Hatcher, *Medieval England: Rural Society and Economic Change*, and their *Medieval England: Towns, Commerce and Crafts*; Dyer, *Making a Living in the Middle Ages*.
4. Miller and Hatcher, *Medieval England: Towns, Commerce and Crafts*, p. 278.
5. M. Allen, 'Volume of the English currency'; Britnell, *Commercialisation of English Society*; Letters, *Gazetteer of Markets and Fairs*.
6. Latimer, 'Early thirteenth-century prices', pp. 42, 69, 70.
7. Coggeshall, p. 151.
8. Margam, pp. 25, 26; Osney, p. 50.
9. This is the hypothesis advanced in Latimer, 'The English inflation reconsidered'.
10. See Bolton, 'The English economy in the early thirteenth century'; and, more generally, his *Money in the Medieval English Economy*, pp. 149–52.
11. P. D. A. Harvey, 'English inflation', p. 14. Harvey was here referring particularly to the inflation which he situated generally in the period 1180–1220.
12. Latimer, 'Early thirteenth-century prices', p. 61.
13. See Maddicott, 'Oath of Marlborough', p. 299 note 84, who takes a low estimate of three million.
14. See Appendix I.
15. See Wilkinson, *Women in Thirteenth-Century Lincolnshire*, pp. 2–3.
16. *Bracton*, ii, pp. 31, 281. It was once thought that the work entitled in modern editions *Bracton on the Laws and Customs of England* was written by a judge of Henry III's, Henry de Bracton, writing in the 1250s. However, S. E. Thorne and Paul Brand have argued persuasively that the work was produced in the 1220s and 1230s by the legal circle around an earlier judge, William of Raleigh. Bracton became part of this circle, and added to the text after 1240, but he did not compose it. See Brand, 'The date and authorship of *Bracton*'.
17. Swanson, *John of Wales*, pp. 125–6.
18. Walter Map, pp. 304–5.
19. *CIM*, no. 2063; *Northumberland Assize Rolls*, p. 98.

20. Tenants-in-chief and under-tenants are discussed in the next chapter.

21. See below, pp. 415, 428, 452.

22. *Glanvill*, p. 85.

23. Holt, *MC*, pp. 452–3, ch. 7. I am grateful for the advice of Paul Brand, Daniel Hadas and Alice Rio on this point.

24. For how the chapter was revised at Runnymede, see below, pp. 346–7.

25. Waugh, *Lordship*, p. 159.

26. Holt, *MC*, p. 53.

27. *PR* 1214, p. 175; *RCh*, p. 203; Holt, *MC*, pp. 199–200. Her son was Roger de Cressy, her first husband having been Hugh de Cressy: Harper-Bill, ed., *Blythburgh Cartulary*, i, p. 7.

28. Paris, v, pp. 336–7; Annesley, 'Isabella, countess of Arundel'.

29. Marshal, lines 16,491–6; *RLP*, 199b; Wilkinson, 'Women as sheriffs'.

30. See below, pp. 353–4.

31. *Glanvill*, pp. 173–6.

32. Meekings, *Surrey Eyre*, pp. 123–5.

33. Meekings, *Wiltshire Eyre*, pp. 88–90.

34. Kosminsky, *Agrarian History*, pp. 203–6, p. xiv note 1; King, *England*, p. 50; Hatcher, 'English serfdom and villeinage', p. 7; Bailey, *Medieval Suffolk*, p. 50. Kosminsky's counties, the only ones for which the 1279 survey survives in whole or part, were Huntingdonshire, Cambridgeshire, Bedfordshire, Buckinghamshire, Oxfordshire and Warwickshire. For the survey, see Raban, *A Second Domesday?*

35. Kosminsky, *Agrarian History*, pp. 91, 205.

36. *Bracton*, ii, p. 89; Hyams, *King, Lords and Peasants*, p. 3.

37. For what is still a good introduction, see Titow, *English Rural Society*, ch. 3. There are detailed calculations of peasant standards of living in Dyer, *Standards of Living*, ch. 5.

38. Dyer, *Standards of Living*, pp. 126–7.

39. See Janken and Sapoznik, 'Spade cultivation'.

40. Tait, 'Studies in Magna Carta'.

41. Hyams, *King, Lords and Peasants*, pp. 143–4.

42. Holt, 'Vernacular-French text', p. 359, ch. 20.

43. In the conventional numbering, this was chapter 16 in the 1217 Charter and chapter 14 in that of 1225.

44. Harrison, *Bridges*, pp. 35–6.

45. For the grievance over bridge building was aggravated under John; see below, pp. 205–6.

46. For further discussion, see below, p. 457.

47. See, for example, Hyams, 'Origins of a peasant land market'; P. D. A. Harvey, ed., *Peasant Land Market*.

48. I owe this collection of names to Abigail Stevenson's doctoral thesis, 'Lordship, landholding and local society'.

49. Richardson and Sayles, *Law and Legislation*, pp. 137–9; and more generally, Hyams, *King, Lords and Peasants*, pp. 151–60.

50. *Dialogus*, pp. 150–53; Hyams, *King, Lords and Peasants*, pp. 261–5 and ch. 9. Lords did, however, get the lands of unfree peasants when they were convicted of a crime, so the stipulation in chapter 32 of the Charter would only have applied to land held freely. Henry Summerson has kindly advised me on this point.

51. For the Jews, see Richardson, *English Jewry*; Mundill, *England's Jewish Solution*; Huscroft, *Expulsion*.

52. O'Brien, *God's Peace*, pp. 183–4, 93–7.

53. *RLP*, p. 33; and *RCh*, p. 93.

54. I have been much helped in this section by Summerson's commentary on chapter 13.

55. Bodleian Library Rawlinson C 641, fos. 21v–29.

56. *Gesta Stephani*, p. 3.

57. Keene, 'Medieval London', p. 107.

58. Howden, *GR*, ii, pp. 213–14; Brooke and Keir, *London*, pp. 45–7; Ramsay, *Angevin Empire*, pp. 313–14, 317. For London's rulers and privileges in the twelfth century, see Reynolds, 'Rulers of London'; there may have been a commune before 1191 (p. 348).

59. *RLC*, p. 64; Round, *Commune of London*, pp. 237–42; 'London municipal collection', pp. 507–8; Reynolds, 'Rulers of London', p. 350; London Metropolitan Archives COL/CH/01/010 (*RCh*, p. 207). London was divided up into twenty-four wards, each under an alderman. There is debate as to whether the 'barons' were synonymous with the aldermen.

60. Ballard, *British Borough Charters*, pp. xxvi–xxxiii. *SC*, pp. 259–62, 305–12, has a useful selection of charters. See in general, Reynolds, *English Medieval Towns*, and Miller and Hatcher, *Medieval England: Towns, Commerce and Crafts*.

61. *EHD 1189–1327*, p. 881.

62. For John's customs, which seem a one-off initiative not related specifically to wool, see *PR 1203*, pp. xii–xiii; *PR 1204*, pp. 218–20; Barratt, 'Revenue of John', p. 838.

63. John of Wallingford, p. 131.

64. Masschaele, 'English economy', p. 158.

65. Goddard, *Coventry*, p. 78.

66. *Basset Charters*, no. 125.

67. *Dialogus*, pp. 162–3.

68. *EHD 1189–1327*, p. 353, ch. 6.

69. *Gesta Stephani*, pp. 3–4.

70. Howden, *GR*, ii, pp. 213–14.
71. 'London municipal collection, p. 726.
72. *SLI*, p. 166.
73. Thomas of Marlborough, pp. 76–479.
74. Helmholz, 'Magna Carta', p. 333.
75. See below, pp. 332–5, 342–52.

5 Magna Carta and Society: Earls, Barons, Knights and Free Tenants

1. *Bracton*, ii, p. 232.
2. *EHD 1042–1189*, p. 970; Keefe, *Feudal Assessments*, pp. 154–88.
3. Sanders, *Feudal Military Service*, ch. 3; Prestwich, *Armies and Warfare*, ch. 3.
4. M. Morris, *Bigod Earls*, p. 2.
5. The young earl of Warwick and the earl of Devon also remained loyal but were not politically very active.
6. Maddicott, '"An infinite multitude"', p. 28, although these estimates include minor barons not receiving personal summonses to parliament.
7. Painter, *Studies*, pp. 170–71, 174; *PR 1212*, pp. 3–4; Maddicott, *Simon de Montfort*, p. 43; Barratt, 'Revenue of John', p. 839; *Building Accounts*, p. 12. The Lacy figure excludes lands in Cheshire itself.
8. *EHD 1042–1189*, pp. 977–9.
9. *RLP*, p. 180b.
10. Faulkner, 'Transformation'.
11. See the court of the fitzGuy family: *Basset Charters*, no. 163, noted by Crouch, *English Aristocracy*, pp. 175, 289 note 46.
12. Holt, *Northerners*, ch. 4.
13. Carpenter, 'Was there a crisis?', p. 355; Faulkner, 'Transformation', pp. 12–13.
14. *CR 1254–6*, p. 293.
15. Crowland, Spalding, pp. 170–71.
16. See Coss, *The Knight*, ch. 2; Faulkner, 'Transformation'. For the debate as to whether the change was related to a social and economic crisis of the knightly class, see Coss, *Origins of the English Gentry*, ch. 4. Coss's book is the key work for the emergence of the late medieval gentry.
17. *MR 1208*, p. 143, no. 130; for the ceremony, see Coss, *Lordship, Knighthood and Locality*, pp. 248–53.
18. Paris, *GA*, pp. 225–6. For knights as baronial stewards, see Coss, 'Knighthood and the early thirteenth-century county court'.

19. For what follows, see Holt, *MC*, pp. 62–7, and Maddicott, 'Magna Carta', pp. 48–9.

20. *CRR*, iii, pp. 129–30.

21. *RF*, pp. 369–70.

22. *PR 1208*, p. 103; *PR 1210*, p. 75.

23. For example, *CFR 1228–9*, no. 261.

24. *CRR*, vii, pp. 158–9; *RLC*, p. 181.

25. White, *Self-Government at the King's Command*.

26. Holt also prefers 'county' to 'county court' in ch. 18.

27. *RLP*, p. 180b.

28. See below, pp. 382–3.

29. For what follows, see Coss, 'Knighthood and the early thirteenth-century county court'. Coss here questions the argument that the court was dominated by the barons of the county through their legal experts, stewards and bailiffs, for which see Palmer, *County Courts*, p. 88, and chs. 4 and 5.

30. *CRR*, vi, pp. 173, 228–31; vii, p. 24; x, pp. 344–6.

31. *CRR*, xii, nos. 2142, 2312; Holt, *MC*, pp. 391–3; Maddicott, 'Magna Carta', pp. 33–4, 49.

32. *RL*, pp. 101–4.

33. Carpenter, 'Sheriffs of Oxfordshire', pp. 181–7.

34. For free men, chapters 15, 16, 20, 27, 30, 34, 39; for earls and barons, chapters 2 and 21.

35. Clanchy, 'Magna Carta, clause 34'.

36. Pollock and Maitland, *History of English Law*, i, pp. 291–6.

37. Kosminsky, *Agrarian History*, pp. 259–60. The landholdings of jurors on hundreds, including those of Blackbourn hundred, are studied in Stevenson, 'Lordship, landholding and local society'. See also Asaji, *Angevin Empire*, ch. 7, Stewart, ed., *1263 Surrey Eyre*, ch. 10, and Masschaelle, *Jury, State and Society*, ch. 5. Masschaele's conclusion (pp. 195–6) from a study of the personnel of various juries from the late thirteenth and early fourteenth centuries, is that they were 'socially integrated bodies', drawing together peasant villagers, members of the gentry, and sometimes even knights and higher lords.

38. For provision for younger sons, see Thomas, *Vassals*, p. 129.

39. Maddicott, 'Oath of Marlborough'; *SC*, pp. 276–7. For serjeants in the rebellion of 1215, see below p. 307. These serjeants are distinct from the serjeants who were professional soldiers.

40. Chapter 3 and see chapter 4 of the Unknown Charter.

41. Alexander and Binski, eds., *Age of Chivalry*, nos. 141, 454.

42. Holt, *Northerners*, p. 110.

43. *PR 1209*, pp. 130–31, 21; Anonymous, p. 145; Holt, *Northerners*, pp. 172–3.

44. See below, pp. 344–5.

45. *Dialogus*, pp. 144–5, 174–5, 180–81; *BF*, p. 144.

46. *RCh*, p. 170; both cited by Summerson, ch. 21, where more evidence is assembled.

47. Marshal, line 13,383.

48. Maddicott, ' "An infinite multitude" ', pp. 21–2, shows that even some of those who did receive personal summonses might be men of small substance.

49. *BF*, pp. 223, 224, 227, 121, 183, 195; *CFR 1220–21*, nos. 70–72.

50. *RCh*, p. 103; see Stewart-Parker, 'The Bassets'.

51. Only the heirs of Thomas Basset would later be charged a baronial relief: *CFR 1219–20*, no. 165; *1220–21*, nos. 70–72; *1232–3*, no. 8.

52. Holt, *Northerners*, pp. 55–7; McKenna, 'Bekerings of Lincolnshire'. Simon's heir was charged a baronial relief: *CFR 1219–20*, no. 91; *PR 1219*, p. 129.

53. The holdings of several are analysed in Holt, *Northerners*, pp. 55–7.

54. See Crouch, *English Aristocracy*, p. 61.

55. For example, *LAR*, nos. 173, 1031, 1082; Summerson, ch. 21.

56. For the later history of this chapter, see below, pp. 453–5.

57. Maddicott, *Parliament*, p. 80 and ch. 2.

58. Carpenter, *Reign of Henry III*, pp. 388–9.

59. *CR 1231–4*, pp. 592–3.

60. *EHD 1042–1189*, pp. 969–70.

61. See particularly Holt, 'Feudal society and the family IV: the heiress and the alien'.

62. Carpenter, 'Second century', pp. 47–54; Golob, 'Ferrers earls of Derby', ch. 5.

63. Carpenter, 'Second century', p. 66. For knights following their lords, see Holt, *Northerners*, pp. 33–53; but see the qualifications in Thomas, *Vassals*, pp. 44–7.

64. Marshal, lines 13,532–44.

65. For further discussion, see below, pp. 217–8.

66. *Glanvill*, p. 84; Hudson, *Oxford History*, p. 809.

67. *RLC*, p. 215b.

68. *CRR*, vi, pp. 135–6; Holt, *MC*, p. 313. For an example (which I owe to Christine Havelock), *Lincs. Worcs. Eyre*, nos. 36, 804.

69. *Dialogus*, pp. 126–7.

70. Crouch, *William Marshal*, pp. 137–42, 161–8.

71. Carpenter, 'Sheriffs of Oxfordshire', chs. 2 and 6; *CRR*, v, p. 210.

72. *RL*, pp. 20–22.

73. *EHD 1189–1327*, p. 353, ch. 6 (the 1236 Statute of Merton on marriage); p. 403, ch. 21 (the 1275 Statute of Westminster on wardships).

74. Peter de Brus Charter, pp. 92–4; *RF*, p. 109; *PR 1207*, pp. 67, 70; Holt, *MC*, pp. 67–70, where the interpretation is far more consensual. For another interpretation, see Thomas, *Vassals*, pp. 203–5.

75. Magna Carta of Cheshire, pp. 101–9.

76. I am indebted to the discussion of aids in Painter, *Studies*, pp. 141–7.

77. See the case of John de Lacy: *RF*, pp. 494–5.

78. *PR 1209*, pp. 139, 21.

79. *CRR*, v, p. 39. For an earlier example of the three customary aids at the level of the under-tenant in 1183–4, see F. M. Stenton, *First Century*, pp. 173–4, 276–7.

80. *Glanvill*, pp. 111–12. Additional aids are also contemplated in the charter from 1183–4 cited in F. M. Stenton, *First Century*, pp. 173–4, 276–7.

81. Summerson, chapter 15, gives a different interpretation of this chapter.

82. See, for example, Jocelin of Brakelond, pp. 65–7; *CRR*, vi, p. 79.

83. *DBM*, pp. 274–5, ch. 4 (a manifesto of 1264); for the legislation on private courts in 1259, see *DBM*, pp. 138–41, chs. 1–3, and discussion in Brand, *Kings, Barons and Justices*, ch. 2.

84. *ERW*, pp. 63, lv; Maddicott, 'Magna Carta', pp. 53–4.

85. Anonymous, p. 150; Hudson, *Oxford History*, pp. 850–51.

86. Carpenter, *Minority*, pp. 387–8.

87. Clanchy, 'Magna Carta, clause 34', p. 545.

88. TNA E 401/1566, r. 3; for the Pirnhows see M. Morris, *Bigod Earls*, pp. 62, 64, 69; P. Brown, *Sibton*, pp. 84–7.

89. See below, pp. 425–6.

90. *SC*, p. 118, chs. 2 and 4.

91. Painter, *Studies*, pp. 146–7; Magna Carta of Cheshire, p. 105, ch. 10.

92. *EHD 1189–1327*, p. 403 (ch. 21) and see p. 417, ch. 5.

93. *SC*, pp. 179–80.

94. See below, p. 427.

95. *Rolls War.*, no. 406.

96. Maddicott, 'Magna Carta', p. 49; see below, p. 426.

97. Maddicott, *Parliament*, pp. 126–34, has an illuminating discussion of Magna Carta and lesser landholders.

98. Lawman, p. 310; see below, pp. 255–6.

99. *RLC*, p. 132; *SC*, p. 282.

6 Magna Carta and the Structure of Royal Government

1. *F*, p. 75.
2. Carpenter, *Minority*, p. 12; *Guala*, no. 140b.
3. Nelson, *Politics and Ritual*, pp. 378, 384–5; *Missale ad usum Ecclesie Westmonasteriensis*, ii, columns 683–4.
4. For the order at Richard's coronation, see Howden, *GR*, ii, pp. 80–83. For a description and discussion of Angevin coronations, see Aurell, *The Plantagenet Empire*, pp. 110–19.
5. *Letters of Grosseteste*, pp. 368–9.
6. Howden, *GR*, ii, pp. 81–2. The quotation is from Roger of Howden's description of Richard's coronation.
7. The evidence is not conclusive, but Richardson argued this clause of the coronation oath was introduced in 1154 with the accession of Henry II: Richardson, 'The coronation', pp. 153–61.
8. Walter Map, pp. 3–4, 24–5, 500–501.
9. For the household, see Church, *Constitutio*, text and introduction.
10. See below, p. 362.
11. For the appearance of the term, see Church, *Constitutio*, p. li note 64.
12. These figures will be updated by the Magna Carta Project.
13. *RLC*, pp. 175, 177, 214–214b; and see Chaplais, *Royal Documents*, pp. 16–18.
14. For a spirited and (I hope) amusing debate about when the rolls started, see Carpenter, 'Origins of the English chancery rolls', challenging and challenged by Vincent, '"Why 1199?"', and in his *Records, Administration and Aristocratic Society*, pp. xvi–xviii.
15. *RLC*, p. 196b; *RLP*, p. 137b; Galbraith, *Studies*, p. 80.
16. Church, *Constitutio*, pp. 206–7.
17. *DI*, p. 259.
18. For a view that sees the wardrobe gaining more independence from the chamber later in the reign, see Kaye, 'Serving the man that ruled', pp. 60–62.
19. *RLJ*, pp. 109–71; *DI*, pp. 231–69. That this is expenditure out of the wardrobe is shown by the marginal annotation at p. 237. It is possible that letters, not found on the close rolls, were written by chamber-wardrobe clerks and sealed by the small seal. It may, however, be a mistake to make any hard and fast distinction between chamber and chancery clerks. See Tout, *Chapters*, i, pp. 158–69.
20. *RLJ*, pp. 114, 118, 128, 138, 145, 155, 162, 170.
21. *RLJ*, p. 231. This money was in loans to the knights and serjeants in the army. See Church, 'The 1210 campaign in Ireland'.

22. Carpenter, 'Household rolls', pp. 33–41. These figures include the costs of the stables and feeding paupers.

23. *RLC*, p. 157. I have lifted these details from Ambler 'Christmas at the court of King John': http://magnacarta.research.blogspot.co.uk/2013/12/christmas-at-court-of-king-john.html.

24. Carpenter, 'Household rolls', pp. 29–30; Under Edward I the issue gained a new dimension by the use of purveyance to supply royal armies: Prestwich, *Edward I*, 407–10.

25. Coggeshall, p. 97; Kantorowicz, *Laudes Regiae*, pp. 174–7.

26. *DI*, p. 237.

27. *RLJ*, pp. 110, 170.

28. For John's itinerary, see below, pp. 204–6.

29. *DI*, pp. 245, 255, 261.

30. The role of the steward is discussed in Kaye, 'Serving the man that ruled', ch. 4.

31. See Church, *Household Knights*, and 'The knights of the household: a question of numbers'.

32. Paris, *GA*, pp. 227–8.

33. See above, pp. 84–5.

34. See West, *Justiciarship in England*.

35. Adam of Eynsham, pp. 101–9; *Election of Abbot Hugh*, pp. 38–9.

36. Maddicott, *Parliament*, pp. 75–6, 80, 143, 206, 388; Anonymous, pp. 145, 149; *CR 1242–7*, p. 242. See above, pp. 142–3.

37. *Pipe Roll 31 Henry I*, ed. J. A. Green; and see Hagger, 'A pipe roll for 25 Henry'.

38. See above, p. 88.

39. See above, pp. 119–20.

40. *Dialogus*, pp. 90–91.

41. For the tax of 1207, see below, p. 210. For a rather confusing discussion of aids, see *Bracton*, ii, p. 116.

42. Barratt, 'Revenue of John', pp. 840–41, 847. The percentages are not of total revenue but of the £19,728 actually paid into the exchequer, leaving out local expenditure.

43. *Dialogus*, p. 70.

44. *Dialogus*, pp. 69–70.

45. *Dialogus*, p. 116.

46. The exceptions were Cheshire, under the earl of Chester, and Durham under its bishop. John made Robert de Vieuxpont hereditary sheriff of Westmorland.

47. Crowland, p. 222.

48. Newburgh, p. 331.

49. Brown, 'A list of castles', p. 90.

50. Brown, 'Royal castle-building', p. 30, citing *RLC*, i, p. 6b.
51. The revised version became chapter 19 in the 1225 Charter.
52. For the forest, see *SPF*, with an excellent introduction by G. J. Turner; Young, *Royal Forests*; and Crook, 'Forest eyre'.
53. Bazeley, 'Extent of the English forest'.
54. *CR 1231–4*, pp. 588–9.
55. For this chapter, see Clanchy, 'Magna Carta and the common pleas'.
56. Gallagher, ed., *Suffolk Eyre*, pp. xiv–xvi.
57. *RCh*, p. 93b.
58. Cam, *The Hundred and the Hundred Rolls*, pp. 124–8.
59. See above, pp. 106–7.
60. The intellectual and institutional changes in the twelfth century that led to the abolition of the ordeal are explored in Bartlett, *Trial by Fire and Water*.
61. For the procedure, see Meekings, *Wiltshire Eyre*, p. 108.
62. Brand, *Making of the Common Law*, pp. 453–4; *ERW*, p. 1; Hudson, *Formation*, p. 239. I have adapted here a writ for Ireland.
63. Hudson, *Oxford History*, part III, gives a comprehensive account of these developments.
64. *Glanvill*, pp. 137, 148.
65. *MR 1199*, p. xlix and note 1 (Richardson's introduction).
66. *Glanvill*, p. 28. See Hudson, *Oxford History*, p. 534.
67. For the writ of right by which legal actions in the lord's court over tenure had to be commenced, see *Glanvill*, pp. 137, 148.
68. For a discussion of honorial courts, see Hudson, *Oxford History*, pp. 556–61.
69. Crouch, *English Aristocracy*, p. 169; Thomas, *Vassals*, pp. 72–3.
70. For this hypothesis, see Milsom, *Legal Framework*, ch. 1.
71. This is from Garnier de Pont-Sainte-Maxence's Life of Becket. The false oath referred to was one secured by the plaintiff affirming that he had not received justice in his lord's court: Hudson, *Oxford History*, p. 512, citing *English Lawsuits*, ii, p. 431.
72. For what follows, see Cam, *The Hundred and the Hundred Rolls*, pp. 137–45 and Appendix IV.
73. Golob, 'Ferrers earls of Derby', pp. 224–5; *RCh*, p. 108b; *RH*, ii, pp. 30, 291, 297; *CRR*, xix, no. 1188; *Basset Charters*, no. 199.
74. Clanchy, 'The franchise of return of writs', and more generally, Cam, *The Hundred and the Hundred Rolls*.
75. For a good example of such liberties, see John's charters to Northampton and Lincoln, *RCh*, pp. 45, 56.
76. For this perspective, see Crouch, *English Aristocracy*, pp. 167–9, where chs. 9 and 10 discuss seigneurial justice and liberties as a whole. The importance of liberties emerges powerfully in Stringer,

'States, liberties and communities', and Holford and Stringer, eds. *Border Liberties and Loyalties*.

77. See Cam, 'The king's government as administered by the greater abbots of East Anglia'.

78. Sutherland, *Quo Warranto*.

79. Vincent, 'A roll of knights'.

80. *PR 1214*, p. 153; *RLJ*, p. 177; *PR 1215*, pp. 81, 94.

81. Sanders, *Feudal Military Service*, ch. 4; Prestwich, *Armies and Warfare*, pp. 63, 68–71.

82. For this hypothesis and the details of the Irish campaign, see Church, 'The 1210 campaign', and also Holt, in *PR 1215*, p. 80.

83. Church, 'Earliest English muster roll'.

7 The Rule of the King: John and His Predecessors

1. Coggeshall, p. 170.

2. *SC*, pp. 117–19; J. A. Green, 'Charter of liberties'; Sharpe, 'Charters of liberties'.

3. Barratt, 'Revenue of John', p. 853; Green, 'Earliest surviving pipe roll'.

4. Keefe, 'Henry II and the earls', pp. 191–221, and at p. 214. Holt missed this article.

5. For an account of the revolt, see Carpenter, *Struggle for Mastery*, pp. 223–7.

6. Vincent, 'Did Henry II have a policy towards the earls?', p. 5.

7. Cokayne, *Complete Peerage*, vii, pp. 672–5.

8. Brown, 'A list of castles', p. 90.

9. The Articles put other arrangements in place should John enjoy the crusader's respite. See below, pp. 316, 347–8. For Henry's disseisins, see Holt, *MC*, pp. 82, 90–91, 104–5, 135–6, and Summerson, ch. 39.

10. *F*, p. 129.

11. Young, *Royal Forests*, p. 39.

12. Young, *Royal Forests*, p. 21.

13. Langton's seal was developed from that of Hubert Walter: Binski, *Becket's Crown*, pp. 40, 64, with pp. 36–40 and 62–5 for both men.

14. Coggeshall, pp. 91, 97; for a modern assessment, see Turner, 'Richard and English episcopal elections'.

15. Newburgh, pp. 305–6.

16. Barratt, 'English revenue of Richard', p. 637; Ramsay, *Revenues*, p. 191.

17. Howden, iii, pp. 210–11, 225; Mitchell, *Taxation*, p. 607; Maddicott, *Parliament*, p. 123; Gillingham, *Richard I*, p. 248 note 94.

18. Barratt, 'English revenue of Richard', p. 649.

19. *F*, p. 129.

20. Crook, 'Forest eyre', p. 70; Waugh, *Lordship of England*, p. 159.

21. *PR 1191–2*, p. 98; *PR 1190*, p. 21.

22. *PR 1196*, pp. 248–9; *PR 1197*, p. 61; *PR 1198*, pp. 213–14; Gillingham, *Richard I*, p. 262.

23. *PR 1190*, p. 101; *MR 1199*, p. 86; *PR 1196*, p. 138.

24. Coggeshall, pp. 91–3, 97.

25. Coggeshall, p. 93; Carpenter, 'Coggeshall', p. 1,219.

26. Howden, iv, p. 88.

27. *F*, pp. 75–6.

28. Coggeshall, pp. 107–10; Carpenter, 'Coggeshall', p. 1220.

29. *SC*, pp. 283–4; for discussion, see K. Harvey, *Episcopal Appointments*, pp. 19–28.

30. Coggeshall, pp. 112–13.

31. Carpenter, 'Coggeshall', pp. 1228–9. Fuller light will be shed on Coggeshall here in a forthcoming paper by James Willoughby.

32. For the end of the quarrel, see below, pp. 279–80.

33. Coggeshall, p. 101.

34. Powicke, *Loss of Normandy*, p. 326.

35. Norgate, *John Lackland*, p. 86.

36. Crouch, 'Normans and Anglo-Normans', pp. 62–3.

37. For revenues, see the detailed calculations and comparisons in Barratt, 'Revenues of John and Philip Augustus', especially at pp. 81–5.

38. For Philip's gains, see Power, *Norman Frontier*, pp. 414–15.

39. For a description of both Gisors and Chateau Gaillard, see Carpenter, *Struggle for Mastery*, pp. 253, 262.

40. Stevenson, 'England and Normandy', p. 202.

41. See below, pp. 234–5.

42. For the actions of the Norman barons, see Power, 'King John and the Norman aristocracy', and *Norman Frontier*, pp. 438–45.

43. *DD*, no. 206. For the last seneschal, William le Gros, see Vincent, 'Chipping Sodbury'.

44. Power, *Norman Frontier*, pp. 448–53.

45. Moore, 'Loss of Normandy', p. 1090. Much of what follows comes from this article, which draws on Moore's work with Daniel Power for 'The Lands of the Normans' project.

46. For the detail in what follows, see Kanter, 'Peripatetic and sedentary kingship', especially pp. 12–17. Church, 'Some aspects of the royal itinerary', reflects on the 'chaotic scramble' involved in such an itinerary.

47. Holt, *Magna Carta and Medieval Government*, ch. 6; Warren, *King John*, pp. 278–85.

48. Holt, *Northerners*, pp. 196–7.
49. Much of what follows is taken from Summerson, ch. 23.
50. *PR 1214*, p. 69.
51. See above, p. 99.
52. For what follows, see Barratt, 'Revenue of John'.
53. For the way later tallages were very fully paid, see Stacey, '1240–1260: a watershed?', p. 139.
54. Jolliffe, 'Chamber and castle treasuries', pp. 133–5; Gillingham, 'Coer de Lion in captivity', p. 78; Barratt, 'Revenue of John', p. 855, with detailed calculations of income in real terms on p. 853.
55. Barratt, 'Revenue of John', pp. 848–51.
56. Harris, 'King John and the sheriffs' farms', p. 533. For the farms, see above, p. 168.
57. Harris, 'King John and the sheriffs' farms', at p. 542; Holt, *Northerners*, p. 154.
58. For this view, see Holt, *MC*, p. 337.
59. It was thus merely as a convenient way of presenting the accounts that, in the pipe rolls, a custodial sheriff answered first for the farm and increment and then the profit above it (which might vary from year to year). For the detailed lists of all their revenue, which custodial sheriffs later presented (and may well have presented in John's reign), see Cassidy, 'Bad sheriffs, custodial sheriffs'.
60. Crowland, p. 215; chapters 28, 30, 31, 38. See above, pp. 180–1
61. Barratt, 'Revenue of John', pp. 846, 849; *PR 1210*, pp. xv–xvi.
62. For discussion of the word, see Hudson, 'Magna Carta', pp. 104, 109–10, although the suggestion here is my own.
63. Faulkner, 'Knights', p. 4; Summerson, ch. 20.
64. Cerne Cartulary, pp. 195–6, 206.
65. For the figures that follow, see Crook, 'Forest eyre', pp. 72–80; Barratt, 'Revenue of John', p. 846.
66. *RF*, p. 365; *PR 1206*, p. 73; Summerson, ch. 20.
67. Holt, *Northerners*, p. 159.
68. Clasby, 'The abbot of St Albans'.
69. *RLP*, p. 73; *RF*, p. 459; Mitchell, *Taxation*, pp. 84–92.
70. Barratt's guess ('Revenue of John', p. 839) is £15,000.
71. *PR 1208*, p. 72.
72. *PR 1208*, p. 169; *PR 1211*, p. 135; *PR 1214*, p. 81. For much of this and what follows I am indebted to Summerson, ch. 13.
73. Stacey, 'English Jews', p. 42.
74. £40,000 is the figure given in a case before the Jewish exchequer in 1219: *CPREJ*, p. 4. Chroniclers give the figure of £44,000; Richardson, *English Jewry*, pp. 168–72; Mitchell, *Taxation*, pp. 105–6;

Holt, *Northerners*, pp. 167–8; for an explanation of the discrepancy, see Stacey, 'English Jews', p. 43 note 10.

75. Wendover, p. 537; *RLP*, p. 102b; *RLC*, p. 459; Mitchell, *Taxation*, p. 106 note 64; *CFR 1222–3*, no. 183.

76. TNA E 401/1564; *RF*, p. 588; *PR 1216–25*, pp. 179–80.

77. *PR 1211*, p. 61; *PR 1212*, p. 109. I owe the point about the forfeiture to a King's College London MA essay by Elizabeth Holsgrove on Gant's debts.

78. *F*, p. 51; *RCh*, p. 93. Paul Brand pointed out to me this contrast.

79. The Articles and the Charter broadened the protection to include under-tenants; see above, p. 321.

80. No interest was taken while Jewish debts were in the king's hands.

81. TNA E 163/1/8B, m. 4.

82. Holt, *MC*, pp. 335–6 and note 180. I do not think that the later legislation cited proves the meaning of the chapter in this sense: *CR 1234–7*, pp. 214, 338 (the 1236 Statute of Merton).

83. *RLP*, p. 132. Earls and barons were not to be summoned, but John may have intended to make separate concessions to them.

84. *RF*, pp. 483–4, 494–5.

85. *RF*, p. 372; Holt, *Northerners*, pp. 52n, 75, 190.

86. *PR 1211*, p. 63; cited by Tilley, 'Magna Carta and the honour of Wallingford'.

87. *PR 1212*, pp. 3–4.

88. *PR 1209*, pp. 64, 108; *PR 1210*, pp. 97, 273; *PR 1211*, p. 68; *RLC*, p. 168.

89. *PR 1212*, p. 37.

90. Waugh, *Lordship*, p. 159; *RF*, pp. 430, 432; *PR 1208*, p. 100–1.

91. Keefe, *Feudal Assessments*, p. 30; Barratt, 'Revenue of John', p. 847.

92. *PR 1211*, p. 2; *PR 1212*, pp. 179, 172–3; M. Morris, *Bigod Earls*, p. 15.

93. Howden, iv, p. 152. John seems largely to be affirming and enforcing the procedures outlined in *Dialogus*, pp. 173–9.

94. Barratt, 'Revenue of John', p. 851.

95. *PR 1208*, p. 5; *PR 1209*, p. 42; *PR 1210*, p. 45, where just £20 remains unpaid. The debts of the earl of Clare have been explored in a King's College London MA essay by Jacob Ninan.

96. *PR 1208*, p. 143; *PR 1209*, p. 129; *PR 1210*, p. 151; *PR 1211*, p. 46.

97. *PR 1201*, p. 157; *PR 1208*, p. 145; *PR 1209*, pp. 130–31; *PR 1210*, p. 152; *PR 1211*, p. 53; Holt, *Northerners*, pp. 170–72.

98. Maddicott, *Parliament*, pp. 127–30, and see above, p. 139.

99. *MR 1208*, pp. 19, 23–68; for sureties being distrained, see *MR 1208*, pp. 23 and 63.

100. *RLC*, pp. 61, 67b; *RF*, p. 348; *PR 1205*, pp. 146, 147, 169.

101. *PR 1214*, pp. 52, 118.

102. *RLC*, pp. 61, 67b.

103. *CFR 1224–34*, vii (figures from Paul Dryburgh and Beth Hartland). I have calculated the 1207–8 figure myself. The fine rolls are lost between 1208 and 1213.

104. *MR 1208*, pp. 211–12.

105. Holt, *Northerners*, p. 34.

106. Clanchy, 'Magna Carta, clause 34', p. 545.

107. Hudson, *Oxford History*, pp. 559–60; Hurnard, 'Magna Carta, clause 34'; Clanchy, 'Magna Carta, clause 34'; *Glanvill*, p. 5; *Bracton*, ii, p. 300; *PR 1204*, pp. xxii–xxxiii (Lady Stenton's introduction); *PR 1214*, pp. xxv, 238.

108. Clanchy, 'Magna Carta and the common pleas', pp. 227–32.

109. *SC*, p. 282.

110. Many of the cases mentioned below, together with others unmentioned, are discussed in detail in Henry Summerson's commentary on chapter 40. Summerson also has here a fascinating account of John's quarrel with the Welsh marcher baron Fulk fitzWarin.

111. Holt, *MC*, pp. 150–55, brings together numerous examples.

112. *PR 1211*, p. 177; *PR 1208*, p. 89; Holt, *MC*, pp. 149, 153. Gant's offer was also for writs to begin his actions.

113. *PR 1209*, p. 80; *PR 1210*, p. 39; *PR 1201*, p. 157; *PR 1199*, p. 56; Anonymous, p. 145.

114. Holt, *Northerners*, p. 22; Holt, *MC*, pp. 148–9.

115. *PR 1207*, p. 74; Holt, *MC*, p. 154.

116. *RF*, p. 46; Holt, *MC*, p. 152.

117. *CRR*, i, p. 382; D. M. Stenton, 'King John', p. 93.

118. *RF*, p. 178. For what follows see Holt's ch. 5, 'Justice and jurisdiction', in his *MC*.

119. *CRR*, iv, p. 99; vi, pp. 133–4, 270. The Caldbeck and fitzWalter cases referred to below are analysed in Summerson, ch. 40. For the Say, Mandeville case, see Turner, *Judges*, ch. 16.

120. Marshal, lines 13,159–256.

121. *PR 1208*, p. 89.

122. *RLC*, pp. 33b, 189b; Stringer, *Earl David*, p. 51. For the 'third penny' and earls in general, see Crouch, *English Aristocracy*, pp. 40–48.

123. *PR 1195*, p. 226; *PR 1204*, p. 34; *PR 1208*, pp. 31, 134; *RLP*, p. 122b; *RLC*, pp. 173, 216; *PR 1214*, p. 11; *CRR*, vii, pp. 110–11.

124. Turner, 'Exercise of the king's will', pp. 281–2, 287; Holt, '*Casus Regis*', pp. 320–21. William de Percy was a ward of, and thus backed by, John's great servant William Brewer. Richard's claim against

William, his nephew, mirrored John's claim to the throne against his nephew Arthur. Richard may consequently have felt he should have all the inheritance.

125. Wendover, p. 523.

126. *RLP*, p. 94b; *RLC*, p. 213.

127. Marshal, lines 13,271–6, 13,362–8, 13,377–421, 14,319–88, 14, 445–86, 14,526–78, 14,708–23.

128. *RF*, pp. 389, 447–57. I owe knowledge of the Roger fitzAdam case to Thamar MacIver.

129. Barratt, 'Revenue of John', p. 849.

130. *RF*, p. 398.

131. *LAR*, nos. 1031, 1082; Summerson, ch. 21.

132. *PR 1207*, p. 74; *RF*, p. 413; *PR 1199*, p. 288. For Eustace see below, p. 276.

133. *RF*, p. 372. The fine included four palfreys, a riding horse worth about five marks each.

134. *PR 1212*, pp. 144–5.

135. Summerson, ch. 39.

136. *RLC*, pp. 16, 31.

137. *RLC*, p. 136b; *CRR*, xi, no. 416; Holt, *MC*, pp. 202–3.

138. *CRR*, xi, no. 1195.

139. *CRR*, vi, pp. 320, 344; *RLC*, p. 215; *CRR*, xii, no. 2646; Holt, *MC*, pp. 206–7; Turner, *King and his Courts*, pp. 162–3.

140. See below, pp. 388, 389, 435.

141. See Vincent, 'A roll of knights'.

142. *PR 1207*, pp. 47–8.

143. *RLC*, i, pp. 216b, 217; Tilley, 'Magna Carta and the honour of Wallingford'.

144. Stringer, *Earl David*, p. 50; *RLC*, pp. 216b–217.

145. *RF*, p. 373. FitzRoscelin was a tenant of Cressy's mother and her second husband, Robert fitzRoger: P. Brown, *Sibton*, pp. 90–93.

146. *CRR*, iii, pp. 129–30. This is the Richard Revel case mentioned above, pp. 132–3.

147. See below, pp. 347–8.

148. See Young, *Making of the Neville Family*.

149. Crouch, *William Marshall*, pp. 137, 141, 163, 195.

150. Wendover, pp. 532–3.

151. Carpenter, 'Sheriffs of Oxfordshire', ch. 6.

152. Marshal, lines 14,433–46, 14,463–8, 16,821–4, 18,301–8.

153. S. Lloyd, *English Society and the Crusade*, p. 100.

154. For what follows, see Turner, *English Judiciary*, ch. 4.

155. *PR 1210*, p. 75; Carpenter, *Minority*, pp. 296–7. For fitzPeter and Brewer, see Turner, *Men Raised from the Dust*, chs. 3 and 4.

156. Vincent, *Des Roches*, pp. 22–6.

157. *Political Songs*, p. 10; Clanchy, *England and its Rulers*, p. 129.

158. Vincent, *Des Roches*, pp. 27, 33.

159. For all of them, see Vincent, 'Who's who in Magna Carta clause 50?'

160. *PR 1208*, p. 72.

161. *PCCG*, p. xvii and notes 1 and 2 (Maitland's introduction).

162. *ASL*, no. 6.

163. *PCCG*, no. 154.

164. *PCCG*, p. xiv (Maitland's introduction).

165. Vincent, 'Who's who in Magna Carta clause 50?', pp. 239, 246.

166. There is at least some connection between a leading member of Gerard's group, the sheriff of Nottingham, Philip Marc, and the notorious sheriff of Nottingham in the Robin Hood legends, as David Crook has shown. The most plausible candidate for the real Robin Hood, one Robert of Wetherby (in Yorkshire), was certainly alive in John's reign. In 1225 he was eventually run to ground and beheaded, his body being suspended from a chain for all to see. The person responsible for this was Eustace of Lowdham. Eustace had been Philip Marc's deputy as sheriff of Nottingham. For all this, see Crook, 'Sheriff of Nottingham'.

167. Church, *Household Knights*, p. 88 note 83.

168. *RLC*, pp. 18b, 32b. For Alan Basset and his family, see Stewart-Parker, 'The Bassets'.

169. *RLC*, p. 87.

170. Walter Map, pp. 478–9.

171. See Church, 'The rewards of royal service'.

172. Carpenter, 'Godfrey of Crowcombe'.

173. Carpenter, *Minority*, p. 34; Holden, 'Balance of patronage', pp. 82–5; *RCh*, p. 53; Cokayne, *Complete Peerage*, iv, pp. 194–5; vi, pp. 457–8.

174. Carpenter, 'The struggle to control the Peak'.

175. He appears throughout Vincent, *Des Roches*.

176. Anonymous, p. 180.

177. *PR 1214*, p. 94.

178. *PR 1212*, pp. 157–8; Vincent, 'Hugh de Neville'; *Lost Letters*, pp. 113–15.

179. *RF*, pp. 382, 386; *PR 1207*, p. 149; *RLP*, 74b; Tout, *Chapters*, i, p. 161.

180. *RCh*, p. 191. There is no evidence for the nature of Maulay's offence.

181. Guisborough, p. 144.

182. Prestwich, *Edward I*, p. 422.

183. Waverley, p. 258; *RLP*, p. 72; Summerson, ch. 14; Maddicott, *Parliament*, pp. 125–6; Mitchell, *Taxation*, pp. 84–92.

184. Crowland, p. 203.
185. Articles, ch. 44; Magna Carta, chs. 56 and 57. See below, pp. 347–8.
186. *AWR*, no. 576; Davies, *Conquest*, p. 294.
187. Wendover, p. 534.
188. For different practices across Britain, see Gillingham, 'Killing and mutilating in the British Isles'.
189. *AWR*, no. 233; Smith, 'Magna Carta'.
190. *Gesta Annalia*, p. 277; Bower, pp. 448–9.
191. Duncan, 'John king of England', pp. 260–61.
192. I plan to give a much fuller account of the treaty and the events of 1209 on a future occasion. Teresa Webber has kindly advised me about the date of the hand. Dauvit Broun and Alice Taylor have made many helpful suggestions about the interpretation of the letter.
193. Howden, iv, p. 141.
194. Howden, *GR*, i, p. 95; *ASR*, no. 1.
195. Melrose, fo. 28v; see Broun and Harrison, *Chronicle of Melrose*, p. 131.
196. For this source, see Broun, '*Gesta Annalia*', and Duncan, 'Melrose', p. 170.
197. Duncan, 'John king of England', p. 270.
198. *RRS*, no. 488; Bower, pp. 455, 621. In the event only half of the 15,000 marks were paid: Duncan, 'John king of England', p. 270.
199. For the situation in 1212, see Taylor, 'Robert de Londres', pp. 113–14.
200. *RRS*, no. 305; *ASR*, no. 4; Bower, pp. 468–9.
201. *SAEC*, p. 330.
202. Taylor, 'Robert de Londres', pp. 110–14.
203. Stringer, 'Periphery and core', pp. 85–6.
204. See below, p. 353.
205. For further discussion, see below, pp. 318, 352–3.
206. *F*, p. 91.
207. For Ireland, see Duffy, 'John and Ireland'. I am grateful to Colin Veach for allowing me to see an advance copy of his 'King John and royal control in Ireland', from which some of what follows comes.
208. Holt, *Northerners*, p. 186.
209. *RF*, p. 99; *PR 1207*, p. 38.
210. Duffy, 'John and Ireland', pp. 240–42.
211. Wendover, pp. 523–4.
212. Anonymous, pp. 111–12; Crouch, 'Complaint', p. 174 note 10.
213. See above, p. 81.

214. Holden, *Lords of the Central Marches*, pp. 177–80.
215. Crouch, 'Complaint', pp. 168–79.
216. As Holt, *Northerners*, p. 185.
217. For the custom of outlawry, and whether John observed it, see below, pp. 281–2.

8 Standards of Judgement

1. For the idea of the kingdom, see Reynolds, *Kingdoms and Communities*, ch. 8.
2. Chapters 42, 18, 61, 35.
3. Chapters 42, 45, 12, 14.
4. Preamble and chapters 51, 61 and 42.
5. Chapters 1, 60.
6. Dunstable, p. 43.
7. *CR* 1254–6, pp. 194–5.
8. Holt, *MC*, 448–73, has 'realm' throughout. *EHD* 1189–1327, pp. 316–24, alternates between 'realm' and 'kingdom'.
9. BL Harleian 458, fo. 4.
10. Trinity College Cambridge, O. 76, fos. 6–11; Spalding Gentlemen's Society M.J. 13, fos. 140–43, for images of which I am grateful to Cristian Ispir.
11. Holt, 'Vernacular-French text', pp. 356–64; BL Add. MSS 32085, fos. 102–106v.
12. Chapters 61, 39, 55.
13. Holt, 'Vernacular-French text', p. 361.
14. Chapters 1, 63, 33, 41, 50.
15. Chapters 56, 59.
16. See above, p. 201.
17. Adam of Eynsham, pp. 114–15.
18. A key work on national identity in the century and a half after the Norman Conquest is Thomas, *English and Normans*.
19. Marshal, lines 5,215, 16,204–14, 15,616–20, 16,140–46, 15,564–5.
20. This is stressed in Holt, *King John*, pp. 107–9. For a more detailed discussion, see Thomas, *English and Normans*, pp. 337–43.
21. Newburgh, i, pp. 304–5.
22. Melrose, fo. 31v; Broun and Harrison, *Chronicle of Melrose*, pp. 131–4.
23. Crowland, p. 232.
24. Chapters 39, 42, 45, 55, 56.
25. *Glanvill*, p. 3.
26. Chapters 2, 13, 41, 60, 23, 25, 46.

27. Chapters 40, 52, 53, 57.

28. Chapters 19, 39, 52, 55, 56, 57, 59.

29. *Glanvill*, p. 107; *Bracton*, ii, p. 228.

30. Nelson, 'Bad kingship', pp. 1–26.

31. Ullmann, *Principles*, pp. 162–3.

32. Fulbert of Chartres, no. 51.

33. Fulbert of Chartres, p. 90 note 1.

34. I owe this to Alice Taylor's forthcoming work on homage.

35. Nelson, *Politics and Ritual*, pp. 151–3, 369–70.

36. Wendover, *Flores*, ii, p. 81; Coggeshall, p. 167.

37. Stafford, 'The laws of Cnut', pp. 177–9, 190; *EHD 500–1042*, pp. 428–30, chs. 69–83.

38. Holt, *MC*, pp. 475–6; Sharpe, 'Charters of liberties', p. 47, where all the many texts are analysed.

39. For the tenurial structures introduced by the Conquest, see Garnett, *Conquered England*.

40. *DD*, p. 2; *LHP*, pp. 134–5, ch. 31, p. 7.

41. See Hudson, 'Henry I and counsel'.

42. O'Brien, *God's Peace*, pp. 4, 31–6, 159–60, 192–3.

43. Chapters 2, 4, 11.

44. Lawman, pp. 411, xvi–xxiv (the introduction by Rosamond Allen). I think it unlikely that the work had anything to do with the Fleming, William de Frise. In some editions 'Lawman' is described as 'Layamon'.

45. In what follows, I have drawn on ideas in Ashe, 'William Marshal, Lancelot and Arthur'.

46. Lawman, pp. 254–6, 282–4, 309–10; R. Allen, 'Eorles and Beornes: contextualising Lawman's "Brut"'.

47. Ashe, 'William Marshal, Lancelot and Arthur', pp. 24–5; Geoffrey of Monmouth, p. 212.

48. Marshal, lines 6,941–3, 6,987–8.

49. For John's failures of courtliness, see Gillingham, 'Anonymous', pp. 40–41, and Crouch, 'Baronial paranoia', pp. 49–50.

50. Gervase, ii, pp. 92–3.

51. Marshal, lines 10,273–88.

52. Carpenter, 'From King John to the first English duke', pp. 29–36. For the theory and practice of warfare, see Strickland, *War and Chivalry*.

53. *Dialogus*, pp. 116–17; Marshal, lines 10,271–88.

54. De Zulueta and Stein, *Teaching of Roman Law in England*.

55. John of Salisbury, pp. 25, 28–9, 190–93 (III, 15; IV, 1; VIII, 17).

56. Waverley, p. 282; Crowland, p. 225; Margam, p. 27; Melrose, fo. 31v.

57. For Langton, see Powicke, *Stephen Langton*; Baldwin, *Masters and Princes*, i, pp. 25–31; Baldwin, 'Master Stephen Langton'; D'Avray, 'Magna Carta'; Vincent, 'Stephen Langton'.

58. *C&S*, p. 34, ch. 52; Baldwin, *Masters and Princes*, i, pp. 191–2.

59. Carpenter, *Minority*, pp. 263–5.

60. d'Avray, 'Magna Carta', pp. 426–7.

61. d'Avray, 'Magna Carta', pp. 426–9, 436–8. For comment on Deuteronomy, see also John of Salisbury, p. 36 (IV, 4).

62. Buc, *L'Ambiguïté du Livre*, pp. 281–2. The gloss is on I Samuel 10: 25. I follow Buc in translating 'scriptura' as 'charter'.

63. *F*, p. 75.

64. *Glanvill*, p. 108; see *Dialogus*, pp. 144, 180, where the £5 fee is only for a fee held from the king as part of an escheat.

65. *Dialogus*, p. 144.

66. *Glanvill*, pp. 82–3.

67. *SC*, pp. 179–80, ch. 4; *Glanvill*, pp. 58–69.

68. *Glanvill*, pp. 118–19; *Dialogus*, pp. 161–83.

69. *Glanvill*, pp. 111–12.

70. *Glanvill*, p. 114 and note c; *Dialogus*, pp. 168–9; Hudson, 'Magna Carta', pp. 104, 108–10.

71. *F*, p. 51 (a reference I owe to Paul Brand); *RLC*, p. 132; see above, p. 213.

72. Maddicott, *Parliament*, pp. 80–81.

73. Gervase, ii, pp. 96–7; *SC*, p. 277.

74. For a discussion, see Van Caenegem, *Royal Writs*, pp. 373–9; for dower, *Glanvill*, p. 69.

75. *Dialogus*, pp. 6–9, 219–20.

76. Helmholz, 'Magna Carta', pp. 311–55; and for a critique, Hudson, 'Magna Carta'.

77. D'Avray, *Medieval Marriage*, pp. 124–9; *EHD 500–1042*, p. 429; *Dialogus*, pp. 180–1. Walter Map, pp. 508–9.

78. Helmholz, 'Magna Carta', pp. 317–19, and Hudson, 'Magna Carta', pp. 104–7. I have been helped by Adrienne Showering's commentary on this chapter in a Kings College London MA Essay. For the influence of the *ius commune* on *Glanvill*, see Van Caenegem, *Royal Writs*, pp. 373–9.

79. *Glanvill*, p. 114.

80. Codex Justinianus, 8.16.7pr; Helmholz, 'Magna Carta', p. 328. I am grateful to Alice Rio for helping me interpret the passage in the Codex.

81. The *ius commune* may also have influenced the stipulation about interest on debt not accruing in minorities: Helmholz, 'Magna Carta', pp. 320–21.

82. Howden, *GR*, ii, pp. 213–14; Maddicott, *Parliament*, pp. 119–20.

83. Howden, iii, p. 136.

84. *PR 1198*, p. 222. This is the fine of William de Novo Mercato.

85. See above, pp. 132–3.

86. Ballard, *British Borough Charters*, pp. xxvi–xxxiii, 197–201, 214–16, 220–32; *SC*, pp. 305–10.

87. See above, p. 148.

88. Peter de Brus Charter, pp. 92–4; see above, pp. 146–7.

89. O'Brien, *God's Peace*, pp. 118–19, 121; Holt, *MC*, pp. 93–5, 118–19.

90. *LHP*, pp. 102–3, ch. 8, 1b, p. 317, note to ch. 8, Ib; Holt, *MC*, p. 94.

91. *MGL*, i, pp. 147–51.

92. *SC*, p. 277; J. E. Morris, *Welsh Wars*, p. 229 note 1; *CWR*, p. 336. For a discussion of Angevin ideology, see Aurell, *Plantagenet Empire*, pp. 83–162.

93. *RCh*, pp. 133–4; *Correspondance Administrative* no. 2, 022. I owe this reference to an MA essay by Anais Waag. For the theory of necessity and other Roman law ideas, see *Harriss, King, Parliament and Public Finance*, pp. 21–4.

94. Walter Map, pp. 508–9; *RL*, p. 20; *CRR*, v, pp. 202–4; Turner, *English Judiciary*, pp. 7 and 170. I owe the point about Guestling to Hudson, *Oxford History*, pp. 846–7.

95. *Dialogus*, pp. 2–3.

96. *Dialogus*, pp. 4–5, 20–21, 74–5, 164–5.

97. Vacarius, pp. 296, 12, lx, cxlviii.

98. *Glanvill*, p. 2; *Dialogus*, p. 5.

99. *Rolls of the King's Court*, p. 50; Howden, iii, p. 242; *Dialogus*, p. 169.

100. Mason, 'Hero's invincible weapon', pp. 131–2; see above, p. 97.

101. M. Allen, *Mints and Money*, pp. 54–5, 63; Eaglen, *Abbey and Mint*, plates 6–21.

102. *RLP*, p. 135b.

103. *Glanvill*, p. 108; *Dialogus*, pp. 144–5, 180–81.

104. For 1205, *Gervase*, ii, pp. 97–8.

105. Bisson, *Crisis of the Twelfth Century*, pp. 521, 527.

106. Crouch, 'Complaint', p. 170; Marshal, lines 13,229–32.

107. *PR 1216–25*, p. 10.

108. BL Cotton Julius D ii, fo. 128 (a cartulary of St Augustine's, Canterbury).

109. Marshal, lines 15,873–88; Gillingham, 'Anonymous', p. 37.

110. See below, pp. 299–300.

111. *PR 1210*, p. 120. Note the other punitive fines here.

112. See Garnett, 'The origins of the crown'.

113. *Election of Abbot Hugh*, pp. 163, 117.

114. For the Jews, see above, pp. 115–7.

115. *RCh*, pp. 133–4; addressed to Ireland, but echoing appeals made in England.

116. *SC*, p. 277; *RLP*, pp. 72–3. These examples and others are brought together in Summerson, ch. 12.

117. Wendover, pp. 538–9.

118. *RLP*, p. 76.

119. *Gesetze*, pp. 655–6, cited by Harriss, *King, Parliament and Public Finance*, p. 9.

120. *RLP*, p. 76.

121. D. M. Stenton, 'King John', *passim*.

122. *St Augustine's Canterbury*, pp. 148–9.

123. Holt, *MC*, p. 107; Holt, *Northerners*, p. 192.

124. See Holt, *MC*, pp. 327–31, for his discussion of chapter 39.

125. *RLP*, p. 141.

126. Marshal, lines 13,150–13,154.

127. For some of what follows, see Holt, *MC*, pp. 76–8; Vincent, 'English liberties', pp. 244–6.

128. Altamira, 'Magna Carta', pp. 230–31, and the reference there given.

129. Bisson, 'An "Unknown Charter" for Catalonia', pp. 199–212, quotations at pp. 202 and 211–12.

130. Statute of Pamiers, columns 625–35, chs. i, xv, xvii, xxviii, xxix, xxxi, xxxiii, xliii–v, and column 634.

131. The events of 1212 begin the next chapter.

9 Resistance, 1212–1215

1. Gervase, ii, pp. 96–9; *RLP*, p. 55. See Maddicott, *Parliament*, pp. 142–3.

2. *AWR*, no. 235.

3. *RLC*, p. 165b.

4. Dunstable, p. 33.

5. *RLP*, p. 94.

6. Anonymous, p. 115 (on fitzWalter).

7. Anonymous, p. 119. The evidence is carefully reviewed in Norgate, *John Lackland*, 289–93. There is a good account of fitzWalter by Matthew Strickland in the *ODNB*.

8. Furness, p. 521; Norgate, *John Lackland*, pp. 289–93. The story was specially inserted into a chronicle being copied out at Furness abbey. According to it, Vescy placed a common woman in John's bed. John then broke her finger, thinking it was Vescy's wife.

9. *PR 1203*, pp. 201, 204, 214; *PR 1207*, p. 74; *PR 1211*, p. 34; *CRR*, v, pp. 58–9; vi, pp. 135–6; *RLC*, pp. 99, 215b, 216b.

10. Alexander and Binski, eds., *Age of Chivalry*, no. 454.

11. *RLP*, pp. 17, 144b; *PR 1209*, p. 190. For fitzWalter's claim to Hertford (in right of his wife), see Summerson, ch. 40.

12. Anonymous, pp. 117–18; translation by Matthew Strickland in his 'Robert fitzWalter'.

13. Paris, *GA*, pp. 220–21, 226–7.

14. Wendover, p. 534.

15. *RCh*, pp. 192, 197.

16. *BF*, pp. 52–228. Vincent, 'English liberties', pp. 251–2, recognizes the importance of this inquiry.

17. See below, pp. 398–400.

18. John of Salisbury, pp. 15, 206–13 (III, 15; VIII, 20, 21); for discussion, see Van Laarhoven, 'Thou shall *not* slay a tyrant', p. 328. Aurell, *Plantagenet Empire*, pp. 70–71.

19. O'Brien, *God's Peace*, pp. 175–6.

20. Bémont, *Simon de Montfort*, p. 341; Maddicott, *Simon de Montfort*, pp. 31–2.

21. Cheney, 'Alleged deposition'.

22. Powicke, *Stephen Langton*, p. 97; Fryde, *Why Magna Carta?*, p. 100; Vincent, 'Stephen Langton', pp. 82–7, with a full analysis of biblical references.

23. *SLI*, pp. 128–9.

24. Cheney, 'Alleged deposition', p. 102.

25. *Brut*, pp. 194–5.

26. See above, pp. 272–3.

27. *F*, p. 108.

28. *RLP*, p. 97; Holt, *Northerners*, pp. 85–6.

29. *RLC*, p. 132. John may, however, have made concessions to earls and barons on an individual basis.

30. Crowland, pp. 207, 214–15.

31. *F*, p. 104.

32. This is the episode mentioned above, p. 81.

33. Wendover, p. 550.

34. Rowlands, 'King John', p. 270.

35. For all this, see Carpenter, 'Archbishop Langton', pp. 1057–60.

36. *SLI*, p. 189 and notes 4 and 5; *RBE*, ii, p. 772.

37. *F*, p. 126.

38. Coggeshall, p. 170.

39. *RLC*, 122, pp. 216b–217; *RLP*, p. 94b; Stringer, *Earl David*, pp. 50, 285 note 141.

40. *RLP*, p. 99.

41. *BNB*, ii, p. 666; *RLC*, p. 165b. For the outlawry of fitzWalter and Briouze (evidence is lacking for Vescy), see Summerson, ch. 39. The need for indictment by the 'fama patrie' comes from a judgement given in 1234 by William of Raleigh. Whether in an outlawry process

there was 'judgement by peers' depended on who was present at the final county court when the outlawry was pronounced. Chapter 39 could be read as requiring a baronial presence if the person being outlawed was a baron.

42. Holt, *MC*, pp. 190–91.

43. *PR 1214*, pp. 11, 31, 81, 93, 120, 175, and xiii–xxiv (Patricia Barnes's introduction); *RLP*, p. 129b; *RCh*, p. 203; Holt, *MC*, pp. 199–200; *RLC*, p. 386b; *PR 1218*, p. 93; *RF*, p. 528.

44. Holt, *MC*, pp. 206–7, 495.

45. Turner, 'Mandeville inheritance', pp. 294–8.

46. Dunstable, p. 45; Crowland, p. 225; John's letters about the marriage are the only places where he styles Geoffrey Earl of Essex: *RLC*, p. 162b; *RLP*, p. 109b.

47. *F*, pp. 104–7; *RCh*, p. 186. For the diplomacy of 1212–13, see Vincent, 'A roll of knights'.

48. Wendover, pp. 551–2; Crowland, p. 212; Coggeshall, p. 167.

49. Dunstable, pp. 40, 38; Coggeshall, p. 167; *SC*, p. 282.

50. Vincent, 'English liberties', p. 257.

51. James of Aragon, pp. 24–5.

52. Coggeshall, p. 168.

53. *RLC*, p. 202. Holt, *Northerners*, pp. 98–100, analyses the army.

54. *RLP*, p. 118b.

55. There is a fine account of the campaign in Ramsay, *Angevin Empire*, pp. 451–65.

56. Barratt, 'Revenue of John', p. 839; *PR 1214*, p. 91. The pipe roll for 1213 is lost. See Barratt, 'The 1213 pipe roll'.

57. *PR 1214*, p. 95; *PR 1219*, pp. 205–6; *F*, p. 126; Holt, *Northerners*, pp. 100–102.

58. *RLC*, p. 213; Vincent, *Des Roches*, pp. 107–13; Holt, *King John*, p. 91.

59. *CRR*, vii, pp. 158–9; *F*, p. 89; Holt, *MC*, pp. 61, 66.

60. Coggeshall, p. 168.

61. *SLI*, p. 203.

62. *RLC*, pp. 192b, 198b, 199, 214; Anonymous, pp. 150–51.

63. *SLI*, pp. 194, 213; *RLP*, p. 138b.

64. *SLI*, p. 165; *F*, p. 126; Coggeshall, p. 167. Crouch, 'Baronial paranoia', pp. 58–9, brings out the importance of corporate action in 1212.

65. *Brut*, p. 201.

66. Southwark and Merton, p. 49.

67. Wendover, pp. 582–3.

68. Holt, *MC*, pp. 406–11, criticizing R. M. Thomson in *Election of Abbot Hugh*, pp. 189–92, and Gransden, *Customary of Bury*, p. xxv note 5. My argument differs from all three.

69. *Election of Abbot Hugh*, pp. 112–13, 112 note 1.

70. For what follows see *Election of Abbot Hugh*, pp. 110–29. For this source see above, p. 78

71. *Election of Abbot Hugh*, pp. 128–9, said a little later in proceedings.

72. *RLC*, p. 174. In the event, the visit to Rochester took place after the Bury meeting. A gap in the itinerary of a few days leaves open whether John went on to Canterbury and Dover.

73. *RLC*, pp. 175–7; *RLP*, p. 123.

74. FitzWalter and Mandeville attest on 2 November; *RCh*, p. 202, *RLP*, p. 123.

75. *Election of Abbot Hugh*, pp. 126–7. The quotation was from Deuteronomy 7:19.

76. *RLP*, p. 123. Norfolk's son had married the Marshal's eldest daughter.

77. Norgate, *John Lackland*, p. 192.

78. *SC*, pp. 283–4; *RCh*, p. 202b. For a nuanced discussion of the charter, which brings out its advantages for John, see Harvey, *Episcopal Appointments*, pp. 18–24.

79. *RLC*, p. 179.

80. *CMS*, p. 201; Southwark and Merton, p. 49.

81. *CRR*, vii, p. 315; Sanders, *English Baronies*, pp. 16, 53; Harper-Bill, ed., *Blythburgh Cartulary*, i, p. 7; Holt, *Northerners*, p. 12; *RF*, p. 417.

82. Wendover, p. 584; *SLI*, p. 194.

83. *CRR*, vii, p. 315; *RLP*, p. 126b; *RCh*, pp. 203–5. Ros was also a guarantor of the letters of conduct.

84. *DD*, pp. 28–30; Crowland, pp. 217–18.

85. *SLI*, pp. 198–201.

86. *DD*, pp. 28–30.

87. Gervase, ii, p. 109.

88. Tyerman, *England and the Crusades*, pp. 134–5; S. Lloyd, *English Society and the Crusade*, pp. 163–5.

89. *SLI*, pp. 202–4, 212–13, 217.

90. *Election of Abbot Hugh*, pp. 162–5; *RLC*, p. 193b. For John's protest about the election made at Ely, see *RLP*, pp. 132b–133.

91. *RLC*, p. 197b; Kantorowicz, *Laudes Regiae*, p. 217.

92. Crowland, p. 219.

93. Landon, *Itinerary*, pp. 185–6.

94. *SLI*, pp. 196–7. I agree with Holt's arguments that this was what Innocent described later as the '*triplex forma pacis*': *Magna Carta*, pp. 413–17.

95. *SLI*, pp. 202, 214.

96. Wendover, pp. 585–6; Crowland, pp. 219, 225; *RLC*, p. 189b; Holden, *Lords of the Central Marches*, pp. 178–9. I agree with Holt in doubting Wendover's list of who was at Stamford.

97. Wendover, p. 586.
98. What follows all comes from John's letter to the pope of 29 May: *F*, p. 129; see also *SLI*, pp. 214–15.
99. *SLI*, pp. 196–7.
100. Southwark and Merton, p. 49.
101. *Bracton*, ii, p. 237.
102. For the '*diffidatio*', see Strickland, *War and Chivalry*, pp. 231–5, and Gillingham, 'Introduction of chivalry', pp. 223–4. For theories of resistance between 1215 and 1399 and the events of 1215–7, see Valente, *Theory and Practice of Revolt*, pp. 12–67
103. See above, p. 257.
104. *RCh*, p. 209b; *RLP*, p. 141; *F*, p. 129; *SLI*, p. 215.
105. *RLP*, p. 141.
106. *RLC*, p. 204.
107. *RLP*, p. 135; *RLC*, p. 198b.
108. *RCh*, p. 207. The charter survives in the municipal archives: London Metropolitan Archives, COL/CH01/010.
109. Southwark and Merton, p. 49; Crowland, p. 220; *RLP*, p. 137b.
110. Crowland, p. 220.
111. Paris, *HA*, ii, p. 156.
112. *PR 1214*, p. 93; *RLP*, p. 129b.
113. *RLP*, p. 135; *RLC*, p. 198b.
114. *RLP*, p. 145; Smith, 'Treaty of Lambeth', p. 577 note 11.
115. Holt, *Northerners*, p. 110; Powicke, *Stephen Langton*, pp. 207–13.
116. Crowland, p. 220.
117. For what follows I am indebted to Stringer, 'Alexander II: the war of 1215–1217', and 'Alan, son of Roland, lord of Galloway', pp. 85–9, although my emphasis is slightly different.
118. *RLC*, p. 189b; *RLP*, p. 144. For a different view, see Stringer, *Earl David*, pp. 51–2 and 51 note 154.
119. Gervase, ii, p. 111; *RLC*, p. 216b. David's legitimate son was only a child.
120. Crowland, p. 220; Dunstable, p. 43.
121. *RLP*, p. 132b; Holden, *Lords of the Central Marches*, pp. 187–8.
122. Dunstable, p. 43; Crowland, p. 220; *Brut*, p. 90; *AC*, p. 70; J. E. Lloyd, *History of Wales*, ii, pp. 642–4. Latimer, 'Rebellion', points out that there were rebels amongst the Welsh marcher barons, quite apart from Giles de Briouze, bishop of Hereford.
123. *RLC*, pp. 181, 197; Latimer, 'Rebellion'.
124. Wendover, p. 585.
125. *RLC*, p. 200.
126. Faulkner, 'Knights', pp. 7–8; *RLP*, p. 137b; *CRR*, vi, p. 360.
127. See below, p. 382–5.
128. The returns are for Herefordshire (*CACW*, no. 1); Rutland and

Leicestershire (*F*, p. 144); Shropshire, and Staffordshire (Eyton, *Shropshire*, x, pp. 326–7); and Gloucestershire. This last (TNA X Box 2705) was discovered by Adrian Jobson and is discussed in his forthcoming 'Rebellion in Gloucestershire'.

129. *F*, p. 144; *CRR*, vi, p. 131; v, p. 38; vii, p. 240.
130. Holt, *Northerners*, pp. 43–4; but see Thomas, *Vassals*, pp. 45–6; *CACW*, no. 1.
131. Coggeshall, p. 171.
132. Carpenter, 'Sheriffs of Oxfordshire', pp. 42–6.
133. *PR 1215*, p. 10; *PR 1211*, p. 14; P. Brown, *Sibton*, pp. 90–93; see above, p. 226.
134. See *RLC*, pp. 260, 417b, 622b; *BF*, p. 962.
135. Faulkner, 'Knights', pp. 2, 8.
136. *Hotot Estate Records*, p. 32.
137. Crouch, *English Aristocracy*, pp. 17–18.
138. *CRR*, vi, p. 231; Lapsley, 'Buzones', pp. 80–83; *PCCG*, no. 154.
139. Holt, *Northerners*, p. 47; *RLP*, pp. 132b, 134b, 135b; *RLC*, pp. 216b, 217; Tilley, 'Magna Carta and the honour of Wallingford'.
140. I am grateful to Adrian Jobson for allowing me to see some of the preliminary conclusions in his forthcoming 'Rebellion in Gloucestershire'.
141. See above, pp. 135–7.
142. Wendover, p. 585; see below, p. 441.
143. *PR 1215*, p. 10.
144. *RLP*, pp. 135b–136; Crowland, pp. 220–21.
145. Holt, *Northerners*, pp. 105–6.
146. Gervase, ii, p. 109; *MR 1208*, p. 129; *RLP*, p. 138b.
147. Carpenter, *Minority*, p. 48.
148. *RLP*, p. 136b.
149. *RLP*, pp. 138b, 142.
150. *F*, p. 129.
151. *RLP*, pp. 142–3.

10 The Development of the Opposition Programme

1. Wendover, p. 550; Coggeshall, pp. 167, 170; see also *DD*, no. 19.
2. Wendover, pp. 552, 582–6; *Brut*, pp. 200–201.
3. O'Brien, *God's Peace*, pp. 156–203.
4. Chapter 8 in the 1100 charter and chapter 9 in the Articles.
5. Chapters 2, 4 and 11.
6. See above, p. 258–9.
7. For the roots of this usage, see Holt, 'Magna Carta 1215–1217', pp. 293–6, and Holt, *MC*, pp. 518–22.

8. See above, p. 272–3.

9. Sharpe, 'Charters of liberties', pp. 18–20, 37–8, 46–7, 53–4.

10. *Election of Abbot Hugh*, pp. 166–7.

11. Wendover, pp. 552–4.

12. Coggeshall, p. 170; Crowland, pp. 217–18; Anonymous, pp. 145–6; *Brut*, p. 201.

13. I follow Liebermann here, see Sharpe, 'Charters of liberties', pp. 45–6.

14. For example in BL Cotton Claudius D ii, fos. 68v, 70v. See Ker, 'Liber custumarum', for this source. I am grateful to Hugh Doherty for information about copies of Henry II's charter.

15. Holt, *MC*, p. 224.

16. Chapters 11, 10, 6.

17. For the document, see above, p. 17. It is printed in Holt, *MC*, pp. 427–8.

18. Crowland, p. 218.

19. Chapter 5 in the Unknown Charter and chapter 7 in the 1100 Charter.

20. Chapters 4, 6, 3.

21. Holt, *MC*, p. 419.

22. Chapters 2, 5, 7, 11. Chapter 10 gives the forest privileges to 'knights'.

23. Wendover, p. 586.

24. I owe this point to Summerson's commentary on chapter 20.

25. Smith, 'Magna Carta'.

26. Under the terms of chapter 25, judgement would be by the twenty-five if the disseisin was by John. It was to be by judgement of the complainant's peers in the king's court if it was by Henry II or Richard. John would presumably have argued that it was Henry II who had deprived the king of Scots of the northern counties. If John was to have the delay enjoyed by other crusaders, then judgement was to be by Langton and the bishops See below, p. 552 n.20.

27. Sharpe, 'Charters of liberties', p. 44.

28. *Gesetze*, pp. 656–6.

29. *Gesetze*, pp. 656–7; Bisson, 'An "Unknown Charter" for Catalonia', pp. 211–12.

30. Maddicott, *Simon de Montfort*, p. 157.

31. Burton, p. 471; *DBM*, nos. 3, 11; Brand, *Kings, Barons and Justices*, pp. 43–53. For knights having their own agendas, see Maddicott, *Parliament*, pp. 220–24.

32. For a fuller analysis of what follows, see above, pp. 147–54.

33. *F*, p. 89; *RLC*, p. 131; *SC*, p. 254, ch. 20; Hunnisett, *Medieval Coroner*, p. 151.

34. See above, p. 133.

35. See below, p. 439–40.

36. There is no change of ink at these points, however.
37. This may be another chapter, however, put in after the joining up of London.
38. Holt, 'The making of Magna Carta', pp. 219, 224.
39. Cheney, 'Twenty-five barons', p. 285. The detail was the time John was to have to put right any breaches of the Charter.
40. Galbraith, 'Runnymede', p. 308.
41. Melrose, fo. 31v. I owe the translation to Dauvit Broun. For the date of this portion of the chronicle, see Broun and Harrison, *Chronicle of Melrose*, pp. 131–4.
42. Anonymous, p. 150; Wendover, p. 603.
43. Holt, *MC*, pp. 499–500.
44. For the 1258 oath, see Hey, 'The oaths of 1258'.
45. Altamira, 'Magna Carta', pp. 239–40.
46. Turner, *King and his Courts*, pp. 241–3.
47. *RCh*, p. 45.
48. *CMS*, p. 3. Although the London chronicle where this appears was written in the 1250s, it was here copying from what was a contemporary list of sheriffs. I am indebted for this point to Ian Stone, who is preparing a new edition of Arnold fitzThedmar's London chronicle.
49. *RLC*, p. 64; *SC*, p. 312; Round, *Commune of London*, pp. 237–42; 'London municipal collection', pp. 507–8; Summerson, ch. 13.
50. Gervase, ii, pp. 96–7.
51. Thomas of Marlborough, pp. 438–41; see also Gransden, 'A democratic movement'.
52. Hyams, *Rancor and Reconciliation*, pp. 11, 65, 67, 80; and for later and in a European context see Brunner, *Land and Lordship*, pp. 36, 43, 63, 66, 81–7, 90.
53. Riley-Smith, *Feudal Nobility*, pp. 156–9.
54. *Enchiridion*, pp. 134–43, with the 'resistance' passage between pp. 142 and 143.
55. Rady, 'Right of resistance', argues that the chief concern was not to be accused of infidelity and thus cut off from royal patronage.
56. Gervase, ii, pp. 97–8.
57. *Bracton*, ii, pp. 33, 110; iii, p. 43; iv, pp. 158–9; Carpenter, *Reign of Henry III*, pp. 40–41; Brand, 'Date and authorship'.
58. *RLC*, pp. 200, 244; *RLP*, p. 138; Turner, 'Simon of Pattishall', pp. 212–13.
59. For what follows, see Vincent, 'Twenty-five barons'.
60. I have argued for this view, while setting out the whole debate, in my 'Archbishop Langton'. See Holt, *MC*, pp. 268–70, 280–87.
61. See above, p. 259.
62. *ASL*, pp. 12–13.
63. Wendover, pp. 554, 585.

64. It was in this even-handed spirit that he seems to have offered to excommunicate the barons, if John sent his foreign mercenaries home and the barons then refused to lay down their arms: *F*, p. 129; Carpenter, 'Archbishop Langton', p. 1046 note 21. One wonders whether John's order on 13 March, telling the forces summoned from Poitou that they could go home, followed a request from Langton related to an offer along these lines: *RLP*, pp. 130–130b.

65. Although unnamed, he would also have been involved with the grievances of the Welsh under chapter 44.

66. For the meaning of the clause (25), see Carpenter, 'Archbishop Langton', p. 1046 note 17. See also n.20 to chapter 11 below.

67. Baldwin, 'Master Stephen Langton', pp. 817–19.

68. *SLI*, pp. 201–2.

69. *RLC*, p. 146.

70. Lambeth Palace Library MS 1212, fo. 111. The three were William of Eynsford, William de Ros and Richard of Graveney. See below, p. 384.

71. I am using here the title of ch. 8 in Reynolds, *Kingdoms and Communities*. For discussion see also Maddicott, *Parliament*, pp. 139–47

72. *Dialogus*, pp. 152–3; Hyams, *King, Lords and Peasants*, pp. 260–62; Turner, *English Judiciary*, p. 262; see above, p. 193.

73. Baldwin, *Masters and Princes*, p. 166.

74. Reynolds, *Kingdoms and Communities*, pp. 268–9.

75. See above, p. 111–12.

76. Reynolds, *Kingdoms and Communities*, pp. 268–9. See above, pp. 151–2.

77. *EHD 1189–1327*, pp. 496–7.

78. Paris, *GA*, pp. 225–9.

79. Holt, *Northerners*, pp. 59–60.

11 Runnymede

1. *RLP*, pp. 142b–143.

2. Holt, *MC*, pp. 249–50, gives a good description of the topography.

3. For what follows, *Election of Abbot Hugh*, pp. 168–73.

4. Coggeshall, p. 172.

5. See Holt, *MC*, p. 476.

6. *RLP*, p. 143.

7. Holt, *MC*, pp. 244–8.

8. For what follows, see Hoyt, *Royal Demesne*, pp. 144–5.

9. See Articles, chapter 15.

10. For the copies and how they contain elements of drafts, see above, pp. 19–22. They are fully discussed in my 'Copies of Magna Carta'.

11. Galbraith, 'A draft of Magna Carta', p. 348; and see above p. 19–20.

12. Peterborough Dean and Chapter MS 1, on deposit at Cambridge University Library, fos. 7v–74.

13. Society of Antiquaries, London, MS 60, fo. 226; *Cartularies of Peterborough Abbey*, p. 6; and see above, p. 20. The cartulary is known as the 'Black Book' of Peterborough.

14. Bodleian Library, Oxford, MS Lat. Hist. a.1 (P); Vincent, *The Magna Carta*, p. 74. Here and in the Peterborough copy 'consilium nostrum' evidently means 'our council' rather than 'our counsel'. See above, p. 166. In the Bodleian copy's version of chapter 48, the malpractices revealed by the investigation of the knights are to be 'corrected' – 'emendentur'. This is a reading from the Articles of the Barons, not Magna Carta, so the copy clearly has elements of a draft.

15. Another copy of the Charter, that in a late thirteenth-century statute book, omits the need for consent in chapter 12 altogether: TNA E 164/9, fo. 45.

16. Contrast chapters 25 and 37.

17. This variant appears in the copy of the Charter in the Peterborough cartulary mentioned above, in the copy in the late thirteenth-century statute book that Galbraith found in the Huntington Library in California (Galbraith, 'A draft of Magna Carta') and in a number of other copies. Galbraith dated the statute book to before 1290.

18. See above, p. 224.

19. *CPR 1247–58*, p. 637, for a parallel in 1258.

20. The interpretation given here of chapter 25 of the Articles is, as Holt puts it (*MC*, p. 286 and note 102), 'the obvious construction of the Latin'. If it was intended simply to mean that Langton and the bishops were to decide whether John should have the 'term' enjoyed by other crusaders, it was badly drafted. See also Carpenter, 'Archbishop Langton', p. 1046 and note 17, and for Langton and the Articles see above, pp. 332–5.

21. See Helmholz, 'Magna Carta', pp. 348–9, and Brundage, *Medieval Canon Law and the Crusader*, pp. 172–4.

22. Smith, 'Magna Carta', p. 359. In the light of Smith's paper, Holt altered what he had written between his first and second editions: contrast *MC* (1965), p. 193, and *MC* (1992), p. 288. I think his first formulation is nearer the truth.

23. Smith, 'Magna Carta', pp. 361–2, 345–6. See below, p. 393.

24. Chapter 59; Smith, 'Magna Carta', pp. 349, 359.

25. *SLI*, p. 215.

26. Duggan, *Becket*, p. 44. I owe this point to Nicholas Vincent.

27. Ambler, 'Kingship and tyranny', p. 127, and her 'Peacemakers and partisans', pp. 140–66.

28. *SC*, pp. 117–18, 158; Bisson, 'An "Unknown Charter" for Catalonia', p. 211.

29. *RLP*, p. 100; Lambeth Palace Library MS 1212, fos. 12v, 107 (a reference I owe to Nicholas Vincent).

30. See above, p. 317.

31. See above, pp. 106–7.

32. Turner, *English Judiciary*, pp. 168–71.

33. Klerman, 'Woman prosecutors in thirteenth-century England', pp. 295–6; Wilkinson, *Women in Thirteenth-Century Lincolnshire*, pp. 144–9. In 1202 over seventy appeals were made by women before the justices in Lincolnshire: *LAR*. pp. lvi, 342 and see nos. 630, 673, 690, 847.

34. See above, pp. 111–12.

35. Davis, 'An unknown charter of liberties', p. 723, thus thought the clause showed the author was of 'humble extraction'.

36. Anonymous, p. 150.

37. This is printed as a continuation of chapter 37.

38. *APS*, pp. 111–12; Duncan, 'John king of England', p. 271. See above, p. 121.

39. For a fuller discussion, see above, p. 120. For fitzWalter's military role, see 'London municipal collection', p. 485.

40. Holt, 'Vernacular-French text', p. 361, ch. 45.

41. See Carpenter, 'Copies of Magna Carta'.

42. In chapter 9.

43. Paul Brand has kindly commented on the drafting of chapter 39.

44. It was Henry Summerson who pointed this change out to me.

45. *Sarum Missal*, pp. 220–21; Magdalen College Oxford MS 168, fos. 90–92 (Powicke, *Stephen Langton*, p. 176). I am most grateful to David D'Avray for sending me a commentary on the sermon. For Langton's sermons, see Roberts, *Sermons of Stephen Langton*.

46. See Carpenter, 'The dating and making of Magna Carta'.

47. Holt, *MC*, pp. 250–55; Cheney, 'The eve of Magna Carta', pp. 330, 332–3, and Cheney, 'Twenty-five barons', p. 280.

48. *RCh*, pp. 202–9.

49. Galbraith, 'A draft of Magna Carta'.

50. Holt, *MC*, pp. 248–9, and Holt, 'The making of Magna Carta', p. 230.

51. *RCh*, p. 210b.

52. The second copy retaining the pope is in a late thirteenth-century statute book: TNA E 164/9, fo. 47. The third, which I have only very recently discovered, is in a copy of the beginning and end of the 1215 Charter found in the late fourteenth-century Register of William Cheriton, prior of Llanthony Gloucester: TNA C 115/78, fos. 123–123v. (I am grateful to Jessica Nelson for locating this reference.) As in the Huntington copy, the Charter here is given by John at Windsor on 15 June rather than at Runnymede. The omitted text

makes it impossible to know whether the Cheriton and Huntington copies were the same in other ways.

53. Wendover, p. 603; Anonymous, p. 150.
54. *DBM*, pp. 90–91, 103, 113.
55. Coggeshall, pp. 139–40, 146, 154–6.
56. Vincent, ed., *Episcopal Acta: Winchester*, p. 130.
57. Paris, vi, p. 65. Hubert seems in error in remembering that Earl Ferrers was also there.
58. I follow here Holt, *MC*, pp. 481–3, with the text at pp. 490–91.
59. Holt, *MC*, p. 263.
60. *RLP*, p. 180b; Rowlands, 'Text and distribution', p. 1429.
61. *RLP*, p. 181.
62. *RLP*, p. 150.
63. Anonymous, p. 150.
64. Crowland, p. 222.
65. *RLP*, pp. 180b, 143b.
66. For Henry III developing this argument, see Carpenter, *Minority*, pp. 387–8.
67. Crowland, p. 221; Paris, *HA*, ii, p. 159.
68. *RCh*, p. 210b.

12 The Enforcement and Failure of the Charter

1. *Basset Charters*, no. 238.
2. *RLP*, p. 144; for the departure of some of the Flemings, see Anonymous, p. 151.
3. *Enchiridion*, p. 142.
4. *RLP*, p. 180b; Rowlands, 'Writ for publication', p. 1429.
5. Coggeshall, p. 172.
6. *RLC*, pp. 377–377b.
7. *RLP*, pp. 144–5.
8. *RLP*, pp. 146b, 148b, 149b–150; *RLC*, pp. 218–218b.
9. Fox, 'Originals', p. 333 and note 2.
10. *RLP*, p. 180b; Holt, *MC*, pp. 494–5.
11. See below, note 34.
12. Dunstable, p. 43; Rowlands, 'Writ for publication', p. 1428.
13. For his career, see Vincent, 'Elyas of Dereham'.
14. Collins, 'Documents', p. 238.
15. *Acta Hugh of Wells*, p. 4. I owe this reference to Huw Ridgeway. See also above, p. 230.
16. *RL*, pp. 20–22.
17. For the role of the church in disseminating news, see Maddicott, 'Politics and the people', pp. 8–9.
18. Crowland, p. 222.

19. Burton, pp. 321–2.

20. Holt, 'Vernacular-French text', p. 351. See above, p. 19.

21. But see Clanchy, *Memory to Written Record*, pp. 220–21.

22. Carpenter, 'Copies of Magna Carta'; *DBM*, p. 96. I owe the reference to Byland to Sophie Ambler.

23. See below, p. 432.

24. Anonymous, pp. 149–50.

25. BL Add. MSS 32085, fos. 102–106v.

26. Cheney, 'Twenty-five barons'.

27. Cheney, 'Twenty-five barons'; Holt, *MC*, pp. 478–80. In the legal volume (BL Harleian 746, f.74), the order is the earls of Clare, Aumale, Essex, Winchester, Hereford, Norfolk, and Oxford, William Marshal junior, Robert fitzWalter, Gilbert de Clare, Eustace de Vescy, the mayor of London, William de Mowbray, Geoffrey de Say, Roger de Montbegon, William of Huntingfield, Robert de Ros, John de Lacy, William d'Aubigné, Richard de Percy, William Malet, John fitzRobert, William de Lanvallei, Hugh Bigod, and Richard de Munfichet.

28. Strickland, 'Enforcers of Magna Carta'; Powicke, *Stephen Langton*, pp. 207–13; Holt, *Northerners*, p. 110. Painter, *Reign of John*, pp. 288–90, gives a geographical analysis of the leaders of the revolt.

29. Cheney, 'Twenty-five barons', p. 307; Holt, *MC*, pp. 478–80.

30. Wendover, pp. 605–6.

31. *RLP*, p. 143b.

32. For the survival of the letter to the sheriff of Gloucestershire, which was witnessed on 20 June, not 19 June, see Rowlands, 'Text and distribution'. This may well have been the letter for Engelard, since he was sheriff of both Gloucestershire and Herefordshire. The letter is now in the archives of Hereford cathedral.

33. *RCh*, p. 210. The recipients of the letters are analysed in Rowlands, 'Text and distribution', pp. 1424–6.

34. A royal letter of 27 June, discussed below, which was sent to all the sheriffs, was issued following a judgement with which Langton was associated, so it is not unlikely that Dereham was at court at this time, and then received the twelve 19 June letters, as well as his first batch of four Charters. He may also have received the 27 June letter for Hampshire, since one of the 19 June letters was certainly for that county. It is the 27 June letter for Hampshire, translated into French, which is copied, alongside the French translation of the Charter, in the cartulary of Pont Audemar. One suspects, therefore, that the translation likewise was made from the Charter connected with Hampshire, and thus from the Charter (if the arguments advanced above are correct) sent to Winchester cathedral for the Winchester diocese.

35. Lambeth Palace Library MS 1213, fo. 94.

36. *RLC*, p. 216b.

37. See above, pp. 334–5. There are many references to the Eynsford, Ros and Graveney families in du Boulay, *Lordship of Canterbury*.

38. *RLJ*, pp. 179, 180, 182, 207, 210, 211, 217, 219.

39. *BF*, pp. 687, 239, 242; *CRR*, iv, pp. 21, 97; v, pp. 8, 113, 191, 213, 273.

40. Du Boulay, *Lordship of Canterbury*, p. 107; for the long-running dispute between Becket and Henry II over the overlordship of Ros's seven fees, see Barlow, *Becket*, pp. 83, 89, 136, 193, 196, 213.

41. *PR 1212*, p. 15.

42. Barlow, *Becket*, pp. 93–4, 111; Warren, *Henry II*, pp. 457–8, 478 note 1.

43. *RLC*, pp. 234, 235b, 237b, 295, 325; Gervase, ii, p. 110. In the 1220s, probably through the influence of Hubert de Burgh, Eynsford became briefly a steward of the royal household.

44. For elections in the county court, see above, pp. 133–4.

45. *RLP*, p. 145b; Holt, 'Vernacular-French text', p. 364. The writ sent to Kent is copied in Lambeth Palace Library MS 1213, fo. 195.

46. Crowland, p. 222; Coggeshall, p. 173; Wendover, p. 606.

47. See below, pp. 448–9.

48. *F*, p. 134.

49. Crowland, p. 222; *PR 1215*, p. 10.

50. *RLP*, pp. 143b–145b; *RLC*, pp. 215–18; the figures here come from Holt, *MC*, pp. 360–61.

51. *RLC*, p. 215.

52. *RLC*, p. 218.

53. *RLC*, p. 216b; *RCh*, pp. 29, 186b; Stringer, *Earl David*, pp. 49–50.

54. *RLP*, p. 17b; *PR 1209*, p. 190.

55. *RLC*, p. 216b.

56. *RLC*, pp. 216b, 217; for other 'ifs', see *RLC*, pp. 215b, 216.

57. *RLC*, p. 215. I think this letter does imply that Salisbury was not present at Runnymede, despite John putting him down in the Charter as one of his counsellors. Anonymous, p. 149, suggests the same, but see Holt, 'Making of Magna Carta', pp. 237–8.

58. *RLC*, pp. 216, 216b.

59. Holt, *MC*, p. 490; Crowland, p. 221, whose view was that Geoffrey had no claim save that his father, Geoffrey fitzPeter, enjoyed custody of the Tower as John's justiciar.

60. *RLP*, p. 139b; *RLC*, p. 215; Holt, *MC*, pp. 431–2.

61. Tilley, 'Magna Carta and the honour of Wallingford'.

62. Holt, *MC*, pp. 499–500 (discovered by H. G. Richardson).

63. Wendover, p. 606 (where the council was to meet at Westminster, which is most unlikely); Melrose, fo. 31v; Coggeshall, p. 172.

64. *RLC*, pp. 215, 339b, 614b; *RLP*, pp. 43b, 44, 106, 122; *MR 1208*, p. 138, no. 70.

65. *RLC*, p. 221b.
66. Smith, 'Treaty of Lambeth', p. 577 note 11; *RLP*, p. 145.
67. *RLC*, p. 223.
68. *RLP*, p. 149. The place of the letter is given as between Newbury and Abingdon. It is very unusual for John's instruments not to be dated to a specific place.
69. Richardson, 'Morrow of the Great Charter' and 'Morrow of the Great Charter: addendum'. For Holt's critique, see *MC*, pp. 484–9, which goes much too far, in my view, in reducing the importance of the council.
70. *PR 1215*, p. 10.
71. *RLP*, p. 149.
72. *RLC*, pp. 221b, 222b.
73. *RLP*, p. 141; Crowland, p. 225; Dunstable, p. 45.
74. *RLP*, pp. 149b–50.
75. *RLP*, p. 151; Painter, *Reign of John*, p. 332.
76. *RLP*, p. 150; Smith, 'Magna Carta', pp. 361–2, 345–6. Llywelyn had still not obtained the release of all his hostages as required by the Charter: *RLP*, p. 151. During the council envoys were probably also received from King Alexander, since his letter of credence for them (*RLP*, p. 150) was enrolled just before the letter of conduct for the Welsh rulers.
77. *F*, p. 134 (*RLC*, p. 269). See above, p. 387.
78. *RCh*, pp. 213–15.
79. Anonymous, p. 151; Gillingham, 'Anonymous', p. 43; Wendover, p. 611.
80. *RLP*, pp. 150–50b.
81. Holt, *MC*, pp. 499–500, from Richardson, 'Morrow of the Great Charter', p. 443.
82. Melrose, fo. 31v.
83. *RLP*, pp. 150–150b.
84. *SLI*, pp. 217–19.
85. *SLI*, p. 217 note 1.
86. Anonymous, pp. 151–2.
87. *RLP*, pp. 147, 148; Anonymous, p. 151.
88. *RLP*, pp. 144–50; Jenkinson, 'Jewels lost in the Wash', pp. 163–4.
89. *RLC*, p. 218.
90. *RLP*, pp. 152b, 153b.
91. Crowland, pp. 222–3; *RLP*, p. 153.
92. *SLI*, pp. 207–9; The bull 'Miramur plurimum', pp. 91–2.
93. Crowland, p. 224; Southwark and Merton, p. 50; Coggeshall, p. 173.
94. The bull 'Miramur plurimum', pp. 90–93.
95. Crowland, pp. 224–5; *RLP*, pp. 154b, 155.

96. *F*, p. 75.
97. Crowland, pp. 224–5; Coggeshall, p. 176; *F*, p. 140.
98. *F*, p. 104.
99. Southern, 'England's first entry into Europe', pp. 147–9; see, however, Holt, 'Magna Carta, 1215–1217', pp. 292–3.
100. *SLI*, pp. 212–16.
101. Norgate, *John Lackland*, p. 248.
102. Baldwin, *Masters and Princes*, i, p. 166; Carpenter, 'Archbishop Langton', p. 1042.
103. The whole story is told in Rowlands, 'King John'.
104. Coggeshall, pp. 174–5; *RLC*, p. 228; *RLP*, pp. 138, 181; Wendover, p. 606.
105. *RLP*, pp. 154b–155.
106. Galbraith, *Studies in the Public Records*, pp. 136, 161–2.
107. *F*, pp. 136, 137; Holt, *Northerners*, p. 1.
108. Holt, *MC*, pp. 499–500, from a discovery by H. G. Richardson.
109. Smith, 'Treaty of Lambeth', p. 577 note 15.
110. *APS*, p. 108; Petit-Dutaillis, *Louis VIII*, pp. 115–18.
111. Crowland, pp. 225–6.
112. *F*, p. 140.

13 The Revival of the Charter, 1216–1225

1.   For the military events, see McGlynn, *Blood Cries Afar*.
2.   Church, *Household Knights*, pp. 104–8.
3.   *APS*, pp. 108, 110, 112; Melrose, fo. 33; Coggeshall, p. 183; Anonymous, p. 179; Stringer, 'Alexander II: the war of 1215–1217'. The source for John's remark is Paris, p. 642.
4.   Warren, *King John*, pp. 278–85; Holt, 'King John's disaster in the Wash'.
5.   *Guala*, no. 140b.
6.   *RLP*, p. 199; *CChR*, p. 172.
7.   Coggeshall, pp. 183–4. Coggeshall was a daughter house of Savigny.
8.   *F*, p. 192; Church, 'King John's testament', pp. 516–17; Worcester, pp. 391–2, 395. For a wider context see Draper, 'King John and St Wulfstan', and Mason, 'St Wulfstan's staff'.
9.   Carpenter, *Reign of Henry III*, pp. 435–6.
10. Latin texts and translations of the Charters of 1216, 1217 and 1225, and of the Forest Charters of 1217 and 1225, are in *SR*, pp. 14–27, and translations in *EHD 1189–1327*, pp. 327–49. Text and translations will appear in due course on the website of the Magna Carta Project.
11. *PR 1216–25*, p. 22. For what follows see Carpenter, *Minority*, pp. 31–5.

12. *Political Songs*, p. 22.

13. *PR 1215*, p. 14; Carpenter, *Minority*, p. 29.

14. Crowland, p. 236; *Guala*, pp. xli–ii (Vincent's introduction).

15. Apart from the Marshal, they were Hubert de Burgh, now with his title of justiciar, Matthew fitzHerbert, John Marshal, Alan Basset and Philip d'Aubigné.

16. The change had some significance when it came to deciding who had the right to the crops and stock at the point the wardship ended.

17. See Carpenter, 'Copies of Magna Carta'. A specially worded engrossment of the 1216 Charter, known from a now destroyed copy, was sent to Ireland. It is collated with the Durham engrossment is *SR*, pp. 14–16. The copy in an Abingdon cartulary (*Abingdon*, ii, p. 283, no.C355) turns out to be the Charter of 1217.

18. *Layettes*, pp. 434–7; *Guala*, p. 29.

19. Gervase, ii, p. 111.

20. All four are illustrated in Vincent, *The Magna Carta*, pp. 61–4.

21. *RA*, pp. 148–9, and plate XIX.

22. *SR*, p. 16.

23. Illustrated in Vincent, *The Magna Carta*, p. 75, and in an engraving in *SR*.

24. Carpenter, 'Copies of Magna Carta'. There are no known copies of the Forest Charter or Magna Carta with a 14 or 15 November date. Many have no date at all.

25. Lawlor, 'An unnoticed Charter', p. 525; *Guala*, pp. 30–31; the charters with Marsh as the giver are usually hybrids combining elements from 1217 and 1225.

26. *RL*, pp. 180–81. From the time of his appointment as bishop of Durham in 1217, down to his death in 1226, Marsh was largely a titular chancellor (though taking the revenues of office), and the work was done by Neville.

27. I have not, however, discovered a copy of the 1217 Magna Carta where the 'givers' are Guala and the Marshal as opposed to Marsh, but one may come to light. See Carpenter, 'Copies of Magna Carta'.

28. For the tourn and frankpledge, see above, pp. 178–80.

29. *F*, p. 89. See above, p. 133.

30. Melrose, fo. 36.

31. *RLC*, p. 377b; see above, pp. 4–5. The enrolled letter is to the sheriff of Yorkshire but it probably went to the other sheriffs as well.

32. *RLC*, p. 378; Vincent, *The Magna Carta*, pp. 61–4.

33. Wendover, pp. 75–6; Carpenter, *Minority*, pp. 295–7.

34. Norgate, *Minority*, pp. 225–6; Anonymous, p. 173; *RLC*, p. 139b.

35. Carpenter, *Minority*, p. 389, explains why, in the event, Henry entered full power in January 1227 actually before he was twenty-one.

36. For example in 1264, *DBM*, pp. 268–9.
37. *C&S*, p. 162.
38. See above, pp. 349–51.
39. Carpenter, 'Cerne abbey Magna Carta'. The abbot of Cerne was one of the witnesses. For the assembly that granted the tax, see Maddicott, *Parliament*, pp. 106–8.
40. *C&S*, pp. 137–8, 206–7.
41. Blackstone, *Great Charter*, pp. 27–59; Thompson, *Magna Carta*, p. 148.
42. *Enchiridion*, p. 142.
43. See below, p. 445.
44. In the 1236 Statute of Merton: *CR 1234–7*, p. 338.
45. See above, pp. 151–2.
46. Chapters 32 and 36 in 1225, and chapters 39 and 43 in 1217.
47. Chapter 21 in 1225 and chapter 26 in 1217. The use of 'knights' in a sense which would seem to include barons is also found in chapter 10 of the Unknown Charter.
48. See above, pp. 185–6.
49. All four surviving engrossments of the 1217 Charter have 'or his bailiff' – 'ballivus suus'. However, the Durham and Lacock abbey engrossments of the 1225 Charter omit the 'suus', whereas the other two retain it. I do not think this is significant.
50. *CR 1231–4*, pp. 592–3, 588–9; Maddicott, 'Magna Carta', pp. 49–50.
51. Another change that might seem to buck the baronial trend was that made to Magna Carta 1215's chapter 28 (19 in 1225) about the seizure of corn and other chattels without payment by constables and baliffs. From 1216 the constables and baliffs were no longer specified as those of the king.
52. Carpenter, *Minority*, pp. 90–91, 168–9.
53. *Glanvill*, p. 59; *Bracton*, ii, p. 265; Biancalana, 'Widows at common law', pp. 277–84; Loengard, 'What did Magna Carta mean to widows?', pp. 148–9, and her '*Rationabilis Dos*', pp. 66–8.
54. For what follows, see above, pp. 111–13.
55. Chapters 16 and 35 in 1217, chapters 14 and 29 in 1225.
56. See 'Magna Carta repeals'.

14 Did Magna Carta Make a Difference?

1. I am grateful to Paul Brand for commenting on a draft of the chapter.
2. *SR*, p. 28; *CChR*, pp. 225–6.
3. Holt, *MC*, p. 394.

4. Poole, 'Publication of Charters', pp. 451–2, touches briefly on this subject. For a recent discussion of the dissemination of information, see Maddicott, 'Politics and the people'.

5. *RLC*, p. 377b; *RLC*, ii, pp. 70, 73b; Wendover, pp. 91–2; Crowland, p. 256; Carpenter, *Minority*, pp. 73–4, 383–4.

6. *CR 1254–6*, pp. 194–5; *DBM*, pp. 312–15.

7. *EHD 1189–1327*, pp. 485–8, 496–7.

8. Carpenter, 'Copies of Magna Carta'.

9. Burton, p. 322; *Rishanger*, p. 405. For proclamations in English in 1258, see *DBM*, pp. 116–23; *EHD 1189–1327*, pp. 367–70.

10. Vincent, *The Magna Carta*, pp. 49–71.

11. Burton, p. 322; *C&S*, p. 851; *CCR 1272–9*, p. 582; Maddicott, 'Politics and the people', p. 9; Thompson, *First Century*, pp. 96–7.

12. See Carpenter, 'Copies of Magna Carta'. I plan there to update the figures given below. I am most grateful to Paul Brand and Susan Reynolds for sharing their knowledge of copies with me.

13. Most of these are accompanied by the Forest Charter.

14. *Hotot Estate Records*, pp. 14, 32.

15. Reynolds, 'Magna Carta 1297'.

16. Carpenter, 'Copies of Magna Carta'; Lawlor, 'An unnoticed Charter'. For a printed example, Guisborough, pp. 162–79.

17. Carpenter, 'Cerne abbey Magna Carta'.

18. Holt, 'St Albans chroniclers'; Reynolds, 'Magna Carta 1297', p. 241 and note 54; Carpenter, 'Matthew Paris and the *Chronica Majora*', p. 7 note 43.

19. *SR*, pp. 28–31; Vincent, *The Magna Carta*, p. 78.

20. It was copied at St Albans, however: Wendover, pp. 616–20.

21. Paris, v, pp. 520–21; Maddicott, *Parliament*, pp. 198–9.

22. Thompson, *First Century*, p. 65.

23. *RL*, pp. 20–22; Carpenter, *Minority*, pp. 73–4, 102–3.

24. *RL*, pp. 151–2; Carpenter, *Minority*, pp. 210–11.

25. *CRR*, x, p. 7. For references to what may or may not be the same man, see *RLC*, p. 333; *CRR*, viii, pp. 179, 236, 254; *CRR*, xi, no. 1019.

26. *CRR*, xi, nos. 2142, 2312; *RLC*, ii, pp. 153–4, 212–13; Maddicott, 'Magna Carta', pp. 33–4.

27. Thompson, *First Century*, ch. 4, with the figures on p. 64. The subject will be explored more fully by Paul Brand in a forthcoming paper.

28. *CRR*, xvi, no. 136C.

29. Nichols, 'An early fourteenth-century petition'; Razi and Smith, eds., *Medieval Society*, pp. 179–80; for another example of knowledge of the Charter at the peasant level, see Thompson, *Magna Carta*, p. 71.

30. For what follows, see Thompson, *First Century*, ch. 4; Holt, *MC*, ch. 11; Carpenter, *Minority*, ch. 12; and most especially Maddicott, 'Magna Carta'.

31. The 'henceforth' is only found in the Durham engrossment.

32. *CRR*, xii, no. 2646; xiv, no. 751; for litigation in the minority in general, see Carpenter, *Reign of Henry III*, pp. 26–9.

33. *CFR 1231–2*, no. 94; Clasby, 'The abbot of St Albans'; *CChR*, pp. 99–100.

34. Carpenter, 'Archbishop Langton', pp. 1062–4; and for fitzAlan, *CFR 1256–7*, no. 934.

35. *PR 1219*, p. 43; *PR 1222*, p. 168 (as Margaret de Cressy). The subject of what happened to the fines made by widows under John has been explored by Abigail Armstrong in a King's College London MA essay.

36. Paris, iv, p. 385. For Henry's itinerary, see Kanter, 'Peripatetic and sedentary kingship', pp. 22–6.

37. Ridgeway, 'The Lord Edward', 'Henry III and the "aliens"' and his 'Foreign favourites'.

38. *EHD 1189–1327*, pp. 359–67; *DBM*, pp. 96–113.

39. *DBM*, p. 81, chs. 4–6; Carpenter, *Reign of Henry III*, ch. 14.

40. Carpenter, 'Magna Carta 1253', p. 182.

41. See above, p. 208.

42. Carpenter, *Reign of Henry III*, pp. 171–4; Cassidy, 'Bad sheriffs, custodial sheriffs'. In fact the salary plan never really functioned, and the solution from 1259 was to reduce the size of the increments.

43. *DBM*, pp. 275–7.

44. *DBM*, pp. 108–9, 155. For the sheriffs of the period of reform, see Ridgeway, 'Sheriffs of the baronial regime'.

45. *DBM*, pp. 146–7, ch. 21; Maddicott, 'Magna Carta', pp. 47–8; Brand, *Kings, Barons and Justices*, pp. 81–2.

46. Maddicott, 'Magna Carta', pp. 48–61, and for the weakness of Henry's rule that allowed such oppression, see Carpenter, *Reign of Henry III*, ch. 5.

47. See above, pp. 185–6.

48. Brand, *Kings, Barons and Justices*, pp. 43–53.

49. *DBM*, pp. 138–43; Brand, *Kings, Barons and Justices*, pp. 42–53, 87–90, 295–301; see above, p. 426.

50. *DBM*, pp. 142–5, chs. 9 and 10; Brand, *Kings, Barons, and Justices*, pp. 54–7.

51. *DBM*, pp. 99, 115, 131–7, 160–63; *Special Eyre*, pp. lii–lxiii (Andrew Hershey's introduction.)

52. Carpenter, *Reign of Henry III*, ch. 5.

53. For these changes, see above, pp. 129–37, 144–5.

54. Burton, p. 471.

55.   Maddicott, *Simon de Montfort*, p. 176.

56.   *SCWR*, p. 43; Carpenter, *Reign of Henry III*, pp. 309 and 325–39, for what follows.

57.   The reforms of 1258–9 did nothing, however, to overturn the legal disabilities of villeinage. See, for example, the case of the villeins of Bampton in Oxfordshire in *SCWR*, p. 106.

58.   *DBM*, pp. 134–5; *FH*, ii, pp. 426–7.

59.   Brand, *Kings, Barons and Justices*, pp. 77–82, 87–90.

60.   *RH*, ii, p. 485.

61.   *DBM*, pp. 116–19; *EHD 1189–1327*, pp. 367–8.

62.   Maddicott, *Simon de Montfort*, is the classic biography.

63.   Eleanor is brought alive for the first time in Wilkinson, *Eleanor de Montfort*.

64.   *DBM*, pp. 312–13; *SR*, table of contents XV; Ambler, 'Magna Carta 1265'.

65.   *CR 1264–8*, p. 100.

66.   For the way his episcopal supporters justified the revolution, see Ambler, 'The Montfortian bishops'. Jobson, *First English Revolution*, provides an excellent narrative of the period.

67.   Maddicott, *Parliament*, pp. 210–18 and ch. 5.

68.   Chapters 19 and 21 in 1225; efo chapters 28 and 30 in 1215.

69.   *EHD 1189–1327*, nos. 74 and 85, ch. 2.

70.   *DBM*, no. 36C.

71.   For how fair the accusations were, see Howell, *Regalian Right*, p. 145, and Harvey, *Episcopal Appointments*, pp. 76–88.

72.   Paris, v, p. 738; Hershey, 'William de Bussey'.

73.   *DBM*, pp. 270–5; Maddicott, 'Magna Carta', pp. 54–61; Carpenter, *Reign of Henry III*, pp. 30–6, 98–106; Moore, 'Thorrington dispute'; *Special Eyre*, pp. liv–lxiii. Carpenter, *Reign of Henry III*, ch. 2, questions Holt's hypothesis that baronial litigation went through more smoothly after 1215.

74.   *RL*, ii, p. 102.

75.   *DBM*, pp. 108–9, ch. 18; pp. 270–71, ch. 2; *C&S*, p. 543, ch. 24; Waugh, 'Origins of the articles of the escheator'; Thompson, *Magna Carta*, p. 19. For examples of procedure other than by letters patent, see *CFR 1270–71*, no. 408; *CFR 1271–2*, nos. 123, 136.

76.   *Mirror*, p. 178. For the question of date and authorship see Maitland's beautifully written introduction. *The Mirror of Justices* is an imaginative work and no guide to precise law, but it can make interesting and acute observations.

77.   *ERW*, pp. lv, 63; Maddicott, 'Magna Carta', pp. 53–4; *RH*, i, p. 169.

78.   Maddicott, 'Magna Carta', pp. 36–40; *DBM*, pp. 80–81, no. 9; Prestwich, *Edward I*, pp. 518–19, 534–7, 548.

79.   *CR 1231–4*, pp. 592–3, 588–9.
80.   *CRR*, xvi, nos. 31, 46, 112.
81.   *Northumberland Pleas*, pp. 163–4; Cassidy, 'William Heron'. See also *DBM*, pp. 126–9, ch. 16, where again the charter is misinterpreted.
82.   *Special Eyre*, pp. xlix, li, lii, lv, lvii, lix, and nos. 56, 74, 76, 129 (for the Lucy wardship), 152, 173, 312, 340.
83.   Examples are brought together by Julia Barrow in *Hereford Acta*, pp. 43–7.
84.   *EHD 1189–1327*, p. 359.
85.   *Letters of Grosseteste*, pp. 253–4.
86.   *F*, pp. 289–90; Carpenter, 'Magna Carta 1253'. New light will be thrown on this subject by Felicity Hill's doctoral thesis on excommunication and Magna Carta.
87.   Thompson, *First Century*, p. 64.
88.   *EHD 1189–1327*, p. 485, ch. 1.
89.   *ERW*, p. 363; for writs available, see also Thompson, *Magna Carta*, pp. 42–51.
90.   *ERW*, lv, p. 63; Maddicott, 'Magna Carta', pp. 53–4; Thompson, *Magna Carta*, pp. 44–6.
91.   *Mirror*, p. 176.
92.   Cam, *Studies in the Hundred Rolls*, pp. 20–22, 92–100.
93.   For the difficulties of procedure by writ, see Hershey, 'Justice and bureaucracy'.
94.   *DBM*, pp. 162–3, ch. 7; Cam, *Studies in the Hundred Rolls*, p. 96, ch. 20, p. 98, ch. 11.
95.   *Northumberland Assize Rolls*, pp. 163–4.
96.   Paris, *GA*, p. 340; *EHD 1189–1327*, p. 497.
97.   *DBM*, pp. 150–55, chs. 5 and 20.
98.   *CCR 1272–9*, p. 582.
99.   *DBM*, pp. 150–51, ch. 6.
100. Maddicott, 'Magna Carta', p. 33, here about Lincolnshire.
101. *DBM*, no. 37C; Stacey, 'Crusades, Crusaders', pp. 138–42.
102. Howell, *Regalian Right*, pp. 142–6, where the emphasis is on the exploitation.
103. Harvey, *Episcopal Appointments*, pp. 97–8, and more generally pp. 76–99; Huscroft, 'Robert Burnel', pp. 85–6.
104. For significant early examples, see Carpenter, *Minority*, pp. 63, 191, 197, 204. There are occasional exceptions that I hope to write about elsewhere. They are sometimes explained by the heir buying himself out of a period of wardship or purchasing the king's stock in the manor. There were occasions when Henry III levied scutage at 3 marks a fee, the same rate as in 1214, and thus could be deemed to be in breach of the 1217/1225 Charter's stipulation that scutage should be taken as under Henry II. However he secured consent for

such levies: Mitchell, *Taxation*, pp. 186, 191, 232, 248 note 90, 285 note 142.

105. Waugh, *Lordship of England*, p. 86.
106. *CFR 1218–19*, no. 367.
107. *CPR 1232–47*, p. 352.
108. Waugh, *Lordship of England*, pp. 159–60, where the decline in the number and value of fines for permission to marry freely is also set out. See discussion in Ray, 'The lady is not for turning'; Annesley, 'The impact of Magna Carta on widows'; Carpenter, 'Hubert de Burgh, Matilda de Mowbray'.
109. Carpenter, *Struggle for Mastery*, pp. 420–21; Paris, v, p. 336; Annesley, 'Isabella countess of Arundel'.
110. The eventual practice was simply to take an oath from the widow not to marry without the king's licence: *CFR 1255–6*, no. 627; Waugh, *Lordship of England*, pp. 116–7.
111. Coss, *The Lady*, pp. 121–3; *CR 1242–7*, p. 61. Between 1236 and 1258 the fine rolls have a dozen fines imposed for having married women without the king's licence.
112. *CFR 1226–7*, no. 125.
113. Biancalana, 'Widows at common law', pp. 284–8, 313–16; Loengard, 'What did Magna Carta mean to widows?', pp. 149–50.
114. Klerman, 'Women prosecutors in thirteenth-century England'; Stewart, ed., *1263 Surrey Eyre*, p. cx; Klerman, 'Settlement and decline of private prosecution'.
115. Carpenter, *Reign of Henry III*, pp. 79–80.
116. Carpenter, *Reign of Henry III*, pp. 38–42.
117. The disseisins consequent on the reforms in 1236 to the running of royal manors were quickly reversed: Stacey, *Politics, Policy*, pp. 101–3. See also Carpenter, 'Robert de Ros'.
118. Carpenter, 'Roger Mortimer'.
119. For what follows, see Holt, *MC*, pp. 332–3; Harcourt, 'Amercement of barons'; Carpenter, 'Robert de Ros', pp. 7–9.
120. *Bracton*, ii, p. 330.
121. PRO E 370/1/6, m. 2. I am grateful to Paul Dryburgh and Jessica Nelson for transcribing this for me.
122. *CRR*, vi, pp. 289–90; *CFR 1255–6*, no. 657.
123. Carpenter, 'Magna Carta 1253', p. 186.
124. Holt, *MC*, pp. 332–3; *Bracton*, ii, pp. 330; Carpenter, 'Robert de Ros' and 'Magna Carta 1253'.
125. Brand, *Origins of the Legal Profession*, p. 24.
126. Musson, 'Local administration of justice'; Kanter, 'The four knights' system'; *CFR 1256–7*; *RF*, pp. 371–464.
127. *Mirror*, p. 179; Clanchy, 'Magna Carta, clause 34', pp. 543–4; Thompson, *Magna Carta*, pp. 49–51.

128. Carpenter, *Minority*, pp. 392–3; Maddicott, 'Edward I and the lessons of baronial reform', pp. 26–7.

129. Williams, *From Commune to Capital*, pp. 207–8, 255–60.

130. *MGL*, i, pp. 500–502; John of Wallingford, p. 131; Thompson, *First Century*, p. 39.

131. Meekings, *Wiltshire Eyre*, pp. 108–9; *Fleta*, pp. 103–4.

132. For what follows, see Hyams, *King, Lords and Peasants*, pp. 143–5.

133. *Walter of Henley*, pp. 310–11; Poole, *From Domesday Book to Magna Carta*, p. 476 note 2; Razi and Smith, eds., *Medieval Society*, p. 49; *SPMC*, p. 44.

134. *Bracton*, ii, p. 34; Hyams, *King, Lords and Peasants*, p. 143.

135. *ERW*, pp. lv, 63; but see *Fleta*, p. 103.

136. Nichols, 'Early fourteenth-century petition', p. 306. Since the Charter actually had amercements, other than for earls and barons, assessed by the men of the neighbourhood, rather than explicitly by peers, the peasants may also have been influenced here by the Statute of Westminster of 1275, which stipulated judgement by peers for everyone including villeins: *EHD 1181–1827*, p. 399, ch. 6.

137. Hyams, *King, Lords and Peasants*, pp. 144–5.

138. *Mirror*, p. 177, and see p. 79.

139. I have calculated the 1207–8 and 1256–7 figures myself. The other figures were calculated by Beth Hartland and Paul Dryburgh, 'Development of the fine rolls', 194–5: see *CFR 1224–34*, pp. vii–ix; *CFR 1234–42*, pp. xii–xiii. For the fines to recover the king's grace and benevolence between 1236 and 1258, see *CFR 1235–6*, no. 152; *CFR 1250–1*, nos. 359, 822; *CFR 1256–7*, no.894; *CFR 1257–8*, no. 37. I have not included the dozen fines for having married women (mostly widows) without the king's licence. Their total value was only £746. The largest was the 500 marks imposed on John de Grey for having married the widow of Paulinus Peyvr: *CFR 1250–1*, no. 1213. The £500 fine in 1257 was made by John de Balliol. For Henry's treatment of him and Robert de Ros, one of the few occasions when he acted like King John, see Carpenter, 'Robert de Ros'. For the general nature of Henry III's personal rule see Carpenter, *Reign of Henry III*, ch.5.

140. Carpenter, 'English royal chancery', pp. 54–5.

141. Carpenter, *Minority*, pp. 206, 210–11.

142. Mitchell, *Taxation*, pp. 186, 191, 208–9, 241–2, 253–4.

143. *EHD 1189–1327*, p. 486, ch. 6.

144. Stacey, 'Parliamentary negotiation'.

Glossary of Terms

1.   I have found particularly helpful John Hudson's Glossary in his *Formation of the English Common Law*, pp. 240–48.

Index

Many of the terms in the index will be found defined in the Glossary.

In the sub headings Magna Carta has been abbreviated to MC and all references are to the 1215 Charter unless stated. AB stands for the Articles of the Barons. In my labelling of the chapters of Magna Carta, I have largely followed that in Holt, Magna Carta, 543–5. I am most grateful to Richard Cassidy for constructing the peoples and places side of the index.

PENGUIN CLASSICS

THE KORAN

> 'God is the light of the heavens and the earth ...
> God guides to His light whom he will'

The Koran is universally accepted by Muslims to be the infallible Word of God as first revealed to the Prophet Muhammad by the Angel Gabriel nearly fourteen hundred years ago. Its 114 chapters, or *surahs*, recount the narratives central to Muslim belief, and together they form one of the world's most influential prophetic works and a literary masterpiece in its own right. Above all, the Koran provides the rules of conduct that remain fundamental to the Muslim faith today: prayer, fasting, pilgrimage to Mecca and absolute faith in God.

N. J. Dawood's masterly translation is the result of his life-long study of the Koran's language and style, and presents the English reader with a fluent and authoritative rendering, while reflecting the flavour and rhythm of the original. This edition follows the traditional sequence of the Koranic *surahs*.

'Across the language barrier Dawood captures the thunder and poetry of the original' *The Times*

Over a million copies sold worldwide.

Revised translation with an introduction and notes by N. J. Dawood

PENGUIN CLASSICS

THE CAMPAIGNS OF ALEXANDER
ARRIAN

'His passion was for glory only, and in that he was insatiable'

Although written over four hundred years after Alexander's death, Arrian's
Campaigns of Alexander is the most reliable account of the man and his
achievements we have. Arrian's own experience as a military commander gave
him unique insights into the life of the world's greatest conqueror. He tells of
Alexander's violent suppression of the Theban rebellion, his total defeat of Persia,
and his campaigns through Egypt, India and Babylon – establishing new cities
and destroying others in his path. While Alexander emerges from this record as
an unparalleled and charismatic leader, Arrian succeeds brilliantly in creating an
objective and fully rounded portrait of a man of boundless ambition, who was
exposed to the temptations of power and worshipped as a god in his own lifetime.

Aubrey de Sélincourt's vivid translation is accompanied by J. R. Hamilton's
introduction, which discusses Arrian's life and times, his synthesis of other
classical sources and the composition of Alexander's army. This edition also
includes maps, a list for further reading and a detailed index.

Translated by Aubrey de Sélincourt

Revised, with a new introduction and notes by J. R. Hamilton

Penguin Classics

THE LETTERS OF THE YOUNGER PLINY

> 'Of course these details are not important enough for history …
> you have only yourself to blame for asking for them'

A prominent lawyer and administrator, Pliny (*c.* AD 61–113) was also a prolific letter-writer, who numbered among his correspondents such eminent figures as Tacitus, Suetonius and the Emperor Trajan, as well as a wide circle of friends and family. His lively and very personal letters address an astonishing range of topics, from a deeply moving account of his uncle's death in the eruption that engulfed Pompeii and observations on the early Christians – 'a desperate sort of cult carried to extravagant lengths' – to descriptions of everyday life in Rome, with its scandals and court cases, and of his own life in the country. Providing a series of fascinating views of imperial Rome, his letters also offer one of the fullest self-portraits to survive from classical times.

Betty Radice's definitive edition was the first complete modern translation of Pliny's letters. In her introduction, she examines the shrewd, tolerant and occasionally pompous man who emerges from these.

Translated with an introduction by Betty Radice

PENGUIN CLASSICS

THE HISTORY OF THE CHURCH
EUSEBIUS

'Could I do better than start from the beginning of the dispensation
of our Saviour and Lord, Jesus the Christ of God?'

Eusebius's account is the only surviving historical record of the Church during
its crucial first 300 years. Bishop Eusebius (c. 260–339 AD), a learned scholar
who lived most of his life in Caesarea in Palestine, broke new ground in writing
the *History* and provided a model for all later ecclesiastical historians. In tracing
the history of the Church from the time of Christ to the Great Persecution at the
beginning of the fourth century and ending with the conversion of the Emperor
Constantine, his aim was to show the purity and continuity of the doctrinal
tradition of Christianity and its struggle against persecutors and heretics. He
supported his account by extensive quotations from original sources.

This edition of G. A. Williamson's clear, fluid translation is accompanied by an
introduction by Andrew Louth discussing the life and works of Eusebius, together
with notes, a bibliography, a map of the world of Eusebius and brief biographies of
the figures who appear in the work.

Translated by G. A. Williamson
Revised and edited with a new introduction by Andrew Louth

PENGUIN CLASSICS

ECCLESIASTICAL HISTORY OF THE ENGLISH PEOPLE
BEDE

'With God's help, I, Bede ... have assembled these facts about the history of
the Church in Britain ... from the traditions of our forebears, and from my own
personal knowledge'

Written in ad 731, Bede's *Ecclesiastical History of the English People* is the
first account of Anglo-Saxon England ever written, and remains our single most
valuable source for this period. It begins with Julius Caesar's invasion in the first
century bc and goes on to tell of the kings and bishops, monks and nuns who
helped to develop government and convert the people to Christianity during these
crucial formative years. This is a rich, vivid portrait of an emerging church and
nation by the 'Father of English History'.

Leo Sherley-Price's translation from the Latin brings us an accurate and readable
version of Bede's *History*. This edition includes *Bede's Letter to Egbert*, denouncing
false monasteries; and *The Death of Bede*, an admirable eye-witness account by
Cuthbert, monk and later Abbot of Jarrow, both translated by D. H. Farmer.

Translated by Leo Sherley-Price
Edited with an introduction and notes by D. H. Farmer

PENGUIN CLASSICS

THE FEDERALIST PAPERS
JAMES MADISON, ALEXANDER HAMILTON AND JOHN JAY

> 'The establishment of a Constitution, in a time of profound peace,
> by the voluntary consent of a whole people, is a PRODIGY'

Written at a time when furious arguments were raging about the best way to govern America, *The Federalist Papers* had the immediate practical aim of persuading New Yorkers to accept the newly drafted Constitution in 1787. In this they were supremely successful, but their influence also transcended contemporary debate to win them a lasting place in discussions of American political theory. Acclaimed by Thomas Jefferson as 'the best commentary on the principles of government which ever was written', *The Federalist Papers* make a powerful case for power-sharing between State and Federal authorities and for a Constitution that has endured largely unchanged for two hundred years.

In a brilliantly detailed introduction Isaac Kramnick sets the *Papers* in their historical and political context. This edition also contains the American Constitution as an appendix.

'The introduction is an outstanding piece of work. I am strongly recommending its reading' Warren Burger, the former Chief Justice, Supreme Court of the United States

Edited with an introduction by Isaac Kramnick

PENGUIN CLASSICS

THE LIFE OF SAMUEL JOHNSON
JAMES BOSWELL

**'Johnson, to be sure, has a roughness in his manner,
but no man alive has a more tender heart'**

In Boswell's *Life of Samuel Johnson*, one of the towering figures of English literature is revealed with unparalleled immediacy and originality, in a biography to which we owe much of our knowledge of the man himself. Through a series of richly detailed anecdotes, Johnson emerges as a sociable figure, vigorously engaging and fencing with great contemporaries such as Garrick, Goldsmith, Burney and Burke, and of course with Boswell himself. Yet anxieties and obsessions also darkened Johnson's private hours, and Boswell's attentiveness to every facet of Johnson's character makes this biography as moving as it is entertaining.

In this entirely new and unabridged edition, David Womersley's introduction examines the motives behind Boswell's work, and the differences between the two men that drew them to each other. It also contains chronologies of Boswell and Johnson, appendices and comprehensive indexes, including biographical details.

Edited with notes and an introduction by David Womersley

PENGUIN CLASSICS

LEGENDS FROM THE ANCIENT NORTH

BEOWULF

THE ELDER EDDA

THE SAGA OF THE VOLSUNGS

SIR GAWAIN AND THE GREEN KNIGHT

THE WANDERER: ELEGIES, EPICS, RIDDLES

J. R. R. Tolkien spent much of his life studying, translating and teaching the great epic stories of northern Europe, filled with heroes, dragons, trolls, dwarves and magic. He was hugely influential for his advocacy of *Beowulf* as a great work of literature and, even if he had never written *The Hobbit* and *The Lord of the Rings*, would be recognised today as a significant figure in the rediscovery of these extraordinary tales.

Legends from the Ancient North brings together from Penguin Classics five of the key works behind Tolkien's fiction. They are startling, brutal, strange pieces of writing, with an elemental power brilliantly preserved in these translations. They plunge the reader into a world of treachery, quests, chivalry, trials of strength. They are the most ancient narratives that exist from northern Europe and bring us as near as we will ever get to the origins of the magical landscape of Middle-earth (Midgard) which Tolkien remade in the 20th century.

PENGUIN CLASSICS

MEDIEVAL WRITINGS ON SECULAR WOMEN

'Woman, who is equal to the moon in the flower of youth,
Is equal to a little old ape after the onset of old age'

This remarkable collection brings together a host of writings from across different regions and cultures of the Middle Ages, from the ninth to the fifteenth century. They are arranged to follow the life stages of a Medieval woman living a secular existence, from infancy and girlhood, through marriage and motherhood, to widowhood and old age. Some women are captured in exceptional circumstances, such as the transcript from Joan of Arc's trial describing her rural childhood, or a letter written by Edward I's mother. Many others are anonymous or humble: an account of an abandoned baby in Italy, a disturbing description of a slave girl by a Baghdad diplomat, an epitaph for the female leader of a Synagogue. Speaking across the ages, here are wry, moving voices that were written out of history.

Containing many newly translated pieces, this selection is accompanied by an introduction discussing the Medieval woman's life and legal status. There are also separate introductions to each chapter, background information on each piece, notes and a bibliography.

Edited with introductions by Patricia Skinner and Elisabeth van Houts

---

PENGUIN CLASSICS

IVANHOE
WALTER SCOTT

'Fight on, brave knights! Man dies, but glory lives!'

Banished from England for seeking to marry against his father's wishes, Ivanhoe
joins Richard the Lion Heart on a crusade in the Holy Land. On his return, his
passionate desire is to be reunited with the beautiful but forbidden lady Rowena,
but he soon finds himself playing a more dangerous game as he is drawn into a
bitter power struggle between the noble King Richard and his evil and scheming
brother John. The first of Scott's novels to address a purely English subject,
Ivanhoe is set in a highly romanticized medieval world of tournaments and sieges,
chivalry and adventure, where dispossessed Saxons are pitted against their Norman
overlords, and where the historical and fictional seamlessly merge.

This volume is based on the acclaimed Edinburgh Edition of the Waverley
Novels whose first edition was drawn from Scott's original texts. It contains an
introduction that examines Scott's use of history in the light of contemporary ideas,
a chronology, bibliography, glossary and extensive notes.

'It remains one of the most exciting stories in the language' A. N. Wilson

Edited with an introduction by Graham Tulloch

PENGUIN CLASSICS

A JOURNAL OF THE PLAGUE YEAR
DANIEL DEFOE

> 'It was a most surprising thing, to see those Streets,
> which were usually so thronged, now grown desolate'

In 1665 the Great Plague swept through London, claiming nearly 100,000 lives. In *A Journal*, written nearly sixty years later, Defoe vividly chronicled the progress of the epidemic. We follow his fictional narrator through a city transformed: the streets and alleyways deserted; the houses of death with crosses daubed on their doors; the dead-carts on their way to the pits. And he recounts the horrifying stories of the citizens he encounters, as fear, isolation and hysteria take hold. *A Journal* is both a fascinating historical document and a supreme work of imaginative reconstruction.

This edition contains a new introduction, an appendix on the Plague, a topographical index and maps of contemporary London, and reproduces Anthony Burgess's original introduction.

'The most reliable and comprehensive account of the Great Plague that we possess'
Anthony Burgess

'Within the texture of Defoe's prose London becomes a living and suffering being'
Peter Ackroyd

Edited with an introduction by Cynthia Wall

PENGUIN CLASSICS

THE DEATH OF KING ARTHUR

'Lancelot has brought me such great shame as to dishonour me through my wife, I shall never rest till they are caught together'

Recounting the final days of Arthur, this thirteenth-century French version of the Camelot legend, written by an unknown author, is set in a world of fading chivalric glory. It depicts the Round Table diminished in strength after the Quest for the Holy Grail, and with its integrity threatened by the weakness of Arthur's own knights. Whispers of Queen Guinevere's infidelity with his beloved comrade-at-arms Sir Lancelot profoundly distress the trusting King, leaving him no match for the machinations of the treacherous Sir Mordred. The human tragedy of *The Death of King Arthur* so impressed Malory that he built his own Arthurian legend on this view of the court – a view that profoundly influenced the English conception of the 'great' King.

James Cable's translation brilliantly captures all the narrative urgency and spare immediacy of style. In his introduction, he examines characterization, narrative style, authorship and the work's place among the different versions of the Arthur myth.

Translated by James Cable

He just wanted a decent book to read ...

Not too much to ask, is it? It was in 1935 when Allen Lane, Managing Director of Bodley Head Publishers, stood on a platform at Exeter railway station looking for something good to read on his journey back to London. His choice was limited to popular magazines and poor-quality paperbacks – the same choice faced every day by the vast majority of readers, few of whom could afford hardbacks. Lane's disappointment and subsequent anger at the range of books generally available led him to found a company – and change the world.

'We believed in the existence in this country of a vast reading public for intelligent books at a low price, and staked everything on it'
Sir Allen Lane, 1902–1970, founder of Penguin Books

The quality paperback had arrived – and not just in bookshops. Lane was adamant that his Penguins should appear in chain stores and tobacconists, and should cost no more than a packet of cigarettes.

Reading habits (and cigarette prices) have changed since 1935, but Penguin still believes in publishing the best books for everybody to enjoy. We still believe that good design costs no more than bad design, and we still believe that quality books published passionately and responsibly make the world a better place.

So wherever you see the little bird – whether it's on a piece of prize-winning literary fiction or a celebrity autobiography, political tour de force or historical masterpiece, a serial-killer thriller, reference book, world classic or a piece of pure escapism – you can bet that it represents the very best that the genre has to offer.

Whatever you like to read – trust Penguin.